MW00389691

THE REFORMATION

ERNEST G. SCHWIEBERT

THE REFORMATION

Volume I
The Setting of the Reformation

Volume II
*The Reformation
as a University Movement*

FORTRESS PRESS   MINNEAPOLIS

THE REFORMATION
Volume I: The Setting of the Reformation
Volume II: The Reformation as a University Movement

Cover design: Ellen Maly
Internal design: The HK Scriptorium, Inc.

Library of Congress Cataloging-in-Publication Data

Schwiebert, Ernest G. (Ernest George), b. 1895.
    The Reformation / Ernest G. Schwiebert.
        p.   cm.
    Includes bibliographical references and index.
    Contents: The setting of the Reformation — The Reformation as a
university movement.
    ISBN 0-8006-2836-5
    1. Reformation—Germany.   2. Lutheran Church—Germany—
History—16th century.   3. Martin-Luther-Universität Halle—
Wittenberg—History—16th century.   4. Luther, Martin, 1483–1546.
5. Melanchthon, Philipp, 1497–1560.   6. Germany—Church
history—16th century.   I. Title.
BR307.S436   1996
274.3'06—dc20   96-26063
                                                                              CIP

The paper used in this publication meets the minimum requirements of American National Standard for Information Sciences—Permanence of Paper for Printed Library Materials, ANSI Z329.48-1984.

Manufactured in the U.S.A.   AF 1-2836
00   99   98   97   96   1   2   3   4   5   6   7   8   9   10

To my wife, Billie,
without whose long labors
in typing, editing, and loyal support
this work could not have been completed

Castle Church of Wittenberg

Contents

Preface

During the years 1927–1930, when I was a teaching fellow at Cornell University, my mentor, Preserved Smith, introduced me to my life's work. He asked me to write a doctoral thesis on "The University of Wittenberg and Other Universities in Relationship to the Reformation." My point of departure was to be the *Matrikel* of the University of Wittenberg, in which its students had registered upon entry. I was to investigate student registrations, by decades, from 1520–1560, the period in which the Reformation was in full bloom under Luther and Melanchthon. My tasks were: to determine students' places of origin, lengths of stay, and later activities after their return to their home territories; to record their numbers on a map of Europe by decades; and to create a statistical table for comparative study of what transpired in their homelands. In the course of these statistical studies, I discovered how wrong many scholars had been in believing that the students came largely from the cities. it became clear that the Reformation was a very complex movement, and that it involved as many as 16,292 students from Wittenberg. My investigation also revealed that in no two places did the Reformation proceed in the same way, ranging as it did from mild transformations (as in Breslau) to quite stormy ones (in Magdeburg, for example). Luther and the rest of the Wittenberg faculty thus became the center around which this complex reform movement revolved, guiding hundreds of fellow reformers in various regions of Europe.

Of course, Preserved Smith recognized the great complexity of the study on which I had embarked. He often spoke of my thesis as only a beginning, an initiation into a lifetime of study. This is in fact what happened, for I spent sixty additional years teaching, writing, participating in academic meetings, and gathering material in the leading libraries in this country and abroad. I then decided to publish my unique approach to the Reformation. Thus in 1970, as a fellow at the Princeton Theological Seminary, I began to write the manuscript that now encompasses the present two volumes.

During my lifetime there has been a trend among Reformation scholars to place more emphasis on the climate out of which the Reformation emerged. Thus the first volume of this study begins with an introduction to the physical conditions in the German lands, the Germanic westward movement, and the coming of the Slavs into the later Wittenberg region. Chapter 2 is based on the reports of excavations in the Sorben lands around Wittenberg. I encountered these reports while working in the Firestone Library of Princeton University. Considerable attention is then given to the origin of Electoral Saxony. Since, during the days of the Reformation, Thuringia formed a large part of Ernestine Saxony, its background—based on medieval chronicles—is also treated in detail. The volume concludes with an account of the rule of Frederick the Wise, based on new findings.

I would like to express my indebtedness to a number of institutions and scholars, dating back to my parochial school days, when a German pastor, Jacobus Bomgarten, taught me, at the age of five, to write German script. At Capital University, Dr. R. C. H. Lenski taught me my first Greek and gave me my introduction to the Greek New Testament. I also owe a large debt to the distinguished medievalist James Westfall Thompson, at Chicago, for introducing me to the Middle Ages and making possible my study at Cornell. I have the fondest memories of Preserved Smith, my mentor, who introduced me to this study. Nor is my thankfulness any less for being privileged for three years to sit at the feet of Carl Becker in his lectures and seminars. A president of the American Historical Association, he taught us how difficult it is to rediscover historical reality. I am also deeply appreciative of the help offered by Oskar Thulin, the custodian of the *Lutherhalle* in Wittenberg, as well as the many local scholars who assisted me in reconstructing sixteenth-century Wittenberg and describing life in Electoral Saxony. While in Germany, I had a fine discussion with Walter Friedensburg, whose history of the University of Wittenberg and source book were invaluable for my studies. My gratitude also goes to Johannes Ficker, who taught me how to decipher texts in paleography. Later I used his methodology to decipher the handwriting of some thirty different Reformation figures. In 1936 I also visited Heidelberg and discussed the Reformation with Walther Köhler and wife. His many contributions to Reformation studies have proved to be very helpful.

During the postwar years, 1947–1950, I was invited to serve as guest professor at the University of Erlangen, where I learned to know Walther von Loewenich and Paul Althaus. I wish to express my gratitude to both of them for their help in my research and teaching while at Erlangen. Von Loewenich and I have since become warm friends during our meetings at many *Luther-kongresses.*

I am also very grateful to a number of institutions for their hospitality and assistance. I owe my lasting gratitude to the Seminary and Firestone Library of Princeton University for permitting me to borrow and use some of their rare holdings, especially volumes from the Firestone Slavic collection and its many monks' chronicles of Thuringia. President McCord of Princeton Theological Seminary deserves special mention. A similar debt of gratitude is extended to the Folger Shakespeare Library, under its director, O. B. Hardison, Jr., and also to Philip Nagel, for making their facilities available during many summers. Nor would my acknowledgments be complete without offering my thanks to Folger's acquisition librarian, Elizabeth Niemeyer, and her staff, for building and cataloging a fine Reformation library. Also I wish to express my gratitude to the staff of the Perkins Library of Duke University. Dr. Clarence Gohdes, professor of English at Duke and one of my classmates at Capital University, arranged for research facilities and provided much rare and valuable material. And my thanks go to the library's computer experts, Johannan Sherrer and Ken Berger, for their gracious assistance.

Most of all, I wish to express my indebtedness to my wife, Billie, who has typed most of these chapters, checked them, and encouraged me while I prepared the various drafts.

University of Wittenberg

1. Old monastery in which Luther did all his instruction   4. Melanchthon home
2. Old Frederici College building   5. The Augusteium
3. New Frederici College building   6. The Tozen House

In these buildings of the University of Wittenberg there blossomed forth the Reformation as a University Movement.

Abbreviations

Note: Unless otherwise indicated, English translations of quotations from primary and secondary sources are by Ernest G. Schwiebert.

Adam   Adam of Bremen. *History of the Archbishopric of Hamburg-Bremen.* Francis J. Tschan, ed. New York, 1959.

Adams   Adams, C. *The March of Democracy.* New York, 1932.

Album   *Album Academiae Vitebergensis,* ed. C. E. Förestemann. 3 vols. Leipzig, 1841ff.

AR   Wegele, Franz X., ed. *Annalen Reinhardsbrunnes.* Thüringische Geschichtsquellen. Vol. 1. Jena, 1854.

Aristotle   *Aristotle Dictionary,* ed. Thomas E. Kiernan, intro. Theodore E. James. New York: Philosophical Society, 1962.

Luther   *Martin Luther.* Berlin: Atlantis Verlag, 1933.

Barge   Barge, Hermann. *Andreas Bodenstein von Karlstadt.* 2 vols. Leipzig, 1905.

Baron   Baron, Hans. "Imperial Reform and the Hapsburgs, 1586–1504." *American Historical Review* 44 (1939): 298–303.

Barraclough   Barraclough, Geoffrey. *Medieval Germany, 911–1250.* Studies in Medieval History. 2 vols. Oxford, 1948.

Bauch, "Anfänge"   Bauch, Gustav. "Die Anfänge des Studiums der griechischen Sprache und Literatur in Norddeutschland." *Metteilungen der Geschichte für deutsche Erziehung und Schulwesen.*

Bauch, *CaS*   Bauch, Gustav. *Andreas Carlstadt als Scholastiker, Zeitschrift für Kirchengeschichte.* Gotha, 1896.

Bauch, *Erfurt*	Bauch, Gustav. *Die Universität Erfurt im Zeitalter des Frühhumanismus.* Breslau, 1904.
Bauch, *Geschichte*	Bauch, Gustav. *Geschichte des Vereins für Geschichte und Altertums Schelesians.*
Bauch, *Leipziger*	Bauch, Gustav. *Leipziger Frühhumanismus mit besonderer Rücksicht auf die Streitigkeiten zwischen Konrad Wimpina und Martin Mellichstadt.* Leipzig, 1897.
Bauch, *Monatschrift*	Bauch, Gustav. "Die Einführung de Hebräischen in Wittenberg." *Monatschrift für Geschichte und Wissenschaft des Judentums* (1914).
Bauch, Rhegius	Bauch, Gustav. "Die Vertreibung des Johannes Rhegius Aesticampianus aus Leipzig." *Archiv für Litteraturgeschichte.* Leipzig, 1885.
Bauch, Scheurl	Bauch, Gustav. "Christoph Scheurl in Wittenberg." *Neue Mitteilungen aus dem Gebiet historisch-antiquarischer Forschungen.* Band 21. Halle, 1903.
Bauch, WudS	Bauch, Gustav. "Wittenberg und die Scholastik." *Neues Archiv für Sachsische Geschichte.* Dresden, 1887.
Bauer	Bauer, Karl. *Die Wittenberger Universitätstheologie und die Anfänge der Deutschen Reformation.* Tübingen, 1928.
Berendt	Berendt, Friedrich. *Die Beziehungen Anhalts zu Kursachsen von 1212 bis 1485.* Halle a.d.S., 1907.
Berkowitz	Berkowitz, D. S. *In Remembrance of Creation.* Waltham, Mass., 1968.
Berthold	Berthold. *Das Leben des heiligen Ludwig, Landgrafen in Thüringen, Gemahls der heiligen Elizabeth.* H. Rückert, ed. Friedrich Kodiz von Salfeld, trans. Leipzig, 1851.
Blaschke	Blaschke, Karlheinz. "Sachsen im Zeitalter der Reformation." *Schriften des Vereins für Reformationsgeschichte.* Vols. 75–76. No. 185. Gütersloh, 1970.
Boedler	Boedler, Karl E. F. *Die Gewalt der Askanischen Herzöge in Westfalen und Engern bis zum Ausgang des 14. Jahrhunderts.* Halle a.d.S., 1912.
Boehmer, *LLRR*	Boehmer, Heinrich. *Luther in the Light of Recent Research.* New York, 1916.
Boehmer, *Luther*	Boehmer, Heinrich. *Der Junge Luther.* Gotha, 1925.
Böttiger	Böttiger, C. M. *Geschichte von Sachsen.* Theodore Flathe, ed. Gotha, 1867.
Bouwsma	Bouwsma, William J. *The Interpretation of Renaissance Humanism.* Washington, D.C., 1959.

Burdach	Burdach, Konrad. *Reformation, Renaissance, Humanismus.* Berlin, 1918.
Burkhardt	Burkhardt, C. A. H. *Geschichte der Sächsischen Kirchen und Schulvisitationen von 1524 bis 1545.* Leipzig, 1879.
Cary	Cary, Max. *A History of Rome.* London, 1954.
Chappell	Chappell, Warren. *Short History of the Printed Word.* New York, 1970.
Charitius	Charitius, M. D. Andreas. *Chronik der Wittenberger Archidiakonus.* Ca. 1740. Unpublished. In 1936 this manuscript was part of the Max Senf collection in Wittenberg.
Clark, *Care of Books*	Clark, J. W. *The Care of Books: An Essay on the Development of Libraries and Their Fittings, from Their Earliest Times to the End of the Eighteenth Century.* Cambridge, 1901.
Clark, *Libraries*	Clark, J. W. *Libraries in the Medieval and Renaissance Periods.* Cambridge, 1894.
CR	Melanchthon, Philip. *Corpus Reformatorum.*
Cranach	Cranach, Lucas. *Wittemberger Heiligthumsbuch.* Munich, 1884.
Dialogus of 1507	*Dialogus illustrate ac Augustissime urbis Albiorene vulgo Vittenberg dicte Situm Amenitatem ac Illustrationem docens Tirocinia nobilium artium iacentibus Editus.*
Drews	Drews. "Spalatiana." *ZKG* 19:506.
Dungern	Dungern, Otto von. *Adelsherrschaft im Mittelalter.* Aachen, 1927.
Eisenstein	Eisenstein, Elizabeth. *The Printing Press as an Agent of Change.* Cambridge, 1979.
Enders	Enders, E. L., and G. Kauwerau, eds. *Dr. Martin Luthers Briefwechsel.* 19 vols. Stuttgart and Leipzig, 1884–.
Erdmann	Erdmann, G. *Kaisertum und herzogs Gewalt im Zeitalter Friedrich II.* Theodor Mayer, ed. Leipzig, 1944.
Eschenhagen	Eschenhagen, Edith. "Wittenberger Studien, Beiträge zur Social und Wirtschaftgeschichte der Stadt Wittenberg in der Reformationzeit." *Jahrbuch der Luthergesellschaft.* Munich, 1927.
Fay	Fay, Theodore S. *The Three Germanies.* New York, 1889.
Ferguson	Ferguson, Wallace K. *Renaissance in Historical Thought.* Cambridge, 1948.
Ficker, *Exposition*	Ficker, Johannes. *Ansprache zur Eröffnung der*

	Lutherbildnis-Ausstellung im Provinzial-museum zu Halle, Luther, Vierteljahrschrift der Luthergesellschaft. Munich, 1931.
Friedensburg, *G. U. W.*	Friedensburg, Walter. *Geschichte der Universität Wittenberg.* Halle, 1917.
Friedensburg, *Urkundenbuch*	Friedensburg, Walter. *Urkundenbuch der Universität Wittenberg.* 2 vols. Magdeburg, 1926.
Fuchs	Fuchs, C. H. *Die ältesten Schriftsteller über die Lustseuche in Deutschland.* Göttingen, 1813.
Geanakopolos	Geanakopolos, D. J. *Greek Scholars in Venice.* Cambridge, Mass., 1962.
Gess	Gess, Felican. "Leipzig und Wittenberg." *Neues Archiv für Sächsische Geschichte und Altertum.* Dresden, 1895.
Giesebrecht	Giesebrecht, Wilhelm von. *Geschichte der Deutschen Kaiserzeit.* 5th ed. 6 vols. Leipzig, 1881–1895.
Gillert	Gillert, K. *Der Briefwechsel des Conradus Mutianus.* Halle, 1890.
Gimbutas	Gimbutas, Marija. *The Slavs.* London, Thames and Hudson, 1971.
Goodyear	Goodyear, F. R. D. *The Annals of Tacitus.* Cambridge, 1972.
Grandaur	*Chronik van Sanct Peter zu Erfurt, 1100–1215.* Georg Grandaur, trans. Leipzig, 1893.
Grane	Grane, Leif. *Contra Gabrielem, Luthers Ausandersetzung mit Gabriel Biel in der Disputatio contra Scholasticam Theologicam 1517.* Gyldendal, 1962.
Grohmann	Grohmann, J. C. A., ed. *Annalen der Universität Wittenberg.* 2 vols. Meissen, 1801.
Gronen	Gronen, Edita. *Die Machtpolitik Heinrich des Löwen.* Vaduz, 1915.
Güterbock, *Gelnhauser*	Güterbock, Ferdinand. *Die Gelnhauser Urkunde und der Prozess Heinrich des Löwen.* Quellen und Darstellungen zur Geschichte Niedersachsens. Vol. 32. Hildesheim and Leipzig, 1920.
Güterbock, *Schisma*	Güterbock, Ferdinand. *Zum Schisma unter Alexander III.* Munich, 1926.
Hagen, *Hebrews*	Hagen, Kenneth. *A Theology of Testament in the Young Luther: The Lectures on Hebrews.* Leiden, 1974.
Hahn	Hahn, H. "Die Söhne Albrecht des Bären." *Jahresbericht über die Louisenstädtische Realschule.* Berlin, 1869.
Haller, *Politik*	Haller, Johannes. "Auswärtige Politik und Krieg."

	Morgenrot der Reformation. Julius von Pflugk-Hartung, ed. hersefeld, 1916.
Haller, *Sturz*	Haller, Johannes. "Der Sturz Heinrich des Löwen." *Archiv für Urkundenforschung* 3:295–450. Reprint.
Harnack	Harnak, O. *Das Kurfürstenkollegium.* Giessen, 1883.
Hartfelder	Hartfelder, Karl. *Philip Melanchthon als Praeceptor Germaniae.* Berlin, 1889; reprint 1964, Nieukoop B. De Graaf.
Haskins	Haskins, Charles Homer. *The Normans in European History.* London, 1919.
Haskins, *Rise*	Haskins, Charles H. *The Rise of Universities.* New York, 1949.
Haskins, *Renaissance*	Haskins, Charles H. *The Renaissance of the Twelfth Century.* Cambridge, 1928.
Haskins, *Science*	Haskins, Charles H. *Medieval Science.*
Hausleiter	Hausleiter, J. *Die Universität Wittenberg vor dem Eintritt Luthers.* Leipzig, 1903.
Haywood	Haywood, Richard M. *The Myth of Rome's Fall,* reprint of 1959 ed. Westport, Conn." Greenwood Press, 1979.
Heer	Heer, Friedrich. *The Holy Roman Empire.* Janet Sonderheimer, trans. London, 1986.
Heinemann	Heinemann, Otto von. *Albrecht der Bär.* Darmstadt, 1864.
Helbig	Helbig, Herbert. *Der Wettinische Ständestaat.* Münster and Cologne, 1955.
Helmold	Helmold. *The Chronicle of the Slavs.* Francis J. Tschan, ed. New York: Octagon Books, 1935.
Hensel	Hensel, Witold. *Die Slawen im Frühen Mittelalter: Ihre Materielle Kultur.* Waldemar Hein, trans. Berlin, 1965. Original title: *Slowianszezyzna Wezennosrednicwieczna.* Warsaw, 1956.
Herrmann	Herrmann, Joachim. *Die Slawen in Deutschland: Ein Handbuch.* Berlin, 1970.
Herte, *Lutherbild*	Herte, Adolf. *Das katholische Lutherbild in Bann der Lutherkommentare des Cochlaeus.* 3 vols. Münster, 1943.
Herte, *Lutherbiographie*	Herte, Adolf. *Die Lutherbiographie des Johannes Cochlaeus, eine Quellenkritische Untersuchung.* Diss. Münster, 1915.
Heubner	Heubner, H. *Der Bau des kurfürstlichen Schloszes.* Wittenberg, 1937.
Hildebrandt	Hildebrandt, Ernst. "Die kurfürstliche Schloss und Universitätsbibliothek zu Wittenberg 1512–1547." *Zeitschrift für Buchkunde* 2 (1952): 40.

Hildesheim	*Die Jahrbücher von Hildesheim.* Eduard Winckelmann, trans. Leipzig, 1893.
Hoest	*Stephen Hoest, Reden und Briefe, Quellen zur Geschichte der Scholastik und des Humanismus.* Ed. and trans. Frank Baron. Munich, 1971.
Huizenga	Huizinga, J. "Das Problem der Renaissance." *Wege der Kulturgeschichte.* Munich, 1930.
Israël	Israël, Friedrich. *Das Wittenberger Universitätsarchiv, seine Geschichte und Bestände.* Halle, 1913.
Joachimsen	Joachimsen, Paul. "Der Humanismus und die Entwicklung des deutschen Geistes." *Deutsche Vierteljahrschrift für Literaturwissenschaft und Geistesgeschichte.* Halle, 1930.
Johnson	Johnson, E. N., and J. W. Thompson. *An Introduction to Medieval Europe.* New York, 1937.
Jordan	Jordan, Julius. "Aus der Lutherhalle Geschichte des Lutherhauses nach 1564." *Luther Jahrbuch.* 1921–1922.
Jordan, "Luthers Bild"	Jordan, Julius. "Luthers Bild." *Luther Mitteilungen der Luthergesellschaft.* 1919.
Junghans	Junghans, Helmar. "Die Einfluss des Humanismus auf Luthers Entwicklung bis 1518." *Luther Jahrbuch* 37. Hamburg, 1970.
Kaegi	Kaegi, Werner. *The Renaissance Investigations of Ernst Walser.*
Kaufmann	Kaufmann, Georg. *Geschichte der deutschen Universitäten.* 2 vols. Graz, 1958.
Kaufmann, "Universitätsprivilegien"	Kaufmann, Georg. "Die Universitätsprivilegien der Kaiser." *Deutsche Zeitschrift für Geschichteswissenschaft.* 1889.
Kibre, *Nations*	Kibre, Pearl. *The Nations in Medieval Universities.* Cambridge, Mass., 1948.
Kibre, *Scholarly Privileges*	Kibre, Pearl. *Scholarly Privileges in the Middle Ages.* Cambridge, Mass., 1962.
Kirn	Kirn, Paul. *Friedrich der Weise und die Kirche.* Leipzig and Berlin, 1926.
K&K[1]	Kötzschke, Rudolf, and Helmut Kretzschmar. *Sächsische Geschichte: Werden und Wandlungen eines Deutschen Stammes und seiner Heimat im Rahmen der Deutschen Geschichte.* Frankfurt a.M.: Verlag Wolfgang Weidlich, 1965.
K&K[2]	Kötzschke, Rudolf, and Helmut Kretzschmar. *Sächsische Geschichte: "Vor" und Frühgeschichte, Mittelalter und Reformationszeit.* Frankfurt a.M.: Weidlich, 1965.

Kleineidem	Kleineidem, Erich. "Die Universität Erfurt in den Jahren 1501–1505." *Reformata Reformanda*. Münster, 1965.
Knapton	Knapton, Ernest John. *Europe, 1450–1815*. New York, 1958.
Knochenhauer	Knochenhauer, Theodor. *Geschichte Thüringens zur Zeit des Ersten Landgrafenhauses (1039–1247)*. Gotha, 1871.
Kolde, *Analecta*	Kolde, Theodor. *Analecta Lutherana*. Gotha, 1883.
Kolde, *Friedrich*	Kolde, Theodor. *Friedrich der Weise und die Anfänge der Reformation*. Erlangen, 1881.
Kristeller	Kristeller, P. O. *Die italienischen Universitäten der Renaissance*. Krefeld: Scherpe Verlag.
Kroker	Kroker, Ernst. *Katharina von Bora. D. Martin Luthers Frau*. Zwickau.
Krüger, *Lutherstadt*	Krüger, Gottfried. *Die Lutherstadt Wittenberg im Wandel der Jahrhunderte*. Wittenberg, 1939
Krüger, *V.d.L.*	Krüger, Gottfried, et al. "Wie sah die Stadt Wittenberg zu Luther's Lebzeiten aus?" *Vierteljahrschaft der Luthergesellschaft* (1933) 13–14.
Lamprecht	Lamprecht, Karl. *Deutsche Geschichte*. 5 vols. Berlin, 1891–1895.
Langer, *Einzugsbereich*	Langer, Gottfried, et al. *Einzugsbereich der Universität Wittenberg*. 2 vols. Halle, 1967.
Lauterbach	Lauterbach, M. Anton. *Diaconi zu Wittenberg. Tagebuch auf das Jahr 1538, die Hauptquelle der Tischreden Luthers*. Ed. Johann Karl Seidemann.
Liber Decanorum	*Liber Decanorum Facultatis Theologicae Academiae Vitebergensis*. Ed. C. D. Förstemann. Leipzig, 1838.
Lissner	Lissner, Ivan. *The Caesars' Might and Madness*. J. Maxwell Brownjohn, trans. New York, 1958.
Lortz, *HRC*	Lortz, Joseph. *How the Reformation Came*. New York, 1964.
Lortz, "Martin Luther"	Lortz, Joseph. "Martin Luther." In *Reformata Reformanda*, ed. Irwin Iserloh and Konrad Repgen. 2 vols. Münster, 1965.
Löwenich	Löwenich, Walther von. *Martin Luther, Der Mann und das Werk*. Munich, 1983.
Macmullan	Macmullen, Ramsay. *Soldiers and Civilians in the Later Roman Empire*. Cambridge, 1963.
Mariotte	Mariotte, Jean Yves. *Le Conte de Bourgogne sous les Hohenstaufen*. Paris, 1963.
Maurer	Maurer, Wilhelm. *Der junge Melanchthon zwischen Humanismus und Reformation*. 2 vols. Göttingen, 1967–1969.

Mentz, *Friedrich*	Mentz, Georg. *Friedrich der Grossmutige, Beiträge zur neueren Geschichte Thüringens.* Jena, 1908.
Mentz, *Johann Friedrich*	Mentz, Georg. *Johann Friedrich der Grossmutige, 1503–1554.* Jena, 1903.
Merian	Merian, Matthaeus. *Topographia Superioris Saxoniae, Thuringiae, Misniae, etc.* Frankfurt, 1650.
Michelson	Michelson, A. L. J. "Über die ungedruckte thüringische Chronik von Conrad Stolle." *Zeitschrift des Vereins für thüringische Geschichte und Altertums kunde.*
Müller	Müller, Sebastian. *Annalen des Chur-Fürstlichen Hauses Sachsen Ernestin- und Albertiner Linien, von Anno 1400 bis 1700.* Weimar, 1700.
Munz	Munz, Peter. *FrederickBarbarossa.* Ithaca: Cornell Univ. Press, 1969.
Musset	Musset, Lucien. *The Germanic Invasions.* University Park, Penn.: Pennsylvania State Univ. Press, 1975.
Myconius	Myconius. *Historia Reformationis,* 35.
Mylius	Mylius, M. J. C. *Memorabilia Bibliothecae Academiae Jenensis.* Jena and Weisenfels, 1746.
Obermann	Obermann, Heiko. *The Harvest of Medieval Theology.* Cambridge, 1963.
Pagaviensis	*Chronici Pagaviensis.*
Patze, *Entstehung*	Patze, Hans. *Die Entstehung der Landesherrschaft in Thüringen.* Cologne and Graz, 1962.
Patze, *Geschichte*	Patze, Hans and Walter Schlesinger. *Geschichte Thüringens.* Cologne and Vienna, 1974.
Paulsen	Paulsen, Friedrich. *Geschichte des gelehrten Unterrichts.* Berlin, 1919.
Plitt	Plitt, G. *Jodocus Trutfetter von Eisenach, der Lehrer Luthers.* Erlangen, 1876.
Portal	Portal, Roger. *The Slavs.* London, 1969.
Post	Post, R. R. *The Modern Devotion: Confrontation with Reformation and Humanism.* Leiden, 1968.
Prantl	Prantl, C. *Geschichte der Logic im Abendlande.* 4 vols. Leipzig, 1870.
Rait	Rait, Robert S. *Life in the Medieval University.* Cambridge, 1912. Reprint, New York, 1969.
Rashdall	Rashdall, Hastings. *The Universities of Europe in the Middle Ages.* 3 vols. Oxford, 1936. New rev. ed., ed. F. M. Powicke and A. B. Emden, 1951.
Reu	Reu, M. *Luther's German Bible.* Columbus, 1934.
Rietschel	Rietschel, George. *Luther und die Ordination.* Wittenberg, 1883.

Rinke, *Oratio*	Nicoli Marscalei Thurii oratio habita albiori akademia in alemania iam nuperrima ad promotionem primorum baccalauriorum numero quattuor et viginti anno domino mcccccciii.
Rommel	Rommel, Christoph von. *Geschichte von Hessen.* 2 vols. Kassel, 1823.
Rost	Rost, Julius R. *Die Pädagogische Bedeutung Bugenhagen.*
Roth	Roth, Rudolf. *Urkunden zur Geschichte der Universität Tübingen aus de Jahren 1476–1550.*
Rothe	Rothe, Johann. *Düringische Chronik des Johann Rothe.* Thüringische Geschichtsquellen. Vol. 3. R. von Lilienchron, ed. Jena: Friedrich Fromann, 1859.
Russell, "Celts"	Russell, Jeffrey B. "Celts and Teutons: A Joint Study." *The Transformation of the Roman World.* Lynn White, Jr., ed. Berkeley: Univ. of California Press, 1966.
S&A	Slater, O., and O. August. *Atlas der Saale und Mittleren Elbesgebieten.* Leipzig, 1959. *annalista Saxo.* Eduard Winckelmann, trans. 2nd ed. Leipzig, 1894.
S. Petri	Menckenius, Johannes. *Chronicum S. Petri Vulgo Sampetrinum Erfurtense, ab Anno MXXXVI usque ad MCCCLV.* Scriptores Rerum Germanicarum Praecipve. Vol. 3. Leipzig, 1730.
Schachner	Schachner, Nathan. *The Medieval Universities.* London, 1938.
Schalscheleth	Schalscheleth, P. (P. Heynig). *Historisch-geographische Beschreibung Wittenbergs und seiner Universität.* Frankfurt und Leipzig, 1795.
Scheurl	Scheurl, Christopher. *Briefbuch.*
Schlesinger, *Burgen*	Schlesinger, Walter. *Burgen und Burgbezirke.* 3 vols.
Schlesinger, *Beiträge*	Schlesinger, Walter. *Mitteldeutsche Beiträge zur deutschen Verfassungsgeschichte des Mittelalters.* Göttingen, 1961.
Schuchhart	Schuchhart, Carl. *Ankona, Rethra, Vineta.* Berlin, 1926.
Schwiebert, E.T.W.	Schwiebert, Ernest G. "The Electoral Town of Wittenberg." *Medievalia et Humanistica* 3 (1945): 104–5.
Schwiebert, *Luther*	Schwiebert, Ernest G. *Luther and His Times.* St. Louis: Concordia, 1950.
Schwiebert, "Library"	Schwiebert, Ernest G. "Remnants of a Reformation Library." *The Library Quarterly* 10 (October 1940): 494–531.

Schwiebert, *Theses* — Schwiebert, Ernest G. "The Theses and Wittenberg." *Luther for an Ecumenical Age.* St. Louis, 1950.

Schwiebert, *Wittenberg and Other Universities* — Schwiebert, Ernest G. *The University of Wittenberg and Some Other Universities in Their Relation to the German Reformation.* Dissertation, Cornell University, 1929.

Schwiebert, *Wittenberg Library* — Schwiebert, Ernest G."Remnants of a Reformation Library." *The Library Quarterly* 10 (Chicago, 1940): 494–531.

Sennertus, *Athenae* — Sennertus, Andreas. *Athenae Inscriptiones Wittenbergensis.* Wittenberg, 1665.

Smith, *Reformation* — Smith, Preserved. *The Age of the Reformation.* New York, 1920.

Spalatin — Berbig, G. "Georgii Spalatini Ephemerides, inchoatae anno MCCCCLXXX," *Quellen und Darstellungen aus der Geschichte des Reformationsjahrhunderts.* Leipzig, 1908.

Spalatin, *Chronik* — Klee, Alfred, ed. *Spalatins Chronik für die Jahre 1513 bis 1523.* Borna and Leipzig, 1919.

Spalatin, *Friedrich* — Spalatin, Georg. *Das Leben und Zeitgeschichte Friedrichs des Weisen.* C. G. Neudecker and Ludwig Preller, eds. Jena, 1851.

Spitz — Spitz, Lewis W. *The Religious Renaissance of the German Humanists.* Cambridge, 1963.

Starke — Starke, Heinz D. "Die Pfalzgrafen von Sommerschenburg." *Jahrbuch für die Geschichte Mittel- und Ostdeutschlands.* 4 vols. Friedrich Meinecke, ed. *Institute der Freien Universität Berlin.* Tübingen, 1955.

Stein — Stein, Hermann. *Geschichte des Lutherhauses.* Wittenber, 1883.

Steinmetz — Steinmetz, David. *Misericordia Dei: The Theology of Johannes von Staupitz in Its Late Medieval Setting.* Leiden, 1968.

Stier — Stier, C. *Inscriptiones Viteberegae latinae.* Wittenberg, 1856.

Stocki — Stocki, Roman Smal. *Slavs and Teutons: The Oldest German Slav Relations.* Milwaukee, 1950.

Strauss — Strauss, Gerald. *Manifestations of Discontent in Germany on the Eve of the Reformation.* Bloomington, Ind.: Indiana Univ. Press, 1971.

Stupperich — Stupperich, Robert. *Melanchthon.* Trans. Robert Fisher. London.

Suevus	Suevus, Gottfridus. *Academia Wittebergensis ab Anno Fundationis 1502 usque ad annum 1655.* Wittenberg, 1655.
Thiele	Thiele, R. "Thüringische-erfurtische Chronik von Konrad Stolle." *Geschichtsquellen der Provinz Sachsen.* Vol. 39. Halle, 1900.
Thietmar	Holzmann, Robert, ed. *Die Chronik des Thietmar von Merseburg.* 4th ed. Leipzig, 1939.
Thompson	Thompson, E. A. *The Early Germans.* Oxford: Clarendon Press, 1965.
Thompson, *Feudal*	Thompson, James W. *Feudal Germany,* reprint of 1928 ed. New York: AMS, 1980.
Thompson, *Medieval*	Thompson, James Westfall, and Edgar Johnson. *An Introduction to Medieval Europe, 300–1500.* New York: W. W. Norton, 1937.
Thompson, *Medieval Library*	Thompson, James W. *The Medieval Library.* New York, 1957.
Thompson, *Middle*	Thompson, James W. *The Middle Ages.* 2 vols. New York: Knopf, 1932.
Thomson, *Renaissance*	Thomson, S. Harrison. *Europe in the Renaissance. 1963.*
Thulin, *Lutherstadt*	Thulin, Oskar. *Die Lutherstadt und Wittenberg.* Berlin, 1932.
Thulin, *Martin Luther*	Thulin, Oskar. *Martin Luther, Sein Leben in Bilden und Zeitdokumenten.* Munich, 1958.
Tierney, *Sources*	Tierney, Brian. *The Middle Ages: Sources of Medieval History.* New York, 1970.
Troeltsch	Troeltsch, Ernst. *Historische Zeitschrift.* 1906.
Vogt, *Johannes Bugenhagen*	Vogt, K. A. F. *Johannes Bugenhagen, Pomeranus.* 1867.
Voigt	Voigt, Georg. *The Revival of Classical Antiquity.* Berlin, 1859.
WA	Luther, Martin. *Werke.* Kritische Gesamtausgabe ("Weimarer Ausgabe"). Weimar: Böhlau, 1883–.
WA Br	Weimarer Ausgabe, Briefwechsel.
WA Tr.	Martin Luther's "Table Talk," in WA.
Walser	Walser, Ernst. *Studien zur Geistesgeschichte der Renaissance.* Basel, 1932.
Wartburg	Baumgärtel, Max, ed. *Die Wartburg: Ein Denkmal deutscher geschichte und Kunst.* Berlin, 1907.
Weisheipl	Weisheipl, James A. *Friar Thomas D'Aquino.* New York, 1974.
Wernle	Wernle, Paul. *Die Renaissance.*

Widukind   Widukind. *Sächsische Geschichten.* Paul Hirsch,
                       ed. 5th ed. New York: Johann Reprint Corp.,
                       1965.
Zeumer   Zeumer, Karl. "Die Goldene Bulle Kaiser Karls
                       IV." *Quellen und Studien der Verfassungs-*
                       geschichte des deutschen Reiches im Mittelalter
                       und Neuzeit. 2 vols. Tübingen, 1908.

THE REFORMATION

❖

Volume I

The Setting of the Reformation

1

The Geography and Topography of Germany

Americans, who are accustomed to tremendous distances, are often mis-led when they look at maps of Germany. The five so-called Stem Duchies (Sax-ony, Franconia, Bavaria, Swabia, and Lotharingia), which together stretched from the Alps to the North Sea, covered an expanse of less than four hundred miles from north to south, and were not much larger in width. Of course, one must note that the political and geographical boundaries of the Holy Roman Empire of the German Nation, as defined by Rainald von Dassel, did not co-incide with the duchies of Henry the Fowler, and even included portions of northern Italy. However, the present study is limited to the German lands.

Geographically, the whole of northern Germany is merely a continuation of the Baltic plain, which embraces the Netherlands, parts of Denmark and Swe-den, and the coast of Poland. Much of this terrain is very low and flat, dotted here and there with large glacial deposits known as terminal moraines. During the Ice Age, the area was a coastal plain covered by a southern lobe of the conti-nental ice sheet. This sheet left a series of moraines as it retreated. It also estab-lished the courses of the rivers that run northwest into the North and Baltic seas, which flow almost parallel to one another between the moraines. It is thought that the ice sheet forced these streams to flow in a northwesterly direc-tion along its retreating edge. In this way the present courses of the Rhine, Ems, Weser, Elbe, Oder, and Vistula were gradually fixed. Because of a lack of drainage, the flat territory was originally covered with many lakes and swamps and was initially not well-suited for settlement.

In the western part of Germany we encounter quite different geographical conditions. The two outstanding features are the Slate Mountains and the Rhine *Graben* (rift valley). The Slate Mountains are a trapezium-shaped area that, according to Alfred Hettner, are the remains of a single mountain that broke into parts as it gradually rose. This high, flat surface, with its occasional ridges in the less eroded parts, is practically cut through the middle by the

3

Rhine gorge. Other breaks form the Moselle, Meuse, and Lahn gorges, dividing the region into six parts. The climate here is affected by the sea, which results in much rain in the summer and snow in the winter. In the lower basins, such as the one surrounding Cologne, the winters are mild. The whole area is well-suited for forests and pasturelands. In the river gorges there is some agriculture, and along the Rhine and Moselle there are also many vineyards. In view of the terrain, it is not surprising that Germany's three leading archbishoprics—Mainz, Trier, and Cologne—had their principal holdings here. Each was located in a river valley. Cologne, with its strategic position on the Rhine, was built by the Romans and was one of the most flourishing commercial centers of the early Middle Ages.

To the south of the Slate Mountains is the Rhine *Graben*. This area is part of a single geological formation in the earth's crust that extends from Paris to Vienna. A cross-section of the formation, viewed from the southern side, would show that the Rhine Valley is almost at the center, with the Vosges Mountains forming a high mountain ridge on the French side and the Black Forest making up a German counterpart in the west. Passing beyond the Black Forest, the land slopes gradually down to form the Bavarian plateau, the eastern equivalent of the Paris basin. This region of sedimentary rock is bisected by two rows of bold, westward-facing escarpments, the Swabian Alps and the Franconian Alps. The Bavarian plateau is high tableland formed from the deposits washed from the higher Alpine glaciers. The broad alluvial plains have forced the Danube, which drains most of the Bavarian plateau, to flow along the northern extremity of the highlands near the Swabian Alps and then eastward around the foothills of the Bohemian Massive. The land westward from the Vosges Mountains is a counterpart to the eastern formation, with six or seven less bold escarpments tapering gradually toward the central French highlands, "Isle de France."

Structurally, the Rhine Valley is a fallen segment of the earth's surface; the crust pulled apart, causing the upper layers to drop down. It is quite evident that the Black Forest and the Vosges were once two pieces that fitted together. Nor was this break in the earth's crust a small one, for the Rhine Valley is 30 kilometers wide at some places, and its length from Basel (where the river enters the valley) to Mainz is approximately 300 kilometers. Nor does the Rhine *Graben* end there, where the river turns eastward through the Slate Mountains; it continues on through the Hessian highlands.

Since the Rhine is fed year-round from Alpine glaciers, and is the only river to cut through the central highlands, its importance as a passageway and trade route may be readily discerned. The river channel, with its meandering course and numerous oxbow lakes and swamps, presents many difficulties to navigation. Even with human effort in straightening its course, dredging its channel, and building numerous canals, larger vessels can progress only as far as Mainz.

Many of the cities along the Rhine date to Roman times, especially on the west bank; many also played important roles in medieval history. Numerous high spires and domes testify to the location of old ecclesiastical centers, mostly seats of bishops. Here are Basel, Strasbourg, Speyer, nearby Heidelberg (on the

Neckar), Worms, and finally Mainz. Except the Luther lands themselves, there is not another region in Germany so closely associated with key events of the Reformation.

The climate of the Rhine Valley has also played a role in the making of this highly developed region. In winter, the temperature seldom falls below freezing, nor in the summer rises above seventy. Perhaps this is why the Romans were interested in developing the area and contributed to its early cultural blossoming.

Among the cities of the Bavarian plateau, the most important during the Reformation were Frankfurt a.M., Tübingen, Constance, Ulm, Ingolstadt, Würzburg, Bamberg, Nürnberg, and Coburg. Adjacent to the Bavarian plateau, on the northeast side, is the Bohemian Massive, sometimes called the "citadel of Europe" because of its strategic position. In some respects its appearance is that of a huge bowl with an uneven bottom and the sides formed of bulky masses of granite and crystalline rocks. The northern rim is composed of the *Erzgebirge* (Ore Mountains) on the one side and the Sudeten ranges on the other; the southern and western rims are covered by the *Böhmerwald* (Bohemian Forest). There is one break through the northern rim, used by the Elbe to drain the plateau; while tributaries of the Danube and Oder make use of the partial opening on the eastern side. Perhaps the reference to Bohemia as a bowl is not entirely appropriate, because the formation is not homogeneous in structure. The older, southern uplands disappear under the newer limestone deposits to the north, with occasional ridges and peaks, while still other portions are rolling highlands. The only comparatively level part of the bowl is the northeastern part, at the foot of the Sudeten in the Elbe basin. This area enjoys a pleasant climate because, while removed from the sea and enclosed by mountains, it has a fairly stable yearly climate and temperature. Its rainfall is adequate and the soil is productive, making agriculture profitable. Rich mineral resources, combined with accessible trade routes, have made the region one of the most highly developed in Europe.

The name *Bohemia* is derived from the name of an old Celtic tribe, called the *Bojern*, that occupied the area before the Germans. During the barbarian invasions the land became greatly depopulated and fell into the hands of Slavic tribes, the Czechs. While never conquered by the Germans, they were greatly influenced by their Teutonic neighbors. The Elbe was a common waterway for both peoples.

Having completed a survey of geographical conditions along the outer ring of the German lands, we now turn to the central highlands and the Luther lands. The Hessian highlands, which form the western half of the central highlands, are the most irregular region of all Germany. Geologically, the country is a continuation of the Rhine *Graben*. However, its appearance has been greatly altered by volcanic formations such as the Vogelsberg and Rhön, at the southern end near Fulda, and a number of smaller ones to the north. The region has no orderly arrangement of ranges, but consists of irregular ridges and isolated peaks. Many of these volcanic remains are covered with forests, as was already the case when the missionary Boniface established an ecclesiastical center at Fulda. Practically the entire Hessian highlands are drained by the Weser and its tributaries. Marburg and Fulda were the only towns of importance in the region during the sixteenth century.

The eastern part of the central highlands is fundamentally quite different from the western part. The general direction of the Harz and the Thuringian Forest seems to indicate that the region is merely an extension of the Bohemian Massive. Between these two mountain ridges lies the Thuringian basin, a slightly elevated and somewhat uneven country. Here and there, on the old basin, are more recent deposits of rich, fertile soils, where such cities as Erfurt and Weimar are located. The whole Thuringian high plain *(Hochfläche)* is without forests, except the eastern end, and so forms a fertile farming region. The Unstrut, Gera, Ilm, and Saale rivers have cut rather deep valleys through this territory. Erfurt and Weimar are the most important cities of the basin for a study of the Reformation, as are also Jena, Naumburg and Merseburg—all three of which are located on the Saale River in the eastern part. The lowlands, which surround the central basin, are the widest and most productive areas in the north, especially around Nordhausen. This region became known to Germans as the *Goldene Aue* (Golden Meadow) because of its productivity. To the east of Nordhausen is the Kyffhäuser, a smaller promontory presenting an impressive view as it towers from the lowlands.

Rich in association with medieval history is the Harz mountain region, which separates the Thuringian basin from "Old Saxony." Here, at Goslar, the Franconian emperors had their capital, and from the Rommelsberg they obtained much of their silver. The Harz forms a real barrier between the Thuringian region and the Baltic plain. On top of the Harz are flat areas that lead off into scenic valleys, many of which are covered with forests. The Brocken, a majestic, granite peak, is the highest point in northern Germany. To the northwest, the Harz slopes into an uneven landscape covered for a great distance by forest. To the southeast is the Mansfelder mountain region. Here and around nearby Eisleben, the mineral resources of copper led to mining, which in the sixteenth century attracted Martin Luther's father. Although this whole region was not part of the Saxon lands, it is closely related to the Reformation.

On the south side of the Thuringian basin is another extension of the Bohemian Massive, made up of the Vogtland, the Frankenwald, and the Thuringian Forest. Here, on its western end, is the Wartburg. The Thuringian Forest forms a sharp ridge that breaks off into small, sloping valleys on all sides. The extension looks somewhat like a finger pointing to the northwest, widening into a hand at the Frankenwald. The ridge is not of even height, for peaks such as the Inselberg in the north and the wooded Schneeberg in the south stand out above the remaining ridges. The Thuringian Forest did not present a real barrier. As a result, early in the Middle Ages the country was settled by people from the west, who pushed into these more open, undeveloped regions. The forest barrier widened with the Frankenwald and formed a division between Franconia and Saxony.

In a sense the Saxon lands may be regarded as a counterpart to the Thuringian basin. The Thuringian country slopes to the southeast, where it is met by the generally northwestward slope of the southern highlands in the Saale and Elster valleys. During the early medieval period this land was occupied by Slavic peoples known as the Sorben. The southern part of these central highlands is almost entirely mountainous. Next to the Vogtland and the Frankenwald we come upon the *Erzgebirge*, formed of granite, slate, and gneiss. This mountain formation is really a huge plain that extends as far as the Elbe area and gradually rises toward the south. In parts, ridges such as Keilberg and Fichtelberg rise high above the general plain, and deep valleys have been cut through it by the Mulde and its tributaries. Since the Slavs were not particularly attracted to the *Erzgebirge*, it remained forestland until it was settled by Germans. Later the minerals around Freiberg were mined and the region increased in importance. North of these mountains lies an important basin through which, early in the Middle Ages, the principal east–west highway passed. Zwickau and Chemnitz are in this area.

To the north of the *Erzgebirge* are highlands that are met in the Elbe region by the Lausitzer plateau. Between these two ranges lies the Dresden basin, a cretaceous formation that at one time may have been a lake, from which the Elbe worked its way through the narrow valley to the north. Early in the Middle Ages, Henry I built Meissen at the end of this basin. In time, the entire region came to be known by this name. The area had its counterpoint along the Elbe in Bohemia. During the Reformation, Dresden lay on the same east–west highway as Zwickau.

Passing along the Elbe to the north, the lands along the river are at first very low, but then they rise in a westerly direction. This is especially noticeable at the entrance to the Leipzig basin, where quite early in the Middle Ages that city was founded at the confluence of the Elster and the Pleisse.

North of these Albertine lands is the region that during the Reformation period belonged to the elector of Saxony, Frederick the Wise. The important towns were Torgau, the residence of the elector, and Wittenberg. Around Wittenberg, where the Elbe bends westward, the land is very level, although it becomes more rolling as one travels southwest. The climate of the area may be called continental. It is mildest in the valleys of the Elbe, Mulde, and Pleisse, while in the *Erzgebirge* the temperature is at least ten degrees lower in both summer and winter. The summer average runs between 62 degrees and 64 degrees F. in the valleys, and the winter about 30 degrees. The rainiest part of the central highlands is the *Erzgebirge*, while Leipzig typically has the least rainfall.

2

The Decline of Rome and
the German Invasions

The decline of Rome did not occur quickly, but happened over a period of about five hundred years. A gradual infiltration of the empire by the Teutons occurred for centuries before en masse invasions by the Goths, Vandals, Lombards, Alemanni, Burgundians, and Franks. Jeffrey Russell has stressed that in the decline of Rome and the rise of the West, both "assimilation" and "synthesis" were involved.[1] The transformation began as early as the third century and did not reach its fruition until the age of Charlemagne.[2]

The early history of the Teutonic tribes will forever remain shrouded in mystery. Historians know little about the Germans prior to the records left by Julius Caesar in 55 B.C. The tribes of Caesar's day were eventually destabilized by the aggressiveness of their neighbors. The stronger tribes conducted raids against the weaker ones, took booty and slaves, and drafted the younger warriors into military service. This makes it even more difficult to determine exactly where a specific tribe resided at a certain time. Since none of the Germanic tribes had a written language, details of tribal life were never recorded.

It was not until the Gothic missionary Ulfilas created an alphabet for the Germanic language, in order to translate the Bible for the Visigoths, that we obtain the first German script.[3] But he left us little knowledge about the people themselves; most of our information about the Visigoths and Ostrogoths has been derived from Roman historical sources. In his excellent study *The Caesars' Might and Madness*,[4] Ivan Lissner concluded that in those early days four Teutonic tribes resided in Scandinavia, while in Germany proper, eleven other tribal units could be identified. These conditions seem to have remained constant during the "golden age" of Rome, from Caesar Augustus to Marcus Aurelius.

The first Roman historians to describe the early Germans were Julius Caesar, Pliny, Tacitus, and Ptolemy. To what extent Caesar's *Memoirs of the Gallic Wars* are based on actual observations is difficult to determine. No doubt most of Caesar's impressions came from contacts with the tribes nearest the Roman frontiers on the Rhine and the Danube. Even though Roman coins have been dug up as far inland as the Elbe River (at Wittenberg), it remains doubtful that Caesar was acquainted with these people. E. A. Thompson explored all the extant data for his book *The Early Germans*,[5] where he treats the Teutons some one hundred and fifty years before Tacitus' famous *Germania*. Thompson also described later changes among the Teutons up to the time of Tacitus.

Modern historians believe that the German tribes of Caesar's time were still primarily pastoralists, possessing flocks of cattle and sheep in common. In this early period the Teutons made little use of iron, but frequently used bronze. There was some Latin correspondence from German tribes to Roman officials; no doubt such letters were drafted for tribal chiefs by mercenary soldiers or Roman hostages.[6]

There was no private ownership of land among Germanic tribes in Caesar's day; everything was possessed by the tribe as a whole. However, Thompson found that private ownership of herds of cattle began quite early. The tribes nearest the Roman frontier developed individual ownership of land as well. The evidence suggests there was considerable freedom within clans and tribes.[7]

During wartime, however, the German tribes underwent considerable change. When Caesar crossed the Rhine in 55 B.C. on a pontoon bridge, the nearby Suebi tribe became alarmed. All their women and children, as well as movable property, were transported deeper into the woods. Meanwhile the warriors assembled and chose a number of chieftains of equal rank to lead them in battle. After the war, however, the tribal structure reverted to its former basis.[8]

There was a span of one hundred and fifty years between Caesar and Tacitus, and during that time German tribal life underwent significant change. Whereas in Caesar's day there had been poverty, want, and hardship, conditions were now much improved. The potter's wheel had come into more general use, and iron was being smelted. Trade with the Romans had grown, especially in the border provinces. Although much of the trade was limited to the frontiers, by the time of Caesar Augustus traders had begun to penetrate deep into German forests, selling Roman goods and luxury items. Some Roman merchants even settled deep within *Germania*, carrying on trade and even loaning the Germans money. Though much of the exchange was still by means of barter, Roman coins have turned up throughout the German lands. In Tacitus' time individual ownership of glass, textiles, pottery, wine, and weapons had become common among the German tribes. The arable land had by now become prized private property, on which owners cultivated their own crops. From the middle of the first century, during the reigns of Claudius and Nero, some Germanic tribes began to fertilize their fields. By then wealth among the Teutons was measured by the size of their herds of cattle.[9]

In Caesar's day a Germanic tribe would gather a council of leading men only in time of war, but in Tacitus' time such a council also functioned in peacetime.[10] At the age of puberty, Germanic boys from leading families were admitted into the general assembly. Able young men often rose rapidly in rank; the

Cherusci tribe chose Arminius as a chief at the age of twenty-six. Tribal issues were first discussed by its council, after which they were brought before the general assembly. The council's recommendations, however, carried considerable weight. By Tacitus' time the military leader of the tribe also remained during peacetime. Subsequently kings appeared, also elected by their tribes. The Batavians, Cherusci, and Heruls all had kings by the sixth century. The king of the Cherusci presented tribal problems before the assembly of warriors, and was no doubt elected for life. His title implied more wisdom than authority; in the sixteenth century the king of the Herule still ate with his warriors, which implied that he commanded no privileged treatment.[11]

Tacitus claimed that until A.D. 9, the Roman general Varus controlled all of *Germania* up to the Elbe River. Subsequently the young Cherusci commander Arminius met and defeated the Roman legions in the Teutoburger Wald, prompting Varus to kill himself. This defeat created a very dangerous situation for Rome, because a German victory over the "invincible" Roman legions could give the Teutonic grandiose ideas. But Rome knew how to defeat the Cherusci by fostering internal dissension, as it had done with other tribes.[12] It could count on the help of many traitors. Even though Arminius had the Roman army at his mercy in A.D. 5, there were a number of Cherusci leaders who pleaded for peace with the Eternal City. The tribe chose to follow the advice of Inguiomerus, the young commander's relative. Upon the older man's advice, the Cherusci elected Segestes, a strong pro-Roman, as their military chieftain. This disloyal commander had Arminius thrown into chains.[13]

According to Tacitus, the Romans used many other clever methods to control the internal affairs of Germanic tribes. A favorite technique was to capture young boys from noble families, offer them the advantages of Roman culture, and educate them as members of the Roman nobility. After this they were returned to their respective tribes as chieftains. Arminius himself had been reared as a Roman; he had even commanded a company of German auxiliaries for them, achieving such distinction that he had been knighted. Other methods used to keep the Teutons under Roman control included: leaving an uninhabited strip of land several miles wide along the German border; forbidding all German boat traffic on the Rhine and the Danube; limiting the number of trading posts between the Germans and the Romans along the rivers; prohibiting Germans from crossing the Rhine after dark; requiring Germans carrying arms to have a Roman escort; the assassination and abduction of German military leaders; and the indiscriminate burning of Teutonic fields.[14]

Toward the end of the first century, during the reign of Emperor Domitian, the Romans began to realize that their defenses against the Teutonic tribes were inadequate. In A.D. 83 Domitian built the first *limes*, a no-man's-land guarded by an earthen embankment, originating near Mainz on the Rhine and running south, diagonally, to the Danube. The emperor had already annexed the German lands that later became Württemberg and Baden so that he could construct the original line of defense further inland. J. W. Thompson claims this original *limes* ran from near Regensburg in the south toward Lorch, and then northwest to the steep hills of Taunus between the Main and Lahn Rivers. To properly defend the new fortifications, Domitian settled the region with Roman veterans, who supported themselves from their lands.[15]

The original construction of the *limes* was somewhat primitive, consisting of an earthen embankment or boundary limit from which enemy formations could be observed if they entered a strip of cleared land facing it. At that time the Chatti tribe, located just north of the *limes*, seemed to the Romans to be the most dangerous.[16] Later emperors did not regard the original *limes* as sophisticated enough to be a real deterrent to the Teutons. The able and aggressive Hadrian decided to strengthen the *limes* by constructing a wall with a palisade in front and a deep ditch on the German side. About the middle of the second century his successor, Antonius Pius, straightened the *limes* by pushing it forward. Thus the fortification ran from the Rhine, near what is now Bad Hönningen and Rheinbrohl, to the southeast, toward Regensburg on the Danube, a distance of 350 miles. This barricade did not come any too soon. By the year 213 the Romans experienced Teutonic pressure along the middle Rhine and on the Danube. The Alemanni in southwestern Germany had formed an alliance with the Chatti, who resided in the region above the Main. These two aggressive tribes broke through the *limes* and entered the empire.[17]

In the second and third centuries, Roman military camps sprang up in all parts of the empire, and in time soldiers were given farms and tilled them with their own slaves. These conditions prevailed even on the Roman side of the *limes*, which meant that by the fourth century the legions had been reduced to a militia. The best part of the army had been removed and was quartered in the towns, leaving the frontier exposed. As raids by Germanic tribes increased, large stone towers were erected to serve as places of refuge. These were roughly a thousand feet square, with walls about three feet thick, narrow windows, and heavy, solid doors. Hilltops and crests were now chosen by Romans for residences. These villas were protected by earthworks, moats, and stockades, while the neighboring territory in the countryside served for agriculture.[18]

Macmullen concluded that after Septimius Severus the Roman army was civilian turned soldier and soldier turned civilian. By the fourth century the army's chances of winning battles against difficult foes such as the Huns or the Parthians had declined to about fifty-fifty. In the later centuries Rome actually had more troops under arms, but the guards of the German *limes* were too conscious of their farms and houses to be good soldiers. Often the army's ranks were filled mostly with Germans. There were no regular drills, for the troops spent much of their time on their estates.[19] After Septimius Severus the barriers were let down; soldiers could marry, take up trades, and even participate in off-duty clubs.[20]

In the fourth century, Emperor Valentinian built new fortifications all along the Rhine. The Visigoths had been unpleasant neighbors across the Danube and were beginning to molest the Balkans. There was good reason for this pressure. Behind the Visigoths were the Huns, a fierce tribe that lived practically on horseback. The Huns had originally migrated from the region of the Great Wall of China, moving westward toward the Black Sea. They had practically wiped out the Alans and the east Germans, and the frightened Visigoths asked Co-emperor Valens for permission to seek refuge in the empire. The emperor permitted them to enter peacefully, settle on farms, and serve in the Roman army. He made one further provision, that they give up their arms. But later the Romans abused the German settlers, and war broke out between the Visigoths and Rome.[21] During the battle of Adrianople in A.D. 378, Valens was defeated and killed. But under Theodosius I the Goths once again settled down peacefully in the Balkans, and the threat to the Danube region receded.[22]

Theodosius governed the eastern part of the empire, and he recruited the Visigoths to fight against the Persians as well as defend the empire against renewed German attacks. He enrolled many more Teutons in the ranks of the overextended Roman army. Whole units now had both Teutonic officers and men, who used their own weapons and tactics.[23]

Under Theodosius II, in A.D. 438, the empire received its first great law code. From that point on its eastern part began evolving in a way quite different from the western part. Part of this was due to the influence of a renewed Hellenism and the use of Roman law. Greek Christianity also gave the East a unique character. Meanwhile the West bled to death because of internal disturbances and the Germanic invasions. Rome had no reserve of strength to stop the Teutons.

During A.D. 429, the Vandals were permitted to pass through the empire and settle in North Africa, where they began to establish pirate bases and close trade on the Mediterranean.[24] Meanwhile the Visigoths became dissatisfied with their conditions in the Balkans and migrated in search of a better home. They invaded Italy, and in A.D. 410 their leader Alaric sacked Rome. After some wandering, the Visigoths were permitted to settle in Acquitania; with full Roman approval they established a new kingdom there.[25]

It is generally granted that the barbarian invasions played a vital role in the final decline of the western empire. In this the Visigoths and Ostrogoths played prominent roles. But behind them was the pressure of the Huns. Under their leader, Attila, they practically wiped out the Ostrogoths. This caused the Slavs in the Danube region to migrate northward and the Visigoths to seek entry into the empire.[26]

For a long time the Roman rulers saw in the Huns an asset in their engagements with the threatening Gothic tribes. For some fifty years they treated them as allies. According to Priscus, during A.D. 449 the Huns even sent an ambassador to Constantinople.[27]

After being repelled by the Huns, the Slavic tribes moved northward into Moravia, Bohemia, and beyond. These lands had been left unpopulated by the migrating Germans. The significance of this for our study is that the so-called Luther lands were left behind, making it possible for the Sorben to move into those regions.

J. W. Thompson claimed that there was considerable regrouping and amalgamation of Germanic tribes between the days of Julius Caesar and the mass invasions of the fifth century. This makes it difficult to locate tribes at a given time with any degree of accuracy.[28] However, if Lissner's findings prove to be correct, a number of Germanic tribes dwelt and moved around in the later Slavic lands during the "golden age" of Rome. According to his chart, in the north near the eastern side of the Elbe were the Suebi, while to the east were the Rugii. In the region where Wittenberg was later located were the Burgundians and the Vandals, both of whom later moved into the empire. In the lands of Meissen, east of the Saale, were the Mermenduren, who later disappear from the record. In Bohemia was the once prosperous Marcommani tribe, which was first destroyed internally and later wiped out by the Romans.

The Goths that had migrated from Gotland, Östergötland, and Västergötland in southern Sweden were dwelling east of the Vistula in the days of Trajan and Hadrian. From there, around A.D. 250, they started to the southeast, across the Carpathian mountains and toward the Black Sea region. Thus they vacated the lands for the Slavs in later Pomerania and Poland.[29] The invasion of the various Slavic tribes will be examined in the next chapter.

3

The Sorben
in Electoral Saxony

It was long assumed by historians that the Wittenberg region (which in A.D. 1180 became Electoral Saxony) had previously been an undeveloped territory—much like the western prairies of the United States prior to the Civil War. Accounts led readers to believe that the sand hill where the Elbe bends westward had been but an overnight stopping place for river traffic, halfway between the markets of Torgau and Magdeburg. It was believed that travelers stopped here on their journeys north and south along the river road, while in time a market with temporary structures developed there. This rationale assumed that the surrounding region was covered with forests and had no population. Little was it realized that a Slavic people, known as the Sorben, had settled there, in the land between the Saale and the Elbe, as early as the seventh century, and had cleared much of the land in the Elbe valley.

Today we know that the Sorben began to move into the region as the Teutonic tribes migrated westward, leaving behind only a few German stragglers. Thus, between the seventh and the twelfth centuries, the Sorben cleared the lands of the later *Kurkreis* (electoral circle), built their *Rundwalle* (bulwarks of refuge and defense), and started their own villages (where no doubt they had markets on the Wittenberg sand hill and traded farm products with river travelers long before Wittenberg existed).

Misconceptions about the early history of Electoral Saxony developed for good reason. In the nineteenth century, two famous students of Leopold von Ranke, Karl Lamprecht and Wilhelm Giesebrecht, wrote their monumental histories of the *Kaiserzeit* (era of the Kaisers) based on the medieval annals and chronicles. Their sources were written by clergy who were neither properly informed nor lacking in bias against earlier settlers. Catholic chroniclers such as Widukind, Thietmar, Adam of Bremen, and Helmold had but limited knowledge of the Slavs in the eastern marks, who spoke a strange language and, in

14

their estimation, were far below them in civilization and culture. Before the spade had unearthed so much new evidence, Karl Lamprecht could write with patriotic pride that for the Germans, conquering the Slavs and bringing these "inferior" peoples into the orbit of German feudalism was "the great deed of the Middle Ages."[1] Since in later centuries the Slavs became an integral part of feudal society, it became difficult distinguish what was Slavic from what was German. In addition, extreme Prussian patriotism tended to glorify everything German and play down any Slavic contributions. For example, many specialized studies on the *Burgwarden* systems—the castle fortresses believed to have been created by Henry I and Otto the Great, and built in the Sorben lands between the Saale and the Elbe—considered them to have been created by the Germans exclusively for defense. The medieval chroniclers helped to create this misconception. They claimed that the early Saxon emperors dotted the river valleys of the Saale, Mulde, and Elbe with whole chains of *Burgwarden*, to protect their newly conquered lands from more distant Slavic tribes and the Hungarian Avars, who periodically raided and plundered these regions. Little was it realized that the conquest of the Sorben by the Franks, and later the Saxons, had made it possible for the Germans to acquire these Slavic strongholds and convert them into a new *Burgward* system for regional defense.[2]

Just as in the nineteenth century the spade of Heinrich Schliemann unlocked the secrets of old Troy, and the excavations of Sir Arthur John Evans revealed a lost Cretan civilization, the spade of Carl Schuchhart in his diggings near Ankina, Rethra, and Vineta in the early twenties was to reveal to the modern world a "lost" Slavic civilization in the north. In more recent decades, excavations in some five thousand other places have unearthed unimagined treasures in Moravia and Bohemia, as well as in the Sorben lands.[3] Out of this has grown an entirely new picture of the role of the Slavs in German history. We can no longer say that the villages of Electoral Saxony, including Wittenberg, were principally Flemish-German creations.[4] Even the town plan of Wittenberg, which closely resembles numerous Wendish patterns of excavated hamlets, seems to point to a very significant Sorben influence.[5] Since there must have been a significant melding of Slavic, German, and Flemish cultures in the Wittenberg region, historians can no longer claim that a definitive influence was exerted by any one group. But since, according to Herrmann, the Slavs formed nine-tenths of the area's population as early as the thirteenth century, doubtless the influence of the Slavic element remained very strong.

In this chapter we shall seek answers to the following questions: Who were the Sorben? From whence did they migrate into the Saxon lands? What type of civilization had they established by the time Bernhard took over the Wittenberg region in 1180? And finally, what role did these elements play in the building of Wittenberg?

Today the literature concerning these Slavic peoples is tremendous; source materials occupy an entire section in the Firestone Library of Princeton University. That collection includes accounts in many languages. Roman Smal Stocki believes that Slavic languages are definitely Indo-European in origin.

Loan-words in Slavic indicate that there was an earlier, close connection to proto-Germanic.[6] However, opinions diverge in this area. Two Russian historians, George Vernasky and Michael Karpowich, disagree with equally competent historians from the West. The Russians do not grant that western Slavs had any influence on the Slavs in Asia.[7] But western scholars such as Alfred Senn and Roman Smal Stocki hold that there were originally three groups of Slavic tribes, namely, the West Slavs, the Middle Slavs, and the East Slavs.[8] There has also been a significant difference in the methodologies employed by the two groups of scholars. In the West, historians have tried to penetrate the Paleolithic Age of these peoples. Orthodox Marxists have regarded the Indo-European philology employed by the West to establish Slavic origins as "bourgeois deceit."[9] By means of this approach, western scholars have attempted to prove the existence of a common ancestry for all three Slavic types.[10] Such scholars claim that originally there existed a Slavic *Grundsprache*, or source language, into which, during migrations between 500 B.C. and A.D. 50, Baltic, Germanic, and other "loan words" infiltrated. Later, when the West Slavs moved into the Black Sea region, near the East Goths and West Goths, more "loan words" crept in.[11] When Teutons moved westward into the Roman Empire, some Slavs invaded the Balkans, while others were driven north and migrated through the Moravian Pass into Moravia and Bohemia, finally passing into the Sorben lands up to the Saale River.[12]

The first scholar to establish that the Slavs belonged to the Indo-European family was Francis Bopp, the father of Indo-European philology. He concluded that, linguistically, the Slavs were closer to the Baltic peoples (the Lithuanians, Latvians, and the native Prussians), but that they also showed a kinship with proto-Germans.[13] Stocki said that the West Slavs in particular show that this earlier kinship existed.[14] However, scholars are not in agreement concerning the original Slavic homeland. Roger Portal and Marija Gimbutas both claimed it was somewhere north of the Carpathian Mountains. The Romans referred to the Veneti as a Slavic tribe, dwelling between the Oder and the Vistula during the first and second centuries before the Christian era; they reported that these tribes also had been known by the Greeks.[15] But then the Slavs are lost from our sight until the sixth century A.D., when references are made in Gothic and Byzantine sources. The Gothic historian Jordanes alluded to the Veneti as the *Sclavenes* and *Antae*, dwelling in a vast territory of the upper Vistula.[16] The historian Procopis of Caesarea also mentioned the *Antae* as a numerous people, living somewhere in the area of present-day Ukraine.[17]

Gimbutas held that those members of the Slavic tribes in the Black Sea region were driven toward the north by the Scythians and Samatians, the fierce Iranian tribes of the Pontus region. Like the Teutons, they encountered the Huns in the Danube valley. In fact, he concluded, the Huns, Avars, and Bulgars paved the way for the Slavic migrations into Central Europe and the Balkan Peninsula.[18] Later, in the seventh century, the Slavs pushed on into Moravia, Czechoslovakia, and up the Elbe River valley.

During the seventh century the Sorben lands east of the Saale River were still a vast forest with many lakes and swamps. But for those willing to clear the land, the soil was rich and suitable for agriculture. The earlier westward German migrations had left behind few original settlers. Much of the land around rivers and lakes could be claimed by these Slavic tribesmen. The Sorben were divided into many smaller groups ruled by dukes and kings.[19] A Frankish leader named Samo was cited by medieval chroniclers as the one who organized the Slavs in Bohemia and the Sorben lands to repel the Hungarian Avars in 623; in 631 he led a successful campaign against the Franks and defeated them.[20] But the Franks soon rallied and established a *Limes Sorabicus*, a defensive boundary on the Saale River. Later the Germans reinforced this line by erecting new fortresses along the stream.[21] Later research has shown that there were some peaceful penetrations into Thuringia in the form of farm settlements, but these were not lands that in the early days were regarded as Slavic.[22] Herrmann stated that it was Fredigar who, in 631, designated these Slavs as Sorben, adding that the Slavs dwelt in very productive lands between the Saale and the Elbe rivers.[23]

We will now take a closer look at the Sorben settlements to ascertain what type of civilization these Slavs had developed prior to their subjugation by the Germans in the later feudal system.

Historians such as Walter Schlesinger[24] and Joachim Herrmann[25] have given us excellent descriptions of and insights into what scholars have gained from recent excavations. Scholars maintain that the Slavic tribes were divided into nineteen separate groups that settled in and around the Wittenberg region (the later *Kurkreis*), arriving from Bohemia by way of the Elbe River. By contrast with the Germans, the Slavs practiced cremation of the dead. In every case where excavators have discovered burial urns containing human ashes beneath homes, dwellings, and castles, it is evident that the dwellers were Slavs and not Germans. The urns of all these settlers were the same simple, unadorned type, done without the potter's wheel. Herrmann concluded that the original settlers did not migrate to mountainous territory, but instead chose more level areas along streams and lakes, suitable for agriculture. Not only did the Slavs regard water as absolutely essential, but a stream or a lake formed the simplest type of enclosure. Historians claim that the Elbe River once flowed much closer to Wittenberg and its old river road than it does today. Wittenberg's semicircular town plan resembles other Sorben town plans that have recently been excavated. Thus it seems most likely that, in its *Stadtplan*, the original Wittenberg was Slavic. In time there arose a much more complex system of defenses, as we shall see, especially after the Franks in Merovingian days tried to subjugate these peoples. In larger communities, the common settlers were protected by *Fluchtburgen*, large areas surrounded by high earthen walls, where the inhabitants could flee in times of danger.[26]

Soon after their arrival, the Sorben settlers chose for their new homes the favorable forest locations that were along water. Then they began the process of clearing away part of the forest around them, just as American settlers would later do in the state of Ohio. Trees had to be felled, rolled into piles, and burned. With seventh-century tools this must have been quite a task. Once the trees were out of the way, the stumps had to be cleared and their roots dug out. The region around later Wittenberg was cleared of forests quite early. Much of this work must have been done in the Merovingian days. The Sorben plows had wooden plowshares that only scratched the surface of the soil, but wooden shafts enabled them to be pulled by a horse or a team of oxen. Such plowing was most effective when the soil was crossed from both directions; hence the Slavs laid out their fields in squares.[27] All the stones and roots of stumps had to be eradicated; otherwise a farmer might break a plowshare. Later, metal plowshares were imported from the Carpathian region; eventually the Sorben built charcoal-fired blast furnaces and made their own steel plows. In addition to strength, metal plowshares had the advantage of actually turning the soil over. Therefore a field needed to be plowed in only one direction, and the square field became obsolete. In the later land redistribution under feudalism, the Slavs began to cultivate longer fields.

In time, Sorben villages such as Torgau and Wittenberg appeared, with their markets. In fact, in Slavic the word *Torgau* means "marketplace." Thus travelers on the Elbe and along the river road from Torgau to Magdeburg could purchase farm products and supplies along the way in the Slavic marketplaces. Later, as Sorben culture advanced, such markets also offered outlets for furs, fish, chickens, ducks, clothing, rugs, and other flax and wool products produced in Slavic communities.[28]

Wheat and rye were staple necessities for Slavic family life. Grain was harvested with sickles, brought to a threshing floor, and threshed out by means of wooden clubs or paddles. Grain was normally stored in silos and used later as needed; but due to the danger of it being stolen by invaders, they often buried their grain underground.[29] In time, communities also had flour mills, in which they used grindstones that were often shipped from Scandinavia or the Rhine region. Millet was also cultivated, ground, and baked into a type of flat cake-bread. In their gardens the Slavs grew onions, peas, carrots, beets, poppies and hemp.[30]

The Sorben raised sheep both for food and wool, practiced spinning and weaving, and made extensive use of animal hides.[31] Formerly it was believed that beef played only a minor role in the Slavic diet, in the belief that conditions were primitive and hunting supplied most of the meat. But after excavations in more settled regions, Herrmann claims that beef comprised about ninety percent of the household meat.[32] Domesticated animals included both cows and goats, pigs, sheep, and oxen.[33]

Horse raising was an advanced, proud profession among the Slavs, dating as far back as their northward migrations.[34] As a result, cavalry played a significant role in the stubborn Slavic resistance to German conquest. The value of a horse was very high, even more than that of a slave. Ibrahim ibn Jakub, a merchant who traveled in the lands of the Slavs, found in 965 that the Obodriten were particularly blessed with fine horses.[35] Excavations have revealed that a Slavic horse was sometimes buried with its rider.[36]

Since the Catholic Church observed 150 fast-days, when fish was regarded as the proper substitute for beef or pork, in later times fishing became a regular profession among the Sorben. Their lands were full of rivers and lakes, where fish could be caught and sold at the market. Fish were salted or smoked when not eaten immediately.[37]

Another profession in Sorben society that was closely related to the life of the medieval church was the production of honey and its by-products. According to Herrmann,[38] the beekeepers had been a special class in Slavic society from the very beginning. They not only gathered honey and prepared the wax for future use in the church, they also brewed an intoxicating honey-wine drink called *Met*. Since there was a great demand for wax candles, their place in society became all the more important. After the Sorben converted to Christianity, honey and beeswax were part of the prescribed tithe. During the reign of emperor Henry IV, a law was passed requiring that the Slavs pay the honey tithe or face the prospect of going into captivity.[39]

All evidence gained from recent findings points toward nuclear family life among the Sorben, even prior to the takeover of their lands. Such a family seems to have consisted of the grandfather as the titular head, while below him in rank were the father and the grandchildren.[40] The father's home furnished the central gathering place, and the homes of the sons were grouped around it in semicircular fashion.[41] Before any major action was undertaken by the family, the titular head assembled all the sons and adult grandsons to consult with them as to the appropriate course to be taken.[42] Sorben women were completely in charge of life in and around the home, the *Zadrunge*. The grandmother, mother, and mother-in-law managed all the household chores. If the grandmother was too old or died, the mother took over.[43]

The nuclear family formed the smallest unit in a larger social organization of Sorben settlers living east of the *limes Sorabicus*, drawn by the Franks.[44] In 631 Fredigar called the Sorben a *Gens*, subdivided into smaller tribal groups presided over by kings or dukes. The sources contain references to specific kings who were killed, such as Milito in 806, Cimuscle in 839, and Zistobobo in 858.[45] The Slavs definitely had kings and dukes before the German conquest.[46] Herrmann asked what happened to these rulers, and the answer seems to be that they were exterminated by the Germans.[47]

Gimbutas claims that the individual villages in the Sorben settlements formed a part of an exogamous clan, known in Slavic as a *Rodu*, that jointly controlled forests, pastures, and wider settlements. If an act of violence was committed against a family or the clan as a whole, blood vengeance was called for as a matter of natural defense.[48]

According to Roman sources, the Sorben tribes were governed by kings and dukes. Below these were another class of *primores*, or "prominent people."[49] According to Widukind, Markgraf Gero invited thirty-eight of these chieftains to a banquet, got them thoroughly inebriated, and then had them all slain.[50] Schlesinger believes that these upper classes among the Sorben were all eliminated during the Frankish and Saxon conquests, but in time a new feudal leadership emerged from within the Sorben ranks. This was a natural development,

since the Germans did not know the Sorben language, and were initially interested mainly in tribute and in tithes paid to the church. Thus somewhat by
default the Slavs continued to live under their own laws and customs. The Sorben were allowed to govern their own settlements, collect the necessary
Abgaben (the agreed tribute), and the tithe.[51]

There were variations in Slavic home construction and systems of defense.
Most of the Sorben built their houses of logs, while the nobility used stone as
building material. In the common dwellings, which were square in shape, the
roofs were supported by central posts. The size of a house was about 16 meters
square, with an entrance to the south or east. At first these homes were partly
subterranean; in later periods they built them above ground. Inside the average
house, in one corner they had a partly sunken hearth built of stones, which
heated the whole structure.[52]

The Sorben learned to build strong, well-constructed castles long before they
settled in the Saale, Mulde, and Elbe valleys. Schlesinger believes they may
have learned much about castle construction from the Romans during their
migration through the Danube valley. The *Mühlhauser Reichsrechtbuch*,
edited by Herbert Meyer, reveals that there were Sorben east of the Saale as of
A.D. 632.[53] Grimm claims that Wogatisburg existed in Bohemia as early as 631,
and the specialized studies of Schwarz and Käubler have confirmed this.[54] The
Frankish leader of the Slavs, Samo, also mentioned this fortress in his description of the defeat of Frankish king Dagobert near Kaaden.[55] Gimbutas has
described extensive excavations which show that the eastern branch of the Sorben built large hilltop forts that provided refuge for up to five thousand people.
A fortress on the banks of the Morava River controlled all the neighboring
lands, and even sent envoys to the imperial assembly in Frankfurt in 822.[56]
Later, the great Moravian Empire expanded its sovereignty into the Nitra
region of Slovakia, and between the year 875 and 884 extended its power into
Bohemia, Lusatia, Silesia, and the Kraków region of Poland. Its furthest eastern
penetration was into western Hungary, up to Lake Balaton.[57] Recent excavations have shown that the Moravian Empire flourished at a very advanced level
between the seventh and ninth centuries.[58]

Schlesinger claims that the Sorben between the Saale and the Elbe rivers
were well-defended by a number of *Burgen* in the early days of their settlement. When the Saxons besieged the Sorben castle of Kesigesburg, they took
possession of not only it, but also eleven other Slavic fortresses.[59] Doubtless the
early Sorben had many types of *Fluchtburgen*, strongholds for refuge in times
of emergency, though today few can be identified with any degree of accuracy.[60]

There may have been some direct relationship between early Slavic fortress-
building and that by the Franks in the later Merovingian and early Carolingian
periods. The Slavic fortresses must have seemed quite formidable, and this may
have caused the Franks to fear western expansion by the Sorben and build their
own strongholds. Charlemagne extended the line of defensive positions, which
have been identified by the excavator Schuchhart.[61] We can understand why
protection was necessary, for Erfurt was already a trade center in 805, while

Magdeburg's marketplace began in 806. Charlemagne built a bridge over the Elbe near Magdeburg and protected it with two castles. After that the emperor built additional castles near Magdeburg and Halle.[62] In 839 Thuringia was set up as a mark, which by the middle of the century was ruled by a Markgraf named Thakulf, whom contemporaries called "the duke of Sorben limits."[63] All this seems to point to the fact that later Carolingians feared further westward expansion by the Slavs.

During the reign of the Saxon emperors in the early *Kaiserzeit*, when the Avars overran the Slavic and German lands with their swift cavalry, there was a further impulse among the Sorben to protect their property and homes with additional *Burgen*.[64] This was also the motivation that sparked construction of the formidable German *Burgward* system, which soon dotted the river valleys of the Saale, Mulde, and Elbe. Herrmann published an excellent chart which reveals that, between the tenth and twelfth centuries, many of the former Slavic *Burgen* had been integrated into the new *Burgward* system of the German Kaisers, through which they now controlled all the Sorben lands. The chart shows that just below the site of Wittenberg on the Elbe stood three of these *Burgwarden*, while close by was a cluster of six more castles. As one turns south from Wittenberg, ten more *Burgen* controlled the Mulde valleys, while on the eastern banks of the Saale, twenty-two *Burgwarden* were scattered along its shores, up to Magdeburg. Besides these, five more *Burgen* were placed in Thuringia west of the Saale. This adds up to a chain of twenty-seven fortresses that protected the older part of the *Reich* all along the Saale River. Two additional fortresses can be observed that guarded the juncture of the Mulde with the Elbe, while a cluster of five controlled the confluence of the Saale with the Elbe further north. By A.D. 1200 an additional thirty *Burgwarden* controlled the upper part of Electoral Saxony, guarding it from hostile attacks from the Slavic tribes of the north.[65] This offered a strong system of defense, and may explain why the Sorben did not get involved in the later Slavic uprisings in the north.

Schlesinger's study also contains an excellent chart of the *Burgen* that existed in Sorben lands around the year 1000.[66] One notes on this map that vast regions south of Wittenberg and to the west, especially in the Mulde River valley, were still covered with forests. But the lands along the banks of the Elbe, where Wittenberg was soon to emerge as the capital of the *Kurkreis*, had been cleared. Since the Sorben had arrived in the area around A.D. 600, the region must have been under cultivation for centuries before Wittenberg was founded. The lands would have been filled with scattered hamlets that later clustered around the *Lutherstadt*. By 1040, a wide strip of land had been cleared all along the Elbe, even up to Dohna castle, below Meissen. By 1004 Torgau had its own castle. Doubtless there was Elbe River communication along the Elbe between the Torgau market and an even older one in Magdeburg, which existed as early as A.D. 806. The river road between these two must also have been in use by merchants. Coming up from Torgau, the Elbe makes a sharp bend to the west at Wittenberg. Here an early market must have been located on the white sand hill for which the later Wittenberg was named.

The names of the *Burgen* that existed in the *Kurkreis* around the year 1000 have been placed on a chart by Heinz Quirin; these assist us to form a mental picture of conditions in this region at that date. According to Quirin's findings, in the year 1004, a few miles west of later Wittenberg, stood the *Burg* Wöelitz; a bit to the south stood Pratau, Eutzsch, Rakith, and Trebitz; then, to the east of the Elbe, before its confluence with the Schwarze Elster, stood Klöden. It is of interest that Quirin did not date the first Wittenberg castle prior to 1187. Around Torgau, by the year 1004, there was the castle Supitz, while the castle Graditz was located on the right bank of the Elbe River. Nearby, the Slavs had two more: Elsnig, which had been built in 981, and Zwethau, dating to the same period.[67]

In the beginning, Sorben kings had their own fortresses; then came the *Herrenburgen* of the nobility, and finally the *Landesburgen* or *Fluchtburgen* of the *Bauern* (larger landowners) and the rest of the population.[68] *Burgen* may also be classified according to time periods. Thus from A.D. 700 to 900 we can designate Slavic *Burgen* as fortified settlements. This applied to communities before they enjoyed much protection from their kings and nobility. In the beginning, castle construction was often simple, consisting of an embankment with a moat in front. Since such *Burgwallen* could be constructed by using earth excavated from the moat to build the embankment, the enclosures were often quite extensive, protecting both fields and hamlets. A second type of *Burg*, the supervisory type, arose between A.D. 800 and 900. These fortresses were built for Slavic kings and ranking dukes, after the Sorben became governed by sovereign princes. In the age of feudalism, the Germans integrated the Slavic defenses into their new *Burgward* system. Slavic officials were now employed as nobles, knights, craftsmen, merchants, and menial servants, residing near the nobles' *Burgen*. Before long these dwellings formed a regular town attached to the castle. Such "suburb"-type *Burgen* flourished between A.D. 1000 and 1100. After that, feudalism underwent further changes, as the nobility built their own castles, from which they could defy the king or any Markgraf who challenged their territorial claims. In this system, Slavic nobles and knights maintained their place in the region, and their castles continued to serve an auxiliary purpose.[69]

German historians do not agree on how the Sorben reacted to German conquests. They had enjoyed an independent existence for more than four hundred years, so it must have been difficult for them to have been slowly melded into a new and strange feudal system during the tenth and eleventh centuries. H. Helbig claims that there was little conflict between older Slavic and later German settlements, that there was a gradual compromise in ways of life. Herrmann's investigations have led to a different conclusion: that the Sorben *Bauern*, the larger landowners, resisted feudalism, which they regarded as an attempt to overthrow their institutions. It was one thing to conquer a Sorben army, but quite another to send officials into a hostile community to collect taxes and tithes. Some were driven out of Sorben villages, others were murdered. Tensions grew to the point which the bishopric of Meissen even repurchased some villages in which the feudal lords had been overly aggressive. The Sorben tribes insisted on their centuries-old settlement rights (*Stamm-*

rechte), so the German *Sachsenspiegel* (the old Saxon law code) was not easily applied to them.[70] The Slavs, the Flemish, and the Germans all lived in the Sorben lands, and each of these peoples lived under a different type of legal system. They operated with the law codes based on the conditions under which they originally settled. Over all of them was the church's canon law—at least once the settlers had become Catholic.[71] The *Sachsenspiegel* classified the Sorben into two groups: the "free upper classes" and the "unfree lower classes." The law also required that trials among Slavs be conducted in their own language.[72]

The word *Villa* appears quite often in the sources, especially in ecclesiastical documents covering land grants. In Schlesinger's findings, the word seems to have been the equivalent of the German word *Dorf.* But he points out that among the Franks, the word *Villa* meant a group of settlements by different families that cooperated with one another. The land the Sorben tilled lay all around the inner settlement of a Slavic village. This arrangement continued prior to the changes made by the Germans under feudalism.[73] A resurvey of Slavic lands after 1100 was ordered by the ruling lords, bringing a basic transformation in Slavic life.[74] Whole regions made up of many *Dörfer* were reassigned and moved by feudal lords. This took place in the bishopric of Meissen and involved many *Villae.* At Altkirchen, in the *Reich's* Pleiszengau, such a transaction occurred under Bishop Udo, involving 33 villages.[75]

The studies of H. P. Schmid have revealed an interesting form of ecclesiastical organization, which was later reintroduced during the Reformation. Prior to this the Germans had financed their clergy by tithes based on *Hufen*, while the Slavs had used the *Dorf* to establish a *Pfarrkirche*, in which the *Pfarrer*, or pastor, was financed by the Slavic *Dorf.* Among the Sorben the union of homes formed a small economic unity, a kind of farmers' union of families, who together supported their *Pfarrkirche.*[76]

In the early *Kaiserzeit*, when the Sorben *Villa* had been brought into the orbit of the church, the Slavic community was only obligated to pay a lump sum, called a *Solidus*; but by 1162 the church would no longer allow lump-sum payments, because too much income was lost for the church. The result was the forced land survey that divided the Slavic lands into *Hufen*, so that a direct return could be exacted for every unit involved. This increased the tithe tremendously and made it necessary to appoint new officials for the villages. These were made responsible for specified sums, even when a town failed to meet its quota.[77]

The new *Hufen* surveys must have been made in the twelfth century. In the royal *Fiskus* of the *Pleiszengau*, the first reference to such a land division was in 1119, at the cloister of Bosau; a similar survey was undertaken at that time at Zwickau. The Altenburg tithe was also collected on the basis of *Hufen.* The records of the bishopric of Naumburg show that sometime after 1200 the Sorben were making payments in kind and not in lump sums as they had formerly done.[78] This system still prevailed in the days of the Reformation with regard to the *Stift* of the Castle Church at Wittenberg. The elector used the income to finance the University of Wittenberg.[79]

In the later period the Slavic community was also required to give service (German, *Wachdienst*; Latin, *publicae vigiliae*) to the Markgraf or to the immediate nobility. This was still the common practice in Wittenberg in Luther's day; men were posted at specific places on the town walls at night, and at the tower gates.[80]

Under feudalism, the German nobility seems to have used Slavic lawyers and knights to carry out tax collections and handle legal battles. By 1181 there was an official known as the *Supane* (German, *Eldesten*), a senior legal assessor who presided over the Sorben court sessions, known as *Landdings*.[81] Bernhard of Ascania, the first elector of the new Saxony, used these officials to settle land disputes. They seem to have presided over court sessions held at the seats of *Burggrafen*. Such courts had extensive powers, involving even corporal punishment. Both German and Slavic defendants appeared before them.[82] Closely related to these courts were Slavic officials known as the *Withasii* (German, *Witsessen*). These seem to have been knights who rendered equestrian service in the marks, possibly serving as assessors and military controllers in land disputes.[83]

The existence of lay legal assessors such as the *Supane* and *Witsessen* implies the existence of an assessors court. Land in the *Dörfer* was divided by fiefs, which were held in feudal obligation. Such a setup was controlled by the *Supane* and the *Witsessen*, who exercised legal service for the government over both free and unfree *Bauern*. Those officials seem to have been the regional chairmen in the assessors court.[84]

With the destruction of Sorben tribal organizations, the *Bauern* came under the control of the feudal lords. Some seem to have remained free farmers, but by the eleventh century, a lower class known as *Smurden* appears, who were the "unfree *Bauern*."[85] Perhaps the number of *Abgaben* had something to do with their impoverishment. Where formerly the *Bauern* may have gotten off fairly easily, later the only interest the nobility had in them was tribute, tithes, and whatever else they could collect. The emphasis had been placed on the acquisition of territory and power. After the year 1100, in the Saale, Mulde, and Elbe valleys, the *Bauern* were obligated to pay thirty kinds of taxes as *Abgaben*; on top of that the church also collected its tithes.[86] It is little wonder that some of the less successful *Bauern* became *Smurden*, that is, the "stinking ones."[87] By 1057 the *Bauern* were spoken of as forming two strata of Sorben society, those who were their own bosses and managed their own farms, the "free *Bauern*," and the *Smurden*, who were no longer their own bosses.[88]

To gain a correct picture of the *Bauern* in the *Kurkreis*, where the Ascanier ruled from 1180 until 1422, we must keep in mind that there were three types of farmers, though living apart in different individual communities: (a) the Sorben, the native settlers (who were by far the most numerous); (b) the Flemish settlers, who migrated into the region in the twelfth century; and (c) the Germans, who settled there, clearing parts of unclaimed forests after 1200 and later. The Slavic settlers, who had lived in the region since 600, were no doubt well-established. For at least three hundred years, from 600 to 900, they had lived there quite independently, under their own nobility. After the German conquest and the imposition of feudalism, things changed, though Sorben communities continued to exist under the supervision of the *Supane* and *Witsessen*. These, in turn, were accountable to the new feudal overlords, first the *Burggraf* and later the territorial prince.[89] The Flemish settlers, brought in during the rule of Albrecht the Bear, were regarded as latecomers. James W. Thompson has a very descriptive chapter on how the Flemish settlers were recruited and settled in the Slavic lands. The enticement of colonists resulted in quite a competition between Adolf of Holstein, Henry the Lion, Albrecht the Bear, and the highest-ranking clergy. The settlers were promised land that had been surveyed and laid out along streets, with new homes near the road and gardens, farmland, and woods behind. They were guaranteed their own legal system, imported from their homeland, as well as plows, axes, shovels, and other tools. They were given lowlands, for these Dutch and Flemish settlers knew how to drain swampy land that the Sorben had left untouched. The Slavs naturally looked down upon these recent immigrants. The *Fläming*, not too far north of Wittenberg, gives evidence of their settlement by the early Ascanier. However, from all the evidence available, the Slavic, Flemish, and German settlers lived peacefully, side-by-side, in different localities.[90]

Most of the German *Bauern* were also, relatively speaking, recent arrivals in the Wittenberg region. Before 1200 the German settlers were few. But as feudalism began to restrict the rights and movements of farmers in the already crowded west, many of them sought their fortunes in the unclaimed lands of the eastern marks. Often these settlers were welcomed by the Markgrafen of Meissen and the electors of Saxony to reclaim wild forest land. There is no real evidence that Germans, at this late date, were offered privileged treatment. By now the Sorben were well-acclimated to the feudal system, and to make a distinction between them and the Germans would have been abnormal.[91]

The average *Bauer* had at least two *Hufen* of land; but the more prosperous ones possessed from four to twelve *Hufen*.[92] A *Hufen* could vary from fifteen to one hundred and twenty *Morgen*, but was normally at least thirty *Morgen*. A *Morgen* represented a morning's work—the amount of land an ox could plow in a forenoon.[93]

A free *Bauer* was not obligated to do road service, or to perform duties around the lord's castle; neither was he asked to serve in the *Landding*. In comparison to the *Bauern*, the *Supane* possessed from two to four *Hufenland* (which seems to have been from twelve to twenty *Hacken* lands), and had relatively few obligations in *Abgaben*; however, like the *Witsessen*, they had duties to supervise the population and settle legal problems in the *Landding*.[94] Below the relatively prosperous *Bauern* were the *Smurden*, who had sunken into a status of less land and the carrying out of a number of duties. However, they were relatively free to manage their own farms.[95] These Sorben were tied to the soil, while in time the free *Bauern* also acquired the *Erbrecht*, the inheritance of their rights, which they could pass on to their children.[96]

Among the Slavs in the early period was another class of settlers, known as *dediti* (German *Deditzen*), who in the earliest period were beekeepers and fishermen. In pre-feudal days they seem to have been a class closely associated with the kings and nobility, and were ranked as important subjects. They cannot be called *Bauern*, as their land possessions were relatively small. They were assigned regions in which they collected honey and paid their tithe to the church.[97] The right of being an *Imker* (beekeeper) became hereditary. If there were a number of sons, the professions were divided, both as to location and the nature of their work. If the chief *Imker* died, the supervisory position often passed to a brother, a practice that even continued in the cloisters of Slavic origin.[98] The *Deditzen* were freemen, making them equal in rank to the *Bauern*. Schlesinger claims the *Imkers* were later organized into four guilds covering the Slavic lands, referred to in Slavic as *Starastien*. Membership in the guilds was not hereditary. In some places these beekeepers may also have ranked as *Supane*.[99] There is evidence that, during later centuries, the *Deditzen* class possessed a few *Hufen* of land, and that some even served as judges and vassals in the feudal system.[100] The guild under which they operated was designated as the *Starastie*, and it controlled all aspects of their profession.[101]

As of A.D. 1426, each St. Martin's day, certain fishermen in Lower Lausitz were obliged to pay their lord a tax on their fisher's trade; but these fishermen are also classified as *Deditzen*, which indicated a double profession of some *Imkers*. But in the same region these *Deditzen* were already living in the suburbs. This may mean that some *Imkers* by the fifteenth century were already moving to the suburbs of rapidly growing cities, where "unfree Slavs" also had an opportunity to rise as freemen.[102]

It is still unclear exactly how the original Sorben society was organized before the Frankish and later German conquests. Did the Sorben live in small tribal groups after their original settlement? Was there a king or duke over each one of these units? We do not know whether the original government extended beyond the village confines, or whether, at the time of the migrations in the seventh century, the rulers directed the forest clearings and the formation of villages. Neither do we know how these hundreds of Slavic *Dörfer*, the little hamlets scattered throughout the woods, were related to the *Fluchtburgen*. Without a doubt, in the formative period, the influence of the kings and dukes must have been very strong; but how the chiefs became their leaders is also unknown. Did their rise result from superior might, or was it brought about by an election? One thing seems clear: judging by their relations with the Franks, the kings governed whole settlements of villages, and offered them defense in times of attack. Their relationship may have been similar to that which existed among the Teutons during the early *Kaiserzeit*, under Henry I and Otto the Great, where the right of inheritance and right of election were taken for granted.[103]

Even though we lack definite information on many aspects of early and later Sorben society, much information has been extrapolated from evidence. Herrmann, in his long study of written records and excavations, has tried to give us a view of the various layers of Sorben society as it may have existed prior to and after its absorption into feudalism. His finds indicate that: (1) there existed during the migrations and some time afterward in the Slavic settlements an upper layer of tribal chiefs, referred to in contemporary sources as kings and dukes; (2) immediately below these chiefs existed a layer of Sorben nobility, who were the kings' officials and who lived, like the kings and dukes, from the *Abgaben*, payments in kind made by the villages below them; (3) still another layer, smaller in size, were the elders and knights in the days of feudalism, who had risen from the ranks and controlled the villages and regions to which they had been assigned. This class was able to take over after the upper layers had been wiped out by the German conquests. The German nobility placed the members of the lower classes in *Dörfer* as *Supane* and *Witsessen*, to collect *tithes* and taxes in kind from the *Bauern*, the *Smurden* and the *Deditzen*; (4) below them was quite a large layer of free *Bauern*, men who owned their lands and were quite free in that they were exempt from duties outside of farming; (5) then came the *Deditzen*, the beekeepers and fishermen, who were quite free during the pre-conquest period, but later declined to a lower level during feudalism; (6) below them was a level of poor farmers, known as the *Smurden*, who had no doubt once been free, but were no longer; they had many assigned duties on roads and around the castles of the nobility; finally, (7) there were "unfree" house servants and slaves, who performed menial tasks around the homes and castles of the *Burggrafen* and the feudal lords. One should add that, during high feudalism, with the growth of cities around the *Burgen*, a new class of craftsmen, merchants, and townsmen arose, many of whom were Slavic in origin. Together these classes composed a mixed population in the later Middle Ages.[104]

The assessment of the relative advancement of a people in civilization and culture is not simple. It presupposes having a standard of comparison in the form of an exact knowledge of related, neighboring peoples. After decades of excavations in this century, the need for a reevaluation of the Sorben civilization cannot be disputed. A few balanced attempts have been made in this direction. The fine book by the Polish historian Witold Hensel, *Die Slawen im frühen Mittelalter: Ihre materielle Kultur,* is just such an attempt.[105] The emphasis is placed on Polish and Russian Slavs, but the author also displays a mastery of Slavic civilizations in the Balkans, Moravia, Slovakia, Bohemia, and even the Sorben lands. This volume is filled with detailed data of Slavic accomplishments in the many professional crafts, which he profusely illustrates with photographs of excavated sites and objects. He makes the claim that, in their civilization and culture, the Slavs in the Balkans, Poland, Moravia, Bohemia, and the Elbe valley were equally advanced as—and, in many professions, even surpassing—their German conquerors. Since the book was originally written in Slavic, the author is familiar with early Slavic expressions and terms, throwing much light on institutions and culture. One also detects a slight national bias in favor of Polish and Russian accomplishments. But this does not detract from the singular merits of the work.

The reader is already familiar with two equally fine German attempts at a reassessment of Slavic culture, the works by Herrmann and Schlesinger, whose

merit for us consists in the fact that they are thoroughly familiar with the literature and have likewise mastered, to a remarkable degree, the contributions of
recent excavations. They offer the added advantage of concentrating on the
Sorben civilization and culture that existed in the Saale and Elbe River valleys.

Joachim Herrmann's *Die Slawen in Deutschland: Ein Handbuch*, is a classic in
its interpretation of Sorben culture.[106] Its balanced approach and profuse illustrations of excavated evidence make it an invaluable asset to anyone wanting to
obtain an accurate impression of what Sorben life was like from A.D. 600 until its
melding with feudal medieval culture. Finally, there is Walter Schlesinger's
interpretation of Slavic institutions, *Mitteldeutsche Beiträge zur deutschen Ver-
fassungsgeschichte*.[107] This is an excellent supplement to Herrmann's volume. To
the best of our knowledge, these three scholars offer the most balanced, well-
rounded picture available of Sorben civilization.

What is now known about Sorben civilization and culture requires an entirely
new assessment as to the origin of Wittenberg, the city that became the center
of the Reformation in the sixteenth century. We can no longer consider the
Lutherstadt to have been a previously undeveloped region in which Albrecht
the Bear had planted a few Flemish settlements. The Sorben had occupied
hundreds of *Dörfer* and many fortresses in that region for more than three centuries. This also makes it more understandable why Bernhard of Ascania, after
becoming the new elector of Saxony, decided to attach his new title to the
region that was to become the future *Kurkreis*.[108] That the civilization of the
Slavs had become as advanced in this region as it had elsewhere may safely be
assumed, for it had been more than three hundred years since the first settlers
had arrived there. Until the thirteenth century the Sorben made up nine-tenths
of the population; therefore they must have played a vital role in the layout and
development of the electoral town of Wittenberg. In this process they would
have brought to bear much of the cultural heritage of their eastern ancestors.
Of particular note are the impressive accomplishments of the Moravian civilization, referred to earlier in this chapter.[109] There is now ample evidence to prove
that the Moravian Empire was extremely advanced.

The question might naturally be asked, Was the culture and civilization that
flourished both in Moravia and Bohemia also found in the lands that later
became Electoral Saxony? The answer must be in the affirmative. Herrmann
reports how excavations in the Dessau-Mosigkau region have established that
the Sorben around Saxony had made similar progress. Both Hensel[110] and
Herrmann[111] claim that Slavic civilization developed quite uniformly throughout the eastern lands. Herrmann believes that the original settlements were
only a beginning of the migrations from Bohemia. Although it is impossible to
reconstruct the exact state of advancement of Sorben culture at specific dates,
there can be no question that the Slavs played a vital role in the creation of the
environmental conditions in Electoral Saxony and Wittenberg that existed by
the time of the Reformation.[112] The Sorben must have played an important role
in the original layout of the *Lutherstadt*, in the erection of the first *Rathaus*, and
in the construction of the castle and the *Pfarrkirche*.

4

The Origins
of Electoral Saxony

Electoral Saxony was that region of the Ernestine lands in which the city and university of Wittenberg were located. In the early Middle Ages it was inhabited mostly by the Sorben. For a long time the Germans called the rather poorly defined area the *Ostmark*. It was controlled by the military might of the Saxon emperors, exercised through their resident feudal lords. After the region became Electoral Saxony (under the Ascanier, in the days of Frederick Barbarossa), the decentralizing tendencies of territorialism resulted in the disintegration of the medieval empire. This transformation permitted a shift in the center of gravity of the German *Reich* from the Rhine valley to the lands of the new territorial princes of the Slavic north. This was especially observable in Brandenburg, Bohemia, and the later Saxon lands.[1] Only by taking this change into account can one comprehend how, in 1521, Martin Luther could both be excommunicated by the papal bull *Decet* and condemned by the imperial Edict of Worms, yet still, after a short stay at the Wartburg, return to his university to live and work in relative peace. The "Luther problem" was discussed at the diets of Augsburg, Worms, and Speyer, yet both Maximilian I and Charles V hesitated to invade the electoral lands to arrest him. As elector and *Reichsvikar*, Frederick the Wise was practically an independent sovereign over his own lands, even as the margrave of Brandenburg and the duke of Albertine Saxony were over theirs. Circumstances in England and Bohemia prior to the sixteenth century made it impossible for similar protection to have been considered for John Wycliffe and Jan Hus. Martin Luther did not escape a violent end simply because Frederick the Wise accepted the Reformation, but because territorialism had become so powerful a force in the Holy Roman Empire that neither pope nor emperor could control an individual prince's actions.[2]

The Electorate of Saxony was established by Frederick Barbarossa at Gelnhausen in 1180. On that occasion Henry the Lion ceased to be duke over the duchies of Saxony and Bavaria, and the title was bestowed on Bernhard, the youngest son of Albrecht the Bear. In this chapter we will consider how "old Saxony" suddenly disappeared from the map of Germany and how the "new Saxony," which included the Wittenberg region, emerged.

In the *Staatsarchiv* in Düsseldorf lie the remains of a faded old parchment document known to scholars as the *Gelnhauser Urkunde*.[3] Its ornate red lettering, beautiful script, red ribbon, and golden seal all contribute to the conviction that it is an authentic document which originated in the chancellory of Frederick Barbarossa.[4] It is dated 13 April 1180, which indicates the exact date of the official dissolution of the old duchy of Saxony.[5] The document formalizes the actions taken by the emperor at Würzburg, when the Kaiser stripped Henry the Lion of his ducal titles, fiefs, and feudal privileges and gave them to other princes, leaving him only his allodial lands.

Unfortunately, through use, exposure, and neglect, the original copy of the *Gelnhauser Urkunde* soon began to fade. By 1375 its custodian in Cologne already had difficulty reading the faded sections; later, perhaps in the seventeenth century, some scribe took the liberty of retracing the faded, red letters with black ink.[6] The ink must have been of a poor quality, for soon the two inks faded into each other. The folds of the parchment also became badly worn, making the document scarcely legible.[7] In spite of these difficulties, scholars have recently done a marvelous job of reconstructing the text.[8] They treated the document with *Gallus* tincture and reconstructed the text with ultraviolet photography.[9]

Some background is necessary before discussing the fall of Henry the Lion. The period of the medieval empire from 919 to 1254, which includes the Saxon, Franconian, and Hohenstaufen dynasties, is known by Germans as the *Kaiserzeit*. The German Kaisers fought for centralization, while the princes struggled to preserve their Stem Duchies. The former represented the kingship, the latter the rights of princes. Since the kingship became hereditary, the rulers gained some advantage. But the growth of feudalism—if properly controlled—also offered real advantages to the king. Feudal lords assisted the monarchs in battles with the Slavic tribes in the north, went on expeditions into Italy to help subdue the cities of Lombardy, and, at times, even assisted the Kaisers in their struggles with the papacy.

The power of the clergy presented a problem for the emperors, as exemplified by the Investiture Controversy in the days of Henry IV.[10] During the early Middle Ages the emperor used the clergy and nobility as counterweights to balance one another. As feudalism progressed, kings started to use a new group of officials known as *ministeriales* in their crown lands. These were lay officials who represented the royal house in the various duchies.[11] The *ministeriales* usually occupied royal castles, were immune from the control of the nobility, and were generally disliked.

The Saxon dynasty began with Henry the Fowler in A.D. 919 and ended with the death of Henry II in 1024. The *Reich* was continued by the Franconian or Salien line of emperors, beginning with Conrad II in 1024 and ending with the death of Lothair II in 1139. Finally came the Hohenstaufen line, which began with Conrad III and ended with the death of Frederick II in 1254. Much of our attention in this chapter is focused on Frederick Barbarossa, the second Hohenstaufen king, who reigned from 1152 to 1190.

In the early *Kaiserzeit*, the German *Reich* was divided into six Stem Duchies. The duchies were ruled by dukes on behalf of the emperor.[12] At times, however, royal houses took over duchies themselves and ruled them through members of the royal families. In prehistoric times these dukes had been tribal chiefs; now they aimed to become princes. Accordingly, they tried many ways to liberate themselves from royal sovereignty.[13] Thus in the twelfth century Henry the Lion regarded himself more as a territorial prince than as a king's official.[14]

Such struggles for ducal independence increased during the conflict Henry III and Henry IV had with the papacy, a struggle that reached its summit at Canossa in 1077 under Pope Gregory VII.[15] But that struggle was limited to the upper layer of feudalism, for the Investiture Controversy was a contest between the pope and the emperor that left the territorial princes untouched.[16] Since the Concordat of Worms in 1122 did not even settle the controversy at the royal level, it hardly applied to the lands of the feudal lords. The same was true of the ecclesiastical and lay princes. Thus the real victors in the investiture struggle were the territorial princes, for they could now curb even the power of the church in their lands. In general, the emphasis in the *Reich* was now on the acquisition of lands and castles, the control of courts, and the coinage of money; in short, the goal was to acquire enough power to establish princes on an independent footing and give them real control. This territorialism applied not only to the older parts of the *Reich*, but also to the Slavic north.[17]

The conflict between Frederick Barbarossa and Henry the Lion had its roots far back in the German empire.[18] The real cause was a disagreement over how much kings could meddle in ducal affairs. The rivalry grew out of an earlier struggle between the Guelfs and Ghibellines in Lombardy; it had an Italian counterpart, and this was the reason the Staufer also had his troubles there. In the previous Franconian period, under King Lothair II, the Welf leader was Henry the Proud, the son-in-law of the Kaiser. Since Lothair II had no male heirs, he designated Henry the Proud as his successor. Henry was already duke of both Saxony and Bavaria; in addition, he possessed the Matildan Tuscan lands. The German electorate feared the Welf because of his wealth and power. Accordingly, when Lothair died, they chose Conrad III of Hohenstaufen—a Swabian—as his successor. Conrad soon began to cut Henry the Proud down to size.

First he separated Brandenburg from "old Saxony," and later, Austria from Bavaria. At a later *Reichstag* in Würzburg the *Reich* decided that a duke could rule over only one duchy, and Henry was given a choice between Saxony and Bavaria. He refused, took to the sword, and was killed in battle. At the time of Duke Henry's death, Henry the Lion was a mere boy. Before Conrad III died (from exposure, while participating in the Second Crusade), he designated Frederick Barbarossa as his successor. The German electorate granted the dead Kaiser's wish.[19]

The eminent nineteenth-century historian Wilhelm von Giesebrecht devoted an entire volume of his monumental series *The History of the German Kaisers* to the period of Frederick Barbarossa.[20] He states that in Frankfurt a.M. on 4 March 1152 there was great rejoicing over the Staufer's election. Frederick's uncle was Henry the Proud, and many saw in his choice the termination of the Welf-Ghibelline struggle. His contemporaries were agreed on Frederick's qualifications and expected that he would bear the crown in glorious fashion. The young Staufer was gifted and decisive, possessing a keen intellect and expressing himself with eloquence. He had a magnetic personality and was a religious man. James Westfall Thompson adds that Frederick was an expert horseman.[21]

The principal figures involved in the downfall of Henry the Lion were Conrad of Wettin, Albrecht the Bear, Archbishop Philip of Cologne, Bishop Ulrich of Halberstadt, and Bernhard and Siegfried of Ascania.[22] Several of these men were unusually strong historical figures, which was noted in the contemporary adage:

> Heinrich der Leuw und Albrecht der Bär
> Dartho Frederick, de mit dem roden Haar
> Dat waren dree Heeren
> Die Kunden de Welt verkehren.[23]

Behind Henry the Lion's truculent attitude toward the crown lay much Saxon history. Saxony had even rebelled against Henry IV in 1075, and had met with a humiliating defeat. But this was only round one in the contest between Saxony and the future emperors.

In the late Franconian and early Hohenstaufen era, the contestants in Saxony were Henry the Proud, of the Welf family, and Albrecht the Bear of the house of Ballenstedt. The latter was related to the centuries-old Billung family through his mother.[24] Albrecht's father was Otto the Rich, the count of Ballenstedt, and his mother was Eilika, the daughter of Magnus Billung. Otto the Rich had been duke of Saxony for a while under King Conrad II, and Albrecht held that position for a short while under Conrad III of Hohenstaufen.[25] The Billung and Welf families were really interrelated.[26] Albrecht the Bear married Sophia of Hohenstaufen, who is believed to have been a sister of Frederick Barbarossa.[27] Albrecht the Bear was not given his nickname because of his outstanding courage, but to distinguish him from Henry the Lion.[28] Albrecht was awarded Brandenburg because of his loyal support for Frederick's Italian campaigns.[29] His family was large, numbering seven boys and five girls. Of the seven boys, only three are known to history: Otto, the oldest, who became margrave of Brandenburg; Siegfried, the archbishop of Bremen; and Bernhard, the youngest, duke of Saxony.[30] Albrecht's sons were rewarded for their loyalty to the Kaiser; they attended him on campaigns and visited the *Reichstagen*, where Henry's fate was discussed and finally settled.[31]

Since Albrecht the Bear died in 1170, he was spared the conflict that determined the fate of his long, bitter rival. Albrecht spent his later days cultivating good relations with Christian Slavic chiefs and subduing hostile forces in Pomerania and Brandenburg.[32]

Early in the Middle Ages, the divisional lines between marks were not well-fixed, but by Albrecht's day the boundaries between the eastern marks were more carefully distinguished. A keen rivalry had developed between the counts of Meissen and Thuringia and the officials who supervised Albrecht's lands.[33] The struggle involved Bernhard's lands in the Saale-Elbe region, which he had inherited from his grandfather Otto and his father.[34] We have also seen that he had legal claim to a region around Wittenberg.[35]

The relatives of Henry the Proud, the father of Henry the Lion, were known in their Italian lands as the Guelfs; but they were called Welfs in German lands. Their opponents are known as the Ghibellines. The Welfs were supported by the pope in their contest with the emperors. Because Henry the Proud was the son-in-law of Emperor Lothair II, he was made duke of both Saxony and Bavaria, and expected to become emperor upon the death of Lothair II, whom Henry had enthusiastically supported. But territorialism was already making itself felt, and rival nobles feared him. So upon the death of Lothair, Conrad III of Hohenstaufen was elected Kaiser. At a packed diet presided over by Conrad III, Henry was also deprived of Bavaria.[36] He then challenged his opponents, and in a civil war Henry the Proud was killed.[37] This was very unfortunate for the Welf family, because at the time Henry the Lion was a mere boy.[38] Conrad III was then succeeded by his nephew, Frederick Barbarossa.

Space does not permit a detailed account of the complicated history of Frederick Barbarossa's reign. It involved changes in internal policy, the subduing of the Slavs in the Rügen region, and five Italian campaigns. We are principally interested in seeing why "old Saxony" fell apart with the downfall of Henry the Lion. Even more puzzling is how this breakup resulted in the historical transplantation of the title to the "new Saxony," located on the Elbe River around what later became Wittenberg.

Henry the Lion, son of Henry the Proud, was Frederick Barbarossa's cousin. He was considerably younger than the Staufer.[39] Frederick was a keen judge of human nature and fully aware of the devastating effect of the former strife between Henry the Proud and Conrad III over the duchies of Saxony and Bavaria. Accordingly, he decided to befriend his cousin rather than continue the old Welf-Waibeling strife.[40] He attempted to placate his young Welf cousin by returning both duchies and working closely with him. After that, Henry proved loyal for twenty years, accompanying the Kaiser on the first four Italian campaigns (between 1154 and 1168). He also played a vital role in the conquest of the northern Slavic tribes.[41]

After 1168 Henry went on a trip to the Holy Land;[42] but upon his return, Henry's attitude had changed.[43] The reasons are not clear from contemporary evidence.[44] A recent historian, Edita Gronen, believes it was partly due to the fact that Henry had become a powerful territorial prince. He had even enhanced his prestige by marrying the oldest daughter of King Henry II, the most powerful of the medieval English monarchs. Through these connections

Henry might have become involved in English foreign policy, attempting to circumvent Frederick's control over Lombardy by blocking the Alpine passes.[45] How much validity such a thesis has is difficult to assess, for most of the basic evidence is lacking.[46] Henry's problem may have been that his attitude became similar to that of his father, Henry the Proud. It could well be that King Henry II of England encouraged his son-in-law to defy the emperor, for he offered the duke a haven after he was expelled from the *Reich*.[47]

That Henry the Lion had built up a powerful territorial state in old Saxony and the eastern Slavic lands must have been evident not only to neighboring princes but also to Frederick Barbarossa.[48] Judging from Helmold's descriptions of Henry in *The Chronicle of the Slavs* and the complaints of rival feudal lords, there emerges a picture of a rather ruthless, modern-type territorial prince, with little regard or respect for his German and Slavic subjects or for his neighbors.[49]

One of Frederick's problems grew out of an attempt to force his "Grand Design" for the Holy Roman Empire upon the culturally advanced Lombard cities. They resented this and engaged in a struggle for their own independence.[50] The barrier of the Alps made control of the rival Guelf-Ghibelline factions in Lombardy even more difficult. Since the days of the Saxon Ottos, this ambition had proved costly to the German empire in both men and resources. This was intensified with Frederick's revival of the old ambitions of the Kaisers to force the Italian cities into submission.[51]

We noted that Frederick had received the enthusiastic support of his Welf cousin on four Italian expeditions.[52] Henry the Lion and Albrecht the Bear had also combined forces to help the *Reich* subdue the last of the Slavic tribes. During this period the temple of Rethra was captured and destroyed, a site that was recently excavated by Carl Schuchhart.[53] Thus in the days of the Hohenstaufen the final Slavic resistance was broken. Accordingly, the Kaiser had every reason to count on Henry's cooperation and to be well-satisfied with his cousin's loyalty.[54]

Upon the termination of the fourth Italian expedition in 1166, Henry ventured on a private crusade to the Holy Land. There he was honored with the pomp and splendor of a king, which must have increased his arrogance.[55] Upon his return from the Middle East, his marriage to the daughter of Henry II of England may have added to his high-handedness, for now he even dared to criticize Frederick's Lombard policies.[56] Some historians also accuse Frederick of political maneuvering while Henry was in the Holy Land, aspiring to take over his possessions.[57]

One of the principal challenges that faced the German emperors after the Investiture Controversy was the papacy. Generally speaking it had been Welf in its outlook, for it strongly opposed the ambitious plans of Frederick's "Grand Design."[58] The pope had aroused the Lombard cities to erect Alexandria, which even assumed the name of the pontiff.[59] To force the cities into submission, the Staufer embarked on his fifth Italian expedition, and also the so-called Chiavenna affair, in which Henry is reputed to have refused to participate.

The chroniclers of the Staufer's day were hardly historians. They were familiar with the Guelf-Ghibelline strife from the time of Henry the Proud, which they felt continued to smolder beneath the surface. Various versions of the Chiavenna affair were being turned into a series of legends. The next generation of chroniclers wrote during the civil war that broke out between the Kaiser's sons after his death. These added still more legends, while embellishing the older ones. This episode has now been completely rejected by modern historians.[60]

The story, according to the legends, was used as an explanation of the *Gelnhauser Urkunde* until modern times. In brief, the account goes as follows. Before Frederick Barbarossa embarked on his fifth Italian campaign, he realized he needed more troops. Accordingly, in 1175 he summoned Henry to Chiavenna for help in subduing the Lombard League. Supposedly Frederick asked Henry personally, but the Welf remained cool and indifferent. Some sources claim that after this Frederick even fell on his knees and begged Henry to support him with his Saxon forces. It was also said that Henry asked the emperor to cede Goslar and the silver mine at the Rommelsberg to him as the price of his cooperation.[61]

Modern historians began exploring the evidence and slowly rejected one aspect of this tradition after another. Von Sybel stressed that, according to feudal law, Henry was not obligated to go on any Italian expedition. Furthermore, both von Sybel and Ficker concluded that Henry was actually opposed to both the fruitless Italian campaigns and Frederick's Grand Design.[62] Peter Munz, in his fine recent biography, *Frederick Barbarossa*, has thoroughly exploded the old thesis that Henry the Lion's fall was due to the Chiavenna affair, which may not have happened at all.[63]

Modern historians believe that the defeat at Legnano forced the Kaiser to make his peace with Pope Alexander III in Venice. It gave Frederick cause for much soul-searching that, in time, led to his discarding of the Grand Design.[64] His representatives then engaged in some preliminary skirmishing at Anagni for a favorable settlement with the pope,[65] while the troops of Christian of Mainz occupied and held Frederick's Matildan lands.[66] Meanwhile, by the time of the Peace of Venice in 1177, Frederick had developed a new peace plan that fit much better into the developing scheme of feudalism. The emperor decided to make his peace with the pope, grant the Lombard League a truce of six years, and grant Sicily peace for fifteen years. But the Kaiser insisted, in a secret agreement, that the pope allow him to continue his rule over the Matildan lands.[67]

Since such a settlement granted the pope's demands and gave the Lombard cities quite a breathing spell, the proposal was accepted. A strong element of Frederick's bargaining power was the fact that the Matildan lands lay outside the boundaries of the Lombard League; besides, they were already being occupied by Christian of Mainz's troops.[68] After a draft document was signed and sworn to by both representatives, Frederick came to Venice in the doge's galley and was received with great pomp and splendor by Pope Alexander III. The emperor removed his purple coat, prostrated himself, and kissed the pope's feet; they then embraced while the crowd sang the *Te Deum*. Thus, with bells ringing, the Staufer was received back into the bosom of the Roman church. On

1 August 1177 oaths were made in the patriarch's palace, and the schism was again healed.[69]

Frederick was now free to return to Germany. Though somewhat humbled, he was determined to set his German house in order in accordance with his revised feudal plans. To do this required several steps. He would have to determine which feudal lords to deprive of power and decide which noble families to cultivate in the future. Dungern's research led to the conclusion that some three hundred families had controlled feudalism for roughly three centuries, but many of the old blood lines had become impoverished and were hardly worthy of serious support by the crown. Meanwhile a new type of feudal lord had risen from the ranks of the *ministeriales*; these had become knights and acquired their own castles and manors; often they accomplished this by marrying the daughters of the dukes, counts, and barons who had originally employed them.[70]

On his return to Germany, Frederick stopped for a while in Burgundy to cement his hold on his wife Beatrix's lands; thus, before departing, the Staufer also had himself crowned as king of Burgundy. Later, in 1186, the emperor made his son Otto the count of Palatine, a transaction which implied that with the countship also went the Beatrix heritage.[71]

When Frederick finally arrived at Speyer on 11 November 1178, he was welcomed by many princes and feudal lords. At Speyer the Kaiser held his next *Reichstag*, during which many nobles who had been offended by Henry the Lion's actions brought charges against him. At the close of the meeting, Frederick summoned Henry to another *Reichstag*, at Worms in January 1179, to answer the charges. But Henry failed to appear at Worms. Frederick, perhaps remembering their years of friendship, decided to give Henry another chance. He summoned him to another meeting, to be held in June 1179 at Magdeburg. There his case was to be heard by a court in which his own Swabian tribesmen would be sitting as judges and his northern neighbors would be the accusers.[72]

It is doubtful that the Kaiser realized what Henry's reaction to his earlier summons would be, though he must have been fully aware of the duke's pride and power. The first hearings were not really trials. But the one scheduled for Magdeburg in June 1179 was to be a real trial, conducted in accordance with old tribal customs.[73] But Henry had been in Swabia not long before, and he had done extensive politicking behind the scenes. When the trial was to take place, to Frederick's surprise both Henry and his Swabians failed to appear. Thus there could be no trial. However, now Margrave Dietrich of Landsberg charged Henry with high treason and challenged him to a duel.[74]

Even though the Kaiser was aware of Henry's conspiracy with his Swabian tribesmen to circumvent the trial at Magdeburg, the Staufer seems to have wanted to give him another chance to clear himself. Accordingly, the king arranged for yet another meeting, at Kayna, a small place in the eastern Swabian region where Dietrich had many relatives. But even though, under feudal law, failure to appear for a duel amounted to an establishment of guilt, Henry disregarded the summons. The princes who were present were now ready to proclaim the defiant duke an outlaw; but because there were no Swabian judges present, no official proclamation could be made. Frederick was not ready for a military campaign to capture Henry, which such a proclamation would have implied.[75]

But Frederick was determined to bring the obstreperous Welf to justice. When Frederick summoned a new court hearing at Würzburg in January 1180, the judges were a new body composed of tenants-in-chief, holding fiefs directly under the king; they were a body of nobility who had to participate in the trial or else forfeit their vassalage. The Würzburg court was composed of new nobles of the territorial type from Swabia, Franconia, and Saxony. Since the emperor was now the plaintiff, he brought a variety of charges against Henry, including high treason.[76]

Meanwhile, reports had reached the king that Henry was engaged in new feuds with his ecclesiastical neighbors. At the Peace of Venice in 1177, Frederick and Pope Alexander III had agreed on a clause that angered Henry. During the long schism before 1177, Henry had removed Udalric of Halberstadt from his bishopric and replaced him with Gero, a personal appointee. Henry had also favored Gero with additional fiefs. Now that Pope Alexander III was in the saddle, he implemented the Venice clause, which deposed Gero and replaced him with Henry's enemy, Udalric. Udalric, in turn, claimed the additional lands that Gero had meanwhile acquired. At this point Henry attacked Udalric. Archbishop Philip of Cologne, who had also feuded with the Welf, entered the struggle, and now the duke was faced by a formidable alliance.[77]

At this point it was clear that the old tribal system of justice would not suffice.[78] There needed to be a new assessment of the German nobility, ecclesiastical and lay. Old families with much territory, prestige, and power—even with the titles of dukes and counts—could be made new tenants-in-chief; while those of old blood lines who had fallen into a state of dissolution would now be replaced by new territorial princes. In this new society that Frederick created, the tenants-in-chief and the counts and barons at lower levels were vassals of the crown, bound directly to Frederick by feudal oaths.[79] Under such a system the tenants-in-chiefs formed the new *Curia regis*, which was the body that met at Würzburg in January 1180. Quite naturally, Henry did not qualify for Frederick's new feudal state.[80]

Thus at Würzburg, Henry's whole status had changed; according to Erdmann, he was now being charged before the new *Curia regis* of the empire, a feudal court as opposed to the old tribal court. Under feudal law (still imperfectly formed), this court could deprive the Saxon duke of his title and all his fiefs, but could not touch his allodial lands. Henry had actually played into the Kaiser's hands through his "Swabian conspiracy."[81] The *Curia regis* decided that Henry was guilty of high treason, and that henceforth he should be deprived of his title, as well as the fiefs he held under the feudal system.[82] They were to revert back to the Kaiser, for his redistribution to other deserving feudal lords.[83]

But the verdict was not to be enforced immediately. Frederick extended his period of grace until the April meeting at *Gelnhausen*. According to Haller, under feudal law Henry had a year and a day during which he could renew his feudal oath. That period terminated at Gelnhausen.[84]

At the new Kaiserpfalz at Gelnhausen on 13 April 1180, the fate of Henry the Lion was to be settled. At Würzburg the emperor had already given his *Urteilsspruch*, the sentence that deprived Henry of his ducal titles and acquired his ducal fiefs in order to redistribute them—provided Henry did not appear at *Gelnhausen* to make his peace with the emperor. The *Gelnhauser Urkunde* states that Henry was guilty of defying a court summons and a number of different offenses.[85] Therefore judgment had finally been pronounced on the offender.

The Gelnhauser charter reveals that Bernhard of Ascania was designated the future duke of Saxony. The clause read as follows:

> Also by agreement with our favorite blood relative, Duke Bernhard, upon whom, in the presence of all, we bestowed the remaining part of the Duchy of Saxony, under the imperial seal, we have solemnly invested the aforementioned Archbishop Philip [of Cologne] with that portion of the former duchy, which of long standing had been gathered by his own church.[86]

Some modern historians have argued that Ducal Saxony, which had once been one of the original Stem Duchies, did not really exist any longer. They have claimed that the Saxony of the days of Hermann Billung and Otto the Great had already been broken into pieces by feudalism, and that apart from Henry the Lion's allodial lands, Saxony was being held together by Henry's power politics.[87] Be that as it may, says Güterbock, the Ascanier now reaped their reward:

> Especially the two brothers, who in the battle against Henry the Lion had advanced most vigorously, Bernhard and Siegfried, now plucked the fruits of their politics at *Gelnhausen* in April, 1180; both obtained their desired goals; Bernhard received what his father and grandfather had longed for, Ducal Saxony—of course in somewhat shrunken size; while Siegfried was made the Archbishop of Bremen.[88]

According to the charter, the Weser River was to constitute the dividing line; the lands to the west were to pass to the archbishop of Cologne, while those to the north were to belong to Bernhard of Ascania.[89] But so far the settlement was only on paper. Henry still had to be captured and subdued before the verdict became a reality.

Soon after, in June 1180, the emperor held another *Reichstag*, at Ratisbon, to settle the Bavarian question. There Henry was to have another chance. But once again the proud duke failed to appear. Accordingly, Frederick turned over the major part of Bavaria to his friend and fellow warrior, Otto of Wittelsbach, investing him as the new duke of Bavaria. The Styria part of the former Bavaria was separated and given to the counts of Andechs, who became imperial princes with the titles of dukes.[90]

However, these official court actions did not settle matters with Henry. The proud Welf was quite confident that he could hold his own in spite of his condemnation. In accordance with the *Gelnhausen* verdict, on July 25 an imperial campaign was launched against him.[91] Frederick's forces began to move to the north, but there was no actual confrontation between the two armies. The Kaiser's *Reichsheer* came to the aid of Bishop Adalric of Halberstadt, and neighboring feudal lords became uneasy about their status as vassals in the new feudal system. Giesebrecht, who described the campaign in detail, related that many nobles joined the Kaiser and turned over their castles.[92] Henry II of England tried to persuade France and Flanders to come to Henry's aid, but nothing came of it.[93] Lübeck was besieged by royal forces and capitulated.[94] Even Northalbinga, Henry's stronghold, could not rescue him, and the whole north caved in.[95]

Henry sent messengers to the emperor's camp asking for an interview. But the Kaiser was adamant. He demanded complete surrender and complete submission to the verdict of the princes.[96] The king held a preliminary session with his leaders at the Quedlinburg.[97] Henry tried to soften the terms of his sentence by releasing Ludwig and Hermann of Thuringia, whom he had held captive.[98] Finally Henry arrived at Erfurt, on 11 November 1181, and was led before the emperor as a broken man. He threw himself at the emperor's feet and begged for his mercy and that of the court, which he certainly did not deserve.[99] The Staufer lifted Henry from the floor and kissed him.[100] The Welf rebel could not have expected immediate reinstatement, for his offenses were too grave. Besides, such a decision would rest with the princes, whom he had offended for years. But secretly, no doubt, the duke hoped that day would one day come. At Erfurt the princes' verdict turned out to be severe. Henry lost his title as duke of Saxony, as well as all the lands he held as a vassal of the king. He was permitted to keep his rich allodial lands in Braunschweig and Lüneburg.[101] Frederick did not aim to reduce him to a pauper. As a further penalty, Henry was to be exiled from Germany for three years; even then, he could not return without royal permission. Henry II of England and Philip of Flanders even attended the *Reichstag* at Mainz on 16 May 1182, hoping to expedite Henry's return and give him a chance to be reinstated.[102]

Before Frederick departed on the Third Crusade, Henry tried once more to ingratiate himself and return to Germany; but the Kaiser did not trust him in his absence. He offered his cousin one of three choices: (1) to accompany him on the Crusade; (2) to have his son participate in the journey to the Holy Land; or (3) to remain in England.[103] Henry chose exile. In the meantime, Henry II of England died, as did Henry's wife Matilde.

After Frederick's death in the Near East, Henry the Lion broke his oath and reappeared in Germany. At the *Reichstag* of Merseburg he tried to challenge the new Kaiser, Henry VI, Frederick Barbarossa's son; but due to the continued hostility of many princes, Henry did not get far. Old Saxony was gone forever.

5

The Emergence
of the New Saxony

Precisely what transpired in the northern lands after the death of Frederick Barbarossa and Henry the Lion's return to Germany is difficult to determine. Historians such as Boedler and Hahn have tried to reconstruct this time to determine what happened to Westphalia and Engern, the lands that Bernhard of Ascania had been granted in the Gelnhauser charter; yet even after all their research, the picture is not altogether clear.[1] Hahn studied the pre-Gelnhausen lives of Albrecht the Bear's sons; later he also reconstructed the record of Bernhard and his descendants. He attempted to cast light on the transference of the north to the "new Saxony" on the Elbe, by examining the signatures of Henry the Lion and Bernhard on documents during the period that followed.[2] Boedler concluded that prior to Henry's fall, the original stem duchy of "old Saxony" had already ceased to exist. The concept of a duke being an imperial official of a specific region had perished much earlier. At the height of Henry's power, the duke's strength as a territorial prince lay in several factors: the possession of allodial lands with many castles; a reputation as a military leader; control of commerce and markets in newly founded cities; control of court systems; and actual wealth.[3] Thus it is not strange that the forces of decentralization, at work since the days of Henry IV and given a free hand after the Concordat of Worms in 1122, should also have contributed to the breakup of "old Saxony."[4]

The question might rightly be asked: Did Bernhard actually become the duke of Saxony? The *Gelnhauser Urkunde* granted him—at least on paper—the lands east of the Weser River, along with their title. But why did Bernhard fail to occupy the duchy of Saxony after Henry's departure to England? Stranger still was the transfer of his ducal title to the new Wittenberg region. These are questions that defy complete answers. According to Boedler, the archbishop of Cologne was not given all of Westphalia. His grant was limited to the bishopric of Paderborn, which lay to the south of the Lippe River, extending eastward to the Weser. The considerably larger portion of Westphalia was given to Bernhard of Ascania.[5] The archbishops of Cologne who succeeded Philip soon lost power in the newly acquired regions; accordingly, by the time of the Mainzer *Reichstag* of 1235, the new duchy of Braunschweig-Lüneburg was created, a settlement to which Albrecht of Ascania gave his signature. This, said Boedler, is ample proof that the decentralizing force of territorialism nullified the grant made in the Gelnhauser charter.[6] Henry the Lion had great strength in Engern, Hildesheim, Verden, Bremen, and Minden, where he also controlled the dioceses; but he possessed no allodial lands around Münster and Osnabrück. Thus, in Westphalia, Henry's claims were merely private and territorial.[7] He exerted them through a kind of free-wheeling power politics that also created many enemies, including Philip of Cologne. Since Henry's greatest power had been in the east, there the opposition of the Ascanier and other princes had been most heated; and it was there that Emperor Frederick had received his strongest support. Once Otto, the oldest son of Albrecht the Bear, became margrave of Brandenburg, and Sigfried, the third son, became archbishop of Bremen and Bernhard, Henry had little chance to restore his former role.

It seems that Bernhard learned that he had received little more than the title of duke. Since he lacked both allodial lands and family clout, he could hardly enforce his claims. Hahn concluded that this may have been the very reason why the Staufer selected Bernhard to be Henry's successor. The vassals refused to accept Bernhard as duke of Westphalia and Engern, and at times even the emperor seems to have supported them. When Bernhard tried to assert himself with the city of Lübeck, the Kaiser sided with the citizens. Nor did Bernhard's relations with the Slavs always fare well.[8]

Hahn employed a rather unique approach with regard to sources. He analyzed the records of chroniclers, who quoted contemporary diplomatic documents, in order to ascertain the exact titles attached to the signatures used by Bernhard and Henry the Lion in later years. After Gelnhausen many of the chroniclers referred to Bernhard as duke of Saxony. On 9 October 1180, Bernhard signed a document to which he attached the title "Duke of Saxony."[9] He repeated the same title in a document dated 15 and 16 November 1181.[10] Another investigator, Fritz Hasenritter, has analyzed Henry the Lion's signatures in 1154 and later, after his loss of Saxony and Bavaria. He found that from 1154 to 1180 Henry used several titles: "Duke of Saxony," "Duke of Bavaria and Saxony," and "Duke of Saxony and Bavaria"; but after his fall, he signed all his papers "Duke Henry," or again, "Duke Henry on the basis of being the son of Henry."[11] However, says Hahn, Henry never rejected the idea of being a duke in his own allodial lands.[12]

According to Arnold of Lübeck, Bernhard was an easygoing, peace-loving individual. However, historians believe that Bernhard's fate as elector was determined more by the circumstances of the times than by anything he neglected to do.[13] No matter what territories Bernhard controlled, he regarded himself as the duke of Saxony. That title appears in Italy in 1183 with two of his signatures.[14] Doubtless the many problems connected with enforcement of his title finally caused Bernhard to realize the futility of trying to actually restore "old Saxony." In any event, Bernhard's descendants continued to apply the title to the "new Saxony." That territory he had inherited from his father, Albrecht the Bear.[15] Wittenberg was later to become its principal city.[16] In his work *History of the Electoral States*, the historian Weise adds this comment:

> Since at this time the mentioned land possessions are considered to have been the principal territories of the duchy of Saxony, even the title of the prince went over to it; for, at that time, it was customary to include the personal title of the ruler with the lands that he possessed.[17]

A later University of Wittenberg professor, P. Heynig, writing under the nom de plume Schalscheleth, compared the breakup of "old Saxony" to the shaking of a pear tree with many hungry boys waiting to pounce on the fallen fruit. Thus when the emperor shook the pear tree, the feudal lords who ruled in Henry's lands took advantage of the situation; these princes were more successful than poor Bernhard in garnering the fallen fruit.[18] Schalscheleth further suggested that, like a beggar with his bag, Bernhard wandered around the countryside seeking some land to which he might attach his title. Finally, his father took pity on him and gave him the region around Wittenberg—a territory he had recently wrested from the Wends—and settled it with people from Flanders. Thus, in desperation, Bernhard was finally forced to attach his title to this new region.[19] This is a rather clever analogy, but the story contains many factual errors.

Historians have investigated what lands the Ascanier held in this region prior to Henry's fall. Heinemann claims that Bernhard already possessed territories in the Saale River region that had been given to him by his grandfather, Otto the Rich, before his death in 1122.[20] In addition, he had holdings in the Anhalt region, where the young duke ruled over Aschersleben, Bernburg, and other lands near the Elbe. Bernhard's lands extended to the north and east, up to Brandenburg, where they joined the possessions of his brother Otto. Thus Bernhard's territories already covered a large part of what became Electoral Saxony, the Anhalt region around Zerbst, and the *Grafschaft* Aschersleben—a tract that extended some distance west of the Saale.[21]

On the basis of the Gelnhausen grant Bernhard may at first have rightly regarded the duchy of "old Saxony" as his own. But thirty years of fighting for his rights with the feudal princes of "old Saxony" made him realize the futility of continuing the struggle.[22] By 1208 there was a disputed imperial election in which, according to Arnold of Lübeck, Bernhard supported the Welf candidate Otto IV.[23] There is also evidence that his ducal title continued to be contested until the Mainzer *Reichstag* in 1235.[24]

As noted earlier, Henry the Lion attempted to regain his former status upon his return from England (as well as earlier, after the death of Frederick during the Third Crusade). But he was not very successful in making a comeback.[25] Boedler cited a source in which Bernhard expressed his feelings toward the former Welf potentate, who seems to have been jealous of Bernhard's possession of the "new Saxony":

> How long are you going to open your jaws toward the east? Stop, for you have all you want; turn rather toward the north.[26]

This seems to say that Bernhard was now satisfied being the elector of Saxony, ruling over his own lands in the east, and that Henry should concentrate on regaining his allodial lands in Westphalia and Engern. But even there, Henry could not retake what the neighboring feudal lords had meanwhile appropriated. Soon the dukedom of Braunschweig-Lüneburg would be created amid the Welf's former lands, and Bernhard's younger son, Albrecht, then the elector, was to be one of the signatories.[27] All this proves that the second generation of Ascanier had given up all hope of claiming "old Saxony" as part of their ducal title. Boedler feels the Ascanier never attempted to lord it over their neighboring feudal lords in the north. As in Frederick Barbarossa's new feudalism, the ducal title could be identified only with actual territorial possessions. Bernhard's descendants were satisfied to attach the title of Electoral Saxony to the Wittenberg region.[28] The historian Friedrich Berendt claims that upon his return, Henry tried to gain control over the bishoprics of Minden, Osnabrück, and Münster; but these, like most of his former fiefs, had meanwhile been acquired by their former feudal lords.[29]

According to the new territorialism, each fief strove for its own independence. Accordingly, fiefs soon began to be regarded as independent possessions, no longer held in vassalage to a feudal lord. In time, the strong were able to claim their fiefs as private property.[30] In this way the barons and lords helped bring about the fall of Henry the Lion. The easygoing Bernhard made such plunder by other princes all the easier. Thus, in a broad sense, Schalscheleth was right when he compared the fall of Henry to the shaking of a pear tree, and thus "old Saxony" rapidly disappeared from the map of Europe.[31]

Before his death, Bernhard divided his lands between his two sons, Henry the Elder and Albrecht the Younger. The result of this transaction reminds one of the story of Jacob and Esau.[32] According to common feudal practice, the oldest boy had his choice as to which lands he preferred to inherit. In this territorial division, Bernhard's oldest son Henry was designated a count (*Graf*), while Albrecht and his descendants were from then on referred to as dukes of Electoral Saxony. Henry became the *Graf* of Ascania, while Albrecht was made duke of Inchen.[33] The *Annales Stadenses* tried to rationalize Henry's choice on the grounds that his grant included the *Grafschaft* of Anhalt, while Albrecht's title was attached to the less developed region on the Elbe, and also because the province of Anhalt possessed more allodial lands belonging to the Ascanier. Hence Henry's choice was more promising.[34] Bernhard had additional lands besides the Wittenberg region, and these were included in the grant made to him at the time of the partition.

As to the description of the lands that Bernhard's sons inherited, Henry's territory began just below the Harz mountains, which also included the *Burg* Anhalt; his lands also included the Ballenstedt region and the *Grafschaft* Aschersleben.[35] This region began west of the Saale, crossed the Mulde, and stretched up to the Elbe. The territory inherited by Albrecht (later known as the *Kurkreis*) extended a little to the southwest of the Elbe, but in the main his lands were located to the north and east of later Wittenberg. There the area was bounded by the lands of Ascanier, the margrave of Brandenburg. In 1290 the electoral circle was considerably enlarged by the grant of Brehna, which Emperor Rudolph I made to his grandson, Rudolph I of Saxony. The original *Kurkreis* already had the villages of Seyda, Dobien, Zahna, and Niemegk above Wittenberg, as well as Belzig on the Brandenburg border.

Weise observed that, "Since the time mentioned, [Albrecht's] places were considered the principal possessions of Electoral Saxony and the title of the prince became attached to it, because it was customary to associate a personal title of a ruler with that of his lands."[36] After that the Saxon rulers changed their signatures. Albrecht now signed documents as "Herzog von Sachsen," while Henry referred to himself as "*Graf* von Ascanien und *Fürst* von Anhalt."[37] During Frederick II's election both Ascanier houses preferred Otto IV.[38] But after Otto IV died, Albrecht somehow effected a reconciliation with the emperor.[39]

During this period there were a number of disturbances, especially in "old Saxony," but Albrecht took no part in them.[40] Heinrich of Braunschweig regarded himself as the *Reichsvikar* in the north, and did not want Albrecht around.[41]

In 1244 Henry of Anhalt, Bernhard's older son, died, leaving a large family of five sons and four daughters. As was customary, two of the sons accepted ecclesiastical appointments. But the division of Henry's lands between the remaining three sons left the father's heritage still more splintered, as was typical of territorialism.[42]

Under the rule of Albrecht (1212–1260), the electoral circle began to acquire added importance. Even though the Ascanier did not live in Wittenberg during this early period, they built the town around the original marketplace along the river road. Doubtless the later chancel of the town church dates back to this period, being originally a small chapel. Professor Charitius claimed that Albrecht's wife, Helena, at this time founded the Franciscan monastery just north of the marketplace, an institution that also served as the original burial place for the Ascanier family.[43] During the Reformation, the twenty-seven oaken caskets containing the mortal remains of the electoral family were moved into an underground vault in the main tower of the castle church, where they still resided in 1936.[44]

When Albrecht I died in 1260, both John, the older son, and his younger brother, Albrecht II, were minors, and their mother Helena served as the regent. These two sons became the founders of two branches of the Ascanier house. John became the head of the Lauenburg line, which continued until 1689, while Albrecht II became the founder of the Saxon-Wittenberg line. The latter, through a series of historical accidents, was to become the family which carried the electoral title and the region of the electoral circle. (This line continued until 1419, when the castle of Schweinitz collapsed on the sleeping royal family.[45]) In the struggle between the papacy and Frederick II, Albrecht's line of the Ascanier house chose to be neutral.[46] This proved to be a real advantage. Another stroke of good fortune occurred when Albrecht II married Agnes, the daughter of Rudolf of Hapsburg.[47] Not only did the emperor's son-in-law spend considerable time at the imperial court, but the Hapsburg ruler took a special interest in his grandson and namesake, who later was to become Rudolf I of Saxony. Duke Rudolf was to play a vital role in the building of Wittenberg, turning it into the capital city of the *Kurkreis*.[48] He is believed to have erected the original castle church, after the king of France had bestowed on him a sacred gift—reputedly a thorn from the crown of Christ—for he felt such a treasure needed to be placed in a special chapel.[49]

When Rudolf of Hapsburg died in Speyer on 15 July 1291, once again there arose the matter of which of the two Ascanier lines should cast the electoral vote. Bernhard's oldest son John, of the Lauenburg line, had also died, and his two sons were still minors. Thus Albrecht II was declared eligible to cast his vote for the next emperor, Adolf of Nassau.[50] The same circumstances prevailed in 1298, during the election of Albrecht of Austria, because Albrecht's two nephews were minors. By the time Albert of Austria was murdered in 1308 and Henry was chosen as his successor, Albert III of the Lauenburg line had already died. This meant that the Saxon-Wittenberg line (Rudolf I) again had to cast the Ascanier vote. When Charles IV, emperor of Bohemia, established the German electoral college (in the document known as the Golden Bull of 1356), he had to consider that there were sixty-five years of precedent in emperors being chosen by the Saxon-Wittenberg line rather than the Lauenburg branch.[51] It was also unfortunate for the Lauenburg family that during the election of Charles IV, they supported the king's opponent, Gunther of Schwarzburg. Elector Rudolf I was Charles IV's uncle.[52] Thus, first in the "Saxon Clauses" and later in the Golden Bull, Emperor Charles IV made Rudolf I, his namesake Rudolf the Younger, and their primogenitors the sole possessors of the Ascanier electoral vote (*Kurrecht*).[53]

With the termination of the *Kaiserzeit* in 1254, the Holy Roman Empire underwent two decades of great confusion. The Apostolic See, which had been a strong factor in its downfall, faced even greater problems: Charles of Anjou tried to control all of Italy, while Philip III of France even aspired to obtain the imperial crown. As a result, Pope Gregory X urged the German princes to elect a new king. The electors, too, had found the long *Interregnum* filled with strife, including robber knights who tried to enhance their own holdings. The electors met at Frankfurt a.M., but their vote was divided. Albrecht of Saxony cast the decisive vote in favor of Rudolph of Hapsburg. King Ottocar of Bohemia, Rudolph's powerful opponent, fought against his rival and even papal excommunication, until he was killed in Lower Austria during the battle of Marchfeld. The Austrian lands of Styria, Carinthia, and Carniola became permanent Hapsburg possessions.[54]

During the next half century the empire had five different rulers. Adolf of Nassau was killed in battle after six years; he in turn was followed by Albert I of Austria (son of Rudolf I), assassinated by a nephew after a ten-year reign. The electors then chose Henry VII of Luxembourg, who through the efforts of his brother, Archbishop Baldwin of Trier, was crowned emperor in Rome, only to die the following year in Sienna (during a mass, perhaps from poisoning). During the next thirty years there was a series of struggles between two of the grandsons of Rudolf of Hapsburg and several popes. Four electoral votes were cast for Frederick the Fair, making him the legitimate choice; but Louis of Bavaria declared war and captured him. Louis was then excommunicated by Pope John XXII. Louis crossed the Alps with a large army, deposed the pontiff, and had himself crowned with both the iron crown of Lombardy and the imperial crown.

A later pope, Clement VII, claimed the right to control imperial elections and to make the Holy Roman Empire a vassal state of the Holy See.[55] This interference in German affairs so incensed the seven electors that, in the summer of 1338, they laid a partial foundation for the future German constitution.[56] At that time the papacy was in exile in Avignon. In a meeting at Rhens, the electors asserted that the electoral college had the divine right to nominate and choose future German emperors, acting without nomination, approval, or confirmation by the Apostolic See. On 6 August they held a second session at Frankfurt a.M., where they issued the historic decree, *Licet Juris*, stipulating that: (1) the office of emperor was of divine origin (a view that had been held since the beginning of the German *Reich*); (2) the election of an emperor would be by majority or unanimous vote; and (3) election of a king or "emperor of the Romans" would, ipso facto, make him the ruler, and that such action required no papal approval. These principles were later accepted in toto by Emperor Charles IV and codified in the Golden Bull of 1356. In a sense, therefore, Charles sold out to the territorial princes—the seven German electors—as the determining force in the future German empire.

When Louis of Bavaria was about to accept Clement VI's offer to make Germany a vassal of the Holy See, the German Diet indignantly rejected the proposal. Afterward, Louis was damned by an excommunication that used the strongest possible language, while, by means of bribes and maneuvering behind the scenes, the pope influenced the electoral college to choose, by a narrow margin, Charles IV of Luxembourg-Bohemia. This was the election in which Rudolf I cast the decisive vote.[57] Afterward Charles IV faced great obstacles to win the approval of his opponents. The archbishop of Mainz refused to crown him, while the citizens of Aachen would not permit the coronation to be held in Charlemagne's cathedral. Finally, in desperation, the archbishop of Cologne agreed to perform the coronation at Bonn. Charles' principal obstacle was Louis of Bavaria, whose crown lands extended from the Tirol to Brandenburg, and who had been allied with Edward III of England in the Hundred Years War. In 1346 Charles IV and his father, John of Luxembourg, had fought in the battle of Crécy. The English longbows proved to be too much for their superior number of knights, and Charles' father died on the battlefield. Louis of Bavaria then suddenly died, perhaps from poisoning, and his successor was weak. This ended some of Charles IV's early problems.

Charles IV was the great-grandson of Rudolph of Hapsburg. There was also a relationship between him and the electors of Saxony. This relationship played a role in Charles' drafting of the "Saxon Clauses" of the Golden Bull. The unexpected death of John of Luxembourg in the battle of Crécy gave the Wittels-bachs a new advantage. As a result, Charles' brother Henry was expelled from the Tirol, while Louis of Bavaria started to flex his muscles. Charles then formed an alliance with the new pope of Avignon, Clement VII. The alliance paid off, for the pope vowed to remove the Wittelsbach claimant to the throne. The pope also freed the bishopric of Prague from control by the archbishop of Mainz by elevating it into an archbishopric.[58]

Though elected by the majority of the German electors, it took a ten-year struggle for Charles to win the crown of emperor. Archbishop Baldwin, his great uncle, was constantly working for him behind the scenes. The territorial princes were already very powerful, and the empire was tossed about as in a turbulent sea of competing princes, knights, feudal lords, and cities. Amid the confusion, Charles eventually won out, and after the death of his rival Gunther he was crowned at Aachen. Subsequently, Charles was crowned with the Iron Crown of Lombardy, followed a little later in Rome by the imperial crown.

It was Charles IV and the seven German electors who gave the Holy Roman Empire a new constitution. The so-called Golden Bull (a reference to its golden seal) originally consisted of twenty-three chapters proclaimed by the court chancellor in the presence of the Kaiser, electors, and high officials on 10 January 1356. A few additional clauses were added at the following *Reichstag*, late in 1356, and on Christmas Day these were officially presented by the Kaiser and his electors in the presence of the cardinal legate, the duke of Normandy, and the two oldest sons of the king of France.[59]

Formerly it was believed that the constitutional law book was drafted by Johann von Neumark, but scholars such as Karl Zeumer and Konrad Burdach have rejected this thesis. They hold that the king himself drafted the constitution with the aid of his chancellory and the guidance of the electors.[60] The so-called Saxon Clauses had been drafted before the emperor left Prague for Nürnberg.[61] Historians have shown that, in the main, the Golden Bull only codified and regulated existing constitutional practice, which had gradually evolved since the days of Rudolf of Hapsburg. No doubt the chancellory lawyers studied previous German law books. For the duties of a *Reichsvikar* during an *Interregnum* and the role of the *Erzmarschallamt* (keeper of the royal stables), the lawyers found guidance in the *Schwabenspiegel*, the Swabian law code from the time of Rudolf of Hapsburg, and the *Sachsenspiegel*, the old law code of the Saxon lands.[62]

Charles IV was officially crowned emperor on Easter Day, 1355. Afterward he remained in Italy several months, returning to Germany by way of Augsburg, Nürnberg, Regensburg, and Sulzbach to Prague. There he was met by a number of German princes and electors, among them his uncle Rudolf, the elder of the Saxon-Wittenberg line, and his son, Rudolf the Younger. Before leaving Prague for Nürnberg, the emperor drafted the Saxon Clauses.[63]

The Kaiser may have already decided to hold his next *Reichstag* in Nürnberg when he passed through that city on his return from Rome in July 1355. But he did not send out invitations to the electors until 17 September, announcing 11 November as the official opening of the *Reichstag*. But Charles himself was delayed, not reaching Nürnberg until 25 November. On the day of his arrival, he announced his plan to give Germany a new constitution. But since the three ecclesiastical electors were still absent, he postponed the official opening of the *Reichstag* for two more weeks. Archbishop Gerland of Mainz arrived in Nürnberg on 12 December, but Boemund of Trier and William of Cologne did not get there until 22 December.[64]

The original draft of the Golden Bull was officially presented on 10 January 1356.[65] Since the German constitution was quite detailed, it seems doubtful that the document was read in its entirety at that time.[66] But Charles and/or some of the electors must not have been entirely satisfied with the original draft. For example, prior to this, Bavaria rather than Bohemia had participated in imperial elections. Charles must have decided to summon a second *Reichstag* at Metz to settle such problems.[67] The second draft of the bull made Bohemia a member of the electoral college and established its role in the ceremonies at future *Reichstagen*.[68]

The Golden Bull per se is not our present concern, but rather the decisions made regarding the electoral college of the empire and its influence on the future of Electoral Saxony. That the bull enhanced the power of the seven electors is obvious. But its impact on the future of Electoral Saxony was extraordinary. Charles not only established once and for all that the Saxon-Wittenberg line would possess the *Kurkreis* around Wittenberg, but made the elector of Saxony (1) the emperor's formal sword bearer; (2) imperial *Erzmarschall*; and (3) *Reichsvikar* during an *Interregnum* (ruler of the empire during periods when there was no emperor).

One of the causes of confusion during the time between the reigns of Rudolf of Hapsburg and Charles IV was the tendency for lay electors to equate the *Kurrecht* with their families. Such was the case with the Ascanier, but also in the Pfalz and in Brandenburg.[69] The emperor attempted to correct this. The rights of the Pfalzgraf Ruprecht the Elder and his descendants had already been established by 18 March 1339, but in the case of Electoral Saxony there was a need for an official ruling about which of the two lines would exercise the *Kurrecht*. This problem was carefully resolved at the two *Reichstagen* at Nürnberg and Metz.[70] The *Sachsenspiegel* defined the *Kurrecht* as being tied to a definite territory, not as a family possession. Hence Charles established that the *Kur*, or electorship, would be associated with the possession of specific lands which could not be diminished or changed. In the case of Electoral Saxony, the *Kurland* would be the electoral circle around Wittenberg. Thus the Saxon-Wittenberg line now had the *Kurrecht* under its control.[71]

On 24 August 1355, before leaving for the Nürnberg *Reichstag*, the emperor published a document certifying that from henceforth Rudolf the Elder and his descendants would be the rightful possessors of the *Kurrecht* and the *Erzmarschallamt*; the German text was repeated in a Latin version on 6 October 1355.[72] In the first of these Saxon Clauses, Charles set forth in detail why he and the German princes had decided that the *Kurrecht* and the *Erzmarschallamt*, with all its rights, should properly remain with Rudolf and his descendants. For the previous three-quarters of a century that house had possessed and exercised the *Kurrecht*. The rulers of Electoral Saxony had served in the electoral college ever since the days of Rudolf of Hapsburg, whom Duke Albrecht II of that house had helped to elect "King of the Romans" and later saw safely crowned. This role was continued by his great uncle, Albrecht II, during the elections of Adolf of Nassau and Albert of Hapsburg. Then again, the document adds, after Albrecht II's death, his son, Rudolf the Elder, the uncle of Charles IV, had helped elect Henry VII of Luxembourg, and after him, Frederick the Fair; while in more recent times the same Rudolf had helped elect and crown Charles IV "King of the Romans." In addition, the emperor stated, in this matter he had conferred with and had the full support of the other electors, counts, barons, and feudal lords.[73]

Charles made his official announcement in these words:

> In order that this particular and distinct right and honor may be constantly and immutably preserved and remain unaltered for himself, his heirs, and descendants, we declare herewith, in the form of an imperial edict, to be immediately effective, and for all time to come; furthermore, we make this proclamation upon the certitude of our imperial authority, namely, that the aforementioned Duke Rudolf the Elder, our esteemed uncle, shall be, and no one else, the true elector of Saxony and Erzmarschall of the Holy Roman Empire, and the legitimate elector, now existing, as he has in the past; and, just as agreed upon, let it be understood that he has the right within the empire to cast a vote in the election of a "King of the Romans."
>
> Upon his death, the previously referred to electoral vote and rights with reference to an election, are to pass to his firstborn son; or, if he is no longer alive, to his firstborn son. But if the first born, legitimate, hereditary, masculine line should have died out, then the vote, right, and power in elections would pass to his senior brother in the paternal line of descendants. After that it would progress by the same rule of primogeniture in succession in the right to vote and power as described above about the dukes of Saxony, and it will be henceforth perpetually observed.[74]

Charles' language allowed for no loopholes that could be used by the rival Ascanier line; furthermore, he stated that if anyone were to find any legal ground for annulment of the rule, based on extant public or private extant statutes, that party was duty-bound to report it immediately.[75] If in the future anyone were to pursue a contrary course, that person would not only incur the ill-will of the emperor and face the danger of banishment, but would also be fined 1000 gold Marks, half of which would be paid into the imperial treasury, while the remainder would go to the offended party. Should the offense be repeated, the same fine would again be exacted.[76]

Rudolf the Elder had became ill prior to the opening of the *Reichstag*, and he had delegated his electoral powers to his son, Rudolf the Younger.[77] At Nürnberg on 29 December, the emperor gave a second document to the son, forming another part of the Saxon Clauses. It begins essentially in the same vein, but amplifies the previous agreement on one point. The former document had not allowed for the possible minority of the oldest son. The addition reads as follows:

But if the firstborn son is left a minor, in time of peace, the [previous elector's] eldest brother will serve as his tutor and the administrator of the realm,
until the boy has reached the legitimate age; as a consequence then, the
eldest brother is permitted to assume the dignity, vote, right, and power with
respect to all things falling upon the electoral office. The legitimate age for
assuming the electoral power (for the legitimate heir) we decree to be eighteen. Meanwhile, in governing the electorate during the interim, we decree
that all laws of previous Roman emperors and kings shall be observed.[78]

The second document, also, states that any challenge or attempt to set it aside
is to be regarded as null and void.[79]

At Metz about a year later, on 27 December 1356, Emperor Charles IV
solemnly invested Rudolf the Younger as elector of Saxony, in the presence of
all the dignitaries, granting him the *Kur* and *Erzmarschallamt* that his recently
deceased father had held. At the time the Kaiser issued another document,
which, in its main lines, repeats the previous terms made with his father.[80]

The Golden Bull stated that if an entire house died out, as happened to the
house of Saxon-Wittenberg in 1422, the Kaiser could designate a successor.
This is what Sigismund did when he turned the Electorate of Saxony over to the
House of Wettin.[81] On 2 January 1356 the archbishop of Mainz added his voice
of approval to Charles IV's action in the Saxon Clauses. As chairman of the electoral college, the archbishop no doubt gave his approval in the name of the rest
of the electors.[82]

The bull stipulated that if there were an imperial vacancy, the archbishop of
Mainz would issue a summons for the electors to assemble in Frankfurt a.M., in
the Church of St. Bartholomew; there, after mass, they were to take an oath
before they cast their respective votes for the next "King of the Romans." A
majority vote was to be decisive. In this the bull was only codifying accepted
procedure.[83] In voting, the archbishop of Mainz called upon the electors
according to rank and custom: Trier, Cologne, Bohemia, the Pfalz, Saxony, and
Brandenburg, after which Mainz cast the seventh vote.[84] Such matters as rank
and who sat next to the king during banquets were codified in the bull.[85]

One special honor that was extended the dukes of Saxony was that, because
they were the emperor's sword bearers at *Hoftagen* and *Reichstagen*, they also
held the royal sword part of the time during the king's banquets. Exactly when
this distinction began is no longer certain. Until the middle of the twelfth century, that honor was not extended to any specific person; usually the privilege
was given to the first person that did homage to the king. But in a poem by
Walther von der Vogelweide about the Hoftag at Magdeburg in 1199, the first
elector of Saxony, Bernhard of Ascania, was already privileged to carry the
emperor's sword. Two other sources also support this.[86] Boedler thinks the real
beginning of the *Erzmarschallamt* dates to Emperor Rudolf of Hapsburg,
whose daughter had married Albrecht II of Ascania. He believes that the
emperor took such a liking to his grandchild, Rudolf I of Saxony, that he conferred upon him the title of *Erzmarschall*, or keeper of the royal stables, and
that later the *Kurrecht* and the roles of *Erzmarschall* and *Reichsvikar* all

became interrelated. But Karl Zeumer claims that in the thirteenth century there appears no reference indicating that the sword-bearing privilege went with the *Erzmarschallamt*; yet it seems strange that in describing the duties of the different electors, the *Schwabenspiegel* states, "The Duke of Saxony is to carry the king's sword. Ficker holds that this section of the code was drafted later. Martin of Troppau composed verses about the duties of the electors, stating: "The Saxon is known as the duke that carries the sword." Another source, discussing the establishment of the electoral college, adds: "The Duke of Saxony is he who carries the sword in the presence of the emperor."[87]

But actual practice did not always conform to theory. In 1338 Kaiser Ludwig of Bavaria hosted a gathering of many dignitaries, including Edward III of England. On this occasion the honor of sword bearer was offered to the duke of Brabant, who carried the royal sword in the presence of all the electors. Duke Rudolf of Saxony did not seem to object. But two years later, at Frankfurt a.M., the duke of Saxony made a strong protest to Emperor Ludwig, claiming that his rights under the *Erzmarschallamt* had, at the previous meeting, been usurped by the duke of Brabant.[88] Several sources testify to this rather unusual encounter between elector and king.[89] Yet the first definite action taken to implement the sword-bearing right was in the first draft of the Golden Bull, where in Chapters IV and XXII it states that the elector of Saxony is to exercise his *Erzmarschallamt* on festive occasions, as expressed in the Swabian Law Code; while in Chapter XXII, the law book adds: "The elector of Saxony is to carry the Kaiser's sword in these ceremonial processions."[90]

But even the Golden Bull did not stop the king's ambitious brother, Wenzel, from challenging the right of young Rudolf II to carry the emperor's sword in the procession to the banquet at Metz. He caused a fracas in the cathedral in the presence of the electors and the emperor. However, Rudolf stood his ground, no doubt with the support of the rest of the electors and the emperor. The record shows that Rudolf carried the sword and also held it for a while at the banquet.[91] In a document written two days later, the Kaiser consoled his angry brother, noting that he had not yet been invested with the duchy of Brabant, and hence did not have a rightful claim.[92] But Wenzel must have continued his efforts to influence Charles, which created some concern on the part of the Saxon elector. To resolve the dilemma, the emperor wrote to Rudolf II on 7 January 1357, asking him not to be concerned about the letter he had written to Wenzel the previous month.[93] But for some time the emperor's indecisiveness continued to have an effect. By the fifteenth century, the norm of the Golden Bull was followed. From that time forth the elector of Saxony was in fact the official sword bearer, based on the right of being the *Erzmarschall* of the Holy Roman Empire.[94]

The practice of having two *Reichsvikars* to govern the country during periods when the throne was vacant had been employed since the days of Rudolf of Hapsburg. It was modified somewhat in the regulatory clauses of the Golden Bull. Boedler believes it was Rudolf of Hapsburg who created the system. In the meantime, the *Reichsvikars* had acquired certain powers and rights. There are extant letters from 1328 and 1354 showing that dukes, margraves, barons, nobles, and their vassals all regarded themselves as vassals of the Pfalzgraf and of the elector of Saxony, even when there was no *Interregnum*.[95] Though in the Golden Bull the practice was to be limited somewhat, past practice still had an impact.

The *Reichsvikariat* was established in Chapter V of the new constitution. The bull modified the rights of a *Reichsvikar* during a vacancy, and also during a king's reign, should there be the need to remove an emperor for malfeasance in office. During such a period, the Pfalzgraf of the Rhine was assigned a double function in the *Reich*: (1) he became the head of the supreme court, to try all feudal offenses, or even an emperor, if charges were brought against him; and (2) in the capacity of *Reichsvikar*, he had definite powers in the Rhenish and Swabian lands, where Frankish law continued to be in effect. On the other hand, the elector of Saxony was *Reichsvikar* in the northern German lands where the *Sachsenspiegel* was law. According to Boedler, the duke of Saxony originally obtained the right of *Erzmarschall*, the *Vikariat*, and the *Kurrecht*, from Rudolf of Hapsburg.[96]

Thus, both before and after the Golden Bull, a *Reichsvikar* exercised considerable power during an *Interregnum*, and his prestige and influence naturally carried over into the reign of the next emperor. Someone has called the *Reichsvikar* a "small king" in his respective realm.[97] According to the Golden Bull, during an imperial vacancy the *Reichsvikar* possessed the following powers: (1) the right of *judicia exercendi*, a kind of supreme court power in his lands, to try offenses against the "peace of the land"; (2) control over ecclesiastical prebends, in which allowance for meals and maintenance of services were to be guaranteed; (3) the right to collect the *Reich's* incomes, especially those owed from crown lands; (4) the right to receive feudal oaths from the king's vassals (such oaths had to be renewed within a year and a day); and (5) the distribution of fiefs at the lower level, which was performed in the name of the king. Such distributions did not apply to the level of electors and princes.[98] These functions could also be postponed, for the electoral college was obligated to elect a new king within a year and a day.[99]

That the elector of Saxony received these added powers under the bull was not because of his newly assured *Kurrecht*—an electoral right that Brandenburg and Bohemia also possessed; it resulted rather from his now equalized rights as *Reichsvikar* over all territories that were under Saxon law.[100] It is not strange, therefore, that at Worms in 1521, these lands looked to the elector of Saxony as the ranking figure, and that Charles V treated Frederick the Wise with special respect.

Prior to the Golden Bull, the Pfalzgraf of the Rhine had been the chief judge of the German supreme court. The *Schwabenspiegel* describes the Pfalzgraf as an elector having two distinct, additional functions. He was a *Reichsvikar*, while also being the supreme judge of the *Reich*. The Golden Bull recognized this same distinction. The right of the Pfalzgraf to rule over the Franconian lands during an *Interregnum* had been established long before the bull; but such practice was not applied during the days of Henry the Lion, after 1180, nor with respect to Bernhard of Ascania's lands in the original Saxon stem duchy. This confusion was eliminated at Nürnberg by Charles IV, for now the king gave the elector of Saxony equal rights to that of the Pfalzgraf in his own northern lands.

The bull also tried to improve relations between the German electors and the emperor by having them work more closely with him on problems and planning. Henceforth the electors were to meet with the king each year for four weeks immediately after Easter, after better weather had set in. Locations for *Reichstagen* were to be agreed upon jointly. A rotation of meetings at the most favorable spots was to be followed as long as this seemed agreeable. To lessen the perils involved in traveling to and from meetings, the Kaiser promised his protection for electors through "safe-conducts," similar to the one Luther was offered on his way to Worms. The Kaiser felt that banqueting had been excessive at Nürnberg in 1356; accordingly he placed a ban on inviting too many guests.[101]

Ever since the days of Rudolf of Hapsburg, the German electors had assumed an increasingly important role in the German *Reich*. During the days of Frederick the Fair and Louis of Bavaria, conditions had favored the electors in their rise to greater power. Their prestige was enhanced still more at Rens in 1338, when they had declared their independence from papal and all other outside influences during an imperial election. Charles IV recognized this enhancement and supported that previous decision in the drafting of the Golden Bull, which made the electoral college virtually independent of either papacy or empire. Nor did Charles dispute the electors' right to meet wherever they liked when filling a vacancy. In this new constitution, the kaiser aimed to employ the electors as a kind of "privy council."

The impression one gathers from the Golden Bull is that the Kaiser wanted to make his future *Reichstag* meetings more attractive to the electors. The language of the bull flattered them by calling them the very pillars and foundation of the *Reich*. The emperor spoke of the values that were derived from more frequent meetings and promised to reduce their cost. *Reichstagen* could of course be very useful to the king as sounding boards, to determine the conditions and the feelings of his subjects. But it would be erroneous to hold that the drafting of laws fell into their hands; for in granting the constitution the emperor made it clear that ultimately all powers of lawmaking and the issuing of decrees were vested in him as Holy Roman emperor.[102]

Although not always observed in all details, the basic clauses of the Golden Bull continued to be a guide for the Holy Roman Empire. All the evidence indicates that, by the time of Emperor Maximilian, the German diets had a very high regard for the German constitution. How familiar all were with its contents is another matter.

The Golden Bull's validity was reaffirmed in Charles V's *Wahrkapitulation* of 3 June 1519:

> We are obliged and wish to confirm and renew, on the basis of the Golden Bull, the emperor's peace and other regulations and laws contained therein;

and, wherever it is necessary to improve upon them with the assistance of our counsellors and the electors of the Reich, princes and estates; and to be always well disposed to the convenience of the empire.[103]

The Golden Bull was never abrogated, even though in later *Reichstagen* throughout the centuries there were changes due to new problems and political upheavals.[104]

As observed above, the descendants of Albrecht I, who died in 1260, were of two families. The descendants of Johann formed the Lauenburg line; while descendants of Albrecht II became known as the Saxon-Wittenberg line. We have seen how, through a series of historical circumstances and fortunate marriages, the younger brother's descendants had served for half a century as electors of Saxony, and were firmly established in that office by the Golden Bull. But in spite of the Saxon Clauses of the constitution, Duke Erich, of the Lauenburg line, after 1356 still claimed to be the legitimate elector through the *Reich's* practice of primogeniture. Accordingly, the Kaiser summoned him before his high court of princes. He finally yielded to the *Reich's* decision.[105]

Elector Rudolf II was succeeded in 1370 by his son Wenzel, who ruled until his death in 1388. We know very little about him, but, for some unknown reason, his nephew signed some official documents. This implies that they conducted the business of government together. There was also a claim that the official line should pass to the house of Lüneburg. In 1376 the *Reich* officially reaffirmed the Golden Bull, stressing once more the law of primogeniture. But the proclamation also referred to the passing of the *Kurkreis* to the house of Lüneburg. Some claimed that Wenzel was poisoned by a Prior Bertram, but this charge was never established.[106]

These were stormy times within the empire. By comparison with his father, Wenzel turned out to be a failure. In 1399 the electors assembled at Marburg to correct the problem with reference to the indolent king. During the meeting, many electors were inclined to depose their Kaiser. The Saxon elector Rudolf III urged the replacement of Wenzel by his brother-in-law, Friedrich of Braunschweig. But to this there developed considerable opposition from the elector of Mainz and the Palatinate.[107]

After the meeting, Rudolf accompanied Friedrich of Braunschweig, in the company of a fair-sized bodyguard. But near Fritzlar they were attacked by about two hundred knights and their servants under the leadership of young Henry of Waldeck, the top-ranking official of the archbishop of Mainz. In this encounter Friedrich put up a noble defense, but he was stabbed, captured, and locked up in the Waldeck Castle. After that it took considerable funds to gain his release.[108]

Rudolf III did not support the election of Ruprecht of the Palatinate, Wenzel's successor as emperor, but instead expressed his preference for Jobst of Moravia or Sigismund of Hungary. For this Sigismund rewarded him, after he became emperor in 1410, by investing him with the *Kurkreis* and also the Lüneburg lands. In Rudolf III's struggle with Brabant over sword-carrying rights at *Hoftagen*, Sigismund decided in favor of Saxony. He also granted

Rudolf the right to mint gold coins in his lands.[109] (Emperor Ruprecht is also credited with the construction of the magnificent castle in Heidelberg.)[110]

Rudolf III was married twice, first to Anna, the daughter of Landgraf Balthasar of Thuringia (a marriage that resulted in no children), and, later, to Barbara von Liegnitz, who blessed him with two princes. But in 1406 these two young princes were staying in their Schweinitz castle when a tower collapsed during the night and killed them.[111] Rudolf III himself was killed in 1419 while fighting in the Hussite wars.[112]

The only legitimate successor to the Electorate of Saxony, according to the Saxon Clauses of the Golden Bull, was Rudolf III's brother Albrecht III, who then ruled from 1410 to 1422. His contemporaries referred to him as "the poor," for the family had been completely impoverished by Rudolf III's lavish spending.[113] Albrecht was forced to restrict his court to four officials. Poverty also forced him into a conflict over privileges and taxes with his own city of Wittenberg, in which Elector Friedrich of Brandenburg finally served as arbiter.[114]

Soon after his return from the *Reichstag* at Nürnberg in November 1422, the elector and his wife went on a hunting trip in the Lochauer Heide, where they stayed in a farmhouse. The building caught fire during the night and both Albrecht and his wife Eufemia, daughter of Konrad of Öls, were badly burned. Albrecht was taken to Wittenberg, where he died from shock and burns four days later. Like thirty-six other members of the royal family, he was buried in the Franciscan Monastery, near the high altar, next to his brother Rudolf.[115]

According to the imperial constitution, the electorate was now terminated and reverted back to the Kaiser. This opened it up to the highest bidder. There were several claimants, among them Frederick of Brandenburg. He proposed his brother Johann, because his wife was the daughter of the former Elector Rudolf III, and the margrave was even bold enough to occupy the *Kurkreis* with his troops. Erich von Lauenburg again based his claims for the electorate on the fact that the two families claimed a common ancestor, Albrecht I; by the rule of primogeniture, the Lauenburg line should really have inherited the *Kurkreis* in 1260, for Johann I was the oldest son. Another bidder was Elector Ludwig of the Palatinate, who tried to obtain the prize for his son, also named Ludwig. Finally there was Frederick the Valiant of the Osterland, to whom Emperor Sigismund was deeply indebted for his prominent role in the Hussite wars. Apel von Vitzthum even made a special trip to the Kaiser's court to plead Frederick's case.[116]

The decision about the *Kurkreis* hung in the balance for some time while Sigismund reflected on the wisest course of action. The situation in Saxony demanded a strong personality to protect the *Kurkreis* from further aggression. Sigismund ruled out the Lauenburg line from the very outset. As for Brandenburg and the Palatinate, each already possessed one electoral vote (*Kur*). In the end, Frederick the Valiant's efforts in the Hussite wars made the emperor decide in his favor.[117]

On 6 January 1423, at Presburg, Kaiser Sigismund quietly issued a letter investing Frederick the Valiant with the Electorate of Saxony. He also ordered the margrave of Brandenburg to withdraw his troops from the *Kurkreis*. But to implement this choice effectively, the emperor ordered his Hofmeister Graf, Johann von Lupen, the Landgraf of Stulingen, to transport the new elector to his lands by force. Little is known of what happened behind the scenes, but Margrave Frederick of Brandenburg left Saxony only after the new elector had paid him 10,000 Groschen. After that, Frederick the Valiant was extended the "exemptions and privileges" with the fief of the *Kurkreis*. At Bingen in 1424, Frederick was officially welcomed into the electoral college. On 1 August 1425, at Ofen, Hungary, the Kaiser ceremoniously invested Frederick with the Electorate of Saxony and its distinctive emoluments, in addition to the Pfalz Allstadt, the *Grafschaft* Brene, and the *Burggrafschaft* Magdeburg.[118]

But even these official actions did not stop the determined Erich from trying to further the old family claims. The Lauenburg line prepared a forged letter of investiture, dated 1414, which made them—rather than the Saxon-Wittenberg line—the official electors of Saxony. This issue was to be taken up in a princes' court. But when Erich did not get his way, he took his case to Pope Martin V in 1427. He, in turn, referred the case to the council of Basel in 1434. The council seems to have been impressed by the forged investiture document and considered the case as if Lauenburg were the rightful line. Both Frederick the Gentle (the new elector of Saxony) and the emperor made strong protests to this procedure, and the case was terminated. The following year Erich died, and his successor Bernhard did not resume the longstanding feud. In 1474 the case was raised once more and again brought to the attention of the papacy, but this last attempt also proved to be without success.[119]

6

Sources for Constructing
a History of Thuringia
and Meissen

A glance at the map of Germany during the Reformation era reveals that the Saxon lands, once confined to the electoral circle around Wittenberg, had grown to an immense size. By the time of Frederick the Valiant, they extended from the Werra in the west to the bishopric of Meissen and Oberlausitz in the east and from the Electorate of Brandenburg in the north to the region of Coburg in the south. The two ruling Saxon houses in Luther's day, the Ernestine and Albertine lines, still remained intact from 1485 to 1547. But these were territorial states, governed at a number of levels of jurisdiction. There remained the noble houses of Schwarzenburg, the Henneberg and Kyffhausen, as well as the ecclesiastical lands of Mainz around Erfurt and the bishoprics of Naumburg, Merseburg, and Meissen. All of these were to some degree the acknowledged subjects of the two Saxon houses; yet they possessed their own allodial lands and ecclesiastical bishoprics, in regard to which they were practically independent. To clarify what it meant historically that Electoral Saxony was combined with Thuringia and Meissen after the Ascanier line died out in 1422 necessitates a treatment of the earlier history of these lands. It requires some knowledge of the history of the Saxon lands to perceive the roles of Erfurt, Leipzig, and Wittenberg in the now enlarged Saxon territories.

The historian faces some difficulties in attempting to trace the history of Thuringia and Meissen. Historiography was not yet developed during that period. Most of the historical records of the Middle Ages are ecclesiastical, written by monks, and often not too trustworthy. These *Annalen* were frequently compiled from older sources; often the monks even relied on forgeries. The centers of these early histories of Thuringia and Meissen were Erfurt, Reinhardsbrunn, Eisenach, and Nordhausen. The history of Erfurt's cloister, located on the Petersberg, dates back to Merovingian days, but later this monastery fell into ruin. It was not restored until the Hirsauer Abbot Giselbert took it over in 1085, as well as Reinhardsbrunn, which had been founded by the Ludowinger.[1]

Abbot Giselbert brought his previous *Annalen Lamperts* from Hersfeld, which he then continued under the title *Annales S. Petri Erphesfortenses Antique*. Since the early history of Erfurt was no longer extant, Giselbert extracted the first part, covering the years 1078–1163, from his own *Lampert Annalen* on St. Peters; while the rest he copied from the Pegau *Weltchronik Ekkehards von Aura*, in which he tried to trace the history as far back as Erfurt's founding in 706. The abbot also covered St. Peter's history since its incineration by Henry IV. This initiated the local historical writing in Thuringia.[2]

Wiprecht von Groitzsch, who inherited the Osterland from his uncle, Udo von Stade, founded the Benedictine monastery of Pegau for his Bohemian wife, Judith, daughter of King Wratislav of Bohemia.[3] He brought in Hirsauer reform monks under the abbot Bero, who already possessed the famous *Chronik Ekkehards von Aura*. But instead of continuing the Ekkehard chronicle, Bero started a new cloister history. In this he traced the territorial history from the time of the monastery's founding.[4]

The early theme of *St. Peter's Chronicle* at Erfurt covers the period of Markgraf Ekkehard's rule under Lothar III. This chronicle really constitutes a history of the last of the Salien emperors, viewed from the perspective of his home town. Historians believe there existed an older *Reinhardsbrunn Chronicle*, since lost, which the Erfurt writer used, covering the years 1152–1181. Perhaps even the Erfurt and Reinhardsbrunn monks worked together, which may explain why their accounts seem to agree so well. Out of this background there emerged another series of annals, the *Chronica S. Petri Erfordensis Moderna*, or the *New Erfurt Chronicle*, written between 1208 and 1209. A later, fourteenth-century entry for the year 1070 read: "Notice, here begins the *Modern Chronicle*."[5]

The first part of this *Erfurt Modern Chronicle* also drew heavily on the lost *Reinhardsbrunn Chronicle*; while its second part, written around 1276, likewise made ample use of this old source. In this last part, the histories of the Ludowinger Landgrafen and the Meissen Markgrafen frequently seem to be intertwined. The *Erfurt Modern Chronicle*, however, does not limit its horizon to local or even Thuringian affairs, but becomes European in scope.[6]

The Benedictines of St. Peter's Monastery were not the only historians in old Erfurt. The mendicants, both Franciscans and Dominicans, also drew upon the *Reinhardsbrunn Chronicle* when they wrote their *Chronica minor Minoritae Erphoedensis*, or *A Small Chronicle by an Erfurt Mendicant*. Since both mendicant orders traveled widely, their outlook proved to be less local and more general in scope.[7]

An unknown cleric in Erfurt wrote a history of such merit that it might properly be dignified as the first real historical writing in Thuringia. Its title was *Liber Chronicorum sive annals Erfordensis*, or *A Chronicle Book of the Annals of Erfurt*. At the outset he stated that his aim was to relate the history of the Thuringian *Landgrafschaft*, using Erfurt at his point of departure. Of real advantage to him proved to be the large *Reinhardsbrunn Chronicle*, which had been completed. He drew upon this source for his history of the Ludowinger family.[8] No doubt the close relationship that existed between the town of Erfurt and the Landgrafen explains why the *Book of Chronicles* was terminated in 1345.[9]

There was a decided advance in the historiography of this region in the *Chronicon ecclesiasticum*, which Nikolaus von Siegen began in the Peters-kloster of Erfurt in 1494. But unfortunately he was swept away by the Plague the following year. We still possess an autographed copy of his chronicle, pre-served by Goethe.[10] Siegen really attempted to write a secular history of Thuringia. For the years 1250 to 1355, after the land had passed under the Meissen Landgrafen, he relied heavily on the *St. Peter's Chronicle*, and for the subsequent years he used John Rothe's account.

Naturally, Siegen's historical account of his Benedictine order, covering the ecclesiastical-secular history in relationship to Thuringia, does not resemble the treatises of modern historians; but neither is it any longer a chronological account of the events of his country's past; it manifests real attempts to get at basic reality. At the outset he remarked, "Please observe, my dear reader, as God be my witness, here by means of my own hand, to use the expression, I am writing the following account without the intention of propagating Lothar for-geries and lies."[11]

The fact that Siegen took nothing for granted and examined seals and other marks of authenticity to establish facts was no doubt due to his humanistic train-ing. Of course he still lacked the necessary library tools and modern reference works. Yet he concluded, with reference to the founding of St. Peter's at Erfurt, that the founder of the original Benedictine monastery could not have been Dagobert I but was rather Dagobert III, who lived in that period. Hence he authenticated 706 as the date of St. Peter's founding.[12]

Others contributed to Thuringian history, among them Konrad Stolle, who, in his *Memoriale* or *Remembrances,* also covered faraway themes and events of his day. Yet he wove much local history into these larger accounts. He was edu-cated at St. Severi and lived in Rome and Florence from 1458 to 1462; yet no humanistic influence is traceable in his writing. He drew upon Johannes Rothe's *Düringer Chronik* and covered the tragic "Saxon Brothers War," yet he did not give it a distinct title in his coverage. Instead he wrote about Charles the Bold, the fall of Constantinople, the defense of the island of Rhodes, and even the Pazzi plot against Lorenzo the Magnificent. In his homely, local dialect, he wove many observations, in the form of asides, into his local Erfurt history.[13]

Another historical treatise that emerged from the Erfurt circles was entitled *Erphurdianus Antiquitatum Variloquus incerti auctores*, written in very bad Latin, which historians believe was the work of Master Johann Werlich of Erfurt. This professor rose from a small *Bürger* family, took his master's degree at Erfurt in 1493, became dean of the philosophical faculty in 1503, and died of the Plague in 1521. Werlich was one of Erfurt's old scholastic professors, who first tolerated, but later fought, the humanists. The earlier part of his history is of little worth; but after 1460 he relates events on the basis of personal experi-ence—like the Erfurt revolution of 1509, which he described in some detail. In this struggle the Erfurt *Stift* and the Wettiner under Frederick the Wise fought over potential commercial advantages. So far no historian has explored this from the viewpoint of the Erfurt *Bürger*, which could be profitable.[14]

Finally, in the *Chronicle* of Hartung, the city treasurer of Erfurt, we have the first known German document stemming from the *Bürger* class. In 1431 Hartung was elected by the Landgraf to the office of travel controller. He also served five times as *Bürgermeister* of Erfurt. In his *Chronik* the principal events in the Wettiner lands are recorded, such as the aforementioned Saxon Brothers War as well as the passionate struggles of the Schwarzenburger nobles and other similar contemporary events. He also vividly described Erfurts reception of Cardinal Nicholas of Cusa, as well as the stir created in front of the cathedral by the penance preacher Johannes von Capestrano, whom Hartung brought to the city in a parade composed of the town council and the faculty of the University of Erfurt. After demanding draughts, dice, playing cards, and hair ornaments from the women of Erfurt, the penance preacher also created a great spectacle by publicly burning the treasured ornaments. This account vibrates with the life of the times.[15]

In his last testament, the city treasurer stipulated that the *Chronicle* was to be kept in the choir loft of the Church of Saint George; but the church officials feared that visitors might learn too much of contemporary history. So the *Chronicle* was transferred to the safe custody of the town council, where no one could read it. Hartung's history reveals the world view of a fifteenth-century Erfurt *Bürger*.[16]

As noted in the previous section, the Erfurt historians of St. Peter's drew heavily on the *Reinhardsbrunn Chronicle*. The famous old Thuringian monastery of Reinhardsbrunn is believed to have been founded by Ludwig der Springer, the second-generation ruler of the Ludowinger family.[17] He is said to have brought Hirsauer monks to Reinhardsbrunn, and later it served as a burial place. The monks produced the first *Thüringische Annalen*, covering the years 1100 to 1149, during the reigns of the last two Salien rulers, Henry V and Lothar II, as well as Conrad III of the Hohenstaufen line. The *Chronicle* also shows that these monks kept notes covering part of the reign of Emperor Frederick Barbarossa during the years 1152 to 1181.[18] Since the relationship between the Staufer and the Landgraf was close, one can understand the monks' interest in these eventful years.[19] But of all these earlier drafts, only one manuscript has survived, the *Chronica Reinhardsbrunnensis* of 1338. This work consists of three parts. The first deals with the Thuringian history under Landgraf Hermann I, until his death; the second treats the life and rule of Landgraf Ludwig IV (the Pious), and his wife, the Holy Elizabeth—Ludowinger who made the Wartburg their principal dwelling.[20] The final section, covering the reigns of Heinrich Raspe and the subsequent Wettiner Landgrafen of Thuringia, extends to the year 1338.[21]

For the years 1187 to 1215, the 1338 copyist and editor reproduced rather accurately the text of the lost *Reinhardsbrunner Historien*, including the participation of Ludwig IV and Hermann I in the Crusades. The struggle for the crown between Philip of Swabia and Otto IV, in which the loyalty of Hermann I shifted back and forth, captivated the writer of the second chronicle. The chronicler became deeply concerned with his landgrave's lot in those days, and the annals show that he knew his facts firsthand. The writer showed that he had a mastery of Latin, with which he pictured Hermann I's reign in somewhat dampened tones.[22]

From these *Chronicles* the reader obtains a clear picture of life in towns and castles in the days of Frederick II. Ludwig IV is portrayed as being faithful to his emperor, Frederick II. Berthold's account of Ludwig's life is the best work covering the times of the Ludowinger. The Thuringian dynasty was seen to have reached its peak during the rule of Ludwig V. But in the reign of Ludwig's brother, who succeeded him (after Ludwig had died on a crusade), the writer saw merely the extension of the Ludowinger domains.[23]

The monks of the Reinhardsbrunn cloister were not as intimate with the Wettiner, who acquired Thuringia in 1247, when Heinrich Raspe died without heirs. The *Chronik* reveals the struggle for succession as well as the land divisions after the death of Henry the Illustrious.[24] In 1292 the Reinhardsbrunn cloister fell victim to a fire, which burned it to the ground. After this tragedy the historians horizon narrows, largely confining himself with monastic life.

The Reinhardsbrunn chronicler stated that his objective was to give a faithful account of the phenomenal rise of the Ludowinger from a forest clearing to being the Landgrafen of Thuringia. He claimed that his aim was to show how the Ludowinger reigned through the days of the Saliens, as enemies of the *Reich*, and their loyalty to the Hohenstaufen under Ludwig III. At the same time, it is clear that the original spirit of William of Hirsau lived on at Reinhardsbrunn for 250 years after its founding.[25]

In addition to the *Reinhardsbrunner Chronik*, two smaller histories were written there. It is believed that the same historian prepared a chronicle entitled *Genealogia principium Reinhardsbrunnensis* or *A Genealogy of the Princes of Reinhardsbrunn*, in which he showed his belief that a Carolingian lineage of the Ludowinger could be traced. He began his genealogy with Ludwig the Bearded and traced the family lineage all the way back to its end in 1247.[26]

A number of treatises were written on the lives of Ludwig the Pious and Holy Elizabeth. Caesar of Heisterbach wrote a biography of Elizabeth between 1236 and 1237. In 1289 Dietrich von Apolda, a Dominican Friar in Erfurt, gave us another account of her life. But these contain very little not found in Chaplain Berthold's earlier biography. In 1308 a no longer extant *Vita Ludowici*, or *Life of Ludwig*, was written in Reinhardsbrunn. This is what Friedrich of Saalfeld, the rector of the cloister school in the monastery, used as a basis for his biography, *Das Leben des Heiligen Ludwig*, written sometime between 1314 and 1323. In this the author extolled the signs and wonders that he claimed had occurred during this holy man's lifetime, and he charged that monks had shown so little regard for these events in later years that God had caused the monastery to go up in flames in 1292.[27]

In the nearby town of Eisenach, the Dominicans also kept a *Chronica Thuringorum*, or *Thuringian Chronicle*, published by Pistorius in 1583. It has been designated by historians as *Pistoriana*. This main Dominican chronicle covers the Thuringian history to 1305, after which it becomes spotty, ending in 1412. But the account also offers little that was new. The book was based almost exclusively on the above-cited Erfurt records. What the writers did not find there was extracted from the Reinhardsbrunn chronicle and some older Dominican records in Eisenach.[28]

Not to be outdone, the Franciscans in Eisenach also wrote a history of the landgraves of Thuringia, prepared in 1407 after the death of Markgraf Wilhelm. It appeared under the title *Geschichte über die Landgrafen von Thüringen*. Later, in 1722, this chronicle was published by Eccard. It is commonly known as *Eccardiana*, and much of its content was gleaned from the Dominican *Thuringian Chronicle*. One of the authors was Martin of Troppau. The form of the document is that of a world chronicle, with the contemporary Thuringian history woven into the larger account. This history was terminated sometime between 1476 and 1482. The historical writing of the Franciscans actually contributed little of significance.[29]

However, one encounters something qualitatively different in the writing of Johannes Rothe of Creuzburg, a contemporary of Hartung Kammermeister who could be designated as a half-priest and a half-layman *Bürger* in Eisenach. His life span covered the years between 1350 and 1434. Rothe began as a priest and became vicar of the Liebfrauenkirche, later serving as a teacher in the local *Marienstift*. He then became the town secretary of Eisenach, and finally advanced to secretary of the upper court of the landgraviate of Thuringia. As a former clergyman, he moved freely among the laity of the Thuringian and Meissen courts. Such contacts are plainly reflected in his writings. These included the *Eisenacher Rechtsbuch*, a lawbook that treated the local court activities; the *Meiszner Rechtsbuch*, which parallels the former, treating court activities in the Meissen Slav lands; and, finally, a *Corpus iuris civilis*, a book on Roman civil law. In this massive accumulation of legal data and court procedure, Rothe also did not hesitate to draw freely from the canon law of the Roman Church. Thus there is a strange mixture of antique, German, and Christian elements, in which Rothe is revealed as one who grew up in the piety of the Middle Ages and yet was much attracted by the reform movements evolving in his day. He attempted to offer guidance for all classes in society.[30]

Johannes Rothe may also be the author of the *Chronicum Thuringicum*, or the *Thuringian Chronicle*. This author drew upon the *Eccardiana* as one source, but with much better diction made it more intelligible to his fellow Eisenach citizens. He even used Wendish names such as Zeitz and Scheiplitz, with which his readers were no doubt familiar. In this chronicle Rothe combined the world of the landgraves with that of the *Bürger* of Eisenach. In his chronology he also distinguished between the high Middle Ages and the later period of his own day. In his coverage of the life of Ludwig IV, he omitted the miracle stories and treated his *Vita* in a secular context.[31]

Rothe was no doubt also the author of the *Düringische Chronik*, allegedly dictated to Bruno of Teutleben, the custodian of the Wartburg between 1417 and 1419. This historian is credited with a third history specifically written for

Landgräfin Anna, entitled *Von den Kaisern, Papsten, von dem Lande und der Herrschaft zu Thüringen*, a treatise that terminated with the year 1421. It was really a Thüringien *Weltchronik* in which Rothe combined universal history with local Thuringian events. It drew much of its data from the aforementioned *Eccardiana*. Few of its chapters have any original value, as he, in typical medieval fashion, still combined whole epochs with world history, beginning with creation and continuing through the Greek and Roman periods, about which he knew very little. As a result, there is often too sharp a break between ancient history and that of Thuringia.[32]

The writings of Johannes Rothe and Konrad Stolle furnished the basis for the Adam Ursinus *Chronicum Thuringicum*, or the *Thuringian Chronicle*, in which Ursinus covered the years until 1500. This undertaking was completed in 1547.[33]

Besides these major chronicles there were also some *Stift* chronicles worthy of citation. There appeared the *Chronicon Gozecense* or *Chronicle of the Gosneck Cloister*, which covers the history of counts of the Saxon Palatinate. This really originated in an endowed institution (*Stifte*) such as Reinhardsbrunn. The codex also contains material from the often cited *Pegauer Annalen*. It is strange that we possess no history of the counts of Schwarzenburg, although there are some entries concerning the history of this old family in the *Reinhardsbrunner Chronik*. Equally strange is the fact that there is no known chronicle about the lives of the counts of Henneberg. References to them as existing in the upper Werra region are proof of their existence, but their chronicles may have perished with their libraries when these monasteries were terminated. In Spangenberg's *Chronicon Hennebergense* and Carluss' *Queyenbergische Wallfahrtsannalen*, the *Annales of the Meynigen Cloister* contain references to them. It is believed that the *Veszrei Annalen* were also written contemporaneously with those of Reinhardsbrunn, and that regular genealogies were kept by the Henneberg family.[34]

There did exist historical works about the Henneberg family, partly lost and some extant, which fall into the later period of humanism and the Reformation. Georg Doth wrote a poem about the 1476 pilgrimage of Count Wilhelm III to the Holy Land, while the Heidelberg humanist Adam Wernher of Themar prepared family trees for the various counts. There were also court historians among them, but the quality of their work was jeopardized by too much flattery. There were such men as Johannes Nuhn of Hersfeld, a student at Erfurt in 1461, and who in 1475 entered the service of Count Heinrich II, remaining there until his death. Later this secular clergyman was employed by the landgrave of Hesse, for whom he prepared a Hessian chronicle with a very pretentious title: *A Hessian Chronicle from the Forty-Seventh Year before Christ until the Year after Christ 1520*. This impossible undertaking reflected the same weakness as Rothe's *Düringische Weltchronik*. Nuhn's Hessian history appeared at the very periphery of a universal history. In it a real void existed between the Carolingians and the first Ludowinger ruler of Thuringia, Ludwig the Bearded. What appears even more peculiar is that Nuhn began his history with Ludwig the Bearded, the real founder of the Thuringian dynasty; after that, he immediately passed into the Hessian story.

A similar procedure was followed by Wigand Gerstenberg, who lived between 1457 and 1522. This chronicler was also a secular clergyman, one who had studied at Erfurt about 1473. Gerstenberg wrote a *Frankenberger Stadtgeschichte*. This cleric, likewise, tried to write a Thuringian-Hessian history, but with little more success than Nuhn.[35]

About the same time, an anonymous author wrote a work called the *Chronicon Hennebergense*, or the *Henneberger Chronicle*, which appears to have been finished in 1519. This author wrote in much better Latin and displayed a good knowledge of humanistic rhetoric. The chronicle covers the Henneberger history from 1040 to 1517, treating it in genealogical sequence. For his sources he employed existing annals, chronicles, and family genealogical tables.[36]

We have briefly reviewed the principal sources that modern historians must use to reconstruct the history of Thuringia and Meissen, which we are about to undertake. Our first theme must be the history of Thuringia, since it was a separate *Landgrafschaft* from the Mark of Meissen until 1247, when the Ludowinger family died out. After that date, the lands of Thuringia and Meissen were combined under Henry the Illustrious. These two states were later incorporated with Electoral Saxony in 1422, after the Sachsen-Wittenberg line of Ascanier had died out. For a proper grasp of the setting of the Reformation, the reader needs to become familiar with the historical development of these three lands.

7

Early Thuringian and Meissen History

Like the region between the Saale and the Elbe Rivers, the beautiful hills and valleys of Thuringia were once largely covered by dense forests. Schlesinger claims that the word *mark* (and thus the title "margrave") came from the Slavic *Marka*, meaning "swamps."[1] The Slavic settlers lived largely along lakes and streams, while the feudal lords placed their castles, or *Burgwarden*, in key locations on hillsides. In the early period a mark did not imply a region with definite boundaries; rather it was a vague designation for an area dominated by *Burgwarden*. In the early German empire, counts were royal officials who carried out the emperor's will and protected the lands of the crown. Later they acquired territories of their own ("allodial lands"), the right to hold court, and some control over distribution of land. In time a Graf would even begin to regard his *Markgrafschaft* as hereditary. Such marks passed back to the crown only if a ruling line of counts died out. In the new east the granting of marks was relatively simple, for among the Slavs there were no longer nobles from old family lines with vested interests.[2] By the eleventh century, the territorial boundaries of such marks became more fixed. At that time, according to Thietmar, the empire began to distinguish between the Mark Meissen and the Ostmark (the east mark).[3]

Little is known about the political history of Thuringia during the days of Henry I and Otto the Great. As early as 880, a certain Poppo referred to himself as a Thuringian duke. But his title could not have been comparable to that of the dukes of the old Stem Duchies of the *Reich*, who were royal officials. The Liudolfinger and the Babenberger were present at an early date, and they formed a dangerous coalition against the crown. Prior to the Saxon dynasty under King Arnulf, the Liudolfingers had pushed their way into Thuringia from the Harz Mountains.[4] A number of old-line families existed in the Thuringian hills; however, only four of these concern us: the Ekkehardinger, the counts of Weimar, the Ekberts, and the house of Wettin.

Reference to a Count Ekkehard is made in a document related to Otto the

Great. Where this count's lands were located is unknown. A Saxon annalist claimed his son was Count Günther, margrave of the bishopric of Merseburg. The original Ekkehardinger lands seem to have been located mainly west of the Saale River in Thuringia, somewhere below the Harz Mountains; but the count's influence also extended into the Slavic lands to the east. Count Günther was with Otto I at Ravenna in 968, and Otto the Great commanded him and Count Siegfried to wage a campaign against the Greeks and Saracens in 969.[5]

In 973, however, after the emperor's death, Günther and a group of other princes rallied in support of the election of Henry the Quarrelsome of Bavaria. The Saxon Kaiser who was elected instead of Henry then moved swiftly to deprive the disloyal Günther of the Mark of Meissen. He gave it as a fief to Thietmar I (or Thimo, as he was better known), a close personal friend. Thimo had helped Otto II obtain the crown and had done other personal favors for him. Thietmar already possessed the Ostmark, which generally extended from the confluence of the Saale and the Elbe to Strehla. Now he also became the margrave of Meissen. Since Count Wigger of Zeitz and Count Wicbert of Meissen had both died, Thietmar had no trouble extending his control over their lands as well as Merseburg. In 979, however, Thietmar was dead, and after years of exile Günther was reinstated in the Mark Merseburg. It remains doubtful whether he was able to extend his rule over the marks of Zeitz and Meissen. In 982 Günther died in a battle with the Greeks and Saracens at Capo Colonna, south of Crotone. The Kaiser himself barely escaped the debacle.[6]

Günther had two sons, Ekkehard and Gunzelin. In 983, immediately after Günther's death, the first great Slavic rebellion swept over the northern German lands, but left the Sorben lands to the south relatively undisturbed. No doubt this was due to the vast *Burgward* system.[7]

Ekkehard I was a strong, reliable, level-headed leader. A tremendous advantage for the young man proved to be his marriage to Schwanhild, the daughter of Herman Billung, the powerful duke of Saxony under Otto the Great. Schwanhild's first marriage had been to Markgraf Thietmar. This marriage immediately lifted the Ekkehardinger, already of high rank, into the elite circle of German nobility close to the crown. Schwanhild had a son from her first marriage, Gero II. She also bore Ekkehard seven additional children, of whom Hermann I, Ekkehard II, and Günther II played leading roles in imperial politics. Hermann I and Ekkehard II both became Markgrafen of Meissen, ruling successively until the year 1046. Günther II was made chancellor of the *Reich* in 1009, and then rose to become the archbishop of Salzburg in 1024. Thus from 992 to 1046, covering the reigns of the Kaisers Otto III, Henry II, Conrad II, and part of the rule of Henry III, the Ekkehardinger dynasty reigned almost continuously as margraves of Meissen. During this period the territory of the Mark of Meissen stretched roughly from west of the Saale to the Mulde River.[8] The ruins of their family castle can still be observed today.[9]

After Kaiser Otto II had died, his wife, Queen Theophano—who ruled during the minority of King Otto III—assigned the *Markgrafschaft* Meissen to Ekkehard I. She no doubt expected him to restore order on the confused eastern frontier and bring the Slavic lands in Meissen firmly back into the German orbit.[10]

In a war with Milzener at Bautzen, Ekkehard I defeated the Slavs and forced them to acknowledge German sovereignty. He also gained the respect of Duke Boleslaw of Poland. Thietmar, the chronicler who described this period, claimed Ekkehard I was also made duke over all Thuringia simply by election of the people.[11] But Helbig argues that this control must have been limited to the ruling noble families. Other historians, including Schlesinger, Giesebrecht, Kötzschke/Kretzschmar, and Tille, accepted this view. Yet Posse points out that in the sources, Ekkehard I is never referred to as a *dux*, or duke, but only by such titles as *comes* (count) or *marchio* (margrave).[12] However, no doubt Thietmar knew the ambitions of Ekkehard I as being nothing less than establishing such a duchy of Thuringia, though his death kept it from being realized.[13] Historians agree that such a title would not have equaled the dukedom of the *Reich's* earlier Stem Duchies.[14]

Count Ekkehard I soon won the favor of Otto III, and in time thereby acquired a number of lands that Ekkehard II later tried to convert into allodial territory. Exactly where these lands lay is no longer known, but they must have been on the north bank of the Unstrut River near Groszjena. Ekkehard had settled these regions with farmers and merchants. He constructed a castle on the Kappellenberg, along the Erfurt route passing through the Unstrut valley to Merseburg. Ekkehard also placed the Altenburg on the right side of the Saale, just opposite the entrance of the Unstrut River into the main stream. Later, his uncle Gunzelin and Ekkehard's two sons fought over the possession of this key castle. The Ekkehardinger also erected Steinberg castle as a border fortress on the right side of the Saale. The Naumburg, one of the mightiest of their castles, formed the third leg in their system of defense. The mighty Ekkehardsburg exists today only as a ruin. Upon Ekkehard's death, his wife Schwanhild regarded all these lands and castles as her personal property.

The process by which royal grants of land ultimately came to be regarded as allodial lands played a significant role in the later growth of territorialism as well as in the decline of the medieval empire. Ekkehard I also tried to take advantage of neighboring cloister fiefs. Thietmar related the story about a conflict between the Ekkehardinger and the bishop of Merseburg, who owned a certain forest. Originally it had belonged to the Ekkehardinger; but in the presence of Ekkehard's father, Kaiser Otto II had transferred it to the bishopric of Merseburg. After that the boys of the Ekkehard family began setting up traps, nets, and slings to catch game in the forest. When the bishop came upon them he ordered all the traps sprung and the nets cut. Then the battle began. The bishop finally won the case by means of a forged document presented to his superiors. After describing the forest war in some detail, Patze ended with the observation, "He who can write, can prove his rights."[15]

Ekkehard I was resourceful and possessed a boundless drive to achieve his goals. He also had many powerful enemies. When Otto III died at the fortress of Paterno, Ekkehard began to reach for the crown. But his opponent was

Henry II, a man of royal blood and far better qualified than he. When Otto III's mortal remains arrived at Augsburg, Henry made his bid for the throne. In the west and in other parts of the *Reich* groups began to take sides on the elevation of Henry II. Some princes wanted to wait and see how things developed. A few of the Saxon princes held a meeting in the royal court at Frohse, under their chairman, Count Gunzelin, a meeting in which Ekkehard's candidacy was opposed. In a private meeting there, Markgraf Liuthar pledged that the nobility would support Henry. An angry Ekkehard later asked the Markgraf why he was being opposed, to which Liuthar replied (according to Thietmar): "Do you not notice that you lack the fourth wheel on your wagon?" The editor noted that what Liuthar meant was that Ekkehard was not a relative of the royal family.[16] After that, opposition to Ekkehard mounted, but he decided to continue his campaign in spite of the warnings of his friends. Thietmar claimed that Ekkehard then decided to campaign in the west, where opposition to Henry seemed to be the strongest. There he planned to discuss his campaign with "the mighty in the empire."[17]

First the margrave visited Bishop Bernward of Hildesheim, where he was received like a king. After that he went on to Paderborn, but found the city gates locked. Later the bishop ordered that he be permitted to enter. After worshiping in the local church, the Markgraf went to the bishop's house for a meal and the two sat and talked things over. The bishop informed him that the planned meeting had been cancelled. When Ekkehard let him in on his plans, the bishop became offended. The margrave broke off their meeting and proceeded to Nordheim for an interview with Count Sigifrid. Here, too, the initial reception must have been friendly. But the Countess Ethelind warned Ekkehard that her husband's sons and brothers had vowed to waylay him on his departure and kill him. She begged the Markgraf to stay overnight, or at least to travel by an unexpected route. He replied that he would not alter his plans.[18]

All day Ekkehard and his entourage traveled, looking for possible ambushes, unaware that the young men had decided to wait until nightfall for their attack. The tired group then decided to find shelter in an old wooden structure. The margrave went inside to sleep, and his men slept at the front of the building. They, too, fell asleep, and during the night the assassins fell upon them. Both of Ekkehard's knights were killed right away, and the Kaiser's treasurer was wounded. With four assailants, it was almost impossible for Ekkehard to defend himself. The men decapitated him and mutilated his body. This happened on the night of 30 April, 1002.[19] The local Abbot Alfker said mass over the body. The chronicler reported that it was not known why this act of violence had occurred, but made this observation:

> I know this much, that Margrave Ekkehard I was a real credit to the *Reich*, a pillar of the fatherland, a source of hope for his subjects and a fright to his enemies; and he would have been a complete man had he only been willing to remain humble.[20]

When Ekkehard's oldest son, Hermann I, learned of his father's death he left his siege of Weimar (which had been ordered by his father) and, with Ekkehard's wife Schwanhild, rushed to the scene and took home the remains. Ekkehard I was buried at Groszjena on the Unstrut. The family then went into a thirty-day period of mourning, whereupon the mother took her two sons to Meissen.[21]

The sons of Ekkehard I were far from the equals of their father. The neighboring Slavic tribes realized this and rejoiced that the powerful margrave was gone. Soon the Slavs would be causing real problems for the *Reich*. Nor were Ekkehard I's sons in good standing with Emperor Henry II, for they had assisted their father in opposing his election.

Henry II, the last of the Saxon line of emperors, did not follow the dreams of Otto III in trying to establish a universal empire. Instead he generally confined his attention to German affairs. He displayed a good grasp of reality and took a firm hand in establishing peace in the slavic lands of the east. But Duke Boleslaw of Poland, often referred to as "the Bold," felt the time was right to strike. He would simply annex all the Slavic lands east of the Elbe. If he were successful in doing that, he would press westward to control all the Slavic lands up to the Saale. The *Burg* Meissen was besieged, and saved only by the brave stand of the warrior Thietmar. Boleslaw demanded the whole Elbe region, but instead of giving it to him, Henry made Gunzelin, the brother of Ekkehard I, the new Markgraf of Meissen. Gunzelin also happened to be the brother-in-law of the Polish duke. Boleslaw was so furious that he attacked the fortress of Strehala, and, after capturing it, led all the townspeople (mostly Slavs) into captivity. But the appointment of Gunzelin did not work out well. Within a few years his subjects accused the margrave of selling Slavs to Jews. Henry II held a trial in which Gunzelin was deposed. Mark Meissen was then transferred to Ekkehard I's oldest son, Hermann I.

Margrave Hermann I proved to be an able ruler who established order. He participated in many vital affairs of the crown (to which his signatures bear testimony), and also engaged in a number of imperial military expeditions, going deep into Poland and Silesia. The Markgraf married Regilin, the daughter of Duke Boleslaw. This should have ameliorated family relations, but the effect proved to be of short duration.[22]

Thietmar's *Chronicle* of this period is filled with accounts of Boleslaw and his son Miseco engaging in campaigns up to the Elbe and Meissen regions. They followed Henry II's army at a distance, ambushing and killing Count Gero in a woods. Later they attached the fortress of Meissen, which was only lightly defended by Hermann's men. In the siege that followed, Boleslaw's troops destroyed the part of the town outside of the fortress, but were not immediately able to take the castle itself. Heavy rains broke out during the night and the fortress was saved by flooding of the Elbe. Henry II brought in reinforcements, and the destroyed areas were rebuilt within two weeks.[23]

Nor did this end the Polish invasions. In 1017 they overran the region between the Mulde and the Elbe, and many of the inhabitants were led off into captivity. Finally, in a treaty at Bautzen on 30 January 1013, Hermann and many of his lords were forced to surrender Lower Lausitz and the Milzener lands.

Part of the settlement was that Count Boleslaw would acquire as a bride Hermann's sister Oda, the youngest daughter of Ekkehard I. Hermann's son Otto accompanied her to the castle Seitschen just southwest of Bautzen, where the duke held a large reception. This treaty remained in effect for thirteen years.[24]

After Henry II died, Conrad II of the Salien line succeeded him as emperor. He was made of sterner fiber, and did not like the way Henry had conducted the eastern frontier settlements. He could not immediately apply his energies to that problem, but in 1029 decided to regain past losses. Boleslaw had died in 1025, and Poland had become plagued by internal conflicts. This put campaigns in the west out of the question. But Meissen was once more overrun by a Polish army in 1030. As a result the Kaiser struck back with his forces, assisted by Hermann I. He defeated the Poles in 1031, regaining the lands around Bautzen and Lower Lausitz. In a treaty of 1031, the Lausitz regions once more officially passed into German hands.[25] Hermann I died in 1038. Conrad II, who was much closer to the Ekkehardinger sons than the previous king, made Ekkehard II, the younger brother of Hermann, the new margrave of Meissen.

Though the Polish threat had receded, before long a new menace appeared in the east. Duke Bretislav of Bohemia refused to accept German dominance in his lands. In fact, by annexing Lausitz, he hoped to encircle the Mark Meissen both from the east and the south. Emperor Henry III would not tolerate this. Ekkehard II participated in several of Henry's campaigns against Bretislav, thereby bringing peace to the whole region. Ekkehard had been custodian of the Ostmark since 1032, and he proved to be a faithful vassal of the Salien emperors. The king regarded Meissen as forming a buffer region against Bohemia. Ekkehard II was married to Uta, daughter of the count of Ballenstedt, near the Harz Mountains. But his marriage remained childless, and thus the Ekkehardinger line died out in 1046.[26]

As early as the days of Widukind in the tenth century, the counts of Weimar had become a significant force in Thuringia. Their origin is uncertain. Widukind regarded them as natives to the area,[27] but Posse thinks that dynasty may originally have resided in northern Swabia.[28] They first appear in historical records during the days of Otto the Great. Count William II was no doubt a brother of Poppo, and some historians believe they were related to the famous Babenberger family.[29] Others hold that they obtained their start with the help of the Liudolfingers.[30] In the year 975 the allodial possessions of these counts centered around Weimar, but some of their lands lay around Orlamünde. Bishop Thietmar considered Count William II one of the most powerful lords in Thuringia.[31] It is even possible that Weimar served as the gathering place of the Babenberger family in the days of Poppo II.[32]

When Otto the Great, the second ruler of the Saxon line of German emperors, was elected in 936 and then crowned in Aachen, he faced no simple task. Otto was fully aware that his claim to the throne might be challenged. Eberhard, the brother of the dying King Conrad I, had at Fritzlar presented his father, Henry the Fowler, as the future emperor, to which the assembled crowd had loudly shouted its approval. Thus Otto knew that his father, Henry I, had not been the choice of the five original German tribes, later known as Stem Duchies.[33] When young Otto, who had been designated by his father as his successor, set out to unify these tribal duchies into a single *Reich*, he encountered strong opposition. Much of the difficulty originated with his own family.

One of Otto's problems was that, as emperor, he dreamt of a restoration of the greatness of the Carolingian Empire. This demanded that he at least control northern Italy. Thus continued military campaigns across the Alps were required. To manage things at home while he was abroad, the Kaiser chose Hermann Billung, a member of a powerful noble family of Saxony, to serve as Duke of Saxony. Margrave Gero, an excellent military commander and frontiersman, was placed in charge of the eastern marks to subdue and control the Slavs.[34] Otto's choice of leaders enraged the king's half brother, Thankmar, who was already incensed because he felt deprived of his rightful share of the family inheritance.[35]

When Thankmar gathered disgruntled leaders and troops in various parts of the realm and even among the Slavs, the emperor's younger brother Henry first supported Otto. Later, due to the enticement of some top clergymen and nobles, Henry also aspired to become king. Two medieval chroniclers have related the story of the death of Thankmar in Hersfeld, as he stood next to an altar in St. Peter's Church, to which he had fled for safety after his defeat by Otto's troops.[36] Henry's fate was a little better. He, too, was defeated and fled to the frontier fortress of Merseburg. There he was captured and finally released after the continued pleadings of his mother. After that Otto made Henry duke of Bavaria, and he remained loyal.[37] As if that were not enough, later the king's own son Liudolf, misled by Siegfried, archbishop of Mainz, and other ambitious nobles, also made a failed attempt to depose his father. During this struggle of 963, Count William of Weimar appears on the scene.[38]

The death of Ekkehard I in 1002, as related above, lessened the pressure from the north on the Counts of Weimar. William III ruled as count of Weimar-Orlamünde from 1009 to 1039. The Hildesheimer *Annalen* rated him as one of the "chiefs of Thuringia." William III had four sons, among whom William IV was notable. We know very little about the counts of Weimar who ruled during these years, except that William III and William IV were contemporaries of the Markgrafen of Meissen, Hermann I and Ekkehard II. After that the Ostmark, over which Ekkehard II had ruled, passed to Dedi of the House of Wettin. At this time Kaiser Henry III decided to retain the Mark of Meissen for a while, but later he bestowed it on Count William IV of the house of Weimar Orlamünde. Formerly the counts of Weimar had been very close to the Saxon line of German emperors. With royal assistance, this house had became very powerful in the lands lying west of the Saale. Perhaps this was part of Henry's rationale, that by combining the house of Weimar with the Mark of Meissen, he would create a strong buffer zone against Bohemia and Poland. Military campaigns occupied much of William IV's rule. During a campaign in 1061 he was captured, but because the count had fought so nobly in the battle, King Bela of Hungary offered him his daughter Sophia as a bride. He died the following year, while on the way to receive his Sophia.[39]

The Mark of Meissen now passed to William's brother Otto, who seems to have been much weaker than his predecessor. During this reign a great struggle erupted between Margrave Otto and Siegfried, archbishop of Mainz, relative to church tithes. By giving in to the church, Otto proved to be a great disappointment to his subjects. Formerly they had not paid tithes.[40]

Little is known of what transpired in the Meissen and Weimar-Orlamünde lands during the Weimar line of rulers. However, the great disturbances in the *Reich* during the reign of Henry IV, including the Investiture Controversy with Pope Gregory VII, did not leave these lands unaffected. The churchmen of the Saale region also became involved.[41] Anno, the archbishop of Cologne, was once summoned to make a decision about a piece of property near Saalfeld in the Orlamünde region. This property had been willed to the *Stift* of St. Peters in Cologne by Richeza, the daughter of the Palatinate Count Ezzo, who had been the former wife of the deposed Slavic leader Miseco II.[42] This was also the period of the founding of many new reformed monasteries, patterned after the Hirsau model, which in turn had been influenced by the Cluniac reform movement supported by Pope Gregory VII.[43] Count Otto often fought in the ranks of Henry IV against the pope and his supporters. With Otto's death in 1067, the dynasty of Weimar-Orlamünde came to an end.[44] A lone survivor of the Weimar-Orlamünde line lived until 1122, after which there were no male heirs.

When Otto of Weimar died, Henry IV gave Meissen to Ekbert of Braunschweig, a member of the Brunonen family, which was very close to the Kaiser. Ekbert had assisted Henry during his escape from Kaiserwerth in 1067. On another occasion he had saved the king's life by leaping into the Rhine. Doubtless, another factor was that his wife Irmgard was related to the royal family. In the difficult days of Henry IV's struggle with Rome, Ekbert had been a strong supporter of the monarch. He was also a close friend of Archbishop Anno of Cologne. Thus it is understandable that Henry IV rewarded him with the *Markgrafschaft* of Meissen.[45]

But Ekbert was not Markgraf very long. He died in 1068 and designated his son, Ekbert II (a mere boy) his successor. We do not know who ruled Mark Meissen during Ekbert II's minority, but it may have been Count Dedi, the ruler of the East Mark. Otto's wife, Adelia of Brant, tried to bridge the gap between their houses by arranging an engagement between her daughter Oda and the young Ekbert. When the mark finally passed to Ekbert II, it did not include the lands around Zeitz; these had meanwhile been given as a fief to the count of Stade.[46]

After Canossa, the opponents of Henry IV elected Rudolf of Swabia as an opposition king, and Ekbert II participated in that Swabian opposition. Young Ekbert II, after the death of his wife Adelia, seems to have gone to pieces without her stabilizing influence, and became more or less a weather vane. He vowed allegiance to one person one day and then allowed others to turn him from his pledge the next. The Kaiser was much displeased by this. In 1086 Ekbert II was tried at Wechmar and his lands were given to Wratislav of Bohemia, who had proved to be loyal during Henry's trying times. Young Ekbert II now started to besiege his own castles. Later he made his peace with the emperor and was offered another chance. But the archbishop of Mainz and the bishop of Halberstadt turned Ekbert's head once more by offering him the kingship. War broke out again, after which Ekbert was tried at the Quedlinburg and condemned. Even after that he continued to battle. At a mill on the Selke River, Ekbert finally was killed in a battle on 13 July 1090. His marriage with Adelia had been childless, so the Ekbertinger line died out with him.[47]

After Ekbert's death and the passing of Meissen to Wratislav of Bohemia, a colorful figure appeared who, for a while, served as margrave of Meissen and Lower Lausitz. This was the warrior-knight Wiprecht von Groitzsch. It is from the Pegau records that most of the information about him has come down to us. Because Wiprecht was the founder of the monastery, the praise of their patron is doubtless somewhat overdrawn.[48]

Wiprecht had a distinguished ancestry. The family may have been descended from royalty, as the monks claimed. His father died when Wiprecht was quite young; as a result his uncle, Udo of Stade, raised the boy. Quite early the young man proved to be a capable warrior, destined for knighthood. Later his uncle bequeathed to him the castle of Groitzsch, located in the eastern lands, a gift that included several towns, pastures, and woods. Wiprecht fought nobly in Italy during Henry's campaigns, and even distinguished himself while storming the Lionese City in Rome. Upon his return the young knight's reputation spread. As a result he married Judith, the daughter of Wratislav of Bohemia. For this noble woman he built the Pegau Monastery. In time Wiprecht was given much additional land by Henry V, as well as by archbishops and bishops. In the earlier days he had been very loyal to Henry IV, as well as to Henry V; but he opposed Ekbert II in his dubious campaigns. The Benedictine monastery at Pegau became the first mendicant house established east of the Saale, a monastery that he staffed with monks from Korvey. Later, however, Wiprecht lost his lands for two years. This was due to a squabble with Henry V relative to his second wife Kunigunde, who had previously been married to a count in the House of Weimar. Wiprecht claimed that his wife had a rightful claim to her inheritance. Henry V, on the other hand, was trying to acquire the Weimar-Orlamünde region as crown lands of the king. After losing his private castle of Groitzsch, Wiprecht spent two years in a Kyffhäuser prison cell. Meanwhile his son fought nobly for his father's cause. The Saxon nobility, under the leadership of the young Groitzsch, defeated the emperor's forces at Welfesholze, which brought about the father's liberation and reinstatement. Later Wiprecht also became margrave of Meissen and Lausitz for a time. But Duke Lothar of Supplinburg opposed his elevation. The seventy-year-old Markgraf then fled to Halle, where by accident he was badly burned in a fire. The father returned to his Pegau cloister and became a monk, where he died on 22 May 1124.[49]

We now begin with the house of Wettin, whose dynastic rule extended through eight hundred years of European history. Frederick the Wise—the Elector of Saxony during Luther's day—his brother John the Constant, and his son John Frederick were the Wettiner who ruled over Ernestine Saxony from 1485 to 1547. Some historians believe their beginnings can be traced to Carolingian times. They are certainly traceable to Markgraf Burchard, who died in a battle with the Hungarians in 908.[50] His grandson, Dedi, served as a supervisor of Kaiser Otto I's castles on the Saale (according to Thietmar), and belonged to the family of the Buzini.[51] Later he became known as the count of Hassegau (a region north of the Unstrut, lying east of the Saxon lands). Dedi died in 957, leaving three sons: Burkhard, Dedi, and Dietrich.[52] Böttiger claims that, according to the *Sachsenspiegel*, the Wettiner were Swabians. Their original family *Burg* overlooked the Saale River from a high cliff near Halle.[53]

Burkhard, the oldest of Dedi's three sons, was the ancestral founder (*Stammvater*) of the house of Goseck, later known as the Saxon Pfalzgrafen. The second son, Dedi II, numbered among those who died in the surprise counterattack against Otto II's army by the Greeks and Saracens at Capo Colonna. The third son, Dietrich, became the *Stammvater* of the later house of Wettin.[54] Böttiger points out that this Dietrich is listed in the *Book of the Counts of Wettin* as a free noble, who became a royal vassal only because of his allodial possessions.[55]

Dietrich, the founder of the house of Wettin, had two sons, Dedi and Friedrich. His son Dedi was a capable and proud warrior who was killed in a quarrel in 1009. Friedrich, who ruled over the Eilenburg region, died without male heirs in 1017. Dedi had a son, Dietrich II, who succeeded in pulling the family lands together. He became the count of the Ostmark, and also controlled Lausitz after it had been freed from the Poles. He died in 1034.[56] Dietrich II had three sons: Dedi, Thimo, and Gero. Dedi ruled Lower Lausitz as Saxon margrave for three decades, dying in 1075. His son, Heinrich of Eilenburg, inherited Lower Lausitz and became margrave of Meissen in 1089. He ruled until his death in 1123. The second son, Thimo, together with his younger brother Gero, possessed the region of Brehna. Thimo married Ida, the daughter of the powerful Otto of Nordheim, and was referred to as a count of Meissen. From that marriage came Dedo and Conrad. The latter became the real *Stammvater* of the House of Wettin, and was known as Conrad the Great.[57]

8

The Rise of the Ludowinger

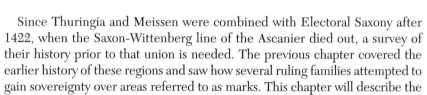

Since Thuringia and Meissen were combined with Electoral Saxony after 1422, when the Saxon-Wittenberg line of the Ascanier died out, a survey of their history prior to that union is needed. The previous chapter covered the earlier history of these regions and saw how several ruling families attempted to gain sovereignty over areas referred to as marks. This chapter will describe the beginnings of the Ludowinger; their rise from Markgrafen in central Thuringia to Landgrafen of the entire region; and their sovereignty over Thuringian and Hessian lands for several centuries.

The story of the Ludowinger rulers begins with Ludwig the Bearded (German: *Ludwig mit dem Bart*), who settled in Thuringia in 1039. Their history terminated with Heinrich Raspe, who died childless in 1247.

As previously indicated, our knowledge of the early history of Thuringia is limited almost exclusively to contemporary and later ecclesiastical annals.[1] Accounts such as those by the monks of Reinhardsbrunn, a monastery founded by the Ludowinger as a family burial ground, would naturally tend to dress up the history of their own noble family. In addition, we do not possess the original monastic record, but a later one compiled from the original (and copies), which was recorded by the monks of St. Peters and the Pegau Monastery.[2] Historians believe that many forgeries were added to the monastic accounts during the Investiture Controversy, as a way of supporting territorial claims.[3]

Hans Patze,[4] a recent historian who worked with the *Reinhardsbrunn Chronicle* and all related sources in considerable detail, admits that it is extremely difficult to bring the early history of the Ludowinger into historical perspective. Unexplained details remain, even though historians have tried for more than a century to establish the facts about the Ludowinger family's origins and the settlement of the Thuringian woods.[5] As early as 1880, Grosz wrote a thesis about the beginnings of the family, but his account was immediately challenged by others.[6] About the same time, Theodore Knochenhauer published an excellent history of Thuringia in which he conceded that early Thuringian history was partly shrouded in folklore and tradition. But he also concluded that the account was essentially reliable.[7]

According to the *Reinhardsbrunn Chronicle*, Kaiser Conrad II returned from Italy shortly before his death in 1039. After delays in Bavaria, Swabia, and Burgundy, he went back to his beloved Goslar to celebrate Christmas. The account says that in the presence of many princes and nobles, Conrad graciously gave Ludwig the Bearded an estate in central Thuringia, thus establishing the Ludowinger dynasty.[8] The original document of this royal grant was supposed to reside in Gotha, but when Knochenhauer went to examine it, he concluded that, like many family records, it was a forgery.[9] Other historians believe that even though there was much embellishment of the story by later writers, basically the account must be factual.[10] But why did Kaiser Conrad II perform this gracious act? The monks attempted to explain it in the *Chronicle*.

The chronicler of the original draft of the *Reinhardsbrunn Chronicle*, written several generations after the events, advanced the explanation that there had been a close relationship between Ludwig the Bearded and the royal family.[11] Knochenhauer, writing one hundred years ago, already judged many of the dressed-up details of the Reinhardsbrunn account as forgeries; yet he granted that the Ludowinger rise to power required explanation.[12] He provided this very simplified version of the monastery's account:

> In the days of Emperor Conrad II there lived two brothers, who had come from the left bank of the Rhine, in the land of the Franks, claiming an ancestry dating back to Charlemagne and Louis the Pious. These brothers, whose names were Count Hugo and Ludwig the Bearded, were blood relatives of Queen Gysela. Hugo was inordinately rich, and refused to serve anyone but the princes of Fulda and Mainz. The only male heir of these vast possessions was a son, Wichmann, who was by nature somewhat simple-minded and difficult. Because of his weakness, Mainz passed a legal sentence that took away his fiefs and gave them to another. Upon learning of this, young Wichmann rushed to Mainz with a band of followers and forced his way into the archbishop's palace. Afterward, either because he was a little crazy or very angry at the loss of his fiefs, he singlehandedly broke into the assembly room and, in the presence of the archbishop and the whole assembly, slew the robber of his estates. But when he tried to rush out of the palace and looked for an avenue of escape, he found the way blocked by a clergyman. A scuffle then occurred in the assembly room and Wichmann was put to death. Later all the allodial lands of young Wichmann passed to his uncle, Ludwig the Bearded.[13]

The chronicle states that since Queen Gysela was Ludwig's sister, it was she who arranged for the contact between him and Emperor Conrad II. As a further explanation, it adds that Ludwig was a prudent, wise, and ingenious man who so carefully guarded the affairs of the empire that in later meetings he even counseled the emperor. The chronicler adds that Ludwig was well-liked by the rest of the staff in the court.[14] The monastic account concludes by saying that Ludwig performed these services for the crown so laudably and proficiently that over time he was drawn more and more into royal deliberations; eventually the king performed no work when Ludwig was absent.[15]

A number of different stories appeared about the origins of the Ludowinger. One account runs as follows. Ludwig and his brother were the sons of Duke Charles of Lotharingia, who for years had fought against the usurpation of France by Hugh Capet, the last of the Carolingian line. In 991, the Lotharingian ruler and his family had been led into captivity by Hugh. According to the account, his two sons, Charles and Ludwig, escaped and fled to the court of the German Kaiser.[16]

Extant Lotharingian sources make the French origin of Ludwig very doubtful. Colorful and romantic as this family tradition may be, it is directly contradicted by another old report in the Lotharingian sources. This one claims that Otto, the oldest son of Duke Charles, had inherited the dukedom in 991, upon the death of his father, while the two younger boys, Ludwig and Charles, had died before that.[17]

Since we do not possess the original *Reinhardsbrunn Chronicle*, let alone whatever original family tradition lay behind it, we are forced to rely on a dressed-up version of the story as it evolved in later centuries. One is puzzled by a number of aspects of this account. Certainly Ludwig, regardless of his origin, must have been a man of considerable means and rank at the time the family appears in history. Otherwise, how do we explain the fact that the *Stammvater* moved into the Thuringian woods with the blessing of Kaiser Conrad II, and that he later received gifts from Henry III? How does one explain that he was favorably received by powerful counts and nobles, and that he was even given royal approval to build a castle in a strategic location? How does one account for his marriage to Cäcelia of Sangerhausen, with a gift of considerable size as a dowry? How else can one explain that he was able to clear stretches of forests, build hamlets and towns, and purchase additional land? All this implies that he was a man of previous prominence. It is of course possible that he was a native Thuringian with an old family history for which we possess no extant record. But this explanation does not fit very well into the story of the family's later circumstances.

Knochenhauer was aware of all these problems. Patze doubted the tale of Ludwig's Rhenish origin, as well as the claim that he had migrated to Thuringia from East Franconia, believing he was a native Thuringian. As evidence he cited the fact that his sons, Ludwig der Springer (or "Leaper") and his brother Beringer, in 1139, possessed a mill and a cloister at Schönrain; the monastery was located in the neighborhood of the counts of Reineck, a line that died out between 1071 and 1108. Patze accepted the Reinhardsbrunn account that they were blood relatives.[18]

One hundred years ago Böttiger claimed that he had reconstructed the Ludowinger background: Charles' two younger boys had been born in prison during the father's captivity; upon their release, they had sold their Lotharingian claims before entering the court of King Conrad II. After that Hugo had gained much wealth in the service of the archbishop of Mainz, and through marriage.

After Wichmann's death, this wealth had gone to his uncle, Ludwig the Bearded. Böttiger further concluded that Conrad II had committed Ludwig to the service of Archbishop Bardo of Mainz, who, in turn, had exchanged Ludwig's Rhenish possessions for new ones in Thuringia and Hesse. Thus, in the main, this historian already accepted the story about the Ludowinger's Carolingian descent.[19]

Even though research has cast doubt on the reliability of the Reinhardsbrunn saga, recent scholars have been inclined to believe that there is more truth to the original story than was thought a century ago. Patze cites two recent studies by Folz[20] and Cramer.[21] The former stressed the reasons why the Reinhardsbrunn writer tied the Ludowinger origin into a distinguished ancestry like the Carolingian, while the latter did not believe that the tale could have been plucked out of thin air. Patze regarded the rise of the Ludowinger as a vital part of territorialism, which also expressed itself in the rise of the Welfs, Ascanier, Wettiner, Zähringer, and Wittelbachs.[22] Thus the Reinhardsbrunn forgeries tried to create an ideal picture of the Ludowinger's small territorial state.[23]

The *Reinhardsbrunn Chronicle* are silent on why Ludwig the Bearded, after a successful court career, suddenly decided to resettle in the Thuringian woods, far away from civilization. There must have been some previous planning for the move, since it was done with the emperor's blessing and with the good will of the archbishop of Mainz. Ludwig had been assigned to the archbishop by the king's court, and he would soon enrich him with further fiefs. The venture would have offered the emperor a defensive flank against aggressors, but the sources are silent on this point. The account merely states that Ludwig the Bearded, accompanied by twelve knights, some nobles, and freemen, was awarded a large stretch of mountain valley land near Loyba in Thuringia.[24] The land was described as lying between the Kathernberg, Alsenberg, and Cornberg. Patze offers us an excellent description of the region. There were many small mountain streams where settlers, dressed in rough sheepskin, began to cut down timber in the forests and build hamlets; the center of this activity was around Friedrichsroda.[25] The original land grant must have been of considerable size, for Ludwig's son offered the church in Sangerhausen six hamlets that his father had erected.[26]

The chronicle speaks of hamlets at Gotha; in the provinces of Tenneberg, Friedrichsroda, Regnherborn, Dinstirberg, Egelspach; and at a number of other places, scattered here and there throughout the forest clearings.[27] Starting with a small estate near Altenburg, Ludwig kept buying land wherever available, until he became quite distinguished in the eyes of neighboring counts and nobles.[28] According to Böttiger, Ludwig had bought land from Count Gunther of Käfernburg, Count Busso of Gliechen, and a number of others. These were woods, villages, and stretches located around his estate. He claims that through Gysela's pleadings Conrad gave Ludwig more of the Thuringian forest, the offices of Tanneberg, Georgenthal, Schwarzwald, and Ichtershausen, and a large part of the dukedom of Gotha. He adds that the Kaiser regarded this area as a firm anchor of the *Reich*.[29] Later, under Henry III, Ludwig also obtained permission from both the king and the neighboring nobles to erect the castle

Schauenburg. In addition, the king granted him more territories from the royal domains.[30] We no longer know the limits of these lands, but Patze observed that they were in strategic locations. The Ludowinger now controlled the entry to Eisenach and the pass to Schmalkalden, leading to Friedrichsroda, Gotha, and Erfurt.[31] Where other feudal lords typically controlled lands only here and there, Ludwig exercised sovereignty over all his possessions. Ludwig made use of every opening that was offered while the political battle raged between the *Reich* and the church.[32]

After Ludwig the Bearded became the vice-chief of the archbishop of Mainz's fiefs in Thuringia, and had been securely established in his own vast estates, he was ready to acquire a suitable wife. The *Reinhardsbrunn Chronicle* tells us that he chose to marry Cäcelia, the daughter of Count Bertold of Sangerhausen, who brought him the rich dowry of 7,000 *Hufen* of land, as well as many other possessions and benefices.[33] There has been some difference of opinion as to who Cäcelia was. Böttiger thought she was a niece of Queen Gysela and the daughter of Ludwig of Braunschweig, which made her a sister of Markgraf Ekbert I of Meissen.[34] Knochenhauer asked: Was she perhaps a member of the Brunonen family of Braunschweig? At first this seems to be a logical tie-in with the royal family, for Queen Gysela's first husband had been Count Bruno of Braunschweig. But Schumacher held that Cäcelia was the daughter of Count Rudolf IV, who was the son of Gisela and Bruno of Braunschweig, a view that Rommel also supported. The genealogy of Cäcelia has created some real headaches for scholars. Knochenhauer concluded that her relationship to the Brunonen is doubtful. He preferred to believe she was a local girl, the daughter of the neighboring *Gaugraf* Hamezo.[35]

The *Reinhardsbrunn Chronicle* claims that Cäcelia was the mother of five children, two boys and three girls. Hildegard was the oldest girl, Uta the second, and Adelheid the third. Ludwig, the oldest boy and named after his father, inherited most of the family estate. Later he added significantly to the family possessions.[36] The youngest son, Beringer, later married Gertrude of Kathalenburg, who inherited the Sangerhausen estate. Her son was Conrad of Hohenstein, whose progeny became the counts of Hohenstein.[37] Knochenhauer claimed that Beringer later married Bertrada, the daughter of Markgraf Conrad of the house of Wettin, and through that marriage acquired the Hohenstein estate, where that family line was established on the border of Thuringia.[38] The *Reinhardsbrunn Chronicle* go into a detailed genealogy of Ludwig's daughters.[39] Perhaps this was to show how, through marriage, the Ludowinger wielded wide influence.

The death of Ludwig the Bearded is reported with but a single sentence in the monastery annals. The chronicler wrote: "an old man, ripe in years, Ludwig spent his last year in the year 1055."[40] But the *Düringische Chronik*, written much later, adds the following details. In 1056 Kaiser Henry III died and was buried in the Cathedral of Speyer. Pope Victor and his cardinals, along with many bishops and princes, were in attendance. Among the nobility was also Ludwig the Bearded from Thuringia, even though as a rule counts were not permitted to be present. For this occasion was not just a burial, but also the election of a successor. In accordance with Henry III's designation, Henry IV was elected. On the way home, when Ludwig and his party entered Mainz, the count became seriously ill and no cure seemed to help. He died and was buried in Mainz next to the grave of St. Alban. The chronicler added that Ludwig's rule in Thuringia had covered a period of thirty years.[41]

By the time that Ludwig the Bearded died in 1056, the Investiture Controversy had begun. Thuringia often became a battleground for it, and the general confusion kept Ludwig's successors from operating freely.[42] Ludwig the Bearded was followed by his sixteen-year-old son, Ludwig III. Knochenhauer regarded him as still only a territorial prince in the eyes of neighboring nobles. But Ludwig the Leaper (German: *Ludwig der Springer*) built the Wartburg (in spite of the counts of Frankenstein), purchased his brother Beringer's Sangerhausen heritage, and in other ways enlarged his father's estate.[43]

The chroniclers' stories about Ludwig the Leaper reveal embellishment by later folklore and tradition. Even the original writer of the *Reinhardsbrunn Chronicle* seems to have confused the marriage of Ludwig II with that of Ulrich of Weimar. He claims that Ludwig had first married a daughter of Ulrich of Saxony, but later repudiated her.[44] This story reflected poorly on him, so several centuries later, in the *Düringische Chronik*, the Eisenach schoolmaster Johann Rothe added that the woman had been overbearing, proud, and difficult. After her return home her parents and friends chided her so much that she became ill and died soon afterward.[45] But the modern editor of the *Reinhardsbrunn Chronicle* doubts the whole tale. It seems very unlikely that Ludwig married twice.

The story of Ludwig's marriage to Adelheid (the date of which is unknown) has also been dressed up. In the chronicle the story of the love affair begins in the middle, when Ludwig was already madly in love. He had secretly become so attached to her, the wife of Count Frederick of the Saxon Palatinate, that he was beside himself. They must have had a rendezvous somewhere, for she also fell in love with young Ludwig. The two hatched a plot to kill Frederick, under the pretext of an accidental death while deer hunting.[46]

The *Düringische Chronik* adds a few details that make the tale all the more plausible. Count Frederick was accustomed to staying at his castle Schiplitz in the Osterland, which was adjacent to Ludwig's lands. Both chroniclers claim that the details of the plot were worked out by Adelheid, since she was very familiar with the habits of her husband. She would get him to bathe and would assist him so that he would be completely unaware of Ludwig's arrival. Ludwig was to blow the huntsman's horn and summon his dogs.[47] Frederick was roused when he heard the horns and commotion. His reaction was all the greater when Adelheid chided him and asked what he was going to do about the fact that a neighboring noble dared hunt right under his nose. He jumped out of the bath and, lightly dressed, ran to the stable, where he leaped on his stallion and rode after Ludwig. Unarmed and unprotected, he shouted and cursed him as he approached. Suddenly Ludwig turned his horse, met the excited count, and ran him through with a blade used for hunting bears. Frederick fell from the horse and died almost immediately.[48] Here the Reinhardsbrunn account ends, but the *Düringische Chronik* adds that he was buried in the Bonzigk Monastery on the Saale River near Naumburg, which Frederick himself had founded.[49]

To what extent the details of Count Frederick III's murder are true, or were made up by later chroniclers to enhance the romance, can no longer be established with any degree of certainty. Böttiger claimed that the murder of Adelheid's husband remained unproved; yet Adelheid's son, born after his father's death, always remained suspicious of his stepfather. He even challenged him to a duel in 1107. But Emperor Henry IV opposed such a test, perhaps because Ludwig was then already advanced in age. However, the emperor did insist that the Saxon Palatinate be returned to the boy.[50] On the other hand, Knochenhauer regarded most of the tale as fictitious, even though the murder itself had a factual basis. He concluded that Ludwig was the culprit behind the scenes, but that the actual killing was carried out by two brothers, Dietrich and Ulrich of Dedeleben, with the assistance of Reinhard of Reinstadt.

After the murder of her husband, Adelheid, being pregnant by Frederick, wore the prescribed veil of the church for a time. There is no evidence that contemporaries suspected any foul play. After the mourning period had passed, Ludwig married her. They held a festive house-warming party at the Schauenburg, the castle that Ludwig's father had recently built.[51] For the ambitious young Ludwig, this marriage constituted quite a prize. Adelheid was the daughter of Udo, the Markgraf of Staden, thus belonging to one of the oldest and highest-ranking families of the Saxon nobility. Udo and her sister Uta could trace their noble blood as far back as Markgraf Thimo, who had served the crown as the first Markgraf of Meissen. The Reinhardsbrunn chronicler proudly observed that Adelheid's sister, Uta, was the mother of Conrad the Great of Meissen. Conrad was in turn the father of Margrave Otto and the grandfather of Theodoric of Meissen. In addition, the chronicler added, the Adelheid marriage immeasurably increased the Ludowinger lands as well as riches. Rothe repeated most of the same story, but added that the Schauenburg party occurred in 1064.[52]

Ludwig's days were not to remain peaceful. The Reinhardsbrunn monks felt that this may have been punishment for his sins. However, modern historians view the struggle between Henry IV and Pope Gregory VII as involving both Saxon and Thuringian nobility, and in the Investiture Controversy Ludwig was held to be an enemy of the Saliens.[53]

There may have been good reasons why only later were there royal repercussions from the murder. Since Emperor Henry IV was not quite six years old when his own father died and he was designated his successor, his mother Agnes served as regent until the lad turned twelve. At that time, while on a visit with his mother to Kaiserswerth on the Rhine, young Henry was enticed onto a boat by some Saxon nobles, kidnapped, and taken to Cologne. In Cologne he was placed under the guardianship of Archbishop Hanno. Later his guardian became Archbishop Adelbert of Bremen. Adelbert happened to be the brother of the murdered Frederick. To the great surprise of the nobility, the archbishop declared Henry IV of age when he was only fifteen.[54] What better opportunity would Emperor Henry IV have had to learn of Ludwig's alleged guilt than from the dead man's own brother? This may explain how Ludwig escaped punishment for his sin until young Henry IV came of age.

Dates in the medieval chronicles are often unreliable and at times downright confusing. Some time after 1065,[55] the Reinhardsbrunn chronicler claims, Ludwig and Adelheid established their household and started raising a family, which grew in time to a total of seven children.[56] They had four boys and three girls. The oldest boy, Hermann, was captured by Henry V's forces. According to the account, "he died in chains in the castle of Hammerstein." The next son, Ludwig, was to become the first Landgraf of Thuringia, while his younger son, Heinrich Raspe (not to be confused with the ruler of the same name who died in A.D. 1247 without heirs), later became ruler over the Hessian lands of the Ludowinger. The youngest son, Udo, entered the church and eventually became the bishop of Naumburg.[57]

Like other territorial princes, the Ludowinger engaged in favorable dynastic marriages with neighboring noble houses as well as with those from other lands. In this way they sought to strengthen their ties with their neighbors and increase their holdings and prestige. The oldest daughter, Kunigunde, was married to a Saxon count named Wichmann of the Nordheim family. They founded the Augustinian monastery at Kaltenburg in 1120, providing it with many temporal furnishings and also ample funds.[58] The second daughter, Cäcelia, married Count Gerlach of Waldensehe, who came from a line that had begun to spread and grow during the Ludowinger period.[59] The third daughter of Ludwig, named after her mother, was married for a while to Count Ulrich of Weimar-Orlamünde; but she was rejected by the count because they had no male offspring. His line died out with him in 1112.[60]

Ludwig the Leaper was Markgraf at a time when knighthood and castle building were the order of the day. During the reign of Henry III, the Franconians had made Goslar the center of the empire, with the Harzburg as their principal castle. By the time of Henry IV, they had built five royal castles in Saxony and two in Thuringia,[61] believing that fortresses were the logical response to the territorial princes of Thuringia and Meissen.[62] Siegfried Asche observed that Ludwig the Leaper had by then expanded the family holdings until they now extended from Freiburg on the Unstrut to Marburg on the Lahn in Hesse. By the end of his reign the Ludowinger castles consisted of the Schauenburg, Wartburg, Weiszensee, Neuenburg, and Eckhardsburg.[63]

The origin and use of the Wartburg by the Ludowinger is of special interest to this study. The Wartburg was Luther's hideout in 1521–1522, after the Diet of Worms. There are many tales about its origin, most of which can be dismissed as pure fiction. Yet it is a fact that the castle looms 174 meters in the air and defied the army of Henry IV in 1080.[64] Professor Wenck, in his excellent study, has also pointed out that from Ludwig's day on, the Wartburg dominated the territory between the Saale and Lahn, and that the castle served as a great unifying force for the Ludowinger throughout Thuringia.[65] But how did it happen that the castle was built there? Our knowledge is limited to the original accounts of the monks of *Reinhardsbrunn* and that of the schoolmaster of Eisenach in his *Düringische Chronik*. Of course these cannot be accepted at face value; yet they no doubt contain insights and elements of truth that are otherwise no longer available to historians. So we must first present the accounts that were believed in the Middle Ages, and then analyze the sources for possible explanations.

The chronicler of the *Reinhardsbrunn Chronicle* related how, shortly after he became margrave, Ludwig the Leaper was out deer hunting one day in the neighborhood of Eisenach, when he and some hunters climbed to the top of what later became known as the Wartburg Mountain. He had not been up there before, so he looked around in all directions and admired the view. He thought, *What a place for a castle*! But the chronicler adds that he also realized the land belonged to a neighbor. This troubled him, but in time he thought up an ingenious plan. He employed twelve knights to dig up soil near Eisenach, on his own land, secretly carry it to the top of the mountain, and spread it in the place where he wanted to build a castle. Upon being challenged, the twelve knights unsheathed their swords, stabbed them into the ground to the hilts, and swore that the ground on which they stood belonged to Ludwig.[66]

In time the story grew. The monks did not dare admit that Ludwig stole the land. In the fifteenth century, Rothe stated that the land around Eisenach had been given to Ludwig's father by his good friend Archbishop Bardo of Mainz, who had baptized Ludwig. The grant included all the wooded area up the Werra River in the west. Ludwig often went deer hunting there, for he was fond of the region. Accordingly, on a certain day, he and some men shot a stag with a bow and arrow. The wounded animal ran to the top of the mountain, with the men in hot pursuit. When Ludwig arrived at the top he was tremendously impressed.[67] Looking around in amazement, he shouted, "*Warte Berg, hier werde ich eine Burg bauen*," or, "Wait Mountain, here I will erect a castle." Ludwig realized he was on the land of the Frankensteiner, and he wondered how it might be acquired. Rothe states that before Ludwig's transfer of soil to the mountaintop, some of his friends actually moved a house up there to serve as a "squatter's claim." To this both the neighboring nobles on the Metelatein and the Frankensteiner objected, claiming that "he took their property against God, against law, and against honor."[68] Ludwig's reply was that the land had originally belonged to the Mainz *Stift* and it had been granted to his father.[69] To prove his claim, he ordered the knights to move the dirt from his own lands up there, so that they could take the oath referred to previously.[70]

To make this story more plausible, perhaps, Rothe digressed a little. He claimed that the land belonging to Eisenach was a stretch lying between the Horsil and Nesser rivers, and that in the middle was the mountain of St. Peters, which in his day was still the old part of town. The region was rich in iron, and Eisenach had received its name from the smelting of iron ore. This land Bardo had given to the Ludowinger[71]

Yet there was still the need to explain how Ludwig moved the material for the massive structure that was built. In 1077, a year after Ludwig's father died, there had supposedly been a great famine in Thuringia. Ludwig gathered wheat and oats from his Sangerhausen estates, which he used to feed the people; in return they gladly worked on the construction of the Wartburg. The *Düringische Chronik* also adds a new version of the origin of the *Burg's* name. Rothe claimed that Ludwig shouted, "Warte Berg, welch ein Berg!" ("Wait mountain, what a mountain!"). From this people began to name the fortress the Wartburg.[72] That name was still in use in the fifteenth century, but by Luther's day Thuringians called it "die Wartburg."

How much of the Wartburg tale is to be believed? How much of it is simply later tradition intended to glorify the Ludowinger? Knochenhauer accepted the *Reinhardsbrunn* claim that the land around Eisenach belonged to Ludwig as an inheritance from his father, but said that the Frankensteiner lands, on the border of Thuringia, were off-limits for him.[73] Karl Wenck, who explored the story some centuries later, regarded the story of Ludwig's hunt as pure fiction. Yet the fact remains that the Wartburg was built by Ludwig the Leaper. Wenck also held that the construction was done by force on the lands of the lords of Frankenstein, who for a long time had been the vassals of Hersfeld monastery.[74] Wenck likewise questioned Rothe's story that the land had been a part of the Mainz *Stift*, that it was given to Ludwig's father, and that the stones in the castle had come from a Gotha quarry.[75] This aspect of the story was examined by J. W. Storch, who compared the stones in the original part of the castle with those in the Eisenach quarry and concluded they came from there.[76] The claim that twelve knights participated in the certification that the Wartburg Mountain belonged to Mainz was also questioned by Wenck. The monks no doubt associated the number twelve with that of the apostles, believing it would make the claim particularly sacred and trustworthy. It seems to be a suspicious coincidence, observed Wenck, that there were twelve knights who originally came to Thuringia with Ludwig's father, the founder of the Ludowinger; that there were also twelve here in the erection of the Wartburg; and later, there were again twelve monks involved in the foundation of the *Reinhardsbrunn* monastery.[77]

Unanswered questions remain. If Ludwig indeed took the site by force, why is there no record of a Frankensteiner challenge? Also, how could any count quarry the stones, transport them to those heights, and build a castle of gigantic size, without employing a very large force? Thus even when we reject the dressed-up elements of the story, the undertaking must have been carefully planned. The fortress is almost centrally located between the Saale and the Lahn on the southern fringe of Thuringia; in fact, it is at the strategic intersection of several important highways. If the Wartburg was begun in 1067 and completed in a short time, Ludwig must have accomplished this by highly organized means, and no doubt with inexpensive labor.

The Wartburg was not the only fortress Ludwig added to the Ludowinger system of defense. The *Reinhardsbrunn Chronicle* also speaks of another fine castle he built on the Unstrut above Freiburg, quite near its confluence with the Saale.[78] The *Düringische Chronik* places this construction in the courtship days of Ludwig and Adelheid, claiming it was built there so that he could be near his lover.[79] But Wenck believes it was built later, during the minority of his stepson Friedrich. This fortress was built on a steep cliff facing the Saale, was narrow at the top, and had very steep inclines on three side.[80] It was an excellent dwelling for the Ludowinger, which in those days they enjoyed as much as the Wartburg.[81] Asche claims that the Neuenburg and the later acquired Eckhardsburg formed the pillars of the imperial defense, while the Wartburg formed its head.[82]

As noted earlier, there was no immediate imperial response to Ludwig's involvement in the murder of his wife's former husband. But papal records from the time indicate that Pfalzgraf Friedrich's relatives repeatedly complained to the guardians of the young emperor.[83] Thus, when Henry IV came of age and perceived that the Ludowinger Graf had cast his lot with his Saxon enemies, he did not hesitate to put him into the political prison of Gibichtenstein. The real grounds for his arrest remain unknown, but the *Reinhardsbrunn* account relates it all to the murder. There may have been other reasons for Ludwig's arrest. The Graf sat in chains for two years, and then the emperor pronounced the death sentence on him for the murder of Frederick.[84]

But Ludwig worked out a plan for his escape. One of his trusted *ministeriales* came to the castle of Gibichtenstein with Ludwig's white stallion and placed it at the edge of the river adjacent to the castle. At a specified time, the official entered the water with the horse and swam with it until they were just below a particular attic window. From there Ludwig made the long leap into the river.[85]

After this escape Ludwig was considered a fugitive within the empire. The *Reinhardsbrunn* chronicler compared him to King David, who had been guilty of both murder and adultery.[86] But the chroniclers tried to demonstrate that, like David, Ludwig came to repentance. The original *Reinhardsbrunn* story is less detailed, but contains the essential elements of the later account by the Eisenach schoolmaster. Ludwig's conversation purportedly occurred on a Good Friday, after his wife Adelheid had prepared a sumptuous meal (which was forbidden by the church). Ludwig inquired about the reason for such a feast. But then he asked why they could not indulge just a little? Adelheid is supposed to have reminded him that Good Friday was the day on which the Savior died cruelly on the cross for Ludwig's past sins. She asked if they could forgo just a little in this life for the sake of heaven. The count is reported to have bowed his head in shame and begun to weep. From that day on, Ludwig wondered how best to make his peace with God and how to make the necessary amends for his murder of the Pfalzgraf.[87]

After Easter Ludwig is alleged to have sent for the bishop of Halberstadt, a close friend, who was a pious and wise father confessor. The two discussed ways in which Ludwig might make amends and improve his life. He and the bishop decided to make a trip to Rome in order to obtain papal absolution and thereby put Ludwig beyond the reach of his enemies and the emperor. In Rome the matter was discussed with Pope Urban II, and a plan of satisfaction by good works was proposed. Later Ludwig did penance before Bishop Stephan of Halberstadt. As his third step of penance, Ludwig was asked to found a monastery. The location was left up to him. Adelheid, also, was required to take similar steps for her own sins.[88]

When Ludwig returned from Rome he decided to set his own house in order. To his oldest living son he willed his two castles, the Wartburg and the Neuenburg. He also stipulated that he would give his son the towns of Eisenach, Freiburg, and Sangerhausen. But Ludwig retained for himself and his wife the Schauenburg and the *Vogtei* rights over the woods.[89]

After Ludwig and Adelheid had personally received absolution from Pope Urban II and thus complete freedom for the future, he was obligated by his pledge to erect a monastery. He began to survey the territory to determine where it should be located. The chronicler of *Reinhardsbrunn* points out that there was a mud hut in the woods not far from the castle of Schauenburg, just below the Loyba Forest, where Ludwig's father had settled. This place was known as Reynhero. Nearby was a freely flowing fountain of the same name.[90] The *Düringische Chronik* adds that the man who occupied the hut at the time was a mentally deficient individual named Reynher. Ludwig visited the spot and learned that this local resident placed candles around the well at night.[91] He concluded that this was the place for his monastery. Before taking the final steps for the construction of the building, he discussed the possibility with his friend, Bishop Stephen of Halberstadt. Out of these discussions rose the famous monastery that the Ludowinger named Reinhardsbrunn. The Graf claimed the construction was made to the honor of God, the Blessed Virgin, and St. John the Evangelist. Once completed, Ludwig staffed the new monastery with twelve regular monks from Hirsau, placed under the Abbot Giselbert. This abbot drew up new rules for the monastery patterned after those in use by other Benedictines at Hirsau.[92]

In 1092 Pope Urban II placed Reinhardsbrunn under direct papal control and, in 1102, Pope Pascal II confirmed this arrangement. This removed the monastery from the reach of neighboring ecclesiastical and secular rulers.[93] The founding of Reinhardsbrunn also received the blessing of Henry IV. Knochenhauer cites evidence that the monastery was actually authorized by the emperor in 1089, who had in front of him the papal authorization that his chancellory had copied.[94]

The *Düringische Chronik* also tries to demonstrate Adelheid's piety after her own conversion. She was deeply stricken with remorse and wanted to make things right with God. She returned to Obersleben, a monastic spot beloved by herself and her first husband, and there engaged in many works of Christian charity. She then converted the castle Shiplitz, where her husband was stabbed, into a nunnery.[95]

In 1106 Henry IV's son became emperor, but rather than improving matters, he merely accentuated the Investiture Controversy. At first it seemed that by 1107, Ludwig had won the heart of young Henry V. He even accompanied the Kaiser on an Italian expedition and fought with him on a campaign against the Slavs.[96] But peace with Henry could not last, for the vested interests of the Franconians were opposed to peace with either Saxony or Thuringia. There seemed to be a deep-seated hostility between the Saliens and the Thuringians, as had become evident during the reign of Henry IV.[97] Ludwig's stepson Friedrich was also disgruntled because he had not obtained his father's inheritance. But Friedrich appears to have been quite close to Hermann, Ludwig's oldest son. Later they became embroiled in a conflict with the Kaiser's field commander, Count Hoyer of Mansfeld, who forced them to seek refuge in the castle of Teuchen near Weizenfels. After a siege they had no choice but to capitulate, after which both were captured and thrown into the dungeon of Hammerstein Castle. In time Friedrich was able to escape by paying a ransom, but poor Hermann lingered on in chains until he finally died.[98]

Ludwig the Leaper faced some more rough times with Emperor Henry V. His second imprisonment grew out of events beyond his control. On 12 May 1112, Count Ulrich of Weimar and Orlamünde had died without any male heirs. Henry V saw in this an excellent opportunity to enlarge the crown lands by adding Count Ulrich's possessions to the royal *Fiskus*.[99] Meanwhile, all the surrounding nobles wondered what the king would do, for these lands were neither part of the royal fiefs nor were they allodial. Yet Henry had forcefully taken them from the wife of Otto of Meissen, one of Ulrich's daughters.[100] Henry seems to have reasoned that the lands, once given to old-line families as fiefs (though later commonly regarded as allodial by the house of Weimar), could rightfully escheat back. This action was in accordance with the general judgment of princes, since the male line of that family had died out.[101]

However, when the Kaiser attempted to appropriate Ulrich's lands, complaints from relatives and nobles on all sides were loud and clear. Some of the strongest opposition came from the bishop of Halberstadt and the daughters of Ulrich.[102] Ludwig remained on the fence for a while, for he had not quite recovered from the shock of Ulrich's rejection of his daughter Adelheid.[103] The ringleader of the opposition was Adelbert, archbishop of Mainz. The king believed that the archbishop had also aroused Ludwig and Wiprecht of Groitzsch (who, in his second marriage, had been wed to Kunigunde, another daughter of the deceased Ulrich). In 1112 the Kaiser had Archbishop Adelbert arrested and cast into Trifels prison.[104]

Henry V celebrated Christmas at Erfurt that year, but none of his invited princes came. He then invaded the nobles' lands, causing widespread devastation. He employed Count Hoyer of Mansfeld as field commander. After the arrest of the archbishop of Mainz, the new leaders of the opposition became Ludwig and Wiprecht. The opponents of the king met at Warnstädt, not far from the Quedlinburg; but Hoyer led a force of three hundred men in a surprise attack on the meeting, catching the small group completely off guard. Pfalzgraf Friedrich was mortally wounded during the encounter; Wiprecht was captured, condemned to death, and locked up in Trifels. Ludwig somehow eluded them and got away.[105] After this Ludwig had some second thoughts, for his son Hermann and stepson Friedrich were already in chains. He chose to capitulate at Dortmund.[106] But the young Henry would neither release the two sons nor Ludwig himself until the count had turned the Wartburg over to the crown.[107] Henry gave Wiprecht the choice of turning over all his lands or being killed.[108]

In 1114 Henry V married Matilde of England at Mainz, and the wedding was a grand affair. Many distinguished guests attended, including a number who had not been invited.[109] Ludwig appears to have been among the latter. He believed that, after the Wartburg turnover, he was now on good terms with the Kaiser. However, the king claimed that the Graf had offended his dignity, and he ordered his arrest. Once more Ludwig found himself in chains.[110] Already in his seventies, Ludwig suffered there for two years and nine months.[111] Meanwhile his sons, Ludwig and Heinrich Raspe, governed the Ludowinger lands. Henry V tried to expel the boys from their territories, and they were saved only by paying a heavy fine.[112]

Eventually the emperor's behavior went too far for the princes and feudal lords of the *Reich*. Under the leadership of Wiprecht's son and Count Lothar, on 11 February 1115 the princes challenged Henry's forces at Welfenholz. In this engagement the Kaiser was completely defeated. He had already begun a siege of Weimar, which he was forced to terminate. Meanwhile Hoyer of Mansfeld had died, leaving the imperial army to a much less experienced leader. The king's forces held Ludwig's castle Neuenburg, which now underwent a siege. The commander of Henry's forces was captured, leaving no other course for the Kaiser but to liberate Ludwig, Wiprecht, and the Burggraf of Meissen. Thus by the end of the year 1116, the Ludowinger family could once again celebrate Christmas in the Wartburg.[113]

After Frederick, Ludwig's stepson, had been liberated from his captivity, he had conversations with the king. The Kaiser agreed to take the young man's rightful title, Count Palatinate of Saxony, from Friedrich of Sommersenburg (a relative of the king), and return it to him. This action made Frederick a staunch supporter of the Kaiser. Ludwig also concluded an agreement with the young man in which, by the payment of a specified sum, he obtained the right to retain the *Vogtei* overlordship of the cloister of Goseck.[114]

Patze observed that in a day when Thuringia was filled with the clamor of weapons, Ludwig was still able to retain his control over the Ludowinger lands. In fact he was able to enlarge and fortify them.[115] Since this was also the period of the Cluniac reforms, when both Rome and the monastic reformers were attempting to expel laypersons from their houses, Ludwig understood how the founding of cloisters such as Reinhardsbrunn was useful both for the purposes of piety and the aggrandizement of princely power.[116]

In 1123, after an active life, Ludwig the Leaper decided to enter Reinhardsbrunn as a lay monk and turn the Ludowinger lands over to his sons.[117] It had been sixty-seven years since his own father had died, and he had ruled from the time he was sixteen.[118] He must have been seventy-six years old when he was released from his last captivity. His beloved Adelheid had died some years earlier, and she was buried in Reinhardsbrunn.[119] Ludwig died in 1123, dressed in simple monk's attire, amid the brothers. He was then buried next to his wife in the monastery they had founded.[120]

After Ludwig the Leaper died, the Ludowinger lands continued to be ruled jointly by his sons Ludwig III and Heinrich Raspe. We noted above how Ludwig II's oldest son Hermann died in chains at the castle of Hammerstein. The father's youngest boy, Udo, in time became the bishop of Naumburg. Knochenhauer observed that the details of the joint rule by the other two sons remain vague. We know that Heinrich Raspe, named after his castle, later exercised *Vogtei* rights over the Goseck cloister and its lands, while Ludwig maintained the same rights over Reinhardsbrunn, along with its vast possessions.[121] This might indicate that there was a division between the rule in the north and in the south. But the situation was far more complicated than that.

Even before Ludwig the Leaper had died, the Ludowinger lands had been considerably enlarged through some very rewarding dynastic marriages. Ludwig III, now regarded as the heir apparent, had married Hedwig, the daughter of Count Giso IV of Gulenburg. This had helped the family expand into Hesse, around Marburg.[122] Later, Giso IV had married an apparently younger woman named Hedwig, whose family connections remain unknown. When Giso died, Heinrich Raspe married this widow, and he seems to have made her lands his center of activity during their reign.[123]

The counts of Gison also owned considerable land around Marburg on the Lahn River. In addition, they were closely related to the Werner family. Werner IV had acquired the county of Maden from Mainz. Patze says there is also the possibility that Heinrich Raspe had acquired some of the Werner lands.[124] There had been a number of generations of Gisons prior to this, and Giso IV named himself the "count of Gudenberg," after his lower Hessian castle. When the last male heir of this line, Giso V, was killed on an Italian expedition, the Ludowinger inherited all these territories in the Marburg region.[125] But the archbishops of Mainz saw to it that the Ludowinger expansion into Hesse remained limited. Mainz strategically planted its fortifications on all sides of the Gison and Werner lands.[126]

Through Ludwig's marriage to Hedwig, the Ludowinger made a third territorial acquisition. As the daughter of Giso's first wife, Kunigunde von Bilstein, Hedwig had also inherited lands on the Rhine. These allodial properties were not extensive, and they were scattered and surrounded on all sides by ambitious territorial princes.[127]

We noted earlier that, when Ulrich of Weimar died in 1112 without any male heirs, Henry V tried to appropriate his holdings. One of his strongest opponents was Adelbert of Mainz, from whom Ulrich had acquired a number of regions as fiefs. Working closely with Ludwig the Leaper, the archbishop had now turned these fiefs over to the Ludowinger. During the father's lifetime the family relationship with Mainz remained good; but after the Concordat of Worms in 1122, Mainz's strong rivals had died. A new archbishop now embarked on an aggressive program of expansion both in Hesse and Thuringia. Erfurt was now acquired and fortified with a wall. Mainz now held the mighty pillars of Mühlberg, Erfurt, and Harburg.[128]

In 1123 Henry of Eilenburg died, who had been the margrave of Meissen and the East Mark. This now exposed these lands to royal intervention. Henry V had hoped to fill these vacancies with his loyal supporters. Such action provoked a challenge from the neighboring princes, led by Lothar of Supplinburg, the duke of Saxony. With the support of Lothar and the Ludowinger, Conrad the Great of the house of Wettin now occupied Meissen, while Albrecht of Ballenstedt, later called Albrecht the Bear, took possession of the East Mark. Meissen had been promised to Hermann von Winzenburg, one of Henry's staunch supporters, but this action was prevented by Lothar and Heinrich Raspe.[129]

Halfway through the reign of Ludwig III and Heinrich Raspe an event occurred that would have far-reaching effects on the Ludowinger and the future history of Thuringia. In 1125 Henry V died. Following the Salien line of succession, the kingship should have passed to Frederick of Hohenstaufen. From the time of the early Saxon rulers, Henry I and Otto the Great, the kingly office had been passed on according to the hereditary line. Royal succession had tended to elevate imperial rule and suppress the original Stem Duchies. But the Investiture Controversy had taught the papacy much about the strength of the German kingship and what was needed to suppress it. If the hereditary principle of succession could be destroyed and the kingship once again put on an elective basis, the papacy would have a powerful role in the election of future German emperors.[130]

Rome possessed a powerful ally in Adelbert of Mainz, Germany's leading ecclesiastical primate. Adelbert must have despised Henry V after being arrested and held in chains in Trifels. Even before Henry's death, he had tried to stir up Rome. To assist the pope Adelbert would now help destroy the hereditary principle of kingship.[131]

The Saxon duke Lothar of Supplinburg had led the opposition to Henry V in his attempts at aggrandizing the royal holdings of the Salien emperors. Lothar was the son of Count Gebhard of Supplinburg. His mother was Hedwig, the daughter of Ordulf Billung. The house of Billung's rule had ended with Magnus Billung in 1106. After that, Henry V would have liked to have had the rich Billung duchy escheat to the crown. According to a contemporary Saxon chronicler, however, Henry feared a Saxon rebellion.[132] Lothar had enhanced his own standing as duke among the princes still more by marrying Richsa, the daughter of Otto of Nordheim.[133]

The death of Henry V in 1125 caused an upheaval in the German *Reich*. The Empress Matilde returned to England, taking with her the crown jewels as if they were her private possessions. The Hohenstaufen thereupon claimed that the Tuscan lands of Countess Matilde belonged to them, as well as the city and castle of Nürnberg, and also everything that had escheated to the crown or been confiscated while the Saliens had been in power.[134] Adelbert of Mainz now favored the election of Lothar of Supplinburg. But by hereditary rights the real claimant to the throne was Frederick of Hohenstaufen.[135] A third candidate was Leopold of Austria.[136]

The Electoral College met at Mainz on 24 August 1125, and held its sessions along the banks of the Rhine.[137] Adelbert and his supporters attempted to revert to the election methods of the early *Reich*. Accordingly, the dukes of Saxony, Franconia, Swabia, and Bavaria arrived with so many subjects that the crowd swelled to some 60,000 people. These masses were to give their final approval to the election.[138] The rivalry was so intense, says Thompson, that the two parties occupied opposite sides of the Rhine.[139]

In choosing an emperor the assembled body employed what we might call a nominating committee. Each of the four Stem Duchies chose ten representatives, who together selected one elector. The vote of these four electors would then determine the outcome.[140] Two of the candidates agreed to this arrangement, but Frederick of Swabia refused to go along with it.[141] He was confident of his claim to the throne based on hereditary principles, and he did not want Adelbert of Mainz to upset his plans.[142]

Frederick was not able to stop the revolution in voting procedure, and the electors chose Lothar as their king. The announcement was loudly applauded by the assembled body, and Lothar was raised on the shoulders of his followers.[143] Rome must have rejoiced, for it regarded Lothar as far more docile than the Hohenstaufen. Soon after, Lothar knelt at the feet of Pope Innocent II and agreed to receive the empire as a fief from Rome.[144] However, according to Thompson, the new king was still a man for whom Germany came first.[145]

After Lothar's election, times were favorable to the Ludowinger. Patze concluded that Mainz now resolved to curb their growing power.[146] The archbishop made Graf Ernst governor of the city of Erfurt.[147] On 13 May 1126 Emperor Lothar invited a number of princes to Merseburg, where he gave his daughter Gertrude in marriage to Henry the Proud of Bavaria.[148] Since the king already possessed lands in Thuringia, he may have regarded the friendship of the Ludowinger as a natural bridge between the two extremities of the *Reich*, Saxony and Bavaria. The first favorable event for the Ludowinger, in which Lothar no doubt played a role, was the elevation of Udo, the younger brother of Ludwig, to the important position of bishop of Naumburg.[149] This must have occurred almost immediately after the king's coronation in 1125. Shortly afterward, Heinrich Raspe was named the future "banner carrier" of the king.[150] It is unknown when Heinrich Raspe was appointed to this honor, but he must not have held the privilege very long, for he died in 1129.[151] Upon the death of his brother Heinrich, Ludwig (Graf of Thuringia) now became the sole ruler of all the Ludowinger lands in Thuringia and Hesse.

During this period of Thuringian history both the church and the nobility became obstreperous, and the Pfalzgrafen of Saxony were also beginning to cause trouble. In 1130 Count Hermann von Winzenburg had his *ministeriales* surround the king's close friend, Burchard of Loccum, and murder him.[152] Most of the details of this plot are no longer known. The Pfalzgraf was tried by King Lothar in the presence of a number of princes, found guilty, and deposed, with his castle of Winzenburg was besieged, taken, and leveled.[153] All the medieval chroniclers associated the fall of Hermann von Winzenburg with another event of great significance for the future of Thuringia. The *Reinhardsbrunn Chronicle*, the original source, adds that after the trial and condemnation of Hermann for the murder, the king proclaimed that he was elevating Ludwig to Landgraf of Thuringia.[154] This decision must have been announced at the same meeting, for the chronicler added that all princes present gave their enthusiastic approval.[155] Hermann must also have possessed lands in the Meissen region, for the chronicle adds that "Count Conrad of Wettin was chosen to replace him in Meissen."[156] As for the lands in Thuringia that Hermann had held, the *Annalista Saxo* notes, "The king gave the Grafschaft of the same to the previously named Ludwig of Thuringia."[157]

Later historians differ in their interpretation of what transpired at Hermann von Winzenburg's trial. Knochenhauer concluded that Hermann may have been a Landgraf prior to the trial, at which point the king merely transferred that title to Ludwig.[158] Patze, after a detailed study of the evidence, concluded that the title did not exist earlier. Furthermore, he separated the two events. According to his view, in 1131 King Lothar held a *Landtag* at Goslar, where he made his official proclamation of Ludwig's advancement to the *Landgrafschaft* of Thuringia.[159]

The demotion of Hermann von Winzenburg by Kaiser Lothar thus led to the elevation of the rulers of Thuringia. Patze regarded the *Landgrafschaft* as a necessity for the times. There was a need in Thuringia for a counterweight to the ambitions of Mainz, and certainly there was a need for greater law and order among the princes. Hermann had slain one of the king's vassals in cold blood, and Ludwig's brother had been poisoned. Thuringia had not been one of the original Stem Duchies, and thus the creation of a dukedom was no longer possible. Yet the king attempted to create an office that placed the Ludowinger above the rest of the counts in the land. In a sense, a Landgraf was halfway between a count and a duke.[160]

After the elevation of the Ludowinger, there followed a period of relative calm in Thuringia. Ludwig III was not ostentatious about his new rank, unless one counts his enlargement of the Wartburg.[161] But while there was peace between the king and the pope, with Thuringia no longer their battleground, there was unrest in the north and south. In Saxony the son-in-law of the king, Henry the Proud, did not rest until Albrecht the Bear had been expelled from his dukedom and he had assumed the title for the rising Welfs.[162] Meanwhile, in the south, Frederick and Conrad of Hohenstaufen refused to acquiesce to Lothar's election as emperor. In this period Ludwig III remained on good terms with the king and made it a point to attend all the gatherings of the princes.[163] His signature appears on some of the official transactions of the *Reich*.

The Kaiser does not appear to have been given much rest during his reign. In 1132 he went on his first Italian expedition, with three goals in mind: to reinstate Pope Innocent II; to administer and conduct necessary business in his Italian dominions; and to have himself crowned emperor in Rome by the restored pope. Meanwhile the Hohenstaufen started causing trouble in the south. While settling matters with them, reports came to the emperor that the Norseman Roger of Sicily was molesting Venetian sailors in the Mediterranean and apparently running roughshod over the people of Apulia and Calabria.[164] Thus the king started on a second Italian expedition in 1135, in which these southern regions were recaptured and returned to the papacy.[165] On his way home the Kaiser became ill and died near the Bavarian border.[166]

After Lothar's death the *Reich* faced more upheaval as the struggle between the Guelfs and Ghibellines flared up anew. Lothar had tried to pass the kingly mantle on to his son-in-law, Henry the Proud.[167] But both the papacy and the German princes feared Henry.[168] The archbishop of Trier now assumed leadership of a group that championed the Hohenstaufen candidate.[169] The *Annalista Saxo*, which offers the most detailed account, states that the German princes assembled at Coblenz during the middle of Lent in the year 1138. There they agreed to hold an imperial election at Mainz to choose whomever God would ordain. When they assembled, the archbishop of Trier and his supporters succeeded in having Conrad III, the brother of Frederick of Swabia, chosen. He was crowned at Aachen on 7 March by Cardinal Thietwin.[170]

Whether Ludwig participated in this election or not, it must have confronted the Ludowinger with some difficult questions: Should they continue to support Lothar's son-in-law? Or was it time to join the Hohenstaufen? Geography no doubt played a role in the answers. Thuringia lay immediately between the two duchies of Henry the Proud. The first to decide for a change seems to have been the younger brother, Udo, bishop of Naumburg. Thompson asserts that Conrad III resorted to an *ex post facto* action to stop Henry the Proud, offering him a choice between ruling over Saxony or Bavaria.[171] In July of that year Conrad III held a meeting at the Quedlinburg. By then it was evident that Ludwig III and the neighboring princes had joined the side of the Staufer.[172] This implied that their lands might now become a battleground between the Welfs and the Staufer. Conrad III, with Ludwig and a number of princes in the royal forces, moved up to Hersfeld to attack Saxony. But even though Henry moved up to Creuzburg on the Werra, the expected battle did not materialize. The entire campaign ended with the mysterious death of Henry the Proud on 20 October 1140.[173]

At the close of Landgraf Ludwig III's life, the relationship between the Ludowinger and the crown must have been fairly close. Otto von Friesing wrote that an engagement was arranged between Emperor Conrad III's niece, Julia (a daughter of Duke Frederick of Swabia), and Ludwig IV, who would become the next Landgraf.[174] This relationship would certainly assure the Ludowinger a continuation of their rule as landgraves of Thuringia. The engagement proved timely, for on 12 January 1140 Ludwig III suddenly died.

Landgrave Ludwig III left behind three sons and four daughters. The oldest son was Ludwig IV, then still a minor; but he had already been invested as landgrave at the Diet of Worms on 2 February 1140. Ludwig's ceremony of investiture had no doubt been performed in conformity with the king's wishes, to which the princes had acquiesced.[175] The second son, Heinrich Raspe II, became the count of Hesse. The third boy later became Ludwig von Thamsbrück, after matters had not proved acceptable at Reinhardsbrunn.[176] There were four daughters in the family: Cäcilia, Jutta, Adelheid, and Machtild. The last of the daughters, Machtild, was later wed to the sixth son of Albrecht the Bear.[177]

Tradition made quite a tale out of young Ludwig's IV's colorful life as landgrave of Thuringia. (The *Düringische Chronik* relates this development in detail and ties it into the origin of his later nickname, "Ludwig the Iron Man.") The landgrave was still a minor in 1140, when his father died, but he must have been almost sixteen. Ludwig attended Conrad III's diets and meetings immediately after his investiture as landgrave at Worms in 1140. He was also at the Diet of Würzburg in 1141.[178] He must have married Jutta, the Kaiser's niece, soon after he became landgrave. His engagement had taken place while his father was still living. Judging by the number of imperial meetings in which he participated, Ludwig must have been fairly close to the Kaiser. There is some disagreement as to whether he accompanied Conrad III on the Second Crusade to the Holy Land, but the record indicates that he attended fourteen of the German *Reichstagen* and *Hoftagen* during the decade when Conrad III was emperor.[179]

At Conrad III's stormy *Reichstagen* at Würzburg in 1141 and Frankfurt a.M. in 1141, the Ludowinger were, as boys, already ushered into the heat of battle with the Saxons and Welfs over an issue that dated back to Henry the Proud: Should Henry the Lion be given back the Duchy of Saxony or should it remain with Albrecht the Bear?[180] Conrad III agreed with the Saxon lords that Saxony should be taken from Albrecht the Bear and returned to the future ruler, young Henry the Proud; the king refused to offer Henry Bavaria as well. This meant that, for the time being at least, peace had been restored in the north between the supporters of the Welfs and the Hohenstaufen.[181]

In 1141 Adelbert of Mainz died; he was replaced by the more peaceful Markulf, the former prior of Aschafenburg. This reduced interference by Mainz in the Thuringian lands.[182] Within a year, Markulf also died and was succeeded by Prior Heinrich of Mainz, a churchman who was likewise kindly disposed toward the Ludowinger.[183]

According to the *Cronicum S. Petri*, in 1542 a large conflagration broke out in Erfurt, which consumed most of the old city. The flames consumed the old monastery of St. Peter and the Church of St. Severn, as well as all the neighboring churches.[184]

Both the *San Petri Annalen* and the *Chronicon Paviensis* relate in considerable detail how Conrad III, stirred up by the sermons of Bernard of Clairveaux, set out with King Louis of France to recapture the Holy Land from the Turks. Ludwig did not participate in the crusade. Knochenhauer believed that his hesitancy may have been due to the fact that his uncle, Bishop Udo of Naumburg, had earlier lost his life on another crusade. He accompanied them as far as Nürnberg and then returned.[185] However, he did erect the monastery of

Ichtershausen.[186] No doubt the arduous expedition broke Conrad III's health, for the Kaiser returned in 1149 and died in 1152.[187]

Upon his return, Conrad III's first problem was to deal with Henry the Lion in the north, who was threatening his neighbors. The king then tried to use Albrecht the Bear as a counterweight against the ambitious Welf. He and Ludwig met with Albrecht at Altenburg, and again at Erfurt. These sessions were followed by further meetings at Goslar and Braunschweig.[188]

Ludwig was no doubt very pleased with the choice of the Conrad's nephew, Frederick Barbarossa, as the next emperor.[189] Letters preserved in Reinhardsbrunn show that the relationship between Ludwig and the young Staufer was already very close.[190]

Ludwig's role during the Kaiser's first Italian expedition remains unclear. Knochenhauer claims he went to Italy, but returned home early with the Kaiser's full blessing because of some special assignment.[191] Patze does not believe that Ludwig went on the expedition, but that instead he was asked to preserve the peace at home.[192] At this time Ludwig was having problems with Archbishop Arnold of Mainz, who had been installed in 1153. This was Arnold of Seelhafen, a native of Worms who had made a special trip to Rome to ascertain his rights as churchman. He seems to have been envious of the landgrave's role in Thuringia, regarding it as his duty to curb both Ludwig IV and his supporters. Knochenhauer cites two letters to the emperor in which Ludwig said that if the Kaiser did not curb the archbishop's ambitious conduct, he might soon "find him to be a beast of prey."[193] The Kaiser wrote a sympathetic reply, in which he stated that the crown would consider this problem at the next German diet in Worms.[194] The archbishop had also become involved in a struggle with Pfalzgraf Hermann of the Rhine. Later the Kaiser seems to have heard the two sides at a diet in Worms and then warned all the parties involved.[195]

Meanwhile, in 1157, the emperor went on another expedition into Poland to bring Duke Boleslav under control. Boleslav had acted in a high-handed manner through the expulsion of his brother Wladislav of Bohemia. Ludwig and his brother Heinrich Raspe accompanied the Kaiser, as did many ranking princes and nobles. The Bohemian Duke Wladislav had married Ludwig IV's sister, Jutta. Frederick forced Boleslav to renew his feudal oath, in which he also had to acknowledge his future obligations to the German *Reich*, Wladislav was now dignified with the title of King of Bohemia, in which ceremony Ludwig witnessed the elevation of his sister to the rank of queen. The Polish king was forced to offer his brother and some nobles as hostages and to promise to remain loyal. But Duke Boleslav does not seem to have been very trustworthy.[196] Ludwig returned home by way of Regensburg. In March 1158 he again appeared in the company of the Kaiser at Frankfurt a.M., and from there he followed him to Kaiserswerth.[197] Shortly after that, the Landgraf again accompanied him on another Italian expedition, where he fought with the king's forces in the siege of Milan.[198] But the Landgraf must not have remained in Italy, because there were pressing problems in his homeland. In 1160 he seems to have become involved in the murder of Archbishop Arnold by his fellow townsmen at Worms, and also in the election of Arnold's successor.[199]

The degree of Ludwig's involvement in the siege of Milan is not clear. On 8 September 1158, Milan capitulated. Later, Pope Alexander III offered continued support to the Milanese, fostering another rebellion. During this period, the existence of two rival popes, Victor IV and Alexander III, resulted in further confusion. By the spring of 1161, Frederick's warriors again arrived in Italy. Among the leaders were Ludwig and his relative Pfalzgraf Conrad of the Rhine, Duke Frederick of Rothenburg, and the archbishop of Cologne, who was Ludwig's brother-in-law. By August the citizens of Milan tried to arrange for an armistice with the emperor. They proposed contact with an imperial committee, consisting of Ludwig, Theobald (the duke of Bohemia, the brother of the king of Bohemia), and the aforementioned Pfalzgraf. A place for the meeting had been arranged, but when the Milanese delegates arrived, they were attacked by Rainald von Dassel's troops, in direct violation of their safe-conduct. The committee was so disgusted with this that they wanted to kill Dassel. But he tried to justify his action before the emperor, and Frederick ordered that he should not be harmed.[200] Ludwig then obtained the emperor's permission to go home and returned to Thuringia.[201]

Emperor Frederick had decided to make Conrad of Bavaria archbishop of Mainz. Once in power, Conrad began to cause trouble for the Landgraf. He planned to make Erfurt a counterweight to Ludwig's rule by erecting a wall around the old city.[202] Barbarossa returned from Italy in 1162, and in April 1163 the Kaiser weighed the interests of Mainz. The result was that Ludwig was ordered to tear down the walls around Erfurt that Conrad had erected.[203]

In a previous chapter we examined the change in Henry the Lion toward the emperor after the first four Italian campaigns. Ludwig's Thuringia lay between Saxony and Bavaria, which forced him to decide which way he should go; he could either join Henry and condone his actions, or he could join his hostile neighbors and fight with them for survival.[204] Ludwig turned away from Henry, but his actions were certainly not condoned by the emperor. In 1166 Henry's castle of Haldenburg was besieged. Henry moved up with his army, but the clergy were able to arrange for an armistice before the opposing forces fought. Then fighting was renewed and Goslar fell.[205] The *Chronicon s. Petri* describes the extensive devastation.[206] The Kaiser's delegates, Christian of Mainz and Duke Berchtold of Zähringen, then arrived from Italy and ordered that peace be restored. Finally, in the spring of 1169, the Kaiser himself returned from Italy.[207] At a Würzburg meeting, some Saxon princes agreed to keep the truce until the next *Reichstag*.[208] The *Reinhardsbrunn Chronicle* relates that after Easter 1168 the emperor held a diet at Regensburg, where Ludwig the Iron Man entered a truce with Henry the Lion in the presence of the rest of the princes.[209] The *Chronicles* adds that Henry himself was permitted to be absent, for other Saxon princes acted in his place.[210] During this period Ludwig remained constantly at the Kaiser's side.[211] By then Ludwig was already an old man, and he faced constant danger from Henry the Lion. Thus in 1168 his son Ludwig V was designated his successor.

The *Chronicon s. Petri* informs us that in 1170 Kaiser Frederick held a general *Reichstag* at Erfurt on the day of John the Baptist, where they agreed to a general conciliation between the Saxon princes and Henry the Lion.[212] In 1168, while Ludwig was with the Kaiser at the *Reichstag* in Regensburg, the Reinhardsbrunn chronicler relates that his wife Jutta, the Kaiser's sister, ventured upon a bold undertaking. She began the construction of a lofty new castle known as Weiszensee. It served as a stopover point halfway between the Wartburg and the distant Neuenburg. But there was one catch to the undertaking. Count Frederick of Beichlingen complained to the emperor that this construction offended his rights. The chronicler claimed that Frederick called Ludwig to task for it. Though he was offended, Ludwig relayed the brother's message to the sister. But the account adds that Ludwig secretly told his wife to go ahead, counting on the good will of the Kaiser. The castle was finished and nothing more was heard by way of objections from Frederick.[213]

The *Reinhardsbrunn Chronicle* relates how, when the Landgraf died, his body was transported with great honor to the family burial place. Ludwig the Iron Man and his wife Jutta had five children, four boys and one girl. The oldest son, as we observed, was made landgrave of Thuringia even prior to his father's death. Friedrich, the second son, became prior of the *Stift* of Saint Stephans in Mainz, but that life did not seem to agree with him. He left the *Stift* in order to marry Luchardis of Ziegenhain. The third son, Heinrich Raspe, named after his uncle, became the count of Maden and of Hesse. He also had the *Vogtei* rights of Hersfeld, lands on the Rhine, and the castle of Windeck. The fourth son, Hermann I, was given the *Pfalzgrafschaft* of Saxony until the death of Ludwig III. Meanwhile Heinrich Raspe III had died and Ludwig became Landgraf. The daughter Jutta married Count Hermann von Ravensburg.[214]

9

The Reigns of Ludwig IV
and Hermann I

Ludwig the Iron Man had carefully planned the transition of power to his son, Ludwig the Pious. The *Düringische Chronik* relates how, in Erfurt in 1170, Frederick Barbarossa had the nephew knighted.[1] As we have seen, during his final years Ludwig also turned over some governmental duties to his son.[2]

According to the chroniclers, young Ludwig was more inclined to rely on God than on human weapons. He was completely dedicated to the Apostolic See. The chronicle also claims he had great concern for the well-being of his family and his subjects, especially the poor.[3]

For twenty years Frederick I and his cousin, Henry the Lion, had been on friendly terms, so relationships between Saxony and Thuringia were just the opposite of what they turned out to be a decade later. Like his father, Ludwig the Pious was a strong supporter of Henry the Lion, and thus had the Kaiser's good will. Albrecht the Bear had been friendly with Conrad I, for their mother is believed to have been a Staufer. The sons often accompanied the Kaiser on his campaigns and fought in his battles. Later they became dissatisfied, because at Goslar the Kaiser had withdrawn Plötzkau castle from them.[4]

Albrecht the Bear had seven sons. The proximity of the Ascanier lands to those of the Ludowinger made these sons dangerous to have as enemies. Count Bernhard's lands extended to the eastern border of Ludwig's holdings, while Hermann was in possession of Weimar-Orlamünde. The territory of Albrecht, the sixth son, extended far into Thuringia.[5] The Ascanier, meanwhile, drove Ludwig out of Plötzkau castle; but young Ludwig, in turn, demolished Weimar with the assistance of the Kaiser.[6]

Frederick Barbarossa must have been at his wit's end to please both sides of the family. It is believed that Sophia, the mother of the Ascanier boys, was a Hohenstaufen, and Ludwig and Hermann I were his sister's sons. The Staufer tried to stay on the good side of both them and the Ascanier. This may explain why another Ascanier, Siegfried, then became bishop of Brandenburg.[7]

In the latter part of August, 1164, the Kaiser started on his fifth Italian expedition, traveling by way of Burgundy and the St. Cenis, to continue his struggle with the Lombard League.[8] Both Ludwig the Pious and Henry remained at home to continue their battle with the Ascanier. Count Bernhard had even invaded Ludwig's lands and attacked Melfingen. Henry rushed north from Bavaria and ran roughshod over Bernhard's lands, leaving his Aschersleben in ruins. This drove Bernhard out of Thuringia, east of the Saale.[9] Meanwhile Henry the Lion was becoming more ambitious. He soon stirred up trouble with Archbishop Philip of Cologne and Bishop Ulrich of Halberstadt, whom the Welf had deposed and replaced with Bishop Gero.[10]

In the summer of 1176, after the Legnano defeat, Ludwig the Pious was in Italy with the Kaiser.[11] There was an uprising at Erfurt during Ludwig's absence, no doubt stirred up by Count Erwin of Gleichen.[12] Patze believes that the culprits were the neighboring counts Erwin II of Tonna and Henry I of Schwarzburg. When Ludwig returned from Italy, he attacked their castle and destroyed three of Henry I's strongholds.[13] After the emperor returned in July 1179, he restored peace in Thuringia.[14]

When Henry the Lion was placed under the ban he stormed Halberstadt, burned its church, and led Ulrich into captivity. This brought the duke's old enemies to the forefront, and Archbishop Philip of Cologne and Henry traded blows.[15] This turn of events made Ludwig wonder what to do. Meanwhile Archbishop Wichmann attempted to mediate between the hostile forces.[16] Patze claims it was Philip of Cologne who brought the Landgraf and Hermann I to opposite sides in the conflict.[17]

After the Kaiser's actions at Würzburg and Gelnhausen, Henry struck back at the emperor and his supporters.[18] This made Ludwig rush to defend his lands. After the fall of Nordhausen the Landgraf went to confront the Welf outlaw at Weiszensee, but most of Ludwig's troops fled. Bernhard, who had come to support the Ludowinger, slipped away, and both Ludwig and Hermann were captured, along with 400 to 600 knights. The rest fled to Mühlhausen, which was then captured and burned.[19]

Henry's eventual release of Ludwig and Hermann from prison came too late to help him in his conflict with the Kaiser. The Ludowinger had managed to remain on good terms with the Hohenstaufen emperor. When the Kaiser had become dissatisfied with Henry the Lion, the Ludowinger had changed their loyalties as well. And when the *Pfalzgrafschaft* of Saxony became vacant, the emperor gave it to Ludwig's brother, Hermann I.[20]

The title "Pfalzgraf of the Palatinate of Saxony" would be highly prized by the future Ludowinger rulers. Starke has given us an insight into its significance.[21] According to the *Sachsenspiegel*, every original stem duchy had such an official. The chief count of the Palatinate even had a court in which to try rulers for malfeasance in office.[22] This Saxon official was not under the duke, but directly under the Kaiser.[23] Not even Henry had been able to make the official subservient to himself.[24] The Kaiser's granting of the title to Hermann I strongly enhanced the standing of the Ludowinger in the *Reich*.[25]

The Ludowinger reached the peak of their power at Gelnhausen and Erfurt.[26] Since the Hessian ruler Heinrich Raspe had died, the Kaiser now made Ludwig IV Landgraf of both Hesse and Thuringia.[27] After Henry's expulsion from the *Reich*, Ludwig was in control of the whole Werra Valley, up to Hannover-Münden.[28] The chroniclers claimed that Ludwig IV graciously offered the *Landgrafschaft* of Saxony to his brother, Hermann I, who was landless. The Kaiser confirmed this at the Erfurt *Reichstag* in 1181.[29]

The archbishops of Mainz did all within their power to curb the rise of the Ludowinger. Both Adelbert I and Adelbert II allied themselves with the Landgraf's enemies in order to enhance their territorial possessions.[30] This limited Ludowinger growth in the Lahn River and the Marburg region, where before they had tried to expand their lands to the Kassel border.[31] Heinrich Raspe had even allied himself with the archbishop of Cologne and his allodial lands.[32] The Ludowinger then attempted to establish a link between Hesse and Thuringia, but the archbishop tried to prevent it. He knew that what they wanted was the entire Werra River valley.[33]

When Archbishop Christian died in Italy in 1183, the pope replaced him with Salzburg's Conrad of Wittelsbach.[34] He made Count Henry of Schwarzburg, Ludwig's old enemy, the vice-regent of Mainz.[35] The two attempted to outmaneuver one another by buying and selling territory. The new archbishop bought Wiverstedt and gave it to Günther von Schwarzburg. This placed one of Mainz's vassals in the castle Eckhartsberge, which was really Ludwig's fief.[36] From various sides, others took advantage of this pressure exerted by Mainz. Otto of Meissen tried to appropriate some Thuringian territory, but in a counter-move, Ludwig captured him and locked him up in the Wartburg. After that, princes complained to the Kaiser that he had violated the peace of the land. In a meeting at Fulda, the emperor made it clear that he did not blame the Landgraf for his action. Frederick I ordered Otto's liberation, and this pacified his neighbors.[37]

German lands breathed easier after the Peace of Constance in 1183. But Frederick Barbarossa was displeased by the continuing strife between the archbishop of Mainz and the Ludowinger. He ordered a meeting at Erfurt to settle matters. A huge crowd gathered in an upper hall, overloading the structure. The floor collapsed, killing some sixty nobles. Among the dead were three of the troublemakers, but young Henry VI and the archbishop remained unhurt. However, the Landgraf was caught under some debris and had to be liberated. It was a sobering experience that ended the strife.[38]

When Pope Alexander III died in 1184, the mending of political fences began all over again under the new Pope Lucius. The Kaiser decided to visit Italy, and was accompanied by Conrad of Mainz, Landgraf Ludwig, and a few ranking nobles and princes. In Verona, Frederick I met with the pope, discussing the Matildan lands in particular, but no settlement seems to have resulted.[39] The archbishop remained with the Kaiser a little longer than did the Landgraf. When a new feud broke out over the castle Eckhartsberge, Conrad returned. This conflict had many repercussions in Hesse and Thuringia, and Conrad demanded that Ludwig return a Mainz fief.[40]

Soon after this, Pope Lucius died and was followed by Urban III. This demanded another goodwill visit to Italy. The Kaiser also wanted his son Henry VI crowned emperor by the pontiff, and he arranged for the marriage of Frederick II to Constancia, the daughter of Roger, the brother of King William. Naturally the pope would not approve of such a marriage, for by means of it Henry VI might become king of all Italy. In spite of papal objections, the marriage was held in Milan on 27 January 1186.[41] To make matters worse, the new pope used Philip of Cologne to divide the German episcopacy. In this the Kaiser kept the upper hand, for at a *Reichstag* in 1186, Conrad of Mainz had the majority of the German clergy in his favor. Here the Landgraf was among Frederick I's strongest supporters. At another *Reichstag*, at Worms in 1187, Philip had to give an account of his action.[42] Soon after that Pope Urban III died, and his successor, Pope Gregory VIII, acted kindly toward the emperor.[43]

The new pope was barely in office when Saladin captured Jerusalem in cooperation with the Turks and the Saracens.[44] At the *Reichstag* of Worms in 1187, the papal legate Albano appeared and called on all the German princes to launch a Third Crusade to liberate the Holy Land. Barbarossa decided to participate, along with kings of France and England. Ludwig was also among those marked with the holy cross by the bishop of Würzburg, in the presence of the papal legate.[45]

Before going on such a journey, Ludwig had to put things in order at home. Since the second brother, Frederick, declined to become ruler during Ludwig's absence, the lot now fell upon Hermann I. Hermann was already Pfalzgraf of Saxony, and now became ruler of all the Saxon lands, as well as Hesse and Thuringia.[46]

By May 1189, at the Regensburg *Reichstag*, the crusaders were ready to depart for the Holy Land by way of Greece.[47] Ludwig left later and traveled via Italy. From Apulia he sailed to Tyre. He was wounded in battle and had difficulties with the French. He decided to return, but became ill on the way back, dying on 16 October 1190. His body was transported to Germany, and he was buried at Reinhardsbrunn next to his ancestors.[48] Though Ludwig was married twice, there were no male heirs. His daughter, Jutta, married Count Dietrich of Wettin, who later also became the count of Groitzsch. The fact that only male heirs could be successors created a problem. Heinrich Raspe, the older brother, died in 1180, and the next son, Frederick, was not interested in becoming Landgraf. This meant that the mantle fell on the younger brother, Hermann I.[49]

Hermann I's mother was Jutta, the sister of Frederick Barbarossa, and she seems to have imparted to her son a desire for learning. He attended the University of Paris, and he loved to be surrounded by poets and scholars. During Hermann's reign the Neuenburg and the Wartburg were cultural centers for traveling minstrels.[50] He also stressed the polished idea of knighthood that flourished in Thuringia at the time.[51] Walther von der Vogelweide of Eisenach and Wolfgang von Eschenbach often entertained at the Wartburg for Hermann and his family and their many guests.[52]

Hermann's cousin Henry VI attempted to take advantage of the scholarly young ruler after Ludwig's death. He refused to recognize Hermann as the rightful male heir. Had Henry been able to acquire Thuringian and Hessian lands, the Hohenstaufen would have controlled central Germany from the Wartburg to the Lahn, as well as Pleiszen lands in the east. But other territorial princes sided with the Ludowinger and stopped the Kaiser's ambitious plans.[53] The emperor's chronicler claimed he was only holding the lands as fiefs until Hermann I returned from the Crusade.[54]

A feud broke out between Markgraf Albrecht of Meissen and his brother Dietrich. This interested Hermann I, for his daughter Jutta was married to Dietrich. The friction was over the profits from the Freiburg silver mines.[55] Hermann I had warned Albrecht that he needed to make peace with his brother or else he would resort to force. After Hermann I's army invaded the Meissen lands, the Markgraf accused him of planning to assassinate the Kaiser.[56] He even challenged Hermann in battle. Hermann replied that he was willing to fight, provided it was in the presence of the king. Henry VI planned such an encounter at Nordhausen, but Albrecht failed to come. Henry held a second meeting at Altenburg, where the accuser was charged with character defamation.[57] After this Bernhard of Saxony brought about their reconciliation.[58] In the settlement, Albrecht was forced to divide the silver mining profits with Dietrich.[59] Subsequently the Kaiser postponed his attempts to acquire the Ludowinger lands.[60]

Pope Clement III died in 1191 and was followed by Pope Celestius, who was installed on Easter Day, 14 April 1191.[61] The pope then crowned Henry VI as emperor and the next day crowned the queen.[62] While the Kaiser was in Apulia and Sicily, a plague broke out and killed many of his best troops, among them Archbishop Philip of Cologne. The Kaiser became very ill as well, and suffered on the way home. But he was able to celebrate Christmas in Hagenau.[63] In 1192, Henry VI feuded with Pope Celestius III on the appointment of new German bishops, after several had died. The Kaiser was also charged with the crime of the murder of the bishop of Lüttich.[64] The question of a successor for Lüttich had been discussed in 1191 at a *Reichstag* in Worms, where the Kaiser rejected both candidates and instead chose Prior Lother of Bonn. His opponent, Adelbert, went to Rome to obtain papal approval. In Reims he was solemnly invested by Archbishop Bruno of Cologne and the archbishop of Reims. The emperor was angered by this, and while in Reims the bishop was murdered, with the king's approval.[65]

Enemies of the Hohenstaufen now raised their heads everywhere. Conrad of Mainz was the ringleader, and he formed an alliance with Hermann I and Ottokar of Bohemia. Henry VI even went to Saxony to placate the opposition, and he seems to have succeeded.[66]

King Richard I (the Lionhearted) of England went on the Third Crusade with Philip Augustus of France and Frederick Barbarossa. On his return Richard was captured by Leopold II of Austria, who soon turned him over to the emperor Henry VI as a political prisoner. Before Richard could be released, England had to pay 100,000 pounds of silver and give England to the Kaiser as a fief. This greatly boosted the emperor's stock, and his enemies were easily pla-

cated. Hermann I also effected his reconciliation with the Kaiser, along with
Bernhard of Saxony. Thus by June 1193, at a *Reichstag* in Worms, all was well
again.[67] Yet at the same *Reichstag* the emperor deposed Ottokar of Bohemia,
who had supported him.[68]

Archbishop Conrad was displeased with Hermann I because of his reconciliation with the crown, and he defamed him among the princes. Markgraf
Albrecht joined Hermann and forced the bishop to restore peace.[69] It is
believed that the Landgraf played a significant role in the reconciliation
between Richard I and the emperor discussed at the *Reichstagen* of 1193 and
1194. In 1194, Richard was brought to Würzburg by the Landgraf to be presented to the Kaiser. At that *Reichstag* it was announced that the English king
had become engaged to the Pfalzgraf's daughter. This helped bring the Welfs
and Hohenstaufen together and led to the liberation of the English king.[70]

After this settlement, the emperor returned to conquer all of southern Italy
and Sicily.[71] During the king's absence, Markgraf Albrecht again feuded with his
brother, breaking his past commitment. He seized the castle Wunnenfels.[72]
When Albrecht refused to listen to the Landgraf, the latter arrived with soldiers
and drove him away.[73] Since Albrecht continued to be truculent, he was invaded
by a larger army. His fortresses fell to his brother Dietrich, and Hermann
departed as conqueror.[74]

While the Landgraf had been occupied with his Meissen problem, the ambitious Archbishop Conrad reopened his Hessian feud. Now a new war broke out,
led by the archbishop of Cologne, who invaded the Hessian lands from the
north.[75] This divested Hermann I's territories and the town Grünberg lay in
ashes.[76] When the Landgraf prepared to meet the threat, Albrecht was again on
the rampage in Meissen, even invading Thuringia. But Hermann reversed his
course and fell upon Albrecht's camp by surprise, defeating him and taking
many prisoners. But the Markgraf himself was able to slip away.[77] The annalist
recorded that God continued to protect the princes of Thuringia.[78] When the
local princes in Hesse continued their battle, and Hermann came to their support, peace was restored.[79]

Since Markgraf Albrecht had gotten nowhere with Hermann I, he went to
Apulia in Italy. After the Nordhausen affair, however, the emperor did not trust
him, and he made no headway with the Kaiser.[80] In fact he feared for his life and
fled back over the Alps. Soon after that the Markgraf died in Leipzig; the Reinhardsbrunn annalist suggests that he was poisoned.[81] With the death of
Albrecht, the *Markgrafschaft* should have passed to his brother Dietrich.[82] But
according to the St. Peter's chronicler, Henry VI was overcome by pride after
his success in Italy, becoming king of Sicily, and being reconciled with the
papacy.[83] Upon his return, he refused to make Dietrich the Markgraf of Meissen, which caused a feud among the Ludowinger. After discussion by the crown
at Mainz and again at Würzburg, the king was still holding onto Meissen. The
Kaiser may have been playing for larger stakes, but Hermann wanted action.[84]

In October 1195, after a large *Reichstag*, the papal legate John of Monte
Celie made a strong appeal for a Fourth Crusade. On 28 October 1195 many

crusaders took up the cross, including Archbishop Conrad and Landgraf Hermann I of Thuringia.[85] But Henry VI never really got started on this attempt to conquer Byzantium.[86] The archbishop had sailed for Acre with an army of crusaders, leaving the Kaiser behind. When in August 1197 the rest were ready, a great heat wave broke out in Messina, and many of the crusaders, among them Henry VI, died.[87] Before his departure, the emperor had managed to get the German princes to agree that his young son Frederick II should be his successor.[88] Hermann I, also, had been concerned that he might not return. Thus at Würzburg, in 1196, he obtained an agreement in writing stating that his daughter would inherit the Ludowinger lands, even though this was opposed by the princes.[89]

When Henry VI died in Messina, young Frederick II was not quite three years old. This meant that for at least a decade, some other regent would have to rule. At this time the strongest pope of the Middle Ages, Innocent III, ruled over the Holy See, and he moved kings and princes across the chessboard of Europe like pawns. He became pope on 22 February 1198.[90] The situation was tense when the king's brother, Philip of Swabia, had himself elected Kaiser by the electors.[91] Meanwhile, Archbishop Conrad of Mainz was still not back from the Holy Land.[92] Adolf, archbishop of Cologne, had Otto IV of Brunswick (son of Henry the Lion) elected as a rival king.[93] Then, on 12 July 1198, Otto IV was officially anointed in Aachen by the archbishop of Cologne.[94] On 5 April 1198 Philip had already been crowned in Worms, but for some unknown reason he was not anointed until 8 September.[95]

In 1198 many crusaders returned, and among the stragglers was Hermann I, who had remained for the founding of the Order of the Teutonic Knights.[96] In the days of Hermann's son, Ludwig V, and Ludwig's wife, Holy Elizabeth, this famous order was located in Marburg on the Lahn. Knochenhauer claims that the landgrave tried to avoid meeting Philip on has way home.[97] Thus he returned by way of Bohemia.[98]

The two rival kings now began bidding for Hermann I's support, for Thuringia's central location made it vital for each candidate. The Reinhardsbrunn annalist says that Philip began promising towns and castles, and Otto tried to trump the Staufer with higher offers.[99] Otto reminded Hermann of his mistreatment by Henry VI over Thuringia.[100] King Otto IV offered Hermann the gift of the two imperial cities of Nordhausen and Saalfeld, and 1800 Marks as well. The encounter ended with Hermann proclaiming Otto king.[101] This was followed by a feudal investiture of Hermann I's lands and the Landgraf's pledge of allegiance.[102] Giving the two cities as gifts was easier said than done, for the cities favored the Hohenstaufen, and capturing them required the use of force. A six-week siege of Nordhausen was begun.[103] Hermann redirected the Helme tributary of the Unstrut, which provided the town's water supply. Then the city capitulated.[104] Next Hermann's forces turned to Saalfeld, which chose to surrender and was devastated, along with its Benedictine monastery.[105]

Upon later reflection, Hermann I wondered about the wisdom of his pledge to Otto IV, for in 1199 the whole picture changed. Otto had besieged Goslar,

and Philip had driven him off, so by 1199 Goslar was under the Staufer's control. Otto had used English gold to buy supporters, but in that year Richard I
was killed, and King Otto lost most of his supporters. Meanwhile Philip still had
his allodial lands as income. In addition, Otto IV failed to pay Hermann I the
1800 Marks he had promised.[106] By Pentecost 1199, the Landgraf had joined
Philip, and as fiefs of the *Reich* he was given Nordhausen, Mühlhausen, Saalfeld, the Orland, and Rania castle.[107]

The devastation of Saalfeld was discussed by the court in Erfurt, and Hermann and his lands were put under the interdict until he made restitution for
the damages. By 2 July 1199 the archbishop of Mainz had returned, and he
stopped to discuss German affairs with Pope Innocent III. He wanted the rival
kings to step down and honor Frederick II as the rightful successor, but he got
nowhere.[108] Soon after that the archbishop died. In the year 1200 Hermann
assisted King Philip in his war with Braunschweig. But his ardor for Philip's rule
seemed to be waning, even though he attended his *Reichstag* in Bamberg. He
felt that Innocent III was dominating affairs in the *Reich*. The pontiff then
placed Philip under the ban and declared Otto IV the legitimate ruler.[109]

When Archbishop Conrad died in 1200, the principal German bishopric
became vacant, and this again started a rivalry. The Staufer Kaiser wanted
Bishop Lupold of Worms, but the electors and Pope Innocent III, along with
Otto IV, wanted Siegfried von Eppenstein, the prior of St. Peters in Erfurt.[110]
Now all the cards were stacked on Frederick's side. The Roman pontiff supplied
the pallium and the installation and investiture were performed by Archbishop
Adolf of Cologne. To finish matters the pope sent his legate, Guido of Palestrina,
in August 1201. He was to officially depose Lupold of Worms and pronounce the
pope's candidate archbishop of Mainz.[111] The Landgraf must have observed that
King Otto IV enjoyed international support while Philip did not.[112]

At the *Reichstag* in Bamberg in 1202, Kaiser Philip indicated that he might
want Hermann I to return the imperial cities as fiefs.[113] While the Landgraf was
in a quandary about this, Otto IV promised that he would make good on his previous promise of the 1800 Marks. Even then the pope threatened Hermann
with dire consequences if he failed to support Siegfried.[114] The Landgraf went
along with the pontiff, and for the first time this put him in serious conflict with
Philip.[115] Hermann I became an ardent supporter of Siegfried and ordered his
subjects to follow his orders. He even expelled Count Lambert von Gleichen
from Erfurt because he was a Staufer supporter.[116]

Such a strong stand by the landgrave did not go unchallenged. The Kaiser
attacked Thuringia from two sides. He invaded from the east with 2000 knights
and lighter troops in order to devastate and burn Hermann's lands; meanwhile
Archbishop Lupold was to invade his lands from the west. The resulting
destruction was terrible, and the chronicler claimed it exceeded that caused by
the Saracens.[117] Hermann I called on his father-in-law, King Ottokar of
Bohemia, who came with a vast army that caused the Kaiser to hide in Erfurt. A
siege of Erfurt by both armies followed, but Philip escaped. The Staufer then
enlisted the support of neighboring nobles. The king and the Landgraf lifted

the siege to attack the Kaiser's forces, but he evaded them and returned to Swabia without engaging in a major battle.[118] However, the Kaiser had succeeded in punishing both Thuringia and Meissen.[119]

At this point Otto IV felt he had triumphed, and he held an elaborate court on St. Bartholomew's Day at the city of Merseburg, with even the papal legate as a guest. There Otto crowned Ottokar of Bohemia as king, and in another ceremony Ottokar pledged his allegiance to the king and received his lands in his name.[120] But changes were coming soon. At harvest time Philip invaded Thuringia, putting ripe fields of grain on fire, devastating and pillaging. Philip tried but failed to take the Ludowinger castle of Weiszenburg, built by Jutta, Frederick I's sister. Hermann asked Ottokar for help, but when he arrived and saw the size of Philip's army, his army fled and Hermann I was captured. He was forced to capitulate and give hostages, and he became Philip's vassal.[121]

With Otto seemingly helpless, the princes rallied around Philip. They even arranged for a second coronation of the Staufer and his wife.[122] Because Philip's opposition was in the north, in 1205 he invaded the lands of Archbishop Adolf of Cologne, and besieged Cologne itself. The people appealed directly to the Staufer, bypassing Adolf. After five days Philip moved on to Reusz on the Rhine.[123]

By 1204 Archbishop Adolf had cooled in his support of Kaiser Otto and had joined Philip. This meant that the Staufer could now be crowned in Aachen, an event that occurred on 6 January 1205. Pope Innocent III then ordered a new election to replace Archbishop Adolf with Archbishop Bruno, to whom he had already sent the pallium.[124] Adolf then retaliated by attacking Kaiser Otto and Bruno. Adolf was familiar with the region and he set a trap for his opponents. By hiding his troops in a woods and having the front line feign a retreat, he encouraged the enemy to charge boldly upon the retreating front until they had passed the ambush. At that point they were completely surrounded and forced into a swamp. Somehow King Otto managed to escape, but Bruno was captured and incarcerated in Trifels prison, near Landau in the Rhenish Palatinate. On 16 October 1206, at the Würzburg *Reichstag*, the citizens of Cologne were extended Philip's pardon, after his enemies had bowed before him and given both hostages and a considerable ransom.[125]

The final years of Hermann I's reign were stormy because of the confused situation regarding the empire. First there was the matter of loyalty toward Otto and Philip, and then, after Philip's death, conflict between Otto and Frederick II.[126] It is difficult to follow the complex game played by Pope Innocent III, who advised Hermann to be only outwardly loyal to Philip, and then support the Welf cause when possible.[127] By 1207 the pope had shifted, sending a large delegation to Worms to crown Philip, and lifting the papal ban. Another delegation was sent to King Otto, stating that the Apostolic See demanded his abdication.[128] The enraged Otto replied that he would never abdicate. A face-to-face meeting was followed by an armistice that lasted until 28 June 1208.[129] Meanwhile Hermann remained loyal to the Staufer and attended his *Hoftagen*.[130]

When King Philip held a *Reichstag* at Würzburg, in November 1507, Archbishop Bruno was liberated from Trifels.[131]

Meanwhile Philip had gone to Bamberg to renew the struggle for the kingship. On 21 June 1208 he retired for a brief rest. He was still awake when Pfalzgraf Otto of Wittelsbach knocked on the door and asked to enter. As the two talked about military matters, the Pfalzgraf suddenly drew his sword and stabbed the defenseless king in the throat. The chroniclers wondered why the trusted Pfalzgraf would have committed this murder. Was it because the king had once offered his daughter's hand to the Pfalzgraf and then later withdrawn it?[132] The motive seems to have been more complicated than that.[133] But the Pfalzgraf did not get very far. Marshal von Kalden caught and killed him on the Danube near Regensburg.[134]

The whole political climate in the *Reich* then changed, and Innocent III called it a judgment of God.[135] King Otto was advised to make his peace with the opposition.[136] But the eastern clergy had their own ideas of straightening out Otto IV's standing with Rome. Meanwhile, Siegfried returned from Rome with the full approval of the pope and was now installed as the legitimate archbishop of Mainz.[137] On 22 September 1208, King Otto held his reconciliation meeting at Halberstadt. Many of the supporters of Philip had their misgivings and wanted to elect Frederick II, as they had pledged to Henry VI before his crusade, but they finally went along with Otto IV.[138]

On 11 November 1208, Otto IV held a large *Reichstag* at Frankfurt a.M., where he conducted an extensive investiture of the *Reich*. He forced his vassals to do homage to him as their accepted "King of the Romans." In turn he agreed to keep the laws of the *Reich* and preserve the peace.[139] The deceased Pfalzgraf Otto of Wittelsbach was charged with Philip's murder, Otto IV pronounced the imperial verdict upon him, and his crown lands were taken away.[140] Otto IV then also became engaged to one of Philip's daughters, offering him a claim to the Staufer crown lands.[141]

Upon his return from the *Reichstag*, Hermann I conducted a series of court meetings at Ekhardtsberge. Siegfried (now an archbishop) cooperated with the Landgraf in order to set his house in order after so much strife.[142] King Otto IV was unacquainted with many parts of the *Reich*, which he now visited. At Easter in 1209 Otto was Hermann's guest in Altenburg, along with many Thuringian nobles; then on Pentecost he met at Braunschweig with those of the north and east.[143] Pope Innocent III also drew closer to the Welf king. He even talked of crowning him in person under the pontiff's conditions: giving up the Matildan lands and no renewal of the Staufer interests in Apulia and Sicily. Perhaps the pope even wanted to obtain control of the *Reich*.[144] Otto IV was finally crowned by Innocent III after meeting these conditions. Ludwig did not attend the coronation. Once crowned, however, the Welf emperor revolted and took the Matildan lands by force. When he entered Apulia he was placed under the papal ban.[145] Strangely, it was Siegfried, the emperor's staunch supporter, who on 2 February 1211 pronounced the ban on him. But at this point Hermann I deserted Otto IV and attended a meeting held by Archbishop Albert of Magde-burg, the king of Bohemia, the Markgraf, and others. These now sent a message to the pope that henceforth they would leave the emperor and regard as bind-ing their pledge to the earlier King Henry VI, that his son Frederick II would be the legitimate successor to the throne.[146]

During this period Philip Augustus of France contacted the Landgraf about marrying his daughter Irmengard, for Philip planned to divorce his Danish wife Ingeborg. However, Rome refused to grant the divorce. The French king was also ready to pay money to support Frederick II as the next Kaiser. Since this offer failed, Irmengard later married Count Heinrich of Anhalt. But the mar-riage offer shows how highly esteemed the Ludowinger had become outside the *Reich*.[147]

Opposition to Otto IV did not die down. A larger meeting took place in Nürn-berg, at which the rulers and nobility took an oath to oppose the emperor. Inno-cent III also sent a message to the princes, stating that Otto IV was an enemy of the Roman church and that Frederick II should be chosen as the future Ger-man emperor. The assembly asked Frederick II to visit Germany.[148] Now the Hohenstaufen were jubilant; however, the Welfs were ready to battle for their emperor.[149] After that, the duke of Brabant, the king's brother, came with force and devastated the *Erzstift* of Mainz and Siegfried's lands. The archbishop took refuge with the Landgraf during the invasion. Then Gunzelin of Wolfenbüttel, Otto's steward, assembled some Saxon nobles at Nordhausen and Mühlhausen, using these cities as armed bases from which he could attack neighboring vil-lages and farms. They also offered barons in the area rich rewards to attack the landgrave's lands.[150] Hermann was not in a position to fight back, except from his castles.[151] The worst offender in carrying out acts of barbarism was the count of Beichlingen.[152] Upon his return, King Otto gathered a large army to attack Thuringia's larger cities and expel the Landgraf. In the face of such odds Hermann fled to the Wartburg.[153] In March 1212 Otto IV was back and started mending fences, winning some support.[154]

In a *Hoftag* at Pentecost that year, Emperor Otto IV announced that he planned to strike Thuringia in harvest time to burn the Landgraf's food sup-plies. He also announced that he would use a catapult to hurl large boulders into cities and against castle walls.[155] Later the emperor used the machine against the town of Langensalza, and it capitulated.[156] Then he turned it against the towering Weiszensee castle built by Hermann's mother, but there the weapon was not as effective.[157]

In Nordhausen the king was married to Beatrice, the daughter of former King Philip. But she died of an illness almost immediately afterward.[158] This tragedy disrupted his campaign against the Landgraf, and he discontinued the siege.[159] It may be that the real reason was that Otto had heard Frederick II was entering the *Reich* with an army. Otto went on to Erfurt, Würzburg, and Con-stance, where he heard that Frederick had just arrived. The gates remained locked against the king.[160] Later he learned that the Staufer was not in the city. It seems rather incongruous that the pope, who fought the Hohenstaufen, should now send the young Frederick II to deprive Otto IV of his kingship.[161] The pope helped the young Staufer en route through Italy and then provided escorts for him across the Alps to Constance. From there Frederick went to Basel, where he was welcomed by Archbishop Siegfried of Mainz, as well as other south German princes.[162] By November the Staufer held his first *Hoftag* at Mainz. From there he went to Frankfurt a.m., where he was elected "King of the Romans" on 5 December 1212, and crowned as the German Kaiser on 9 December 1212.[163] He held another *Hoftag* in Frankfurt a.m., where, says the chronicler, Hermann I was received with great festivity. Upon his arrival he was escorted into the city by 500 of the Kaiser's knights.[164]

During this period, the French king Philip Augustus tried to draw closer to Frederick II as the future Holy Roman emperor. The Erfurt chronicle claims that in Frankfurt a.m. the French king gave the young Staufer 20,000 gold Marks. The young king distributed these among the princes who were present.[165] Knochenhauer claims that Hermann I received his share and that the Kaiser returned Nordhausen to the Landgraf as a fief.[166] Count Berchtold of Zähringen and Lupold VI of Austria joined the young Staufer, and by the time of his investiture they came into the *Reich* as loyal vassals.[167]

After that Hermann I frequently traveled with Frederick II. They went to a *Hoftag* in Regensburg, where Ludwig of Bavaria renounced Otto IV and joined the Staufer's ranks as a vassal with his princes.[168] In February of the following year Hermann I was again with the Kaiser in Nürnberg, and from there went to the court on the Eger, where Frederick II made far-reaching promises to Pope Innocent III, like those Otto IV had made before his coronation.[169] In the fall of 1212, Frederick II held a *Hoftag* in Merseburg, where he aimed to cut the roots of Otto IV's power.[170]

Otto could never recognize that he had been defeated. He attacked anyone he regarded an enemy. Since Archbishop Albert of Mainz had announced Innocent III's ban against him, he attacked his lands and even succeeded in taking the archbishop captive. But he was soon forced to liberate him.[171] Otto failed in his attempt to capture Halle, but he burned the residences of Bishop Engelhard of Zeitz and moved with fire and sword across Thuringia.[172] Frederick II then recruited a large army, and when Otto saw that he was greatly outnumbered, he found refuge in Braunschweig. This was followed by devastation of the Welf's lands in the north. The armies under the Staufer went home for the winter in the Rhineland. Meanwhile, Markgraf Dietrich had also left Otto IV and joined Frederick II's side.[173]

The following year was the turning point in Otto IV's kingship. He sided with the English in the Battle of Bouvines. Frederick II did not get involved in the war, but Otto and the English were decisively beaten by the French. Now Otto's star began to wane, for the devastation of his army left him helpless. Thus Frederick was crowned in Aachen on 25 July 1215 by Archbishop Siegfried of Mainz. He then entered Cologne as the new Kaiser.[174]

More misfortune fell on the Welf king in his personal life. Otto married Maria, daughter of the duke of Brabant, who turned out to be a compulsive gambler. In Cologne she accrued huge debts, and the onus fell on her husband. After that the citizens of Cologne turned from Otto to Frederick II.[175]

In the last days of Hermann I's life, trouble developed when Hermann of Orlamünde took advantage of his brother Albert's absence and seized some of his castles and lands. Since Albert was Hermann I's son-in-law, the Landgraf besieged Weimar. In the course of the siege Count Dietrich and Count Hermann were captured, but the latter escaped.[176] He seems to have had help from the inside. According to the Reinhardsbrunn account, when Hermann learned that his prize prisoner had been allowed to escape, he flew into a rage. The guards would not talk, so he put them through gruesome torture on the rack to get a confession.[177] Meanwhile Archbishop Siegfried of Mainz had excommunicated Hermann I, an action which the Kaiser investigated. He met Hermann at the Neuenburg, where he had the Landgraf and Count Hermann present their differences.[178] There is no account of what transpired there. It is doubtful that after this Hermann I was in trouble with the Kaiser, for a little later the Landgraf was again with the king at Gelnhausen.[179]

There is practically no record of the last part of the Landgraf's life. He seems to have suffered from a chronic illness that confined him to his home. But he was not without problems, including some with Archbishop Siegfried of Mainz. The archbishop is to have remarked that Hermann I was still under the ban when he died.[180] But this is not supported by the Eisenach account, which also claims he was stricken with an epidemic and was ill for eight days. He "was given the Holy Sacrament in Christian custom, and died deeply penitent for his past sins."[181]

When Hermann I died at Gotha, the abbot of Reinhardsbrunn came to claim his body; but to his surprise, the Landgraf's widow Sophia objected to his burial in the family monastery. The reason was that her husband had specified that he wanted to be buried in the Monastery of St. Cathere in Eisenach. He had founded that monastery mainly for this purpose. The Landgraf was buried there in accordance with his wishes.[182]

Under Hermann the Wartburg had been enlarged, and he added the *Rittersal*, which was suitable for elaborate *Minnelied* festivals. The Wartburg scholar, Professor Wenck, points out that from Hermann's time into the fifteenth century, the Wartburg served as the capital of all Thuringia, which stretched from the Oder to the Werra rivers.[183]

10

The Reign of Ludwig V
and Holy Elizabeth

❖

Landgraf Hermann had several sons: Ludwig V, Heinrich Raspe, and Conrad. Ludwig V, the oldest, ruled for only a decade, from 1217 to 1227.
The reign of Ludwig the Pious, as the oldest boy became known in his homeland, and his wife, Holy Elizabeth of Hungary, brought to the Wartburg a style
quite different from that of Ludwig's father, Hermann I. Most of the information we possess about Ludwig's reign comes from the monks of Reinhardsbrunn, who received many gifts from him. We possess some additional evidence
from the chronicle of St. Peters, and later from Rothe of Eisenach. Certainly
tradition has glorified the pious couple. In this study the author is well aware of
his limitations, for the period can be seen only through the concave and convex
lenses of those who lived in it and wrote about it.

The *Reinhardsbrunn Chronicle* states that Ludwig V was born in the year
1200,[1] and the Landgraf's chaplain, Berthold, listed the date of his birth as
28 October, the holy day of St. Simon and St. Jude. Some sources suggest there
was an older brother, Hermann II. Ludwig's life cannot be understood without
considering his wife, Holy Elizabeth. This forces our account to return to the
days of Hermann I.

Karl Wenck pointed out that Elizabeth was one of Germany's most notable
women in the very worldly feudal age.[2] While the previous period had stressed
gaiety and worldly glamour, in the time of Elizabeth the Wartburg experienced
a religious zeal that expressed itself in the care of lepers and the poor. Although
the rule of Frederick II had elevated the status of women, the courtly life of the
great Hohenstaufen did not appeal to the retiring, saintly wife of the Landgraf
of Thuringia.

To understand Elizabeth, we must turn to her childhood. Here our primary
source is the *Reinhardsbrunn Chronicle*.[3] We also possess a later, more embellished account, in the *Düringische Chronik*.[4] In 1211, Hermann I arranged for
the engagement of Ludwig to the four-year-old daughter of the king of Hungary.

The Reinhardsbrunn chronicler tells us that in 1207 the mother of Elizabeth, a descendant of the dukes of Carinthia, had given birth to Elizabeth at their castle in Elzeberg.[5] A contract was drawn up to transport Elizabeth from Hungary to the Wartburg, where she was to be reared as young Ludwig's future wife. The chronicler also described to some extent the situation in Hungary at the time. He claimed that the headstrong queen had alienated some of the nobility, who had quite an influence on the rather quiet, easygoing king. This may have influenced the marriage arrangements with the landgrave of Thuringia.[6] The Reinhardsbrunn chronicler described the gracious reception given the delegation when they arrived at the Wartburg.[7]

The Order of St. Francis came to the Wartburg region in 1212, and this no doubt had a profound effect on Elizabeth.[8] Another influence on her may have been the slaying of her mother by a group of nobles, reportedly on orders from Elizabeth's father. There may have been another woman whom the king had decided to marry.[9]

Ludwig's activity as Landgraf was not always as saintly as has sometimes been depicted.[10] In conflict with the political forces of the day, he was forced to employ the same means as other princes.[11] Even when he was a child, his father had offered him as a hostage to King Philip during the siege of Weiszensee, and he was not released until his father shifted to the Welf rival. Ludwig thus learned a certain toughness quite early, a trait he demonstrated throughout his life.[12]

Because of Hermann I's death, Ludwig V was forced to govern the *Landgraf-schaft* of Thuringia at the young age of seventeen.[13] The transfer of power took place in Eisenach on 7 June 1217.[14] In his struggle with Archbishop Siegfried II, the Landgraf's youth placed him at a disadvantage. Yet he seems to have born up well, exercising both ingenuity and good judgment.[15] When a matter offered two extreme decisions, Ludwig V preferred the middle way; yet when decisions demanded action, he neglected nothing to accomplish his course.[16]

Rothe depicts Ludwig as a clear-headed young man with a likable personality, a man who deserved his nickname.[17] The Landgraf's habits were simple, and his honesty and chastity were known everywhere. He was kind and indulgent to those in need and offered much to charity.[18] He was modest, prudent, eloquent, and religious.[19] But soon friction developed between the Landgraf and the power-hungry Archbishop Siegfried of Mainz, who dared to excommunicate the seventeen-year-old Landgraf for sins committed by his father. He claimed that Hermann I had died while under his ban, and its curse then fell on Ludwig.[20] Knochenhauer believes Ludwig V supported his father's position against the ambitious archbishop, and this did not please the aggressive prelate.[21] The previous conflict had centered in Hesse, where the archbishop had impeded the Ludowinger movement southward.[22] But according to Patze, the archbishop's real motives are no longer known. However, Müller and Ulhorn believe it was to keep the Ludowinger from expansion into southern Hesse, establishing a link from Thuringia.[23] The archbishop of Mainz used fire and the sword in Marienberg and Schaffenstein, and Ludwig replied in kind. He returned to Thuringia as victor.[24] This seems to have silenced the archbishop for the time being, for he met with Ludwig at Fulda and removed the ban, absolving him of all his past sins and transgressions.[25] But in 1220 the conflict broke out anew.[26]

Meanwhile, the young Landgraf had moved closer to the Kaiser. He was a frequent fellow-traveler with Frederick II, and he participated in the coronation of his son, Henry VII. At a *Reichstag* the German princes declared that they wanted the Mainz conflict solved, but it continued nevertheless. After that Frederick II crossed the Alps to Italy in order to obtain his coronation and put his Sicilian lands in order. Since the *Reich* now passed under Henry VII as regent, its power passed into the hands of the German princes. In reality, the regent became Archbishop Engelbert of Cologne, and subsequently the princes played a major role in the government of the *Reich*.[27]

On 16 January 1216, Pope Innocent III died. He was followed by Honorius IV, a gentler and less aggressive man. But Innocent had insisted that Frederick organize a crusade, and this pressure was continued by his successor. Young Henry VII was not in a position to handle the affairs of the *Reich* while his father pursued his interests in southern Italy. Meanwhile Ludwig V attempted to extend his rule from Meissen to Lausitz and the border of Poland. His sister Jutta was married to Dietrich of Meissen, who appeared to have been ill, and she assumed the title of Markgräfin in 1195. We saw earlier how her young son Henry had been placed under the guardianship of Ludwig, a protective measure common in the feudal era. On 17 February 1221, Markgraf Dietrich died, leaving Jutta with her three-year-old son.[28]

When the Landgraf returned from a meeting in Würzburg, he learned that there was danger of attacks in Meissen. He wanted to preserve the peace and protect the three-year-old Henry. Regarding Ludwig's real motives, Patze is not as gracious as Knochenhauer, who claimed that Ludwig acted with Jutta's full approval when he made all the subjects in Dietrich's lands take an oath of allegiance to himself—ostensibly so that he could protect the young boy from outside attacks. Patze saw in this a plot to take advantage of the widow so that Henry could expand his lands. The action implied that, should young Henry die before maturity, Ludwig would inherit the *Markgrafschaft* of Meissen. The Reinhardsbrunn chronicler claimed that Ludwig simply wanted to protect Jutta and the rightful heir of Meissen and Lausitz.[29]

No doubt the papacy regarded Ludwig's actions as quite calculating, for on 18 March 1221 the Markgräfin was brought under the protection of the pontiff. Soon such protection was also extended to Ludwig I's own mother.[30] We know that not even Frederick II was willing to endorse the Landgraf's plans; yet Ludwig moved right along to assure his territorial gains to the east. He governed the affairs of Meissen and conducted its court sessions in person.[31]

In time Jutta became suspicious that her half-brother might be using her son as a political pawn.[32] The only course of action available to her was to marry again, which would remove her son from Ludwig's sponsorship. When Ludwig wanted to conduct a *Landtag*, Jutta opposed it. This resulted in a feud and some hard feelings. He realized that he needed to leave Meissen, and he returned home.[33] Knochenhauer believes there was some verbal agreement between

Jutta's husband and the Landgraf prior to his death that prompted Ludwig's actions. It may be that Jutta was never fully informed about the nature of the guardianship that Ludwig had assumed.

The Landgraf was intent on preserving peace, both in Meissen and Thuringia. There may also have been an agreement as to Ludwig's duties in case Henry died before reaching maturity, namely, that Meissen and Lausitz would become a part of Ludwig's kingdom.[34] The Reinhardsbrunn annalist pointed out that Ludwig stressed peace in Hesse as much as in Jutta's lands.[35] We learn that the conditions in Orlamünde caused the situation to worsen.[36] Ludwig seemed to have engaged in a war of nerves with Count Hermann of Orlamünde. The count had caused trouble before, and Ludwig tried to humble the unruly noble.[37]

Hermann I had become involved in a matter that demanded the Landgraf's attention. In May 1223, Count Heinrich of Schwerin had captured King Waldemar of Denmark. The struggle involved a province in which Hermann I was also involved. Kaiser Frederick II ordered a *Hoftag* to be held at Nordhausen, to be conducted by his regent, Henry VII. On 12 September 1223, Ludwig participated in this discussion of the release of the Danish king.[38] A clash developed over how to handle the problem. At odds were Archbishop Engelbert of Cologne, the *Reich's* administrator, and Bishop Otto of Würzburg, to whom the emperor had given plenipotentiary powers.[39]

In October of that year the Landgraf was in Würzburg, where he signed a document related to the Teutonic Knights.[40] This vital political transaction with the German Kaiser revealed Ludwig V's standing among the princes of the *Reich*. The master of the knights, Hermann von Salza, arrived from Italy with an important message for Ludwig himself.[41] In May 1224, King Henry VII held a *Reichstag*, where Hermann von Salza presented the emperor's message about the Teutonic Order to the assembled body. The message dealt with preparations for another crusade.[42]

In 1224 Ludwig V held a meeting at the Neuenburg, announcing his intentions to enter the Osterland to conduct court at Görschen. Jutta did not like this.[43] About this time the Landgraf had an unexpected visit by Count Poppe of Henneberg, who was on a feigned business trip to Saxony. To Ludwig's complete surprise, Count Poppe announced that he and Jutta had recently been married at Leipzig. Ludwig was invited to accompany them on their homeward journey, but he declined.[44] Jutta had hoped to frighten the Landgraf, but that was a miscalculation. He proceeded with his planned court session.[45] Leipzig citizens were also disturbed by the events, and they invited the Landgraf for a visit. When Ludwig came, on 10 January 1224, the citizens were alarmed about the Markgräfin's secret marriage. Jutta had also replaced the Leipzig city guard with her own men. With her remarriage, they now worried about their safety and asked Ludwig to offer them protection. They promised that if they came under siege, they would support him.[46]

This agreement created real hostility between Jutta and Ludwig, but when they were challenged, Jutta's guard capitulated and their castle was leveled. Now Jutta began to defame her half-brother among the *ministeriales* and lords throughout Meissen. Ludwig sent out messages, justifying his action in Leipzig as preservation of peace in the land.[47] His sister, however, charged him with betrayal and violent actions. The Leipzig citizens supported Ludwig, but the officials and lords supported Jutta.[48] Ludwig then devastated the lands of the hostile nobility and besieged their castles, causing them to capitulate.[49] In May 1224, he attended Henry VII's *Reichstag* and held court in Delitzsch.[50] Toward the end of the month the Landgraf attended King Henry VII's *Reichstag*.[51]

By the middle of June, 1224, Ludwig returned to Meissen, again conducting court sessions between the Saale and Elster rivers. Meanwhile, Groitzsch had capitulated and was held by Ludwig's men. In July he took Rochlibesburg and placed his men there as well.[52] But forces were at work to bring peace between Jutta and Ludwig, and it seems the hostility was terminated.[53] Knochenhauer identifies the peacemaker as Duke Otto of Meran, the uncle of Elizabeth and a relative of Count Poppo. Ludwig of Sangerhausen also attempted to settle the family feud. Another meeting took place on July 20, where the dispute was finally laid to rest. Ludwig then returned to the Neuenburg.[54] The settlement appears to have favored the Landgraf, for he retained the guardianship of young Heinrich.[55] A later report that Poppo was forced out of the mark is doubtful, since there was no political advantage in it for the *Reich*.[56] Ludwig then continued his rule in the mark, even initiating a campaign to the east.[57]

During this period Elizabeth gave birth to Sophia, who eventually married the duke of Brabant.[58] Later, when Heinrich Raspe died, there would be a struggle for succession between Sophia and Henry, the son of Jutta, over who should rule over the Ludowinger lands.[59]

According to the *Reinhardsbrunn Chronicle*, in 1225 Ludwig went on an extensive campaign in the east, as far as Poland. He had recruited a large army from all parts of the Ludowinger lands, which crossed the Elbe river and besieged the castle of Lebus. At the time it belonged to Duke Wladislav Loskongi of Poland.[60] Ludwig's motive for this action is no longer clear, but the *Düringische Chronik* claims it was because the Polish duke was using the castle to rob traveling Thuringian merchants.[61] Ludwig moved to the Elbe with his army, where, according to Berthold, he advanced with three hundred knights and set all the dwellings around Lebus on fire.[62] When his army arrived on 1 September 1225, the sheer size of it frightened the defenders.[63] They sent messengers to Duke Wladislav, who sent a friendly message to the Landgraf, saying he could not understand why he had come with such a huge force when no hostility existed between them.[64] Ludwig's reply was laconic and determined. He stated that he would not leave until forced to do so by the sword. In vain the duke's delegate pleaded for a peaceful settlement. Even Archbishop Gnesen's warnings and threats were ineffective.[65] Instead, Ludwig insisted that he would welcome an engagement with Poland's army.[66] The Landgraf then ordered the siege of Lebus.

Since the duke had offered them no protection, the defenders offered to surrender the fortress to the Landgraf within three days. Wladislav must have realized that on short notice he was unable to engage Ludwig's huge army in battle, so he did nothing. The defenders capitulated and turned over hostages. After that, Ludwig staffed the castle with some of his men.[67] He then dismissed the main body of his army and sent it home.[68]

Within a short time the Landgraf was once more with young King Henry VII, who held a *Hoftag* at Bardowick, north of Lüneburg. Hermann von Salza, grand master of the Teutonic Knights, and other princes were present. There Count Albert of Orlamünde, Ludwig's brother-in-law, represented the Danes, and Ludwig proved useful, for he was familiar with the Danish situation. While there, Ludwig was stricken with a severe cold and high fever, but by 10 October 1225 he had returned to camp at Bleckede, not far from Lüneburg.[69]

Since Frederick II was continually absent, the German princes could maneuver more freely in pursuit of their territorial ambitions. A vital question was who would become the wife of young Henry VII.[70] Until now, the Staufer had been closer to the French than to the English, but the ecclesiastical regent for Henry VII tried to shift the family relationship toward the English side. While in Italy, however, Emperor Frederick II had renewed his ties with King Louis VIII of France. At a *Hoftag* at Ulm in January 1225, when the regent proposed that young Henry should marry the sister of King Henry III of England, his proposal fell on deaf ears.[71] The emperor had already arranged for the engagement of his son Henry to Agnes of the Bohemian royal house. The young girl was already at the court of Duke Leopold of Austria, to be trained as his queen. Since the bride-to-be was also the niece of Duke Ludwig of Bavaria, another powerful prince was involved. In addition, the girl was the daughter of Ludwig's wife's aunt Constantine, which caused Elizabeth to be interested. Thus a formidable group of princes were opposed to the regent's proposal that Henry marry into the English royal line.[72]

But things did not work out as planned, for Duke Leopold, who was to train the young Agnes of Bohemia, changed his mind. He decided that Henry VII's queen should not be Agnes, but rather his own daughter, Margaretha of Austria. Ludwig was also in on the plan, for he sent two of his court officials to Italy to convince the emperor to change his mind. After an extended visit and some maneuvering, they won the emperor to Leopold's plans. The pope also agreed to the change. Ludwig then proposed a double marriage, one between King Henry VII and Margaretha, and another between Ludwig's sister Agnes and the Duke's son Heinrich, provided there was no dowry.[73]

Naturally this change caused bitterness and strong reactions among powerful families. Most vocal in their reactions were King Ottokar of Bohemia and Duke Ludwig of Bavaria. The King of Hungary was also opposed to the changes, and the result was a regrouping of princes. After his return, Leopold sent Agnes back to her father, and Ludwig had to placate his enraged relatives.[74] The young Kaiser seems to have preferred Agnes for a wife, but in this matter the groom's views were secondary. After some pleading, Henry appears to have agreed to a Babenberger marriage, but it took weeks for King Ottokar to come around. The double marriage was held on 29 November 1225.[75]

By his middle twenties, Ludwig was confronted with many new problems. In

1225 Archbishop Engelbert of Cologne was murdered, which required a new regent. The murderer was apprehended, condemned, and expelled from the *Reich*.[76] Soon after that, from Italy, the emperor summoned the German princes of rank to a *Reichstag* in Cremona, to be held by Easter in 1226. There the emperor brought up several problems, but the main one was that the papacy was calling for a crusade. The pontiff had also asked Ludwig V to participate. The Kaiser had promised Ludwig 4,000 Marks, and at a *Hoftag* in 1224, he had raised the amount to 5,000 Marks, including free passage. But before the Landgraf took up the cross, he demanded that Meissen become a fief of Thuringia, with an annual fee of 20,000 Marks.[77] Poppo and Jutta did everything to keep the Kaiser from granting Ludwig's wishes.[78]

Both the Reinhardsbrunn chronicler and Berthold, in his biography of Ludwig, cover the story of his Italian expedition and his meetings with the Kaiser in Ravenna.[79] According to these accounts, the Landgraf's expedition began in the spring of 1225 with a small force. He crossed the Alps around Easter and arrived at the emperor's camp on April 19, where he planned to attend a *Reichstag*.[80] But many princes were late, so the *Reichstag* was delayed until Pentecost.[81] The Landgraf was royally received by the emperor, and the two spent much time falcon hunting, the Kaiser's favorite sport.[82] Since Ludwig was going on the crusade, the Kaiser allowed him to return home to make his final arrangements. When Ludwig departed, Frederick instructed him to persuade his uncle, Duke Ludwig of Bavaria, to accept the post of regent of the German *Reich*, vacant since the death of Archbishop Engelbert. This may also have been to placate the duke about his son's marriage.[83]

After the Landgraf's departure, hostilities broke out between the emperor and the Lombard League, and the Cremona *Reichstag* could not be held. Pope Honorius then became disgusted with the emperor's failure to begin a crusade, and again placed him under a papal ban. Young Henry VI was en route to aid the emperor, but he could not cross the Alps because the Lombard League had blocked the passes. On his way home Ludwig found Henry VII and his troops still waiting in Augsburg.[84]

The Landgraf returned from Italy with the Kaiser's approval of his ambitions regarding Meissen and Lausatia. If young Henry were to die while on a campaign against Prussia, Ludwig could acquire all his lands by conquest.[85] The Kaiser's assignment to the Landgraf was twofold: placating his uncle, Duke Ludwig of Bavaria, and filling the office of regent in the German lands. Ludwig's visit to Italy had given the Landgraf the chance to present the Kaiser's demands within the German *Reich*.[86] When Ludwig arrived in Augsburg on 2 July 1226, he made the Kaiser's mandate known to the assembled princes. But the Landgraf found it was not as easy to placate the strained feelings between Bavaria and Austria. Finally, his Bavarian uncle's feelings softened and he was ready to accept the king's wishes to become regent in Germany.[87] Now Ludwig could return to Thuringia.

On his way back, the Landgraf was accompanied by his brother Heinrich Raspe, and on the way home the two stopped at Schweinfurt.[88] But there Ludwig was tipped off about a plot in which Poppo of Henneberg was planning to ambush the two riders. Killing them would leave no male descendants among the Ludowinger, voiding the Kaiser's promise of land. Since they needed to pass through a dangerous wooded region, the two decided on a fast, all-night ride home. They arrived safely at six o'clock the next morning.[89]

Elizabeth had been brought to the Wartburg as a child and married to Ludwig at the age of fourteen. Elizabeth was deeply influenced by the simple and austere ways of Hermann von Weiszensee and the Franciscans. Worldly possessions did not appeal to her, and the richness of the Wartburg and the life of the troubadours in Hermann I's reign may have had a reverse effect. While Thuringian women among the nobility adorned themselves with beautiful clothes and jewelry, Elizabeth went around barefoot, attired in a simple dress as she performed works of mercy among the poor.[90] The Landgraf's wife often stood barefoot among the poor, listening to Franciscan sermons, her arms loaded with clothing to give away. She even spun wool to make clothes for the needy, and the ideal of St. Francis was ever before her.[91] By her early twenties, Elizabeth was already influenced by Rodegar's extreme ways of living. Ludwig made Conrad of Marburg her new father confessor, in which he no doubt hoped to moderate her excesses of charity.[92]

Since the time of Pope Innocent III there had been a campaign in Germany against what Rome regarded as heresy. There were a number of heresy-hunting movements in various regions, and Conrad of Marburg should be understood in that light. Conrad of Hildesheim was a similar heresy-hunter who engaged in similar excesses.[93] Both theologians had studied at Paris and were masters of theology.[94] Oliverius of Paderborn, a Cologne scholastic, was a witch-hunter of the same stripe.

Conrad of Marburg was a raw individual, and was emaciated due to fasting and self-discipline. He traveled on a small horse, preaching moving sermons to assembled crowds. Prior to 1224, both Conrad of Marburg and Conrad of Hildesheim took persons charged with heresy and converted them into piles of ashes. Pope Gregory IX praised Elizabeth's father confessor for his heresy-hunting and burnings.[95] The most gruesome period of Conrad's witch-hunting came after the deaths of Ludwig and Elizabeth.

Conrad became Elizabeth's father confessor around April 1226. He seems to have been recommended by Conrad of Hildesheim when the Landgraf started on his crusade.[96] Conrad of Marburg has been regarded as one of the darkest characters of the Middle Ages, but the Reinhardsbrunn monks considered him God's chosen vessel to preserve the holy church. The chronicle portrays him as being very fair with orthodox Catholics and as an erudite preacher. It claims he sought no gain, dressed very simply, was very moral and austere in his trials of the wicked, and spoke with apostolic authority.[97]

While the Landgraf had been in Italy with Frederick II, Thuringia had experienced trying times. The winter of 1225 had been exceptionally cold; the Plague had killed many animals; and, because armies had burned the fields at harvest time, there was widespread starvation. When the Plague struck the general population, an additional load was placed on Ludwig's wife, who worked ceaselessly to help the victims. Needy persons assembled daily at the gate of the Wartburg, and Elizabeth fed them with food prepared by her servants. Daily she gave the poor shoes, clothing, and even tools to till their crops. She had a small hospital erected at the foot of the Wartburg with twenty-eight beds, and there she cared for the sick. She washed the wounds of lepers at a nearby well. Such was the state of things at home when Ludwig and Heinrich returned from their Italian journey after an all-night ride.[98]

Before his departure for the Holy Land, the Landgraf had many things to arrange and settle. He did not neglect the *Reich's* business, for, by the end of November, he chaired a *Hoftag* for Henry VII. The new regent, Ludwig of Bavaria, actually conducted the meeting. Ludwig seems to have been in no hurry to leave, for in March 1227 he attended another *Hoftag* in Aachen, where Margaretha was crowned as queen. Ludwig remained at the court until April before returning home.[99]

As noted earlier, there was considerable tension between the pope and the emperor over starting another crusade. This had been the subject of much discussion at *Reichstagen*, and the pope had instructed Conrad of Hildesheim to put some fire under the idea. Though Ludwig had been hesitant, he finally agreed to accept the cross. However, he kept it a secret from his pregnant wife.[100] When Elizabeth accidently found her husband's crusader cross, her response was to dedicate her next child to a monastic life.

When the time for Ludwig's departure arrived, he summoned his servants, nobles, and knights to Creuzburg on the Werra. This group included both those who would accompany him and those who would be left in charge at home. Berthold, his chaplain, left a record of this meeting.[101] Ludwig said he was going on a perilous journey from which he might never return. He warned those left at home to avoid strife and turmoil while he was rendering his services to the Lord. Afterward Ludwig visited the monasteries of his lands, offered improvements, and asked for their benedictions and prayers. The Landgraf also admonished his brother, Heinrich Raspe, not to cease doing at home what was essential to his salvation.

On the Day of St. John, the time for Ludwig's departure arrived. He placed Thuringia in the care of Heinrich Raspe. Then he mounted his armored stallion and rode away on a journey from which he would not return. After traveling with him for two days, Elizabeth returned home.[102]

Many of Ludwig's own household rode off with him on the crusade. The Reinhardsbrunn chronicle mentions twenty-four persons. These Ludwig had employed at his own expense.[103] The riders crossed Franconia and Swabia and entered Bavaria, then crossed the Alps into Italy and went on to the kingdoms of the Two Sicilies. There Frederick II met Ludwig V and his entourage.[104] By 3 August 1227 Ludwig had arrived in Troya, where he remained three days.[105] The emperor and the crusaders had their final meeting and made plans for the

Landgraf's departure. They began a southward march toward Monopoli, with stops in Barletta and Bari.[106] Here the Berthold chronology becomes somewhat confused.[107]

By now there were so many crusaders that there were not enough ships for all, and this caused some delay. Finally, on 9 September 1227, both the emperor and the Landgraf were ready to depart from St. Andrews, an island in front of the harbor of Brindisi.[108]

Ludwig and the Kaiser boarded separate ships, and the Landgraf sailed for Otranto. At that port he left the boat to bid his farewell to Queen Isabella, the daughter of King John of Jerusalem. She gave them a farewell banquet. But the Landgraf became ill and returned to his ship to rest on a cot. When he realized that he might die, he summoned the Patriarch of Jerusalem, who offered him communion and administered the sacrament of extreme unction. In his high fever and delirium Ludwig spoke about doves and said "it behoved him to fly away." [109] In the *Düringische Chronik* Rothe wrote, "Thus departed the virtuous prince in the Christian faith."[110] The crusaders who had accompanied him reversed their course to make a temporary burial of their prince in foreign soil.[111]

The news of Ludwig's unexpected death shocked Thuringia. When Elizabeth was informed, she was speechless for a moment and then rushed out of the room shouting, "Dead, dead, dead!" Later, according to Berthold, she said, "For me now, the world and all that is in it has lost its meaning."[112] Ludwig's death also had a devastating effect on the crusade. Emperor Frederick II himself had likewise been afflicted by fever. Later he took a turn for the worse that forced him to remain behind at Otranto. For this the pope pronounced a ban on him.[113] By now the spirit of the crusade was gone.

In Thuringia, the new Landgraf, Heinrich Raspe, had no use for Ludwig and Elizabeth's piety. He expelled Elizabeth and her three children not only from the Wartburg, but from Thuringia. She found refuge with her uncle, Bishop Egbert of Bamberg.[114] Rothe points out that Heinrich Raspe may have been motivated by the fact that Ludwig's son, Hermann II, would become the legitimate heir to the Thuringian *Landgrafschaft* and could claim both its lands and the Wartburg.[115]

On their journey home from the crusade, Ludwig's former companions stopped at Otranto and exhumed the prince's body. On the way back to Thuringia they kept his bones in churches, under vigils, and morning masses were conducted. People came from far and wide to see the coffin. In Bamberg, Bishop Egbert held a funeral service in the cathedral.[116] There the exiled Elizabeth saw her husband's remains.[117] In the presence of Ludwig's former servants and friends, she also had an opportunity to unburden herself about the harsh treatment given her by Heinrich Raspe and his brother Conrad. The bishop impressed upon the lords that it was their duty to make it possible for Elizabeth to live comfortably and in peace. They made sure that she could return to the Wartburg and attend her husband's funeral at Reinhardsbrunn.[118]

En route from Bamberg to Thuringia, many people assembled to witness the passing of the funeral procession,[119] and at Reinhardsbrunn a huge crowd gathered.[120]

Immediately after the burial, Heinrich Raspe, Conrad, and Sophie discussed the funeral expenses. Meanwhile, Ludwig's fellow crusaders remained to have a private discussion with Heinrich about his treatment of Elizabeth and her children. But who would speak for them? After some discussion, they chose the former tap-room custodian, Rudolf von Varila, because of his dignity and eloquence. This distinguished noble and old friend of Ludwig dressed down the proud new Landgraf. He began by relating how, on their return through Franken and Thuringia, the crusaders had learned how shocked people were by Heinrich's cruelty toward Elizabeth. Varila asked the Landgraf who his advisors were during the shameful episode. He then reminded the Landgraf that he had mistreated his dead brother's wife, Holy Elizabeth, the daughter of the noble King of Hungary, when he should have offered the grieving widow sympathy and comfort. He asked what right the Landgraf had in expelling Elizabeth from the Wartburg. What is worse, he had expelled his brother's widow from Thuringia, leaving her a poor, helpless beggar. Had he not been committed by his dead brother to take good care of the Ludowinger lands? What faithlessness he, in turn, had shown his own brother![121]

Such a strong rebuff, in the presence of Ludwig's fellow crusaders, was too much for the young prince, who was still in his early twenties. While Varila spoke, he hung his head in shame, and afterward the young man remained speechless. Varila pointed out that because of his shameful conduct, no one could foretell what the future fate of Thuringia might be. Unless he did penance and became reconciled with Elizabeth, the wrath of God would remain on him and Thuringia.[122]

The Landgraf wept and expressed sorrow for his conduct. He claimed that he had been misled by his advisors. He said he would mend his ways, find his peace with God, and regain Elizabeth's friendship. He was ready to do whatever she desired.[123] Later there was another meeting, with Elizabeth present, to inform her of what had transpired. Elizabeth replied that she had no desire for castles, cities, or lands, nor did she wish to rule over Thuringia. As for her rightful inheritances, those remained hers. And she should have the right to reside in the lands where she wished, for that was related to her soul's salvation, and she should be able to maintain her relationships with her past friends.[124]

In his account of these events Rothe may have gotten carried away, for he related that there was then a tender meeting between Heinrich and Elizabeth, in which he expressed his regrets for his conduct. Rothe claimed that Heinrich even embraced her and that they both wept in the presence of Sophie and the still assembled nobles. In any case, the crusading companions then separated from the family and went home.[125]

According to the Eisenach chronicle, afterward Heinrich was very gracious with Elizabeth. He brought her back into the Wartburg, where she resided for a year. But according to tradition, she remained very withdrawn. It is reported that she asked Heinrich for a suitable place, in a small town, where she could live with her small household. The Landgraf is said to have offered her Marburg and its outlying villages. She thanked Henry for her stay at the Wartburg, and he offered her five hundred Marks to help her move and get settled. Her father confessor is to have accompanied her in the move. But upon her arrival in Marburg, she was showered with honors, and again became a public figure, which was too much for her. She then retired to a small, neighboring village.[126]

After Elizabeth settled in the Marburg region, she erected a *Spital*, a refuge for the sick and helpless poor, which she staffed with two young women dressed in simple attire. There she displayed great patience and mercy toward invalids and destitute persons. When her father became aware of her less-than-noble style of life, he sent Count Panvas to invite her to return to Hungary. But she refused the offer, for she found her work very satisfying.[127]

In her last days, Conrad, her father confessor, kept her under severe discipline, insisting on exhausting fastings and prayers. He also placed her on a very restricted diet, often no more than bread and water. She contracted various diseases, which caused her death at the early age of twenty-five.[128]

In her Marburg days Elizabeth had acquired the reputation of being a miracle-worker, and sick and lame persons flocked to her *Spital* for cures.[129] As reports came in of healings, Heinrich questioned them. But eventually he became her ardent supporter, as did his brother Conrad. Likewise, Archbishop Siegfried II of Mainz at first ridiculed the stories, fearing these reports would glorify the Ludowinger house.[130] In time Elizabeth's miracle-working became known in Rome, and, after her death, Pope Gregory IX decided to canonize her. Archbishop Siegfried then dedicated two altars to her in Marburg. On Pentecost in 1235, an assembly was held in Perusii, attended by Pope Gregory IX, the patriarchs of Jerusalem and Antioch, and many cardinals, archbishops, and ranking clergy. There Elizabeth was declared a saint of all Christendom.[131] The following year Emperor Frederick II came to Marburg to honor the mortal remains of Elizabeth. In 1236 clergy and laity from all lands assembled there to participate in her glorification. It had been decided to exhume her body, place it in a lead coffin, and transport it to the newly-built St. Elizabeth's Cathedral, where today it rests in an elaborate setting.[132]

11

The Reign of Heinrich Raspe

Thuringia became more turbulent under Heinrich Raspe, who failed to realize his limitations as he tried to reach for the stars. His ambitions were frustrated by the fact that he had no legitimate claim to the *Landgrafschaft*. The rightful claimant was Ludwig V's son Hermann II, born in March 1223, but he was only four years old when his father died.[1] Emperor Frederick II recognized the boy as the legitimate heir to the *Landgrafschaft*, and perhaps even to the *Markgrafschaft* of Meissen. Heinrich did everything he could to interfere. He even tried to break the friendly relationship between the Kaiser and the papacy.[2] In 1230 the authorities in the *Reich* acknowledged Hermann II as the rightful ruler of Thuringia.[3] Heinrich then named himself Landgraf, his brother as Hessian Landgraf, and Hermann II as third Landgraf—a strange new arrangement in Thuringian history. The Kaiser remained silent about this.[4]

When Ludwig's widow Elizabeth relocated to the Marburg region, Hermann II wanted to stay with his uncle at the Wartburg, for under his guardianship he could be trained as a feudal prince. He proudly called himself the "son of Holy Elizabeth," and must have asserted his claims as the future landgrave.[5] But Heinrich asserted himself as head of the family, believing that Hermann II would later be satisfied with ruling over a few towns.[6] When Hermann II was a minor, both Heinrich and his brother Conrad signed official documents with their titles as Landgrafen.[7] Hermann II's first official signature was in 1234, but he possessed no seal.[8]

The strife between Heinrich and the archbishop of Mainz continued. On 21 December 1227, Heinrich made his peace by means of a document signed by the neighboring princes.[9] But this peace was of short duration, for on 9 September Siegfried II died and was followed by his cousin, Siegfried III, who became aggressive. There were church visitations, and in 1230 he visited Erfurt. Before long the struggle with the Landgraf was renewed, especially in Hesse.[10] The archbishop offended the abbot of Reinhardsbrunn by taxing the monastery. In Erfurt, before the bishop's court, Abbot Eckehard defied Mainz's right to levy the tax. The archbishop placed on the abbot a penance of kneeling for three days, totally naked. When Landgraf Conrad learned of it, he entered the chapter, grabbed Archbishop Siegfried III by the hair, drew his knife, and was about to kill him. The archbishop was saved only by his companions, and he fled from Erfurt to escape the Ludowinger wrath.[11] Although this story has no doubt been enhanced by tradition, it shows how the battle with Mainz could become quite bitter.

Conrad and Heinrich then decided to besiege the Mainz city of Fritzlar.[12] After burning suburbs and the town mill, they were ready to lift the siege when some of the women appeared on the city wall, lifted their dresses to expose their buttocks to them, and shouted insults at the troops. At that the brothers decided to begin the siege in earnest. The town went up in flames and there was great loss of life. Among those who capitulated were the bishop of Worms, some priors, and a number of the archbishop's men. This was followed by plundering of the treasuries.

Conrad's treatment of the clergy had its repercussions. Böttiger claims that the pope put Conrad under the ban; Conrad then went to make amends for his conduct and to have Holy Elizabeth canonized.[13] Rothe asserts that the pope made Conrad take the third step of penance by making a gift to a cloister in Eisenach and dedicating a church, for he had burned the Monastery of St. John in Fritzlar.[14] But the angry archbishop wanted more, so he devastated Witzenhausen and its countryside.[15]

Patze regarded these actions as a kind of chess game in which each side used fortresses to block the other's expansion. Earlier Ludowinger, also, had played this game.[16] Such procedures were used by Mainz to keep Hessian and Thuringian lands apart.[17] A peace settlement in 1232 between landgrave Conrad and Siegfried III was concluded by Conrad of Marburg, Elizabeth's father-confessor. The basis was the previous settlement between Ludwig V and Siegfried II, the details of which remain unknown.[18] In that agreement, Heiligenberg was to have remained with the archbishop, but the fortress was to have been destroyed. Yet it had been rebuilt.[19] Conrad was given Wolfhagen as a fief from Mainz. Patze said it was a compromise, reached because Pope Gregory IX was busy with Elizabeth's canonization. It was Conrad of Marburg who drafted the peace, so the pope, rather than the emperor, was the one who signed it.[20]

Conrad's punishment of Fritzlar seems to have been on his conscience, for he tried to find peace with God by acts of mercy. Thus he dedicated one-tenth of Hesse's income to good works.[21] He also made a large gift to the *Spital* that Elizabeth had founded at Marburg.[22] In addition, Conrad joined the Order of the Teutonic Knights while he was in Rome.[23] A document of July 1234, drafted in Frederick II's court, shows his presence there; another, a bull by Pope Gregory IX dated 18 October 1234, stated that he could wear the ring of the Teutonic Knights.[24] According to Böttiger, Conrad also did penance for his awful siege in the presence of the *Bürger* of Fritzlar.[25] In 1236, upon the death of Langensalza, Conrad became the new Hofmeister of the Teutonic Knights.[26] Patze suspects that Frederick II asked Conrad to enter the order because he wanted to elevate the prestige of the Ludowinger among the princes of the *Reich*.[27]

During the period of veneration of Holy Elizabeth there was a heresy hunt in the Rhine valley in which Conrad of Marburg played a leading role. Thuringia was also subjected to heresy hunting.[28] In 1233, while the hunt raged, four victims were burned in Conrad's presence.[29]

The next year, under papal directive, a regular crusade was preached by Conrad of Hildesheim against heretics in the Ludowinger lands.[30] After a meeting called by the archbishop of Mainz, certain heretics were condemned, about whose fate the chroniclers at the time remain silent.[31] According to Rothe, many heretics were tried, of which some were converted, others burned, and some tried and released. Conrad's activity greatly enraged the population. A certain Count von Stein was among the accused, but because of his rank he was permitted to think it over. Yet Conrad allowed the masses no such reprieve, and many were simply burned.

After the Mainz meeting, Conrad started on his way back to Marburg. While en route, he and a Franciscan brother Gerhard, together with twelve priests, were ambushed, tortured, and murdered.[32] After the death of Conrad of Marburg, Conrad of Hildesheim turned witch-hunting into a regular crusade.[33]

During this period a strong papacy helped terminate the medieval empire under the Hohenstaufen line. At a *Reichstag* at Worms in 1231, summoned by the regent and by Kaiser Henry VII, the princes were granted important privileges over the cities. This was made official at Ravenna in December 1231 by Emperor Frederick II.[34] Heinrich Raspe was present, but his name is not among the signatures.[35] However, Heinrich still appears to have been supporting the emperor in his struggle with the Lombard League, for he remained with the Kaiser until March 1232.[36]

During this period, Frederick II involved Heinrich in a meeting in Vienna that named his own son Conrad, then ten years old, as the future Kaiser. But soon the Landgraf got into deep water. In 1238, having been a widower for seven years, he decided to marry Gertrude, the sister of Duke Frederick of Austria. She was hostile toward the emperor. Before long he followed papal advice and supported the Lombard League. He also began dealing with the duke of Bavaria and the king of Bohemia, and even stayed away from an important meeting with the Kaiser at Erfurt.[37]

Heinrich seems not to have known which side to support. He no doubt realized his own shaky position, for Hermann II was about to become of age. Under Salien law, Hermann could take over at the age of twelve. Unfortunately, Frederick II was too deeply occupied with his struggle in Lombardy to devote any time to the Ludowinger succession and help Hermann II assume his rightful place in the *Reich*. Meanwhile, in 1237–1238, Siegfried III tried to separate Hesse from Thuringia, and Heinrich feared the archbishop might use his influence to make Hermann II Landgraf in his place.[38] In addition, the Landgraf aspired to acquire the *Reich*'s cities of Nordhausen and Mühlhausen.[39]

In 1238, Hermann II became engaged to the Kaiser's two-year-old daughter

Margarete, an event formalized the next year in Aschaffenburg. This placed Hermann II directly under the Kaiser's sympathies and protection.[40] Yet Heinrich pretended to remain loyal. Siegfried III played a conciliatory role, which kept Heinrich undecided as to his next move.[41]

Patze asserts that historians such as Caemmerer, and even the papal legate Albert von Beheim, have gone beyond the evidence in analyzing Raspe's actions. He argues that you cannot prove that from the time of Heinrich's marriage to Gertrude of Austria he was under the influence of her brother, for the Erfurt meeting was very sparsely attended. In addition, the engagement of Hermann II may have been another attempt for the Kaiser to hold Raspe to his side.[42] Frederick II also had trouble with his son, Henry VII, who seems to have been somewhat headstrong and overly ambitious. As early as 1232 he showed a lack of loyalty to his father. The future king made a false step against the duke of Austria, his father-in-law.[43] But the ranking German princes did not agree with Henry's plot to divide the German empire, and his father soon learned about it.[44] And so the emperor returned to Germany to put things in order. Soon young Henry was captured and locked up in Heidelberg castle.[45] Then followed the festive marriage of Emperor Frederick II and Isabella of England. In August the Kaiser held a *Reichstag* at Worms, where he tried to solve some of the problems that had arisen in the empire. There, for the first time, young Hermann II participated in the legislation of the German *Reich*.[46]

In the middle of the thirteenth century, Thuringia faced many problems. The territorial princes and emerging cities strove against princely authority. In 1234 a feud broke out between the proud *Bürger* of Erfurt and the archbishop of Mainz. In his conflict with the duke of Bavaria, the archbishop wanted Erfurt to offer the troops and supplies. He also placed a heavy tax on the city. The *Bürger* refused to comply with his demands. No one could settle the feud. Accordingly, when Henry VII held a *Reichstag*, Siegfried III presented his side, and the *Bürger* then presented theirs. When a solution was not forthcoming, the archbishop placed Erfurt under an interdict.[47] The whole problem centered around the recent decree that had strengthened princely controls over the cities. Erfurt remained adamant. The problem was discussed at another *Reichstag*, in Altenburg, and King Henry VII pronounced the imperial ban on the truculent city. Finally, Erfurt agreed to a stiff fine, and the interdict was lifted on 1 August 1234. In this matter Landgraf Heinrich played a conciliatory role, though he failed to sign the final document.[48]

Another feud also broke out, between the Landgraf and Count Heinrich of Gleichen, who was of a very old feudal family. The count was guilty of some minor border offenses. After some toleration, Heinrich Raspe summoned him before the court, but the proud count refused to appear. In response, the Landgraf declared his feudal holdings forfeited. Heinrich then captured his Belsek castle and had twenty-three captives executed.[49] No doubt these events, also, must be viewed in light of the decree at Worms strengthening the power of the princes over the cities in the *Reich*.[50]

Heinrich Raspe talked Hermann II into breaking his engagement to Margarete, the Kaiser's daughter. Hermann then married Helena, the daughter of Duke Otto of Braunschweig. Heinrich had made him the ruler over Hesse and some Ludowinger lands. Then on 2 January 1242, he mysteriously died at home.[51] Rothe refers to an earlier account of the prince's death, which blamed Bertha von Scheche. Others felt that Heinrich himself had tried to eliminate his rival. Still others blamed Heinrich of Meissen, who knew the Landgraf was without male heirs and hoped to succeed him.[52] Hermann II had specified that if he were to die, he should be buried next to his mother. Strangely, Raspe disregarded his wishes and had him buried at Reinhardsbrunn.[53]

An Eger meeting had been called by the emperor to resolve his conflict with Pope Gregory IX, who had placed him under the ban. At the meeting all agreed that Heinrich's brother Conrad, the new Hofmeister of the Teutonic Knights, was the logical person to be sent to the pontiff.[54] But when young Conrad appeared in Rome on his mission, intensely hot weather brought on illness and he died.[55]

After the death of his wife, Gertrude of Austria, almost immediately Heinrich married Meatrix of Brabant.[56] In that year a scare spread through the west about a fierce group of Tartars that had swept through Russia, Poland, and Hungary, and was now threatening the German lands. King Wenzel of Bohemia wrote and pleaded with the Landgraf to come to his aid. The frightened Heinrich wrote his father-in-law that the last judgment was at hand. Strangely, he failed to mention Kaiser Frederick II's duties in this matter. Fortunately Silesia was able to contain the Tartars and they turned back, realizing that they had overextended their drive.[57]

On 21 August 1241 Gregory IX died, the pope with whom the emperor had tried to achieve a settlement. Afterward a disagreement among the cardinals left the papal throne vacant for two years.[58] Before long the old feud was renewed with unusual sharpness, under Innocent IV. Trained in canon law, he saw the struggle between the papacy and the *Reich* in grand perspective. He felt that the emperors had failed in their Christian duties and that the popes needed to correct them in the name of the kingdom of God.

Patze believes that Innocent IV's relations with the Landgraf must be viewed against the wider horizon of the medieval papacy.[59] He had the same goals of dominating Frederick II and the *Reich*, but with greater capability and finesse.[60] The chroniclers state that Frederick II had a blatant disregard for things sacred.[61] But some thought he was guilty of gross heresy and should be excommunicated. The emperor added fuel to the charges by capturing some of the pope's prelates as they traveled to the Council of Lyon. The pope then claimed that the Kaiser's former excommunication had been justified and would continue. Now the battle resumed with fury.

Heinrich Raspe had already been tempted by the offer of kingship as a rival of the Hohenstaufen emperor; in the midst of the new battle, the ambitious prince now saw his opportunity to rise from Landgraf to emperor. The archbishop of Mainz also joined in, on the papal side. The Dominican prior in Eisenach was Heinrich's advisor and father confessor, and he must also have influenced him in his fatal step.[62] The prior and the archbishop were on very close terms. Yet Heinrich seems to have hesitated to desert old friends and the Hohenstaufen emperor, for he hated the curia.[63] Wenck believes that Heinrich must have realized the dangers in cooperating with the papacy, and only slowly acquiesced to pressure. Lonely, and still childless, he was reported already to have been suffering from the effects of the disease that would claim his life.[64]

Emperor Frederick resorted to the most powerful means to oppose the conspiracy. According to Knochenhauer, the Kaiser even returned to Germany in 1242 and held a meeting with the Landgraf and some trusted princes, possibly in Frankfurt a.M.[65] Heinrich came with his father confessor, and it appeared that the Kaiser won Heinrich back to his side. Frederick II even made him procurator of the *Reich*, also entrusting his own son Conrad to Heinrich's guardianship and care.[66] But Heinrich was a wavering type of person. There is no evidence of his guardianship, nor of his tutorial services to young Conrad. He did not participate in the Mainz-Bavarian feud, yet in a document drafted for the cloister in Georgenthal, he signed with the title "Procurator of the Sacred Empire."[67] Wenck believes that Raspe usually reacted to political pressure and then acted on the basis of the greatest political advantage.[68] When, in April 1244, Innocent IV communicated with the Landgrave—while Heinrich was legally the Kaiser's procurator—the pope's communication assumed he was already with the papal party. How much he had shifted his allegiance by this time remains unknown.[69]

After the pope's coronation, he renewed his battle with the *Reich* with unusual vigor. Frederick must have been aware that Heinrich could not be trusted. On 30 June 1243, the *Reich's* chancellor dispatched a document that Heinrich had requested. This stated that the Kaiser had shifted his allegiance to Heinrich the Illustrious, the Markgraf of Meissen and Lausatia. This message guaranteed that if Heinrich died without male heirs, the Markgraf would inherit the *Landgrafschaft* of Thuringia and the *Pfalzgrafschaft* of Saxony. Nearly one hundred years had passed since Markgraf Ludwig III had pledged his allegiance to an earlier Staufer emperor, Conrad II.[70] This was the final communication between the last Ludowinger and the Staufer emperor.

The strategy Rome pursued to get Heinrich to defect is complicated and difficult to trace. Haller claimed that the transactions were covert, while Frederick II tried to extricate himself from the papal ban.[71] On Maundy Thursday 1244, the Kaiser made his peace with Innocent IV, but soon he discovered it was a mirage. The papacy did not want peace, and had not included peace with the Lombard League in the settlement.[72] The *Düringische Chronik* claims Heinrich even connived with some princes who charged the Kaiser with blasphemy and made many false accusations.[73]

Yet Heinrich hesitated to commit himself completely between 4 April and 14 July 1244, when he finally decided. Patze pointed out that meanwhile he had dropped the title of procurator, and on 12 April agreed to be elevated to kingship in the *Reich*.[74] Caemmerer traced Heinrich's decision to Archbishop Siegfried III, who had also deserted the emperor, while Malsch and Fink trace his defection to the influence of Heinrich's father confessor, Elgers von Hohenstein, who had died in 1242.[75] The pope also promised Heinrich that for three years he would be immune from papal bans or interdicts.[76]

Innocent IV was fully aware of the strife that territorialism caused in the Thuringian lands, and the archbishop of Mainz reacted adversely to the promised elevation of Raspe. No longer did he dare to openly attack Thuringia and Hesse, and no attacks were made on the landgrave of Hesse during the prescribed three years. In the beginning even the pope seems to have doubted Heinrich's loyalty. In a letter of 30 April 1244, he complained that though the rival Kaiser had sworn, once crowned, to remain subordinate to the Holy See and accept the church's guidance, he was not trying to evade the mandates of the papacy.[77] The pope urged him to be loyal and elevate his station among princes by loyalty to the apostolic seat.[78] Whether this meant that Rome already regarded Heinrich as an opposition Kaiser is not clear, for as yet he had taken no definite action against Frederick II.[79]

Meanwhile the pope had attempted to create a favorable climate for Heinrich's takeover of the *Reich*. In the interim the tension between the pope and Frederick had risen.[80] Thus the German Kaiser had called a meeting at Verona, and all the German princes attended.[81] The frightened pope had fled to Lyon, where he held a council, mainly with Gallic bishops.[82] There, on 17 June 1244, the pope declared Frederick II deposed.[83] He hoped to elevate Heinrich as the opposition Kaiser when he arrived.[84]

The pope then sent Philip of Ferrara as his envoy, to inform Heinrich of Frederick's removal as Kaiser of the *Reich*. However, even at this late date the landgrave was indecisive. He must have realized—and rightly so—that the German princes would require silver for their support. Rothe says that Heinrich wrote the pope that he was too old, was without children and friends, and that Thuringia was a small country without wealth, so that the cost was beyond his means. But the pope promised to assist him in every way.[85] Nor was this an idle boast on part of the pontiff, for it was claimed that he was the richest pope up to that time. When Heinrich finally accepted the offer, the pope sent him 25,000 Marks of silver.[86]

We might ask, as many others have, why the pope wished to establish the Landgraf as his opposition Kaiser. Patze answered that Heinrich was ideally suited for Innocent IV's larger game of chess. He could not initiate a new dynasty, for he was childless. Thuringia, with its central location, was ideally suited for the new Kaiser, who would be buttressed by the power of Mainz. The pope wanted a pawn on the chessboard and not a man of first-class stature. He would be an ideal *Pfaffenkönig*, a tool of the clergy. Besides, he was from the land of Holy Elizabeth and the Hofmeister of the Teutonic Knights.[87]

Wenck, the standard biographer of the Landgraf, is quite severe in his judgment of Heinrich. The pope kept dangling the Kaiser's crown before him, and Heinrich was too weak and nearsighted to see the pope's larger objectives. He should have feared the power of the Staufer and realized that, apart from bribery, his chances of obtaining the kingship were slight. But when Rome offered silver, the Landgraf succumbed to the temptation.[88] Rothe claims that the pope had large amounts of silver exchanged in Venice, and had the sum of 25,000 Marks transported to Erfurt.[89] But the pope had miscalculated the deal, for the Erfurt merchants would have no part in the transaction. Archbishop Siegfried III had summoned a meeting in Weimar, attended largely by the clergy. The Erfurt refusal proved to be a real obstacle for the pope, so the archbishop resorted to an interdict against the merchants. Through this and other forms of pressure, together with liberal gifts, the merchants were finally brought into line. Wenck claims Heinrich distributed his silver quite liberally to attain the pontiff's goal.[90]

After the deposal of the emperor at Lyon, the pope had dispatched his legate Philip of Ferrara to Germany.[91] Philip, in turn, used Bishop Hermann of Würzburg, the Landgraf's trusted friend, to contact Heinrich in September 1245.[92] They met with Heinrich at a secret place, no doubt in the Wartburg, where they made final arrangements.[93] The pope had prepared a series of letters to the German electors, in which they were asked to choose Heinrich as an opposition Kaiser.[94] But in spite of all the planning, Heinrich failed to get the support of the important princes. Even with the strong support of the bishop of Würzburg, the *Bürger* of that city refused to have a *Pfaffenkönig* elected in their midst. The election therefore had to take place in Veitshöchheim, a small town nearby.[95] Only the three archbishops participated, so Heinrich had to cast the final vote.[96]

Strange as it may seem, it was a valid election.[97] Present were a number of ranking bishops as witnesses.[98] Naturally many of the clergy in Germany rallied to Heinrich's support, but none of the significant princes fell in line. Heinrich's strong opponents were now the king of Bohemia, the dukes of Austria and Bavaria, and Heinrich, the Markgraf of Meissen.[99] Patze claims that the duke of Brabant, Heinrich's father-in-law, accepted him even though he was not at his election.[100] The prince's vassals and the archbishop of Mainz attended out of duty. But in spite of the pope's pressure, Heinrich failed to get a solid foothold. Even the legate Philip, with his plenipotentiary powers, was unable to shake the princes' support for Frederick II. Neither the king of Bohemia nor Duke Otto of Bavaria could be won over.[101] Even sweeping promises proved of no avail.[102]

After the Landgraf's election, a swarm of lower clergy and nobles rushed to his side in Thuringia and Hesse. Thus Heinrich could hold his first *Reichstag* at Frankfurt a.M.[103] In July 1240, Heinrich was still getting ready, gathering an army. But when he started out and came to the Nidda river, the Kaiser's son, Conrad, was on the other side, daring him to cross. For a while they faced each other there. It is believed that the archbishop of Mainz had bribed Conrad's army.[104] As a result, the Swabians joined Heinrich's army, and the new Kaiser captured six hundred knights. But Conrad escaped to Frankfurt a.M.[105] Böttiger says this gave the Landgraf but a temporary advantage, for the stronger princes still failed to go along.[106] But when Heinrich and his army came to Frankfurt a.M., the city would not accept him. He was forced to hold his meeting outside the gates. He even had to dismiss his army for lack of funds. But the pope supplied him with more money.[107]

After this, Heinrich returned to the Wartburg, no doubt to wait for the additional silver the legate had promised in Eisenach. On 30 November 1246, he addressed a letter to Ravenna for more funds. He also informed the Lombard League of his victory over Conrad, which awakened hope in Italy.[108] Heinrich wanted the Italians to continue their opposition to Frederick II.[109] He may have dreamed of an Italian expedition himself, to gain the support of the Lombard League and with them move against the Kaiser.[110]

According to a recent study by Rubesamen, in the fall of 1246 the landgrave marched into Swabia with an army, to hold a *Reichstag* in Nürnberg. But on the way he encountered an army under Conrad. In the ensuing battle he was defeated, and he rushed to Nürnberg.[111] We do not know what transpired in the Kaiserstadt or who attended the *Reichstag*. Rome boasted that Heinrich held his *Reichstag* even after his defeat.[112]

But Heinrich Raspe's fortunes were about to turn against him. After the meeting at Nürnberg he besieged Ulm, and failed because of the city's stubborn resistance. It was the middle of a cold winter, which was too much for Heinrich's failing health. He also faced the possibility of the arrival of Conrad's army. So before long he lifted the siege. After that the sick Heinrich hurried home over wintery roads. He barely made it. It is reported that near the Wartburg he fell off his horse, a broken old man. In bed he had the "red Ruhr," a type of dysentery.[113] On 16 February 1247, Heinrich Raspe died at the Wartburg, and with him perished all papal dreams of an opposition king to Emperor Frederick II.[114]

Although there is some disagreement about the matter, the Reinhardsbrunn chronicler says that Heinrich was buried in Eisenach. The burial was reportedly on such a stormy, wintery day that the pallbearers could barely make it down the Wartburg's icy slopes to that nearby town.[115]

Since Heinrich had no male heirs, his rule ended the Ludowinger dynasty. Between 1039 and 1247 the Ludowinger had given Thuringia the famous Wartburg and a number of other distinctive features.

Patze argues that Heinrich's reign terminated the medieval empire and even extended beyond into the new era—for the reign of Frederick II ended the *Kaiserzeit*. Frederick II could no longer play the role of an Otto the Great, because the world of the great Saxon no longer existed. In the reign of Frederick II, papal power had reached its peak. The papacy was now an advanced legal institution, and the popes were masters of canon law. The emperor of the *Reich* was but one figure, along with the rulers of France and England, with whom the Roman pontiff battled.[116] The Investiture Controversy had been fought at the top and had ruined the medieval empire. The German princes were the victors, and during the period of territorialism they had free reign at the expense of the Hohenstaufen emperors. The popes played this development to good advantage. The Ludowinger rule in Thuringia was really that of the German *Reich* in miniature. It reflected the struggle with the Salien kings and cooperation with the Staufer, swinging between Welf and Ghibilines, finally accepting the kingdom from the hands of the papacy.[117]

During the Investiture Controversy and the Saxon wars, castles sprang up all over the surrounding mountains, so that by the time of the late Ludowinger, Thuringia was a stable *Landesstaat*, even though neighboring princes tried to gain their independence. Thus, after Heinrich's death, the unity of the lands of Thuringia and Hesse was never questioned. In time the *Landgrafschaft* passed over to Henry the Illustrious as a unit, and Henry became Landgraf of Thuringia with the full consent of his subjects.[118]

12

Thuringia under the House of Wettin

❖

Heinrich Raspe, the last Ludowinger Landgraf, died without male heirs. The only two claimants to the Thuringian *Landgrafschaft* were Jutta, the daughter of Hermann I who had married Markgraf Dietrich of the House of Wettin, and Sophie, the daughter of Ludwig V and Holy Elizabeth, who had married the duke of Brabant. Jutta's son became known as Henry the Illustrious, while Sophie's son was referred to as Henry the Child.

A full decade would pass before the succession issue was settled. There were nine years of pillaging and burning, including the Castle War between the Wartburg and the city of Eisenach. One event worthy of note is that Duke Albert of Braunschweig, Sophie's commander, was captured in a surprise attack by Rudolf of Vargula that also resulted in the death of many neighboring nobles.[1] Duke Albert was imprisoned and had to pay a huge ransom of 8,000 silver Marks, as well as give up many castles and lands.[2] Afterward Henry the Illustrious called himself the landgrave of Thuringia.[3] In 1292 his title was officially accepted by the *Reichsfürstenstand*, the official body of princes of the Holy Roman Empire.[4]

After nine years of war and the peaceful settlement of the rivalry between Meissen and Hesse, Henry the Illustrious had significantly widened his possessions. He could now claim the vast territory that extended from the Werra River in the west to the Oder River in the east; in the opposite direction, his lands began in the Harz Mountains in the north and ran to the Bohemian Massive in the south. Because of the silver, gold, and iron mines in the southern part of the Bohemian Massive, Henry was now quite wealthy.[5] He could take pride in his many castles, and near the center of his lands rose the beautiful, impregnable Wartburg. Cities such as Mühlhausen, Nordhausen, Eisenach, Erfurt, and Leipzig began to assume their later prominence. Before long these lands could also take pride in two distinguished universities, Erfurt and Leipzig.

According to the feudal law of primogeniture, Albert the Depraved, the

Landgraf's oldest son, should have inherited the now combined Wettiner lands. Historians have wondered why Henry decided to divide his territories between his three sons. The partition of Thuringia, Meissen, and the eastern lands between Henry's three sons ruined all hopes for Thuringian greatness for more than a century, while marriages into other noble families multiplied the problem and led to what has become known as the "Age of Confusion."[6]

Henry the Illustrious died in 1286, amid constant strife between his sons and grandsons. He was buried at *Altenzelle* with his forefathers. He had been Markgraf for a full fifty years and was an accomplished musician. Today Henry is listed among the 140 Minnesingers Germany produced. Hagen claims he wrote six of the Minnesinger songs.[7] Henry also wrote musical settings for the mass, to be used in his own chapel. The papacy even permitted his settings of the *Kyrie* and the *Gloria* to be used in all of his churches.[8]

During his fifty-year reign, the margrave witnessed tremendous changes: the decline of Danish power in the northern German lands; the fall of the Babenbergers in Austria (1247); the decline of the Hohenstaufen emperors in 1254; the disappearance of the former dukedoms of Bavaria and Franconia; the fall of Ottokar of Bohemia (1278), whose aunt had been Henry's wife; the decline and collapse of the medieval empire; and a decline in interest in the Crusades, even at the level of the German Kaisers.

In 1265 Henry turned the *Landgrafschaft* of Thuringia over to the sixteen-year-old Albert, and divided the rest of the Wettiner lands among his other sons. Albert was married to Emperor Frederick II's daughter Margaretha, but later rejected her in favor of a barmaid in Eisenach named Kunigunde. Albert had a child by Kunigunde, named Apitzen. He loved the boy and tried to elevate him by disinheriting his legitimate sons, Frederick and Dietzmann.

The ensuing family conflict drew the attention of neighboring nobles, who saw opportunities for themselves amid the confusion. Historians believe that even Emperor Rudolf of Hapsburg looked upon the family conflict with greedy eyes. The descendants of Henry the Illustrious fought among themselves while the rulers of the German *Reich* bought the Wettiner lands from Albert the Depraved and his henchmen, who were always in need of funds.

Tuta, the son of Albert's brother Dietrich, had purchased some land from the Landgraf for which he was unable to make payment. This brought him into the maneuvering between the Landgraf and the emperor. In time these lands went to Frederick the Happy, the son of Albert.[9] The emperor himself spent much time in Erfurt, possibly because of his involvements in Thuringia. Eventually the imperial armies arrived in Thuringia to collect debts.

The sons of Landgraf Albert objected to their father's careless treatment of what they regarded as their rights. On 1 January 1289 the father was captured, and in the *Rochlicher Agreement* he was forced to make concessions to his sons. The agreement required him to return the city and castle of Freiburg, the rich silver-mining region of Meissen, and the neighboring mountains and towns. But after obtaining his freedom Albert continued his same old tricks. He attempted to win Tuta's support, implying that he would make him the future Landgraf;

but meanwhile he contemplated making his beloved Apitzen his successor. However, the older sons did not sit idly by.[10] They forced him to accept the *Eisenach Agreement*, drafted on 5 August 1290, forcing him to stop willing cities and fortresses to Kunigunde's son.[11] Albert realized that he was not able to combat his two oldest boys, so he turned to neighboring princes for help. But they demanded gold for their assistance. Therefore he sold the *Landgrafschaft* of Landsberg, which really belonged to his deceased brother Dietrich.[12]

After Rudolf of Hapsburg died in 1482, he was succeeded by Adolf of Nassau, whose rival was the duke of Austria. Meanwhile a tragedy befell the Ludowinger's beloved Reinhardsbrunn Monastery. Ludwig of Hesburg set it on fire and burned it to the ground, together with all its treasures, because a posse had captured his thieving brother and beheaded him.[13] The fire spread to the church and to other buildings, including the Chapel of the Virgin, which had to be rebuilt.[14]

An even greater tragedy took place in 1293, when Albert the Depraved turned to the new Kaiser, Adolf of Nassau, to obtain favors at the expense of his family. In April he met with the emperor in Nürnberg to obtain funds by selling family property. Adolf was interested in buying Mark Meissen and especially the mining regions of Freiburg, an interest that Albert was quick to exploit.[15] Sources from Pisa claim that Albert even made an agreement with his son Dietzmann, granting him the *Landgrafschaft* of Thuringia, fortresses, and joint ownership of Thuringia during his lifetime. But he deceived Dietzmann by making a conflicting agreement with Albert of Nassau. He sold Thuringia for 12,000 silver Marks, provided only that after his death it would escheat back to the crown of Nassau. In this deal he disinherited not only his two legitimate sons, but also Apitzen. Kaiser Adolf used this as a trump card when he tried to arrange a marriage between his son Rupert and Agnes, daughter of King Weszel of Bohemia.[16]

According to the records, Adolf commissioned his conservator, Gerlach von Breuberg, to visit Frederick the Valiant, demanding that Tuta's lands be annexed to the *Reich*. Frederick opposed this, for he regarded them as his lawful inheritance. The Kaiser then resorted to force, and, by September 1294, he invaded Thuringia with a sizable army. He regarded it as the property of the crown.[17]

The *Reinhardsbrunn Chronicle* describe Adolf's campaigns in gruesome detail, as the imperial troops killed, raped, and burned.[18] The army included some cavalry, but in the main it was made up of crude, untrained foot soldiers. The king's strategy was to acquire and control key castles, with the exception of the Wartburg, which was to be left undisturbed during Albert's lifetime, and then revert to the crown.[19] He occupied Eisenach, and fought towns and castles that denied the king's rightful purchase.[20] The troops made no distinction among targets, attacking nunneries, monasteries, and churches. Imperial cities such as Nordhausen and Mühlhausen were singled out for attack. Albert mortgaged the former for 2000 silver Marks, but Mühlhausen refused to go along, nearly costing Kaiser Adolf his life.[21]

When told by older knights how his troops were vandalizing churches, tear-ing down altars, and stealing sacred objects, the emperor was shocked but asked how he could control an entire army.[22] Afterward, however, he appears to have made an example of ten men by ordering that their right hands be cut off. This brought an end to the vandalism.[23]

By January 1295, the Kaiser had returned to the Rhineland, after making Gerlach von Breuberg governor of his conquered territories.[24] But as soon as the king was away, Frederick and Dietzmann recaptured most of the lands they had lost. This prompted a second invasion, in 1296, that was just as devastating as the first. By spring the troops had conquered the silver mines of Freiburg, after which Adolf had sixty of their defenders executed. He established Henry of Nassau as governor over Meissen, the Osterland, and the Pleiszenland, while Gerlach von Breuberg was placed over Thuringia.[25]

The house of Wettin had never seen darker days. Everyone feared deceit and the loss of their freedom or their lives. The landgrave's sons did not risk staying in their own lands. Dietzmann hid for a while in Lausitz, while Frederick visited the Tirol and Lombardy, where the Hohenstaufen honored him as Emperor Frederick II's grandson.[26]

The rule by Governor Gerlach did not go over well with Thuringian counts and nobility, and they struck back. In order to carry out their inspections, the governor's troops had to pass through dense woods; there they encountered raiding parties that killed their horses and then engaged them in hand-to-hand combat. Rothe tells us of five such attacks, resulting in heavy loss of life.[27] Count Henry's troops were resisted as well. Everyone seemed to have turned against the emperor.[28]

Duke Albert of Austria sensed that this was an auspicious time to become Kaiser. No doubt he had received inklings of support from some of the electors. He planned to move into the Rhine region via Bavaria and Swabia, an expedition on which he embarked in the spring of 1298. The Kaiser learned of the invasion and prepared to defend his throne. Albert discussed strategies with the three archbishops of the *Reich*, and they agreed on a plan. The duke's main army would be hidden in a woods, while an advance group would confront the king's army and lead it into the ambush.[29]

As planned, the battle began with a cavalry charge on St. Martin's Day. When the duke's troops turned back, the king and his army rushed headlong after them. Then the trap was sprung. There was no room for escape, and the duke's forces proved victorious. The king was killed and his son was captured.[30]

A number of the electors of the *Reich* seem to have been in the Worms region, awaiting the outcome of the encounter, for in only three days Albert was chosen "King of the Romans" and Kaiser of the *Reich*. Later, in Aachen, he was officially crowned with pomp and ceremony. Thus the second Hapsburger was elected king of the *Reich*, the beginning of the Hapsburg dynasty of the Holy Roman Empire of the German Nation.[31]

One of the first subjects brought up before Albert's 1298 Nürnberg *Reichstag* was the persecution of Jews. The chroniclers reported a gruesome slaughter of Jews at Würzburg and Rothenburg. Jewish homes, schools, and synagogues were broken into, and the men, women, and children slain. There was danger that the violence would spread.[32]

Meanwhile, Albert's lands remained in great confusion. It was difficult for Frederick and Dietzmann to stage a comeback. Nor did the new king's outlook toward the Wettiner appear good. He immediately appointed King Wenceslaus of Bohemia as the *Reich's* governor over Meissen, the Pleiszenland, and the Osterland. As if that weren't bad enough, Albert also sold Meissen to King Wenceslaus for 40,000 silver Marks.[33] But the sons did not give up attempting to recapture the lost territories. Archbishop Gebhardt was on their side at the Diet of Nürnberg, and in vain Dietzmann there offered him 1,000 silver Marks to keep the emperor out of Thuringia. However, Albert was too busy elsewhere.

In the year 1229, King Albert held a wedding at Toul, France, for his son Rudolf and the sister of Philip the Fair of France. Amid the festivities the French king made a remark that gave much offense. He stated that young Rudolf should be designated "King of the Romans," while his father should be crowned emperor in Rome. A great silence followed. Finally, Archbishop Gebhardt criticized the suggestion, for it would make the throne hereditary. King Albert then refused to pay the expenses of the archbishop and his large entourage, which proved to be embarrassing.[34] In revenge, the archbishop asked the other two archbishops and electors to oppose the appointment of Rudolf II as "King of the Romans."[35]

Rothe claims that King Albert later begged the three archbishops to use their influence to elect his son, but they remained noncommittal, arousing the king's wrath.[36] Even though the king then resorted to force against the archbishop's lands and castles, as well as against the Pfalzgraf, the Kaiser's son remained uncrowned.[37] After he had already inflicted massive destruction, the king invaded Trier and Cologne, where he was just as merciless. In Cologne the archbishop left the king to his looting and burning, still refusing to budge.[38]

At the turn of the century, Kaiser Albert was still interested in making Thuringia and the rest of the Wettiner lands part of the Hapsburg empire. In Meissen, however, he encountered a problem. He had entered into a quarrel with King Wenceslaus over the Hungarian throne, and had demanded that Wenceslaus return Meissen to the *Reich*. This was impossible, for he had mortgaged certain castles and cities in Meissen to Markgraf Otto of Brandenburg for 50,000 silver Marks.[39] Wenceslaus's successor tried to get out of this bind by having Brandenburg return these possessions to Meissen, so that he in turn could return them to the *Reich*.[40] But the assassination of King Albert and subsequent developments intervened.

In 1300, the Landgraf faced a double grief. His beloved wife Kunigunde died and was buried in St. Catherine's monastery in Eisenach. Later in the same year their son Apitzen also died.[41] The aged Landgraf soon married his third wife, Elizabeth von Arnschaug. She was the former wife of Count Alheit, and a sober, wealthy woman. She had a fourteen-year-old daughter, also named Elizabeth, whom the Landgraf invited to live in the Wartburg. Apparently Albert and his son were now on better terms, for now that Markgraf Frederick's wife had died,

Albert approved of his marriage to the younger Elizabeth. For a time, relationships in the family approved, and Frederick received some inheritances.[42]

In 1304 the old family strife broke out anew, but peace was soon restored.[43] It did not last long, however. Eisenach had drafted a *Landesfrieden* agreement, signed by Landgraf Albert and King Adolf of Nassau, who were opposed to having the Landgraf's sons assume the rule of Thuringia. This gave the father an excuse to become involved in Thuringian affairs.[44] At the time the landgrave was in the middle of an invasion of Bohemia, due to a feud with King Wenceslaus. He was succeeded by his son Boleslaus, who made peace with the *Reich*. Boleslaus' reign was short, for he died in 1306 after being stabbed by Johann von Bolstent.[45]

Kaiser Albert held a *Hoftag* in Fulda, where the elderly Landgraf made serious charges against his sons, who were absent.[46] The father reaffirmed his deal with the king, making Thuringia and the Wartburg royal property after his death. The Kaiser swore on the chains of St. Peter that he would reign in the sons, and placed them under the *Reich's* interdict, which was essentially a declaration of war.[47] Shortly after the Fulda *Hoftag*, the emperor learned that the king of Bohemia had been slain, and he rushed there to ensure the election of his own son, Rudolf II. He then arranged for a wedding between Rudolf and the former wife of King Wenceslaus.[48]

At this point in the story it becomes difficult to separate truth from fiction. In 1306 Frederick seems to have been waging war in the field against the king's forces, while his wife Elizabeth was with her mother in the Wartburg. She was in the last stage of her pregnancy with her first child, and Landgraf Albert was in the same household. Frederick felt that he should be with them at the time of the baby's delivery. The older Elizabeth let Frederick know how, with their assistance, he could enter the castle. The obstacle was the Landgraf, who needed to be bound. Frederick and a small group of bodyguards hid in a cave in a neighboring mountain for days, awaiting a signal. At an opportune time, he and his guards entered. After the aged father had been captured, they convinced him to take up residence near the town of Eisenach.[49] New living quarters were provided in a small village nearby. Meanwhile, news spread that Frederick was in the Wartburg, and guards from Eisenach cut off entry to the great fortress.[50]

The king's forces and the citizens of Eisenach prepared for a major siege against the Wartburg. The king used the count of Weilau to direct the attack. The count would employ a new weapon, the catapult, to hurl boulders from the mountainside into the fortress.[51] Frederick planned to escape after his wife had had a week's recovery from childbirth. They waited until nightfall, when the guards were asleep, and used ropes and twelve horses for their flight. The group fled to Tannberg via a hunter's route, off the main road. There Frederick left them.

Frederick's immediate task was to bring relief to the besieged defenders of the Wartburg. He asked his brother-in-law, Duke Henry of Braunschweig, to assist him with troops. Friendly Thuringian nobles also provided food and supplies. Many knights were among the force that was recruited, and Frederick's brother, Dietzmann, and his men also participated. They all gathered at Sonndborn with wagonloads of food and supplies. The army was led by 336 well-equipped knights, clad in full armor and helmets. When the besieging troops observed this large force, the guards fled and Eisenach locked its gates. Supplies could then be delivered to the castle.[52]

One wonders what happened to the king's main force. Were they also frightened? When they resumed the siege, Count Weilau was taken prisoner and locked in the Wartburg prison. He suffered greatly there and died. After that the siege collapsed.[53]

But King Albert was determined, so he planned another invasion under Burggraf Henry of Nortenberg. He also began the customary plundering in the Osterland. Frederick and Dietzmann opposed him with their combined forces, and other princes, including the Saxons, also joined in. They defeated the king's forces at Lucka, near Altenburg, leaving hundreds of dead on the field. Three hundred and sixty were taken prisoner, and the Burggraf himself was captured, making it a decisive victory.[54]

Just when the two brothers might have rejoiced, another tragedy befell them. While attending a Matins service with his bodyguard, Dietzmann was stabbed and killed by one of his own men. He was buried in Leipzig.[55] Now Frederick had to battle it alone.

All King Albert's efforts to release the prisoners held by Frederick failed. The king then entered the Wettiner lands with another army, but was forced to break off the attack when his son, Rudolf II, unexpectedly died. His mad rush to retain Bohemia failed, for the Bohemians had already elected Duke Henry of Kärthen to the throne. To the king's surprise, Henry had previously made a treaty with Frederick, and had paid him 2,000 silver Marks.[56]

Frederick was fully aware that the time had arrived to undo the years of damage his father had inflicted on his sons. He assembled all the counts, nobles, and Vögte of his lands, as well as those of his brother, at Erfurt. There he assumed the titles of his father and brother and demanded that they take a feudal oath as his vassals. He then gave them horses and reimbursements for their past losses, and their castles and strongholds now formed his defense.[57]

The chroniclers state that in spite of what happened at Erfurt, King Albert was determined to take the Wettiner lands, and so he kept on recruiting an army. His traveling entourage included his nephew, Johann of Austria, who harbored a secret hatred of the king. Together with a large body of nobles and barons, the king arrived at the River Rezzberg, a little stream with a small ferry enabling one to cross it. The king let Johann and his bodyguards on first, and they took up most of the space. So the Kaiser left his own men behind. On the way Johann caused a fracas with the seated Kaiser, drew his sword, and struck him on the head. The blow had such force that it split the king's skull in two. Johann's guards then stabbed the king and left the corpse on the ferry.[58]

Johann's father was the king's brother, the duke of Austria, who had died while Johann was a child. The son had grown up under the Kaiser's tutelage, but the king had advanced his own son to the dukedom. Because of this Johann had plotted to assassinate his own uncle.[59]

After the king's assassination, Frederick's old enemy, the city of Eisenach, desired to make peace with the landgrave. Upon invitation, the Landgraf arrived with his loyal nobles and officials. As conditions of friendship he called upon the city to rebuild the *Klemme*, which they had torn down during the siege of the Wartburg, and to behave as loyal subjects. This was followed by a feudal ceremony of investiture, held near the Preacher's Tower.[60] A similar reconciliation took place with the Osterland and with Meissen, old enemies that now accepted him as overlord. His father, now in his Erfurt quarters, seemed by now to have lost interest in life.[61]

After the death of King Albert, the German electors selected Henry of Luxembourg as Kaiser. He was crowned in Aachen by the archbishop of Mainz, on the throne of Charlemagne. Henry was expected to continue the effort to incorporate Thuringia, Meissen, and the Osterland into the *Reich* as crown lands. This was of some concern to Frederick.[62] Peace did not last long, thanks to Albert the Depraved, who had sold the Erfurt *Bürger* a number of illegal Vogteien, or judgeships. Frederick notified the Erfurt citizens that he was now their Landgraf and that they had to conform to his demands. They refused, and so he resorted to force. All roads to Erfurt were ordered closed, dealing the city a severe blow. A wagon train tried to get through, but it was captured.

Frederick then summoned the city officials to his court in Mittelhausen. The town council came in a procession, led by praying priests, hoping to make an impression. They were followed by an armed force that intended to break up the court, which caused the lawyers and judges to flee. Once again they were summoned to Frederick's court, but this time a strong defense was put in place to receive them. The officials went to Count Hermann of Weimar for assistance, and also appealed to Mühlhausen and Nordhausen. The soldiers who were recruited proceeded to rob, burn, and plunder Thuringian villages and the countryside. But then Count Hermann refused to proceed. This terminated the outlawry, and Erfurt's troops rushed home.[63]

In 1310 the combined troops of Erfurt, Mühlhausen, and Weimar initiated even worse devastation, not even sparing churches and monasteries, where they dared to quarter their troops. Frederick resolved to put a stop to it. He captured Captain Ludwig von Guttirn, along with one hundred horses. After that the citizens turned on the clergy, attacking the cloister and hospice of St. Peter. They even forbade the monks of St. Peters from going outside and grinding flour at their mill. None of the clergy could supply their patients with food.[64]

In response, Frederick recruited an army of considerable size in Meissen, Bohemia, and the Vogtland. He besieged Weimar and brought proud Count Hermann to his knees, exacting a costly settlement. He established his headquarters in Hochheim, a village outside Erfurt, and during the siege destroyed the houses, gardens, and grape arbors. The Landgraf then lifted the siege, for unknown reasons.[65] The proud *Bürger* of Erfurt then appealed to the new king, Henry of Nassau, but he was preoccupied with larger issues. Erfurt's cause was now hopeless.[66] In the final settlement, the city paid a heavy fine and restored the stolen judgeships. The cities of Mühlhausen and Nordhausen did the same, and paid very dearly. The aftermath of this conflict was vast destruction and great hunger. In Erfurt alone, 8,000 people died of starvation.[67]

Before long it became evident that Henry of Luxembourg was just as ambitious as his predecessors had been in acquiring crown lands. First he wanted to acquire Bohemia, and he achieved full stature by being crowned emperor. Thus he had to depose King Henry of Kärnten.[68] He also refused to recognize Frederick the Courageous as the rightful owner of the Wettiner lands. Frederick then came to Henry of Kärnten's support.[69] While on his coronation journey, the new king appointed the archbishop of Mainz and the count of Henneberg to preserve peace in the Wettiner lands and those of the king of Bohemia.[70] After that, Henry of Kärnten was defeated and had to surrender the crown. However, on 19 December 1310, the Kaiser recognized Frederick as the rightful ruler over the Wettiner lands; but he also stipulated that the king of Bohemia would be the *Reich*'s governor of Frederick's lands and ruler of Moravia and Upper Lausitz. In 1311, the king extended this to the Pleiszenland, adding that the Landgraf could repurchase the lands in a decade for 2,000 Marks.

One wonders why Henry of Luxembourg wanted to invade Italy after many of his predecessors had tried and failed, but perhaps he wanted to be crowned by Pope Clement V. He began with a siege of Brixen, a well-fortified city, and faced strong resistance. The citizens poisoned the water supply used by Henry's troops, and after its surrender Brixen's walls were leveled and many of its leaders beheaded. The king wintered there and remained until 1312. There was much political confusion, and being crowned by the pope was out of the question. When the king arrived in Rome, all the streets were blocked. On 19 June 1312, a designated clergyman sent by Pope Clement crowned him at the Basilica of St. John.[71] Subsequently the emperor attempted a siege against Florence, but it failed.

With the king away in Italy, Landgraf Frederick should have been relieved, but on 7 January 1312, the emperor's son, Johann of Bohemia, altered the previous pact made between the *Reich* and the Landgraf. He charged Frederick with violating his previous oath, and Frederick lost all claims to his land. The new pact even failed to mention the emperor's original agreement.[72]

In his final years, Frederick continued to struggle with the transactions his father had concluded, first with Markgraf Waldemar of Brandenburg, to whom the old man had sold Lower Lausitz. Frederick now took the title of Markgraf of Meissen.[73] However, his tired troops were defeated in battle, and he was locked up as a prisoner in Brandenburg.[74] Frederick's Vögte gathered an army that defeated and captured the count of Kotin, and Frederick was finally liberated.[75]

The Landgraf must have tired of all the fighting. He made peace with Fulda in 1314, then with Mühlhausen, and his relationships with Erfurt improved much. Frederick also found himself impoverished from warfare.[76] In 1311, his brother-in-law Henry brought peace between him and his sons. In 1310 the Landgraf and Elizabeth rejoiced over the birth of Frederick II, no doubt named after Emperor Frederick II, his grandfather. The birth of the child proved fortunate indeed, for Frederick's other son, the youthful Frederick the Lame, was killed near Leipzig by robber barons.

In 1315 Albert the Depraved died in famine-stricken Erfurt, where he had been living on crumbs. In 1318 Landgraf Otto of Hesse arranged for a marriage between Frederick's daughter, Elizabeth, and his son Otto. The marriage did not turn out well, and in 1339 she left, never to return.[77] In 1317, a bolt of lightening struck the central tower of the Wartburg. The resulting conflagration consumed the family coats of arms and many irreplaceable paintings. Frederick had the rooms restored and enlarged and also installed heating facilities. By 1319 the Wartburg was again a family dwelling.[78]

In 1321 Frederick was viewing a play, presented by the Dominicans, based on the story of the wise and foolish virgins in Matthew 25. When the Virgin Mary herself was shown not being able to persuade the bridegroom to show mercy to the foolish virgins, Frederick rose and loudly asked what Christianity was worth if one could not appeal to Mary and the saints, and only through good works could enter eternity.

After suffering a stroke, Frederick the Valiant passed into a coma and died at age 68. He was buried in the Reinhardsbrunn Monastery.[79]

Frederick's second wife, Elizabeth, had given birth to a gifted son who later came to be know as Frederick the Serious. But he was only nine years old when his father died in 1324, so he was put under the tutelage first of Count Henry of Schwarzburg and then Count Henry XII of Reusz and Plauen.[80] Good relations had been established with Bohemia because his father had arranged for Frederick to become engaged to Jutta, daughter of King Johann. Jutta was brought to the Wartburg to live. Yet there were problems with Bavaria, for Kaiser Lewis had wanted Frederick II to marry into his house.[81] Lewis later forced the engagement to be broken so that Frederick could marry his daughter Mechtild. He also promised the boy a dowry. Yet the Bohemian king still presided over the investiture of Frederick as the future Landgraf. Lewis showered Frederick with many gifts; by 1326 he had given him 13,000 Marks, and, when the Burggraf of Altenburg died without heirs, he offered the young Landgraf the *Burggrafschaft* as a fief of the *Reich*. All this was done to protect Lewis' son's territorial lands in the mark of Brandenburg.[82]

After the death of Henry of Luxembourg in 1313, there followed thirty-four years of rival kingship. A disputed election between Frederick of Austria and Lewis of Bavaria led to a challenge on the field of battle.[83] The Austrian was taken prisoner and his troops were routed, ending the strife.[84] But then Pope John XXII excommunicated Lewis, offending not only him but also the electoral college. The king crossed the Alps to depose the pope for his intrusion into the German electoral system. Later he had himself crowned with both the iron crown of Lombardy and the imperial crown of Rome. This failed to end the strife, for later Lewis faced a more powerful opponent in Charles IV.

By arranging the marriage between Frederick II and his daughter, Lewis of Bavaria tried to establish an unbroken territory from the Mark Brandenburg in the north to the Alps in the south, a plan originating with him and not with Charles IV.[85] Now the Brandenburg and Wittelsbach lands were brought together, with friendly Frederick II in between. Lewis wanted the Wettiner to remain neutral, and he appointed Frederick II to be the guardian of his son, with the stipulation that should Frederick die childless, Mark Meissen was to pass over to the *Reich*.[86] In the meantime, a new archbishop, Matthias, stirred up much dissension in Thuringia and in Hesse.[87] In addition, Pope John XXII disregarded the king's declaration that he had been deposed. Through the archbishop of Trier he tried to establish a rival king. A conflict broke out between Mainz and Trier, and nothing came of the scheme.[88]

At the early age of fourteen, Frederick II assumed his responsibilities. After six years of engagement, he and Mechtild were married in an elaborate wedding at Nürnberg.[89] A great number of royalty attended, bringing the prince a rich dowry of 10,000 Marks. The imperial cities of Nordhausen and Mühlhausen were also mortgaged to the prince.[90] Through gifts, King Johann of Bohemia was induced to acquiesce to the jilting of Jutta.[91]

Under the emperor's protection, Frederick II began his reign with much enthusiasm. He made Thuringia the center of his activities, while Meissen remained in the background.[92] He settled a score with the Vogt of Reusz, who had taken advantage of his youth.[93] The Kaiser clashed with Frederick over Henry II of Hesse, but their differences were settled in 1332, with the gift of the castles Triptis, Auma, and Ziegenrück.[94]

However, Henry II disregarded the peace that had been made between the Kaiser, Frederick, and the Vögte, and formed an alliance against the young Landgraf. Meanwhile the counts of Schwarzenburg tried to divide his lands in the Saale valley, and the counts of Orlamünde and the Vögte of Erfurt and Mühlhausen also threatened the reign of the young ruler.[95]

The ruling line in Mark Brandenburg had died out, leaving the *Markgrafschaft* unoccupied. King Lewis claimed it should escheat back to the crown. He designated his son Markgraf of Brandenburg, a title he would assume at maturity. He made two attempts to take over the electorate of Brandenburg, which was protected by Thuringian troops.[96] A third expedition into Brandenburg never materialized, but Frederick still guarded the mark.[97]

As if this confusion were not enough, a great schism also broke out in the archbishopric of Mainz. After Matthias' death there was rivalry between Heinrich von Virneburg and Baldwin of Trier; the former was Pope John XXII's choice as his successor, and the latter was favored by the cathedral chapter of Mainz.[98] Archbishop Baldwin leagued himself with Emperor Lewis and most of the Erfurt clergy; thus it was almost impossible for the papal candidate to establish a solid footing in Thuringia. The nobility supported the archbishop of Trier.

In 1335 the archbishop concluded a ten-year treaty with Erfurt.[99] The Kaiser came to Eisenach to avoid a civil war, and believed it had been settled. But upon his departure, Baldwin unleashed his army. The Vögte of Frederick II were captured at Langensalza, and parts of Thuringia were again ravaged. But, by 12 October 1335, Erfurt had seen enough war and agreed to an armistice lasting until 1 May 1336.[100] Yet Erfurt never completely trusted Baldwin's provost, Hermann von Bibra; for they felt that his booklet, *Bibra Büchlein*, threatened their freedom. In December 1335 the Mainz court was attacked and the provost had to be rescued. Accordingly, Archbishop Baldwin placed Erfurt under a second interdict, even though the one issued by Pope John XXII was still in effect, for they had refused to accept Baldwin's rival candidate.[101]

Frederick II faced another serious problem, namely, the robber barons who attacked and looted commercial transport on the imperial highway from Moravia through his lands to Frankfurt a.M. The nobles in the region were supportive of the Landgraf in this. Emperor Lewis told Frederick II to stop the lawlessness.[102] But the landgrave found that the problem was far more serious than he had thought. Behind the looting were the *Castellans*, the bishop of Naumburg, and the knights of the bishop. Even Bishop Gebhard of Merseburg was found to be involved. The robbers collected much silver, gold, and commercial commodities from merchants. Frederick besieged Naumburg Castle, recovering much stolen property and coins, and restored some of it to its rightful owners.[103] Some nobles from the Saale and Unstrut region refused to return their stolen goods, and were driven from their lands. They were placed under the emperor's interdict and were to be punished if apprehended.[104]

Another nest of robbers was in the Werra region.[105] A joint expedition was planned by the forces of Archbishop Baldwin, Landgrave Philip II of Hesse, and the landgrave of Thuringia, to eliminate the troublemakers. They captured their castle Normannstein and placed the lands under supervision. With Vögte and some Burggrafen on guard, peace finally came to the region.[106] A dispute arose between young Frederick II and his mother involving his father's will and certain cities. Word of this reached Kaiser Lewis. Around Pentecost in 1333, the emperor visited the Wartburg to restore peace between the son and his mother. Count Berthold of Henneberg served as the mediator. In the peaceful settlement, the mother was deeded Gotha, Gene, and Teneberg, including its cities and castles. The Landgraf also gave his mother the monastery of Reynersborn and the town of Weissenfels.[107] Frederick and his wife, Mechtild, built a chapel immediately below the Wartburg, where Holy Elizabeth had performed her works of mercy.[108]

There were also other trials for the young landgrave and his family, for the young Elizabeth had not been happy in her marriage to Landgraf Henry II of Hesse. Rumors of his unfaithfulness spread, and he then circulated false stories about his wife. She unburdened herself to her mother in Gotha, where she later moved.[109] Since Frederick's men had taken Elizabeth to her mother, the Hessian landgrave accused her brother of foul play. Frederick countered by accusing Henry II of spreading false rumors. Henry brought the case before Emperor Lewis, who left the choice to Elizabeth. She refused to go back until the false charges were admitted, so she remained in Gotha until her mother's death. Then the landgrave provided her with necessary quarters and means of support in Eisenach.[110]

The feud between the two archbishops continued through the middle thirties, with alliances changing frequently. After a time, Baldwin, Frederick, and the Vogt of Gera joined together against Erfurt. There was a meeting in the castle of Gelnhausen to sign a six-year agreement, to which they also tried to add the Osterland princes of Reusz and Plauen. In response, Erfurt hired mercenary soldiers, for only Käfernburg was still loyal to their cause.[111]

Frederick II, supported by the bishop of Merseburg, began a siege of Erfurt. He was soon joined by Baldwin and his large army, which brought much destruction of life and property. The citizens of Erfurt, tired of warfare, left the city, and support for the fight began to dwindle. Even Elizabeth, Frederick's mother, tried to restore peace. Erfurt was forced to pay Frederick 3,000 Marks and Baldwin, who had placed the city under the ban, 5,000 Marks. The city also had to terminate all previous alliances.[112]

However, this peace did not end the schism. Upon Pope John's death he was succeeded by Benedict XII, who, at Virneburg's request, excommunicated his rival. Baldwin finally withdrew and returned to his Trier diocese. On 29 June 1337 the Kaiser and the cathedral chapter accepted Henry of Virneburg.[113] This resulted in a change of alliances for Frederick, who made an eight-year alliance with the archbishop of Mainz. But a new problem arose, for the archbishop was unable to control his diocese. That same year, Archbishop Henry terminated the interdict against Erfurt, and peace came to Hesse and Thuringia. Henry also shifted his support to the Kaiser, and the emperor formed an alliance with King Edward III of England against France, just as Adolf of Nassau had done earlier.[114]

King Edward III's war with France over the Flemish weaving cities brought involvement by the German *Reich*, resulting in an English invasion of the region. Edward asked the Kaiser to supply an army, and, upon Lewis' request, Frederick II joined his father-in-law on this expedition.[115] Before departing, the Kaiser warned all the nobles and the cities that if they broke the peace he would punish them with an imperial interdict. He also set up a special court to try offenders.

Frederick II recruited many knights for the campaign. But after their arrival King Philip slipped through their hands, and there was no engagement. All the same, Edward III and the Kaiser felt that Frederick should be knighted for his valor.[116] During Frederick's absence the *Landesfrieden* seems to have been well observed, but upon his return he faced many enemies.[117]

Many of the powerful nobles in Thuringia were the landgrave's rivals; in fact the Schwarzburger in the Saale region had placed a wedge between the landgrave's lands. Another problem was Count Henry of Hohenstein, who was doing all he could to expand his territories.[118]

After the Flanders expedition, Frederick withdrew from broader European politics, for he had ample problems at home.[119] The haughty attitude among the nobility of Thuringia led to a four-year war between Frederick and his vassals. Erfurt now stood with the Landgraf, while Archbishop Virneburg supported the nobles.[120] Patze claims that the archbishop was behind the "Arnstadt Military Union" of some dozen counts and Vögte, all seeking to increase their independence.[121] Frederick visited Arnstadt in an unsuccessful effort to bring about peace.[122]

Rothe claims that Erfurt and the Landgraf recruited their forces in order to level some of the nobles' castles.[123] The nobles themselves engaged in much ravaging and destruction. The Landgraf attacked the Arnstadt stronghold with the most modern equipment available. Erfurt was ready to level the fortress, but Frederick stopped because it belonged to one of his vassals. Erfurt then withdrew and discontinued the war.[124] The nobles concluded that this was an opportune moment to strike Erfurt, but they did not reckon with the fact that Frederick's army was encamped near that city. When the Erfurt troops sallied out to meet them, the enemy became frightened and fled. Frederick's army pursued them, winning the battle. The two counts of Weimar and Schwarzburg were taken prisoner, along with many knights and other prisoners. The knights were incarcerated at Erfurt.[125]

But the battle did not end there. Near Arnsdorf, Count Ruprecht, the archbishop's brother, joined the fight with two hundred well-equipped knights, reversing the tide. Frederick was stabbed while in the saddle, and many of his best knights were killed. But a wagon train of monks arrived playing martial music, and the count and his troops mistook the music for an attack. They rushed back into the fortress, thus saving the Landgraf's life. He was taken to Erfurt for four weeks of convalescence.[126]

By the middle of the century, the Schwarzburgers realized the futility of waging war against great odds, and they signed a peace with Frederick II. On 28 July 1345 they terminated the Nobles' War. Soon the proud counts of Weimar-Orlamünde recognized the Landgraf as overlord in their lands.[127] By 1550, after Frederick II's death, King Charles IV made the counts of Orlamünde vassals of his son, Frederick III. After the counts' death, the lands became a part of the *Landgrafschaft* of Thuringia.[128]

The end of the Nobles' War did not solve all of Frederick II's problems. Heinrich von Stolberg formed a band of robber barons who did much damage. Together with the cities of Erfurt and Mühlhausen, Frederick besieged the outlaws' castle, captured the count, beheaded him, and hanged his henchmen.[129] The territory was now relatively quiet, except that the archbishop was always hungry for more territory, and so tried to acquire the castle of Salsa and its neighboring lands.[130] The Landgraf decided to besiege Salsa, which was held by the archbishop's men. His catapult threw stones that caved in the roofs of houses, and launched incendiary missiles that set the town on fire. The townspeople could not escape, for Heinrich's men kept the gates locked. The archbishop then attempted a settlement by dividing the territory.[131] For a while after the capitulation there was joint rule, but forty years later the region became a part of the *Landgrafschaft* of Thuringia.[132] The next year Frederick II also purchased Landsberg and parts of the Palatinate.[133]

In the year 1346, Count Heinrich von Henneberg, who was then close to the Wettiner, agreed to an engagement between his daughter Katherina and the Landgraf's oldest son, Frederick III. According to custom, the bride to be was brought to the Wartburg for her courtly training.[134] All went well until the principals discussed the dowry. The bride's father did not want to give up the Coburg region. Frederick then requested that his daughter be returned.[135] This angered the count and resulted in a few skirmishes, but in time, and with the assistance of other rulers, the dowry agreement was made with the support of the bride's mother, countess Jutta.[136]

Later, in the Bautzen settlement of February 1350,[137] Frederick III was reassured that Schmalkalden and the Coburg would become his as fiefs of the *Reich*. But a brother-in-law, John, also laid claim to all the Henneberger lands.[138] So when Jutta died in 1353, young Frederick III did not wait for the funeral, but rode cross-country on a fast horse to Prague to be with Charles IV, who agreed to his inheritance of the Coburg and Schmalkalden. Charles also sent letters to his subordinates that effectively blocked the brother-in-law. The Wettiner had now gained a foothold in the old Franconian region.[139]

Contemporary chroniclers were quite dissatisfied with the reign of Kaiser Lewis of Bavaria.[140] Pope Clement VI, his bitter enemy, proposed Charles IV as an opposition king. In this matter archbishop Heinrich of Mainz first supported the pontiff, but later turned to King Lewis. Pope Clement then deposed the archbishop and appointed Count Gerlach von Nassau as the new archbishop. On Maundy Thursday 1346, the pope declared King Lewis deposed and ordered an imperial election. When the electoral college met at Rhens on 11 July 1346, they chose Charles IV but did not depose Lewis, whereupon Archbishop Heinrich resigned.[141] On 11 October 1347, King Lewis died rather mysteriously while hunting. He had just been visited by an Austrian countess, who had ingratiated herself with him. Just before her departure she took two bottles of wine and asked him to drink a farewell toast with her. She drank from one bottle and gave the king the other. After she left he began to feel some discomfort, and when he went bear hunting he fell from his horse and died.[142] In 1147 Frederick II's wife Mechtild died, leaving him with five children.

The Landgraf now had to decide whether to join Charles IV or remain with the Wittelsbach family. Erfurt faced a similar choice. In desperation, the Wittelsbach party asked King Edward III of England to become a rival king. Naturally he declined.[143] There was even some discussion about making Landgrave Frederick II their candidate, but he wisely joined Charles IV. At a meeting in Dresden, Charles paid a large sum to bring the king's son Lewis to his side.[144] This helped the Landgraf make a definite decision to leave the Wittelsbach party.[145]

After all these failures, the Wittelsbachs turned to Count Günther von Schwarzburg as their imperial candidate. Günther must have been puzzled, for he asked for further clarification of what was expected.[146] He was assured of at least three votes, those of Brandenburg, Mainz, and the Palatinate, but what of the rest?[147] Even his own relatives did not favor his election, because he was not well.[148] When Günther arrived in Frankfurt a.M., the *Bürger* refused him entrance because they opposed a double election. Amid some confusion, the electoral college declared Rudolf of Saxony's vote to be invalid and chose the

Schwarzburg count as a rival king. The supporters of Count Günther had won the election by means of the illegitimate vote of the Saxon-Lauenburg line of Saxony.[149]

But in spite of the rigged election, the deposed archbishop immediately elevated Count Günther to the throne as "King of the Romans." In turn, Günther declared Heinrich the legitimate archbishop of Mainz, thus defying the pope's previous action. But the Schwarzburg count had no support in the *Reich*, for all preferred the Luxembourg King Charles IV.[150]

When Charles IV came into the lower Rhine region, five electors awaited his arrival. All knew Günther could not win, for he was too sick to rule. When the wife of Charles IV died, he wisely married into the Palatinate family through Anne, the daughter of the Pfalzgraf Rudolf, who had supported Günther. In 1349, at a meeting in Charles IV's camp, margrave Lewis of Brandenburg appeared to support the Schwarzburg king, yet asked him to step down. The clever Charles displayed no emotion about his triumph, but instead rewarded Günther richly for stepping down.[151] He even had the count buried in *St. Bartholomäuskirche*, where he had been elevated to the kingship—very unusual treatment for a defeated rival.[152]

Perhaps it was wise that Frederick II had stayed out of the imperial election, for he died on 18 November 1349, at the early age of thirty-nine. He was buried in Altenzelle beside Mechtild. They left behind six children, Frederick, Balthasar, Wilhelm, Ludwig, Elizabeth, and Beatrix.

The father had arranged that Frederick III, then seventeen years old, should reign. But since he was still young, the government was turned over to Marschall Timo von Colditz. Elizabeth married Burggraf Friedrich of Nürnberg, later inherited Mark Brandenburg, and became the *Stammutter* of the later kings of Prussia. Beatrix married Count Bernhard IV of Anhalt.[153]

In two decades Frederick II had restored his sovereignty over Thuringia, but his early death left his lands vulnerable to territorialism. Young Frederick III now faced his wife's relatives, all of whom were eager to grab lands.

Even though Archbishop Heinrich von Virneburg had been deposed by Pope Clement VI, he refused to step down and accept the pope's choice of Gerlach von Nassau. Thus the schism was renewed. In this matter Charles IV was uncertain as to whom he should support. Perhaps Charles welcomed the schism so that he could enhance his Bohemian possessions.[154] Charles also favored the growth of cities at the expense of the nobility. He tried to strengthen Erfurt, and asked it to support Gerlach von Nassau in the Mainz schism.[155] Gerlach promised Erfurt that it would never be subject to an interdict. He also offered protection against alliances, and punishment for the recent Jewish persecution.[156] Charles practically elevated Erfurt into an imperial city.[157] The death of the archbishop of Mainz brought relief to Frederick III. On 3 January 1354 the Mainz staff made its peace with Gerlach, ending the schism.[158]

The dispute between Count Heinrich and the Wettiner over the dowry of Catherine was referred to earlier. After the death of Heinrich on 10 September 1347, Catherine's mother favored her son-in-law, Frederick III, in his claim to inheritance of the Coburg region. But upon the death of Jutta, Johann I (the mother's son-in-law) had made his own claim. Before the funeral took place, Frederick III rode on horseback to the court of Charles IV and obtained the Kaiser's approval.

In the final settlement, Frederick III received the Coburg and the river valley of the Itz; Eberhard of Württemberg was given the region around the Harz Mountains, stretching from Königshofen and Irmeishausen up to Münnerstadt and Schweinfurt; and the Burggraf of Nürnberg received the Werra valley from Eisfeld to Hildburghausen.

The second son, Balthasar, wisely married Margarethe, the daughter of the Nürnberg Burggraf. This brought the Wettiner additional lands in the Werra valley. Later, around 1400, these lands were expanded by purchases from Würzburg.[159]

At this time Thuringia entered the period known for the Vogtland Wars. Frederick and Balthasar realized that Charles IV was making moves in the Vogtland and Lausitz to expand the Luxembourger lands in Bohemia. He wanted to make Prague the pride of Europe. The Wettiner Mark Meissen was hemmed in on three sides, with only scattered islands of lands held as fiefs.[160] Charles had even succeeded in bringing Upper Lausitz into the Bohemian orbit.[161] Yet the Wettiner rulers maintained a solid front against partition of their lands.[162]

The Vögte on the Bohemian border had been robbing and killing merchants on highways. They even tried to create wedges of land between the Wettiner territories. The two brothers decided to bring these officials under control.[163] Charles IV agreed with Frederick III that the lords of Schönberg and Hassenstein should be humbled.

In the fifties, Charles IV and Frederick III started the War of the Nobles, in which the power of the Vögte in the Vogtland was completely broken. Afterward both Frederick III and the Kaiser treated them as mere vassals under their control.[164] They also had a natural opponent in the Burggraf of Nürnberg, whose lands formed a natural flank to the south. Charles IV made Nürnberg into his second capital, greatly beautifying it in the process.[165]

The reign of Frederick III and his brothers was almost an "unbroken chain of conquests and wars, often following one after another."[166] Balthasar joined King Edward II in his invasion of Normandy from Southampton.[167] There were also frequent feuds that needed to be stopped by the Wettiner. These were accentuated by the schism within the archbishopric of Mainz.[168]

In the year 1361, the Landgräfin Elizabeth (the grandmother of Frederick III) died, and the Markgraf had her buried in Eisenach, in the *Predigerkirche*, to which she had been liberal donor.[169]

After this the Wettiner lands in Thuringia were frequently invaded by Duke Albert II of Braunschweig. He caused much destruction and refused to listen to reason. Therefore Frederick III and his brothers raised an army of 18,000 men, supported by the archbishop and the leading cities.[170] When the powerful force began to take many strongholds and pillage the duke's lands, he agreed to the hearing of a neutral court. After this the landgrave and his supporters returned home.[171] The settlement gave the Landgraf new castles to guard and supply. But when Frederick sent needed supplies by wagon train, the duke's men captured them. This time the Landgraf's forceful reply was without mercy, and the defeated duke was forced to sign a lasting peace in Eisenach.[172]

A feud broke out between Count Johann II of Schwarzburg-Leuchtenberg and the bishop of Würzburg. Johann II fared poorly in the war and found many of his knights in stocks. In order to liberate them, Johann had to sell three of his castles to Erfurt, places vital to the merchants of the city for guarding the city's highways. Frederick III did not want the transaction to go through. Since they were royal fiefs, the sale required the approval of the emperor, who was in Prague. When Johann and the Erfurt delegation passed through Bavaria with their 9,000 Gulden, they were intercepted and their money confiscated. The Wittelsbacher duke then tried to have the emperor deny Erfurt the right to buy the *Reich's* castles, so that he could sell them to the Wettiner for the higher figure of 12,000 Gulden. The dispute ended with the Wettiner purchasing the castles, angering Erfurt.[173]

The cities had become worried after seeing the growth of the power of the nobility. On 15 February 1371, Erfurt entered a ten-year alliance with Nordhausen, Mühlhausen, and the four powerful counts of noble houses, under the pretense of preserving peace. But when the combined forces of the alliance attacked Hanstein in Eichsfeld, Otto the Square (German: *"der Quade"*) of Braunschweig came to its assistance. The alliance was outnumbered and suffered heavy losses. The final settlement involved fines so heavy that they terminated the league.[174]

In 1371, Landgraf Heinrich of Hesse died without male heirs, and his nephew Hermann assumed the reign. This was contested by Otto the Square, Hermann's cousin. Otto organized an army under the command of Hans von Heringen. Composed largely of outlaws, it began to pillage neighboring lands.[175] Hermann did not dare face the duke and his army alone, so he went to see Frederick III in Eisenach. They reminisced about Hesse and Thuringia in the Ludowinger days and pledged, in typical feudal fashion, that their two lands would once more be united. In this *Erbfolge* pledge they agreed that the lands of the one who died first would be taken over by the other.[176] When Duke Otto learned of the agreement, he attacked and leveled Transfeld. The combined forces of Hermann and Frederick III then attacked Herzberg, which was besieged by Balthasar's troops. Otto's army encountered heavy losses in this war, and broke up in 1375.[177]

The earlier engagement of young Wilhelm and Elizabeth, daughter of the Markgraf of Moravia, had brought the Kaiser Charles IV and the Wettiner closer, and he had invested them with Lower Lausitz. However, in 1363 Charles IV tried to get it back for Bohemia; a year later he succeeded, with the Wettiner receiving some compensation.[178] Later the Wettiner felt the same tension in the Vogtland. Frederick III continued to battle for control of the Vögte of Weida and Gera, but Charles IV finally took back the lands of Gera.

Even though Charles had created the new electoral college by means of his

Golden Bull of 1356, he began to worry about his successor. He was determined to have his son Wenzel made "King of the Romans" prior to his death. To this end Charles was concerned with who occupied the senior electoral position in the empire, the archbishopric of Mainz.[179] He began to make overtures to both the pope and the electoral college in an attempt to control the succession in Mainz. However, the previous archbishop had played a similar game and had pushed his own nephew as his successor.[180]

In the Middle Ages the youngest sons of the nobility usually entered the service of the church, where they often quickly rose through the ecclesiastical ranks. This was the case with Ludwig, the youngest brother of the Landgraf. By the age of sixteen he was already the bishop of Halberstadt. By 1373, Charles IV had advanced him to the rich bishopric of Bamberg, with its fine Romanesque cathedral. When Archbishop Gerlach died in 1371, the cathedral chapter of Mainz became divided over whom to chose, Adolf of Nassau or Kuno of Trier, while the pope wanted Johann of Strassburg. In this confused situation the Kaiser feared that his son Wenzel would not be chosen "King of the Romans." Therefore he made plans to fill the Mainz position with a different candidate whom he could control, young Ludwig, bishop of Bamberg.[181] In 1373 the Kaiser and Wenzel met with the three older brothers of Bishop Ludwig, and in that meeting he offered the Wettiner eight castles.[182]

Frederick III must have been surprised when, in the same year, the Kaiser purchased Blankenberg castle from Heinrich the Younger of Gera and added it to the crown of Bohemia.[183] But they met again and considered Bishop Ludwig's promotion to the archbishopric of Mainz. The appointment required papal approval, and the pontiff had his own purposes to consider. He had already decided to make Ludwig archbishop of Mainz at a later date.[184] Ludwig was sent to Avignon to obtain the pontiff's goodwill. But the pope had to deal with some complications before he could elevate the bishop of Bamberg. By the time he made his move in 1474, Adolf of Nassau had in the meantime been invested in the Mainz archbishopric by the cathedral chapter, the *castellans*, and the council of the Mainz *Stift*, and they refused to comply with the papal orders.[185] In fact, the new archbishop had become active in his office and had even leagued himself with the outlaw army of Otto of Brunswick-Göttingen, who was active in his cause.[186] Yet Charles IV was determined to have Adolf of Nassau replaced by Ludwig. The Kaiser now doubted that young Ludwig could swing Wenzel's election. Even though the archbishops of Cologne and Trier had shifted from Adolf, they were just as lukewarm toward Ludwig. However, Ludwig could still cast a vote, and for Charles that was all that mattered.

A conflict then began, centering around Thuringia and involving Erfurt, Nordhausen, Mühlhausen, and several noble houses.[187] The feud even split the Wettiner lands. The former participants in the Nobles War joined the fray, and archbishop Ludwig placed Erfurt under the ban. This caused its cathedral chapter, monks, and clergy to depart for six years, leaving the *Bürger* without religious services.[188]

The situation around Wenzel's election had become very complicated.[189] In

1375 much diplomatic maneuvering took place, with the different sides each trying to gain the advantage. Adolf of Nassau failed in his attempt to make a deal with Charles IV, and the Wettiner began attacking Erfurt's holdings with mercenaries. Adolf had a large army, which joined Erfurt's at Gebesee.[190]

Not far away, on the opposite side of the Unstrut river, Markgraf Balthasar lay encamped. He had learned much about the art of warfare from the English. He ordered a bridge to be erected across the river to surprise Adolf's army. But spies in Balthasar's army alerted Adolf's forces, causing Balthasar to delay his attack. In the morning the Erfurters and the archbishop's troops fled back to Erfurt, while Duke Otto the Square moved on toward Mühlberg. When the citizens of Gebesee saw the flight of Adolf's army, they gave a signal from the town towers and Balthasar crossed the Unstrut in hot pursuit. Part of Balthasar's army followed Duke Otto's men as far as Langensalza, but they slipped into Mühlhausen.[191]

Frederick III's army of 30,000 men then joined that of Balthasar, and the siege of Erfurt began with intensity. The large force was encamped outside Erfurt's walls. There was much foraging and destruction, and Erfurt's vineyards and fruit trees fell prey to the army. Then the Kaiser and his son Wenzel arrived with their Bohemian army. In the siege many soldiers died on both sides.[192]

Eventually Charles decided that he did not want to destroy the city completely. He wanted to save it for Wenzel's reign. Thus, to the great disappointment of Frederick III and his brothers, in 1375 the emperor withdrew his troops. This was soon followed by the armistice of Tonna.[193] The Wettiner felt that the Kaiser had let them down, and they signed a treaty with Bamberg and Würzburg. Pope Gregory IX was also disappointed, and he refused to accept the Tonna armistice. This placed Erfurt between the two rival archbishops of Mainz.

On 7 January 1376, no doubt to avoid more strife, the pope placed Erfurt directly under the chair of St. Peter. This action also removed its papal ban.[194] This action did not affect the Erfurters' choice, for in 1377 they stated that Erfurt would accept Ludwig as archbishop, provided the Mainz cathedral chapter nominated him. This was an impossible condition, and so their hostility continued. But the counts of Gleichen already supported the Wettiner attempt to make their brother the archbishop.[195]

Charles IV did not approve of the pope's action toward Erfurt, and he placed the city under a "double interdict," making it the worst type of outlaw.[196] In spite of papal coolness, the seven German electors, meeting in Frankfurt a.M., elected Wenzel "King of the Romans." Thus Charles IV accomplished his driving ambition. After the pope's death, his successor, Clement VII, also recognized Wenzel as king elect. But Charles IV had died in the meantime, on 29 November 1378.[197] Earlier that year, the two brothers had buried Ludwig after a tragic accident in which he fell from a stair during a fire at a *Fastnacht* dance. Thus Adolf of Nassau was firmly established as archbishop of Mainz.[198]

Although Frederick II had stipulated before his death that his oldest son, Frederick III, should be in control of Thuringia, Balthasar wanted a larger share in government. This led to tension between them, which their mother tried to control. On 3 July 1379, at Neustadt on the Orla, a first attempt at division of the Thuringian government was made. They agreed that Wilhelm I would be Markgraf, while Frederick and Balthasar would divide the Osterland and Thuringia between themselves. But the division was to be only territorial, and not in industry, courts, sovereignty, vassal servitude, and investiture, all of which the three would hold in common.[199]

When Frederick III died on 26 May 1381, he left three minor sons: Frederick IV, Wilhelm II, and Georg. The Orla agreement was no longer tenable, because by feudal law, Frederick III and Katherina's sons had rights of inheritance. Out of this situation came the 13 November 1382 *Chemnitz Teilung*.[200] In this settlement Katherina and her sons ably presented their rights, and the family divided the Wettiner lands in three ways. The aggressive Balthasar received Thuringia; Wilhelm I received Meissen, some of the Osterland, the Pleiszenland, and the Vogtland; and Katherina's sons received the lands in between. All officials, *castellans*, and cities did homage to the new sovereign. But in the mining town of Freiburg, which produced silver and coinage, they held their rights in common, managed by its courts. The control of officials was also a right held in common.[201]

The *Chemnitz Teilung* was not acceptable to Balthasar and Wilhelm I. In 1383 they began to talk about making changes. Balthasar met with Frederick IV and Wilhelm II to combine the Wettiner lands, but that proposal left Wilhelm I out of the picture. Then Wilhelm and Balthasar discussed another plan, which would combine Thuringia and Meissen and thus create a unity. This meant that the 1387 agreement would favor the uncles. But Katherina stood her ground, and in 1390 she insisted that the Chemnitz settlement remain intact.[202]

Thus the *Chemnitz Teilung* remained in force for two more decades, when the *Freiburger Vertrag* of 1404 named Frederick IV (Frederick the Valiant) and his brother Wilhelm II as the legitimate claimants of the future Wettiner lands. Frederick the Valiant was by then twenty-four years old. According to the *Freiburger Vertrag*, Thuringia, Meissen, and the Osterland formed a basic unity; but this agreement provided also for the Vogtland and the Coburg regions, as well as the lands in Hesse around Eschwege and Sontra. Thus this settlement allowed for a whole new grouping of the Wettiner lands. It even spelled out what would happen when Balthasar and Wilhelm II died, as well as if Frederick III's sons had no male heirs. The different rulers were to be mutually cooperative and assist one other, should the male descendants of different lines terminate. The agreement also provided for the welfare of the daughters of the lines. By means of the agreement of 1404, the Wettiner assured the unity of their lands after the death of the uncles.[203] Balthasar died in 1406, soon after the *Freiburger Vertrag*. In between he tried in every way to have his son made ruler of all Thuringia.[204]

During this period, landgraves and margraves began to assign important legal and political responsibilities to lower officials, often selected from among university-trained specialists.[205] This trend had begun in the late Ludowinger period, and did not yet involve a civil service, though some of the officials were of the *ministeriales* class from the cities.[206] In 1280, during the reign of the Wettiner, a new body of *consiliari* emerged, an advisory body that Albert the Depraved recruited from the Eisenach region.[207]

By the time of Frederick II and Frederick III, however, there were a number of officials with definite posts and duties. The court official was known as a Marschall; he managed fief regulations, traveled with the Landgraf, and paid his debts. Next in rank was the *Hofmeister*, who managed court life. He was held in high esteem because he held the ruler's official seal and managed the finances.

By the year 1250 a chancellory was beginning to emerge, which kept the official records that placed business on a more regulated basis.[208] Between 1250 and 1300, the rulers had a group of advisors, among whom was a *Hofmeister*, who had charge of the court, and a *Protonotar*, who supervised the chancellory. The *Protonotar* had two scribes under him and also a number of trusted knights in his service.[209] Frederick II had a rather defiant official named Albert Knute, a *ministeriales*-class type, who had defied the Landgraf. This had prompted Frederick to revert back to the nobility as advisors.[210]

Frederick III experimented somewhat with an advisory body, the "Secret Council," which was assigned specific responsibilities in the court system and with regard to finances. When Frederick III was a minor, his mother asked Marschall Timo to govern, with officials overseeing mining, coinage, tributes, and urban life. This meant that a new system was emerging, which in time would include a kind of civil service at the lower level of Wettiner rule. Thus Frederick III already had, in embryonic form, a top officialdom; the prince relied heavily on trusted officials and their records.[211]

Frederick III appointed an outstanding individual, Konrad von Kirchberg, to handle the Wettiner business transactions. He had studied law at Bologna, and for a while was the procurator of the empire. His goal was to create a more efficient record keeping system. Closely related to this was the work of Chancellor Heinrich von Kottwitz, who conducted the Landgraf's correspondence and prepared his financial reports. They kept running accounts of the Landgraf's business, and even made copies of the financial register. This office even prepared an important *Lehnbuch*, a record of all the fiefs, listing both incomes and expenditures.[212]

The Ludowinger and Wettiner had dotted their lands with castles that were about two days' ride apart. As dwellings they used the Wartburg, Weiszensee, and the Neuenburg. In the days of Ludwig the Leaper, the Wartburg was but a feudal fortress, but by the time of Ludwig V and Holy Elizabeth, it was more like an ornately decorated home. It remained that for the early Wettiner. Weiszensee, built by Jutta, Ludwig II's wife, had a large hall and was warmed by heated air. The Neuenburg, erected around 1200, with its square tower and double chapel, was the Ludowinger pride and joy. These castles were centers of pleasant relaxation for the princes' families. The Ludowinger also had castles in Hesse, but they preferred the Thuringian ones. In addition they had the

Klemme, a dwelling in Eisenach to keep the *Bürger* in check. Albert the Depraved had ordered it torn down, but Frederick I had it restored.[213]

Under Wettiner rule, Henry the Illustrious made the Wartburg the central attraction and symbol of his princely power. Albert and Frederick I made the Wartburg their residence for many years. In the Ludowinger days, the Wartburg lay right in the middle of their lands; but under the Wettiner its location was at the end of their lands. Frederick I died there, in 1324, as well as Frederick II, in 1349, and Balthasar in 1406. By the end of the fourteenth century the Wettiner seem to have made the Wartburg their permanent residence.[214]

Although most of the tax revenue was still paid in kind, by now the mining industry was in full bloom. The silver mines in Freiburg were a real source of income. Since the Wettiner lived luxuriously, during the fourteenth and fifteenth centuries they were often in debt. Balthasar was not satisfied with Freiburg silver income, but turned to Count Stolberg to mine in his lands. His *Münzmeister*, Nickel von Magdeburg, established the new mining system and fixed the price of silver. Then, with the guidance of Nickel, he expanded the mining to the Harz mountains. But the Harz mining proved to be less profitable, so Nickel had him shift to the Sangerhausen region. When Nickel died in 1401, Balthasar expressed his gratitude by providing his wife and children with a pension. After that, Gabriel von Magdeburg and Perter Hoeberg became his *Bergmeister*, or mining specialists. Count Stolberg and Balthasar decided to divide the mining gains evenly, while Sangerhausen was to receive a stipulated amount.[215]

Frederick IV and Wilhelm II also engaged in mining. In 1394 their *Münzmeister* was Kudenbier, and in 1403 this mint headquarters was consolidated with that in Jena. There was also some mining in the Coburg region, where Markgräfin Katherina, Frederick III's wife, had Friedrich von Owe as her mint master. In 1392 Landgraf Balthasar issued a mint directive, which was to regulate the weight and value of all Wettiner coinage. Patze claims that as a result of this standard regulation, all coins in the Wettiner lands were of equal value, both at home and for purposes of exchange.[216]

13

Frederick the Valiant
and His Successors

By the beginning of the fifteenth century, profound changes had come over the German *Reich*. The Holy Roman Empire had lost its glamour. The later emperors could not revitalize the medieval empire, for the papacy had sapped its vigor; the future now belonged to the territorial princes in their own lands. The lavish spending of the princes had impoverished the lower nobility and the Bauern in their regions. The emerging cities offered a haven for many fleeing from their lands, hoping to find a place for themselves amid the expanding urban economy. Through commerce and trade the *Bürger* had a distinct advantage over the rural population. They were able to create a new urban civilization of their own.[1]

During the *Kaiserzeit*, the *Reich*'s center of gravity had been in the Rhine valley; but by now it had shifted to the east, placing Saxony and Meissen in the middle of the empire. In the Bohemian Massive, the Przemysliden, Hapsburgs, and Luxembourgers had established a strong nation-state; on the northern plains, the Ascanier had accomplished the same thing in Mark Brandenburg. In the fifteenth century, the Hohenzollern began to lay the foundations for a future German empire. Between these lay Electoral Saxony, Thuringia, and Meissen, with their hopes of eastward expansion.[2]

During the fourteenth century, Charles IV had worked to build a powerful Slavic civilization in the east, with Poland and Hungary blocking most German colonization. In 1410, German knights suffered a major defeat at Tannenberg. The Polish leader Wladislaw Jaguello conquered the Litts, and Polish pressure was felt in the Elbe region and in the Sudetenland. Czech religious fervor and power caused the house of Wettin to be restrained in its actions toward its Slavic neighbors.[3]

Frederick III's brother Balthasar had a son named Frederick (Frederick the Peaceful), whom he tried to groom as the future Landgraf of Thuringia. This demanded a proper marriage. Patze reported to what lengths Balthasar went in

156

a search for a suitable wife. He approached the king of Bohemia, the Visconti of Milan, and even the papacy, but met with no success. His son then married the neighboring Anna von Schwarzburg, whose family had been a rival of the Wettiner for centuries.[4] In the Freiburger settlement of 1403, the sons of Frederick III forced Balthasar and his brother Wilhelm to recognize their rights.[5] But Balthasar was aggressive and wanted his son to attain knighthood. Rothe's chronicle relates that King Wenceslaus of Bohemia held a jousting tournament in the Prague *Tiergarten*, in which Frederick participated. He was then dubbed a knight.[6]

In the year 1406 landgrave Balthasar died, and his brother Wilhelm died the next year. By then Frederick the Valiant and Wilhelm II, the sons of Frederick III, were grown men in their thirties. They were no longer satisfied ruling over a narrow strip of land between Thuringia and Meissen.[7] But there would be much strife as they sought control over the Wettiner lands.[8]

Frederick the Peaceful's marriage to Anna of Schwarzburg did not work out well. His father-in-law, Count Gunther XXIX of Schwarzburg-Blankenberg, became very demanding, forcing Frederick to release several of his own lawyers and use some who were more amenable to the Schwarzburger wishes. Tile von Seebach therefore assumed control. Next the young Landgraf offered the count the Kyffhäuser mountain, with its *Burg*, as a fief. The two Markgrafen of the Osterland naturally watched these developments with concern.[9] The two lawyers who had been dismissed were very able, so Frederick the Valiant immediately made Apel Vitzthum his advisor. Wilhelm employed Busse as his director. Patze has noted that Apel Vitzthum succeeded in bringing many powerful vassals to Frederick's side. These became known as "the Lions," and they helped expel the Schwarzburger from the Wettiner Court.[10]

A brief review of the Wettiner in Meissen may be useful. Wilhelm I was the brother-in-law of King Wenceslaus of Bohemia. His ambitions centered more around Bohemia and Mark Brandenburg than in the west. He acquired some Bohemian fiefs that were scattered throughout his lands, and made travel somewhat safer by acquiring key locations. He also obtained Pirna, which pushed his Elbe possessions further to the south, even up to the Bohemian Mountains.[11]

Markgraf Wilhelm I also fared quite well with the church. In 1399 he succeeded in getting Pope Boniface IX to free the bishops of Meissen from outside control and establish four new bishoprics. The papal bull forbade the University of Prague from summoning citizens of Meissen, which meant that the land was practically exempt from religious control, except from Rome.[12]

The sons of Frederick III ruled in the Osterland from 1382 to 1410, about a quarter of a century. But they played lesser roles than their two uncles.[13] After the deaths of the uncles, the older Wettiner line surged forward under Frederick the Valiant, a development made possible by the Naumburg settlements of 1410 and 1415. In these Frederick was given rule over most of Meissen, while Wilhelm II ruled over the Osterland. Frederick the Valiant looked after the needs of the Wettiner lands and kept his eye on the future *Reich*. He was born on 11 April 1370, and while he and his brother were boys, their line was suppressed. But as they matured, the picture began to change and they gained respect in the *Reich*. In time Frederick became known as the "valiant warrior" who laid the foundations for the Saxon lands during the Reformation; he was able to combine the Wettiner lands with those of Electoral Saxony.[14]

In their younger days, in the Osterland, the two brothers had become involved in a conflict with the Schwarzburger family, which was trying to control the Saale valley. The brothers became aggressive opponents of the noble family and achieved some success. In 1380 Gunther XXVIII sold them Saalfeld, with the mortgaged castle of Leuchtenberg, and the town Kahla. However, Erfurt objected, and so did Balthasar and Johann II of Schwarzburg. Balthasar ordered the two brothers to leave Leuchtenberg, but they defied him, and Kahla remained with them. Then the Schwarzburgers besieged the Coburg and entered the Henneberger lands. The bishop of Würzburg became involved, and with the count of Henneberg he came to the support of the two Wettiner. Soon the Burggraf of Nürnberg and the bishop of Bamberg did the same, and they insisted on peace in the Frankenland. They declared the Schwarzburg siege of the Coburg to be outlawry. The two brothers also purchased Altenburg, and finally, in 1396, settled with Johann II of Schwarzburg the formerly contested Leuchtenberg, Kahla, Altenburg, and Saalfeld.[15] In the settlement of 1410, Frederick received most of Meissen, and his brother the Osterland. In the extreme east Frederick IV also acquired many cities and the contested Nürnberg lands, which previously had been mortgaged. Meissen remained the capital and Erbzelle the family burial place. Because of its mines Freiburg was, as in 1382, still to be owned jointly.[16]

The two brothers worked together to make the best of the Naumburg agreements. They even decided to give Leipzig a new image through a four-year plan of alterations. Wilhelm II had been assigned some of the land around the Coburg. Thus he established his residence in Altenburg. This arrangement continued until Wilhelm II's death in 1425, after which Frederick the Valiant took over his lands. This continued until 1445.[17] After the Naumburg agreement of 1410, all legal settlements and all mortgage settlements in the Wettiner lands were handled jointly by the three rulers. It was also agreed there were to be no territorial settlements with other lands and princes. If the Wettiner faced feuds, they would face the opposition together. In 1411, all three rulers signed a peace treaty involving the bishops of Bamberg, Würzburg, and the Burggraf of Nürnberg. They also signed a four-year peace agreement with Count Friedrich of Henneberg.[18]

Frederick the Valiant and his brother Wilhelm were distrustful of Frederick the Peaceful, due to his marriage to Anna von Schwarzburg. The two cousins were concerned about the dominance of the powerful Schwarzburger counts. The family also felt the Landgraf had married a woman unworthy of his rank.

Shortly after taking over the *Landgrafschaft*, young Frederick held court at Sangerhausen; his aggressive cousins took the opportunity to invade Thuringia up to Gotha. War seemed imminent, but the lawyers established the Peace of

Gotha, with terms so severe that they practically demanded a coup d'etat against Frederick the Peaceful. A new government was established under Frederick von Reichlingen, Burggraf Albrecht von Kirchberg, and Dietrich von Witzleben zum Wendelstein. Meanwhile Gunther von Schwarzburg, the previous governor, and Tile von Seebach had disappeared. The Vögte of Thuringia were also replaced by new ones who pledged allegiance to Frederick the Valiant and Wilhelm II. After this first shock, the young Landgraf realized he needed forceful allies. He then concluded a year's truce with Archbishop Johann II of Mainz and Landgraf Hermann II of Hesse, and later did the same with Erich of Braunschweig and with many endowed *Stifte*.[19] However, the young Landgraf was charged with violating the 1403 Freiburger Settlement. The two brothers also concluded a peace treaty with Rudolf III and Albrecht III of Saxony, and they were on good terms with the Burggrafen of Nürnberg.[20]

The lawyers Vitzthum and Busse, who had been re-employed by the two brothers, later returned to the Schwarzburgers. Stranger still, the three Schwarzburgers made an alliance with Frederick the Valiant, expecting in turn to receive Plauen as a fief. They also promised never to enter into a partnership with young Frederick and his heirs, and in the future to conduct state transactions only with the two brothers.[21]

Frederick and Wilhelm were suspicious of Schwarzburger motives, including those of the ecclesiastical member of the family, Günther of Magdeburg. The two brothers made him promise not to accept guardianship of any of Anna's children, nor to accept any Wettiner lands. All this no doubt frightened Frederick the Peaceful, who now turned for assistance to Erfurt, Mühlhausen, and Nordhausen. He also had his misgivings about Landgraf Hermann of Hesse, because of the Wettiner acquisitions of Eschwege and Sontra. To protect his western flank, therefore, in 1410 he formed a defensive alliance with Archbishop Johann of Mainz. That year the three Wettiner signed a peace treaty in Franconia. But to control the Schwarzburgers, the two brothers also formed an alliance with Markgraf Otto of Brandenburg, the counts of Boyneburg, and the city of Mühlberg. The brothers suspected that the Schwarzburger family was attempting to separate Landgraf Frederick from his cousins.[22]

Amid such bewildering transactions, it is clear that the Naumburg Settlement of 1410 was far from satisfying to anyone. It had divided the Wettiner lands, making government difficult. Things improved somewhat when Wilhelm II died in 1425, without heirs, and his brother could take over his lands.

Frederick the Valiant lived in a period in which several far-reaching events occurred that set the stage for the origin of the Saxon lands of the German Reformation. The first event was the mock trial and burning of the Prague Professor Jan Hus at the Council of Constance in 1414–1418. This so enraged his followers that it resulted in the fierce Hussite wars. The second event was the Schweinitz tower collapse in 1419 that killed the electoral family of the Ascanier. Finally, in 1422, the next ruler and his wife were killed by a fire at their hunting lodge in the Lochauer Heide. This event terminated the line of the Saxon-Wittenberg rulers. The extinction of the male line of the Ascanier prompted Emperor Sigismund to award Frederick the Valiant the rule of Electoral Saxony, because of the role he had played in the Hussite wars.

Jan Hus was born in 1369 and entered the priesthood at the turn of the century. As a Czech patriot and a zealous reformer, he delivered powerful sermons in the University of Prague, which were as appealing as they were merciless in their attacks on abuses in the church. Hus was soon excommunicated by the archbishop. Prague, founded by Charles IV, was one of the oldest of the German universities. Modeled after the University of Paris, it had four "nations," three of them German and one Czech. King Wenceslaus offended the German nations by giving the Czech nation equal power. The German nations subsequently left Prague, and in 1409 founded the University of Leipzig, in Meissen.[23] Prague had now become a Czech University, and it elected Hus as rector.

When Pope John XXIII sent indulgence agents to Bohemia to raise money for a crusade and Hus opposed them, the pontiff excommunicated him. Hus then retired for two years to complete his book on the church, *de Ecclesia*, which further offended Rome.[24]

When the Council of Constance was announced, Hus regarded it as an opportunity to vindicate himself. Emperor Sigismund even gave him a safe-conduct. However, upon his arrival he met with much hostility. He was soon arrested and incarcerated in a small tower next to the headquarters building. In time there was a mock trial, and in July 1415 he was burned just outside the city. (A year later the same fate would befall Jerome of Prague.) When the news reached Bohemia it stirred up a storm of hatred.[25]

According to Kötzschke, even before Hus's death the Czechs had sent a delegation to Frederick the Valiant, carrying their "Articles of Faith" and asking for his support in their battles.[26] But Frederick, who was at Constance, refused to help. He even agreed to assist Sigismund in stamping out the Bohemian heresy.[27] Later, in the Battle of Prague, Frederick fought valiantly against the Hussites. For this Sigismund rewarded him with some Bohemian fiefs.[28]

After Hus's death, his followers entered battles with fierce religious zeal, unmatched by the armies of the *Reich*. The Hussites were divided into two types, with the more intellectual group called the *Utraquists* or *Calixtines*, the latter name referring to communion in both kinds. The second type was led by a priest named Prokop, who came from Tabor, for which they were called *Taborites*. Prokop's army was a conglomeration of various kinds of people and lacked specific goals. In warfare the Hussites used advanced methods, fighting from behind encircled wagons so as to make it difficult to reach them with the cavalry charges common in the period. They would use poles with hooks to jerk knights from their horses. Then they would emerge from behind their wagon rings and battle the enemy hand-to-hand. No freshly recruited army could face such fierce fighters in a battle.[29]

Even though a crusade was preached against the Hussites, the emperor was unable to engage them. Frederick the Valiant had learned of the situation early on, but was elsewhere in the *Reich's* service when the situation became serious.[30] The first alarm about the Hussites was sounded in 1420. In the early twenties the three archbishops became concerned, and they joined the three Wettiner rulers in a peace pact against the enemies of the faith.[31] In 1422 Emperor Sigismund became somewhat interested in the threat, but not enough to recognize the dangers involved. He passed a warning on to Erfurt and Mühlhausen, who were still not much concerned. But when the news spread that Aussig and Brüx were being besieged, an uneasiness spread throughout Thuringia. By the time of the Naumburg Agreement of 1410, the Landgraf was obligated to come to their defense.[32]

Just what it was that Frederick the Valiant did in the Hussite wars to so impress the emperor remains unclear. Böttiger claims Frederick fought effectively against General Ziska and was assigned the responsibility of suppressing the entire Hussite movement.[33] Since the emperor also faced the Hungarian problem, he may have used him there.[34]

When the Saxon-Wittenberg line of the Ascanier came to a sudden end, there were a number of claimants who coveted the opportunity of becoming members of the electoral college of the German *Reich*. But the prize was awarded to Frederick the Valiant. Undoubtedly the emperor had considered many factors, including Frederick's service against the Hussites; but he may also have realized that a union of Electoral Saxony with Thuringia and Meissen would create, in the area northwest of Bohemia, a powerful bastion against the Hussites. For his part, Frederick did not spare any effort to achieve this end, for he sent his able lawyer, Apel Vitzthum, to Hungary to plead his cause. There may also have been some palm-greasing. On 6 January 1423, a letter of investiture was sent to Frederick's court, granting a *Privilegium de non evocando*, that henceforth the subjects of Electoral Saxony and Meissen were immune from any outside court summons. The letter also informed Frederick IV that he was being elevated to the elite circle of the seven German electors, who were privileged to use the "red wax" of the *Reich* on all official documents. The document also reiterated the Golden Bull privileges, namely, serving as *Erzmarschall* of the *Reich* and as *Reichsvikar* during an *interregnum*.[35]

A short time later the imperial judge, Count Johann von Lupfen, came to the Saxon lands to conduct Frederick into the office of elector of Saxony, which included rule over the Saxon *Ritterschaft* and the towns of the *Kurkreis*. As he had done earlier, the ruler of the Saxon-Lauenburg line tried to challenge this by means of a forged document, but he got nowhere with the *Reich's* officials. Finally, on 1 August 1425, Frederick the Valiant was ceremoniously conducted into the electoral college. Emperor Sigismund invested Frederick with the electorate, the *Pfalzgrafschaft* of Sachsen-Allstedt, the *Grafschaft* of Brehna, and the *Burggrafschaft* of Magdeburg. Since Wilhelm II died the same year, the new elector also took over his lands. Now only Thuringia remained outside Frederick's domain.[36]

After the *Utraquist* leader, Ziska, was killed in 1424, Prokop took over the entire command of the Hussites. The peasant-dominated Bohemian armies were now less doctrinal and more radical. For the most part they were disgruntled masses without specific objectives.[37] After the Germans had lost more than 4,000 men in various battles, they realized the Hussites needed to be taken more seriously. The new elector emphasized this at a Nürnberg meeting that the emperor failed to attend, but the papal envoy was deeply concerned.[38]

Rothe's chronicle gives us the best account of the Battle of Aussig, which took place the following year.[39] In 1426, while Frederick was preoccupied elsewhere, the elector's wife Katharina and the Landgräfin Anna of Thuringia recruited a large army and chose Ernst von Gleichen as commander.[40] This army included many volunteers, nobles, counts, and distinguished knights. With forced marches it then traveled to relieve Aussig. They arrived exhausted, hungry, and hardly ready for battle.[41] Prokop moved his forces to higher ground and chained the Hussite wagons together in the usual ring formation to stop the cavalry charges. Since this was something new to Count von Gleichen, his forces approached the wagon ring cautiously. But as they got closer, the Hussites opened fire on them point-blank. When some of the braver knights approached the wagon ring, they were pulled off their horses and beaten to death on the ground. Soon there was a cloud of dust and much confusion, making it difficult to distinguish friend from foe. Many died in the ensuing battle. Count von Gleichen was stabbed and slain on the ground. The same fate befell his cousin Frederick. At the end of the battle, twelve counts lay on the ground, along with hundreds of knights and *Bürger* from Wettiner and Saxon cities.[42] When the German troops saw this bloodbath, they fled, with the enemy in hot pursuit.[43] Böttiger estimates that some 12,000 Germans and 3,000 Hussites died. After such slaughter the Kaiser wisely refrained from other battles in Bohemia. But the following year Elector Frederick returned from other service to the *Reich* and decided to recruit a new army to attack Miez in Bohemia. However, the Germans had become so frightened of the "black Hussites" that his troops fled in the face of the enemy. The casualties were estimated at 10,000. Not long afterward, on 6 January 1428, Frederick the Valiant died and was buried in the "Princely Chapel" of the Meissen cathedral.[44] The elector and Katharina had four sons, the oldest of whom became known as "Frederick the Gentle." On his deathbed the father had summoned Frederick and Wilhelm, giving them his blessing as well as instructions on governing the Wettiner lands. The elector asked that the oldest son take over the *Kurkreis*, though he was only fourteen, and that the rest of the lands be ruled jointly.[45] Only the two oldest actually became involved in governing, for Heinrich died as a boy in 1435 and Sigismund joined the ranks of the clergy. It is said that he fell in love with a nun in Weida.[46] Like Peter Abelard, he could not marry her, so he lived with her while continuing as a secular priest. Later he was arrested and locked up for the rest of his life.[47]

In the year of Frederick the Valiant's death, the Hussites broke into Lausitz, Silesia, and Austria, while Sigismund was busy with the Turks in Hungary and could do nothing to stop them. The following year Prokop's forces invaded Meissen and carried their destruction to Scharfenberg.[48] They besieged Dresden in 1430, burning the old city to the ground, and then traveled up the Elbe to Magdeburg.[49] Later came the siege of Magdeburg itself, which the young Elector Frederick II had reinforced with thousands of knights. A ferocious gun battle followed;[50] some Hussites hid in a bathhouse, which the German commander set on fire.[51] The Hussites then moved northward up the Elbe, plundering some 400 towns and 1400 villages and filling 300 wagons with their stolen loot.[52] Then came an attack on Grimma on the Mulde.

Eventually an army belonging to Archbishop Günter of Magdeburg arrived, recruited from Saxony, Thuringia, Meissen, and many other places. This large force moved to relieve Grimma, but the raw recruits were not ready for Prokop's professionals. The fight was disastrous for the knights on horseback, and those in the rear of the army fled. The victorious Hussites now feared no German force, and moved on to Altenburg. The defenders of the town fought bravely as their city went up in flames. The Hussite army then moved into the Vogtland and Bavaria, almost to Regensburg.[53] But by then Prokop had lost too many troops, and large-scale invasion stopped.[54]

After many defeats, Emperor Sigismund also became more tolerant toward the Bohemian heresy. When, in 1431, Pope Eugene IV summoned the Council of Basel, the Bohemians were invited to present their demands. Afterward the council concluded that the *Calixtines* were not as heretical as had been pictured. Later, in the Prague Compact of 1433, Rome drew up acceptable terms with the more moderate Hussites.[55]

Later on, strife between the *Utraquists* and the *Taborites* resulted in open warfare; in this the Catholics of Bohemia supported the *Calixtines*. At Lipan in 1334, Prokop was killed, after which his followers ceased to be a threat. In 1436 an independent Hussite church was created, the "New Unity of the Brotherhood." Thus the terrible Hussite wars ended.[56]

When Frederick the Valiant died, the Wettiner lands were deeply in debt.[57] The sons, Elector Frederick II and Wilhelm, ruled jointly for five years. But this joint rule did not apply to the territory of Electoral Saxony, which always passed to the oldest son. To establish friendly relations with Landgrave Ludwig of Hesse, the rulers renewed the Thuringian-Hessian inheritance agreement. The territories also agreed to open their cities and castles to one another, except for the *Kurkreis*, which did not allow such relations with the rest of the *Reich*. At a meeting in Rothenburg, Anna, the daughter of Elector Frederick, was engaged to Ludwig of Hesse.[58]

Frederick's sons also tried to improve their relationship with Mark Brandenburg. On 5 January 1435, Frederick II and his brother signed an inheritance agreement with Elector Johann the Alchemist, just in case the Wettiner line should die out.[59]

On 7 May 1440, Landgrave Frederick of Thuringia died childless. Frederick II and Wilhelm had prepared for this in a Coburg Agreement that provided for the union of Thuringia and Meissen.[60] But that agreement did not work well because of the differences between them. Wilhelm could not tolerate the fact that his older brother was the elector of Saxony. The Golden Bull stipulated that the older boy should divide the lands, and then the younger should select what he desired. But Wilhelm's lawyer attempted to reverse this method, and even tried to divide Electoral Saxony—an open violation of the Golden Bull. This was an impossible proposal, since the *Reich* had but seven electors.[61]

During their joint rule after 1440, Wilhelm III was Landgraf of Thuringia and the Frankish lands, while Elector Frederick II kept the *Kurkreis* and the eastern part of Meissen, to Altenburg and the Zwickau region.[62] In the meantime, Frederick strengthened his relations with the crown and supported Kaiser Albert II of Austria, but he soon died in a war with Hungary. The next king was Frederick III of Austria, whom the elector also supported. Relations became even closer when Frederick married Frederick III's sister, Margaret. The elector was also on friendly terms with the papacy, and, in 1444, Pope Felix V offered Frederick control over the cathedrals of Naumburg, Merseburg, and Meissen, including the power to appoint their bishops. But Pope Eugene IV tried to undo these privileges.[63]

Frederick II made some important changes in the field of government. Burggraf Henry II had been slain on the Aussig battlefield in 1426, a significant event for Mark Meissen. The position had once been important, but what about now? The Burggrafen had been vassals of the Markgrafen, but the Burggrafen often claimed they held their privileges directly under the *Reich*. During the Hussite wars, this *Burggrafschaft* was given to Count Heinrich von Plauen, one of the Meissen Vögte. This created a new line of Burggrafen. But in the settlement of 1428, the *Burggrafschaft* was given to the Markgraf of Meissen. Later Vögte were to accept it as a fief of the Wettiner.[64] Heinrich von Plauen complained in 1435, insisting on the restoration of his position directly under the Markgraf.[65]

Apel von Vitzthum did everything he could to get Wilhelm to oppose his brother. Frederick II did not like the first Wettiner division, and the estates were to work out a better plan. This plan was issued under the Halle *Machtspruch* of 11 December 1445. Even in this the old lawyer succeeded in having changes made.[66] Apel even attempted to bring King Ladislav of Bohemia, Wilhelm's brother-in-law, into the Saxon line of succession. All this would eventually result in a civil war in the Saxon lands.[67]

Meanwhile, after the death of Landgrave Frederick of Thuringia, Wilhelm had spent two years in the service of King Albert, the new "King of the Romans." He was also interested in Albert's daughter, Anna of Austria. After King Albert died in the Hungarian War, the romance continued. When Kaiser Frederick III came to Frankfurt a.M., he confirmed the engagement between the two.[68] Anna's dowry was to be Luxembourg and a *Grafschaft*, but Philip the Good, of Brabant, refused to go along. The impetuous Wilhelm then sent troops to occupy Luxembourg, but Philip stopped him and Wilhelm remained empty-handed and deeply in debt.[69]

There were two meetings to resolve the division of the Saxon lands, held at Rochlitz and Altenburg. Meanwhile Wilhelm's lawyers maneuvered behind the scenes. The first plan was to give Wilhelm Thuringia and the Frankenland, while the elector would have the *Kurkreis* and Meissen. But where would the boundaries be drawn? Wilhelm presented this plan to the elector for his approval on

10 September 1445. But he attempted to intimidate Frederick by arriving with an army, led by many nobles. The elector called his bluff. He appeared in Leipzig and told the citizens that he was choosing that area for the Wettiner partition, a region that the Vitzthum lawyers wanted. Wilhelm looked for ways to get around this, and the Meissen estates actively worked to preserve peace.[70]

On 11 December 1445, the three supreme judges met in the cloister of Neumark to discuss the whole matter. They then recommended that the elector have the *Kurkreis* and the eastern regions of the Wettiner lands of Meissen, and also Altenburg, Burgau, and Zwickau.[71] Frederick did not like the plan, because it would give Wilhelm exactly what his lawyers wanted. The proposal also stated that if Frederick II's line died out, the electorate would pass to Wilhelm and then to his descendants. Frederick was bitter about this, and war looked inevitable.

Wilhelm now thought that he had things his way, so he married Anna of Austria. The wedding at Jena was a big affair, with about 4,000 guests. But the elector stayed away, and instead invaded the Vitzthum lawyer's own property. The news reached Jena in the middle of the banquet, which ended abruptly as Wilhelm rushed to save Eiszenfels. The elector withdrew his troops, but the matter was not forgotten.[72]

Gradually the Thuringian nobility were won over to the elector's side. Frederick accused the lawyers of having enriched themselves at Wilhelm's expense, and said that peace was not possible until they were banished. However, by this time the bitterness between the two brothers was so great that war could not be avoided.[73]

The elector now made the necessary preparations, and even hired Bohemian mercenaries. With Altenburg as a base, his troops burned the regions of Naumburg and the lower Roszla, where Apel Vitzthum's lands were located. On 7 December 1446, Frederick exacted an oath from the leading bishops of Meissen, the archbishop of Magdeburg, and the counts and lords of Stolberg, Mansfeld, Honstein, Querfurt, Tautenburg, Bunau, and Witzleben, that they would oppose Wilhelm and his lawyers. But the forces of the bishop of Naumburg were met with a defeat by Wilhelm's forces in January 1447, and the war spread into the Saale region.[74] There were a number of meetings in 1447 where attempts were made to restore peace, but these failed.[75] To recruit Bohemians troops for himself, Wilhelm mortgaged six Wettiner towns.[76]

Meanwhile, Archbishop Dietrich II of Cologne got into a feud with the city of Soest and asked the elector for troops. When the request was denied by the elector, Wilhelm and Apel agreed to the use of their mercenaries. On 22 May 1447 the two agreed to furnish 12,000 men for the siege of Soest. They failed, and Wilhelm had to send his Bohemian troops home.[77] So far Apel's lands had suffered little, but the astute lawyer felt he was in for trouble, so he worked out a deal with Wilhelm to trade his lands in Thuringia for some in Franken.[78] He made an arrangement to exchange his Roszla estate, Silsa, and 42,000 Gulden for the Frankenland, but the Kaiser later refused to give his approval to such a ridiculous trade.[79]

As if the Brothers' War was not enough, a "House War" broke out between the families of the Schwarzburger, which in time also involved Frederick II. Apel Vitzthum also had a hand in this feud. The fight dragged on until 1450.[80]

The Brothers War began to spread to the east, where the elector had hoped to acquire the Lausitz region, which had once been Wettiner territory but was now a part of Bohemia. Wilhelm realized that the elector of Mark Brandenburg had similar ambitions, so he set out to spoil his brother's plans by getting together with the Brandenburg ruler and making a deal with the Bohemian King, Georg Podiebrad. Amid this maneuvering the city of Erfurt came to Frederick II's support.[81] To get even, Wilhelm then devastated Erfurt's *hinterland*. The elector's attempt to capture the castle Kettenburg failed.[82] When Frederick learned that the margrave of Brandenburg had invaded Lausitz, he withdrew his troops to Leipzig. Much maneuvering followed, but on 15 October 1450, Gera, which had been defended by Frederick II's forces, fell and many were captured.[83] A number of the elector's able knights also went into captivity.[84]

In 1451 conditions improved somewhat, for the troublemaking Apel von Vitzthum had left Germany for papal service. Now Elector Frederick, Wilhelm III, and many ranking clergy attempted to establish peace in the Wettiner lands. While Apel was away, the elector and officials in Erfurt discovered and exposed a plan by the Vitzthumer that eventually resulted in his exile.[85] Duke Wilhelm accidentally captured a man who had been a spy for Apel. After torture on the rack, he revealed how Apel had never been true to the landgrave and had double-crossed him in order to conclude other deals. He revealed that behind the "Soester feud" of the archbishop of Cologne was a plot to get Wilhelm III killed and then bring Thuringia into a secret union.[86]

Angered by this, Wilhelm demanded the restoration of the Wettiner lands. When Bernhard Vitzthum tried to transport some troops, a feud broke out between the landgrave's troops and the lawyers and guards. Wilhelm then had Bernhard and the others locked up. Later he offered them safe-conduct abroad.[87] The landgrave then appeared before the Erfurt city council, admitting that he had been completely duped by his lawyers. They agreed to assist him in regaining his losses. Erfurt troops besieged and captured Apel's Wachenhausen castle, and Wilhelm began a siege of Kapellendorf. Count Adolf von Gleichen fought until its capitulation, and later took Dornburg castle with the assistance of the *Reich*'s cities. Others that were captured included Gleiszberg, Isserstedt, and lesser fortresses, leaving the Vitzthum family defenseless. They fled to Bohemia,[88] and as far as the house of Wettin was concerned, they were out of the picture until the reign of Ernest and Albert.

A peace settlement was concluded between the two brothers on 27 January 1451, which left the land divisions unchanged.[89] Among the German knights who had been captured at Gera was Kunz von Kauffungen, formerly a ranking official of the court of Frederick at Altenburg. This knight demanded reparations from the elector for his losses. He had an estate at Schweikershein, which, in the peace settlement, had gone to the Vitzthumer. The elector offered him an estate at Milowitz, but it failed to satisfy him. In a trial in the royal court he charged the elector with unfair treatment and also questioned the court's procedure. The angry Kunz then tried to even the score by hiring an assassin, but his plan failed. He resolved to capture the elector's two sons, Ernst and Albrecht, ages twelve and fourteen, and force the prince's hand. Another disgruntled knight, Moses von Schönfeld, agreed to join him. So they waited for favorable circumstances.[90] Kunz developed his plot along with others in Bohemia. Some claim that Apel von Vitzthum masterminded the whole thing. In the Altenburg castle, where the boys were living, a cook named Hans Schalbe became an accomplice. She provided detailed information on means of entry, the location of the boys' bedroom, and the elector's travels. The kidnappers are said to have hidden in the nearby, empty Kohren castle. Then, on the night of 7 July 1455, Kunz and his assistants entered the elector's castle through an upper window. They tied up and gagged an elderly guard. Kunz then took the younger Albrecht and fled south toward Bohemia, while Moses and Schönfeld took Ernst toward Bohemia via Zwickau. The plan was that if either fleeing party were captured, the other would still be able to demand a ransom. The boys' mother sounded the alarm, and soon a posse from Altenburg was in pursuit.

The two groups of kidnappers were without food. When Kunz arrived in Elsterstein, near the Bohemian border, the frightened young Albrecht was very weak. Nearby they saw a strawberry patch, and Kunz told the boy to pick some berries and eat some. But not far away was a group of workers. When the young prince saw them, he ran to the foreman and told him about the kidnapping. When the group approached the sleeping Kunz, he became tangled in his own spurs, fell, and was captured. They turned him over to the troops of the abbot of Grunheim, who took the knight and returned the elector's son to Altenburg.

When Moses and Schönfeld arrived in Stein near Bohemia with Prince Ernst, they were surprised to find that the people were all excited about the kidnapping and fate of the boys. They hid in nearby "Devil's Hole," and soon learned of Kunz's fate. They agreed to turn over Prince Ernst and not kill him, provided that they were not charged with their crime. Count Frederick von Schönberg, the ruler there, accepted the terms, and Ernst, who would become the father of Frederick the Wise, returned to Altenburg unharmed. On 14 July 1451, Kunz was publicly executed in the Freiburg marketplace, and his other accomplices were quartered.[91]

In 1459 Archbishop Dieter of Mainz died, and his successor's election resulted in another schism that enmeshed Erfurt and the Wettiner. The humanistic pope at the time was Aeneas Silvius Piccolomini, who had assumed the papal throne as Pius II. Pope Pius was a crafty schemer. For the Mainz archbishopric he proposed Dieter von Isen-Büdingen, but his military action in the Rhine valley made Dieter the superior of Erfurt as well. In 1462, Dieter's rival Adolf of Nassau tried to control the territorial changes, which also involved the *Landgraf*. Amid much opposition, Adolf stepped down. In 1464, Pope Pius II died, and the year after that Adolf of Nassau, but Erfurt still had tension with Dieter. Then Erfurt was practically destroyed by a large fire that Apel von

Vitzthum and some nobles had hired a monk to start. The fire resulted in a tremendous loss of property and the city's decline in stature.[92]

The loss in Erfurt did not stop Archbishop Dieter from opposing the Wettiner, playing the two branches against each other. He turned from Wilhelm III and offered protective rights to Elector Ernst of Saxony, and made Ernst's brother Albert *provisor* over Erfurt and Eichsfeld. He also promised the electoral succession to members of Albert's family. Erfurt did not want the bishop to acquire that much control, and objected to the Wettiner as *provisor* over their city. It erected a castle within its walls to prohibit Dieter's entry. The archbishop then closed all of Erfurt's trade routes. The city did not resort to force, but sent its town recorder, Dr. Hermann Steinbeck, to Rome. A direct attack on Mainz was impossible due to a lack of troops. But then in May 1482, Dieter died, shortly before the death of the Landgraf himself, who had no male heirs. Thus the two brothers, Albrecht and Elector Ernst, ruled jointly. After that the Mainz cathedral chapter made Duke Albert the administrator over Erfurt.[93]

The new relationship of Erfurt with Mainz under Duke Albert was redefined in an *Amerbach Agreement* and the *Concordia Alberti* of Weimar, which made Albert the protector of Erfurt's rights. For these rights the Erfurt *Bürger* paid 1500 Gulden a year, a large sum for the time.[94]

When the Brothers' War ended and peace was established in 1451, efforts were made to improve relationships between the two houses. Elector Frederick II worked out an inheritance agreement between Saxony and Mark Brandenburg. Frederick wanted to expand toward the east into Lausitz, but failed because of Polish opposition. Yet he did acquire Liegnitz in 1451.[95]

When King Albert II of Bohemia and Hungary died without a male heir, the ever-ambitious Wilhelm III wanted to become the king of Bohemia so that he could outrank his older brother. He attempted an inheritance claim through Anna in 1457–1458, which was supported by some subjects but not by the Hussite Bohemian nobles. Instead, they chose Georg von Podiebrad of Poland. Strife broke out between Wilhelm III and Podiebrad, but Markgraf Achilles of Brandenburg-Ansbach restored peace between them. Later, Kaiser Frederick III also supported King Podiebrad. In April and May 1459, Saxony and Bohemia reestablished peaceful relations, and the elector's young son Albert was married to Podiebrad's daughter Zedena, while the king's son married Duke Wilhelm III's daughter. Now the king released his claims to lands north of the Elster river and the Erzgebirge, which were offered to Albert as a Bohemian fief, including Plauen, Olsnitz, and Colditz. The Wettiner returned Brüx, Duz, and the Riesenberg to Bohemia. Not everyone was happy with these changes, but they brought them closer to the German Kaiser and the now powerful Hapsburg family.

Elector Frederick and his Austrian wife Margaret had a very peaceful home life together. By contrast, after Wilhelm's interrupted wedding to Anna, he had an affair with a prostitute named Katherine. The duke locked his wife up in the Eckhardsburg castle while he visited his mistress secretly in Roszla. Anna died on 13 November 1462. The Landgraf then moved Katherine to Weimar, where they were married by the archbishop of Mainz. But he was soon to learn that she was not welcome there, for the public made degrading remarks about her.[96] At the end of his life, Wilhelm joined a religious order to make his peace with God. He died in a cloister in 1482, and Erfurt lost its most staunch defender against Mainz.[97]

After the death of Frederick II, his oldest son, Ernst, became the new elector of Saxony. Ernst had three sons, Frederick the Wise, John the Constant, and Ernst. Frederick II's second son, Albert, established the Albertine line, and his sons were Duke George and Duke Henry the Pious. In his last testament of 1447, Frederick II had stipulated that the Wettiner lands should never again be divided. But in 1459 he somewhat modified the testament, making Albert an advisor to his brother in the lands they ruled jointly. This opened the door to division. In 1465, Kaiser Frederick III invested the brothers with their respective rights: Ernst would be the elector of Saxony and the *Kurkreis*, the *Erzmarschall* of the *Reich*, and serve as the *Reichsvikar* during an *Interregnum*, as stipulated in the Golden Bull of 1356. The remainder of the Wettiner Lands were to be ruled jointly.[98]

The two brothers widened their lands in the east somewhat by purchasing Sagan from Silesia in 1472. They obtained the Bieberstein lands in 1477 and also acquired some Bohemian fiefs. For a while, Duke Albert was the administrator for Hungary in Lausitz and Silesia.

As their families grew, the two brothers agreed on separate households and two separate courts. Elector Ernst continued to reside in Dresden, while in 1482 Albert transferred his court to Torgau. But they learned that the distance between the courts made joint rule difficult. Since Ernst was the elector, Albert's role as joint ruler diminished. Accordingly, on 7 July 1484, they decided to terminate their joint rule for a decade. Meanwhile, Kaiser Frederick III employed Albert in his Turkish War with Hungary, for which he promised him lands in the Rhine region.[99]

On 4 July 1484, Hugold von Schleinitz, the elector's chief advisor, proposed to divide the lands in a manner consistent with the Golden Bull. The elector would do the dividing, while Albert would do the choosing. According to the German Constitution, the electoral circle was not subject to division, nor were the privileges that went with the electorate. According to the Schleinitz plan, the division was to be different from the customary one of Thuringia, Meissen, the Osterland, and Frankenland. Instead, the lands were to be divided according to their basic yields in income and defensibility. As in the past, mining regions were to be under joint rule, as was the bishopric of Meissen, due to its historic significance. According to Hugold's proposal, the recently acquired lands were to remain untouched. These were Sagan, Trebus, Naumburg, Sorau, Beskow, and Storkow.[100] For a proper division of the Wettiner lands, Elector Ernst employed professionally trained tax assessors. The drafting task took nine weeks.[101]

When Ernst's fiscal experts had completed the plan, it resulted in these statistics: the Osterland and Meissen had thirty-four cities, while the upper Thuringian lands had but twenty-two cities. In this northern Thuringian area, the plan included the feudal states of the lords of Stolberg, Honstein, Mansfeld, Arnstadt, and Beichlingen, as well as the lands of the counts of Schwarzburg. Below these regions lay Erfurt, with its neighboring territories under the archbishop of Mainz. In lower Thuringia, the region had seventy cities, as well as the Schwarzburger lands as Wettiner feudal fiefs. There were the cities of Schwarzburg, Arnstadt, Rudolstadt, Ilmenau, and the Leutenberg. Whoever received these regions would acquire strong vassals in Einsiedel, Brandenstein, Plantis, Bunau, Vitzthum, Wangerheim, and Metzsch. Whoever ruled Meissen would have to pay his brother 100,000 Gulden annually for four years. Conversely, the one who ruled Thuringia had to award the other with 75,000 Gulden. The elector had hoped that Albert would select Thuringia, as had previous Wettiner.[102]

When the two brothers met in the castle at Leipzig, Albert remarked that to thus divide the Wettiner lands would cause confusion and damage. But his choice surprised Ernst and his advisors, for he chose Meissen and Upper Thuringia.[103] This separated the *Kurkreis* from Lower Thuringia, and a border region between Upper Thuringia and Meissen had to be established where the brothers would rule jointly. A simplified explanation of the territorial distribution of the future Saxon lands might be the following: the new Saxon lands now formed the shape of the letter X, or, perhaps, a four-leaf clover. In a general way, Albertine Saxony extended from the Harz in the northwest to the Erzgebirge in the southeast; while, the lands of Ernst, or Ernestine Saxony, extended from the Kurkreis around Wittenberg in the northeast to lower Thuringia south of the Wartburg, and even to the castle Coburg to the southeast.[104]

This territorial arrangement of Ernestine and Albertine Saxony, established in the Leipzig settlement, was in force throughout Martin Luther's lifetime.

14

The Prosperous Reign
of Frederick the Wise

The two Wettiner families lived together harmoniously in Dresden for twenty-one years. Meanwhile, Ernst reared three sons: Frederick III, John, and Ernest. Frederick (who later became known as Frederick the Wise) and John continued the pattern of governing together, except for Electoral Saxony, which was known as the Ernestine lands. The youngest brother, Ernest, rose to become the archbishop of Magdeburg and the administrator of Halberstadt.

After the Leipzig Settlement of 1485, Duke Albert ruled his newly acquired lands as best he could, though he was quite active in the service of the empire. He reared two sons, George and Henry, both of whom were to have profound influence on the course of the German Reformation.

Blaschke offers an excellent analysis of this period.[1] In Luther's day, Saxony was still expanding, and such growth could only be at the expense of its neighbors. As noted earlier, the territorial lands had been greatly altered in the Leipzig Settlement. Ernest continued to rule the *Kurkreis*, the area encompassing Wittenberg and extending to the south of Torgau; the elector also obtained the Mulde region around Grimma, Leisnig, and Colditz, as well as the Thuringian lands between Eisenach and Altenburg. In addition, the Ernestine lands included the mountainous regions of Zwickau, the Schwarzberg, and the Vogtland. Erfurt remained under the sovereignty of the archbishop of Mainz, though Ernest's dominance still made itself felt.

Under the new arrangement, the territorial domains of Duke Albert covered the former Meissen, as far south as the *Erzgebirge* at Annaberg, and stretched from Leipzig through northern Thuringia, up to the Werra River. Travelers on the road from Dresden to Leipzig, following the Mulde, crossed the Ernestine lands to Döbeln; but as they continued westward they again reentered Albertine Saxony. This was to create many problems during the Reformation.[2]

It would be wrong to assume that, under Ernest and Albert, the Saxon lands formed a sovereign state as in later centuries. Within the Wettiner lands lay the bishoprics of Meissen, Merseburg, and Naumburg, which were in reality highly endowed territorial estates. In the largest and most independent of the three, the *Stift* of Meissen, resided the castle of Stolpen, and later, the new fortress at Wurzen. The bishop of Merseburg's domain extended up to the castle in Leipzig, while the domain of the Naumburg-Zeitz *Stiftsgebiet* was the weakest of the three.[3]

Independent nobles and powerful knights presented no end of problems for the Wettiner. For example, the lords of Reusz had at one time been important officials of the empire, known as *Reichsvögtei*. After 1356 they were forced to vacate the Voigtsberg, and in 1466 they lost Plauen; but these nobles still remained in command in the Schleiz, Greiz, Weida, and Gera regions. Still, the Wettiner had a degree of sovereignty over them. The lords of Schönberg also had a unique status; that family was in possession of a small territory in the region of Glauchau, Waldenburg, Lichtenstein, and Hartenstein, even including Geringswalde. These nobles ruled their villages and lands under Bohemian protection.

Even more unusual was the status of Wildenfels, located at the end of the Westergebirge. The counts of this small, almost forgotten region proudly sat next to the Frankish, Swabian, and Rhenish counts at *Reichstagen*. Since Upper Lausitz was under Bohemian sovereignty at this time, it was likewise independent of Wettiner control. Ernest and Albert did not welcome a clash with the powerful Hapsburger, so for the most part they left Lausitz to its independent way of life. Yet it was clear that, sooner or later, Saxon expansion would affect all these territories.[4]

Meanwhile, the sumptuous castle of Albrechtsburg was built in Dresden to accommodate both families.[5] To no small degree their amicable relationship must be credited to their mother, but, in addition, Ernest was the one who actually ruled the Wettiner lands, while Albert went on expeditions in all parts of Europe.[6] Later, they decided to separate their residences, with the former transferring his seat of government to Weimar, and the latter remaining in Dresden.

Ernest lived only one year after the Leipzig Settlement, while Albert remained active in affairs of the *Reich* until 1500. This meant that young Frederick the Wise ruled at home for fourteen years, while his uncle was acquiring a reputation as a commander over the armies of Emperor Frederick III. At the *Reichstag* in Nürnberg in 1487, the emperor had made Albert the commander of his forces fighting against Hungary, in which campaign the *Reichsheer* recaptured the city of Vienna.[7]

Later, when Emperor Maximilian I was captured at Bruges, in Flanders, Albert rushed there to liberate him. Maximilian was so grateful that he elevated Albert to *Statthalter* of the Netherlands in 1488. Later, Albert captured Brussels, Bruges, and Haarlem. In 1492, he also took Sluys, for which he was given the "Golden Fleece." The pope even offered him the "Golden Rose" as a comparable award. Finally, in 1494, Albert was made the governor of Friesland.[8] The father left his son, Duke George, in charge there. But George became endangered by an uprising, and Albert had to come to his rescue. With great difficulty, their forces captured the fortress of Gröningen. But the siege proved to be too severe for the aging father, who retired to Emden and died there on 12 September 1500.[9]

During George's childhood, the Wettiner family had become involved in a feud in Bohemia that involved the Hussites, the pope, and King Podiebrad. There was one point at which the Wettiner feared that they, too, might fall under the pontiff's interdict.[10] Duke Albert was married to Sidonia, daughter of King Podiebrad. At the time of her father's excommunication, she was only sixteen years old. Duke George's mother impressed upon him how tragic it had been for the family to have his grandfather saddled with an interdict. She even urged the boy to study for the priesthood. George was taught to regard the old Catholic practices as sacred, and was instilled with a great fear of the wrath of God. These formative experiences shed light on his later attitude toward Luther and the Reformation.[11]

Little is known about the youth of Frederick III. Most of what we possess as source material comes from the pen of Georg Spalatin.[12] Frederick was born in 1463, at Torgau in Schloss Hartenfels, one of Ernest's favorite residences. According to Kolde, the Augustinian convent in Grimma was at that time blossoming with fine educational possibilities.[13] Frederick and his two brothers were sent there to receive a good education under the guidance of Master Ulrich Kemmerlin. There he learned Latin and the fundamentals as taught in Latin schools of the day.[14] Frederick seems to have enjoyed his time there.[15] However, good Latin schools were quite rare, and it is doubtful that his education at Grimma compared favorably with that offered by schools such as the one Spalatin attended at St. Sebaldus in Nürnberg or the Latin school in Eisenach where Luther completed his preparatory work for later study at the University of Erfurt. Even so, Frederick and his younger brother John learned to read Latin, though they were unable to converse in it equally well. In 1521, when the elector was engaged in conversation with Erasmus at Cologne, he hesitated to answer the great Latin scholar directly, but instead used Spalatin as his interpreter. Frederick learned little French and no Italian. Yet he received a better education than did his father Ernest or his uncle Albert.[16]

When Frederick's father died in 1486, the new elector was only twenty-three years old. Though never quite as strong and robust as his uncle Albert, in his youth Frederick was not without vitality. He was ready to play the role of a knight, and loved to participate in tournaments. The Saxon prince enjoyed hunting throughout his many years. He seems also to have enjoyed shooting events. In 1493, at the age of twenty-nine, he went on a pilgrimage to the Holy Land; this appears to have been related to both his piety and his passion for collecting relics.

By nature Frederick was the type of prince who wanted to know and master things for himself. Often he remained silent, lost in reflection, before expressing himself. But once he had made up his mind, nothing could swerve him from that position. Frederick had a very strong sense of right and wrong. He relied

174 The Setting of the Reformation

heavily on trusted and faithful advisors such as Minkwitz, Planitz, and Feilitzsch to give him the facts, and then made his own decisions.[17]

When Frederick began his rule in 1486, his brother, John, was still a minor. Once John came of age, Frederick continued to rule the *Kurkreis* by himself, but in the rest of the lands the brothers ruled jointly. They remained very close. There can be no doubt that John often influenced the elector at critical moments. Later in life Frederick said that his brother was the only real friend he had.[18] John disapproved of Frederick's love affair with Anna Weller, who bore him two illegitimate sons, Bastel and Fritz. His younger brother, the archbishop of Magdeburg, urged him to marry, while many of Frederick's subjects believed there had been a secret marriage.[19]

In the days of Frederick the Wise, it was customary for princes and emperors to select maxims that befitted their life's goals. Emperor Maximilian, who so frequently overplayed his capabilities, had the motto, "Halt Mass," or "Keep yourself in check."[20] His successor, Charles V, pulled out all the stops, for on his sword and arm band, surrounded by the pillars of Hercules, was placed the motto, "Plus Ultra," or "Go beyond the ultimate."[21] In this regard Frederick was more realistic. He chose as his life's maxim, *"Tantum quantum possum,"* or, "Do all you can." In addition, his coins bore the letters CCSN, the initials for "The cross of Christ is our salvation."[22]

Frederick must have subjected his chancellery to many anxious moments, for he was very meticulous in drafting official papers, documents, and letters. Spalatin reported that the prince was extremely exacting as to the language used. Though he employed a large and able staff, it was often overworked. At times Frederick had a letter drafted and refined twenty times before it was acceptable to him.

The elector was said to have had friends in almost every court, and they tipped him off as to how the wind was blowing. He also possessed a strong sense of when the moment was ripe to act or speak up. Emperor Maximilian, his uncle with whom he frequently associated at imperial diets, found him difficult to analyze. Frederick often participated little in discussions, but when he did make a remark it was usually to the point. At a time when Erfurt was giving Frederick trouble, his advisors remarked that he would lose no more than five men if he were to put them in their place; the prince said that would be four too many.[23]

Frederick agreed that the *Reich* should be honored by its territorial states, but denied that the emperor should govern them as a sovereign ruler. He did not favor strengthening the emperor's powers, but wanted rather to increase the authority of the electors. He also wanted a *Reichsrat* to be established for supervising the Kaiser's activities and limiting his powers. To put the *Reich* on a firmer financial basis, Frederick favored the exaction of the "common penny" as a collective tax from the subjects of the German lands. That the *Reich* might deal adequately with larger political questions, the elector also favored the establishment of a supreme court, the *Reichskannergericht*. In addition, he supported the establishment of a national army.[24]

Frederick was convinced that the German *Reich* should be redivided into *Kreise* to facilitate more efficient supervision. This question was first discussed at the Diet of Augsburg in 1500, and was debated at later *Reichstagen* at Trier and Cologne; but the division of the German lands was not initiated until the Diet of Worms in 1521. This new division also reclassified the Wettiner lands. The Saxon lands were renamed Upper and Lower Saxony. The *Kurkreis* and Brandenburg were joined, constituting part of Upper Saxony, which also embraced the dukedom around Pomerania. The remainder of the Wettiner lands were designated as Lower Saxony, including the archbishopric of Magdeburg and Halle. Control of Erfurt shifted from Mainz to the Electorate of the Rhine. However, this territorial regrouping was not finalized until the Peace of Augsburg in 1555.[25]

When Electoral Saxony had passed to Frederick I, the country had been deeply involved in the Hussite wars. In return for the support of warrior knights and the *Bürger* of the larger cities, the elector had promised them greater participation in his government. Since the cost of the Hussite wars had been high, the elector became obligated to grant the estates further rights. In 1438, the first *Landtag* was summoned to meet at Leipzig. The estates of this first assembly represented the various classes of society: the counts and nobility, the clergy, the knights, and the *Bürger*.[26] This was followed by the division of the Wettiner lands in the Altenburg *Teilung*, which created chaos. Because of the confusion at the top, the estates were summoned again. They met at Leipzig in 1446, Grimma in 1451, and Leipzig again in 1454.[27]

The status of members of the Saxon *Landtag* varied greatly, but none of the classes was eager to become involved in the payment of regular taxes. The upper clergy, the nobility, and the *Bürger* regarded a regular system of taxation as too binding. The knights were divided on the tax issue. Knighthood possessed a special status in the land because of the requirements of constant readiness for battle and the possession of adequate weapons and a charger. The more independent nobles possessed their own lands, conducted their own courts, and maintained a local system of taxation paid mainly in kind. The knights also conducted their own "saddle courts" for minor offenses, but their status was different. They were regarded as "duty-bound freemen." Many cities were also represented in these estates through their city councils. The larger cities possessed their own courts, which included the right of taxation. During a war the townsmen were obligated to supply the prince with troops and wagons, as well as to render certain logistical services. Such cities often possessed a non-service status; some were known as *Amtstädten*, with implied duties, and others as *Adelsstädten*, those exempt from the usual requirements of service. Though the *Bauern* were the most numerous group, they were not yet represented.[28]

Even though the estates began to take a lively interest in the affairs of the land, the princes still maintained the reigns of government. In fact, the rulers' ability to govern had been greatly enhanced. They now employed trained lawyers, educated in the universities, who were quite familiar with current legal and business affairs. Many were skilled in coping with the newly evolving capitalism. Thus the princes came to depend on the *Bürger* of the professional class.[29]

In the days of Frederick III's father, the head of the elector's government had been Obermarschall Hugold von Scheinitz, an extremely capable official who was astute in managing both internal and external affairs of the state. Below him stood the chancellor, Johann von Morganthal, the official in charge of both the political as well as the jurisdictional activities of the land. This man also became somewhat involved in the management of financial affairs. The staff prepared a register and kept account books. In 1469 the two princes elevated Morganthal to the new position of *Land Rentmeister*, because silver mining had begun to boom in the *Erzgebirge* region. He was placed in charge of the Wettiner *Schatzkammer*, the princely treasury, to manage the mining operation. The new treasury included the Saxon coinage mint, which exacted a ten percent cut from the yield in mining for the Saxon princes.[30]

In 1478 another fiscal reorganization took place. The management of funds was now divided between two account offices. This resulted in a definite decline in efficiency. A decade later Jacob Blasbalg, an experienced banker of the merchant class, was placed in charge of the financial office. He managed the collection of the prince's tenth from mining, and also supervised Saxon silver exports. When he died in 1490, his relatives were asked to manage the office. His wife, Appollonia, was experienced in banking and continued the work of her husband. But she soon married George von Wiedebach, a banker from Leipzig, who then assumed the duties of *Rentmeister*.[31] Frederick's advisors were of two types: those who offered the elector advice in his private and religious life, and the court *Räte*, who advised him in the management of the affairs of state.[32]

The elector was a very conscientious Catholic. He attended mass every day, when possible, and used a Franciscan friar as his father confessor. During the early years of the Reformation this *Beichtvater* was Jacob Vogt. He served until his death in 1522, when Frederick selected a second Franciscan, named Johann. Another churchman and trusted friend was Johann von Staupitz, the vicar general of the Congregation of Observant Augustinian Hermits, who served him in a number of ways. Staupitz assisted the elector in his contacts with Rome at the time of his brother Ernest's appointment as archbishop of Magdeburg and administrator of Halberstadt; later he even helped the elector advance his brother for the position of archbishop of Mainz. When Frederick decided to found the University of Wittenberg in 1502, he called on Staupitz and his private physician, Polich von Mellerstadt, to serve as the key pillars.[33]

Georg Spalatin was engaged as tutor for the elector's nephew, John Frederick. He was soon to become indispensable to the court as the prince's private secretary, historian, and court preacher. Spalatin later became the elector's librarian, purchasing thousands of fine manuscripts and books for the University of Wittenberg.[34] It was also Spalatin who served as liaison between Luther and the elector.

The elector's advisors were, on the whole, able lawyers with university degrees. Several professors at Wittenberg stood ready to provide expert legal opinions in the form of *Gutachten*. Among them was Dr. Henning Göde of Havelsberg, a member of the law faculty and prior of the *Stift* of All Saints Church.[35] He had been in the elector's service since 1509. Göde opposed Luther's burning of the canon law and the papal bull *Exsurge Domine* at the Elster Gate in 1520.[36] Another legal professor of conservative leanings was Dr. Wolfgang Stähelin, whom Luther once called a "miserable, blind blockhead."[37] A third Wittenberg lawyer in the elector's service was Dr. Reiszenbush, who was sent on a mission to Rome in 1512. He supported Luther but did not profess it publicly.[38] In 1515 he gave up his professorship at Wittenberg to become preceptor of the *Antoniterhaus* of the monks at Lichtenberg, and later became the chancellor of the university.[39] Two other lawyers, Dr. Hieronymus Schurff, Luther's lawyer at Worms, and Dr. Christian Beyer, were frequently called upon for legal advice. The latter became part of the electoral court and served for a while as the prince's chancellor. Before that Dr. Beyer had also served several times as *Bürgermeister* of Wittenberg.[40] In this same category falls another lawyer, Dr. Gregor Brück.[41]

A number of Frederick's officials served him on missions at home and abroad, first and foremost Hans von Dolzig. He grew up in the region between Zwickau and the Schneeberg mines, entered Leipzig in 1491, went to Ingolstadt, and from there to Bologna in 1498; before long he was made rector and delivered lectures on legal subjects. At Bologna he received degrees in both civil and canon law. In 1501 he entered the elector's service, and by 1513 was elevated to *Oberhofmarschall*.[42] During the early days of the Reformation this able lawyer had a very strong influence in the court.[43] Other men in the field were Bernard von Hirschfeld, Hugo von Einsiedel, Count Philip von Sohms, and Degenhardt Pfeffinger.[44]

Due to mining, cloth production, and other economic expansion within Frederick III's lands, he became one of the wealthier princes of his day and the Saxon lands were greatly enhanced within the *Reich*.[45] This also made it possible for Frederick and Duke George to be leaders in architecture, art, and cultural advancement. They could jointly erect the Albrechtsburg in Dresden, and, later, Frederick could build the castle church in Wittenberg, even as he rebuilt and beautified the castle itself.[46]

Late in the fifteenth century, mining in the Saxon lands took a tremendous upward swing; in fact, it more than equaled agriculture in importance.[47] Of course, silver mining had been done around Freiburg for a long time. After the dangers of the Hussite wars subsided, prospectors began to search for new mines in the *Erzgebirge*.[48] During the rest of the century there was a tremendous expansion of silver output. A "silver rush" of people arrived soon after mining was extended into the eastern and western mountains of the Bohemian Massive.[49] The next important mineral discovery was tin, found in the mountains near Altenburg and Geising.[50] New iron mines were also established, and the discovery of the use of charcoal around 1515 provided new opportunities for capitalism.[51] In the Mansfeld and Sangerhausen regions there were also copper mines, which began to be prosperous; it was here that Luther's father moved as a young man to seek his fortune.[52]

In earlier days, when silver mining had principally been in the Freiburg region, it had been done primarily by assistants to the princes. But by the sixteenth century mining had advanced into big business. Miners employed better tools, dug deeper, and the output became much larger. Often the employers were not even miners, but businessmen who managed large corporations. In time, the corporations even began to sell shares in their mines, which were purchased mostly by rich *Bürger* from the larger cities. The nobility likewise became interested in mining in the *Erzgebirge*; bishops, abbots, monks, and even the elector invested in mining stock.[53]

Investors in Leipzig became tremendously wealthy and independent thanks to their role in the new capitalistic revolution. They even challenged Nürnberg in a business war in which they attempted to make themselves independent of the old Kaiser's city. Leipzig also leagued itself with the city of Frankfurt in gaining control of some of the cities of the old Hanseatic League. New monopolistic cartels were formed, involving the powerful Welser and Fugger families in Augsburg. In Zwickau the Welser set up a branch business on Silver Street, while in Leipzig both the Welser and Fugger houses established branch offices. Other firms came from the Rhine region and Franken to establish large operations in Leipzig. Book merchants and printers followed, with the first press being founded by 1481. In 1497 Leipzig was permitted by the Kaiser to begin its annual book *Messe*. After 1507 no other *Messe* was permitted within fifteen miles of Leipzig.[54]

Yet during Frederick's reign the mining prospectors and corporations were not entirely on their own; all mining was carefully supervised by the Saxon prince. The Wettiner had established their own regulations, through which mining was conducted jointly by the two Saxon lines. The digging, distribution, and selling of shares were carefully regulated by the rulers' officials. Special offices had been established to determine the princes' total profits. The rulers even controlled the formation of monopolies by regulating the mints and the flow of money to shareholders. Frederick III and Duke George were each paid one-fifth of the profits. Blaschke claims that between 1500 and 1540 the income from mining increased twelve times.[55] Most of the silver was converted into coins of varying sizes at their mints.[56] Thus there was a tendency toward coin debasement within the *Reich*. Speculation also entered the capitalistic market, in which nobles, *Bürger*, and lawyers often participated. Duke Albert is reported to have speculated in the silver market, in which he sometimes won but many times lost.[57]

Under the aegis of capitalism, textile production in Saxony had also swollen into a mighty industry.[58] In Frederick's day, linen from Saxony was sold not only throughout Europe, but was shipped from Spain to the New World.

Though the waves of the Italian Renaissance could be observed in Saxony prior to this time, Frederick's reign was contemporaneous with the high Renaissance in Italy. The elector was a lover of beautiful things and a patron of art and culture. Albert, Ernest, and Frederick all employed excellent architects and artists, such as Arnold Westfalen and his pupil Konrad Pflüger. They erected new churches, castles, and town halls in order to beautify their Saxon cities. The construction of the castle church in Wittenberg was begun in 1490, but the interior was not adorned with altars and paintings until 1509.[59] It was a good example of the new type of church construction, with three balconies suspended from the walls, offering a greater seating capacity for large academic gatherings. It also provided ample space for the elector's relics, displayed there once a year, during the week following All Saints Day. The castle church served as a chapel for students and as a site for special academic disputations.[60] The elector spared no expense in its erection and beautification. Spalatin reported that it cost Frederick 200,000 Gulden.[61]

The elector of Saxony must have thought of founding the University of Wittenberg long before it was established in 1502. No doubt the Leipzig Settlement of 1485 influenced Frederick's decision. That partition left the elector without an institution of higher learning in his lands. When, in 1490, Frederick began building a new castle and castle church to replace the previous Ascanier buildings, he must have had in mind their potential for service to the new university. The castle was meant to serve as his dwelling when he visited Wittenberg, but many of its rooms were also meant to serve as classrooms for the university's graduate school of law. There is a difference of opinion as to the length of time it took to complete the two structures. The architectural layout and basic erection of the buildings was completed by 1499.

The castle church became the university chapel by 1503, but its interior was not finished until 1509.[62] Lucas Cranach the Elder, Frederick's *Hofmaler*, may have done much of the internal painting; but the altars and other pictures were mainly done elsewhere. In the nineties Frederick ordered art pieces from Albrecht Dürer in Nürnberg, and he ordered new works after that artist's return from his second trip to Venice in 1507. Oskar Thulin used the term *"überreich"* with reference to the castle church's adornments.[63] Frederick's biographer wrote that there were few *Stifte* in all Germany so richly endowed.[64] One of the real adornments of the church was its relics collection. Cranach prepared a guide for the worshipers in his *Wittenberger Heiligtumsbuch of 1509*, which offers an excellent view of the casements in which these relics were displayed.[65] Hausleiter claims that the number of aisles of relics had swollen to twelve by 1518. A total of 17,443 articles could be venerated, offering 127,709 years and 116 days of indulgences.[66]

Kolde and Köstlin state that the elector continued his relic collecting until 1522, but Kalkoff claims that the relics delivered between 1517 and 1520 had been purchased in 1512.[67] He concluded that the elector later began to have misgivings as he occupied himself with his own personal salvation.

The life of Frederick the Wise falls quite naturally into two periods. The first was typically medieval and continued until 1517. During the subsequent period the elector had to adjust to and maneuver amid events that occurred as a result of Martin Luther's activities and the progress of the German Reformation. How the elector felt and adjusted to these events has presented problems for scholars ever since the development of the Leopold von Ranke school of historical criticism in the nineteenth century.

One of the challenges in our penetration of the thought world of Frederick the Wise comes from viewing the elector from a twentieth-century perspective. Scholars have frequently made Luther out to be a Lutheran and Frederick a Catholic. This immediately confuses the issue. The formative events of the Reformation did not involve Catholics and Lutherans, but rather two types of Catholics. There were the *Altgläubigen*, old-style believers such as Duke George, Cardinal Cajetan, and Tetzel, and the *Neugläubigen*, who aimed to reform the church's errors in the light of the Scriptures.

Just as Luther underwent a tremendous change between 1512 and 1520, so the Frederick who attended the Diet of Augsburg in 1518 was not the same as the Frederick who protected Luther at Worms in 1521. As the recent biography by Höss has shown, Frederick's actions revealed a far deeper involvement in the Reformation than mere political maneuvering on his part to protect the honor of his Wittenberg faculty.[68]

Frederick's attitude toward Luther and the Reformation has been a matter of much controversy for more than a century. An excellent discussion of this debate can be found in the study by Koch, "The Controversy about Frederick the Wise's Position towards the Reformation."[69] A sincere attempt to understand the elector was made by Kolde in 1881.[70] However, a much broader and deeper study of the problem was undertaken by Kalkoff, who wrote a number of treatises covering the period before and during the *Reichstag* of Worms in 1521.[71] This was followed by an excellent study by Kirn in 1926.[72] Perhaps the best insight can still be gained from the historical sources left by Georg Spalatin.[73]

The monastic reforms initiated by the elector centered around morality, not doctrine. Later, however, Frederick was confronted with Luther's "New Theology," which demanded a complete reorientation of his entire religious life. It made Frederick's relics in Wittenberg, and all attendant veneration of saints, obsolete. This must have puzzled the elector, for it contradicted all that he had been taught during his boyhood at the Grimma monastery. But Spalatin, who remained in constant contact with Luther through frequent letters and visits to Wittenberg, often engaged the elector in discussions of the "New Theology." In his biography of Frederick, he observed that the "closer and closer Frederick came to the gospel, the less he wished to have it hidden again or that any harm befall the reformer."[74] Besides, the elector was similar to Luther in the sense that he wanted no halfway measures; when something was right, he insisted that it be carried out. He once told Spalatin that matters of faith should "be as clean as water in the eye."[75] Another similarity between Frederick and Luther was that once they had thoroughly examined a matter, neither one was easily swayed from his views.[76]

Spalatin related how the prince matured in his understanding of the Reformation. Though the elector was steeped profoundly in ceremonies, he never criticized Luther for attacking them, and finally even tolerated the changes that were made in the Wittenberg *Stift*. Spalatin added that shortly before his death, the elector received "the Holy Sacrament of the true body and blood of Christ with great devotion."[77] The court preacher was also at Frederick's bedside when the elector received his final Lord's Supper:

> On the Sunday before his final departure, the elector attended a Lenten sermon. He, also before his death, confessed with great devotion before the holy divine Christ and then received the sacrament in both kinds with such inward devotion, that we, who were there, were all moved to tears, for we were surprised that God had brought him to that point. Had he lived a little longer, he would no doubt have permitted his subjects to have the new gospel in his lands, with both body and soul. Such sincerity we all experienced from an honorable and gracious Christian prince.[78]

However, an important distinction must be made between Luther and Frederick the Wise. The reformer was a scholar of unusual dimensions. The elector, on the other hand, was but an intelligent layman. He greatly admired what Luther wrote, especially the reformer's devotional literature. Frederick loved sermons that Luther had preached, even though he may not have always understood the "New Theology" in its finer distinctions. On one occasion, Frederick expressed his views about Erasmus' theology when he offered his reactions to the Dutchman's treatise *On the Freedom of the Will*. The elector observed that he could not understand Erasmus' view, for the Scriptures said: "Without me you can do nothing."[79] Thus, he concluded, Erasmus contradicted Christ himself.

Though Frederick was much interested in Luther and his reforms, he followed the professor only from a distance. It cannot be doubted that he was shocked at times by Luther's boldness in attacking Rome. Yet at Worms the elector was so pleased with Luther's stand that he summoned Spalatin into his quarters and said to him in private, "The monk, Doctor Martin, conducted himself in a way that amazed everyone, by the way he spoke in the presence of the Kaiser, the princes, and the estates, addressing them in Latin and in German. He is far too sharp for me."[80]

THE REFORMATION

❖

Volume II
The Reformation
as a University Movement

15

The Models for the University
of Wittenberg

❖

The *Stiftungsbrief*, the imperial letter dated 6 July 1502 that founded the
University of Wittenberg, enumerates in a very detailed and flowery way the
many privileges and immunities the new school on the Elbe was to enjoy,
putting it on a footing with the oldest and most revered universities in Europe.
But the document also states that the new university, in all of its rights and privileges, was to be modeled after the universities of Bologna, Siena, Padua, Pavia,
Perugia, Paris, and Leipzig.[1] A proper evaluation of the University of Wittenberg therefore requires a survey of the medieval background of these institutions. For the sake of brevity, the present study will be limited to the two
institutions after which Wittenberg was most closely modeled: Paris and
Bologna.

The modern university had its origin in the Middle Ages and grew out of the
twelfth-century renaissance. Though the Greeks and Romans had some fine
specialized schools, they had no comparable institutions.[2] Their schools had no
licensed masters, formal courses, examinations, or final examinations; neither
did they offer degrees.[3]

There were two distinguished universities on the European continent during
the Middle Ages, and these were Paris and Bologna. They were separate and
distinct institutions in almost every respect. The University of Paris grew out of
the Cathedral School of Notre Dame, where thousands of young clerics flocked
to study theology and philosophy. Since Paris regarded itself as a defender of
Catholic dogma, the papacy took a keen interest in it. While other twelfth-
century cathedral schools (such as Chartres and Lyons) were flourishing centers
of classical learning, the schools at Paris, Rheims, Laon, and Bec turned to theology. They emphasized the use of dialectic and philosophy to expound church
dogma. The great influx of knowledge from the East between 1100 and 1200,
via southern Italy, Sicily, and Spain, made hitherto unknown Greek and Arabic
sources available. Students after Abelard had access to Latin translations of the

185

works of Aristotle, Euclid, Ptolemy, Hippocrates, and Galen. Much new material also became available from the eastern Fathers. These sources were a significant influence on the founding of institutions of higher learning.[4]

However, during the remarkable period that Charles Homer Haskins called
the "renaissance of the twelfth century," students in Paris were mainly interested in Aristotle's dialectical reasoning. Even at Chartres, interest in rhetoric
and the classics was of short duration. Northern scholars became obsessed with
the application of Aristotle's *Prior Analytics* and *Posterior Analytics* to theological disputation.[5] Schachner points out that humanism, which seemed to blos-
som everywhere else during the twelfth century, did not interest the students of
Paris; by 1149, scholasticism was definitely in the saddle.[6]

Peter Abelard's name is often rightly associated with the origin of the University of Paris, though he lived a half century before the Cathedral School of
Notre Dame became a regular university.[7] There can be little doubt that
Abelard's presence in Paris, which drew thousands of students from all over
Europe, helped develop its fame as a cultural center and hastened its rise as a
university. Sometime between the closing days of Abelard and the beginning of
the next century, the Cathedral School evolved into a university. The exact time
when this happened is unclear, but the university's existence can definitely be
discerned around 1200.[8] It seems to have emerged between 1170 and 1175.[9]

The curriculum of the cathedral school had stressed the liberal arts; but with
the influx of new learning in the West, the school's program widened. There was
now a strong emphasis on logic and dialectics, in pursuit of philosophical
themes in theology and canon law.[10] Leff does not believe that the earlier
schools of St. Victor and Ste. Genevieve played a vital role in the evolution of
the university.[11] Yet he admits that both added to the reputation of Paris as an
educational center.[12] By the beginning of the twelfth century, the Cathedral
School of Notre Dame was the only place where secular clergy received a
higher education. It was under the broad control of the bishop of Paris, but the
actual control of teaching and the granting of licenses was under the university
chancellor. When students in Abelard's day swarmed to Paris in ever larger
numbers, lecturers began to offer courses at St. Victor as well, and students
crossed the river to Ste. Genevieve. During this period no special licenses were
needed to teach; all that a teacher such as Abelard needed to do was find a
building and offer lectures.[13]

At the outset, the chancellor supervised the school at Notre Dame and
looked after the needs and care of its library. Before long, however, his sovereignty expanded. In time, teachers came to the chancellor, seeking opportunities; as a result, there was an increase in his ability to grant *licentia docendi*, a
kind of teacher's certificate and the forerunner of the later academic diploma.
This meant that the chancellor gradually assumed control of all the licenses of
future teachers. He learned to charge for this service, which became a lucrative
source of income. Often candidates appeared who were unfit to be licensed,
and palm-greasing became a common practice. At the same time, worthy candidates who refused to engage in under-the-table deals might not be licensed.

After the university was organized, the details of such abuses were reported to Rome. They were even discussed by the Third Lateran Council, in 1179, where Pope Alexander III ruled that future chancellors at Paris were forbidden to charge for the granting of teachers' permits. This decision turned the chancellor into a kind of ecclesiastical superintendent.[14]

The way in which the cathedral school at Paris was organized prior to the thirteenth century can no longer be determined. There is evidence that, before 1200, there were shifting tides of students and peripatetic teachers.[15] These masters must have found it advantageous to organize and thus be recognized as an academic institution by both the French crown and the papacy.

Etymologically, the word *university* means "the whole" of something.[16] The term had long been used by medieval guilds to define trade unions or lodges, which had formed associations for common enterprises. At Paris, the masters banded themselves together in a union and students came and attended their lectures. The motivation for forming the association appears to have been self-protection.[17] Haskins claimed that the word *universitas* originally meant a corporation, but that, in time, it was applied to a learned body of men, known in Latin as the *Universitas societas magistrorum discipularumque*, or "Society of Masters and Scholars."[18] In time, a body of persons at Paris—masters and scholars—were regarded as a legal corporation.

There were a number of reasons why students needed to form such a union for common protection. Citizens of Paris were loath to recognize that students needed to have special rights, even though most were foreigners.[19] It took the thundering and threats of kings and popes to make citizens realize that students needed to be regarded as a group apart, having special privileges, immunities, and exemptions, which, according to civil law, were designated as *Authentica Habita*. Pope Celestius III placed all the clerks of Paris under the control of either the bishop of the diocese or the abbot of Ste. Genevieve, which meant that any member of the school, if arrested, could be tried only under canon law in the bishop's court. King Louis VII of France likewise came to the defense of students against the often overly aggressive provosts and their officials.[20] In Paris, a foreign student was regarded as a *persona non grata*. Students possessed practically no rights and were in constant danger of being seized and mistreated. They could be incarcerated for practically no cause at all. Thus the Paris masters found it advantageous to form associations, so that they and their students could band together for safety and strength. Such an organization had a double advantage; it protected the *universitas* from citizens' molestation, and it also gave the professors control over their students.[21]

A disturbance erupted in the year 1200, during the reign of King Philip Augustus. As a result, the king granted the University of Paris its first official charter.[22] A group of German students had gone to a tavern for an evening. Among them was a young noble, the bishop-elect of Liege, who (for unknown reasons) was assaulted; a brawl then occurred, during which the tavern host was severely beaten. This was reported to the provost of Paris, who gathered a posse of armed citizens and stormed the hostel where the German students lived.

Several of the students died in the encounter, including the bishop-elect of Liege. The masters of the university appealed to the king of France, warning him that there would be an exodus of the entire student body (which constituted one-half the population of Paris) if no redress were forthcoming. The king took decisive action, severely punishing the provost and the participants in the raid on the hostel, and issuing a charter to protect the university.

The charter contains a number of provisions. Its first directive states that, in the future, any arrested student was to be turned over immediately to the ecclesiastical authorities, for masters and scholars were not subject to punishment by civil courts. Also, all citizens were to protect the rights of scholars in their midst and report any mistreatment of students. The newly-appointed provost and his successors were obligated to swear that they would respect the scholarly privileges of the university. The king's directive also denied citizens the right to seize student property in civil courts.[23]

Kibre points out that the charter of Philip Augustus did not terminate all student arrests, for these were often related to the seriousness of the offenses. Arrests became a matter of the degree of the offense. A second royal decree allowed arrests only in the cases of homicide, adultery, and attacks with sticks, stones, or other weapons. But even then, unless the offense occurred late at night, the offenders were immediately to be turned over to the bishop of the diocese or to his officials.[24]

In their early transactions with the papacy, whose support they badly needed, the masters elected a proctor to represent them.[25] The school did not possess its own statutes, have any officials, or have a common seal. The masters of Paris still needed to create a well-organized legal corporation.[26] An obstacle to the creation of such a corporation was the chancellor of Notre Dame.

In the early days, the chancellor had been a subordinate of the bishop of Paris with but limited powers. In time, and for a variety of reasons, he had acquired tremendous power. The chancellor worked constantly to keep the cathedral school from becoming an autonomous institution. By the year 1200 he controlled all student admissions to the university as well as the granting of the *licentia decendi*. The masters became outraged by the oath of obedience that the chancellor exacted from every licensed teacher, for an oath was regarded as sacred and irrevocable.[27] He was able to expel masters from their profession and annul the academic degrees that scholars had previously acquired. This made the chancellor the *Iudex Ordinarius* over all scholars in the bishop's court. He could excommunicate, imprison, and discipline masters of the faculty even though he was not part of the academic organization.

The Paris masters appealed to Pope Innocent III, who had himself been a student at Paris and who understood the faculty's problems. The pontiff reduced the chancellor's power by prohibiting the swearing of oaths by the masters or scholars; he also decreed that no more fees were to be exacted by the chancellor for licensing students to teach.[28] But the masters still wanted the right to draft their own statutes, through which they could regulate university life and be free of all external interference. Their wishes became a reality in

1210. The masters now referred to themselves as a *universitas* that regulated lectures and disputations, faculty and student attire, and other matters. They also followed Innocent III's suggestion that they appoint a proctor to represent the university as a corporate body in the papal court. Such action also implied that the school should become a recognized corporate body with legal powers to sue and be sued.[29]

It was one thing for the masters to draft statutes and declare themselves independent, and quite another to enforce these changes. The chancellor and the bishop of Paris now joined forces, even defying the Holy See. Their new weapon was to excommunicate the new corporate body *en masse*. The chancellor attempted to make many arrests, but the papal bulls of 1219 and 1222 abolished the chancellor's prison and forbade all excommunications that had not first been approved by Rome.[30]

Previously the Cathedral School of Notre Dame had operated under the seal of the cathedral's canons. Now the university, as a separate corporation, needed a new seal with which to certify its official documents. The masters prepared one, an action to which the canons of Notre Dame strenuously objected. They appealed to the papal legate, Cardinal Romano, who happened to be in Paris. The cardinal demanded to see the seal, smashed it in the presence of the masters, and threatened them with a papal anathema if they made another one.[31] The outcry at the university was tremendous. The students and some faculty members stormed the episcopal palace, where the cardinal was residing, forcing the retainers to close the gates. The angry crowd of scholars became so furious that King Louis VIII had to use troops to disperse them, thus saving the legate from being mobbed. Amid the melee, several of the retainers were wounded, one of them mortally; this caused the legate to excommunicate all the university members who had participated.

Eighty masters who had been involved in this action were later absolved by the church, and by 1246 the university was granted its own seal, with full papal blessing. Its four nations were also permitted to have their separate seals.[32] When, on 30 October 1246, Pope Innocent IV granted the university its private seal, he stated that the papacy regretted the previous action taken by Cardinal Romano.[33]

By 1222 the students of Paris were divided into four nations: the French, Norman, Picard, and English. The French nation embraced students from the south, the Latin races; the Normans were mainly from northern France; the Picards included students from the low countries; while the English also included those who were German-speaking. This division was somewhat arbitrary, for later the French nation often outnumbered the other three put together. In the beginning, however, the division may have been somewhat more fair.[34]

"Town and gown" relationships at Paris remained trying. Frequently scholars were mistreated, while the masters would threaten to leave the city and locate the university elsewhere.[35] One squabble was over potatoes; the masters appealed to the queen mother, Blanche of Castile, but she ordered the provost to punish the culprits. The provost took special delight in getting even with the students. On another occasion, some university clerks were engaged in sport outside the city when they were attacked and beaten by townsmen. Several were killed outright, others drowned in the Seine while attempting to escape, and many others were pursued and wounded. The masters suspended classes and departed *en masse* to complain to the queen, the bishop, and the papal legate, but they were met everywhere by sneers and mockery.[36] That was the last straw. The masters and scholars left Paris and dispersed in all directions; many went to Toulouse, Orleans, Bologna, and Angern; some even went to England. With all the students gone, Paris was left shattered, mourning over its past glories.[37]

King Louis IX immediately attempted to make amends for his mother's blunders. The pope also began to thunder at the Paris bishop for his conduct, and the pontiff ordered an inquiry into the matter. He contacted the king and the queen mother, asking them to make amends. In the meantime, however, two years had elapsed, during which there was no assurance that the university would return. The king of England even made overtures to have the school moved to Britain. Finally, in 1231, Pope Gregory IX issued the papal bull *Pares Scientiarum*. It not only restated the university privileges granted by previous pontiffs, but significantly reduced the powers of the chancellor. It forbade him to license students unless they were qualified, and even then, he could do so only upon the masters' approval. The chancellor was to be stripped of his prison. If students were accused of serious crimes, they were to be arrested and held by the bishop. The pope also reaffirmed the university's rights to terminate lectures and declare a strike. However, the university students were obligated to take an oath to uphold the masters' statutes.[38] Denifle has called the papal bull *Pares Scientiarum* the *Magna Charta* of the University of Paris, giving the university apostolic sanction for all its rights and privileges.[39]

In spite of all this, the chancellor remained a problem for the masters until the end of the thirteenth century. After that time, he exercised only those functions specifically delegated to him by the Holy See. Though he still played some role in licensing students (after the faculty had pronounced them qualified), gradually even that function became obsolete.[40]

There were still frequent altercations between the bishop of Paris and the masters, resulting in flagrant violation of university privileges that had been guaranteed by the bull. Thus, on 7 September 1237, another bull reaffirmed the masters' rights to license candidates in the higher faculties of theology and canon law, while the pope ordered the bishop of Paris to refrain from meddling in the licensing of candidates for higher degrees. Later, Pope Innocent IV reaffirmed all the privileges granted by his predecessor; in addition, he exempted masters and scholars from making excommunications without having received prior permission from the Holy See.[41] This pope, however, made it clear that there were crimes punishable by the Paris officials; these included homicide, the abduction of women, roaming the streets at night with weapons, or breaking into houses and stealing property. The pope added that because such conditions existed, the university should really divide its student body into two groups, those who were orderly and those who were not.[42]

To further curb the authority of the chancellor, Pope Gregory IX ordered that henceforth the abbots of Ste. Genevieve could license masters in theology, canon law, and arts to teach within their jurisdictions. Accordingly, the masters of arts gradually transferred themselves to the Latin Quarter, on the *Rue du Fouarre*—the "street of straw" (where straw was strewn on the floor of the lecture rooms)—because they could now acquire their licenses there.[43] The Ste. Genevieve chancellorship was established in 1255, and it was managed by one of its canons in that abbey. By 1246 Pope Innocent IV sought further protection for the university by the establishment of a *Conservator Apostolic*, establishing the archbishop of Reims and the bishop and dean of Senlis as protectors of the University of Paris from ecclesiastical censure. In time, this organization developed into a regular "Court of Conservation," with extraordinary powers.[44]

The institution of rectorships in medieval universities, which developed in Paris around the middle of the thirteenth century, became an important part of European university life. Since this office was copied during the founding of the University of Wittenberg, its origin is of special interest for this study. The oldest reference to such an official at Paris is found in the papal bulls of 1237 and 1244. At the time, this official was employed only by the faculty of liberal arts and served exclusively in the philosophical faculty; that faculty's membership far outnumbered those of the upper divisions, and some type of centralized control was demanded to resolve the conflicts between the nations. Meanwhile, the graduate schools of theology, law, and medicine began to choose their own deans, who would conduct their academic business.[45] Rashdall and Kaufmann agree that in the early days the arts faculty had two officials to control academic life; the records indicate that each nation had its proctor, and these officials chose a rector. Students who got into trouble had to make their peace with both officials. In the beginning the proctors were the chief officials of the respective nations, while the rector was elected head of the whole arts faculty.

Since the schools of Paris were somewhat widely scattered, gathering all four faculties for an assembly required some kind of messenger service. Out of this grew the use of beadles, who carried messages back and forth from the rector and deans of the upper faculties.[46] This practice was later adopted by German universities.

Rashdall is not certain when the system of nations emerged. In the beginning they were opposed by Rome, but they were fully accepted by the end of the great dispersion in 1231. This may have been because, at the time, the Holy See did everything possible to entice the masters to return to Paris. Also, during the period from 1222 to 1249, the rectorship was accepted by the whole university.[47]

When the upper faculties were still small and somewhat disorganized, the rector of liberal arts began to assume that he was the head of the entire university, something to which the graduate school deans, in time, seem to have con-sented. The nations often became quite disorderly when a proposal failed to agree with their wishes.[48] Three votes from the four nations could even block a proposal made by members of the higher faculties.[49]

In 1219 Pope Honorius III terminated the teaching of civil law at Paris; he feared that its popularity might extinguish the study of theology. Prior to the thirteenth century, there is also no mention of a graduate school of medicine, which limited Paris' upper faculties to theology and canon law. By 1213 a reference to such a school appears in the records.[50]

Whenever there was to be a meeting of the entire congregation of the university, it became the duty of the rector to notify the various schools through the beadles. The rector was usually a young master, who at times had considerable trouble in controlling the turbulent nations. There was also a substantial amount of ill-will between the different groups of foreign students, and young scholars often expressed their opposition to measures by shouts, hissing, and the shaking of fists. At times, such opposition resulted in brawls. Fortunately, the carrying of weapons was forbidden.[51] The chest containing the precious institutional seal, without which no action was regarded as official, was secured with seven locks. Since the keys were scattered within the four nations and the three upper faculties, this could prove to be a real obstacle to university action; an opposition group could conveniently claim that it had misplaced or lost its key. Such behavior could block any undesirable legislation, for a document needed to be certified by the institutional seal before it became official.[52]

A rector of a medieval university had many duties: collecting student fees, conducting litigation, executing decrees, adjusting student rentals, settling student conflicts and complaints, and punishing those who violated university statutes.[53] In a university convocation, the rector presided and presented the issues before the school; he then called on the entire student body for discussion. In these discussions, faculty and students of liberal arts as well as members of the three graduate schools expressed their views, pro and con. After the discussion, they voted by faculties. In this manner most of the university's problems were resolved.[54]

During these years, another academic official emerged, a dean of the faculty, who transacted most of its official business. Paris had deans of theology, law, medicine, and liberal arts, a practice later copied by other institutions. By 1252 the higher faculties of Paris were in possession of their individual statutes, while by 1270, both canon law and medicine also possessed their own corporate seals.[55]

Thus by the end of the thirteenth century, most of the academic structure of the University of Paris had come into existence. In the beginning, the graduate school deans seem to have operated side by side with the rector of the arts college, rather than being subservient to him. The arrival of the mendicants, who were quite set in their ways, contributed much to the development of a single rector for the whole university. In the early days, the higher faculties attempted to avoid becoming too subservient to the rector's dominance; they wanted to maintain their own independence, since they already possessed their own deans and corporate seals.[56] Strife broke out between the arts rector and the faculties of canon law and medicine over what was the proper academic protocol between schools. The two superior faculties maintained that the rector of arts could not summon them directly through his beadles, but that this needed to be done through the channels of their own respective deans. A similar protest was made by the faculty of theology in 1279, and again in 1283–84. When the rector of arts asserted his rights to summon any school in the university through his beadles, the theologians replied that they could only be summoned to a congregational meeting of the entire institution, and only through the channel of their academic dean. But the faculty of liberal arts at Paris was too large and too dominating to be opposed for long. In time, the rector won. By the end of the thirteenth century, he summoned all four faculties through his beadles without opposition.[57]

Thus the rise of rectorships in medieval universities was a gradual one. By 1244, there is evidence of the existence of a single rector in the faculty of arts—an elected official chosen by the four proctors of the nations—who carried out the decrees of the entire institution. At this early date, the graduate faculties, being very small, may have been little aware of the importance of the liberal arts rector. In 1259 the pope addressed the rector of Paris concerning the enforcement of debts throughout the institution. A deed, written in 1276, was signed by the deans of canon law and medicine, the rector, and, finally, by the proctors of the four nations. However, by 1289 the prestige of the rectorship seems to have risen to first rank; from then on the name of the rector appears first in signatures, succeeded by the deans of the higher faculties (theology, law, and medicine), and, finally, by the proctors of the four nations. Thus between 1280 and 1290, the rector finally became the official head of the University of Paris.[58]

In the upper faculties, especially in theology, the final recognition of the rector as the official head of the institution ran directly contrary to the will of the officials of Notre Dame. The chancellor claimed that he was still *ex officio* the head of the theological faculty, and, as such, refused to accept the rector's status. It seems that the chancellor, as the ranking professor in theology, continued to preside over meetings, even after the existence of an academic dean. The masters of arts, however, remained independent of the chancellor. This was especially true after they had migrated to the Latin Quarter outside the city. Thus a single rectorship evolved among them much earlier. For the graduate schools this presented an additional problem. The fact that, originally, the rector was chosen by the four proctors of the undergraduate faculties made it somewhat awkward, if not humiliating, for the three graduate deans to acknowledge their subservience.

With the arrival of the friars, the institution was soon to face another challenge. The struggle that ensued lasted more than a decade and became a test of strength between the Paris masters and Pope Alexander IV, the supporter of the friars.[59] The Dominicans and the Franciscans, the principal forces in the conflict, were monks who had dropped the rule of being localized in monasteries. They began to invade the Paris theological faculty during the great dispersion of

1229. The secular clergy became quite concerned about their arrival, for the Dominicans regarded themselves as "the watchdogs of the Lord."[60] They were learned men, educated and trained by gifted lectors and priors, for the order had established schools and faculties in leading universities. With their persuasive oratory, the Dominicans had gained educational footholds throughout Europe. Their greatest educational center was soon to become St. Jacques at Paris; from there they would challenge the entire university.[61]

Even in Abelard's day there had been some battles with Aristotelian dialectic when applied to the Trinity and other realms of revealed truths, but these had been mild in comparison with what transpired among Paris students before the arrival of the first Dominicans and Franciscans. The quality of theological study had declined tremendously, with young men having no appreciation of the sacredness of dogma. Much of the academic confusion resulted from the nature of the "new Aristotle" with which these students had become acquainted, as new translations of the philosopher's works had traveled north via southern Italy, Sicily, and Spain. These texts had arrived via a long, circuitous route, and in the process Aristotle had become hardly recognizable.[62] Schachner expressed in one clever sentence the nature of the strange pabulum that students in Paris had to digest: These were "Latin translations of Spanish translations of Hebrew translations of Arabic translations of Syriac translations from the original Greek!"[63]

If these corrupted texts were confusing, the Paris masters and their students were even more misled by the extensive commentaries and paraphrases by Avicenna and Averroes. Avicenna had paraphrased many Aristotelian tomes that were later translated into Latin by the Toledo school. Some were not even authentic works of Aristotle, but merely works passed under his name. These reemphasized what Arabic philosophy claimed that the philosopher had taught. The most misleading assertions by Averroes and Avicenna were the assertions that Aristotle had taught the eternity of matter and had denied the Christian doctrines of creation, the individuality of the human soul, personal immortality, and the final judgment.[64] In addition, the compilation known as the *Liber de Causis* appeared, which had been translated under the name of Aristotle.[65] At Paris all this new material was studied, debated, twisted, and expounded.

The newly arrived, corrupted version of Aristotle had now become, among dialecticians, a philosopher placed practically on a par with the Bible.[66] The result was much bolder theological speculation than what the church had experienced in Abelard's day. Young and impressionable students, with a limited knowledge of Latin, engaged in the hair-splitting technical jargon of the schools.[67] It is no wonder that Stephen of Tournai groaned as he wrote:

> Beardless youth sit in the chairs of old professors; and they who are scarcely pupils are anxious to be called masters. Neglecting the rules of the arts, and discarding the books of good authority, with their sophistications they catch the flies of senseless verbiage as in the webs of spiders.[68]

Rashdall cites the boldness of one particular Parisian master, Simon of Tournai. He employed such dialectical skill in a public defense of the Trinity, and did it so lucidly, with such elegance and catholicity, that his listeners responded with great applause. He then turned to the admiring audience and remarked that he could have *disproved* his thesis just as ably.[69]

Students now felt no need for literature or culture. In science, there was no need for observation, since Aristotle had done it all for them. Hence, out of Paris flowed a strange, un-Christian doctrine, set forth boldly by infidels, agnostics, and actual heretics. Such a state of affairs shocked Christendom, and Rome could not sit idly by. Offenders began to be anathematized, excommunicated, and forced to retract or burn their works.[70] In 1210, David of Dinant's writings were condemned to the flames by the Synod of Paris. The books of Aristotle on natural philosophy and his commentaries were banned, initially for three years.[71] In 1215, when the first Paris statutes were drafted by the papal legate Courcon, the physical and metaphysical works of Aristotle were banned. Students in the arts faculty were forced to take an oath not to read Dinant's writings or those of other heretics.[72]

In 1231, Pope Gregory IX renewed the condemnation of Aristotle's books until they could be examined more thoroughly and purged of all heresy. But the Paris masters soon learned to distinguish between what was useful in Aristotle and what was to be rejected. By 1248, a Parisian doctor, William of Auvergne, began to make full use of the forbidden books of the Stagirite, seeking, where possible, to refute his errors. By 1255 the works of Aristotle were fully tolerated.[73] Yet the complete purging of the philosopher's works and the task of making them useful to theology was not accomplished until the coming of the friars.

The papacy realized in time that Aristotle could not be suppressed and that there was only one way to deal with him, namely, to disarm him. In this the Dominicans and Franciscans proved to be very useful.[74] The first Dominicans arrived in Paris in 1217, and the first Franciscans two years later. The friars did not begin teaching until the great dispersion in 1229. In that year, Roland of Cremona became the Dominican pioneer on the university faculty.[75] While the masters were away, the chancellor had evened the score by recognizing the friar as an official member of the faculty. When the masters returned, the presence of one Dominican did not seem too significant. But the action had opened the floodgates. Now other orders demanded representation. To stop the invasion, the secular clergy on the theological faculty ruled that no theologian would be licensed to teach at Paris unless he had attained the rank of a *Biblicus* in their school.[76] Now the battle was on. The Dominicans refused to recognize any need for a *Licentia docendi* from Paris in order to become qualified members of the theological staff. Soon John of Giles took a second chair; after him came the distinguished Alexander of Hales. However, the third member soon went over to the Franciscans.[77]

By 1231 the Paris theological faculty possessed twelve chairs, three of which were occupied by mendicants; later came the Cistercians, the Augustinians, and other orders that also wanted chairs in theology. By 1254 the faculty had swollen to fifteen chairs, but only three of these were old-time secular clerics. Yet the theological faculty could boast of two distinguished men within its ranks, Thomas Aquinas, a Dominican, and Bonaventura, a Franciscan. The secular clergy felt they were not only outnumbered, but also surpassed in theological acumen. They appealed to the neighboring clergy in France for support.[78] The Dominicans appealed to Rome, where at first they received a sympathetic hearing. But then Pope Innocent IV issued the bull *Etsi animarum effectantes*, which curbed the rights of the Dominicans.[79]

Just when the advances by the friars seemed under control, Pope Innocent IV died. He was succeeded by Pope Alexander VI, who viewed the additions to the Paris faculty with favor. The university then ruled that one member of each order could be admitted to the theological faculty. The school stipulated that each of these representatives would have to obtain permission from the faculty before his entry. To this the pope added that no action on the part of the faculty would be binding without a two-thirds vote.[80]

At this point the king of France stepped into the fray, claiming that the monks should be removed from the university. He suggested that the friars establish their own school at Paris, so that students would be free to attend both institutions. But the pope was not receptive to this. In 1259 the Dominicans were back in the Paris faculty; however, they had been demoted in rank to one step below the secular clergy, Minorites, Carmelites, Augustinians, and Cistercians.[81]

As we have seen, among the ranks of the early friars were some distinguished names.[82] Then, during the middle of the century, came Albertus Magnus, Thomas Aquinas, and Bonaventura.[83] Rome supported the work of men such as Albertus Magnus (Albert the Great) and Thomas Aquinas. They were capable of controlling the Aristotelian problem.

It was Albert the Great's life goal to refute Arabic philosophy. Although his Latin was somewhat primitive and awkward, his prodigious bulk of material was extremely useful for beginners. When he died, he left the Paris theologians with twenty-one huge tomes of paraphrases of Aristotle's writings.[84] It took Thomas Aquinas, Albert's greatest pupil, to put the master's spadework into finished form.[85] The unimpeachable orthodoxy of these two scholars dissipated all prejudice against scholastic philosophy and its method. But this victory had been achieved at a price. Theologians now placed Aristotle and the church Fathers side by side, except when the former was not in harmony with revelation.[86]

Aquinas knew no Greek; fortunately, at the papal court there was a Greek scholar, William Moerbake, who could offer him a fresh translation of Aristotle. These two scholars labored together, the former serving as the translator and the latter as the commentator, on the new Latin translations. In this way new versions were made available of Aristotle's *De Anima*, *De Caelo*, and his *Metaphysica*. Thomas also conceived his *Opus magnum*, the *Summa Theologicae*, while he was in the papal service.[87]

In his *Summa Theologicae* Aquinas developed a complete catholic system in which the Holy Fathers and Aristotle became fully amalgamated.[88] However, it should be stressed that Thomas made a distinction between truth offered to human beings through revelation and truth discovered by the human intellect.

He added that these two categories must not be made incompatible, as both ultimately emanate from God.[89] For Paris, Aristotle had now become a Christian and a member of the Catholic fold. The Franciscans remained dubious about all this subtlety, but Thomistic philosophy now came into grace.

A medieval university consisted of four divisions. The first was an arts or philosophical faculty, which offered courses toward the bachelor's and master's degrees, preparatory for specialized graduate studies in one of three disciplines. The bachelor of arts degree could be acquired in a matter of two years; the attainment of a master of arts degree usually needed an additional four years. Upon acquiring the master's degree in philosophy, the student could enter one of the three graduate schools—theology, canon law, or medicine—where he worked many years before becoming a master.

The papacy was quite apprehensive about permitting the University of Paris to offer a course in civil law, fearing that it would be too competitive with the study of theology. Therefore it was banned from the curriculum in 1215. Yet courses in canon law were acceptable, and these continued to be taught.[90] Initially Paris did not have regular curricula of studies in the various disciplines. The idea of a definite curriculum in philosophy, theology, canon law, and medicine may have originated in Italy.[91]

Prior to matriculation at Paris, a student was obligated to demonstrate a mastery of Latin. Thus, in the beginning, the burser examined the student as to his linguistic qualification, a task later assumed by the rector. Young students who failed to qualify might be turned over to a master for instruction in Latin grammar. By 1328, students matriculated with the rector of the university and made their applications in Latin.[92] The Paris curriculum in liberal arts fails to mention the disciplines of poetry, oratory, and history.[93] Rhetoric was studied, usually on festival days, in which the professor stressed the rhetoric *Barbarismus*, the third book of Donatus's *Ars maior*, and the *Topics*.[94] The main courses in the philosophical faculty, however, concerned logic, the old and the new Aristotle, and his *Organon*, for which they used an introduction, the *Isagoge* of Porphyry. Later, students were also offered some instruction in the *Quadrivium*, though no specific texts are mentioned.[95] The *Quadrivium* must have been regarded as of limited importance. Geometry and music received little attention, while arithmetic and astronomy were considered useful only as a means of calculating the date of Easter in the church calendar. Later the introduction of Arabic numbering enhanced the attractiveness of mathematics, and there were also some courses in algebra.[96]

While the classics were neglected in the thirteenth century, vernacular French had already made its entry. However, the main interest was in the logic and dialectic of Aristotle. According to the new Paris statutes of 1255, full instruction in Aristotle was permitted, covering both the *Old* and *New Logic* and even the *Ethics*. Rashdall cited fourteen works of the philosopher that were taught, among them a few spurious ones; these formed the basic curriculum in the arts faculty. Among these were the series offered in liberal arts: the *Physics* and *Metaphysics*, *De Anima*, *De Animalibus*, *De Caelo et de Mundo*, *Meteorica*,

De Generatione, De Sensu et Senato, De Somne et Vigilia, De Memoria et Reminiscentia, De Morte et Vita. Among the books covered were also the spurious *De Plantis* and the very dubious *Liber de Causes,* which Thomas translated from an Arabic source. Also studied were the criticism of Aristotle's *Categories* by Gilbert de la Porree, known also as the *Sex Principia,* and the *Summulae Logicales* by Petrus Hispanus (Pope John XXI). The *Barbarismus* of Donatus and Priscian's *De Accentu* were often studied in the same lecture series.[97]

In 1366, changes were made in the curriculum by two papal legates. For the mastery of Latin, the two parts of Priscian were dropped, and in their place Eberhard of Bethune's new *Grecimus,* and a new grammar, the *Doctrinale* of Alexander of Villedieu, were to be used. The latter taught Latin in a doggerel verse, using rhyme to simplify the memorization of the Latin forms of syntax. It proved so popular that it continued to be used until the sixteenth century.[98] Master of arts candidates had to attend all disputations for one year, from October until Lent, and also participate in at least two of them.

During the later Middle Ages some of the newer books were required by students in liberal arts. Marsilius of Inghen gave Paris his *Parva Logicala;* they also studied Eberhard's *Labyrinthus* and *Grecismus;* also, Nicolaus de Lyra's scriptural commentaries were used, and John Holywood's *Tractatus* offered them an astronomical work, the *Tractatus de Sphaera.* By 1431 Paris also made use of a *Nova Rhetorica* of Cicero and the *Metamorphoses* of Ovid. Those who preferred the change could read the works of Virgil in place of Boethius' early work, *Tropica.*[99]

Courses at Paris and Bologna, the two model schools under our consideration, were classified as two types: *ordinary,* delivered by an ordinarius, or regular doctor, and *cursory,* usually delivered by a bachelor who was a graduate student. At Paris the ordinarius was known as a master, while at Bologna they referred to him as a doctor. The ordinary lectures were prescribed by the statutes as required for the degrees, while the cursory lectures were often optional. The former were often delivered by distinguished faculty members, such as Thomas Aquinas or Bonaventura; these were privileged courses, and offered a choice place in the schedule. The required courses were usually given in the morning, while the cursory ones were given in the afternoons or evenings. Since lighting was a problem for both the students and the professors, they both went to bed very early. The ordinary lectures during the summers began at five o'clock, and at six o'clock during the winter months.[100] The entire morning was usually used by regular doctors. The cursory lectures were also called extraordinary; they were given in the afternoon, usually by graduate students who were quite advanced in their studies. They lectured on books of their own choice. Those lectures were more superficial and were delivered in a freer, slower style. Students were permitted to ask questions and there was some discussion.

Since ordinary lectures at Paris and Bologna were delivered by regular resident masters or doctors to whom students were answerable in their degree requirements, they were held in high esteem. No student questions were permitted, for professors were under oath to cover thoroughly a specific amount of material, as well as any *Glossen* added by distinguished scholars. To safeguard against any deviations, *Puncta*, or stops, were often employed to establish the divisions between the material covered in each lecture. At Bologna, professors who failed to comply with their oaths by covering the required material were severely fined.[101]

The lectures by an ordinarius were delivered by the master or doctor from an elevated platform, covered with a canopy, which was in clear view of all the students. In the later Middle Ages the platform was replaced by a specially-built *Katheder*, such as Luther used in the *Grosse Hörsaal* of the Black Cloister at Wittenberg. Such a *Katheder* served well both for lecturing and for disputations. The structure had two elevated rows of seats. At the top sat the master in charge of a class, elevated some nine feet above the students, while for disputations the row below provided seats for three participating faculty members.[102]

During the Middle Ages at the University of Paris, the acquisition of a doctorate in theology was a long and arduous undertaking. Only those who were rich enough, or blessed with rich relatives, could hope to attain that goal. The basic requirement in the statutes was an age of at least thirty-five, while the length of time required in residence varied somewhat. In the beginning, the academic steps that the candidate had to ascend were somewhat less demanding; however, by 1366, the time required to complete the entire program was about sixteen years.[103] The prospective theologian attended Bible lectures for four years, and then for two more years he attended lectures on Lombard's *Sentences*—the famous medieval four-volume treatise on dogmatics that covered Catholic doctrine from creation to the final judgment. After that, if the student felt he was sufficiently prepared, he could approach his master and request to be examined as to his fitness for teaching. The student then appeared before a group of masters. If they found him to be qualified, he was promoted to a degree of *Baccalareus Biblicus*—also called *Biblicus Ordinarius*—which was the first step toward the doctorate.[104]

The exercise through which a candidate had to go to become a *Biblicus Ordinarius* was called, in Paris terminology, the *introitus*. In his *primo cursu*, or first course, the young student lectured from a prescribed book of the Bible for one year; these lectures were delivered under the dean's supervision. If the *Biblicus* conducted himself well, he continued his studies the next year on another assigned book of the Bible. Then the student was obligated to participate in a disputation on a specific thesis assigned to him by the theological faculty.[105] He engaged in a dialectical debate with other graduate students who had already advanced to the *Baccalareus Formatus* degree. In the earlier days of the university this disputation was taken quite seriously, but in time it seems to have turned into a farce. In later centuries it consisted largely of flattering speeches about the doctorate in theology, the Catholic Church, and the University of Paris.[106] If the student fared well in his knowledge of Lombard and in a public demonstration of his skill, he was now advanced to a *Baccalareus Sententiarius*, one fully qualified to begin a lecture series on Peter Lombard's *Sentences*, which he did for the next three or four years.

Before beginning his lectures on the *Sentences*, the student delivered a public address, called the *principium*, in which he expounded on the problems involved in a course on Lombard. After the student achieved maturity as a dogmatician and dialectician, he was permitted to demonstrate his skill in a public disputation; if the faculty was impressed, he advanced to the third step and became a *Baccalareus Formatus*. This meant that he had now fully arrived as a lecturer on Lombard.[107] Later he gained further experience in disputations, responding to some of the masters in annual debates, and taking part in at least one examination of a new master. Meanwhile, he might occasionally be asked to preach a sermon that would be observed by the faculty. Between his rise to a *Baccalareus Formatus* and the attainment of a master of theology, the candidate was to remain in Paris.[108]

During the Middle Ages, academic disputation was regarded as a powerful teaching tool; it continued to be so viewed until the time of the German Reformation. At Paris, the theological disputations (just as they were later, in German universities) were of several kinds. There were the student practice disputations, in which a professor instructed students in methodology; then there were promotional disputations, held in connection with academic degrees; finally, there were faculty disputations such as those engaged in by Thomas and Bonaventura, which the students attended by statutory controls. The latter were used to instruct students in their respective disciplines. In the years of a student's rise, the second type was used to determine a student's mental and intellectual maturity. But the crowning disputation occurred at the close of the theologian's education, held in the lecture hall of the Sorbonne. This was also a kind of endurance test. During this final disputation, the candidate stood on a platform for an entire day, from five in the morning until five at night, with only an hour for lunch, facing a battery of successive opponents, eager to distinguish themselves. In this dialectical dual, the opponents fought like fencers, with the audience stamping or cheering as the rivals scored their points.[109]

Once a candidate in theology had met all the statutory requirements, there came a time for the great "Jubilee Day" of inception as a master. Eventually, at Paris, the licensing of a doctoral candidate turned into quite an affair. It is said that in Paris thousands of citizens would line the streets to witness an academic parade of the distinguished theologians from Methurine Convent to the Bishop's Hall. Since theological doctorates were granted only in alternate years, and on All Saints Day, the affair proved to be all the more impressive.

The University of Bologna was, in its organization, practically the opposite of Paris. While Paris remained in frequent contact with the papacy, Bologna did not wish to become too involved with Rome.[110] In Paris, prior to the university's origin, there existed a body of teachers that drew students from great distances; at Bologna, mature lawyers came from all parts of Europe, organized themselves as a body of students, and then employed distinguished teachers to instruct them. There the students were mostly in their thirties, and were already well-established in a profession at home. They prescribed what courses should be offered, at what hours the lectures were to be delivered, exactly how many absences the faculty would be permitted, and what fines would be assessed if a teacher failed to comply.[111]

In France, Roman civilization had been practically wiped out through the barbarian invasions; the education that later emerged under the Merovingian and Carolingian rulers was centered in monasteries and cathedral schools. In Italy, by contrast, Roman education had never completely been destroyed, and the church did not have a monopoly on learning. It was from Italy that Charlemagne had recruited some of his first teachers.[112] Prior to the rise of the Italian universities, northern Italy had a variety of preparatory schools. There were monastic and cathedral schools, which stressed the liberal arts, as well as secular schools and city schools that provided training for professions and business.[113]

A fierce civic pride existed within Italian towns, expressing itself in a struggle for independence from the Holy Roman Empire. The Italians were administrators, organizers, warriors, traders, and dealers in grain and oil. All this demanded persons who were trained in letter writing, the drafting of contracts and legal documents, and the preparation of materials for legal suits.[114] Students were taught that rhetoric was essential to the art of persuasion in court.[115]

The Romans had left a rich legal legacy to western civilization. The invading barbarians used their own Teutonic law codes for their own tribes, but permitted the native Italians in the cities to continue using their own Roman codes.[116] Beneath the changes in Italian urban life, the continuity of Roman legal institutions had never completely been broken.

The revival of Roman law at Ravenna and Pavia dates to the Carolingian renaissance. By the eleventh century, Bologna also experienced a revival of interest in its legal past. As students flocked to Paris to study theology, others went to Bologna to learn more about the great Roman institutions of antiquity. Schools in the liberal arts now developed into schools of law.[117]

During the Investiture Controversy between the papacy and the empire, many difficult legal problems arose. Bishops, archbishops, cardinals, and popes needed experts trained in the complexities of canon law. And these experts needed reliable textbooks. In 1142, a Camaldunensian monk and manuscript copyist named Gratian, in the monastery of St. Felix in Bologna, published his *Decretum*, or *Concordantia discordantium Canorum*.[118] Gratian used a method similar to that of Abelard in his *Sic et Non*; he placed contradictory opinions of different authorities side by side, then refuted them with answers drawn from past decisions of the church. This volume soon became the definitive university textbook on canon law. The University of Bologna became famous for both civil law and canon law, and often a scholar would take a doctorate in both disciplines. Such a recipient was usually given the title of *iuris utriusque doctor*.[119]

The great migration of students to Bologna must have begun sometime before Emperor Frederick Barbarossa issued his *Habita* of 1158.[120] This document represents the earliest granting of privileges to university faculties and students in western Europe.[121] There was no specific mention of Bologna in the *Habita*, but it referred to students at foreign schools, and Bologna's students interpreted it as applying especially to that institution. The emperor assured students' safety in traveling between their homelands and the university. The document also assured protection against arrest for debts incurred by others.[122] While they were at the university, students were to be considered under the emperor's protection. The document also decreed that, should a student be charged with misconduct, he was to bring the charge to his master, or, if he preferred, to a bishop whom the emperor had assigned to try such cases.[123] Since the masters at Bologna were generally citizens of the town, they did not face the same legal problems as did students.

The many foreign students took a lesson from Bologna's guilds and decided to organize themselves. They held mass meetings for this purpose, and when the city officials refused to comply with the terms of the *Habita*, the students threatened to move elsewhere. As a result, a special board was appointed to look into complaints about housing and food; it was composed of two city officials and two student provosts.[124]

In the early days at Bologna, a teacher such as Irnerius did not need a license. All he needed was a good reputation as a legal scholar and the willingness of the foreign students to accept him as their lecturer. Tradition claims that Irnerius drew such crowds of students that no building could accommodate them; accordingly, he lectured from an open-air pulpit in the town square.[125] Another doctor who drew large crowds, Albericus, lectured in the Pallazo Publico.[126] This indicates that even prior to the great influx of foreign students, professors had organized their own college. The emperor's *Habita* proves the existence of a professors' *Collegia* prior to 1158.[127] By the year 1215, Buoncompagno had produced his *Rhetorica Antiqua*, from which he read in the presence of Bologna's "university professors of civil and canon law and other doctors and a large body of scholars."[128] This earliest evidence of Bologna's existence as a university would put its emergence at about the same date as that of the University of Paris.

Sometime between the *Habita* of 1158 and the *Rhetorica Antiqua* in 1215, the student body organization divided itself into two separate guilds or universities. The one representing the students from the northern lands of Europe was known as the *Ultramontane* university; it included Germans, Gascons, Provençals, Spaniards, Normans, and some English students; while those from Italy were part of the *Cisalpine* university, including Lombards, Tuscans, and Romans.[129] Both sides elected rectors and proctors to represent them in official matters.

At first glance, it seems strange that Bologna's Podesta (a ruler who, in the cities of Lombardy, was usually a dictator) would permit such a guild of students to develop. But its growth was gradual. Even though the two original student organizations used the term *Universitas*, the name was misleading. In the beginning, the students had not organized as academic institutions. Their principal concern was self-protection. They laid no claim to controlling the professors, nor the academic side of the *studium*, which was regarded as the professors' priority. It would take some three decades, and a number of fortuitous circumstances, for the new university to evolve.[130]

The basic unit out of which the later institution emerged was called the nation, which seems to have originated at Bologna. The term is of Latin origin, and originally referred to a foreigner.[131] In 1265 the *Ultramontane* university consisted of fourteen nations, but by 1432 it had increased to sixteen.[132] In 1323 the *Cisalpine* university was divided into the Lombard, Tuscan, and Roman nations, which, in turn, were subdivided into *consiliarii*, which also made up the rector's executive council.

The nations were each governed by a number of officials.[133] According to the German constitution, the German nation was governed by two proctors, while the remaining nations had but one. The German proctors ranked higher than the rector of the *Ultramontane* university and were exempt from giving oaths to anyone. These proctors had one-year terms and kept careful records of the transactions within the nation, which were recorded in their *Annals*.[134]

Another official in the nation was called the *Syndict*. When the proctors took their office they appointed two students to serve them. These were the guardians of the records and funds. At the end of their terms, the proctors turned everything over to the *Syndicts* for checking. The nation had a treasure chest, called the *archa* or *capsa*, for which each proctor held one key while in office. This chest contained the seal of the nation and its vestments, missals, statutes, and matriculation rolls, all of which were stored in the proctor's house. By 1427 there were two chests: a large one for daily use, and a smaller one for special treasures.[135]

Another official used by the proctors was the errand boy, known as the university beadle. There were several types of beadles used at different levels. Assemblies of the nation were held in S. Frediano Church, and all the matriculated nation members were obligated to attend. There students could present petitions to the proctors requesting changes in the nation's statutes; these proposals could be adopted by a two-thirds vote.[136]

The congregation of the university, representing both the *Ultramontane* and *Cisalpine* bodies, was the supreme governing body. Since it was a large organization, it usually met in the cathedral.[137] At such a meeting, where the rectors presided, the university selected thirty-eight *consiliarii* officials, nineteen from each school, who advised the two rectors on matters of governance during their six-month terms. These *consiliarii* were chosen by ballot and formed the rector's executive council, or senate.[138]

Since the rector was the chief executive officer of the University of Bologna during the early Middle Ages, his duties were widespread and numerous. He was responsible for proper student housing and necessary repair of their premises. He also had both civil and criminal jurisdiction. By 1405, the records indicate that this jurisdiction extended to professors as well as students. When litigation occurred between the two jurist universities, the two rectors supervised its outcome. The same also applied to disputes between students at the two institutions. The rector took an oath to help elect his successor. If the rector wanted to leave Bologna, he had to obtain the consent of the majority of his *consiliarii* in the executive council. He even had to post a bond to guarantee his return.[139]

After the student universities became sovereign, their rectors employed four students to report on how courses were managed. Their identities were kept secret so that they could attend courses without being recognized. The rectors were very concerned about the methods employed by teachers in the presentation of their material. These had been prescribed at the beginning of a course, where beadles read the instruction about the proper procedure. Bells were rung at stated intervals during the lecture, guiding the professor in the cadence of his delivery. Complaints could be brought before the executive council, which was composed of the rector and the *consiliarii*. The degree of violation of university requirements helped determine how much an instructor would be asked to forfeit from his salary.[140] Like the nations, each of the two jurist universities also had *Syndicts*, who were appointed to check the work of the rectors; they would perform a careful audit at the end of a rector's term.[141]

Instruction in medicine had originally flourished at the University of Salerno, where Arabic influence had been strong. But soon medicine also began to be studied at other Italian universities, including Bologna. By the fourteenth century, medicine had assumed such importance that its professors agreed to found a new university of arts and medicine within the framework of a double school system.[142] They elected their own rector to run the new school. In this new academic institution, the liberal arts were to prepare students for the study of medicine, but were also to serve the other jurist universities. In the beginning the rector of the school of medicine had jurisdiction over both civil and criminal cases; by 1405 this included both students and professors.[143]

Liberal arts students in the school of medicine were given preparatory courses emphasizing philosophy, logic, and natural science. For this they used the works of Aristotle and the commentaries of Averroes. Before long the liberal arts were influenced by the Renaissance, and the courses began to emphasize poetry and the study of the Latin classics. The college also offered instruction in grammar and rhetoric to improve students' ability in elocution. By the close of the fourteenth century, they offered courses in Greek language and literature. Arts students were also given courses in astronomy and astrology.[144]

By the fourteenth century, Bologna was granted the privilege of offering a doctorate in theology. The theological courses were similar to those at Paris. In preparation for the *Biblicus* degree, lectures on the Bible were offered. There were also lectures based on Lombard's *Sentences*, covering the dogma of the church from creation to the last judgment. By the close of the fifteenth century, Thomistic theology was also being taught.[145]

The influence of the Italian Renaissance was evident in the later history of the liberal arts at Bologna. The courses attempted to teach an appreciation of the Latin classics. Kristeller points out that such courses were not meant for the *Dilettantes*, but for future teachers, secretaries, and chancellors in courts. By then, Greek had become a regular discipline. Moral philosophy was frequently offered by professors of rhetoric and poetry. What was taught there, in northern Italy, soon became known as the *Studia Humanitatis*.[146]

The two universities of law offered courses in canon law (based, in the main, on Gratian's *Decretum*), which were turned over to the ordinary professors; but the extraordinary lectures also covered the decretals of later popes, especially those of Pope Gregory IX. In the late Middle Ages there was also a rich body of canonistic literature and many marginal glosses on which the professors could expound.[147]

The promotion of students at Bologna was similar to that of students in theology and canon law at the University of Paris. After a student had attended classes in civil or canon law (or both), he might approach the rector for permission to try for a bachelor's degree. To demonstrate his maturity, he might be asked to lecture on a single title of civil or canon law or on an entire book. If he were a canonist he might be asked to give a lecture on a single title after four years, or a whole decretal after five years. In addition, the student would engage in a *repetition* with opponents, after which he was solemnly admitted to the bachelors' ranks. To gain experience he now became a teacher in the masters school. In canon law the student engaged in a *repetition* on a book of canon law. To obtain a doctorate in civil law, the student had to complete at least eight years of study; in the case of canon law, the requirement was at least six years. Some students attended law courses for ten years, in which case they could be awarded a degree of *Doctor utriusque iuris*, according to the statutes of 1432. No formal examination was required for a bachelor of laws.[148]

In the early days at Bologna, students in law were not very restricted in obtaining doctorates. They were merely examined by the faculty, and, if found to be qualified, were granted the *licentia docendi*. At that time the doctors controlled the entire ceremony for the conferral of degrees. Later, however, Rome felt that the church should control education. Bologna seemed out of line with Paris, where the chancellor conferred the *licentia docendi*. Thus Pope Honorius III, a former archdeacon at Bologna, placed the Bologna *studium* under ecclesiastical control. After that, the archdeacon of Bologna presided at all graduation exercises.[149]

16

The Electoral Town
of Wittenberg

Old woodcuts and etchings are invaluable aids in visualizing the electoral town of Wittenberg. It would have been extremely useful had Lucas Cranach the Elder prepared one, as he did of the Castle Church, but unfortunately neither he nor anyone else has given us an image of the town in the early sixteenth century. A number of later woodcuts, etchings, and pen sketches of the *Lutherstadt* have been preserved, some of which are misleading or have been misdated. Most of the artists restricted their views to the river side, which left one without much knowledge of the actual buildings in Wittenberg.

In 1936, on the basis of extant drawings of individual buildings and a real estate plat from 1623 (the one Edith Eschenhagen used in her doctoral study[1]), Heinrich Heubner, O. H. Heubner, and I were able to create an "aerial" view of Wittenberg, ca. 1546. A black and white copy of this view appeared in my book *Luther and His Times*.[2]

The electorate of Saxony changed after the defeat of Elector John Frederick at Mühlberg in 1547, and Elector August made profound changes in the *Lutherhaus* area of town. This necessitated the preparation of a second aerial view, completed with the assistance of Wilbert Seidel, depicting that part of town as it would have appeared in 1580.[3] The numbering of the buildings is the same as on the *Plan of Wittenberg in 1623* and *Churstadt Wittenberg* A.D. 1546.[4]

An inquiry into the appearance of sixteenth-century Wittenberg is also aided by nine descriptions of the *Lutherstadt* by eyewitnesses, written between 1508 and 1650. One must be cautious in using them, however, because they reflect a variety of biases.

In the early sixteenth century, an obscure traveler visited Wittenberg, drawn no doubt by the fame of its university. He evidently felt some disappointment at the sights in the city, for he has left us with this impression: it was a "poor, unattractive town, with old, small, low, ugly, wooden houses, more like a village than a town."[5] Even more disparaging is the description from the pen of Luther's ardent opponent Johannes Cochlaeus, who wrote the following comment on Wittenberg to Johann Dietenberg in 1524:

> A miserable, poor, dirty village, in comparison with Prague, hardly worth three farthings; yes, in fact, it is not worthy to be called a town in Germany. It has an unhealthy, disagreeable climate, is without vineyards, orchards, or fruitbearing trees of any kind; it is a regular beer chamber; on account of its cold and smoke it is not an enjoyable place; it is very dirty; in fact, what would there be in Wittenberg were it not for the castle, the *Stift*, and the university? One sees nothing else but Lutheran, that is, dirty homes, unclean alleys; all roads, paths, and streets are full of filth. It has a barbarous people that make their living from breweries and saloons; and a body of merchants not worth three cents. Its marketplace is empty; its town is without better citizens. The people dress as those of the lower middle class. There is great poverty in all the homes of the town.[6]

How much of Wittenberg Cochlaeus actually saw when he visited it in 1524 cannot be established, but his patron, Duke George, agreed with him: "That a single monk, out of such a hole, should undertake a reformation is not to be tolerated."[7]

There appears to have been some ground for such opinions. Valentin von Mellerstadt, son of the cofounder of the University of Wittenberg, once remarked that he felt as though he were sitting on top of a flaying ground.[8] This was, no doubt, due to the close proximity of the university to the stockyards, which were located on the Elbe near the Elster Gate.[9] When the wind blew from a northeasterly direction, the smell may have been quite offensive. Philip Melanchthon, who grew up at Bretten in the Rhine valley, once wrote his former student Camerarius that Wittenberg was a "spot that has no houses, but only tiny cottages, mere huts built of clay and covered with hay and straw."[10]

A more positive view of the town exists in the form of a dialogue between a professor and a student, generally known as the *Dialogus of 1507*.[11] It was written in 1502 by Meinhard, a young, humanistic liberal arts professor, at the request of Mellerstadt, Wittenberg's first rector.[12] In the *Dialogus* we encounter frequent references to specific buildings that aid the reader to form a mental picture of what the town was really like. Even though the document was meant as a *Lockschrift*, to draw students to the elector's new university, it is quite useful, especially chapter sixteen, which is a tour through the city. Eschenhagen's research has shown that this volume has real value.[13] In the summer of 1898, Johannes Hausleiter, in a search for rare books in the former ducal library, happened upon the Jena original of the *Dialogus*,[14] which then appeared in print in 1903.[15]

At this point, a survey of the town plan would be helpful. The market was at the center; from there the streets moved at right angles, fanning out in all directions toward the city gates and the town walls.[16] The river road, formerly the *Langengasse*, became known as the *Collegiengasse* and *Schloszgasse*. This was the long street that ran from the front of the Black Cloister to the Castle Church.

According to Kruger, the inhabitants and the Ascanier decided as early as 1306 to enclose the electoral town with a wall, and this was completed in 1323.[17] The first fortifications consisted of the wall with wooden breastworks, with some kind of earth-embankments added by 1409; these turned Wittenberg into a rather securely fortified electoral center for the Ascanier family.[18] Later a deep, wide moat was added. There were also three elaborate city gates and seven watchmen's towers.[19] The Elster Gate was named after the nearby Black Elster River. Another gate was the Elb Thor, controlling traffic from the south after it crossed Frederick's river bridge into town. Coswiger Thor controlled all traffic to and from the west on the river highway; it derived its name from a nearby village.[20]

Elector John Frederick, fearing the outbreak of war with Charles V, began refortifying Wittenberg in 1542. Charitius tells us that he gave the city a new wall, with high earthworks and an improved moat. This forced some changes in the neighborhood of Luther's home.[21] Schalscheleth has left us this description of the elector's fortifications:

> In the year 1542 he [John Frederick] had the town of Wittenberg surrounded with high breastworks and a deep moat, and he had it thoroughly fortified with a double wall. Prior to this the town had but a single wall and a moat. Also, a dam was created to protect the city from floods from the Elbe. In order to fortify Wittenberg more strongly and more advantageously, he had the eastern part around Elster Gate narrowed. For this a number of buildings had to be removed in that vicinity. Among these was the small chapel that belonged to the neighboring Augustinian Cloister, in which Luther had often preached and said mass. About this Luther complained as bitterly as Jonah over his withered vine. The stones of the buildings were used in the fortifications. This made Wittenberg on the eastern end more rounded, where formerly it was more pointed.[22]

The narrowing of the city wall next to the *Lutherhaus*, with the danger that the high embankment would cause the wall to cave in, gave Luther much cause for concern. But Sennert's *Athenae* claims that all the reformer's complaints were in vain.[23] Charitius quotes the reformer as once remarking at his table that,

> If I should live another year, my little room, from which I stormed the Pope, will disappear; which, because of its significance, would be worthy of being preserved forever. But the large breastwork, main wall, and principal defense will destroy it.[24]

Hortleder also provided these interesting observations:

> The town of Wittenberg is well-fortified and laid out in rectangular form; but its length is greater than its width. On the widest side the Elbe flows just four hundred steps away. There the terrain is level, making it difficult for an enemy to hide.
>
> The town is completely surrounded by a deep, wide moat that remains filled with water; behind it is a nice, thick breastwork that is sixty feet wide. . . . It also has five powerful bastions, which, with the sixth bullwork, permit

the defenders to strike and shoot over the entire area. In Wittenberg there are 120 pieces of artillery, not including smaller firearms.[25]

In 1547 Bugenhagen, the city pastor, also left us his impressions:

> Our fortifications, humanly speaking, are not to be weighed lightly, for there is a large quantity of supplies, provisions of guns, powder, and lead. When, on the Thursday following the festival of St. Martin, Duke Moritz sent the Roman king with his barbarous hordes against the city, our defenders were prepared and shot at them from the walls. Then his grace concluded, after some consultation with his key men, that it would not be so easy to approach the city without great losses, and that he would not attempt to besiege it, and he pulled back. In fact, I have read that the Kaiser is to have remarked that it was fortunate that the city was occupied the way it was; otherwise his people could have racked their heads as to how they would have captured the town.[26]

The city of Wittenberg was laid out in quarters. These were named after the principal streets and were known as the *Coswiger, Markt, Juden,* and *Elster* quarters. Eschenhagen, who examined the town records in detail, claims that the division of the city into quarters was made for purposes of tax assessments and for military service recruitments, but that they also served as precincts for elections.[27] Exactly when Jews lived in the northern part of Wittenberg can no longer be established. Apparently they were gone by the time of the *Dialogus*:

> R: From what quarter of town does the Rische Bach flow swiftly?
> M: It is the Jewish Quarter, named after the Jews who once lived there.
> R: But who have since been expelled?
> M: Completely.[28]

The streets of the city were kept in good repair, especially those bearing most of the public traffic. The *Collegian Gasse* and *Schlosz Gasse*, in particular, were regularly kept paved with cobblestones. The town records speak of funds paid, "to improve the stone-paved streets," for which the citizens were taxed, each paying for those parts in front of their property.[29] Failure to sweep the streets in front of your dwelling would result in fines.[30] The area around the *Rathaus* and *Pfarrkirche* must certainly have been covered with cobblestones, for with weekly markets, those places were in frequent use.

Wittenberg had a curfew of 10:00 P.M. By then there were guards above the three city gates and the seven protected turrets in the city walls. An additional guard was in the *Pfarrkirche*. The town was usually unlit at night, but for special occasions the streetcorners were lit with *Pechkranzen*, or tar-rings. On dark nights the *Pfarrer* of the *Stadtkirche*, the *Bürgermeister* of the town, and a few other privileged individuals were preceded by "lantern boys" at city expense.[31] The darkness was not without its hazards, for the Rische Bach and the Faule Bach were two streams that students had to cross on planks in order to get to their homes or dorms.[32]

For comparative purposes, we can cite Eschenhagen's population statistics about other Saxon and Thuringian cities of the time (the year or years of the available figures are in parentheses):[33]

Mühlhausen (1504–1542)	7,750–8,500
Freiburg in Saxony (1474)	5,000
Leipzig (1474)	4,000
Dresden (1474)	3,200
Chemitz (1474)	2,000–3,000
Meiszen	2,000
Eisleben	4,000

There were, of course, cities in other parts of Germany that were considerably larger. Of these we list just a few:[34]

Strassburg (1474)	20,700
Augsburg (1475)	18,000
Basel (1475)	9,000
Hamburg (1524)	12,000
Magdeburg (1550)	40,000
Berlin	12,000
Halle (1450–1680)	10,000–20,000

Wittenberg experienced some growth between 1500 and 1550. At the beginning of the century it had 392 houses and 2,146 people, but by 1550 this had increased to 446 houses and 2,400 people.[35] An old register also lists the numbers in each of the four quarters. In that list of 2,216 inhabitants there were 403 houses, of which the Coswiger Quarter had 77, with 487 people living there; the Markt Quarter had 71 houses with 410 occupants; the Juden Quarter had 123 houses with 613 persons; and the Elster Quarter had 132 houses with 716 individuals.[36]

The most heavily populated quarter of Wittenberg was the Coswiger, with an average of more than six persons per dwelling; this was followed by the Markt quarter, with about five and a half people per home; next came the Elster Quarter, with more than five persons per dwelling; the Jewish Quarter had fewer than five persons in each dwelling. The Jewish Quarter had most of the small wooden dwellings, occupied by people with low incomes; the rest of the Wittenberg was composed of stone and brick dwellings with slate roofs.

We have little information about the homes of the university faculty, for the professors and academic officials were exempt from taxes and from the supervision of the town council. They reported directly to the elector of Saxony. Around the middle of the century, the city archives listed some 44 professors, with their wives and children, having dwellings with an estimated 242 occupants. They must be counted among the city's wealthier citizens.[37]

The *Dialogus of 1507* concerned an imaginary visit to Wittenberg by a student named Reinhard, who was looking for a university at which to begin his studies. He conversed with Meinhard, a faculty member of the newly founded University of Wittenberg. In the *Dialogus*, Professor Meinhard conducted the prospective student through the city, pointing out the places of interest and leaving us with some impression of what the town looked like at the onset of the sixteenth century.[38]

Meinhard and Reinhard crossed the Elbe on the sturdy oaken bridge that had recently been erected by Frederick the Wise, then turned to the left through the *Vorstadt*, where they entered the city from the south, through the Elbe Gate.[39] As they passed through the Elbe Gasse to the Schlosz Gasse, Meinhard pointed out a large, attractive house on the corner, to the right. At the time, this house was the property of Kasper Treuschel, the town judge. After the judge's death in 1513, it became known as the *Cranachhaus*.[40] As they crossed to the Schlosz Gasse, they turned to the right and admired a large dwelling on Collegian Gasse, the home of one of the founders of the university, Polich von Mellerstadt.[41] In common parlance this was called the "Electoral Palace," which Polich had received from Frederick the Wise as a gift, in appreciation of his service.[42]

As they stood in the *Markt*, in front of the *Rathaus*, Reinhard's eyes were immediately focused on the *Apotheke*, the drugstore at the corner of the *Markt* and Coswiger Street:

R: Where is that very pleasant fragrance coming from?
M: From the apothecary, or paint shop.
R: Where is the drugstore?
M: In the building on the corner.
R: Is that a new building? Was it constructed recently?
M: The apothecary was erected the same year as the college.
R: An elaborate drugstore indeed, but no less so than this building.[43]

From there the two moved on Coswiger Gasse, into the neighborhood of the castle and the castle church, which Meinhard designated as the *arces Jovis*. Here Reinhard was attracted to a fine building, known as the "Bath of Jove," which was near the castle church. What struck the prospective student was that a basin was hung on the entrance of the house. Thus he asked:

R: Why is the basin hung outside?
M: Because there is a bathhouse here, and today it is open for bathing.
R: But why is it named after Jove?
M: Because it is near the castle of Jove, as you notice by its location.[44]

As they moved on toward the Coswiger Gate on the west end of town, which Meinhard called the Gates of Apollo, they passed the famous town mill, driven by the two small streams that flowed through the city. The student began:

R: What is that noise here, the strange sound?
M: It is a mill.
R: In that building? Whose is it?
M: It belongs to the famous princes.
R: How many wheels are spinning?
M: Five, but now a change is planned; four more are to be added to help clean the water.
R: Notice how far the wheels extend beneath the surface. Each is con-

212 *The Reformation as a University Movement*

structed of solid oak. He who built this mill was certainly a master. Where else in town do you see the like? It certainly cost much to build it.[45]

As they moved closer to the city walls, Reinhard observed that part of the wall was crumbling and holes permitted passageways in and out of the city.[46] He then asked:

R: Why are there so many holes in the town walls here, permitting entry into the streets? It appears to me such accesses are frought with much danger from invading enemies or the escape of criminals.
M: That is none of our concern. Let us enter this small chapel.[47]

Meinhard now explained that they had passed through the small Street of Goats, later called Ritter Strasse, and into the Coswiger Quarter, where he wanted him to see a fine church, the *Antoniterkappelle*.

M: Let us enter this small chapel.
R: How ornate and beautiful, adorned with ironworks in front of the altar! But whose is that high dwelling adjacent to the chapel?
M: It is the residence of the Father Lord Goswin, the prior of the house and curia in Lichtenberg, the most worthy chancellor of our school.[48]

From there they followed the path along the city wall until they came to an open site in front of the Franciscan monastery. Here stood a row of linden trees that obscured the monastery, and Reinhard became curious about the open lot:

R: What is this building site?
M: If the reports are right, a law school is to be erected here.
R: It appears to be a most convenient location, for it will be free of all disturbances.
M: You have observed correctly. This section that we just passed through is known as the new part of the city, extending to the Coswiger Quarter. But now we are walking in the direction of the Mendicant Brothers' district.[49]

As they walked in the street, around the lot, on Kloster Gasse, another line of linden trees had obscured Reinhard's view, so he could not see the *Fransiscaner Kloster*. At that time the street in front of the cloister was called the Bruder Gasse, but after the law school was erected the name was changed to Juristen Gasse. Reinhard asked:

R: Where is the monastery?
M: Are you completely blind? Don't you have eyes?
R: The linden trees obscured my view. Can we enter the monastery?
M: Since it is about seven in the evening, entry will hardly be possible.[50]

In passing, Meinhard pointed out that a small street there was where the former humanist, Petrus of Ravenna, had lived, when he was on the Wittenberg faculty, and was now called Ravenna Street. As they passed by, Reinhard saw another bathhouse, and remarked:

R: Look, there is another bath! What is its name?
M: It is the Bath of Mendicants.

From here they walked down Bürgermeister Gasse toward the *Pfarrkirche* of Wittenberg. Reinhard was much impressed, and asked:

R: What is that holy temple facing us?
M: It is the town church.
R: May we enter the edifice?
M: Certainly we may.
R: Shall we enter?
M: You may see it later on your own.[51]

Meinhard did not seem to regard the interior of the *Pfarrkirche* as suitable material for a *Lockschrift*. Reinhard's attention shifted to the small stream flowing along Juden Gasse and Coswiger Gasse to the town mill.

R: What an attractive, clear-water stream glides by here! What is its name?
M: It is the Rische Bach, named after the swift flow of its water.
R: Does any other stream flow by here?
M: Yes, there is another one on the other side of the town church.
R: Those two streams are quite useful and very attractive. Do they converge somewhere?
M: Indeed, down by the mill, prior to driving its wheels. Later, the Faule Bach yields its name to the Rische Bach.[52]

After that they walked through the northern part of town, still somewhat undeveloped at the time, crossing Potter and Coppersmith Streets, until they neared the Elster Gate. There Reinhard noticed the gate they were approaching.

R: What is the name of the gate just ahead?
M: The Elster Gate.
R: Through which we originally entered the city?
M: Exactly.
R: Where does it gets its name?
M: It was named for the Elster River.[53]

As they pass the Black Cloister, which was in the process of being rebuilt, not much was said about it, except that it would be a wonderful dwelling once completed. Nor was much said about the chapel that the Augustinians had in the courtyard. Then the student noticed another bathhouse:

R: Look, there is another bathhouse.
M: It is called the Elster Bath, named after the Elster Quarter and Gate.
R: This is really a spacious city. If I have observed the configuration correctly, it is semicircular in shape.
M: Your observation is correct.[54]

The area where they now stood was still quite open. The Old Frederick College building, known as the *Alte Collegium*, already stood near the town wall. But the *Melanchthonhaus* had not yet been erected, nor the New Friderici College near the Collegien Gasse. Reinhard asked:

R: Are there any *Bursen* here?
M: Certainly.
R: What is the name?
M: That one is the *Bursa Sophiae*, which the illustrious prince and lord, Lord John, Duke of Saxony, etc., has built in the lasting memory of his beloved princess and lady, Sophiae, his deceased wife. The dorm was named after her.
R: The building on the corner, is that not a *Bursa*?
M: It is the *Bursa Merkurii*.
R: Are lectures held in there?
M: Indeed, there are.
R: By what faculty?
M: By the law faculty.
R: To be sure, since professors of law are generally noted for their eloquence and fluency, they are always cultivating that, and Mercury, the god of eloquence, is properly their patron.[55]

Like many European cities, Wittenberg underwent considerable change after its university was founded. These changes can be observed from Plate II in *Churstadt Wittenberg in 1546*, by O. H. Heubner, in the town plan of 1623, and in the Wilbert Seidel etching of the university in 1586.[56] For later changes, see also the aerial view mentioned above.[57]

When Luther arrived in 1508, the university was only six years old and its facilities were quite limited. Like most German universities, its buildings were scattered here and there throughout the city. In the early days, most of the theological lectures were delivered in the monastery, the majority of the law lectures were given in the rooms of the castle, and the remainder were delivered in the *Bursa Merkurii*.[58]

Before long, Konrad Pfleuger, the elector's architect, began to erect the second college building in front of the old one, known as the *Collegium Friderici*, which offered additional lecture rooms and a large auditorium. The space above was a dorm for students. Later, another wing was added to unite the two buildings on the east side. During the early period, the Augustinian monastery had an open space in front, with a board wall separating the Augustinians from the colleges, while in the middle stood a little chapel, surrounded by a graveyard and a few pear trees. This was the chapel referred to earlier, where Luther preached his early sermons and conducted mass. Along the south end of the cloister was a small extension, where, as *Regens Studii*, Luther later occupied a small room on the second floor. Underneath it was a narrow driveway to a monastic garden in the rear.

Between 1539 and 1541, the elector erected a Renaissance-style house for Melanchthon, located on Collegien Gasse; he also gave him an open space extending to the monastic walls.

The Black Cloister, next door to the *Melanchthonhaus*, dates to 1365, when the electoral prince Rudolf II erected a small *Terminierhaus* for monks from Herzberg.[59] It was easy for the monks to arrive there without being noticed. A tunnel where they could keep a boat on the moat still exists. The lower floor of the cloister was used for a kitchen, while another side had a large refectory and some storerooms. The monks' sleeping quarters were mostly on the main floor, but some were housed in upper cells. On the east side of this level were two large lecture rooms, the *Grosse Hörsaal*. It was here that Luther lectured to monks and regular theological students in 1516.[60]

On the west side of this first floor was the long *Kreutzgang*, along which monks walked in pairs, silently, wearing their black-belted Augustinian robes. At dawn they would attend devotions and mass in the small chapel in the court-yard. Then they quietly went to the basement refectory for breakfast. After evening devotions they returned to their cells. As a monk, Luther lived in the square tower, and it was here that he had his famous "tower experience."

It was quite an undertaking to convert the Black Cloister into a family resi-dence for Luther in 1525. Stein has described the physical changes that took place.[61] The elector not only gave Luther the cloister as a wedding gift, but also supplied the materials for its complete renovation and for the construction of a number of rooms on the main floor. In 1936 the present author, using the avail-able sources and with the assistance of Oskar Thulin and his staff, made an attempt to reconstruct the circumstances in which the Luther family lived.[62] The Black Cloister was about 160 feet in length, 40 feet in width, and 45 feet in height. It did not have the later tower entrance, for that was not erected until after 1564. But evidence indicates that the *Lutherzimmer*, Luther's study, was preserved unchanged.[63]

Originally, during the monastic days, the *Erdgeschosz*, or ground floor on the north side, had a kitchen and some additional storerooms, while a large refectory offered dining facilities for monks, located on the south side of the basement. As far as one can determine, this arrangement continued also during later years. The monastic *Kreutzgang* extended to the east exit by way of a *Wendeltreppe*, a winding stairway to the courtyard of the little chapel. This part of the building underwent drastic changes to provide a home for Luther and Katherine. Kath-erine adorned the north entrance with the *Katherinenportal*, which she gave to Luther as a birthday present in 1540.[64] Passing from Collegien Gasse through the courtyard, the family entered by this north door to the basement or by a small stairs to the main floor. To enter the family quarters, one turned to the right. There a door opened into a long, narrow, reception room. Next came the *Lutherzimmer*, with an oak floor and paneled ceiling and walls. On the north side was a large double window with sixteenth-century-type bullseye glass. The furniture arrangement was quite simple; during the restoration of the rooms in 1842, it appears to have undergone little or no change. According to Schalscheleth, the size of the room was exactly eight meters square. On the east wall were some benches for students or visitors, while in the middle stood a sixteenth-century-style oak table, around which companions frequently gath-ered after dinner for table talk. Here also sat the "Sanhedrin," the able scholars in Hebrew, Greek, and Aramaic who assisted Luther in polishing later editions of his translation of the German Bible. In the southwest corner of the room was a built-in *Kachelofen*, a tile radiator that used hot water from a fire in a small room to the rear. Apparently Katie frequently sat and worked at a small sewing table next to the double window, while Luther wrote or did his research.[65] If we had visited the Luther dwelling after 1525, we would have observed that beyond the *Lutherzimmer* were the three bedrooms, two located on the north side and one on the southwest corner. A narrow hallway offered passage from the Luther quarters to the two lecture rooms on the south side on the main floor. They were already there in monastic days and appear not to have been altered.

Of special interest to Reformation scholars has been the *Grosse Hörsaal*, near the southeast corner of the building. Beyond that was the *Kleine Hörsaal*, a small lecture room used for smaller classes and family devotions. On the extreme east end, beyond the *Grosse Hörsaal*, was another small room, the use of which is unknown. It was in the *Grosse Hörsaal* that the young Luther started to lecture between 1515 and 1518 on the Psalms, Romans, Galatians, and Hebrews. There he also gave his lectures on the Pentateuch from 1535 until almost the time of his death. The room was of considerable size and was illuminated by four windows facing south; Luther's chair stood on the east end facing the audience.[66]

The New Friderici College accommodated some twenty students with upper story and dormer rooms. Women were forbidden to enter either of the college buildings; neither could they serve as cooks or workers in the kitchen. Of the thirty-two rooms in the two colleges, six were occupied by supervisors.[67]

In 1535, Elector John Frederick had decided that Philip Melanchthon and his family needed a more comfortable dwelling. Accordingly, he built them a Renaissance-style home.[68] The elector also purchased a garden directly behind the new home. However, since Melanchthon was the leader of the liberal arts faculty and a very busy man, the prince ordered doctors of medicine Augustine Schurff and Hieronymus Krapp to assume supervision of the project.[69]

The *Melanchthonhaus* is perhaps the best-preserved building in Wittenberg. His study has been kept in its original state. In 1936 the present author made the following note:

> It is surprising how easy one finds the experience to write at Melanchthon's desk, with the three double windows illuminating the room. I cannot but observe the contrast between this room and the dark *Lutherzimmer*.

Prior to the founding of the University of Wittenberg, the city had led a relatively simple existence. German society in the sixteenth century was heavily agrarian, and this was also true of the Wittenberg region. The many small towns and villages were surrounded by the farmers' three-field systems. Those seeking a sense of the German countryside in that era should consult Wilhelm Dilich's *Federzeichnungen* of 1627, which he did of Wittenberg and the neighboring region from all four sides of the city.[70] Dilich was a student at the University of Wittenberg during the late sixteenth century. He majored in art and was taught by former pupils of the Cranachs. Doubtless he also had some training in cartography.[71] The east view by Dilich includes the famous oak bridge built by

Frederick the Wise.[72] Not only did Dilich reproduce larger cities with remarkable accuracy, but also such little villages as Niemegk, Brück, Belzig, Jessen, and Düben, enabling the historian to obtain a fairly complete picture of the villages in the *Kurkreis* around Wittenberg. In the etchings Wittenberg thus becomes the principal city, with these little villages surrounding it like a brood of chicks around the mother hen.

The Town Council was the principal organ of government in Wittenberg, and its powers were extensive. Before the university was founded, the town *Rat* numbered eighteen members, but with the added work it increased its membership by the addition of six more seats. Responsibilities were often delegated to committees with specific assigned duties.[73]

The Town Council was really three councils functioning as one. The term of rule for a *Rat* was only one year. Thus the council was set up in thirds, one called the *Alte Rat*, because the members had governed the past year; a second third was the group actually in power, hence known as the *"regierende Rat"*; while the final third, those who would rule next year, were called the *"neue Rat."* Thus the membership rotated, with one-third dropping out and another third coming in every year. Each *Rat* had its own *Bürgermeister*, whose membership in the body is of uncertain origin. *Rat* members were, of course, eligible for reelection, so that often a prominent *Bürgermeister* was frequently the mayor of the city.[74]

Membership in the Town Council was theoretically limited to *Bürger*, taxpaying citizens; but the *Bürgerrecht* could also be purchased through payment of an annual tax of seven silver *Groschen* and four *Pfennige*. Election to the council made service mandatory, and failure to execute the required duties could result in a fine.[75] Membership was also subject to the approval of the chancellory lawyers at the electoral court, and this required a fee.[76]

The *Bürgermeister* was the principal official of the city, although within the circle of the ruling *Rat* his status was that of first among equals.[77] The *Bürgermeister* also represented the town at the elector's *Landtagen*.[78] There he became the official spokesperson for Wittenberg and the electoral circle.

The governing functions of the council were quite wide and general. They included such disparate matters as military defense of the town, the cleaning of the streets and public buildings, sanitation and waste collection, fire brigades, management of potable water, collection of duties and taxes, care for the poor and the infirm, and regulation of the guilds and educational facilities.[79]

Legislative duties were also varied. Short-term regulations were distinct from the written ordinances, which controlled the long-term civic life of the town. Typical of such ordinances were the *Armenkasse*, enacted in 1520.[80] These involved the legal secularization of the Franciscan monastery and the exhuming of the twenty-seven coffins that contained the remains of the royal Ascanier family, which were moved to the *Schloszturm* of the Castle Church. This was necessary before the monastery could become a center for welfare and serve as the town infirmary.[81] Such complex problems often required consultation with the university theologians, the law faculty, the town pastor, and the militia leaders.[82]

The council also served as a court of justice. Its powers in this respect were quite extensive and dated back to 1441, when Wittenberg formally purchased the right to become a court of justice for 1000 Rhenish Gulden.[83] The council had all the powers of a court of law, except those involving capital punishment. However, in criminal cases the nobility still enjoyed the right to be tried before the elector's *Hofgericht*, which was presided over by the elector.[84]

After the founding of the university, the problems of town governance grew more complex. Most of the *Rat's* work had to be carried out by committees. There was a military committee empowered to inspect and maintain Wittenberg's defenses and stores of food and medicine. The council also appointed officials for law enforcement. These civil duties were financed through *Wachtergeld*, guard money assessed against the citizenry, or in some instances, by a *Bürger* performing volunteer duties himself.

Such guards and officials were obligated to preserve order and warn against any surprise attack on the town; they were also to investigate crimes such as arson and robbery, and to quell student disorders. Sometimes, during epidemics, council members were obligated to quarantine travelers, cordon off infected neighborhoods, and isolate infected houses. Failure of the council members to perform their committee assignments was a serious offense.[85] The employment of fire brigades was another responsibility of the Town Council.[86] The council established various fire regulations, for the thatched roofs and half-timbered dwellings required preventive measures.[87]

Citizens were required to keep the cobblestones in front of their dwellings washed and swept. Trash was removed from alleys and millraces. Pigs had to be corralled. Stray dogs and cats were caught and removed by officials. Goats had to be kept outside the city because of their offensive odor.[88] In their supervision of the streets, the police were quite strict. Strangers wandering about in the darkened streets were challenged, stopped, and interrogated.

Wittenberg also had a *Baumeister*, who functioned as general engineer, architect, town planner, and building inspector. This official authorized new construction, supervised replacement of sites in the older quarters of town, and served an inspector.[89]

Epidemics were a constant threat because of the crowded conditions in Wittenberg. Although the *Krankenhaus* and cloisters served in times of ordinary sickness, the dreadful bacilli of cholera, bubonic plague, and typhus were more difficult to control. Isolation of the victims appears to have been the only known solution. An exodus occurred in 1527, when an epidemic caused the university to be moved to Jena. During such periods the guards at the town gates permitted only the most necessary traffic to enter or leave, and no afflicted citizens were allowed to depart. During particularly virulent epidemics, houses and even whole neighborhoods were cordoned off. The council closely supervised the *Apotheke*, which after 1521 belonged to the Cranach family.[90]

Guilds were supervised by the council as well.[91] Weights and measures were carefully regulated. Monthly inspections of scales were typical, and sizes of bread loaves and grain baskets were commonly checked. Guild meetings were not permitted without the approval of the council, and guild by-laws and regulations were subject to its review. Goldsmiths and other artisans were likewise licensed. Prices of foodstuffs such as meat, fish, poultry, and vegetables were determined by the council; penalties for offenses were severe. A baker by the name of Galle Tylen was once heavily fined because his loaves were too small.[92]

The council also had the *Financewesen*, the whole fiscal system of the city, under its control. Two treasurers disbursed city funds, paid outstanding debts, and paid the taxes due to the elector. It was also their duty to collect taxes and debts owed to the town. These officials exercised supervision over the records office, and they made sure that the entries were correctly recorded by the office of the city secretary.[93] The city secretary was apparently a person of considerable importance, and his term of office continued for many years.

Many other officials helped administer the affairs of Wittenberg. There was a *Bauknecht* who was in charge of construction and urban development. He had an assistant called the *Ziegelmeister*, the slate-master, whose duties included the management of the Wittenberg slate quarries and storehouses. The city had attained a monopoly in the acquisition of slate. The riverkeepers were responsible for the quality of water in the streams that supplied the town; they cleaned the millraces and managed the fisheries. In the town *Marstall* there was also a *Reitknecht*, who was responsible for horses and riding; a *Karrenknecht*, in charge of vehicles; and a *Fuhrknecht* and his assistants, who controlled travel in the town. For the city's supervision of the surrounding forests, as well as the supply of lumber for construction and cordwood for stoves, the *Rat* had appointed a *Holzforster*. The town also managed the *Ratskeller* in the basement of the *Rathaus*, which employed a *Bierrufer* to stand in the street and attract customers. Within the *Keller* were the men who served the drinks. The custodians of the *Ratskeller* became quite wealthy.[94]

The livestock of the citizenry were herded daily to and from Wittenberg to the outlying pastures by the *Hirtsmann*, who was employed by the council. None of the council officials, except for the secretary and the *Syndicus*, had permanent jobs. They were employed on a weekly basis and could be dismissed at any time. Each official wore a distinctive dress provided by the council, designed for both winter and summer. New uniforms were issued annually. However, the Hausmann who stood guard in the tower of the *Pfarrkirche* wore a fur coat so as to protect himself against the cold of winter.[95]

Wittenberg paid the elector annual taxes totaling ninety-nine *Schock*, or nearly three hundred Gulden per year. The citizens could be drafted for military service, although some of them were exempt from this duty.[96] The elector proclaimed ordinances to control civic strife; thus his troops were at times required to restore order.[97] Since the elector considered the university his personal institution, the use of royal troops to quiet student disorders was deemed appropriate.[98] There was close and unique relationship between the *Kurstadt* and the Saxon electors. In the medieval sense, the sovereignty of the princes had its feudal seat there. The reign of a new elector had its genesis in the ceremony of investiture, in which the Wittenberg town leaders became the principal officials.[99]

17

The Founding
of the University

The German universities of the Middle Ages were often founded on the authorization of the emperors or the papacy. Frequently, princes founded schools with the support of wealthy *Bürger*. Nine German universities were started by rulers, while seven others were founded by cities.[1] Four institutions, Prague (1348), Vienna (1365), Erfurt (1382), and Cologne (1384), date to the fourteenth century; eleven fall into the period between 1402 and 1477.[2] All existed prior to the founding of the University of Wittenberg.[3]

The German universities were founded by *Stiftungsbriefe*, letters of foundation, and used the Paris professorial method of government. The University of Prague, the original German university, was founded by Emperor Charles IV, who had studied in France in his younger days. Its statutes were modeled after both Paris and Bologna.[4]

Cologne modeled its statutes after Prague.[5] Prague and Cologne were significant influences on Leipzig and Erfurt, and they, in turn, influenced the statutes of Rostock, Basel, Greifswald, and Tübingen.[6]

There were no doubt many reasons why Frederick the Wise decided to found a new university in Electoral Saxony in 1502.[7] Friedensburg points out that in the time of Maximilian I, German princes who did not have universities within their lands were urged to establish such institutions.[8] Scholars have also stressed the influence of, among others, Frederick's family physician, Mellerstadt.

Martin Polich von Mellerstadt, of Franconia, was one of the two key figures involved in the establishment of the University of Wittenberg. The other was Johann von Staupitz. Mellerstadt matriculated at the University of Leipzig in 1470, where he received his A.B. in 1472 and his M.A. in 1475. Gustav Bauch, who has offered us a detailed account of Mellerstadt, classified him as a strict Thomist who was not very original in his lectures.[9] Later Mellerstadt continued his graduate studies in medicine at Leipzig. He acquired his doctorate in 1487, and by 1493 he became a Leipzig professor.[10] In the meantime, he became quite famous for his medical knowledge and served as the family physician of Frederick the Wise.[11] Mellerstadt lectured at Leipzig in the *Via Antiqua* interpretations of professors from Paris, Cologne, and Leipzig.[12] He became an ardent defender of Greco-Roman medicine as opposed to Arabian.[13] He also became interested in astronomy and the horoscope, as related to medicine. He prepared a compendium of predictions of events that attracted the attention of Frederick the Wise. Through Pico in Italy he also became interested in the relationship between medicine and astrology, which caused him to study the *Kabbala*.[14]

Toward the close of the fifteenth century, Europe was stricken with a fearful plague of syphilis, or "the French Disease," as it was called by many doctors in Germany. The previously undocumented disease baffled the medical world.[15] From reading the astrological works of Leoninceno of Vicenza, Mellerstadt came to believe that he knew how this terrible disease might be combatted, and he could not resist displaying his new learning in a public disputation at Leipzig. This aroused opposition among certain members of the conservative faculty. His first challenger was one of his own students, Simon Pistoris. Pistoris drafted a set of theses against Leoninceno of Vicenza and Mellerstadt; this resulted in a pamphlet war in which Mellerstadt appears to have been the victor. But the Leipzig faculty was on Pistoris' side.[16] Mellerstadt's secondhand knowledge of classical sources was now met by an able challenger, his former student Konrad Koch, known as Wimpina (after his native town, Wimpfen in Swabia).[17] Wimpina and Mellerstadt engaged in a heated battle that began with medicine and flared into a contest of poetry versus theology. Neither participant was a real humanist. Mellerstadt tried to show that poetry was a source of divine wisdom.[18] Wimpina accused Mellerstadt of being a heretic, and sent his accusations to Duke George. He tagged Mellerstadt as an idiot, a physician who knew no theology and who should remain in his own field.[19] Mellerstadt then charged Wimpina with belittling humanism, and blamed him for Leipzig's barbarism. The dispute became intensely personal, and no course was left but for both of them to leave Leipzig.[20]

Mellerstadt realized that he was no longer welcome, so he contacted Frederick the Wise and offered his services to help found the University of Wittenberg. The two of them discussed ways in which Mellerstadt could recruit students and faculty, and methods by which the school could be financed.

Mellerstadt looked for support from the famous humanist Hermann von Busche, the doctor of medicine Erasmus Stuler, and the Scotist Herman Kaiser of Stolberg. He promised Stolberg that he would become the Probst of the Castle Church, which was already highly endowed. In a letter to Herman Kaiser, he wrote:

> You will be, in such a post, Probst [or prior], and will be the head of the student body, also the future chancellor of the university, in which capacity you will have things as you wish.[21]

Mellerstadt wrote a second letter to Kaiser in which he tried to assure him that the Wittenberg university foundation was being well planned:

> We will recruit a stately group by the addition of more scholars, for the elec-

tor plans to enlarge the *Stift* by the addition of a large number of ecclesiastical benefices and parishes in Ducal Saxony, which he plans to incorporate with the university; these being in the land of Ducal Saxony, and in addition, several in lands outside at Altenburg, Gotha, and parishes in Orlamünde, Eisfeld, and additional ones.[22]

Kaiser was ready to accept the position as *Probst* in the Castle Church, but not the additional duty to serve as the university chancellor.

A second founder of the University of Wittenberg was Johann von Staupitz of Tübingen, who later became vicar general of the Augustinian Hermits.[23] Staupitz and the elector had been boyhood friends, no doubt while the young Frederick was a student in the monastery at Grimma. Staupitz had received his university education at Cologne and Leipzig, receiving an M.A. in liberal arts in 1489. By 1497 he began his graduate studies in theology at Tübingen, where he was exposed to the *Via Moderna*, which had become entrenched there through Gabriel Biel. Biel had died two years before Staupitz's arrival. At Tübingen, Staupitz no doubt studied under Biel's successors, Wendel Steinbach, Konrad Summenhardt, and Paul Pistoris.[24] By 1498 Staupitz had advanced to his degree of *biblicus* in theology, which qualified him to lecture on a book in the Bible that he had studied under a master. He could also lecture on the first two books of Lombard's *Sentences*. By the middle of 1499 he had advanced to a *Sententiarius*, which meant he was now authorized to lecture on all four of Lombard's books. Staupitz advanced rapidly through the *Formatus* degree to that of *Licentiatus*, which, according to the statutes, made him a licensed master of theology. After that it was not long before one could qualify for a doctorate by engaging in a public, circular disputation. In that same year Staupitz left Tübingen to become the prior of the Augustinian monastery in Munich, a position he occupied for two years.[25]

In 1502 Frederick the Wise contacted Staupitz and asked him to assist in founding the new university on the Elbe. He was to fill the two chairs of Bible and moral philosophy.[26] Tübingen served as a model for Staupitz in organizing the new institution.[27] Staupitz recruited three graduates in theology as members of the faculty: Sigismund Epp, Wolfgang Stähelin, and Ambrosius Vollant.[28]

Frederick the Wise contacted Emperor Maximilian I during the summer of 1502 and asked him to authorize the university's foundation by means of a *Stiftungsbrief*. The emperor complied on July 6. This document is still extant.[29] Usually it was the papacy, rather than the emperor, that founded a university.[30] The use of imperial authorization by Frederick was, no doubt, to lift the school beyond papal control. The elector later requested a papal blessing.[31]

The new school was to be organized into a liberal arts undergraduate school, offering the A.B. and M.A. degrees, and three graduate schools teaching theology, law, and medicine. The regular faculty would be privileged to instruct in medieval philosophy without restrictions on their points of view.[32] According to its *Stiftungsbrief,* Wittenberg was to be a *Studium Generale*, similar to Paris and Bologna and other European universities, having the same rank and dignity in the academic world.[33]

On 24 August, Frederick the Wise announced to the public that he and his brother, Duke John, were opening the University of Wittenberg on 18 October 1502.[34] Frederick ordered that for three years all students would be permitted to attend and be promoted without paying tuition.[35]

The elector's charter from Maximilian I was adequate authorization for the founding of the university. However, the prince regarded it as desirable to request papal confirmation for his new institution. A few months after the founding, on 2 February 1503, the papal legate, Cardinal Raymund of Gurk, wrote his letter of confirmation to the *Stiftungsbrief*.[36]

The elector was fully aware that his institution required some type of permanent endowment. Thus in 1507 he requested from Pope Julius II the incorporation of the endowed *Stift* of the Castle Church with the new university. Grohmann points out that during the first five years the cost of financing the new institution came from the elector's own pocket, but that this incorporation of the university with the *Stift* offered many new sources of income from Saxon villages.[37]

The elector of Saxony wanted the university to draft statutes governing its academic life. According to Friedensburg, little is known about the control of the institution during the first few years.[38] The first Wittenberg statutes were for the most part copies of those from Tübingen, with minor changes in style.[39]

By 1508 the elector felt the university needed a new set of regulations governing its academic life. An able scholar named Christopher Scheurl had recently joined the law faculty. A native of Nürnberg, he had taken a degree in both civil and canon law at Bologna. Scheurl was asked to write the first draft of the *Statutes of 1508*.[40] After the original draft of each set of statutes was completed, it went to a newly appointed group of university "reformers,"[41] who revised and finished them for the elector. The elector, in turn, had his court officials review the final draft prior to publication.[42]

Frederick stated that he wanted to prevent anything that might be divisive in the faculty or student body. Hence he was opposed to having any nations in the University of Wittenberg, which had been such a problem elsewhere. He was also against having conventicles of religious organizations, such as *Heiligengenossenschaften*. The university was to be under the Immaculate Mother of God, the Virgin Mary, and her protective saint, Augustine, in whose honor the 28th of August each year would be a special holiday.[43]

The university statutes begin by stating that there were to be four reformers to control the academic life of the school. These included the rector and the representatives from the four faculties, to be appointed by the elector. The original reformers were Johannes Morgenhofer, chairman, Staupitz, representing theology, Mellerstadt, representing medicine, and Rector Scheurl, representing both law and liberal arts. These were to reform the studies of the four faculties, propose needed improvements, and interpret the statutes as necessary.[44]

The establishment of a system of reformers was new in German universities, but it had been common in Italian schools. According to Scheurl, Bologna had served as his model.[45] The reformers were the elector's representatives. They regulated the system of instruction, softened the conflicts between faculty members, preserved peace and tranquility within the school and town, controlled the distribution of university funds, paid the professors and made official settlements, and solved problems that arose in the institution. In severe cases this might mean the expulsion of a student from school or the withholding of a professor's salary.[46]

Two other types of university officials were the chancellor and the conservators. As chancellor, Frederick chose Goswin von Orsoy, the praeceptor of the Antoniter monastery in Lichtenberg. He, in turn, used Mellerstadt as his vice-chancellor. The office of chancellor of a university had by now declined in stature; he presented candidates at the time of promotions and presided at some public examinations.[47] The conservators were even less important. They had been created by Julius II's papal bull of 1507, which incorporated the funds of the *Stiftskirche* with the school. The conservators were honorary officials who were to keep the peace. Those named to serve in this capacity were the bishops of Meissen and Brandenberg. These conservators were obligated to guard the school's endowment funds and defend the institution against any possible aggression. The services of these officials were never really necessary.[48]

According to the *Statutes of 1508*, the real governing body of Frederick's original university had been the Senate. It made the basic decisions as to how academic life was to be conducted. The Senate was composed of the rector, the masters of theology (both secular and regular), the professors of law and medicine, the dean and two masters of the liberal arts faculty, and the five canons of the Castle Church.[49] When the university faced a problem, or the rector felt that he should convoke the Senate, the members were to be notified by beadles the day before and informed of the order of business. If a member failed to attend, except for good cause, he would be fined. At the meeting, the rector would present the problem facing them and express his views on the matter; he would then call on the members, in order of seniority, each of whom was permitted to address the problem only once. When as many as wished had contributed their reaction, the rector would ask for an official roll call. The members of the Senate were forbidden from revealing to the outside what had transpired at these meetings, upon the threat of being banished from the institution.[50]

The head of the university was the rector, on whom much honor and dignity were bestowed by both faculty and students. The rector was chosen by the Senate in a special session called by the previous rector. The term of office was for only one semester, which permitted little time for centralization of authority. The election of rectors occurred twice a year, once on 18 October, the festival of St. Luke, and again on 1 May, the festival of Saints Philip and Jacob. The eligibility list for the rectorship was quite limited, as it was restricted to individuals of some standing and distinction within the faculty. Occasionally the honor fell upon a young nobleman, at which time a substitute rector might be elected as his assistant. Most rectors chosen were professors from the three upper faculties, but a master of arts with four years of membership in that college was eligible. Married men, the prior and dean of the Castle Church, and professors of theology were not required to serve. Once chosen, a rector was obligated to serve or else pay a fine.[51]

The duties of a new rector were many and somewhat demanding. At an early date, he held a convocation of the entire university, at which the statutes were publicly read. The rector registered all new faculty members and students in the university *Matrikel*, or registration book, collected a registration fee, and administered the oath of membership in the school.[52] The rector was to conduct disciplinary action against those who violated the statutes, and in serious cases could convoke the Senate for guidance and assistance. If a student were arrested and jailed, the town officials were expected to turn him over for trial by the rector's court.[53]

The rector served as the symbol of the whole institution and was dressed with much dignity. He led the parades on festive occasions, accompanied on either side by two beadles, carrying the university maces, symbolizing his power and authority. During disputations, he was seated in the *Katheder* of the Castle Church, where he could be seen, honored, and admired by all. On official missions he was always accompanied by bodyguards. The rector was forbidden to be out of town overnight, except by special permission of the reformers. To send official mail, the rector needed the approval of the respective deans. He presided over all Senate meetings. If a Senate vote resulted in a tie, the rector was given two votes to settle the matter.[54]

The bursar's office was housed in a lower room of the large, west tower of the Castle Church, where it could be securely guarded.[55] Since this office managed the combined funds of both the *Stift* of the Castle Church and the university, the sums involved could be quite large. Entry to the office was possible only by a winding stairway. A complicated system of four locks had to be opened in order to gain access to the treasury chest. The keys to the locks were kept in the possession of the four university deans.[56]

The *Syndicus*, as the bursar of the university was called, played quite an important role in academic affairs. He was in charge of the disbursement of funds and assisted the rector in the collection of matriculation fees. On festival days and at larger university banquets, the *Syndicus* served as the *Erzmarschall*.[57]

Students at Wittenberg acquired mastery of the prescribed lectures and textbooks by means of note-taking and memorization. In theology, for example, students had to memorize the essentials of Peter Lombard's four volumes of the *Sentences*. Closely related to classroom instruction were the disputations that were required of both professors and students. These were of three different kinds: (1) student practice disputations in the dorms; (2) student promotional disputations; and (3) faculty disputations closely related to current classroom instruction, delivered once a year on timely subjects. For the third type, professors drafted their own theses. Failure to participate in the disputation resulted in a fine.[58]

As in all medieval institutions of higher learning, the faculty was very conscious of rank. At the beginning of each rectorship, the reformers prepared a list of rank in the various faculties. This applied to processions as well as to seating in the Castle Church.[59] For processions, the rector was assigned the highest rank, followed by the chancellor and the prior of the Castle Church. Then came the dean of theology, the dean of All Saints Church, and the masters of theology, all marching in order of seniority. Next came the doctors of canon and civil law, the professors of medicine, the dean of arts, the *Licentiates* in theology, masters of arts, and bachelors in the higher faculties. Visitors—such as abbots, counts, barons, and deans from other places—and ranking clergy were seated behind the faculty members.[60]

For circular disputations of doctoral candidates or the installation of a new rector, the faculty would march to the rear of the Castle Church, where the beadles directed them to their preassigned seats. The three higher faculties were seated on the right, in the rear of the chapel, according to schools and seniority, while the deans and masters of arts sat on the left side along with the poet laureates. Guests of note in theology were seated behind the theologians, while others were assigned seats behind the dean and masters of arts. The student body was seated in the center nave, facing the participants in the debate. In front of them was an empty space used for the disputations. At opposite sides in the rear of the church stood two *Katheders*; the one on the left was occupied by the rector, and the other, near the large castle pillar, was used by the professors who participated in disputations.[61]

In the *Statutes of 1508*, the elector directed that during the period when students were completing their academic studies they would pay no tuition. Payments were reserved for the day when they were promoted; they then paid in a lump sum.

It was taken for granted that no student could enter a Wittenberg graduate school without having attained the A.B. and M.A. degrees.[62] Most students did not enter graduate studies; instead, they terminated their academic life with an M.A. degree. When students began graduate work in theology, law, or medicine, the fees paid were much higher for regular students than for monks, who paid a third less upon promotion.[63]

In the Wittenberg statutes, the elector also specified certain small favors or niceties that students undergoing promotion were expected to extend to their superiors. The new masters and doctors of theology, as well as the masters of arts, were to give the rector a gift of a *Piretha*, or a jar of ointment made of crushed flowers, and a pair of gloves; the rest of their superiors connected with their examinations were each to receive a pair of gloves.[64]

In another section of the statutes, Frederick stated that the university would no longer permit *prandas* to be demanded from advanced students. These doctoral banquets were usually given for the faculty members connected with a student's promotion. Such banquets had proven to be extremely costly, since students tried to outdo one another, and only the wealthy could afford them. Instead, the elector instituted two ducal banquets a year connected with the rector's installation, held in the spring and autumn. On those occasions there were also to be vigils, masses, and a public procession. The whole university was to participate in these and help pay for them.[65]

The statutes also define student attire while in classes and in the *Bursen*. Clergy were to be dressed in their customary garb, while the rest were to wear only dark clothes.[66] In the *Bursen* the students were supervised; not all of them could be housed there, however. Therefore it was stipulated that the university had to approve a dwelling before a student could move in.

Students were required to attend at least one lecture a day. Gambling was forbidden, as was association with women. Visits to taverns were prohibited, but students could drink moderately in their dwellings. If students accrued debts, they were turned over to the university's reformers. Acts of violence were reported to the deans and the rector. Punishment in most cases was by fines, and the destruction of property required restoration. Severe offenders were often locked up until their fate was determined.[67]

Courses in the school of liberal arts—or of philosophy, as it was more correctly designated—centered mainly around Aristotle. So much emphasis had been placed on dialectic and syllogistic reasoning that the seven liberal arts had become subservient to the development of logic.

There were no fewer than three hours of lectures in the morning devoted to Aristotle's works, delivered by Wittenberg's full professors. These stressed the *Organon*, *Physics*, and *On the Soul*.[68] Then, in the afternoon, students listened to lectures in *Nicomachean Ethics*, *Metaphysics*, and the logic of Petrus Hispanus' *Summula*, which the statutes called "Minor Logic."[69]

In the *Statutes of 1508*, the elector defined how the courses in Aristotle were to be taught at Wittenberg.[70] In the summer semester, classes were to begin at 5:00 A.M., while in the winter semester, they started at 6:00 A.M.

The ranking professors in the three different schools of philosophy were: Nicholas Amsdorf, already a bachelor in theology, who taught the Aristotelian *Organon* in Logic *in via Scoti*; Andreas von Carlstadt, also a bachelor in theology, who offered the same course in *via sancti Thome*;[71] and the distinguished Master Jodocus Trutfetter, who taught Aristotle's logic *in viam Occam*.[72]

A student had to decide, at the beginning, under what system of thought he wished to graduate and then attend the corresponding courses offered in the curriculum. A lecturer began by reading a portion of a text by Aristotle, while the students took notes. Then he would explain the text in a clear and distinct voice. When he came to difficult points he might add his own *Glossen*, further elaborations of what he thought Aristotle meant. As in earlier universities, each course was divided into points, marking for the lecturer exactly where to close each part under consideration. But in the Wittenberg statutes the elector gave the following direction:

> Let each professor freely teach his course in the way of St. Thomas, Duns Scotus, or Gregory [the latter name was later struck out and the name of Occam written in], and present his views without prejudice. At five during the summer and six during the winter, let the major logic [of Aristotle] be taught in those three ways [in separate courses].[73]

At seven o'clock in the summer, another series of lectures was offered by three professors, using the same three ways of interpreting Aristotle's *Physics* and *Psychology*.[74] Petrus Lupinus offered the courses in natural philosophy as St. Thomas had taught them, while Wolfgangus of Zwickau gave them as interpreted by Duns Scotus. Later, with the arrival of Occam's *Via Moderna* from Erfurt, that course was added to the curriculum.[75]

At noon, Chilianus de Mellerstadt offered a Thomistic course in *minori logica* as taught in the work of Peter Hispanus, while Sebastianus of Freiburg gave the same course according to the teachings of Duns Scotus. By 1508 this subject matter was also treated at that hour by an Occamist.[76] The Wittenberg lectures continued into the afternoon, when, in the second hour, the Scotist master, Konrad Koenig, held his lectures on Aristotle's *De Caelo*.[77] A course in moral philosophy was offered in the early afternoon and taught by Wolfgang Ostermeyer.[78] Another course used Aristotle's *De Anima*.

The *Rotulus* of 1507 is not quite clear about when the additional courses were offered. They must have rotated them, for they also had to give courses on *On Generation and Corruption* and *Meteorology*.[79]

During the third hour in the afternoon, the dean of the arts faculty, Dr. Simon Stein, taught a course in Latin grammar in which he used the text of the Roman humanist Johannes Sulpitius Verulanus.[80] During this same hour, Bodenstein von Carlstadt offered a course in Aristotle's *Metaphysics*.[81]

During the eighth hour, students could also attend a class in Virgil's *Aeneid*, or *Valerium Maximum*, taught by Balthasar Phacchus; in the following hour Dr. Christopher Scheurl offered a course dealing with Suetonius Tranquillius.[82]

The dean of liberal arts was the custodian of the seal of the arts faculty and entrusted with its keys and its statutes, and he was to keep records of all the bachelors and masters transferred to him by the previous dean. He was also to record additional registrations during his term. Every dean was obligated to read the statutes of his college to his members within ten days after entering office. The dean arranged for all disputations and served as chair in all Senate meetings in his department. Prior to any student promotions, bachelors and masters had to deposit their required fees with the dean. At the end of his term, he gave a report to the reformers. The dean was also obligated to visit the courses of his masters, noting attendance. He posted the names of students who were ready for promotions on the doors of the churches, listing the names of the faculty members serving as promoters.[83]

Students in German universities were usually graduates of preparatory schools. The bachelor of liberal arts normally required two years at a university, and a master of arts an additional four or five years. Advancement depended on the faculty's judgment.[84] Besides the course requirements, students had to attend at least thirty practice disputations and participate in four of them.[85]

The statutes established specific times for the examinations of both bachelors and masters candidates. When a student felt he was properly prepared, he contacted the dean and announced his candidacy for the bachelors degree. The dean then summoned the Senate of the arts faculty, in whose presence the candidate took an oath. He promised that he would not be vengeful if he failed or was given a lower rating, and promised to serve as an instructor for a year and a half after his promotion. The student was scheduled for an intensive examination by the faculty. The dean posted the names of the students involved, and their promoters, on all the doors of the churches. At this time the candidate also paid the required fees. If the faculty found the student qualified, the dean notified the lord chancellor, and in due time the student became a bachelor of arts.[86]

The Wittenberg *Statutes of 1508* required masters candidates to have covered courses in the old and the new logic, and also Aristotle's books on *Physics, The Soul, Generation and Death, Meteorology, Nature (Parvia Naturalia), Ethics, Metaphysics,* and *Mathematics.*[87] After that the student was carefully examined by five masters.[88] Candidates also swore to honor the dean and masters of the arts faculty and support the best interests of the university. The elector also required this rather unusual addition to the oath:

> Let the masters candidate add that, if anyone should appear who questions our fundamental beliefs, we shall respond and hold fast to the basic convictions of our faith, and, on the other hand, destroy the opposition in accordance with our strength, that God may favor us and the authors of the holy gospels.[89]

Since the professors in liberal arts were obligated, in their courses on Aristotle, to lecture in accordance with the way their schools had interpreted his teachings, the statutes stipulated that in this they were not to express any prejudice against another school. The danger for this existed especially in the *Via Moderna.*[90]

When an *ordinarius* professor in liberal arts began a new course, using the prescribed texts in Aristotle, the statutes required that he first record the names of his auditors, and at the end evaluate their performance.[91] Student disputations were to be held for three hours in the afternoon every Saturday.[92] All the masters were obligated to engage in such disputations, to widen a students' knowledge of their classroom work. These faculty performances were to be scheduled by the dean of arts, in accordance with the order of faculty promotions. The statutes also prescribed the amounts that the professors were to be paid for their participation.[93] Such debates were conducted with great dignity, and the dean stressed the proper deportment and obedience to his directives.[94]

Students also had the opportunity to learn how to engage in a disputation. They were taught in the dorms by some of the faculty, where beginners debated for an hour after dinner.[95]

Wittenberg had a relatively small faculty, thirty-seven in number. Twenty-two of these were regular professors, while the remainder were graduate students working for advanced degrees. According to the *Rotulus of 1507,* by Christopher Scheurl, there were twenty-one teachers in liberal arts, of whom eleven were fully ranked as professors.[96] In 1507 Carlstadt was head of those faculty members teaching Aristotle's courses in *via Thome,* while Petrus Wolf, Chilian Reuter, and Mathäus Beckau taught other courses under him. Nicolaus von Amsdorf was the head of another branch of the *Via Antiqua* that taught Aristotle's courses *via Scoti*; his fellow professors were Wolfgang Kannegieszer, Sebastian Kuchenmeister, and Konrad Koenig.[97] In 1507 Joducus Trutfetter arrived in Wittenberg to teach the *Via Moderna*. However, Mellerstadt and his supporters did not appreciate the rival philosophy, which dared to question the basic assumptions of the *Via Antiqua*; he made it so uncomfortable for Trutfetter that by 1510 he had returned to Erfurt.[98]

In its final chapter on the arts faculty, the statutes state that the dean shall be assisted by two *conventors*, appointed by the four reformers. These learned members of the staff would keep a record of the activities of the lecturers, supervise the disputations, and control dorm life. If there were major problems in discipline among students, or in town and gown relationships, the conventors could seek the assistance of the reformers.[99]

During Wittenberg's formative years, the medical school was relatively small and weak. Frederick the Wise's strong interest in the school no doubt had something to do with the fact that he suffered from gout and kidney stones.

The elector also gave the school of law a new set of statutes in 1508, beginning with a description of its structure and the role of the two schools. The law school was relatively large, as noted in the Scheurl *Rotulus* of 1507, which lists eleven *ordinarius* masters on its faculty, seven of whom were in canon law.[100]

The student who aimed to acquire a bachelor of canon law degree was required to have attended a year of lectures under an ordinarius professor in the *Liber Sextus*, the five books by Pope Gregory IX, forming a continuation of Gratian's *Decretum*.[101] He also attended lectures under a ranking faculty member for a year, lecturing on the *Clementinae*, the later decisions of Pope Clement VII dating to 1317.[102] If a student wished to restrict his studies to the acquisition of a degree in civil law, however, he was required to hear lectures for one year, on the *Digest* that dealt with excerpts of writings of Roman jurists; or he might choose to attend the *Codex*, on fifty diverse excerpts from Roman law.[103]

The advanced degrees in law were three, the *baccalaureus*, the *licentiatus*, and the *doctor* of jurisprudence in civil or canon law. Once the student had acquired his bachelor of laws degree, canon or civil, he was ready for further instruction toward either of the two types of law. The student now spent two years attending lectures by a professor on the *Liber Sixtus* and the *Clementinae*.[104]

Among the three advanced studies, theology was the most popular, especially for the members of the religious orders, after which came canon law and civil law.

Any student aiming to obtain a doctorate in theology had to complete four steps. The first degree was a *baccalaureus biblicus*, more generally referred to as a *biblicus*, which was followed by the degrees of *sententiarius*, *formatus*, *licentiatus*, and finally the *doctorate*. The length of time required for each of these varied, depending on a student's ability and the faculty estimate of his readiness. A study of the *Liber Decanorum* entries indicates that a number of theologians obtained promotions much earlier than the usual time required: Carlstadt, Link, Lupinus, and Luther.[105] Usually it took from five to seven years simply to qualify for the *biblicus* degree. To finance his studies, one had to be either wealthy or have a rich relative. A student's readiness for examination and possible promotion was left to the dean's judgment. The *Statutes of 1508* required that the work for the *biblicus* degree begin with courses in the Bible and Lombard's *Sentences*, which formed the heart and core of all later advancement.[106]

The student working toward a *biblicus* degree attended lectures on those parts of the Bible that he would later be obligated to teach. After a period of study, the candidate was examined privately and also engaged in a disputation in the *Aula* of the New Friderici College. If the student was found qualified and paid the required fee, he was granted the *biblicus* degree by the chancellor. Now he could teach those books of the New or Old Testament that he had studied and start on the road toward the more difficult *sententiarius* degree. Some exceptionally qualified students appear to have begun to teach the first two books of Lombard's *Sentences* while they continued to study the material of the great dogmatist.[107]

When a student felt ready to try for the *sententiarius* degree, he contacted the dean. After the dean had consulted with the Senate and the student had been subjected to a private examination, he was asked to display his mastery of Lombard in a disputation. If the Senate found him worthy it asked for his promotion.

As usual, the student had to pay the necessary fees. The dean then asked him to debate some assigned theses, in which he could prove his mastery of the required fields.[108] The new *sententiarius* now widened his knowledge of the Bible by attending courses on other books, and also increased his mastery of Lombard. At the same time he delivered his own lectures on the entire Lombard. After the *sententiarius* had lectured on the first two books of Lombard, he was regarded as ready for his promotion to the degree of *formatus*. However, prior to this promotion, the candidate had to prove his dialectical skill in a public disputation. If he did well in the public performance, and if the majority of the Senate felt he was ready, the dean presented him to the chancellor for promotion to the *formatus* degree.[109]

After this came the maturing period of the student, during which he attended many lecture courses on the Bible, completed his own studies, and delivered lectures on the *Sentences*. Once he had done all this he was ready to appear before the Senate to be examined for an entire day. He also engaged in a disputation based on Lombard's *Sentences*. If most of the Senate believed he should be promoted, the dean again presented him to the chancellor, or the vice-chancellor, to grant him the degree of *licentiatus*. This gave one full license to teach in any European university.[110]

The degree of doctor of theology was to be bestowed only on those few who were regarded as worthy of such an honor. The cost of attaining the doctorate was very high, and it was achieved by only twelve people between 1508 and 1517.[111] The doctoral oath expressed the customary loyalty to the dean and faculty of the university, but the elector's *Statutes of 1508* include the following statement: "I will swear obedience to the Roman Church and I will further the peace among the masters and the students, secular or regular. . . ."[112]

18

The University's Staff and Students

THE RECTORSHIP OF WITTENBERG

As in the medieval universities and the earlier German universities, Wittenberg was placed under the control of a rector, chosen by its Senate and ranking faculty of the Liberal Arts College and the three graduate schools. As prescribed by the *Statutes of 1508*, the rectorship was to be rotated among the four faculties; yet in practice, this did not happen, for a variety of reasons.[1] The rectors of medieval universities were held in highest esteem, and this attitude continued in the earlier German universities. Members of the high-ranking graduate schools and staff of the *Stift* of the Collegiate Church were regarded as better qualified for this distinguished office than mere members of the philosophical faculty. The medieval ranking of the graduate schools of theology, law, and medicine was respected and also seems to have played a role in the choice of rectors. In addition, the personal distinctions of faculty members, or their relationship to the elector of Saxony, seems to have influenced early selections for this distinguished office. Now and then a distinguished faculty member like Dr. Christopher Scheurl of Nürnberg, who held degrees in both civil and canon law from the University of Bologna, or the famous Erfurt professor in the *Via Moderna*, Jodocus Trutfetter, after joining the faculty, was made rector upon his arrival.[2] Exceptions were sometimes also made when sons of high-ranking noble families matriculated at Wittenberg, who then were honored with the rectorship. In those cases a faculty member was delegated to carry out the actual functions of the university rector. It may be of interest to present a review of those who occupied the office of rector during the formative years of the University of Wittenberg.

Since theology was regarded as the ranking discipline in the Middle Ages, it is not strange that among the 26 rectorships during the period from 1502 and

1517, 10 were chosen from the faculty of theology, 8 from canon and civil law, 5 from medicine, and only 3 from the arts faculty. Their duties as rectors have been covered in the previous chapter in connection with the *Statutes of 1508*.[3] At the head of the entire university there was a chancellor. In medieval times this official had been quite a powerful figure, but through the centuries he lost his power. At Wittenberg he was more or less an honorary functionary, who participated in student promotions, while the real work of the office was performed by the vice-chancellor, a position occupied during most of the early period by Polich von Mellerstadt, the elector's former physician and personal friend.[4]

The elector must have realized that his university, in its actual operation, would be confronted with problems. These could arise at different levels, including an undesirable rector, faculty problems, and conflict between students in the *Bursen*, or in homes, and by disturbances in the streets with townsmen. Even the *Statutes of 1508* might prove inadequate and need revision. Therefore the prince ordered that the new university should be supervised by four reformers. This also constituted a body of men to whom the rector might turn for advice and guidance, should a serious problem arise. In the beginning the first reformers were composed of the rector, the prior of the Stift of All Saints Church (Morgenhofer), the vice-chancellor (von Mellerstadt) and the dean of the theological faculty (Johann von Staupitz).[5] Walter Friedensburg regarded these reformers as the representatives of the elector on the campus, and as a unique creation of Frederick the Wise. Other German universities did not have such an organization.[6] This may be an overstatement, since Christopher Scheurl had come from the University of Bologna, where he had taken his doctorate, and reformers were common in Italian schools and Bologna, since this had been the law professor's model.[7] Scheurl even wrote to Wolfgang Mellerstadt, son of Polich, on January 5, 1509:

> We are changing the appearance of our Republic of Letters in accordance with the practice at Bologna, by the delegation of all authority to the doctors.[8]

Another organization was created by the papal bull of Julius II in 1507, when he incorporated the university with the *Stift* of the Castle Church in Wittenberg.[9] In reality this organization played a lesser role in the actual management of the University of Wittenberg. In a decree dated December 21, 1507, Julius II dispatched a directive from Bologna, empowering the bishops of Meissen and Brandenburg to preserve the freedom of the newly founded institution. They were to protect the revenues and privileges of the school, as well as its jurisdiction, against anyone wishing it harm. A little later, on October 12, 1513, Pope Leo X also made the Probst of St. Moritz in Naumburg a *Subconsurvator* of Wittenberg University.[10]

The actual academic supervisors and executives in the institutions were the deans of the four faculties. The deanship in Wittenberg, according to its *Statutes*, was to rotate in all four faculties. In the main this pattern was followed, but a few exceptions were made. For example, in 1506 and 1507 the Pest broke out in Wittenberg, and the university was moved to a safer place. Sometimes, when a distinguished member of the nobility matriculated in the institution, he might be honored with the deanship for a semester. Since the upper faculties were small, there had to be frequent repetition in their selection of deans; ambitious younger faculty members were called to serve several times. In this connection the records preserved for posterity by Sennert[11] and Suevus[12] are very useful for a reconstruction of how the deanships in the four schools of the university functioned, and what promotions took place during the respective period of their deanships. Since in this study we are concerned principally with the theological faculty, and also with students' preparatory background in the philosophical faculty, we will highlight this aspect.

During the period of the original Wittenberg, between 1502 and 1517, while the medieval type of university was still in operation, there were 21 deanships; some of these were repetitions, as the theological faculty never had more than six members on the teaching staff. During this first fifteen years, 31 candidates received the degree of *Baccalaureus Biblicus*; 27 continued to take the *Sententiarius* degree; 24 were advanced to the *Formatus* degree; and then 17 received the *Licentiatus* degree, after which 16 were finally promoted to the high honor of doctors of theology.[13] The respective deans of theology and the number of students promoted during their respective deanships, from 1502 to 1517, were tabulated as follows by Suevus:[14]

Dean Johann von Staupitz, 1502–1504	6
Dean Paul Canifices (soon recalled)	0
Dean Ludwig Renning, Winter, 1505–1506	5
Dean Polich von Mellerstadt (1506–1507, Pest)	19
Dean Jodocus Trutfetter, 1507–1508	19
Dean Johann Staupitz, Winter, 1508–1509	4
Dean Jodocus Trutfetter, Summer and Winter (1509–1510)	4
Dean Wolfgang of Monaco, Summer, 1510	1
Dean Polich von Mellerstadt, Summer, 1511	17
Dean Peter Lupinis, Winter Semester, 1511–1512	4
Dean Bodenstein von Carlstadt, Summer, 1514	5
Dean Winceslaus Linck, Winter, 1512–1513	4
Dean Polich von Mellerstadt, Summer, 1513	6
Dean Peter Lupinus, Winter, 1513–1514	2
Dean Bodenstein von Carlstadt, Summer, 1514	1
Dean Winceslaus Linck, Winter, 1514–1515	3
Dean Martin Luther, Summer, 1515	4
Dean Peter Lupinus, Winter, 1515–1516	4
Dean Bodenstein von Carlstadt, Summer, 1516	4
Dean Johann Hergott, Winter, 1516–1517	1
Dean Martin Luther, Summer, 1517	1

The available evidence does not give any information as to who was teaching in the theological faculty during this period. Even Sennert or Suevus in the seventeenth century appears to have been without that information. Christopher Scheurl, in his *Rotulus of 1507*, lists five professors that were on the regular faculty.[15] These were the following:

D. Johann von Staupitz, from Tübingen, Ordinarius
D. Martin Polich de Mellerstadt, Dean and Ordinarius
D. Jodocus Trutfetter from Erfurt, Ordinarius
D. Ludovicus Henning from Pavia, Ordinarius
D. Johannes Mantel of Augustinan Hermits, Ordinarius.[16]

The University of Wittenberg, like other German universities covered in the previous chapter, offered two kinds of courses in theology. Since the school had 22 regular, fully salaried professors on its staff, in a body of 37 faculty members, many of the graduate students served as part of the teaching staff. The regular professors taught the basic courses required toward degrees, and hence were designated as *Ordinarius* professors, as at other schools. They offered their courses at preferred times in the morning, in accordance with rank. The younger, budding professors were called *Extraordinarii*. They taught the elective courses that were not as vital toward earning degrees and taught in a freer style. The supervision of these courses and the progress of the students in their promotions became two basic requirements of the deans.[17]

In regard to the deanships in law and their activities, we are even less informed by the extant records. In the earlier years, the Law School did not keep a *Liber Decanorum* like that of theology. Sennert made no reference to that department, and Suevus merely records that two men acquired the degrees of *juris utriusque doctor*, or a doctorate in both civil and canon law, during this period, namely, Conradus Dulcis of Hamburg and Andreas Ezuldorff, both taken in 1508. But there must have been many students in the law department who received degrees in either civil or canon law.[18] This apparently was never recorded. From the *Rotulus of 1507* it is clear that in Scheurl's day, the faculty of law was quite large, especially in canon law; all were doctors of law, teaching the fundamental course of civil and canon law. The *Rotulus* lists both *Ordinarius* and *Extraordinarius* professors, of which there were seven teaching canon law, but there were only two teaching Roman law and one feudal law. Christopher Scheurl, who was an ordinarius professor in both kinds of law, in his *Rotulus of 1507* made the following list of his fellow canon law professors.

D. Frederick Kitscher, juris utriusque, doctor Senensis, Probst
D. Johannes Monhofer, juris utriusque, doctor, Perusinus, Decanus
D. Wolfgangus Stähelin, juris utriuaque doctor Tubingensis
D. Laurentius Schlamaw, decretum doctor, Pastor Vitembergensis
D. Udalricus Denstadt, cantor Vitembergensis
D. Christophorus Scheurl Nurimbergensis, juris utriusque doctor, Bonensis
D. Christophorus Gross, jurius utriusque doctor, Vitembergensis[19]

This large staff of seven well trained doctors, five of whom were graduates of both canon and civil law, implies that a number of graduate students went into canon law. Unfortunately, we do not know the size of this enrollment in canon law.

The faculty in what Scheurl calls "the Caesar's Law," namely, civil law according to the *Code of Justinian*, was not as heavily staffed. Here the graduate students must not have been as numerous, for only two professors, trained in both canon and civil law, represented the ordinarius professors, which were:

> D. Iheronymus Schurff, juris utriusque doctor, in Codice
> D. Wolfgangus Reisempusch, juris utriusque, in institutionibus.[20]

According to *Rotulus*, the Ordinarius Professor Hieronymous Schurff taught courses in the *Code of Justinian*, while another ordinarius professor taught the *Institutes*, the practices of Roman lawyers, which meant a rather thorough training in Roman law.

To make the law school courses complete, training in customary, feudal law was also required, for the German lands under Frederick the Wise also used it. Customary law had been taught under the *Sachsenspiegel*, an old law code that had come down from the *usus feudorum*, as Scheurl lists it. This part is not too explicit, but the *usus feudus* legal codes also included the *Schwabenspiegel*, the law code during feudalism in southern Germany. This law course was not a regular requirement, but is listed as *Extraordinary*. It was offered by the distinguished Christopher Scheurl of Nürnberg, who no doubt was thoroughly familiar with German feudal law as practiced in that region. Scheurl lists this course in feudal law as: *In jure civili extraordinarie, id est diebus feriatis. D. Christopherus Schewrl . . . usus feudorum*.[21] One wonders how popular this course was since it was given as an elective and during holiday periods. Frederick the Wise may have been interested in such legal training, since he was the *Reichsvikar* during an *Interregnum*, as at the time of Emperor Maximilian I's death, during the election of Charles V, in 1519–1521. At that time feudal strife broke out in the north, in the lands of the *Sachsenspiegel*, resulting in quite a problem.[22]

Concerning the deanship of the school of medicine in this early period we are kept equally in the dark. Even Walter Friedensburg, who had all German sources at his disposal, had little success in his research. Sennert did not attempt to offer any statistics, while Suevus had little new to offer. Apparently no record was kept in the early days. The problem was that outside of Professor Polich von Mellerstadt, few teachers continued to remain any length of time; the old doctor was also busy in theology as well as with his duties as vice chancellor, and his work on his publications offered little time to record other events that were happening. Under these conditions a rotation in such a small faculty was hardly practical. Walter Friedensburg claims that Erasmus Stuler had come to Wittenberg with Polich von Mellerstadt, but for some unknown reason went back to his former school, the University of Krakau, and would not return to the institution on the Elbe.[23] This left Mellerstadt to provide for the needs of a few graduate students in medicine. However, by 1506, Johannes Schwabe is listed as an ordinarius professor of medicine, with Simon Stein and Theodore

Eschaus serving as his student assistants. Whether Schwabe was dean of medicine is not known, but soon this ordinarius professor also departed and was replaced by Professor Dietrich Block of Hildesheim, who likewise did not stay. In 1511 the school was in dire straits, as it had no one to fill the professorship while a student was promoted to the doctorate, so the students coming up in medicine could be examined.[24] According to this record of the school of medicine, it is clear that the situation was not impressive, but as subsequent history reveals, by the twenties the medical school took on new life.

Since this study of the German Reformation aims to show the contrast between the original Wittenberg and the changes that came over it through the reforms made by Martin Luther and Philip Melanchthon in the twenties and thirties, a description of the original philosophical faculty will be necessary, for it formed the background for advanced study in the upper faculties of the graduate schools. Today the student is fortunate that Sennert compiled a list of the deans of the period, from 1502 to 1518, which is as follows:[25]

Sigismund Epp, of Tubingen, Winter Semester, 1502–1503	14
Dyonisius Bickel, *Biblicus* in Theology, Summer, 1503	12
Caspar Grunheim, *Biblicus* in Theology, Winter Semester, 1503	4
Succeeded by Thomas Kollin, *Biblicus* in Theology	9
Simon Buckon, Summer, 1504	8
Georg Zimmerman, Prutenus	9
Petrus Lupinus, *Biblicus* in Theology, Winter, 1504–1505	13
Sebastian Kuchenmeister, Summer of 1505	11
Mathäus Beckau, J.U. Lic., Winter Semester, 1506–1507	6
Simon Stein, Medicine Bachelor (during Pest)	0
Bodenstein von Carlstadt, *Biblicus*, Summer, 1507	5
Nicholaus de Amsdorf, *Biblicus*, Winter, 1508–1509	5
Chilian Reuter of Mellerstadt, Summer, 1509	4
Conradus Konig of Stuttgard, Winter, 1509–1510	8
Mathäus Beckau, J.U. Lic., Summer, 1509	4
Sebastian Archimagirtis of Freiburg, Winter, 1510–1511	8
Nicholaus von Amsdorf, Summer, 1511	11
Georgius Elner De Stafelstein, Biblicus, Winter, 1511–1512	1
Johann Dolst de Feldkirchen, *Biblicus*, Summer, 1512	7
Johan Stob, Winter Semester, 1512–1513	0
Bartholomeus Bernhardi, Feldkirchen, *Biblicus*, Summer	7
Simon Heins de Brug, Winter, 1513–1514	0
Otto Beckmann de Wartenberg, Summer, 1514	9
Johann Reube, J.U. Baccal., Winter, 1514–1515	0
Bonefacius de Rode, Zorwig, Summer, 1515	8
Henricus Stackmann of Brunschweig, Winter, 1515–1516	0
Urbanus Sprecher de Jessen, Summer, 1516	7
Jodocus Morlyn de Feldkirche, Winter, 1516–1517	0
Sebastian Kuchenmeister, Freiberg, Lic. Theol., 1517	4
Jacobus Premsel of Torgau, Winter, 1517–1518	0

The Wittenberg Students

Since all students and new professors had to appear before the rector of the University of Wittenberg and be examined about their academic background and reasons for wanting to enter the institution before they matriculated, the rectors kept a careful record of their entry. This included their names and places of birth. All this remained a carefully guarded record in what was known as the *Album* of the University of Wittenberg. In Germany the authorities were kind enough to make a microfilmed copy of the original *Matrikel* of its Reformation period, which, in turn, was enlarged by the *Firestone Library* for me. This original differs a little from the printed copy I used at Cornell University when I did my doctoral thesis, covering student matriculations from 1520 to 1560 during the Reformation. A printed three-volume reproduction, it was printed in Leipzig in 1841ff.[26] There also appeared a comparative enrollment study of a number of universities in chart form, prepared in 1967 by Gottfried Langer, with the assistance of Charlotte Prokert and Walter Schmidt, covering the years 1502–1648, in which a student can compare Wittenberg's enrollments with its contemporaries like Leipzig, Ingolstadt, Heidelberg, and Tübingen, or the number of students enrolled.[27]

The enrollment in a German university at a given time is difficult to establish, for students and faculty were matriculated only once, at the time of their entry. One can get an accurate count of matriculations by semesters; however, there is no way of knowing how long a period the student remained in Wittenberg. Professor Friedensburg estimated that the average length was five years. Thus a grouping of five-year periods gives one some estimate as to how many students were at the university at a given time.

The establishment of the University of Wittenberg by the elector of Saxony in 1502 may have been seen as a novelty, for on October 18, 1502, no fewer than 416 students had their names inscribed by Polich von Mellerstadt, the first rector, into the *Album* of Wittenberg, but by 1503 the enrollment had dropped to 376 for the next two semesters; then, in 1504, only 152 students entered during two semesters, while in 1505 only 127 came, and by 1506 the enrollments had dropped to 111. It was at this point that Polich von Mellerstadt had Meinhard write his *Lockschrift*, the *Dialogus of 1507*, to entice students to flock to Wittenberg in larger numbers.[28]

Whether the biggest difference was made by the *Dialogus of 1507* or the arrival of Christopher Scheurl of Nürnberg, that able, humanistically minded patrician, we do not know. He was a lawyer from the University of Bologna, who possessed degrees in civil and canon law, and was elected Rector in the summer of that year. The arrival of the distinguished Erfurt scholar Jodocus Trutfetter may also have added to Wittenberg's appeal. In any case, enrollment was stimulated. As we shall see, Christopher Scheurl added color to the academic life, while Trutfetter gave the philosophical faculty a new dimension offering the school the *Via Moderna*. Enrollments began to increase somewhat after their arrival. In 1507, 169 new students came to the campus, while by 1508 the rectors matriculated 179, and 193 the year after. By 1510 the registrations of new students had swollen by 303 new entries, by 247 in 1511. However, for some strange, unknown reason, by 1512 the Wittenberg matriculations had dropped again to 119.[29] After that the matriculation curve moves up and down. This may have been for several reasons. Polich von Mellerstadt had died and first Christopher Scheurl and then Jodocus Trutfetter had left, which may have made the school less attractive. In 1513 the matriculations declined to 151; however, by 1514 they were up again to 213; in 1515 they were nearly the same, at 218. However, in 1516 the new registrations had again declined to 162; while in 1517 the new entries had risen again to 246. The latter was soon to swing upwards, probably due to the spread of Luther's popularity after the posting of the *Ninety-Five Theses* in 1517.

As stated above, we have no knowledge of Wittenberg's enrollment at any given time, but a summary of the number who entered the school may be of interest here. During the first five years a total of 1351 students were enrolled by the rectors; in the second period, from 1507 to 1512, an additional 963 entered the school; and, in the last years, from 1512 to 1517, another 990 students entered the university on the Elbe. When these registrations are broken down on charts and tabulated annually from the two semester registrations, they total:

1502	416
1503	376
1504	152
1505	127
1506	111
1507	169
1508	179
1509	193
1510	303
1511	247
1512	119
1513	151
1514	213
1515	218
1516	162
1517	246

The scholar may find it of interest to refer to the Langer chart for a comparison of Wittenberg's matriculations in this period with two other universities, Tübingen and Leipzig. Since the university on the Elbe was deeply influenced by Tübingen in its early period, due to John Staupitz and the members he recruited to join the new school, a few statistics may be of interest. Tübingen University was not a large institution. During the years from 1502 to 1506, its matriculations per year were not more than 75 students; however, after 1510 the enrollment of new students increased to around 150 to 160. But then it dropped again to fewer than 100 per year.[30] The University of Leipzig, however, had a much larger enrollment during this period. Its matriculations in 1502-1503 exceeded 500 students; but by 1508, while the Pest was raging in Saxon lands, Leipzig's matriculations dropped to 320 students; after the Pest, its enrollments rose again, so that by 1515 its entries were up again to 575. Soon after that Leipzig's yearly registrations were surpassed by those of Wittenberg because of the rising popularity of Martin Luther. By 1519-1520, with the assistance of Luther, Wittenberg's matriculations had risen to 552 students.[31]

THE WITTENBERG FACULTY

There is perhaps no body of men and women with a wider range of viewpoints and philosophies than a university faculty. Thus any hasty generalization as to the kind of teaching staff the elector employed during the formative period would be unwise and perhaps even misleading. Generally speaking, the institution might be called typically medieval in tone and in its offerings, as it was modeled after Paris and Bologna. What complicates the situation is that there were frequent changes due to departures and various other reasons. Another factor is that they were recruited from all over Europe and often brought with them their own local viewpoints of education. In the beginning the university had but the medieval scholastic systems of the *Via Antiqua*, with faculties to interpret dogmatics as Thomists or Scotists; but from 1507 on the school also offered the philosophy of the *Via Moderna* according to its founder, William Occam. With three different philosophies being offered, side by side, some prejudices were bound to result in friction, as all interpreted Lombard's *Sentences* in different ways. To avoid such friction within the philosophical staff, the elector stipulated in his *Statutes of 1508* that courses in the Arts Faculty should be taught by the respective faculties on Lombard's *Sentences*, *Viam Thome*, *Viam Scoti* and *Viam Occam*, but that they were to teach their views without prejudice.[32] But this was not always realized, for when Jodocus Trutfetter arrived in 1507, his *Via Moderna* immediately came under fire, as will be seen later.

In theology, students at the very outset had to make a choice as to which route they wanted to travel, to take courses in the desired faculty and later obtain their doctorates as Thomists, Scotists, or Occamists. As a *Biblicus, Sententiarius, Formatus*, and a *Licentiatus* they would be examined in the steps toward the doctorate, in accordance with the type of training they had received. Thus, as at other institutions, theological education in scholastic philosophy was far from being in agreement prior to the Council of Trent in 1563. It might be compared to a large, three-ring circus, where under the same tent three different views existed side by side. The *Via Antiqua* views of Thomas and Scotus dated much further back than the *Via Moderna* of William Occam, and its arrival at Wittenberg through Trutfetter was a kind of challenge to the older views.[33] But students who had begun their theological studies at Erfurt, Tübingen, and Heidelberg could now continue their studies in the *Via Moderna* at Wittenberg, as

was the case of Martin Luther when he arrived there in 1508–1509 and
1511–1512.

The Wittenberg faculty had 22 regular professors, plus additional graduate
students, to make a total of 37 members. This total applies to all the faculties in
latter years, when the school was fully established in the *Rotulus of 1507*, and
was a number they attempted to maintain. As noticed in the previous chapter,
students who had completed their A.B. degrees in their preparatory training
were obligated to teach while they were graduate students, which maintained
the total. However, the number of full professors, who were in charge of the
courses of the institution, as well as their student assistants, varied somewhat in
different periods. Exact numbers cannot then be established with certainty during this time. In the graduate school of theology there were usually five or six
with doctorates, several of which were regular members of the *Stift* of the
Castle Church of All Saints, such as its prior, the dean, and some canons. At the
same time, graduate students, after they had acquired their degrees of *Biblicus,
Sententiarius*, and *Formatus*, were also obligated to offer courses in the Bible,
and Lombard's *Sentences*, while at the same time they might also teach courses
in the *Philosophical College*. Thus the deans could supervise their development
and know when they were ready to be promoted. The graduate schools of law
and of medicine, though they do not directly concern our Reformation theme,
were similar in organization and practice. Even though we do not possess all the
names, as observed above, there were seven ordinarius doctors teaching different aspects of canon law, and three teaching civil and feudal law. Meanwhile,
there must have been a number of student instructors who were working
toward doctorates in law; while at the same time, this was true in the graduate
school of medicine. Members of the two graduate schools also taught in the liberal arts college.

The philosophical school, or liberal arts college, as it was also called at the
University of Wittenberg, was closely related to the main theme in this study;
for there the students received the philosophical background training for the
later study of theology, law, and medicine. Here a distinction needs to be made
between student requirements for the A.B. and M.A. degrees *per se* and the
electives, which were available in humanistic studies, or poetry, as it was called
at Tübingen and later at Wittenberg.[34] Walter Friedensburg stressed that in the
arts college, in the courses required for degrees, Aristotle was the main star, and
everything circulated around him. The courses students were required to study
for their undergraduate degrees have already been treated in the chapter covering the elector's *Statutes of 1508*. Throughout the week no fewer than three
hours each morning were devoted to Aristotle; ordinarius professors, with doctorates in specific fields, covered the *Organum* of Aristotle, his *Physics*, and his
Psychology in the *De Anima*. All of these taught according to the three ways
cited before. In the afternoons students were introduced to *Nichomachean
Ethics*, concerning the good life, his *Metaphysics* and *Logic*, or the *Summula* of
Petrus Hispanus of Paris. All these courses were interpreted in accordance with
the great scholastics of the Middle Ages—Aquinas, Scotus, and Occam. If you

wished to graduate from Wittenberg with a bachelors or masters degree, you had to be thoroughly familiar with the writings of the Stagirite.[35] There were also private courses offered as electives, but those did not count toward degrees. There were also courses in grammar, which will be covered later along with their instructors.

The way the academic program was set up, dialectics served as the very core and center of instruction; it was drilled into the students so that it became a distinctive part of their life. Not only the courses they attended but also the disputations they engaged in employed the finespun reasoning of the medieval scholastics. The liberal arts program was under the direction of nine professors and a number of student graduates. According to the *Rotulus of 1507*, Andreas de Carlstadt was the chairman of the four Thomists in philosophy, with Petrus Wolf, Chilian Reuter, and Mathäus Beckau being the staff under him; Nicholaus Amsdorf was the head of the Scotists, with Wolfgang Kannegieszer, Sebastian Kuchenmeister, and Konrad Koenig under him.[36] After Professor Jodocus Trutfetter was brought to Wittenberg by the elector in 1507, this specialist in William Occam and Gabriel Biel gave the school an additional dimension, by offering courses in the *Via Moderna* as another approach to philosophy. Each of these men deserves separate treatment.

In an analysis of the individual professors, we must point out that for us today many are but names, even though they were influential professors like members of the *Stift* of the Castle Church. Among these ordinarius professors, three need special treatment: Polich von Mellerstadt, Johann von Staupitz, and Jodocus Trutfetter. But instead of treating their lives and accomplishments, the emphasis must be placed on the type of individuals they were and what impact they must have had through their instructional activity at the original institution.

As a scholar and professor, Polich von Mellerstadt is somewhat difficult to assess. He appears to have been on excellent terms with the students, but he was much disliked by many of the able professors.[37] Karl Bauer claims that Mellerstadt's ambitions far exceeded his actual accomplishments.[38] The prominent scholar on humanism, Gustav Bauch, described Polich as self-willed, headstrong, and domineering toward his peers in the faculty. He granted that in his earlier years, during the Leipzig days, he may have been an influential spirit; but by the time he came to Wittenberg, Polich had become a conservative Thomist, who drove able humanists and professors away from Wittenberg. His aforementioned strife with Wimpina at Leipzig, which continued into the Wittenberg days, doubtless contributed to his later dislike.[39] Stier points out that Mellerstadt, who at Leipzig had claimed to be such a Humanist, certainly did not use his influence to promote the new learning that lay so near.[40] In this he is certainly correct, for at the time Conrad Celtis came to Leipzig, he became one of his ardent admirers and claimed to be one of his *Sodalitas litteraria*; he then began to study poetry and the classics. He boasted about his accomplishments as a humanistic scholar, but Bauch adds that the real spirit of humanism remained foreign to him.[41] Mellerstadt later felt that humanism was placing pressure on scholasticism, and in his earlier days, he had attempted to combine the two philosophies, but without success.[42] Thus Mellerstadt drove away the able humanists who came to Wittenberg, such as Hermann von Bushe, Petrus of Ravenna, and Marschalk. They seem to have resented his intolerance as they did all old-type Thomists.[43] Another ground for resentment by others in the theological faculty may have been the favoritism shown him on the part of the elector of Saxony. He was regarded as an old friend, for he had been the elector's personal physician in earlier days, had accompanied him to the Holy Land in 1493, and had then been asked to be one of the founders of the new university on the Elbe. He was made the first rector when the new school opened with much pomp, was given a nice home for himself and family, and then, when his rival, Wimpina of Leipzig, was promoted to a doctorate in theology, Mellerstadt became very jealous. After that all Wittenberg's promotional standards were dropped in his case, and with the elector's goodwill and funds, Mellerstadt was promoted to the doctorate by Dean Johann von Staupitz—while others took five years to reach the top of that difficult doctrinal ladder.[44] How capable members of the rest of the faculty must have reacted to this dubious transaction one can well imagine. Besides this, during the next decade, and by the desire of the electoral court, Mellerstadt played the role of vice-chancellor of the university. On promotional days he sat in place of the absent chancellor, on the *Katheder* in the *Aula* of the Castle Church, granting promotional certificates to students coming up for their promotions. Thus it is not surprising that this dominant, bigoted scholastic would drive prominent professors out of the institution. He could not tolerate others who held theological views that failed to agree with his Thomistic philosophy. Meanwhile the elector had made him one of the university's four reformers, a body that had been created to stand guard over the newly founded institution.[45]

How able a scholar was Mellerstadt in his own field? Modern researchers have asked this question, as well as, no doubt, his contemporaries. As he became older, under the pressure of so many studies, he taught as professor neither in the theological nor in the medical faculties, for in his many posts his activities were too divided. The aged Mellerstadt could not tolerate the new humanistic trend that was in the air at Wittenberg, and he was determined that Thomism would reign supreme after his death. Friedensburg tells us that Polich hardened in his scholasticism and decided to publish his philosophical lectures *in via Thome*, which he had delivered at Leipzig in his younger days.[46] He claimed these offered students new insight into Aristotle. The sources he used were works from Paris and Cologne, from which he expounded their views in scholastic fashion *à la Saint Thomas*.[47] Mellerstadt, unable to produce anything original, led students to believe his findings were full of precious insight and wisdom.[48] His first publication was entitled *Cursus Logici*, and by 1512 was already printed by Melchior Lotter at Leipzig.[49] The modern scholar C. Prantl, an authority on the logic of the Middle Ages, claims Mellerstadt slavishly copied others in his *Cursus Logici*. Polich worked frantically on his Aristotle's *Natural Philosophy*, claiming its production was an absolute necessity for the Wittenberg students. He even contacted Georg Spalatin at the electoral court and asked him to use his influence with the publisher, assuring him the printer need not fear a loss.[50] But Mellerstadt died in 1513 before the book was in print. However, the Wittenberg reformers felt they should have it printed in memory of the old man, and they published it in 1514. However, the course in Aristotle's *Metaphysics*, for which it was intended, was never offered after his death.[51] That Polich von Mellerstadt, because of his close relationship to Frederick the Wise, wielded quite an influence in the original University of Wittenberg, for better or for worse, cannot be doubted. It will be shown in the next chapter that Mellerstadt represented a further continuation of the *Via Antiqua*, as opposed to the budding humanism represented by capable scholars like Hermann von Busche, Petrus of Ravenna, and Nicholaus Marschalk, all of whom left because they could not tolerate him.

As previously shown in connection with the founding of the university in 1502, the second pillar of the new institution was Doctor Johann von Staupitz, from the University of Tübingen, the later vicar of the Augustinian Hermits in Germany, after 1503.[52] Staupitz had been a boyhood friend of the elector, when they had attended school together.[53] The opening description of Wittenberg, with its many festivities, described in the *Liber Decanorum*, tells how Doctor Johann von Staupitz was chosen the first academic dean of Theology at the opening session in the *Stadtkirche* at Wittenberg.[54] But his deanship and pro-fessorship of "Lectura in Biblia" was soon terminated, for on May 7, 1503, he became the vicar general of the Augustinian Hermits in Germany, which involved much travel and absence from the school.[55] John Staupitz returned to Wittenberg once more and served as dean in 1508-1509, when, during the win-ter semester, he promoted four students. After Luther's *Romfahrt* (1512), Staupitz terminated his post of *Lectura in Biblia* and promoted Luther to the doctorate to make him his successor.[56]

Professor Johann von Staupitz was a very different type of man from Polich von Mellerstadt. He was a kind, fatherly type as an Augustinian prior and had much patience with his fellow monks. In his later years Luther admitted that in his soul struggle he could go to the vicar and confess, "Oh my sins, my sins, my sins,"[57] and that he owed everything to Staupitz for his later development as a theologian. Even though the vicar general remained busy with other affairs in his travels in the Netherlands and Brabant, and to other parts of Germany, including recruiting for the school on the Elbe, Luther's struggle remained on his mind. During the university's formative period, he is said to have brought 100 students to Wittenberg.[58] Academically speaking, what contributions he may have made through his courses remains unknown. Perhaps his greatest contribution to the later institution was his recognition of Luther's promise as a reformer in the German Reformation. He sent Luther to Rome during the win-ter of 1510-1511, in the interest of the union of the Augustinian Hermits. Prior to that, he had brought Luther to Wittenberg to teach the *Nichomachean Ethics* of Aristotle, in place of Master Wolf-Ostemeyer, who was meanwhile attempt-ing to acquire his *Licentiatus* degree.[59] Through these contacts, Staupitz must have recognized the future promise in the young Augustinian. He practically pushed Luther into being promoted to the doctorate in theology in 1512, so he might offer him his teaching position of *Lectura in Biblia*.[60] Had the vicar of the Augustinian hermits not taken these steps, the German Reformation might never have happened.[61]

Another distinguished addition to the Wittenberg faculty, in 1507, was the Erfurt professor Jodocus Trutfetter, teacher of Martin Luther while he was an undergraduate at that school. The electoral court of Frederick III must have been fully aware that Wittenberg's curriculum of philosophy was incomplete without a representative of the *Via Moderna*. He may have learned through his close friend, Johann von Staupitz, that schools like his old Tübingen University taught all three medieval systems of philosophy: the Thomistic, Scotistic, and Occamistic ways of interpretation; that Wittenberg would not be complete by offering courses confined to the *Via Antiqua*, interpreted by the commentaries of St. Thomas and Duns Scotus; and that the *Via Moderna* would widen their course offering to those who preferred to follow *in Viam Occam* and the later commentaries of Gabriel Biel of Tübingen.[62] This new philosophy widened the course offerings in both the philosophical undergraduate school, and also in the graduate school of theology, as Trutfetter had had training in both fields.

In southern Germany the *Via Moderna* was quite strong. In the early years the two schools of philosophy, Thomism and Scotism, had become quite well entrenched at Wittenberg, and the *Via Antiqua* did not welcome a rival philosophy.[63]

The two great Schoolmen of the Middle Ages, St. Thomas and Duns Scotus, placed great emphasis on logic and dialectic, dissecting and analyzing everything in this world and the next. With the assistance of Aristotelian syllogistic reasoning, although somewhat different in their basic approaches, they believed it possible to penetrate the mysteries of God and the kingdom of the world beyond. They even subordinated biblical revelation to human reason. In their world Aristotle reigned supreme.[64] The school of William Occam, in its philosophy of the *Via Moderna*, used just the opposite approach to the problems of philosophy and religion; it assumed that human beings cannot penetrate the mysterious realms of God by means of logic, but held that divine truth was revealed in the Holy Scriptures, which must be accepted through faith, even though much of it humans cannot understand.[65] On the other hand, the Occamists, in the realms of nature, were much more advanced and modern than the *Via Antiqua*. Here, according to the *Via Moderna*, the human mind is free to reason on the basis of induction. They believed the world was round, the moon had an effect on tides, thunderstorms and lightening were due to natural causes, and astrology was no longer applicable to their natural world.[66]

At Erfurt, Jodocus Trutfetter had built up quite a reputation as to its teachings. He had been at Erfurt since 1476, had risen to a doctorate in theology by 1504, and was regarded as a very learned man. In his lectures he used materials from the classics and the Italian humanists, and was a dedicated student of the philosophy of Occam, Buridan, and Gabriel Biel.[67] He was on friendly terms with Nicholaus Marschalk and the younger Wittenberg humanists. After Trutfetter arrived and published his new book on *Logic*, the Wittenberg Poet Laureate, Georg Sibrutus, wrote a *Lobgedict*, in praise of Trutfetter, which served as the opening part of the printed text.[68]

After Frederick the Wise invited Jodocus Trutfetter to join the faculty of Wittenberg and round out his liberal arts curriculum by teaching the third type of interpretation of Aristotle's *Logic* and *Ethics*, according to the *Via Moderna* of Occam, Trutfetter was the first to matriculate after the university was moved back from Hergberg, where it had been moved during the Pest, on December 6, 1506. Frederick must have directed that the faculty bestow upon the Erfurt professor all due honors while he was in their midst.[69] He was made archdeacon to the *Stift* of the Castle Church, immediately elected rector of the institution, and later served twice as dean, first upon his arrival (Winter semester, 1507–1508) and then again in the Summer and Winter semesters of 1509–1510.[70]

Professor Trutfetter began his assignments at the institution with great enthusiasm and vigor. He used his new *Kompendium der Logic*, just published by Schenck of Erfurt in 1507, to good advantage, for he attempted to put the *Via Moderna* on the map within the student body.[71] He must have made quite an impression on the students and many of the open-minded members of the faculty. Meinhard, in his *Dialogus of 1507*, described him as a "humble, just man, who was quite withdrawn from the world and dedicated to God."[72] Even the famous Nürnberger, Christopher Scheurl, has recorded in his *Briefbuch* the following view about his classroom activities:

> Jodocus Trutfetter, in instituting the *Via Moderna*, lectures, zealously advances, instructs, proclaims and pleads.[73]

As to what reception Jodocus had with his students, we are not informed. Bauch observed that in the midst of the climate prevailing at the time, due to the *Via Antiqua* at Wittenberg, the school was not ready for Trutfetter.[74] No doubt he was liked by the young humanists, but hardly at all by the "dyed in the wool" Thomists like Carlstadt and Mellerstadt. Freidensburg points out that Mellerstadt found him to be an uncomfortable *Nebenbühler*, and he adds that what made matters worse, Jodocus Trutfetter was also a somewhat combative personality. Polich wanted to get rid of him by making matters unpleasant, as he had done with his earlier humanistic rivals.[75] No doubt Trutfetter did not feel comfortable under those conditions, when the old combative warrior Mellerstadt felt his Thomism was being threatened by another philosophy, which made him push all the more to get his works on Aristotle into print.[76]

Jodocus Trutfetter was far too famous a man to put up with such jealous Thomistic and Scotistic rivals as the ambitious Bodenstein von Carlstadt and his promoter, the Wittenberg vice-chancellor, Polich von Mellerstadt. Erfurt must have been kept informed about Trutfetter's problems at Wittenberg, for by 1510 he returned to his Erfurt metropolis, whereupon he was made archdeacon of the Erfurt Cathedral. The elector was very disappointed with the course of events at Wittenberg and attempted to persuade him to return; but Jodocus had had his fill and refused to do so.[77] With Polich's support, Carlstadt then acquired his post in the Castle Church, in which dubious arrangement the departed Erfurt professor was even deprived of funds due him. But Karl Bauer points out that the *Via Moderna* did not terminate with Trutfetter's departure, for a revision of the Wittenberg *Statutes* in 1513 continued what had been established by those of 1508.[78]

THE PHILOSOPHICAL FACULTY PROFESSORS

Since none of the graduate schools were left unaffected by the work done in the philosophical faculty of the university, its background preparation for students in theology, so vital to our theme, now needs to be analyzed in some detail. As stated above, the course requirements of liberal arts were very scholastically oriented, as Gustav Bauch has so effectively demonstrated.[79] In a faculty of 22 full professors, 12 were in liberal arts. Since there were quite a number of changes in the faculty during the first fifteen years, with some departing after a short stay and new ones replacing them, it is impossible to reconstruct the complete picture. Besides, after their acquisition of a master of arts, students were expected to teach for a period of time upon graduation, according to the *Statutes of 1508*. This added to the complexity of the Staff. In addition, when graduates of the philosophical faculty continued their studies for advanced degrees, they were employed as instructors in extraordinary courses of liberal arts. The only complete picture we possess is for the year when Christopher Scheurl did his *Rotulus of 1507*, patterned after Bologna. It lists most of the younger instructors, about whom no further information is available. In this coverage of the liberal arts faculty, therefore, we plan to base our treatment on the well-known, most influential scholars for the history of the German Reformation. These views need to be balanced with the subsequent history of the University of Wittenberg, with reference to the inroads of humanism in German universities. This treatment will be reserved for the next chapter.

The first distinguished professor in the philosophical faculty was its dean, Sigismund Epp, who had been brought to Wittenberg by Dr. Johann von Staupitz. Dean Epp was a fellow Augustinian, of the University of Tübingen. Although he did not remain long, Dean Epp had quite an impact on the future study of Aristotle. In the curriculm he lectured as a Scotist, and he was quite an expert of Tartaretus, a late medieval scholar on Aristotle. This field he taught as an ordinarius professor *Viam Scoti*, which was the counterpart of those who taught Aristotle *Viam Thome*, the two divisions of the medieval *Via Antiqua*. Epp was not satisfied with the older commentaries on Aristotle, *Viam Scoti*. He preferred to use the newer works as textbooks, written by Petrus Tartaretus. Those works he wished to have printed for his students. Thus he approached the prior of the Castle Church, Dr. Frederick Kitscher, for an expenditure of 500 Gulden to carry out the project. The prior contacted Polich von Mellerstadt, who agreed to have this done. But the funds would have come from the Saxon court, and a printer had to be found, for at Wittenberg there was only

Nicholaus Marschalk, who had brought his press from Erfurt.[80] The press Epp
wanted to use was that of Wolfgang Stöckel of Munich, who had recently moved
to Wittenberg. But the printing of his texts had to be delayed, as at the time
Stöckel was busy printing a *Compendium* on canon law for Petrus of Ravenna.
This work by the fine Italian humanist, who was also a lawyer of canon law, was
such an elegantly written work, combining fine quotations from the classics
with the basic textual material, that the scholar was anxious to see it in print.[81]

Petrus Tartaretus, Epp's authority on the proposed texts, was one of the
younger scholars in late medieval scholasticism, and had taught at the Sorbonne
in Paris between 11480 and 1490. Bauch does not classify Tartaretus as a voluminous author, but as a sharp thinker in his reworking of the material of Duns
Scotus. In his writings, Tartaretus pedagogically had also kept his students in
mind. The first volume that Epp wanted Stöckel to print covered the *Tractatus
des Petrus Hispanus*, with summaries for the students. In the second textbook
there was a treatment of the *Logic* of Aristotle, covering the *Isagoge des Porphyrius* of Aristotle's *Organum*, which for students would prove useful in the
study of *The Sentences*, as Tartaretus offered his explanations about dubious
points. Bauch, as a humanist, made an interesting observation about the
author's style. Tartaretus, though thoroughly scholastic in content, is different;
for a foreign air blows through the material.[82] In the text, now and then verses
from the classics are interspersed, as in the writings of Petrus of Ravenna's text
on canon law, which appears to have been the new way of philosophical writing
in the later fifteenth century.[83] According to these studies of Stephan Hoest, the
died-in-the-wool scholastics at Heidelberg at first fought the humanists, but
under his reign began to find real merit in combining humanistic style and even
citations from the classics to liven up their own treatises.[84] No doubt Epp, in his
Tübingen training as a scholar, had the same view as Stephan Hoest and wanted
to treat the Aristotelian logic, like Tartaretus, with a humanistic style and flavor.
The same spirit was displayed by other professors in the liberal arts faculty,
where poetry had made some inroads, as we shall see.

However, Sigismund Epp did not remain at Wittenberg long enough to see
those new Tartaretus textbooks in print, for by the time they came off the press,
in 1504, he had returned to Tübingen, where in 1505 he was chosen as their
rector. Perhaps that was a factor in his early departure, for the school was more
than ready to comply with his wishes about the printing of new Tartaretus
texts.[85] The undertaking to have the texts printed was very significant, for had
he also done the Tartaretus works on the *Ethics* of Aristotle, says Bauch, it
would have covered the entire bachelors and masters lecture series, *Viam Scoti*
for the arts students, which was lacking at that time. But, Bauch adds, that it
may have been done and the work has since been lost.

There is no further record about the purchase of the Epp textbooks by the
Wittenberg faculty, nor about who followed him, until we come to the *Rotulus
of 1507*, when the noble, Nicholas von Amsdorf, then the chief of the Scotists at
Wittenberg, is listed as the ordinarius professor, who lectured at 6:00 A.M. on
Aristotle's courses *Viam Scoti*. But we do not know whether he used the Epp

texts. This Christopher Scheurl fails to record.[86] Under Amsdorf, as the chief of the Scotists, were assistants Chilian Reuter from Mellerstadt, Mathäus Beckau of Torgau, and Wolfgang of Zwickau. It also lists Sebastian of Freiburg as another Scotist lecturer.[87] Both Scotists and Thomists, Konrad Koenig, the former, and Master Matheus of Torgau, offered lectures on natural philosophy under Master Amsdorf, which included books *On the Heavens and the World* and *On Generation and Corruption*, which they called the Small Books about Nature.[88]

In 1508, Nicholas von Amsdorf, who during the deanship of Doctor Symon von Stern was a canon of the Stift of All Saints Church, and a *Baccalaureus Biblicus* in theology since 1507, was promoted to *Sententiarius* under rector Trutfetter of Erfurt.[89] Meanwhile, Nicholas Amsdorf advanced through the *Formatus* step in theology, so that in 1511 he engaged in a disputation for the *Licentiatus* degree in theology, which made him qualified to teach in both fields, philosophy and theology.[90] Later he must have joined the theological faculty, for in 1516, when Bartholomaeus Bernhardi came up for a *Sententiarius* degree, a Luther student, we find Amsdorf involved in his promotion. Luther presided over the disputation, while Carlstadt and Lupinus provided the opposition, and Amsdorf appeared to agree with the scholastic's side. But Luther's student, Bernhardi, was so well versed in Scripture that he left a deep impression on the faculty. Lupinus agreed with Luther's new approach, but Carlstadt felt humiliated; however, his reactions belong below with his story.[91]

On September 4, 1517, Francis Gunther tried for his *Biblicus* degree in theology and engaged in a disputation for the degree in the Castle Church.[92] He was one of Luther's students who was already thoroughly oriented in Luther's "New Theology." Luther had drafted theses for the debate on Augustine and "Free Will." The disputation theses were clearly directed against Scotus, Occam, D'Ailly, and Biel, claiming that their views were Pelagian.[93] In this debate Amsdorf became convinced that Luther's teachings were right, and he dropped his Scotism and joined in the cause of the Reformation. After that, Amsdorf became an ardent champion of Luther's cause, and later even accompanied him to Worms. It was in Amsdorf's *Probstei* rooms, near the Castle Gate, where Luther stayed upon his brief, secret visit from the Wartburg in 1521; and in 1525 he became pastor in a disturbed Magdeburg, about which much will be said later. Finally, after the reformer's death, Nicholas Amsdorf defended Luther's views of the Reformation.[94]

A second member of the *Via Antiqua* team on the Wittenberg faculty, who needs to be described in the light of modern scholarship, is Bodenstein von Carlstadt. Since he later became such a controversial figure in the German Reformation, and caused such disturbances, his role in the original University of Wittenberg deserves a more thorough treatment.

An account of Carlstadt's actual role in the formative years of the University of Wittenberg becomes somewhat difficult to present, for he has become a changeable character. Karl Bauer is quite critical of Carlstadt as a man, and views him doctrinally in the light of the Reformation itself.[95] Gustav Bauch, the most thorough investigator of his life and works,[96] does not have a high estimate of him as a scholar, but as an individual who always attempted to be what he was not. Finally, Walter Friedensburg was somewhat kinder in his judgments, but he also was critical of Carlstadt's tendency to try to impress his students and others with his importance.[97] These views of the three historians were often based on findings by more recent scholars, as will be observed from the coverage of Professor Carlstadt.

According to Karl Bauer, Carlstadt had an overbearing arrogance about himself and in relationship to faculty members around him. He apparently could not tolerate rivalry and being outdone, even in fields where he seems to have been less qualified than his rivals. He even compares him to the lines in *Wallenstein's Tod*, II, 6:

> I am a jealous person, I could never tolerate to be looked down upon.[98]

He himself admitted that he loved to be honored, and that he could not bear it later when he was outstripped in honor by young Martin Luther.[99] Karl Bauer claims that when Luther first arrived at Wittenberg in 1509, Carlstadt did not regard him very highly.[100]

Historians fail to agree on the date of Carlstadt's birth, but they feel he must have been considerably older than Luther, which might explain his low estimate of the young Augustinian, who was but 26 years old when he taught the moral philosophy of Aristotle in 1509.[101] Scholars differ up to thirteen years in their estimate of Carlstadt's birth. Barge, a biographer of his, places the date of his birth at 1480, while Karl Bauer thinks it was around 1470,[102] and Friedensburg holds that it was about 1475, or at least in the last quarter of the fifteenth century.[103] Bauer may be closer to being correct, for in 1522 he married Anna von Mochau, when he was reported to be a man of 54, while his bride was a mere child of 14. His contemporaries regarded the marriage as ridiculous. It turned out to be an unfortunate marriage at the time of the Peasants War in 1525. Luther, in a letter to Melanchthon, called her a *novi puellam*.[104]

Carlstadt's academic career began at Erfurt, where he had matriculated in 1499, and he completed his bachelor of philosophy degree in 1502; whereupon he continued his studies of the *Via Moderna* under its distinguished professors of that discipline, Doctors Usingen and Trutfetter, and became an ardent student of Occam and Biel.[105] As there was a similarity between medieval universities, there was a tendency among students to migrate to different schools. For some reason Carlstadt did not remain long at Erfurt, for already in 1503 he was at Cologne, where he matriculated as Andreas Karlstadt, on June 17, 1503. While there he stayed in the *Montanerburse*, which was a Thomistic stronghold. Amid this influence he soon became a Thomist. Bauch adds that whether Carlstadt was already a Thomist when he arrived, or soon became one after his arrival, remains unknown.[106] Karl Bauer sees this change in a different light. He claims it was Carlstadt's arrogance and pride that drove him from one thing to another, always grabbing the newest, in case it offered him advantages, and often without considering the long-term consequences.[107] When he came to

Wittenberg he matriculated during the winter semester of 1504-1505 as a Thomist, where he continued his liberal arts work and philosophy to complete his masters of arts degree, under Dean Petrus Lupinus, on August 12, 1505.[108] The most influential figure in his promotion was Polich von Mellerstadt, who now took Carlstadt under his wing.[109] He assisted him in his promotions, appointments to offices, and rapid rise.[110] In the winter semester of 1507-1508, Carlstadt became dean of arts, during which period he recorded in the philosophical *Matrikel* that he was a distinguished master of arts and a *Baccalaureus* in theology.[111] Bauch points out that it is strange that the *Liber Decanorum* does not even record his promotion to the first step of *Biblicus* in theology. But Bauch says that the original did not begin until 1509, and the first part had to be filled in later, which may explain the omission.[112] Like Mellerstadt, the young Thomist advanced unusually quickly toward the doctorate in theology. Already by August 11, 1508, he became a *Sententiarius*, and shortly after Pentecost, 1509, he was advanced to *Formatus*, while a year later he was granted the *Licentiatus* (October 31, 1510), and then was promoted to the doctorate in November 1510. However, his ambitions were insatiable, for by the summer semester of 1512, Carlstadt was dean of theology for the first time, which honor was repeated five times by 1522.[113]

By 1509 Carlstadt had become an *ordinarius* professor of the arts faculty,[114] was the head of the Thomists at Wittenberg, and also a *Biblicus* in theology; he by now was a regular member of the Senate of the philosophical faculty, in which he interpreted the *Metaphysics* of Aristotle *in via Thome*;[115] while with Mellerstadt's help, he had become a canon of the Castle Church.[116] But this was not enough for the ambitious professor, for he also had gone prematurely into print, upon the request of a few of his students.

In 1507 Carlstadt, while lecturing on Aristotle, had made the statement that he had analyzed the *dialectics* of philosophy by use of the *Intentions*, which was not quite clear to his students. Two of his students, a bachelor, Vitus Trumetarius from Stuttgart, and another, Johann Ruhel, asked him to write a small treatise on *Logic* explaining his new approach.[117] Instead of preparing a solid, well-balanced treatise, he began the work on July 10, finished it by August 10. Bauch says Carlstadt must have worked with feverish speed, as it turned out to be good-sized, with many abbreviations.[118] It is fortunate for Carlstadt, says Bauch, that Prantl, in his *History of Logic,* did not cover that work, for then Carlstadt's weaknesses and errors would have been ruthlessly exposed.[119] Bauer claims it was an interpretation of Thomas Aquinas's theology, according to Capreolus and other Thomists; but Carlstadt also did not hesitate to plunder some of his material from Duns Scotus, by claiming Scotus had learned his wisdom from St. Thomas.[120]

One would have thought, observed Bauch, that in trying to clarify his *Intentiones*, Carlstadt would have begun with an analytical approach to them. Thus, instead of clarifying his definitions of *Intentiones*, he began with some of their implications in his interpretations, without first having clarified what he was really discussing. He advanced arguments between scholars of the Middle Ages without first having clarified what he is talking about. It was apparently a line of reasoning from a major premise in *Logic* to a conclusion, but how his *Intentiones* are involved is not clear. In his treatment he attacks the *Via Moderna* of Occam, then the Thomist Petrus Nigrus and his views of *Nominalism*, and later, Petrus Tartaretus and Thomanus Thomistus, whose lines of thinking, he asserted, do not square with those of St. Thomas. Carlstadt claimed that in the second part he would present the true views of St. Thomas.[121]

In that part, he begins with a citation of Armand von Beauvoir, who he claims was a distinguished Thomist, using a questionable citation as an assertion, as Prantl states his works were heavily colored with he views of Duns Scotus.[122] Then follow an unbelievable line of citations about Petrus Nigrus and many others, raising questions and offering his replies, so that even Bauch admits the treatise can hardly be followed.[123] Bauch concluded that Carlstadt so confused the views of Armand and Nigrus, and so praised Polich von Mellerstadt and Capreolus, employing pseudo-Thomistic sources, that it becomes evident that Carlstadt, after being a master for two years, and meanwhile the head of all the *Viam Thome* courses given at the university, was still not quite clear on the actual teachings of the Blessed St. Thomas Aquinas. A year later Carlstadt barely acknowledged that this was his first literary product.[124]

But apparently Carlstadt's contemporaries failed to realize what a confused philosophical treatise it was, for it did not even distinguish between real and pseudo authors. Frederick the Wise's poet, Richardus Sbrulius, permitted him to use his special *Lobgedicht*, a poem of praise, to be printed at the beginning of Carlstadt's first publication.[125] A second public reference to Carlstadt's first publication came during a farewell address of the law professor, Christopher Scheurl, on November 16, 1507, while he was rector and turned over the office of rector to his successor, the archdeacon of All Saints Church, Jodocus Trutfetter of Erfurt. In this he praised Carlstadt as an author, a sharp and well-informed Thomist, and a distinguished philosopher.[126] He even added that had Wittenberg many Carlstadts, it would have to take no second place even to Paris. He added that he was also a "man very erudite in Latin, Greek and Hebrew, a great philosopher, an even greater theologian, and the highest ranking Thomist."[127] Even Carlstadt must have been embarrassed, or perhaps he had been chided by others, for he admitted in another publication that in his first work he had written much that he later regretted.[128]

How many early works Carlstadt published can no longer be determined. He later announced that he planned to produce a sequel to his first publication in 1508, but the work never seems to have materialized. It was the *Praedicabilia, des Porphyrius*, which also fell in the field of the Old Logic. He claimed the book would deal with *Aristotle's Peri Hermeneias*, which was something entirely new. None of his fellow professors refer to it later, and the *Wolfenbüttler Anonymous* knew nothing of it.[129]

But a second work did appear, with the title *Distintiones sive formalitates Thomistarum*, a work, according to the later scholars in the field, that serves as a dead giveaway as to how little Carlstadt really understood the difference between the teachings of the philosophical schools of Duns Scotus and St. Thomas. He even announced that it was an unusual work, something that was distinctly new. Without Carlstadt realizing it, the *Formalitates* really stemmed from Duns Scotus, according to Prantl, the modern scholastic authority on medieval *Logic*.[130] It did not become an independent work until prepared by a later Scotist, Franciscus Mayron, who treated it in a separate publication.[131] But it entered into the Thomistic stream, by the use of Duns Scotus' *Formalitates*, in a pseudo work of St. Thomas, *De Natura generis*.[132] This Carlstadt thought was a genuine work of Thomas Aquinas by a reliable authority.[133] Later the views of Duns Scotus' *Formalitates* were further presented by the Thomist Thomas of Strassburg.[134]

After a detailed analysis of Carlstadt's work, Gustav Bauch finally concludes that the thinking of Carlstadt, based on these false premises, was that the thinking of Scotus on *Formalitates* and that of St. Thomas were not far apart, little realizing that those were not the views of the former Paris professor at all. He claimed the rational and formal distinctions were very similar, but those of his Holy St. Thomas were superior.[135]

Bauch claims that even though Christopher Scheurl praised Carlstadt's accomplishments in 1508, they passed into history. Meanwhile his thinking about Carlstadt's scholastic attainments had changed. The *Wolfenbüttel Anonymous* claims that later Scheurl regarded Carlstadt to be at the same time a follower of Duns Scotus and St. Thomas, a praise that implies a double meaning. It could also imply that Carlstadt did not know the difference between the teachings of the two scholastics.[136]

Both Mellerstadt and Carlstadt had a strong dislike for Jodocus Trutfetter, the new head of the *Via Moderna*, because he was a distinguished scholar and the representative of a rival philosophical school. In fact they were so jealous of the honor that the elector had bestowed upon him when he brought him to Wittenberg, that they forced him to leave by 1510. Christopher Scheurl, who also soon returned to Nürnberg to accept an important legal post, had a very high regard for Trutfetter, and carried on a long correspondence with him in later years. Scheurl's *Briefbuch* contains many letters between the two men after they were apart, and from that it is clear he had no high regard for Carlstadt. Another able humanist, Otto Beckmann, stated that Carlstadt was a sharp dialectician, but made no reference to his other scholastic attainments.[137]

As will be observed in the next chapter, humanism had made some inroads into the universities in spite of the opposition of the conservative scholastics. This also did not leave Carlstadt untouched, as he was anxious to excel there also above all other rivals. We saw how Scheurl praised Carlstadt as an erudite linguist, who was learned in Latin, Greek, and Hebrew, while the *Wolfenbüttel Anonymous* claimed he was not ignorant of these languages. But how much Scheurl's remarks, made in a public address, as a retiring rector, are to be taken seriously is debatable. Scheurl had been at the institution only a short time and one wonders how well informed he was about Carlstadt's scholarship. The fact that, when Martin Luther introduced courses at Wittenberg in Greek and

Hebrew during 1517–18, there is no reference about the role of Carlstadt during Luther's dealings with the Electoral Court. Where had Carlstadt learned these languages? It is more likely he consulted some of the young humanistic poets at Wittenberg, who then may have assisted him in finding suitable quotations from the classics for his works.

Gustav Bauch, who was dubious about Carlstadt's attainments as a humanist, adds that he introduced a few epigrams in his work on *Intertiones*, on the title page, and also in the index; while in his battles with Petrus Tartaretus he used some classical materials to defend the Holy St. Thomas. In his logic are also some references to the classics, as well as in his lectures on *Metaphysics*. In his *Logic*, with its Thomistic background—which incidentally, he dedicated to Frederick the Wise— he displays little knowledge of Greek, but what appears more amazing, in his work, he wrote in Hebrew, "The Son of God Jesus, the son of Mary and David," printed in block print. This was the first Hebrew to appear at the University of Wittenberg.[138]

Karl Bauer pointed out that Carlstadt's *Ehrgeisz* or ambition never permitted him to allow himself to be surpassed by others. The fact that a Scotist professor, Ludwig Henning, of the minor orders from Padua, came out in print, influenced Carlstadt to write his early books. He had published the Scotus *Formalitates* of the Paris Professor Antonius Sirectus and some additions by a teacher from Padua, Mauritius, which occurred while Henning was dean of the arts faculty.[139] Carlstadt could not permit any philosophical system to outdo his Thomists in honor. Karl Bauer points out that when young Martin Luther began to lecture on Augustine, Carlstadt, not to be outdone, then began lecturing to the Franciscans. When Carlstadt wanted to enter the *Probstei* of the Wittenberg *Stift*, the requirement was a degree in law. Carlstadt hurried from Wittenberg to Siena in Italy. All that transpired there is no longer known. However, we know that a student at an Italian university like Bologna usually took from five to seven years to earn a doctorate in both civil and canon law. The ambitious Carlstadt took a few courses at Siena, and by 1516 he was back, proudly wearing a doctoral gown with the degree of *Juris utriusque doctor* from Siena, which made him eligible to enter the Wittenberg *Stift* as a doctor in both civil and canon law.[140]

As will be observed in a later chapter, this was not the end of Carlstadt's strange and twisted life. When, later, in a disputation with two of Luther's theological students, he was humiliated for not knowing the doctrines of Augustine, he was furious. He went to Leipzig, purchased a complete set of Augustine's works, became convinced that scholasticism was in error, and became an ardent Augustinian, more so than Luther himself.[141]

Carlstadt's later involvement in the Leipzig Debate with John Eck was another example of being jealous about Luther's rapid rise, and wanting himself to remain in the spotlight. Here he suffered another humiliation during the debate, when the clever Ingolstadt professor had Duke George change the rules of procedure from the use of notes to the free-style Italian method of using no references. Later, when the Zwickau Prophets came to Wittenberg to reform the Town Church by force, in order to remain in control he joined them and became such an extremist in reforms that the elector expelled him from his lands.[142]

Even though he did not remain long in Wittenberg, a noteworthy member of the arts and law faculty was Christopher Scheurl, about whom we have already heard much. Scheurl gave Wittenberg the *Rotulus of 1507* and the *Statutes of 1508* and was an effective *ordinarius* professor of both kinds of law. He also gave a course in *Suetonius*. The law professor also appears to have encouraged the younger humanists on the faculty.

Christopher Scheurl was a descendant from a commercial family in the prominent city of Nürnberg, whose lineage extended back to this grandfather, a successful merchant in Breslau.[143] His father, however, had moved to Nürnberg, where he married into the Tucher family, which added to his prestige. Christopher Scheurl was born November 11, 1481. Young Christopher was asked to study law. As a lad he had an excellent Nürnberg upbringing, like other patricians of the city. In time he went to Heidelberg, where he spent a year of his liberal arts training. After that the ambitious family sent him to Italy, where he began his studies at the University of Bologna. There he was intrigued by humanism, but that did not turn him from his goal as a lawyer.

Two years later, in 1501, Scheurl's father lost much of the family's wealth, a situation that was aggravated by giving bail for a fellow-citizen, who failed to pay. The debt fell upon his father. The Tucher relatives came to his assistance, as did the City Council. Now there was talk of Christopher's termination of his Bologna studies and going to Wittenberg in 1505; but, fortunately, he was able to complete a doctorate in both civil and canon law on December 22, 1506, which meant he was ready to follow the family suggestion of becoming part of the Wittenberg faculty. In the spring of 1507 young Scheurl presented himself to the electoral court in Weimar. The elector agreed that he would teach as the *ordinarious* professor of canon law on the *Liber Sixtus*, and offered him a salary of 80 Gulden per year. The elector also wanted him to teach some classical courses in liberal arts, which pleased Scheurl very much.[144]

Prior to Scheurl's coming to Wittenberg he had written a treatise in praise of the German Lands and the Saxon Court, which gave him an excellent reception upon his arrival at Wittenberg. He dedicated the *Libelus* to Frederick the Wise, in which he praised the City of Wittenberg, the elector who, he said, had converted the town from one of thatched roofs to a city of marble. This work he had given as an address at Bologna, and repeated at Wittenberg upon his entry of the rectorship of the university in 1507.[145]

In the short period that Scheurl remained at Wittenberg, he left his mark on the institution on the Elbe. His *Rotulus of 1507*, modeled after the practice at Bologna, gave us the first complete record of the teaching staff and what courses were offered at the time. From the *Rotulus* we learn that he taught the *nova jura* or the *liber Sixtus*, which was an additional part of the *Corpus iuris canonici*. He offered a course in *Lehnrecht*, and while in humane letters of the arts college, he also taught a course in *Suetonius Tranquillus*.[146] But Scheurl's

most important contribution to the academic life of the university was his drafting of the *Statutes of 1508*, which, with the exception of a few alterations and
modifications, served the institution until new ones were given to the institution
by the Elector John Frederick between 1533 and 1536.[147]

Scheurl had already expressed his doubts about the wisdom of accepting a
professorship at Wittenberg, as it was new and not too well established as an
institution. After his arrival in 1507, in spite of all the honors bestowed upon
him, the young and gifted lawyer was not very happy with his environment. This
does not seem strange for a man who had grown up in the old Kaisertown of
Emperor Charles IV and its patrician environment and culture. The people of
Wittenberg, he felt, lacked refinement and were coarse in their manners.[148] He
may also not have liked the dominance of Polich von Mellerstadt, who had mistreated his friend, Jodocus Trutfetter and driven him back to Erfurt, as well as
the prominent humanists. He was drawn to his students, who seemed to grow in
numbers. Scheurl also worked to raise the standards of the student body, which
did not compare too favorably, in his opinion, with other German universities.
His chief concern remained the law faculty. Here, in 1508, he tried to introduce
a *Liber Decanorum* for law, as was kept by the theological faculty. No doubt to
keep the young man satisfied, the elector made him a legal member of his Saxon
Oberhofgericht, the Supreme Court in the land. This appointment seemed to
please him. To anchor the young lawyer even more, attempts were made to find
a suitable wife for him; however, he did not regard this with favor.[149]

Christopher Scheurl had never thought of himself as remaining a professor at
Wittenberg for the rest of his life. He did, however, think of himself as continuing in the service of the Catholic Church in some form, because of his training
in canon law. While in Italy he had thought of becoming the probst of St. Sebaldus Church in Nürnberg; later, while at Wittenberg, he had remained active in
seeking such an appointment. In the spring of 1512 he was offered the position
of *Rechtkonsul* in Nürnberg, which pleased him. With Scheurl's departure Wittenberg lost its most able scholar in the school of law, and a warm friend of
humanistic learning.[150] But Scheurl did not lose interest in the new university
on the Elbe or his friends there, as will be evident in subsequent Wittenberg
history.

Another scholar worthy of being remembered as playing an important role in
the early years of the University of Wittenberg was Peter Wolf of Badenheim,
more professionally known as Petrus Lupinus. His influence was quite significant, for he remained with the institution until his death in 1521.[151] His first
important assignment came when he was elected to the deanship of liberal arts,
during the winter semester of 1504–1505. His early academic record appears in
the school's *Liber Decanorum*, as he soon entered the theological faculty. As a
fellow Thomist of Carlstadt he advanced the steps toward a doctorate. In the
summer of 1505, under the deanship of Master Ludwig Henning, Lupinus was
granted the degree of *Biblicus* in Theology, after which he rose quite rapidly
through the grades and was granted the Degree of *Licentiatus* in 1508, whereupon he soon became a doctor of theology.[152] He was also made a *Kostus* of All

Saints Church of Wittenberg.[153] Lupinus officiated when Carlstadt was pro-
moted to the doctorate in theology on November 9, 1510, under Dean Bishop
Wolfgang.[154] He is also called a "distinguished professor of theology" in the
Liber Decanorum; we find he served three times as the dean of theology during
his lifetime.[155] During the last period, he was also advanced to the priorship of
All Saints Church.[156]

We saw above, in connection with two of Martin Luther's students, how
Lupinus became convinced that the scholastic philosophy of Aristotle could
never be reconciled with teachings of the Holy Scripture, as interpreted by St.
Augustine;[156] whereupon he joined Martin Luther in support of Wittenberg's
"New Theology."[157]

Another professor of the law department, who remained and left a lasting
impression in this formative period and during the beginning of the German
Reformation, was Hieronymous Schurff, who became the successor of Petrus
of Ravenna in 1505.[158] Dr. Schurff was a Swiss scholar from St. Gallen. Hieronymous was two years older than Luther, who began his academic career as a student at Basel University and later attended the University of Tübingen, where
he took his masters in liberal arts. Here he worked under the distinguished
Scotist Konrad Summenhardt, as had also Johann von Staupitz. Staupitz may
have been influential in the elector bringing Schurff to Wittenberg.[159] There he
entered the Liberal Arts College, where he taught two lectures on the works of
Aristotle as interpreted by Duns Scotus. He entered this work at the very opening of the institution in 1502 and would be active at Wittenberg in various
capacities until 1547. After three years, in 1505, he entered the law faculty,
where he gave courses in canon law, lecturing on the *Liber Sextus* and the
Clementines.[160] Since he now occupied the position of *ordinarius* professor,
vacated by Petrus of Ravenna, his salary was increased from 30 Gulden to 100
Gulden.[161] The Scheurl *Rotulus of 1507* claims he also taught *den Kodex*, while
he was assisted by a student, Wolfgang Reisenpusch, who taught the *Institutes
of the Code of Justinian*.[162]

In later years, the Elector used Schurff as his legal advisor. He also sat in the
elector's Saxon *Obergericht*. Frequently he was summoned to the Electoral
Court to offer legal advice, and his *Rechtsgutachten* and *Consilia* were published after his death.[163] Schurff was quite a sharp, penetrating thinker and a
very fluent lecturer, of whom Luther once later remarked, "He is a sharp lawyer
who loves equity."[164] One day, after Luther's *Ninety-five Theses* had been nailed
to the *Schwarte Brett* of the Castle Church in 1517, Schurff happened to meet
the reformer in the street. He asked him what he thought he was attempting,
trying to challenge Rome! He told Luther, "You will never get by with that!" But
Schurff's greatest hour came when Martin Luther was summoned in 1521 to
appear before the Kaiser and the Diet of Worms. In that moment the elector
needed his best lawyer to serve as Luther's trusted advisor and friend, and he
called upon Schurff to serve in that capacity.[165] This was an excellent choice, as
Schurff was a quiet and calm legal mind. His help proved to be necessary in the
first session before the impressive diet. A clever maneuver had been planned.

All of Luther's books, published by then, lay piled on a table. The Kaiser's presiding officer was Johann von Eck from Trier, who first tried to impress the
young Augustinian with the gravity of the situation he was in. Then he turned to
the pile of Luther's books and asked him whether he was ready to recant what
was in the volumes. Naturally Luther was baffled, as the question came as a
complete surprise. Then the calm Schurff arose, faced Chancellor Eck and said:
"Let the titles be read!" This took quite a while, and Luther could determine by
the titles what books Aleander and his advisors had assembled. By this time the
reformer had his composure and could form his answer, that the books there
were of three kinds, and no *en masse* recantation was possible! He needed time
for an answer to the chancellor's recantation until the next day. Thus Schurff
assisted Luther during an embarrassing moment.

Another distinguished member of the early Wittenberg faculty was Doctor
Henning Göde, who was the probst of the *Stift* of the Castle Church for a long
time. Göde had matriculated at Erfurt in 1464, at which school he had acquired
a doctorate in both civil and canon law. As an *ordinarius* professor of these
disciplines he had served his Alma Mater the rest of that century. However, in
1509 something had happened at Erfurt that made him unhappy. He turned to
the elector for assistance as a practicing legal consultant. His reputation at the
Saxon Court stood very high, and here was an opportunity to add him to the
young Wittenberg faculty. The elector offered Henning Göde two excellent
opportunities. He agreed to make him the probst of the *Stift* of his Castle
Church and offer him the vital faculty position of *ordinarius* professor of canon
law. Göde became the prior of the Stift in 1510 and continued in that position
until his death in 1521, even though meanwhile the Erfurt difficulties had been
straightened out by friends. In time the elector became very fond of Henning
Göde as a friend. He often asked him to accompany him on his journeys, during
which the able lawyer performed many court legal assignments. In later years,
the university gathered Göde's *Gutachten*, known as *Consilia*.[166]

In this chapter there has been a coverage of the Wittenberg faculty, namely,
its more distinguished members, about whom historical records have been preserved. However, it must be remembered that there were many other important staff members who were at the institution but a short time and could hardly
have left any significant impact or records. There were also a number of instructors who, after the completion of their masters degree, were obligated to teach
for a specific period, as well as those who continued in their graduate schools
and were obligated to teach courses in the liberal arts faculty. About such persons we have no records except the one year when the *Rotulus of 1507* recorded
their names and some of the courses they taught.

From the details in this chapter, there can be little doubt about the fact that
medieval philosophy dominated the university's studies, just as at Paris,
Bologna, and other German universities. Its requirements for academic
degrees determined students' activities at all levels of the school. Yet it will be
observed in the next chapter that humanism made its inroads at Wittenberg, as
at Heidelberg and other universities in Germany. In fact, many of the scholastic

professors began to realize that, to a degree at least, they needed better methods in the written textbooks, both as to grammar and style, in which the classics could prove to be of value. Thus there remains little doubt that humanism, even though only an elective, prepared the way for the biblical humanism that was introduced in the academic curricula in the next decade by Martin Luther, Philip Melanchthon, and their supporters. Aristotle was dethroned, and biblical humanism began to replace the former scholastic methodology with an emphasis on Latin, Greek, and Hebrew, as the best preparatory instructions for the study of the Holy Scriptures. This new type of interpretation of the Bible gave Wittenberg the "New Theology" that became the core of the German Reformation.

19

Humanism and Wittenberg

THE ROLE OF HUMANISM

In the previous chapters, an attempt was made to trace western culture as a continuous stream, to use the metaphor of Ernst Walser, flowing the Greco-Roman period, through the Middle Ages, and up to the Italian Renaissance. During this period scholars have viewed the Carolingian Renaissance, the Ottonian Renaissance, and the Twelfth Century Renaissance as but peaks in the development of our western culture. We have likewise observed that had not Irish and British missionaries come into Western Europe to establish monasteries with *Scriptoria*, in which well-trained calligraphers copied precious scrolls of antiquity into manuscripts and preserved them in medieval libraries, there would have been no rare books to be discovered by later Renaissance scholars, and the entire Greco-Roman culture would have been lost, as the libraries were lost to flames in later centuries. The stream of culture also had its tributaries, flowing from southern Italy and Spain, which stimulated the growth of learning in monastic and cathedral schools, and in time created the beginnings of the great medieval universities of Paris and Bologna. Thus the influence of the classics and the Christian Fathers became the source of the Christian learning of later centuries.

That this cultural heritage had a direct influence on the Italian Renaissance and the growth of humanism is well realized by scholars, for had Cassiodorus and his successors not preserved the treasures of antiquity there would have been no monastic libraries to explore. As will be seen, there was a very fundamental difference between the scholars who produced the *Via Antiqua*, such as Abelard, Anselm, Scotus, and St. Thomas, in the Middle Ages, and the later ones of the Italian Renaissance, such as Petrarch, Boccaccio, and artists like Cimabue and Giotto. Both drew upon the works of ancient cultures, but for very different purposes, as has already been seen in the cases of the University of Paris and the University of Bologna. They began with very different sets of basic assumptions.

This chapter aims to analyze the degree of influence humanism may have had on the original University of Wittenberg. But this can be done properly only in the light of the Italian Renaissance and its humanistic aspects. This involves analysis of the viewpoints of many European and American scholars during the last century, since Jacob Burckhardt published his epoch-making book in 1860[1]. The prior Voight study had been limited to the revival of the culture of antiquity since the scholastic dominance of the Middle Ages; the Burckhardt approach covered a wider scope, claiming the Renaissance was a cultural epoch in European history, and that it ushered in the modern world by its unique approach.[2] Both approaches were first amplified, then modified, and finally entirely rejected.[3]

Jacob Burckhardt did not need to invent the term *Renaissance*, as it dates far back in the period itself. Huizinga claims the term was first used by Giogio Varsari (1511–1574) with reference to the blossoming of art during the period. Varsari described the arts of the Greeks and Romans as having been a distinctive period, but subsequently art declined to a very low level. After that, he claimed, a great revival of painting and sculpture occurred during the *Quatrocento*, with men like Leonardo da Vinci, Raphael, Botticelli, and Michelangelo, which meant a rebirth of the art of painting and sculpture. Vasari used the Latin word *renasci* and the Italian *Rinascita*, both of which are the equivalent of Renaissance, the sprouts of which date back to Cimabue and Giotto, who stopped copying the Byzantine style of painting and began to paint from nature.[4] A similar view was expressed in 1543 by Lorenzo Valla, as an introduction to his *Elegantia Linguae Latinae*, only he widened his approach to the humanistic aspect of the movement:

> That those arts, closest to the Liberal Arts, for example, painting, sculpture and architecture, have degenerated for so long and to such a low ebb that they almost died with culture, but are now reborn and begin to live again; and *that now* such a rich crop of good and well-trained literary artists has grown up, fortunate are these our times, if we still put forth a little more effort; for I sincerely believe that the Latin language will flourish more before long than the town itself, and with it all the sciences will be restored.[5]

Since Jacob Burckhardt had made the Renaissance a cultural epoch, it soon became evident that the line between the Renaissance and the Middle Ages had been too sharply drawn. Besides this he had tried to limit the revival to Italy, while similar movements had taken place in the French and German countries. It was quite clear that Burckhardt was not acquainted with the inherent richness of medieval life, which denied any sharp break with its culture. If the Burckhardt thesis were accepted, scholars like Dante and Petrarch would become mere forerunners of the Italian Renaissance.[6] Men such as Emile Gebhardt, Heinrich Thode, and Louis Courejod began to push the Renaissance back into the Middle Ages.[7] Emile Gebhardt still agreed with Burckhardt in his main thesis, but felt he did not define his border with great precision.[8] He pointed out that the Renaissance began much before Petrarch, as observed by the sculptors of Pisa and artists like Giotto, though he granted that the culture of the twelfth and thirteenth centuries could not be compared with that of the learned men of the sixteenth century. However, just three years later, Emile Gebhardt came out with another book in which the beginning of the Renaissance was placed into the twelfth century with Joachim von Flora and St. Francis of Assisi.[9] By now another work, by Heinrich Thode,[10] stressed the role of St. Francis as a mystic and his influence in the art of the Renaissance. Huizinga points out how Thode practically wiped out the border between the Renaissance and the Middle Ages.[11]

Now scholars began to ask: What was the Renaissance? If it was not an epoch, an abrupt significant change, which could not likewise be discovered in the Middle Ages, then why call it a Renaissance? As it had now spread so far back, why should it end there? Why stop with St. Francis? How about St. Bernard? Had the word any particular significance when separated entirely from the revival of the culture of antiquity?[12] There were others who stressed new aspects of the Renaissance problem. Louis Courejod asked the question: What was the true origin of the Renaissance? In this he argued that Gothic architecture was a style responsible for its own reorganization by a complete return to absolute naturalism, out of which the Renaissance was born. Neither the pattern of the ancients, as the originators, like Burckhardt and his many cited successors had claimed, nor Italy had any fundamental significance in its unfolding, as had formerly been stressed. He claimed that in all parts of Europe there were evidences of the Renaissance spirit. In France he cited the influence of Flemish artists, who had sown the seeds of naturalism, which created an appreciation of nature. The almost painful realism of Jan van Eyck (1385–1440), Courejod claimed, demonstrated a true Renaissance spirit, independent of the Italians.[13]

At this point scholars began to ask: What shall we do now, give up the revival of antiquity idea? Can we limit the *Quatrocento* to certain distinctive aspects as being new? There were also other aspects of the use of the term, meaning rebirth. The relationship between the Renaissance and the Middle Ages had by now been somewhat clarified, but many other aspects were still unclear, like the relationship between the Renaissance and the modern world. What was its relationship to the Baroque Age? Or the Age of Rationalism? And, finally, what was its relationship to the German Reformation? For all these questions there were but vague answers.[14]

Later in the twentieth century, additional light began to be shed. Charles Homer Haskins, the distinguished Harvard professor, became interested in the theme of the Renaissance and its place in European history. After years of research into its relationship to the Middle Ages, as we have observed in past chapters, he wrote his classic, *The Renaissance of the Twelfth Century*, published by the Harvard Press in 1927.[15] He begins with the observation that it has been customary to picture the Middle Ages as an "epoch of ignorance, stagnation and gloom," which stood in real contrast with that of the Renaissance, when people had an eye for the beauty and joy of life in a wonderful world of today. To this the professor replied with this observation:

> The answer is that the continuity of history rejects such sharp and violent contrasts between successive periods, and that modern research shows us the Middle Ages less dark and less static, the Renaissance less bright and less sudden, than was once supposed. The Middle Ages exhibit life and color and change, much eager search after knowledge and beauty, much creative accomplishment in art, in literature, in institutions. The Italian Renaissance was preceded by similar, if less wide-reaching movements, indeed it came out of the Middle Ages so gradually that historians are not agreed when it began, and some would go so far as to abolish the name, and, perhaps even the fact, of a renaissance in the Quatrocento.[16]

Professor William Bouwsma, in his article on the Renaissance, pointed out that later F. Renucci, in 1931, made a similar claim that we could not maintain that the revival of antiquity was peculiar only to the Italian Renaissance.

THE MODERN VIEWS OF THE RENAISSANCE

Since the period of Haskins' epoch-making book of previous Renaissances in the Middle Ages, many new views have been expressed, but in this chapter we will treat those that are most unique.

The first scholar to cover the later period is Konrad Burdach, who presented a rather novel view of the relationship between the Renaissance and the Reformation.[17] His unique contribution to the Renaissance literature was his claim that the Reformation and the Renaissance came out of the same *Ideenspäre*, the same root of ideas in the Middle Ages. Both periods, he claims, had the same *Heilserwartung*, the same religious feeling of need for renovation; both grew from the same complex religious, cultural, and political unfolding of life in the Middle Ages. According to Burdach, the ultimate cause of a rebirth was the New Testament of the Latin Vulgate, quoted by Joachim of Flora, who used expressions like *renasci, regeneratio,* and *reformari*, signifying rebirth, regeneration, and reformation, which played quite a role in the life of the medieval sacramental system in his period.[18] According to Burdach, the Renaissance had its origin in the cultural development of southern France during the later Middle Ages, due to the troubadours; from there it had passed into Italy. In this view he does not overemphasize Florence, but gives Naples, Padua, Avignon, and Rome a due share of the credit. He viewed the Renaissance as a passionate movement against the intellectual approach of late scholasticism, with its Aristotelianism, colored through an Arabic medium, with its soulless systematic reasoning. The return to antiquity, according to Burdach, became the root from which both the Renaissance and the Reformation sprang as new shoots and developed into the modern world.[19]

According to Burdach, the Italian Renaissance had far-reaching influences. He saw the Reformation as an outgrowth of the same spiritual and cultural development of the late Middle Ages as the Renaissance, and that the former was the peak in its unfolding by its return to the early Catholic Church in the days of the Fathers.[20]

Another Renaissance scholar who made important contributions to the views of the movement was Ernst Troeltsch.[21] He held that in the past, attempts had been made to make a vertical division between the Renaissance and the Middle Ages, when in fact the division should be horizontal. Troeltsch, claimed the major part of the population during the Renaissance remained medieval in their outlook, while an upper strata of scholars, the elite in the population, produced the great cultural advance in so many fields. Thus, according to Troeltsch, the medieval culture continued to flow underneath this upper strata on into the modern period. For him the German Reformation was something different in kind. This upper strata view also left room for the previous Renaissance during the Middle Ages; in those cases, too, it had been an upper strata movement. For Troeltsch the high Renaissance of the *Quatrocento* had been a kind of "Sunday Dress," which applied to but a small part of the population. Nor would we dare, claimed Troeltsch, to draw too sharp a contrast between the Renaissance and the Reformation.[22]

An outstanding Swiss scholar of the origin of the Renaissance was Ernst Walser, who is not too well known in English-speaking circles. He was born in the beautiful Aagau at Wohlem in 1778. His father was an international businessman with considerable means.[23] He appears to have grown among scholar friends, for his mother's brother, Albert Dubler, was a professor of pathology at Basel, who wielded quite an influence on him; while a Professor Roth, a Basel doctor of medicine, was another influential scholar who had just completed a biography of Andreas Vesalius, in which he opposed the views of Galen.[24]

Ernst Walser received an excellent education, as his wealthy father could send him to the best schools, beginning with the *École des Hautes Études* and the *Sorbonne*, which was followed by the *College de France*.[25] After that he went to Zurich, Florence, and Rome. In Rome the young Walser came under the influence of many prominent men, which helped round out his background on the Italian Renaissance, where his environment was anti-curia minded. This may explain why he left the Catholic Church and began to examine Harnach's *Dogmengeschichte*, which helped him get a more balanced view of the past history of the Catholic Church during the Middle Ages.[26]

During the years that Walser was working on his doctorate, Roth came out with a book on Leonardo da Vinci in which he asked: Was Leonardo the real founder of modern anatomy? Roth's thesis was that da Vinci had never dissected human bodies, but had employed surgeons to do it for him, while he made the drawings. Burckhardt had referred to Leonardo as the "founder" or "discoverer" of anatomy, which caused Walser to be much impressed, and this became his later view.[27] But Walser's growth as a Renaissance scholar came during the years he spent in Florence and Rome, when he began to make a thorough examination of the validity of the original Jacob Burckhardt thesis as a cultural epoch in European history. The half dozen years spent in that atmosphere made the Renaissance very real, as he saw it was also woven into the lay-man's culture; while in the Middle Ages he found the heavenly sphere com-bined with the beauty of earth.[28] He made a very thorough source study of Poggio, for which he had gathered his sources from all over Italy, Paris, and in the German libraries. This study also introduced him to the views of Petrarch, Salutati, Bruni, and Poggio, which made the latter a character of flesh and blood and tied into the affairs of his day.[29]

In 1912 Ernst Walser, now a famous Renaissance scholar, returned to Basel and became a professor at the University in 1918. By now his views had spread to the entire Renaissance, the medieval aspects and its continuance into modern history, to determine what fruits it had also borne in later centuries.[30] In the light of such knowledge the Burckhardt thesis fell apart. Walser had now conceived the Renaissance man as a kind of *Januskopf*, a double-faced man, looking in two directions at the same time, like the Roman god Janus. The Renaissance looked back into antiquity for ideas, and at the same time looked forward to determine what applications it might make in the life of the future.[31]

Now Walser began to ask two basic questions: Can we really claim that mod-ern culture, in its basic essence, is also found in the Renaissance? What, in its essence was the Renaissance really like? In his studies he had found that there was an unusual degree of striving toward inner harmony and toward many-sidedness. He had found the same striving in the Middle Ages, but in the Renaissance it was found to be present to a greater degree.[32]

The Swiss professor stressed in his lectures at Basel that Jacob Burckhardt had been much misrepresented in the later nineteenth century; however, he also could not see how the Renaissance could be viewed as a cultural epoch. Rather, Walser had concluded that the Renaissance should be studied length-wise, but he also felt Troeltsch's "cultural elite" theory of the Renaissance and the Middle Ages was misleading. Instead he believed the Renaissance could be traced back to the culture of the ancients. Walser wrote:

> The complete treatises to the present by Burckhardt, Monnier, Voigt, all say: the Renaissance believed, the Renaissance wills, as though a belief, a com-mon will, a plan dominated these two centuries and inspired these thousands of learned men, priests, soldiers and politicians. Had they but faithfully traced these ideas and found how they were born in the Ancient World, dis-tributed themselves during the Middle Ages, lived on in the vernacular litera-ture of the 14th and 15th centuries, and how they were finally translated into Latin by the Humanists, they would certainly have used more sparingly such attributes as "the originator" and "the rediscoverer," or the "Franciscan Renaissance" or similar beautiful rags. These discoveries rest more upon the ignorance of the commentator than on the genius of the discoverer.[33]

Ernst Walser also explored the claims of Burckhardt about individualism and found it applied as well to the Middle Ages. Was there such a thing as a "collec-tive *Volksseele*"? Was the average man in Florence a *microcosmos* of culture? Whereupon he rather humorously asked whether, in the Middle Ages, it required a whole crowd of people to come up with a new idea. He was willing to

grant, however, that in the Renaissance there was the early soil for later individualism.[34] But even Burckhardt, later in life, talked with Walser and made this
interesting observation:

> You know with respect to individualism (in the Renaissance) I do not com-
> pletely believe that anymore, but do not claim that you do not have the right
> answer.[35]

On this same theme, the Netherlands scholar Huizinga made a very strong
statement against this same cultural epoch thesis of the Burckhardt school:

> How could one ever defend the individualistic theory of the Renaissance,
> when on the other side of the line were men like Abelard, Guilbert de
> Nogent, John of Salisbury, Bertrand de Horn, Chrestien de Troyes, Wolfran
> von Eschenbach, Villard de Honnecourt and a hundred others.[36]

Huizinga also held that same view as Walser, that no one who knew the
period which had preceded the Renaissance could possibly cling to the original
Burckhardt thesis.

One of Walser's interesting observations about the transmission of culture
through the Middle Ages from antiquity is well expressed in the following quotation:

> Italian literature may be compared with a stream, which suddenly comes out
> of the ground, which after a brief and glorious flow disappears almost com-
> pletely under a huge ice-sheet, then however comes to the fore again with a
> clearer and cooled freshness to rise rapidly to its highest point of power and to
> express itself in widening, fruitful productivity. It shall be the purpose of this
> thesis to find the clearer places in the ice, through which one may see the
> waters flowing deeply below, and to find thinner spots through which a care-
> ful, listening ear may hear its rushing flow below in order to prove that it is
> always the same old stream, now gray and later becoming more blue, which
> holds up the whole ice-sheet.[37]

This statement in his thesis can also easily be misunderstood by believing that
Walser meant all aspects of culture moved along simultaneously throughout the
stream's flow from antiquity. He expressed another unique idea by advancing
his "Cultural-Historical Plurality Thesis," in which he pointed out that now all
aspects of the later Renaissance culture had flowed side-by-side throughout the
ages; nay rather that there were many separate tributaries into the river system.
Some continued through from the Roman period, and others entered the flow
of the stream later, which necessitated a study of art, literature, philosophy, and
other aspects of culture separately.[38] Since Walser, says Kaegi, Schneider and
Schramm have proven that the ancient imperial and Roman ideas play through
every phase of medieval life, while the Italian scholar G. Volpi has arrived at the
same conclusion.[39]

The recent modern view of the Italian Renaissance tends to lean toward the
view that there was a classical transmutation in culture during the age, placing
more of an emphasis on the classical theme, and the development of perspec-

tive. But this was not a cultural epoch, but merely a change in kind, as it grew out of the "mother soil" of the Middle Ages quite naturally. As we shall see, below, in an analysis of humanism in German universities, like Heidelberg, Leipzig, Erfurt, and later Wittenberg, its nature was bound to be different. Pioneers like Peter Luder and Stephan Hoest in the early period of the fifteenth century and men like Petrus of Ravenna, Nicholas Marschalk and Hermann von Busche were bound to have an impact on the scholastically oriented curriculum of the University of Wittenberg, which in time led to the triumph of biblical humanism under Luther and Melanchthon, which profoundly influenced the German Reformation in the twenties and thirties.

HUMANISM IN GERMAN UNIVERSITIES

As in the case of the Renaissance, there is also a wide diversity of opinion about humanism, which varied in different parts of Europe during the sixteenth century. Also, there has developed a wide range of opinions as to the relationship between scholasticism and humanism in German universities, which was modified during the last half century, after scholars came up with new findings. Italian humanism had a very different orientation from the German Humanism, which we plan to explore with reference to the University of Wittenberg. In the case of Italian humanism, it was less institutional and individually oriented, while in German universities it was used more as academic discipline, a *studia humanitatis* woven into the university curriculum. At Tübingen they called it poetry, which is also the designation at the original university on the Elbe.

In this chapter we will treat Italian humanism as a background prior to its coverage in relationship to that of the German lands; after that we will cover the origin and nature of German humanism in its institutions of higher learning. Later, an attempt will be made to show how recent research has modified our view as to the infiltration at Heidelberg, Erfurt, and Leipzig of an early humanism into their scholastic strongholds, and resulted in a melding of the two disciplines, which led the way for the triumph, of "biblical humanism" at the University of Wittenberg under the leadership of Luther and Melanchthon, with the complete support of the faculty and students, from 1516 to 1519.

Paul Joachimsen had defined humanism as a spiritual movement that had its roots in the revival of classical antiquity. For the Italian humanists this was a part of their past that could be relived to enrich the need of their present way of life.[40] Joachimsen defined humanism as being of two kinds: romantic humanism, with its unattainable ideals, and classical humanism, aiming at needs that already existed.[41] Most scholars agree that Italian humanism began with Francesco Petrarch of Florence (1304–1374), who by nature was an artist, an eager traveler, a voluminous correspondent, and man of affairs.[42] For him Dante was too medieval to be a forerunner of later humanists, but it would be misleading to think that Petrarch was not highly indebted to a number of troubadours who preceded him.[43]

While Paris was the great scholastic center of the North, the Rhone Valley and Province produced its traveling troubadours, with their love of poetry and delight in things of nature. These poets also penetrated the Po Valley, entertaining princes and despots in the Lombard Valley with their love songs. This caused a spreading of the vernacular language through the entire region. People loved lyrics, epics, and heroic poems, combined with science, medicine, and travel. Later there was a revival of the classics in the very regions which the troubadour had visited, which first was centered in Padua and Verona.[44]

Professor Thomson says Petrarch had three such forerunners who paved the way for the later Petrarch. The first early humanist he cited was Lovato de'Lovati (1241–1309), who carried on a lively correspondence with Bellini, claiming vernacular literature was realistic, flexible, and living as compared to Latin poetry, which he said was abstruse and often irrelevant. Lovati sensed the public interest in Rome's past and the classics. He based his poems on *Tristan and Isolde*, and the strife between the Guelfs and the Ghibellines. A second forerunner was Geremia da Montägnone (1260–1321), who, by profession, was an examiner of law graduates at Padua. He was familiar with Catullus' delicate lyric poetry. Geremia prepared a *Compendium Moralium Notalium*, which had quotations from the Bible, the classics, the Fathers, and medievalists.[45] The third forerunner of Petrarch was Alberto Mussato (1262–1329). Though of humble origin, Mussato soon rose to prominence because of his ability. By 1296 he was knighted and became a member of Padua's Great Council. He soon was also used in an ambassadorial capacity in support of Henry VII's Italian campaigns, and sent to Italian cities and the papacy. He was familiar with Livy's Roman history and Caesar's *Gallic Wars*, and in 1313 wrote an account of Henry VII's campaign, *De gestis Henrici*, in which he, like Livy, used the third person and interspersed the text with speeches and documentary, as part of the narrative. He wrote letters, soliloquies, elegies, and epics. In 1315 Mussato was honored with the laurel crown by the city of Padua. As its poet he performed *Eccerinis* and, as in the case of Seneca, a public holiday was declared by the city. He married the daughter of Frederick II, and he played quite a role in the political scene of that day. In poetry he quoted freely from Ovid, Catullus, and Virgil's *Eclogues*, and stressed the Roman past. He helped Petrarch much during his formative period, using the library of the Cathedral of Verona. Mussato had done much in spreading a growing interest in Latin letters, which paved the way for the flowering of the Renaissance.[46] It was in this new type of world that Petrarch and Boccaccio were born, and out of that climate they emerged as humanists.

Francesco Petrarca (1304–1374) has often been proclaimed as the first modern man. This may be an overstatement, but he loomed above predecessors and contemporaries in stature, finish, effectiveness, influence, and productivity.[47] Where Dante definitely still lived in the Middle Ages, showing but traces of the new age, Petrarch was new and different, observed Joachimsen, who created a whole new *Umwelt* for himself. He spoke of another age, antiquity, in which symbolism could no longer satisfy; his Laura was a real person, not a type, like Dante's Beatrice. In Augustine he believed he saw the ancients, like Scipio, St. Peter, and St. Paul. For him heroes, poets, and saints became fused as being part of the same antiquity he sought.[48]

Petrarch was from a very prominent Florentine family. His father, Ser Petracco, was a notary in the Florentine Republic and a member of the Guelf family; however, later his father was driven out by his opponents. In 1311 he moved the family to Pisa, and finally to near Avignon in France. There, under Convenevole da Prato, Petrarch was taught his Latin grammar and rhetoric, which prepared him for entering the University of Montpellier in preparation for the legal profession. However, Petrarch preferred Cicero and Virgil to studying law. Later his father sent him to the famous University of Bologna, where he studied both civil and canon law. Here again the future humanist deepened his knowledge of the classics.[49] Upon the father's death, Petrarch drifted until he met Laura de Sade, whom he loved for the rest of his life. His financial worries were over when a prominent Roman Senatorial family became his patron and offered him opportunities to travel through funds from the Colonna family; whereupon he traveled in Flanders and Germany, searching for manuscripts of Roman authors and forming many friendships. After that he settled at Vaucluse near Avignon, in which idyllic spot on the Sorgue river, from 1337 to 1353, he wrote love lyrics to Laura. By then his reputation had become European in scope, and he was admired by many distinguished people. In September 1340, he was crowned Poet Laureate by the Roman Senate, because of his epic poem *Africa*, on Scipio's defeat of Hannibal. The crowning of Petrarch at Rome became the peak of his career.[50]

The life of Petrarch was also not without its tragedies. In 1343, the young Italian, Cola di' Rienzo (1313–1554), then but 30 years of age, was all fired up by a wild dream to end the violence in Rome by establishing a democracy and making the Eternal City the capital of all Italy.[51] With his nostalgic feeling for everything Roman, as revealed in his *De viris illustribus*, and his hatred for the age of the barbarism that followed Rome's decline, Petrarch felt that a political rebirth of an Italian Republic might be possible and supported Cola di' Rienzo in his dreams of revolution. It all ended with the murder of Rienzo in a popular uprising. Because of his involvement, Petrarch lost the support of the Colonna family.[52]

In 1348 the "Black Death" swept over Europe and one of its victims was his beloved Laura, after which the joy passed out of his life. He then entered into the service of the Visconti family in Milan, where he stayed till 1361. Meanwhile, Emperor Charles IV, in 1356, invited Petrarch to visit him in Prague where, during his visit he was impressed by the culture of Bohemia and that of Prague. His closing years were spent in Padua and Venice, to which he also dedicated his rich library. He died on July 19, 1374, with his head bent over his precious Augustine.[53]

Petrarch's success can without doubt be ascribed to many factors besides his

native ability, namely, his wide travels, passion for learning, and fortunate connections with princes, prelates, scholars, and states. Petrarch possessed a
many-sided personality with a deep interest in Cicero and the classics, combined with a deep Italian patriotism and a veneration for Augustine. His *Canzoniere* is a great love poem covering his beloved in life and in death. His Latin
writings were extensive, including his great unfinished epic poem *Africa*. Of
great importance as a source is his vast correspondence with peoples of many
professions, offering insights into his age of kings, nobles, and statesmen. Nor
must one omit his *De viris illustribus*, cited above, covering the writings of
Caesar, Pliny, Livy, and Suetonius.[54]

Though never a Greek scholar himself, Petrarch was just as interested in
Greek classics as in those of Rome, though he had to limit his appreciation to
translations. A friend from Constantinople sent a Greek text of Homer and sixteen dialogues of Plato. Boccaccio, who was a very poor Greek scholar, sent
Petrarch a translation of the *Iliad and the Odessey*. Petrarch loved the classics
as models of style and because of their joyous approach to life.[55]

Though not a native Florentine, Petrarch was so closely identified with the
Tuscan city in later years that he is regarded as such. His close friend in Florence
was Giovanni Boccaccio (1313–1375). In literary circles Dante, Petrarch, and
Boccaccio are regarded as the creators of Italian humanism and later as an inspiration to German humanists in many universities. Boccaccio was the son of a
traveling merchant from Florence, while his mother was a French woman of
noble birth. He was probably born in Paris, but regarded himself as a Florentine.[56] He studied law at the University of Naples, but it really never interested
him. He became a friend of the king of Naples, the royal chancellor Barttato, and
the librarian, Paul of Perugia, which offered him access to a rich collection of the
classics.[57] It has been reported that when Boccaccio visited Virgil's tomb on the
heights of Posilippo it had such a lasting impact on the young man that he
became a poet.[58] While at the king's court in Naples, he fell in love with Maria
d'Aquino, the ruler's daughter, who was already married to a noble, which turned
out to be a somewhat banal and sordid affair.[59]

There soon came the revelation that Boccaccio would be a tremendous versi-
fier in the native tongue, as some half dozen early minor works appeared, but
his fame came later when he produced his *Decameron*, a most impressive body
of literary activity, much of which was really original pioneering. The
Decameron pictures Florence in 1348, when the "Black Death" was raging in
Italy. In the works, young men and women go into the country and tell stories
covering a space of two weeks. This resulted in some 100 tales.[60] The participants played the roles of kings and queens in the stories they related, which
made it a rare collection of world literature.[61] Later, Geoffrey Chaucer drew
upon this source for *The Canterbury Tales*. This typical Tuscan prose, set forth
in his *Decameron*, pictured a somewhat scandalous world of sensuous enjoy-
ment in the face of the existing ecclesiastical authority.[62]

On one of his travels, Petrarch visited the court of the king of Naples, where
he met Boccaccio. Being a decade older than Boccaccio, the humanist wielded

quite an influence on the younger man, and from that time they became close friends. It is believed that Petrarch's influence caused Boccaccio to turn into a classicist. In 1350 Petrarch, on the way to a jubilee in Rome, stopped in Florence and the younger man claimed the vernacular no longer satisfied his taste; he even expressed an apology for having written his *Decameron*. Boccaccio then purchased works by Terence, Livy, Tacitus, Cicero, Varro, and Boethius and began a search for more. His attempts to learn Greek from a Calabrian, Leonzio Pilato, brought there by the city fathers, did not turn out too well.[63]

In his last 20 years as a classicist, Boccaccio produced a number of works, among them *On the Vicissitudes of Famous Men, On Famous Women, On the Genealogies of the Pagan Gods*, and *The Mountains*.[64] Both Petrarch and Boccaccio must be regarded as transitional humanists, for Petrarch's *Canzoniere* reflects the influence of provincial troubadours from France, just as Boccaccio's *Decameron* is indebted to the cruder medieval predecessors. Petrarch's revealing *Secrets* are in a Latin dialogue between himself and St. Augustine, in which the church father turns his attention from earthly love to divine love; he even questions the value of pagan studies for far better it would be to reflect on the end. Nor did the vernacular of Boccaccio really take hold among scholars until a century later, but instead there was the stress on the revival of the Ciceronian Latin to unlock the study of the classics. And the search for manuscripts continued all over Europe, to build richer collections of the classics for future studies.[65]

Although Florence had no university during the early period, it had cultural centers for the gathering of scholars and the reading of scholarly papers. Such a cultural circle was established by Antonio degli Alberta in his spacious villa, known as the *Paradiso*, where nobles, burghers, churchmen, and scholars assembled for learned discussions. The owner spread a fine table and had musicians who entertained people in gardens while they listened to lectures and poetry, which introduced them to the classics. Another center frequented by Boccaccio and other scholars was the *Santo Spirito* circle, established by the Augustinian Hermit's monk Luigi de'Marsigli, who attempted to make his church a center of the new learning. Boccaccio was buried there and left his fine library to Santo Spirito. The monk was an excellent preacher, drawing freely upon the Bible, the Fathers, and even Cicero, Seneca, and Virgil for illustrations. The tone of this assembly was more serious than *Paradiso*, as its members were predominantly clerical.[66]

A next-generation humanist, friend, and correspondent of Petrarch and Boccaccio was Coluccio di Piero di Salutati, who served as the secretary of the Florentine Republic for 30 years. He was a frequent visitor to the *Paradiso* and the *Santo Spirito*, where he must have met with his fellow humanists.[67] He also followed Petrarch in his attempts to train young humanists in the Ciceronian style of writing. Among these was Leonardo Bruni, the first true historian of the Renaissance, as reflected in his *History of the Florentine People*. He later had also taught Chrysolarus in the Ciceronian style, so that then Aneas Silvius might rightly claim that Bruni was the greatest among the early Italian humanists.[68]

Another of the younger men was Poggio, who became a famous searcher after lost classics. Poggio Bracciolini (1380–1459), as papal secretary during the Reform Council, was offered unusual opportunities to search for rare lost manuscripts tucked away in old monasteries. While he attended the Council of Constance (1414–1417) he took advantage of searches in Switzerland and Germany for rare books. Among his unusual finds was a complete text of Quintilian's *Institutes of Oratory*, a work until then imperfectly known, that later wielded great influence at Wittenberg in the days of Philip Melanchthon, during reforms initiated in the Reformation.[69] Poggio also discovered works by Lucretius, Plautus, and Pliny the Younger, Ammeianus Marcellinus, Columella and some of Cicero's orations.[70]

By this time Italian merchants also began to build up fine libraries. Nicoli, a Florentine merchant, was an example. When students went on trips, Nicoli employed them to buy books for his library; many of these purchases were financed by Cosimo de'Medici. An example is the purchase of a fine copy of Pliny, which was located in Lübeck, Germany. The monks hated to sell it; however, the purchase was finally made with 100 Rhenish Ducats, which in that day was a sizable sum. Many Greek manuscripts also began to be brought to Italy by traveling scholars. This took place long before the fall of Constantinople in 1453, when many Greek scholars fled to Venice and the West.[71] Giovanni Aurisps brought Greek texts of Sophocles, Euripides, and Thucydides to Italy in 1413, a half century before the Greek migrations; a decade later 238 more manuscripts arrived. Guarino of Verona brought 54 manuscripts himself, and Francesco Filelfo brought 40 additional ones.[72]

No doubt the claim that Greek manuscripts arrived in Italy prior to the fall of Constantinople in 1453 has been overdone by some scholars. It is difficult to assess the spread of the Greek language except among a few who attempted to learn it. A great number of Greek scholars came and attended the sessions of the Council of 1438, and some remained who stimulated others. Among them was Bessarion, who later was elevated to a cardinal by the Roman Church, and led other students and induced some to translate the Greek classics into Latin. By the turn of the century most of the Latin and Greek classics were available in printed form.[73]

The concept of founding libraries in Italy was expressed by the Malatesta family and especially by Carlo Malatesta (1386–1429), an idea he shared with Nicoli and Cosimo de'Medici. His idea was to found a library for poor scholars, but death kept him from seeing the fruition of his plan. They had a collection of books which were from Sampierino, a canon of the Cathedral and the teacher of grammar. But the plan was later carried out by Carlo's nephew, Sigismond (1417–1468), who founded this library at Riminiein, the Convent of San Francesco. Sigismond, a Greek and Latin scholar, enlarged it even more.[74]

The great library of Italy was the Vatican Library in Rome. J. W. Thompson dates its history to Pope Eugene IV (1431–1447). In 1443 it contained 340 theological and philosophical volumes; among these were also some of the classics such as Ovid, Seneca, Cicero, Livy, Aristotle (in Latin), Xenophon, and Demosthenes.[75] But the real founder of the Vatican Library was Pope Nicholas V

(1447– 1455), who planned to build a large library and make the Vatican a world shrine for scholars. He began bringing manuscripts from Germany, Denmark, and England. By the end of his reign, the Vatican collection totaled 1,209, of which 795 volumes were written in Latin and 414 in Greek. Meanwhile scholars had been employed by him to translate as many of them as possible from the Greek.[76]

In the interim, the growth of the Vatican Library slowed down but Pope Sixtus IV became its third enthusiastic promoter.[77] In the case of Sixtus IV, there was an enthusiasm not only to enlarge the Vatican but to give it adequate surroundings.[78] By 1475 that library had 2,527 volumes, of which 770 were in Greek and 1,757 were in Latin; by the end of the century, it claimed a grand total of 3,650 volumes.[79]

Leo X, while still a cardinal in Florence, had already quite a library, which he moved to his palace in Rome after becoming pope, and placed at the disposal of scholars. But he also increased the Vatican holdings to 4,070 volumes and took special interest in their care and upkeep. He had agents in other lands, especially Germany and Scandinavia, to collect books or borrow them to be copied. He sometimes used tactics that were somewhat unscrupulous, like offering a plenary indulgence to acquire a special copy of Tacitus. Leo X also became interested in printed books of the Greek and Latin classics. He even gave Aldus Manucius, of the Aldus Press in Venice, a monopoly for 15 years in the printing of Greek texts. He refused to loan books from the Vatican Library without a deposit, and then only to distinguished scholars. Under Pope Clement VII these loans were restricted to John Lascaris and Bessarion. The latter had an excellent library, filled with Greek manuscripts, which later he willed to the Republic of Venice.[80] But in reality Venice did not take advantage in establishing the *Marciana* until much later.[81]

Due to the excellent study of Deno John Geanakopolos, in reference to the Greek scholars in Venice, we now have a much better insight into what role they played in making the Greek language alive once more in the West. He mentions that the more prominent exiles—Chrysolarus, Bessarion, Gaza, Trapezuntios, Argyropoulos, Callistos, Chalcondyles, and Janus Lascaris—have been given attention by scholars, but there are scores of others who have not been investigated, some of whom he has brought to light; in this study he investigates the roles of five scholars who played an important role. The first is Michael Apostolis, a refugee from Constantinople, who offers an insight into the Greek scholarship in Crete; a second is Marcus Musurus, another Cretan émigré, who resided in Venice and in Padua, and later became the editor of a number of Greek first editions published by the Aldus Press, as well as becoming a teacher of a number of western students; a third treated is Arsenios Apostolis, son of Michael Apostolis, who also wielded great influence in Florence and Rome; the fourth, another Cretan, is Zacharias Galliergis, who went from Venice to Rome and established its first Greek press; finally he treats Demetrius Ducas, another Cretan, who went to Alcala University in Spain and contributed to the publication of the Polyglot Bible by Cardinal Ximenis.[82]

Geanakopolos, in summary, points out that in the fourteenth century Greek was known by but a few people in southern Italy; but from the time of Manuel Chrysolarus' Florence lectures in 1397 until Janus Lascaris' death in 1534, Western Europe had advanced from ignorance to a mastery of almost the entire corpus of Greek literature in the original.[83]

When Manuel Chrysolarus delivered his first Greek lectures at Florence in 1397, scholars came from all over, and the first flowering of Greek culture from the East lasted until the collapse of the Medici regime following the French invasion in 1494. Then a number of Greek exiles migrated northward to Venice, where Greek culture became a center of attraction, especially due to the formation of its Academy of Western and Greek scholars and the creation of the Aldus Press with its tremendous productivity. This era ended with the loss of Cambrae in 1509 and the death of Aldus in 1515.[84] This was followed by the age of the Medical popes, Leo X and Clement VII, which terminated with the sack of Rome in 1527. During this later period interest in Greek culture centered in Rome.[85]

But even though Greek studies had flourished elsewhere, such as in Pavia, Naples, Rome, Florence, and Milan, there can be little doubt that the work of the Academy in Venice and its famous press did more to spread the necessary tools and works for the western world than any other place. Geanakopolos also came to this conclusion when he evaluated the Venice Academy:

> The contribution of Aldus' Academy is more difficult to assess precisely than is that of his press. But there can be little doubt that this select intellectual circle, composed of eminent Western as well as Greek Hellenists, was during the period of its existence the chief focus for the development of Greek studies not only in Venice but in the entire western world.[86]

As will be observed in a subsequent chapter, when the elector of Saxony decided to establish a fine ducal library at the University of Wittenberg in 1512, he made Georg Spalatin the superintendent and librarian. Spalatin was a humanist who earlier had been in the Erfurt humanistic circle under the tutelage of Conrad Mutianus, or Mutian, later a canon at Gotha, and Urbanus of Erfurt, and through them had been brought into the electoral court. When the elector wanted to found the new ducal library he and Spalatin used Mutian to arrange an official contact with Aldus Manucius of the famous Aldus Press to fill their new library with humanistic publications, books in Latin, Greek, and Hebrew for the revised Wittenberg curricula, just initiated under the leadership of Luther and Philip Melanchthon. In subsequent years, as seen in chapter 10 of this volume, for the library of the university Spalatin and the Wittenberg faculty purchased freely from works published by the Aldus Press. In fact, Georg Spalatin visited Venice several times to discuss with the printer what new works were available. It is interesting that Mylius, in his later listing of the library holdings, found that no fewer than 307 volumes were from Venice.[87]

What the Aldus Press did for Wittenberg was no doubt repeated in many places in Italy and other European countries. Our account needs to show what a storehouse of knowledge was offered to humanists in Northern Europe in the three sacred languages, Latin, Greek, and Hebrew. Our account would not be complete without discussing the foundation of many private libraries in the larger Italian cities. James Westfall Thompson, in his *The Medieval Library*, has furnished much of the necessary data to complete the picture. Thompson claims one of the largest private libraries in Italy was that of Giovanni Pico della Mirandola, which contained 1000 volumes when he died in 1494 and willed the books to San Marco in Florence; they were later moved to the monastery of San Antonio di Castello in Venice. The library's holdings were largely books on philosophy, astrology, and theology; however, 250 were classics, of which 150 were in Greek and 100 in Hebrew.[88] There were many private scholars who collected classical works by individuals less known, such as Guarino of Verona and Leonardo Bruni; these scholars gathered their own private collections of many classical authors. Thompson cites a Florentine doctor of medicine, Antonio di Pagolo Benivieni, who in 1487 possessed a library of 175 volumes, many of which were in medicine, written in Latin, Greek, and Italian, as well as works in philosophy, poetry, oratory, and theology.[89] Another large library for that day was that of another physician, Bartholò di Fura di Bandizo, who was the possessor of 220 volumes, which were mainly medical, but of the classics there were a few, like Juvenal, Caesar, and Seneca. In Sienna he cites a private collection of Nicolo di Messer Bartolomeo Borghesi, whose library had 368 items in the year 1500, which was comprised mostly of classical material, grammars, rhetoric, logic, dialectics, philosophy, and theology. In Milan there were also several notable private libraries. One was that of Giovanni Corvini Arestino, containing many classics, which were much appreciated by Pilippo Maria Visconti. Another fine library was that of the Trivulzi family, which contained 154 volumes of the classics.[90]

Such an enumeration of private libraries could go on indefinitely, and many are no longer known. For example, Guarino of Verona, later contacted by northern Humanists like Peter Luder, had had a very fine Greek collection of the classics, among which were many rare volumes.[91] Frederick of Urbino also possessed a fine library, of which he prided himself on having original manuscripts in beautiful bindings. He employed an able copyist who reproduced classics on the finest vellum, many of them miniatures, nicely bound and with silver clasps. He refused to add printed copies, for he wanted to have his collection made up entirely of manuscripts.[92]

From the above views expressed on the nature and influence of Italian humanism, it must be quite evident that, regardless of what view of its nature is taken, Italy possessed a vast storehouse of all the classics by the time the University of Wittenberg came into existence, and that any contacts by northern scholars with these wonderful collections could not be without impact. Regardless of what effect it may have had, once the classics were used in northern universities, they would make an impact on even the scholastically minded member of the *Via Antiqua* and the *Via Moderna*, especially when he began to analyze the validity of his assumptions. To determine how northern humanists in Germany differed from the Italian, an analysis of their inner relationship must now be explored in the next section.

THE DEVELOPMENT OF GERMAN HUMANISM

In many respects, German humanism was different from the Italian for a number of reasons. Nor can this be limited to one kind. It varied in humanists due to background, training, and personalities. That it was stimulated by contact with the Italian restoration of the classic Greek, Italian, and Hebrew sources can hardly be doubted; but when it came to its application to life in the German lands it developed into a form that was often fundamentally different in its goals and application as a tool in the academic life of German universities. No doubt German humanism lacked a common heritage of antiquity, which had lived on in Italian cities. Men like Petrarch and Boccaccio discovered, in the lives of men of the Greco-Roman past, kindred spirits; while the Germans regarded them merely as classical scholars whose works they could imitate in their own way, such as Luther and others, as essential tools for an interpretation of the Holy Scriptures; also for the development of well educated teachers and preachers through the media of the classics. Again there were the more deeply motivated German humanists, like Peter Luder, Stephan Hoest, Agricola, Hermann von Busche, Nicholaus Marschalk, Conrad Mutian, and Melanchthon, who were more interested in the *Studia humanitatis* for its own sake.

In this chapter our interest in German humanism is somewhat limited as to the degree it is applicable to the University of Wittenberg and the German Reformation. Also, when applied to the original Wittenberg, founded by Frederick the Wise, we wish to explore the relationship between the early humanism at the new institution and its influence on the strongly entrenched scholasticism at Wittenberg.

For a complete picture, the relationship between humanism and scholasticism needs to be explored at Heidelberg, Leipzig, and Erfurt, as it throws light on what happened at Wittenberg prior to the rise of Martin Luther. Paul Joachimsen, in his contrast between Italian and German humanism, begins with the observation that a basic cause was that in the two countries, there prevailed an entirely different intellectual climate that influenced their development. Where Italy was already a Polis-oriented society, the German lands were still largely rural. Perhaps the only exception was the court of Charles IV, when the first phase of German humanism made its appearance at the imperial court. This court had been visited by both Petrarch and Cola di Rienzo, and the often cited *Ackermann aus Böhmen* stands alone in German culture and had very little influence.[93] Besides, Germany was divided into hundreds of smaller feudal principalities, under princes and lords of various regions. This meant that any humanism that manifested itself appeared largely in the universities. In the fourteenth century, even Bohemis was hardly ready to accept a movement which stressed the *Studia humanitatis*, with a return to the Greco-Roman classics and a culture entirely foreign to them.

German humanism falls into three periods, the first of which came in the days of Emperor Charles IV, who was a rather unusual ruler, with a cultural background. He had studied in France and had been influenced by French culture. It was his goal to make Prague a great cultural center, adorned with a university like the French. He approached Pope Clement VI, in 1346, for a bull to authorize the founding of the University of Prague, modeled after the University of Paris.[94] Thus, for half a century, Prague became the cultural center of Eastern Europe, which continued until the death of John Hus at the Council of Constance in 1415 and the outbreak of the Hussite Wars.

The first period ended with Emperor Wenceslaus, after which the chancellory of the empire was transferred to the son-in-law of Emperor Sigismund, Albert of Austria, in Vienna. The only literary product from this period was Johan von Tepl's *Ackermann aus Böhmen*, a dialogue between a plowman and death, which followed soon after the death of his wife. The chancellor of the empire, Johann von Neurkt, had done some refining of the literary product, which reflects some familiarity with Plato, Seneca, and Boethius and also shows the influence of Petrarch when he visited the court in Prague.[95]

The second phase of German humanism came at the time of the Reform Councils, covering roughly the period between 1409 and 1475, during which the Italian humanists Poggio, Vergerio, and Aeneas Silvius visited Germany. Joachimsen feels the Reform Councils had a definite influence as background to German humanism of the later period. The Reform Councils stressed the need for a reformation of the Christian church. Nicholas von Cusa also wanted to extend the reforms to the state and the German Reich. Under Emperor Sigismund, even popular democratic influences were manifest; the *Gravamina* brought out the need for reform of abuses. These reforms were even supported by the upper clergy, which also included the reforms of monasticism.[96]

German humanism during this period wanted to be different from the Italian; yet when scholars studied the past of antiquity they were, like Peter Luder at Heidelberg, after twenty years of study in Italy, ready to introduce the *studia humanitatis* as a way of improving on the scholastic curricula at Heidelberg. Such scholars learned from Poggio the art of narration, from Bruni the historical and biographical recording of the past. An example is Georg Spalatin, the official biographer of the Saxon princes at the time of Frederick the Wise. Some university teachers also learned from Filelfo the art of speech and letter writing. And in Heidelberg under Stephan Hoest they caught up with Italy in oratory and poetry. Nor did they think that such poetical attainments were to be acquired from rules and norms; but instead they spoke of an ingenious, natural gift, with a natural divine element.[97]

This was really a transitional period, when German humanists began to weigh the appeals of the Italians with that of the importance of their own German past as being equal to that of antiquity. Antiquity to them must have seemed something strange and foreign, for some German humanists now began to appeal to their country's own past. For those familiar with the origin of the Holy Roman Empire, the concept of the Caesars had not been terminated, but through a *tranlatio imperii* had passed over to Charles the Great. Through this action and by papal blessing in the year 800, the empire had become a Holy Roman Empire. Even though it had been truncated by the growth of other nations, Rainald von Dassel called it the *Holy Roman Empire of the German Nation.*[98] There began to develop a definite appeal to the German past, an identification with the days of Tacitus' *Germania* and the days of Charlemagne. The abbot Trithemius was the first to gather sources of the German history. The Elsace school of Geiler, Brant, and Wimpfeling was opposed to his views, for they did not grant that monks were the source of all wisdom. These were the spiritual students of Gerson and Tauler. They returned to the church Fathers, the Bible, and Charlemagne, all of which became a part of this German past. Thus their aesthetic norms were not the ancient Romans. The *Narrenschiff* of Brant was enthusiastically received by the German humanists. Brant wanted order amid confusion, as so much of it was *Zinnlosic*, and did not make sense for him. Even *Sin* was *Narrenverk*, the work of fools on the "Ship of Fools." For these men the restitution of Christianity, though not well oriented, was in primitive Christianity.[99]

Some historians have spoken of German humanism as having a third phase running from 1475 to 1560, but recent research has extended it further back to the middle of the fifteenth century. The studies by R. R. Post[100] and Hans Baron[101] have changed our views of the beginning of humanism. This will be analyzed in another part dealing with humanism in the universities. But this third phase stressed the *Studia humanitatis*, but with more of a religious application.[102] As will be observed in a later connection, the humanism at the University of Wittenberg took on a new turn and became a biblical humanism used by Luther and Melanchthon as tools in biblical exegesis and as a way to develop an excellent style of Ciceronian Latin under the humanistically oriented liberal arts courses. This biblical humanism at the University of Wittenberg did not reach its full maturity until the years 1535–1536.[103]

HUMANISM IN GERMAN UNIVERSITIES

In an earlier period, German scholars were inclined to date real German humanism to the days of Agricola, Celtis, Mutian, and Wimpfeling during the close of the fifteenth century. For Joachimsen the first *Erzhumanist*, real humanist, was Konrad Celtis, who taught in several German universities. Joachimsen claims that had he written in German, he might have been known as its first poetic genius, when, instead, it was Hans Sachs of Nürnberg.[104] Celtis really dug into the German past, and though he was interested in the restitution of the three sacred languages—Latin, Greek, and Hebrew—his chief interest lay in the original Germans of the Druid days and *Tacitus'* treatment of the *Urdeutschen*. Celtis' hero became Armenius, who defeated the Roman army in the *Teutenburger Wald.* This humanism was more romantic, centering around Emperor Maximilian I and the Burgundian knighthood. In this Emperor Maximilian I became associated with Charlemagne, who would give his Germans grammar, law, and a more liberal religion.[105]

During the middle of this century, the common view was that the Brethren of the Common Life had a very profound influence on the development of German humanism. Beginning with P. Meswerdt and followed by Albert Hyma, Lewis W. Spitz, A. Renaudet, and others, it was claimed that their humanism gave it a Christian flavor, and that men like Agricola, Wimpfeling, Erasmus, and even Luther were influenced toward the later biblical humanism at Wittenberg, and that this was a cause of the German Reformation. Meswerdt's thesis was that the *Devotio Moderna* movement began in the southern Netherlands and spread into the Rhine Valley, where German humanism had its real beginning.[106]

This thesis has now been challenged by R. R. Post, a professor in medieval history at the University of Nymegen. Post questions the above claims that humanism could be influential amid a group that stressed simple religious experience and inward piety, that they were the able exponents of the *Studia humanitatis.* How then could their products be men like Cusanus, Agricola, Celtis, Mutian, Hermann von Busche, Erasmus, and even Martin Luther? Post denies that their influence was that pronounced. He challenges the views about John Pupper of Goch and Wessel Gansfort, claiming John Pupper rejected scholasticism, while Gansfort was a nominalist. He also claims that Hegius was only a pious rector of a school, who had some appreciation of the writings of Lorenzo Valla, while Agricola had scarcely any contact with the *Devotio Moderna,* even though he was a friend of Wessel Gansfort. Post states that the Brethren had hospices in Cologne and also for a short time in Louvain and Treves, while they had none in Paris, Heidelberg, Prague, or Vienna. Hegius did not give Agricola his background, which the latter had really acquired in Italy, while Erasmus knew Hegius only a short time, when he was rector of Deventer, and received little instruction from him. Wimpfeling learned of the Brethren though Ludwig Dringenberg, and hence not directly. Post concludes, "The legend that the school of Deventer was an institution of the Brethren dies hard."[107]

The Netherlands professor also questioned the basic assumptions about the "Brethren of the Common Life," by Albert Hyma, set forth in two publications.[108] Hyma had made the *Devotio Moderna* into a renaissance of Christian life. He claimed that Geert Groote and his disciples had revived the Christian life within Christianity and that this had caused the Reformation. This Christian humanism also meant that the reforms of Martin Luther at Wittenberg had been due to Wessel Gansfort. He also held that it had influenced Zwingli and Calvin, through the views of Cornelius Hoen, who in turn had been influenced by Wessel Gansfort. Thus Hyma had made Wessel Gansfort and John Pupper teachers of Agricola and Erasmus.[109]

Post places the Hyma thesis and his facts into the realm of inadequate checking of the sources. Wessel left Zwolle and for 25 years taught in different universities. Thus Hyma had made too much out of the influence of Zwolle and Deventer. Hyma, says Post, also assumed that the Brethren had directed schools in other cities without adequate checking. Hyma made the mistake of ignoring the universities, which were the principal centers of humanism.[110]

In a recent publication, Frank Baron brought out some views with respect to early humanism at the University of Heidelberg, which caused a number of major revisions in accounts of the development of humanism in several German Universities. Since the Baron publications reveal how humanism came from Italy to the University of Heidelberg in the middle of the fifteenth century, our coverage must begin with that institution. Fortunately, the Frank Baron publication of the *Reden und Briefe* of the Heidelberg humanist Stephan Hoest is introduced by an elaborate introduction. This, combined with the actual textual material, offers much new insight as to how humanism in German universities developed long before the previously believed viewpoints of scholars. An additional bonus will become apparent in our later analysis of humanism at the early University of Wittenberg. This study offers insight as to how, in the days of Stephan Hoest, humanism was able to make inroads into the entrenched *Via Antiqua* and *Via Moderna* at Heidleberg.[111]

The early German Universities, as observed above, were modeled after the University of Paris. These began with the University of Prague, founded by Charles IV in 1347–1348, which was followed by the University of Vienna in 1365; the third, the University of Heidelberg, was founded by a papal bull of Pope Urban VI, in 1385.[112] During the middle of the following century, the Pfalzgraf Frederick of the Palatinate became a staunch supporter of humanism at Heidelberg. The chancellor Ludwig von Ast became surrounded by fellow humanists like Matthias Ramung, a master copyist of humanistic documents, and Johann Wildenhertz, the elector's legal advisor. The legal advisor possessed a degree from Ferrara in both civil and canon law, as well as being a humanist. These scholars no doubt wielded quite an influence upon the elector. The Pfalzgraf employed Peter Luder, who had studied the Italian Renaissance for two decades, to join his faculty and restore Latin from medieval barbarism. Luder attempted to do this between 1456 and 1560 by furthering the *Studia humanitatis*. Peter Luder had studied under Guarino of Verona, who, as we saw above, possessed a very fine classical library that Luder must have enjoyed.[113] Luder never worried about giving offense to the scholastic faculty, for he realized that he possessed the good will of the many fellow humanists at the court, and especially the elector of the Palatinate. In his lectures he stressed the importance of rhetoric, poetry, and history, all as ranking high in the academic curriculum. He had many fine students, among whom Stephan Hoest appears to have been his favorite, and they became very close friends. Hoest lectured on Horace, Terence, Seneca, and Ovid.[114] Even after Luder's departure from Heidelberg, when he had been replaced by Stephan Hoest two decades earlier, Peter Luder still remained very close, as seen in a letter to Mathias and notes taken by Conrad Haumolt, the later abbot of Heilbronn. Hoest had continued in his footsteps, in which he combined the *Studia humanitatis* and scholarly lectures, which he later delivered as a theologian and administrator.[115]

The evidence shows there was a fundamental difference between Peter Luder and Stephan Hoest. Peter was much more Italian in his outlook and interested mainly in the classics, while Stephan was both a scholastic and a humanist. The pupil of Peter Luder was a very wide gifted scholar, operating with a wide range of professional activities. Like Georg Spalatin in the next century, Hoest later became the court preacher of the Pfalzgraf, while he continued to preach Luder's courses in the *Studia humanitatis*. At the outset Hoest had been trained in scholasticism, and later began to study theology. By 1567 he reached the *Licentiatus* degree at Heidelberg, in the *Via Moderna*, which meant he was now fully licensed to teach. Later he was even made the vice chancellor and rector of Heidelberg. An address by Hoest has been preserved by Wimpfeling, which he delivered on that occasion at a master of arts commencement. This address reflects how highly Hoest valued the classics as a training tool in liberal arts for students who aimed to continue their studies in the three higher faculties of the University of Heidelberg.[116]

The value of the Frank Baron publication is that he has given the reader a parallel presentation of both the original addresses of Stephan Hoest and also a German translation. Another speech preserved in the Wimpfeling collection was an address delivered by Stephan Hoest when he served as the examiner and was obligated to deliver a sermon in honor of St. Catherine, the patron saint of liberal arts in Heidelberg. This had become an annual affair. All the classes were stopped and the entire faculty and student body were obligated to attend the event. Here the *Examinator* had a captive audience, including some of the conservative scholastics in the *Via Antiqua* and the *Via Moderna*. This was an occasion when Stephan Hoest could draw upon his knowledge of the classics and show why they were not only essential to a liberal education, but also vital even in scholasticism. This insight is valuable for our understanding of what transpired at Wittenberg University a half century later, when humanism made its inroads into the old *Via Antiqua* minded faculty members and paved the way for the later transformation of the university through Luther's "biblical humanism."

In this lecture Hoest stressed the importance of rhetoric, poetry, and history for a student's background in liberal arts, which he claimed had been the philosophy of St. Catherine. In his address he emphasized the need for eloquence even in scholasticism, in which rhetoric was so essential. But Hoest also stressed that in the *Lehrplan*, Aristotle should be but one of the scholars' sources; in fact, he ranked Aristotle as fourth, and stressed that the able scholar should use many sources. In liberal arts the student should become familiar with Plato, Priscian, Cicero, Virgil, Euclid, Pythagoras, but he should also be familiar with Sullust, Seneca, and St. Jerome as well the Holy Scriptures.[117] In the St. Catherine sermon, Hoest quoted Plutarch's *De liberis educandis*, which Guarino had translated into Latin. The educational tracts of Aeneas Silvius were generally known by German institutions, which resembled thoughts of Hoest, as he had also stressed the need of *Studia humanitatis*. No doubt Aeneas Silvius' views were here in the background of Hoest's sermon.[118]

Scholasticism at Heidelberg, in the beginning, taught only a *Via Moderna* that the Pfalzgraf tried to correct by the introduction of a *Via Antiqua* to balance the philosophical curriculum. This necessitated two separate commencements. After that the *Via Moderna* faculty held their commencement exercises in the summer semester, while those of the *Via Antiqua* came in the winter. Usually it was customary for the deans to preside on such occasions, but between the years 1466 and 1472, the head of the festivities was the vice chancellor, an honor that had been bestowed on Stephan Hoest. In reality the *Domprobst* of Worms was supposed to do these honors. On these occasions the vice-chancellor Hoest conducted a perfunctory examination of the candidates, and then he granted them their degrees. At such commencements, the vice chancellor delivered a festive address in the "Large Hall" of the University. Three such addresses, delivered in 1468, 1469, and 1470 have been preserved. Two of these were identified by Gerhard Ritter as being those of Stephan Hoest. One of them was delivered for *Via Antiqua* graduation exercises while another was given at the *Via Moderna* commencement. These speeches were given in the presence of the scholastic faculty, some of whom no doubt disagreed with his viewpoints.[119] Since Hoest was both a scholastic and a licensed theologian, he was familiar with both systems. Hoest frankly criticized the scholastics for their overemphasis on words and playing with ideas. Since both schools based their philosophy on Aristotle's text, this demanded a working out of many disputed points.[120]

As stated above, Heidelberg had no *Via Antiqua* prior to 1452, but when it was introduced, a battle ensued between the logic of Marsilius von Inghen, founder of Heidelberg, and its original rector. This was due to its terminology in thought, whose views were similar to those of William Occam. The dispute also was related to the medieval method of *Questiones*, or the disputed points. The opposition claimed the original *Parva logicalia* did not use *Questiones*.[121]

In his speeches Hoest entered upon the theme of how scholasticism, whatever type was used, was the best pedagogical method of using Aristotle's works as the sources. He believed one should simply follow the text of Aristotle and avoid all superfluous commentaries, just as Cicero had also stressed in antiquity. In the past, said Hoest, scholasticism had engaged in too many *Questiones*, the arguments about interpretations, and this had resulted in many of the scholastic battles. In the Middle Ages the disputed points had become a problem because even St. Thomas, the doctrinal authority in matters of faith for the *Via Antiqua*, had engaged in discussions of the *Questiones* about Aristotle.[122]

Later Jacob Wimpfeling, his devoted pupil, had used the same type of reasoning in his *Adolescentia* for an introduction of his pedagogical tract. Wimpfeling also pointed out that Cicero did not want you to engage in "the tying of dialectical knots" by use of logic and geometry, but that philosophies develop studies by which the well-being of the soul, the honor of God, and the reputation of the state are furthered. Both Hoest and Wimpfeling were deeply influenced by Cicero's treatise *De Officiis*, which was stressed even more in the second commencement address for the *Via Moderna*.[123]

Next came the graduation exercises, which lasted from March 5 to the 12th, for nine students in the *Via Moderna*. The festive occasion began with the examinations on March 5, which were followed by the graduation on March 12. At this commencement Stephan Hoest again delivered the address praising the *Via Moderna*. This speech offers much light on its impact on Scholasticism. The chancellor, however, began with his praise of the *Via Antiqua* in the scholastic discipline, thus eliminating friction between the two schools. He stated:

> For the ways do not stand in hostile opposition to such a degree that one would deserve praise and the other condemnation. Rather the strong points of one serve as buttresses for the virtue of the other.[124]

After an attempt to quiet his audience over the differences between the two philosophies by minimizing their differences, Hoest then offered a history of the *Via Moderna* by way of explanation of the origin of its name. According to Hoest the word *Moderna* was derived from the adverb *modus*, meaning a new way of interpreting Aristotle's philosophy by way of its simplication. The chancellor pointed out:

> Therefore we must observe that this approach in philosophy was necessary to bring about a lighter style to understand the works of Aristotle, which are excellent and at times very profound, involving mixed and twisted concepts. This method is to lay bare the dark areas and to harmonize the seemingly opposites. It attempts to reduce matters to their actuality, and thus, through unobstructed short texts, to lead to an understanding of the truth.[125]

Here the chancellor made an important distinction between the two opposite views of philosophy. It clarifies why the *Via Antiqua* wanted to retain the *Summulae* of Petrus Hispanus with its claims that "universals" exist *ante rem* and not *post rem*.[126] He made some interesting observations about the founders of the *Via Moderna*. He named Henry of Ghent, Johann Scotus, William Occam, and Marsilius as the founder of Heidelberg and Buridan, the founder of Vienna. But Frank Baron took issue with his views.[127] Hoest pointed out that the modernists had played vital roles at the Councils of Constance and Basel. Wimpfeling claims Hoest started out as a Scotist but later became a new theoretical theologian. Hoest was not opposed to the views of the *Via Antiqua* and was friendly toward the Thomists, but he did not neglect the Bible or the Fathers— Ambrose, Jerome, and Gregory. He preferred Scotus to Marsilius because he was not as abstract and more practical.[128]

If the vice chancellor had limited his address to philosophy, the effect on the old time Realists and Nominalists might not have been impressive, but he also drew upon his humanistic background. He began with the illustration of metals, and stressed that iron, silver, and gold were hidden deep in the earth and difficult to acquire. This he compared to the precious thoughts of persons throughout the ages, upon which others could later build as works of the forefathers. This, he pointed out, applied to art, such as painting and sculpture. The same also, he stressed, applied to intellectual history. Even among the Greeks, thinkers like Aristotle had their predecessors: Demokrit, Anaxagoras, Eudoxus, Empedokles and many others. So did the poet Virgil and the eloquent Cicero have their forerunners. In grammar there was the Donatus and Servius that Priscian surpassed. In all fields, he observed, there were the predecessors of the great men. The decisive thing is much individual effort and labor. In philosophy, however, Hoest told his *Via Moderna* candidates, it was a different situation, as they never should turn their eyes from the Aristotelian text.[129]

Then he made an appeal to the graduates, by pointing to the Greeks as the discoverers of the arts and philosophy, and the Romans of law and oratory, while the church Fathers gave us many books on divine wisdom. How does your generation aim to distinguish itself? Or are you of a generation that thinks nothing new can be attained? Those who copy others are really spiritually bankrupt. But life offers many new fields.[130]

He also cited Salutati, who argued against those placing too much authority of the ancients in the *Studia humanitatis* by offering them too much praise and glory. The Italian humanist offered this advice:

> I hold the view that we put aside the whole reliance on authority, this unworthy high evaluation of Antiquity, and with that once and for all free yourself from the conception about the worth and superiority of the priority of time. The decisive thing in this battle is to be informed and not a matter of age.[131]

This does not mean that Salutati did not honor the ancients, but his view was a beginning, in a late fifteenth-century humanism, of relying more, like German humanism, on setting its own norms.[132]

Peter Luder always stressed the modern times in the *Studia humanitatis*, and in a letter to Hoest he called him the negotiator of the new humanistic preaching. No doubt Hoest's address was deeply influenced by Italian humanism. In this and other speeches, one observes the weaving together of the arguments and traditions of two great disciplines, scholasticism and humanism. Hoest did not take the battle between scholasticism and humanism too seriously, as the hearers appeared to be desirous of a reconciliation between the two ways. However, he always employed humanistic arguments, citing classical authors, which made the scholastic position problematic. He wanted to return to the sources, but among them he rated the classical writers above Aristotle. To what extent the philosophy of Stephan Hoest caused the breakdown of the scholastic dominance in German universities toward the close of the fifteenth and the beginning of the sixteenth century, will be examined in connection with humanism at Leipzig, Erfurt, and finally Wittenberg in the remainder of this chapter.[133]

Another aspect of Stephan Hoest's career, which needs to be touched upon briefly, was his *Brevis modus predicande*, the Brief Method of Preaching, which sets forth the vice chancellor's views on how to sermonize. As a scholastic theologian he departed far from the typical representatives of scholastic theology. In Hoest's case, scholars noted before them a Priscian speech on proper eloquence, used as St. Catherine's ideal in her address on the *Via Moderna*. He took the Priscian text and reworked it into the pattern for a sermon. In the sermon he used material from Virgil, Horace, Sallust, and Seneca. Bishop Matthias Ramung of Speyer, the former humanistic chancellor of Pfalzgraf Frederick, had asked Hoest to address the Speyer clergy on the practical art of preaching. The sermon was more the message of a *Seelsorger*, a pastor of a flock, in which he now and then cited Augustine's *De doctrina Christiana*. In it he stressed the need for rhetorical polish and an acquaintance with Holy Scriptures, to convey divine wisdom in a polished address. In the sermon, vice chancellor Hoest did not reveal any scholastic orientation, but is more like Johannes Wenck's "Booklet on the Soul," in which the Heidelberg theologian stressed Christian piety. He tried to bring the clergy back to the moral teachings of the Fathers and the oratory and rhetoric of the *Studia humanitatis*.[134] Wimpfeling was very fond of this sermon on the "Method of Preaching" and cited it several times as being very elegant.

Frank Baron, after translating and studying all the recently rediscovered Stephan Hoest sources, has given us a summary of what influence early humanism at Heidelberg had on Hoest's successor at the close of the fifteenth century. Peter Luder had taken the first significant steps in introducing the *Studia humanitatis* there, and then had passed his mantle on to his most gifted student, Stephan Hoest, who proved to be a very worthy successor in the future of humanism of the German universities.[135]

At the very outset, when Stephan Hoest was a very active and able interpreter of Aristotle and the two schools of scholasticism, he was not too deeply committed to either the *Via Antiqua* or the *Via Moderna*. Thus when he lectured as the vice chancellor of the university, it was not like Peter Luder defending the *Studia humanitatis*, but as a representative of their entire philosophical system. This gave his humanism individual characteristic worthy of serious thought. Italy had its ancients as a frame of reference, but the German universities were church institutions, where the *Studia humanitatis* had to be melded into a more religious climate. Humanism, by its return to the sources, the classics, and the church Fathers, could appeal both to eloquence and to religious reforms. Wimpfeling also strove for a harmonization of the two schools of philosophy. Earlier there was a definite conflict between humanism and scholasticism; however, in this period we gain a different impression. Yet there can be no doubt that Hoest's speeches tended to weaken the authority of the schools of philosophy.[136]

Stephan Hoest had no special way of interpreting the Stagirite's philosophy, which he regarded as vital; but he often gave texts opposite interpretations. However, his apparent neutrality tended to pull the whole bottom out of the two ways. Since the philosophy was based on Aristotelian sources, the philosophers may have been pleased that their views were also supported by Cicero and Horace; but a serious study of Horace would make one question Aristotle in all fields of thought. But in the *Studia humanitatis*, the study of rhetoric, poetry, history, and ethics, there were additional values to be considered. Even the art of the rhetorician might prove useful to make the complex thought of the

schoolmen more comprehensible; while Bible study and that of the Fathers
could add a new dimension to the teachings of the Aristotelians.[137]

Hoest also wrote valuable pedagogical works that added to the instructional
tools in German universities, for which he used material from Terence, Horace,
and Virgil. Peter Luder had already done this in his lectures, but Hoest's offerings caused other German humanists to make similar attempts, like Wimpfeling's *Stylpho* and Jodocus Gallus' *Katherina Dialog*, the forerunner of German
drama. In this Terence gave him real stimulation.[138]

Several decades ago, scholars frequently emphasized that there had been a
real conflict between scholasticism and humanism, which in some schools was
no doubt true. But in Heidelberg we gain quite a different impression. Hoest
seems to have known how to employ rhetoric and poetry in a way that did not
conflict with the scholastic tradition. He was never hostile toward his col-
leagues, for he made them feel that the use of additional disciplines enhanced
their scholastic approaches and made them more acceptable. Frank Baron concluded that Stephan Hoest was already oriented to the entire Renaissance
movement, and that the humanistic tradition, which had its genesis in Petrarch,
continues through Salutati, Bruno, Guarino, Luder, and Hoest.[139] Their teachings were in turn passed on to Wimpfeling, Agricola, Erasmus, and Reuchlin at
the beginning of the sixteenth century. Now it is no longer tenable to claim that
Agricola produced the *Studia humanitatis* at Heidelberg but inherited those
forces set in motion by Luder and Hoest a generation before. These trends
must still have been strong in the beginning of the sixteenth century, when
young Philip Melanchthon began his studies in languages at Heidelberg, which
he completed at Tübingen, to be able to publish his first Greek grammar before
he went to Wittenberg in 1518.[140]

HUMANISM AT LEIPZIG UNIVERSITY

The entry of humanism into German universities was quite common, as after
Heidelberg it also came to Erfurt, Vienna, Ingolstadt, Tübingen, and Leipzig.[141]
In Leipzig, with the entrenched realism of the *Via Antiqua*, Bauch claims the
bitterness toward humanism started quite far back that it continued until the
expulsion of Aesticampanius.[142] As observed previously in an earlier chapter,
the battle raged during the period of Wimpina and Polich von Mellerstadt.[143]

Leipzig University, like Prague and Vienna, was originally founded by
Landesherrn, kings and princes, and then approved by the papacy.[144] In comparison to other universities in German lands, the University of Leipzig had a
rather stormy beginning. The University of Prague had been founded by
Emperor Charles IV in 1547. Its student body was modeled after the University
of Paris, having four nations, three German ones and one Czech. In the early
period the University of Prague gained quite a reputation in Germany.[145]
Prague's problems began when the reformer John Hus began to preach and
teach his reforms, with the approval of King Wenzel and Queen Sophia. The

university became divided amid its struggle. Hus was excommunicated by the bishop of Prague, but the court remained loyal to their reformer. A real academic battle broke out when King Wenzel altered the university statutes, giving the Czech nation equal status with the three German ones. This resulted in a revolt of the three German nations and their students and an exodus of the Germans from Prague. Now the question arose: Where should they move to establish another university? Soon there were rumors of their being welcome in Breslau. Such rumors also reached the Wettiner court of Frederick the Valiant, who had become the new elector of Saxony, and was the Landgraf of Thuringia and the duke of Meiszen. The elector and his brother William II decided in 1409 to found the University of Leipzig, and offered the professors and students the *Grosze Collegium* in Leipzig to settle and found the new institution. This large building was located immediately beyond St. Nicholas Church, and formed the new home for the remnant of the University of Prague.[146]

Before the publication of the Stephan Hoest papers and the publication of the aforementioned Post studies, on the Brethren of the Common Life, scholars had an exaggerated impression of the influence of the Brethren and also of Rudolf Agricola, who was labeled as the "Father of Humanism." He had his beginnings with the school before he went to Italy and became a finished Latin and Greek scholar.[147] Now men like Frank Baron would place men like Agricola and Konrad Celtis as the successors of Stephan Hoest and the Heidelberg humanists, even though it is not quite clear what degree of influence early humanism at Heidelberg may have had on them.

Gustav Bauch was already aware of the influence of early humanism in the middle of the fifteenth century; for through their influence the scholastics began to insert rhymes into their texts even though it created a strange mixture.[148] Then he adds that men like Rudolf Agricola and Wilibald Pichheimer did not take any action but asked others to bring about changes; while men like Konrad Celtis, Jacob Wimpfeling, and Johannes Rhegius Aesticampanius were professors in universities with limited influence. Most of these men did not wish to attack scholasticism and its theology, no doubt because they lacked the depth in those fields to meet them on their own ground.[149]

As at a number of German universities, humanism at Leipzig also went far back into the fifteenth century. Here the *Via Antiqua* of St. Thomas was deeply entrenched, which caused them to refer to the earliest humanists as the *Lustigen Poeten*, the happy poets, which they could tolerate, but later they began to regard them as *Parasiten*, men who were parasites in the institution.[150]

Yet in the closing years of the fifteenth century, Leipzig was frequented by humanists, though they remained but a short duration. Peter Luder, after teaching at Heidelberg, went to Erfurt in 1460, and in 1462 he was for a while at Leipzig. Another name in the roster of the faculty was the poet Samuel Karoch.[151]

According to the studies of Felican Gess, an authority on the conditions at the University of Leipzig, the academic climate at that institution was not very scholarly. The professors often neglected their lectures, as in Konrad Celtis'

288   *The Reformation as a University Movement*

day, when Duke George twice had to rectify matters.[152] Often the older faculty members set the worst example.[153] There was also a strong trend of jealousy toward newly founded institutions like the universities of Wittenberg and Frankfurt a.d. Oder, for they regarded them as rivals in student matriculations. In the case of the University of Wittenberg, this problem has already been treated in the previous chapter of this study. Leipzig remained a problem during the Reformation as long as Duke George lived. When he died in 1539, his successor was Duke Henry, who was the brother-in-law of Philip of Hesse and a friend of John Frederick. This fundamentally altered the situation in the Saxon lands, as he also favored reforms. Thus the Saxon Visitations in Ernestine Saxony could also be carried into the Albertine lands, and the University of Leipzig now supported the German Reformation.[154]

The reader is already familiar with the role of Polich von Mellerstadt and his battles with Simon Pistoris and Wimpina over the French Disease, as the Germans called syphillis. This debate had in time turned into a battle over humanism, as to who was the best informed in regard to the *Studia humanitatis*. To clarify this, that aspect of the battle needs some elaboration.

Polich von Mellerstadt had, as a young man, aspired to be a master of anything distinctive that might enhance his fame. He was really not a master of anything he had tried. However, in the beginning he was a Thomist who lectured on Aristotle's *Organum*. According to Prantl, Polich was largely a copyist and not too original as a thinker. He used the *logica nova* based on the philosophy of Paris and Cologne. His *Lehrbuch* of 1511 and his commentary on Aristotle's *Physics*, printed in 1514 after his death, offer scholars a basis for their analysis.[155] Even though in his younger days Mellerstadt claimed to be a humanist, scholars feel his style remained unrefined medieval Latin. Later Mellerstadt also studied medicine, in which study he accepted the views of Avicenna rather that Galen. When the archhumanist, Konrad Celtis, joined the Leipzig faculty, Mellerstadt became one of his *Sodalitas litteraria*, or staunch supporters.

Paul Joachimsen called Konrad Celtis the first archhumanist among the Germans at Heidelberg after Hoest's period. He dug deep into the German past, after which he glorified the accomplishments of the *Urdeutschen*, the early Germans who had defeated a Roman army under the leadership of Armenius. He was interested in the three sacred languages, Latin, Greek, and Hebrew; but his principal interest lay in the early German past. On the other hand, with the Italians the return movement had centered around the time of their Roman forefathers; Celtis had his ideals too, by going back to the days of Tacitus' *Germania* and the church Fathers.[156]

Konrad Celtis was born in 1459, a year before Peter Luder left for Erfurt and Stephan Hoest began his lectures at Heidelberg. One of our most informative chapters about Celtis as a humanist is that of Lewis Spitz, in his volume on humanism.[157] Celtis studied at several universities, among which was Heidelberg, so he may have attended some of the later lectures by Stephan Hoest.[158] He traveled much, which he regarded as being as educational as books. Gustav Bauch also claims that Celtis came in contact with Rudolf Agricola.[159]

After his university years as a student, Konrad Celtis traveled extensively and crossed the Alps in 1487; he visited Venice, Padua, Bologna, Florence, and Rome. He developed a dislike for the Italians because they tended to regard the Germans as culturally inferior. Upon his return he visited Cracau and Nürnberg, where he was crowned "Poet Laureate," the first to be given that honor. Later he aspired to be the best lyric poet in Germany and wanted to be known as the German Horace.[160] Had he written in German instead of Latin, observed Paul Joachimsen, he might have been regarded as the first poetic genius in Germany rather than Hans Sachs.[161]

Konrad Celtis taught in a number of German universities. Just when he came to Leipzig is not known, but he was already the mature humanist, with all the fire for the improvement of German higher education through the *Studia humanitatis* and emphasis on German nationalism. There was much in the scholastic Thomism for him to criticize. He wanted the Germans to rise and equal the Italians, whom he disliked. He did not like the fact that professors were still using Alexander Gallus' *Doctrinale*. He attempted to introduce instead the art of poetic writing, and in 1486 he published his *Ars versificandi* and then his *Ars poetica*. In this he used source material from Virgil, Horace, Ovid, Juvenal, and Seneca.[162]

An elaboration of the scholarly productivity of Konrad Celtis would lead too far from our major theme of Leipzig's attitude toward humanism, which resembled that of early Wittenberg. There is an aspect, however, which is germane to what happened at Leipzig due to his visit and its effect on some of the faculty. No matter where Celtis went, he attempted to organize his fellow humanists to engage in patriotic tasks to make Germany culturally as distinguished as Italy. He had a Rhenish Sodality, a Danubian Sodality, and also ones in Linz and Strassburg, attempting to inspire them to patriotic goals that would make Germany great. This explains why, during the Reuchlin struggle, the great Hebrew scholar was not alone, and that later the humanists rallied about Martin Luther after the Leipzig Debate.[163]

As in other places, some of the members of the Leipzig faculty were fascinated by Celtis' learning and his romantic nationalism. Even the medical doctor, Polich von Mellerstadt, became a part of his *Sodalitas litteraria*. He began to study the classics and regarded himself as a humanist, though Bauch observed that his Latin remained that of a poor Latinist. Polich loved to engage in controversies with fellow faculty members, in which he attempted to refute them in disputations. In a previous chapter we saw Polich and Wimpina engaged in a bitter strife, which began with a battle over syphilis, but ended with an attempt to prove his superiority over Wimpina as a humanist, a student of Konrad Celtis.[164]

The conservative scholastic faculty of Leipzig could not tolerate such a group of humanists as Celtis' *Sodalitas litteraria*, whereupon friction developed that caused Konrad Celtis to leave. Rhegius Aesticampanius, an able humanist, who later was himself driven from Leipzig, claims Celtis left because of hostility. Polich von Mellerstadt, however, praised him even though he himself was one of the died-in-the-wool Thomists. Hassenstein of Bohemia, a famous humanist, became critical of Celtis, claiming the poet stole some of his verses and copied from Virgil and Homer without giving them due credit.[165] After that, a number of Celtis' supporters also left Leipzig, among them Wittich, a Livy scholar, who went to Mainz, where Schoeffer printed his translation of Livy. Prianus Capotius, an able Latinist, also followed his master.[166]

During the stay of Konrad Celtis at Leipzig and shortly thereafter, a number of humanistic scholars came to the university, which Gustav Bauch barely mentions in passing. Meanwhile Celtis had gone on to Vienna to continue the cause of humanism. The sheer numbers of humanistic scholars that came to Leipzig during Celtis' stay may have irritated the conservative scholastics. Meanwhile, Prianus Capotius, like Celtis, left Leipzig. Capotius was a Latinist who wrote a poem about the Great Saxons, Frederick IV and Frederick II.[167] Unfortunately, Capotius, while in Italy, died in a rebellion. Even a Greek scholar, Jacobus de Candia, visited Leipzig in 1488–1489; while the Album of the school contains among its entries the name of the Italian *Sixtus de Veniciis*, in the year 1491. Among the lawyers was also Johann Fabri, or Obermayr de Werden, who possessed a wide range of humanistic literature. He wrote a history of Leipzig and also a song concerning the "New Music" of that day.[168] Fabri died in 1505. Faulus Niavis, or Schneevogel aus Eger, was not a gifted Latinist, but he wrote an introduction to Ficinus' *Dialogue of the Philosophy of Socrates*. Even though not a distinguished scholar, he loved Cicero, Quintilian, and Sallust, and he stressed that correct Latin and eloquence were not alike. Among the Leipzig students at the time of Celtis was Erasmus Stuler, who completed his liberal arts training for the masters in 1483. He later took on the name Johannes Trithemius.[169] Among the students was also the noble Frederick Kitscher, who later went to Sienna, took a doctorate in both kinds of law, and then returned to Leipzig to edit Cicero's works. Through Frederick the Wise's influence he was later brought to Wittenberg and became the Probst of the Castle Church and the ordinarius professor of canon law in the new school.[170] Another of the humanists belonging to Celtis' *Sodalitas litteraria*, later much respected in the literary world, was Etelwolf von Stein, who matriculated in the summer of 1482 and later became the Rat of Albert of Mainz and Joachim von Brandenberg. Then among the Celtis students was also the later humanistic activist Ulrich von Hutten.[171]

Celtis had attracted a number of other students at Leipzig, who joined his company of ambitious poets and humanistic scholars. Bauch cites Johann Honorius Cripus, really John Erhard from Ellenbogen, who became a bachelor of theology in 1500, dean of liberal arts during the winter of 1503–1504, and finally rector of the University of Leipzig. Other students were Johannes May from Römhilt and George Dottanius from Meiningen, who also attained many honors at Leipzig, among them becoming its rector and even vice-chancellor. Nicolaus Fabri from Grünbarg, in Silesia, became another of Celtis' followers, who later studied theology and was chosen as rector of the school. Raimund

Peraudi promoted Fabri to a doctorate in theology like Wimpina; during the summer semester of 1518 he then joined the Wittenberg faculty. A somewhat younger scholar was Hermann Kaiser, who was a friend of Andreas Proles, Hermann von Busche, and Georg Symler, who later became a teacher of Philip Melanchthon.

It is strange, says Bauch, that these young humanistic followers of Konrad Celtis produced so little in 1489–1491, but in 1491 Conrad Kochelouen produced a work of Poggio of Florence. At Wittenberg even canon lawyers may not have been as scholastic, for they were more humanistically inclined. Frederick von Kitscher, the later Probst of All Saints Church at Wittenberg, while at Leipzig in 1492, published an edition of Cicero's *Parodoxes*, with a commentary. The students of Leipzig had asked for an interpretation, and he added a commentary of his old teacher, Johann Gabriel, a learned scholar of Sienna. In this work Cicero received ample praise as a philosopher. It really appealed to the students of Cicero at Leipzig.[172] In another field, a Leipzig professor by the name of Jacob Illuminatoris taught lyric poetry; he made Ovid's *Art of Love* and Catullus' *Son of Vesper* come to life. He used Ovid to teach them the *Dichtkunst*, the art of poetic composition.[173]

In 1493 Emperor Frederick III died, on which occasion a professor Barinus wrote an oration, which was printed. Later it was delivered by Bernhard Perger in Vienna. This is very interesting, as it drew its main materials from Livy, Lucannus, Valerius Maximus, Justin, Pliny, Orosius, St. Augustine, Ovid, and Fastus. Barinus also lectured on Ovid's *Ars Amandi*, for which his commentary on Book I is still extant.[174]

Johannes Landsberger, a canon law professor at Leipzig, wrote a treatise on the *Battle of Humanism*, which really pokes fun at some of the remarks of medievalism. In this treatise there were two *Interlocutors*, Emulus and Fautor. During the interlocution Emulus attacked humanism. He asked whether the studies of the *Donatus Minor* and *Alexander Gallus* were silly, to which Fautor replied, "No, unless studied too long." Then Emulus wanted to know whether the *Grammatica Doctrinalis* is not vital to the study of the Holy Scriptures, since it has grammar and philosophy mixed together. After some discussion they agreed that proper learning must draw on many fields; that grammar must come first and then logic, without which students are at a loss in studies and their disputations. Emulus argued that poetry can lead students down false paths, but Fautor cites St. Jerome and Seneca as opponents of dialectics. Then he asked: Why did St. Augustine praise Virgil? The art of poetry encourages good *Sitten* and helps students in all fields. St. Basel had also praised poetry, while Aristotle had regarded poetry and ethics as vital to learning. Cicero praised it as well, and Pliny regarded it as essential for a proper expression of one's diction. Then he added that the classics had sucked out the honey from the flowers for us. He continued that it was God who gave us poetry, but today it is looked down upon, where in antiquity it was regarded as important for the youth. Besides, he added, there is always the "Laurel Wreath" to be attained. It is interesting, says Bauch, that the Ficino stress on the importance of Plato also had its impact on Leipzig students. Barinus' speech, though still stylistically somewhat weak, reveals this, and he was one of their best writers.[175]

In the introduction to the address of Barinus, Andreas Hishelburn praised the fortunate age at Leipzig, when barbarism could be terminated, and the poets could become immortal. Yet Barinus did not leave much of a lasting impact. He was attacked from within the faculty, in defense of the old ways of scholasticism. They called the poets heathens, yet Barinus published a rhetorical *Lehrbuch*, a text in humanistic style for the students. In 1495 there was a whole series of humanistic publications. There was Virgil's *Bucolica*, published by Petrus Eolicus, and Prosperez's *Carmina, Liber de mundi gubernatione*. In 1496 George Dottanius taught that the Donatus and Alexander's grammatical poetry did not teach students the barbarism of the Middle Ages. But in the faculty there still was a weakness for the *Doctrinale* of Alexander Gallus, which early humanism could not budge. It took the next generation to throw off medievalism in their style of writing.[176]

In another study of the early humanism at Leipzig, Gustav Bauch treated the example of the expulsion of Johannes Rhegius from the faculty of the University of Leipzig.[177] He begins with the observation that scholasticism was so strongly entrenched at Leipzig that humanism still met opposition from its Thomistic theologians. This created such an unhappy climate that Konrad Celtis stayed but a short time. Polich von Mellerstadt went to Wittenberg, and Johannes Rhegius also became deeply involved in the institution's humanistic struggle.[178]

Rhegius had studied in Krakau and then visited Italy in 1501, after which he had taught four years at the University of Mainz. Meanwhile, as seen in a previous chapter, Konrad Wimpina had also left Leipzig and founded the University of Frankfurt (an der Oder). He had joined his school in 1506, where he was highly honored by marching in front with the beadles in a solemn procession. There Ulrich von Hutten was one of his pupils.[179] Rhegius was a student of Sullust, Virgil, Cicero, and the classics. He was opposed to the grammar of Marcianus Cappella and was disappointed when Frankfurt became so conservative that there was no room for the classics, and he decided to leave. Duke George offered Rhegius a position at Leipzig, where he registered as a professor of rhetoric. He began offering a course in St. Jerome as a theologian rather than a classicist, but he could not help but note that the scholastics lacked a poetic style. This he began to criticize. Among his students were Ulrich von Hutten and Johannes Hess, the later friend of Luther and Melanchthon, and later, the reformer of Breslau. Another student of Rhegius was Caspar Ursinus. The humanist now began teaching Greek at Leipzig.[180] Before long Johannes Rhegius incurred the wrath of the conservative theologians who regarded him as a "fifth wheel on the wagon," as well as their opponent.[181] Now the Leipzig humanist began to criticize the opponents for their opposition to the poets and the classics, the lawyers for their bad Latin, and the medics for attempting to adorn themselves with empty boasts. Soon the atmosphere became too heated, and Rhegius departed for Rome, where he acquired his doctorate. The pope ordered the lawyer Göde to act as the judge in the strife, and that terminated matters. Rhegius now joined the faculty of the University of Freiburg in Breis-gau, where he remained for awhile. When the University of Wittenberg became a center of biblical humanism under Luther and Melanchthon and Aristotle was dethroned, Johannes Rhegius was asked to join the faculty to teach Pliny. He soon became a friend of Luther and Melanchthon, as he fitted well into the new "New Theology" at Wittenberg.[182]

EARLY HUMANISM AT ERFURT UNIVERSITY

In my book *The Setting of the Reformation*, the historical role of Erfurt in the Ludowinger and Wettiner periods has been treated in some detail. In that age one of the problems the landgraves faced was this large metropolitan center, which lived under the sovereignty of the grasping and ambitious archbishops of Mainz.[183] The city was ideally located on the main trade artery from the Hanseatic League cities in the north to the Italian cities via Nürnberg, and also the route connecting the trade centers from east to west. Hence its burghers became quite prosperous in an early period. As a result Erfurt soon grew into one of the great metropolitan cities of the north, with a population of about 32,000 at the time of the founding of the University of Erfurt in the fourteenth century.[184]

Prior to Erfurt's founding by Pope Clement VII in 1379, the city had schools in liberal arts but did not possess any upper faculties. In 1362 the German masters, led by a Master Henry Totting, appealed to Pope Urban V to assist their institution of higher learning. Then a bull of Pope Clememt VII in 1379 authorized the founding of the University of Erfurt, which after Prague and Vienna became the third German university. But the Erfurt plans were delayed, and meanwhile the universities of Heidelberg and Cologne had already been founded in 1385 and 1386. The school finally came into existence in 1392.[185] In some respects Erfurt was patterned after Paris, but it had no nations; its statutes were somewhat modeled after Bologna. The rector was head of the institution, chosen for only one semester, while four deans supervised the School of Liberal Arts and its three graduate schools.[186]

During the first forty years, between 1430 and 1470, while it became well established, Erfurt was the largest of the German universities; however, by the end of the century it had declined to a third in size, for a variety of reasons.[187] Not only did it recruit its students from Thuringia and Hessen, but during its prosperous years, the school drew many students from Lübeck, Hamburg, Bremen, Braunschweig, Hildesheim, and Einbeck, as these cities were combined with Erfurt in trade. A few matriculated from the Franken region and Nürnberg, but most from those regions attended Leipzig. Kleineidem thinks Erfurt reached its peak in the period between 1450 and 1460. After that the university was retarded by several misfortunes. There came the Great Pest, which hurt the institution, and then the city was leveled by a devastating fire, and recovery was quite slow.[188]

Earlier we noted that Peter Luder had taught and introduced the *Studia humanitatis* at the University of Heidelberg between 1456 and 1560, and produced students like Stephan Hoest, who was both a scholastic and a humanist. Later Peter Luder entered Erfurt, where during the winter semester of 1460–1461, he continued his labors as a promoter of the humanistic causes.[189] Whom he taught there, and the courses he offered, can no longer be determined. But it seems difficult to claim any longer, as Scheel and Böhmer have done, that they had no humanism at Erfurt while Luther was a student there from 1502 to 1504, and that he thus experienced no humanistic influence there. Luther already had been under humanistic influence in the *Trivialschule* at Eisenach, where he had excellent linguistic training under Trebonius. Luther later claimed this teacher rounded out his Latin background.[190]

There is strong evidence that humanism flourished in all the five *Bursen*, the dormitories in which the students of liberal arts were housed. Exactly where Luther stayed is not known for certain, but it is generally held that it was in the *Georgenburse*, the statutes of which no longer exist. Others claim he stayed at the Burse *Porta Caeli*, also called *Himmelspforte*, or the *Alte Collegium*.[191] We do possess some of the statutes of the dorms and know what kind of a life was lived by students under the masters who supervised them. In all the dormitories humanistic training was part of the student's preparation for the scholastic courses. Gustav Bauch claims that Konrad Celtis stayed in the *Neue Burse*, which was under the *Collegium Maius*, where for two semesters he trained men like the later humanist Conrad Mutian of Gotha and others, thus wielding a lasting humanistic influence.[192] The humanistic trends existed in all the *Bursen*.

No doubt it was through the humanistic life in the Bursen that the Humanism kindled by Peter Luder, and later by his pupil, Konrad Celtis, lived on at Erfurt until Luther. A letter of Petrus Petz, written by a relative of Celtis, was later cited as proof of this. In 1499 Konrad Schechter willed a library to the university, with an abundance of humanistic material. Shortly after Konrad Celtis' departure, a Master Biermost was in charge of the Burse where the great humanist had stayed and taught. At the close of the century two humanistically minded rectors supervised the *Neue Burse*, a Master Maternus Pistoris from Inquiter and a Master Heinrich Loit from Lich.[193]

Similar humanistic conditions were reported to have existed in *Porta Caeli*, for which we possess records. There was a traveling poet with whom Johannes Knaes worked, the Florentine humanist Jacobus Publicius, who willed his classical library later to the Amplonianschen Library in Erfurt. Besides this there was Heinrich Leonis of Bercka, who also made his works available to the university.[194] At the turn of the century similar conditions prevailed at the *Georgenburse* where Luther is reported to have stayed. Its rector was a Jacob Scholl from Strassburg, whose leanings toward humanism are well known.[195]

In the Burse *Alba rota* was Master Gunther Haupt from Heiligenstadt, who

even used the Latin name Gentherus Hieropolitanus. Thus in all five Erfurt
Bursen the philosophical faculty offered its students the same humanistic environment, teaching them better Latin and becoming acquainted with the classics even though in their basic philosophy they were believers in the *Via
Moderna*, which had recently blossomed forth under its two able professors,
Trutfetter and Usingen, both of whom took advantage of the printing press to
prepare new material for their courses. In 1495 Bartholomäus Usingen had
already started printing texts, but those had to be printed by Arnold of Cologne
in Leipzig; shortly after that Wolfgang Schenck came and took over the printing
in Erfurt. He had a fine feel for quality work; he also made Marschalk's publications possible.

Jodocus Trutfetter, or Doctor Eisenach, as he was sometimes called, after his
native town, deplored a "hair-splitting" type of the old *Via Antiqua;* he even
tried to simplify the dialectics of the *Via Moderna* as represented by Occam and
Biel. Trutfetter even drew upon the humanistic style and poetic verse to make
his scholastic material more popular and effective with the students.[196]
Bartholomäus von Usingen was the second *Via Moderna* professor at Erfurt,
who must have influenced Martin Luther, as he later admired him very much.
In his theology Usingen distinguished between Aristotle as a source and the
Holy Scriptures. In matters of faith he accepted the Bible as the unerring
truth;[197] while in regard to the Fathers and tradition, he evaluated them in relationship to the revealed Word. Usingen's criticism of Aristotle must have deeply
influenced Martin Luther during his rejection of scholasticism at Wittenberg,
as Usingen was up-to-date and progressive in his acceptance of new ideas.[198]
Nor is there evidence of any hostility, during Luther's Erfurt days, between the
poets and scholastic professors, who praised better rhetoric and the art of fine
diction in letter writing.

There can be little doubt that in the Erfurt faculty there were humanistic tendencies, even though students pursued the regular curriculum requirements
for academic degrees. No doubt scholars like Peter Luder, Rudolf von Langen,
Konrad Celtis, Hermann von Busche, Jacob Wimpfeling, and Maternus Pistoris
left their impressions on the students, even though many did not attend their
lectures as they were too busy with their own courses in scholasticism; for, as
Rommel points out, there existed a scholastic humanism at Erfurt, in which the
ordinarius professors like Trutfetter and Usingen used the treasures of antiquity, "as an arsenal of epigrams and proverbs," and even frequently quoted the
classics in scholasticism which they attempted to establish.[199]

More recently Helmar Junghans expressed a similar view about the relationship between early humanism at Erfurt and its *Via Moderna*. He observed that
there was no conflict between the two schools prior to the arrival of Nicholas
Marschalk. The poets were honored by the scholastics, by being exempted from
the customary fees, and were assigned lecture rooms to teach rhetoric and the
art of letter writing. The scholastic professors wanted to use better Latin in their
courses. In fact, he points out that between 1460 and 1500, among its 80 rectorships, 17 of those chosen were from the ranks of *Frühhumanismus*. He feels

that while Luther was there, friendly relations existed between the two schools.[200]

STRIFE WITHIN THE FACULTY

Early humanism at Erfurt appears to have been very similar to that at Heidel-berg from 1460 and 1475, while humanism and scholasticism flourished together. This may have been due to a number of similar factors. Stephan Hoest, the pupil of Peter Luder, was both a member of the *Via Moderna* and stressed the *Studia humanitatis* in order to produce well-rounded scholars. Peter Luder had also been a year at Erfurt by 1460, and taught students how to improve their rhetoric and style of writing letters in fluent diction by the use of the *Studia humanitatis*. Then a number of names follow the Luder period, humanistically minded masters who guided young students in the *Bursen* and led them into the classics. Nor did the two professors of the *Via Moderna*, the only philosophical system taught there, Trutfetter and Usingen, object to a humanism that improved the diction of their students; in fact, that even embellished their style and strengthened their claims, provided it did not interfere with their basic theo-logical views supported by Aristotelian logic and philosophy.

At the turn of the century, we witness the arrivals in Erfurt of Nicholaus Marschalk and the printing press of Wolfgang Schenck. The two worked very closely together in furthering Marschalk's publications. Helmar Junghans, in an able study of Marschalk, claims that he started the battles with the Erfurt scholastics by his attacks upon them in his early publications. This was initiated by the printing of a cookbook, *De Victus ratione*, which Georg Valla had trans-lated into Latin from an original printed at Venice in 1498. For this he added a *Lexicon*, in which he defined Latin and some Greek words by way of an expla-nation. In order to print this *Lexicon* Schenck needed some special Greek let-ters cut; thus he introduced Greek at Erfurt in publications for the first time in 1499.[201] Initially Bauch thought this was the first Greek printing in Germany, but later he learned that Antonius Koburger of Nürnberg had already done some Greek printing by 1497.[202]

Gustav Bauch made a special study of Nicholaus Marschalk with reference to the introduction of Greek in the North, in which he calls Marschalk the *Bannenträger des Hellenismus* in Erfurt and Wittenberg.[203] This designation as the banner carrier of Hellenism is perhaps overdone. It would exclude several others, like Hermann von Busche and Petrus of Ravenna, who were also among the standard bearers, though the credit may belong to Marschalk when the ref-erence is limited to the introduction of Greek and Hebrew at these schools. In 1967 a *Festschrift* was published by O. P. Kretzmann, president of Valparaiso University, to celebrate the 450th anniversary of Martin Luther's nailing of the *Ninety-five Theses*. The text for the occasion was prepared by their professor of classics, Edgar C. Reinke, with the assistance of historian Gottfried G. Krodel.[204] Fortunately, the authors were able to procure a microfilm copy of the original *Oratio* from the University of Halle with the assistance of Hans Müller, the Oberstudienrat of Nördlingen, Germany.[205]

This present study has used most of the material that Bauch, Junghans, Kleineidem, and others have found and thrown the spotlight on Nicholaus Marschalk, who was instrumental in training young humanists at both Erfurt and Wittenberg, and aided in removing the stronghold of scholasticsm. Many of the lawyers and doctors on the Erfurt faculty were already quite favorably inclined toward humanism. Exactly how many students came under the influence of Marschalk is not known, but two young men appear to have been his favorites, Petrus and Heinrich Eberbach, whom Marschalk had instructed in Latin and Greek. Their father was a member of the Erfurt medical faculty, Georg Eberbach from Rothenburg, the ordinarius professor of medicine, who had studied in Italy and had become an archhumanist himself. He was quite a classical scholar who corresponded with Trithemius and other humanists of the day. It was to his able son Petrus that Marschalk dedicated several of his works.[206]

There was something unusual about this first publication, for in it Marschalk did his first printing in Greek, which was unique for Erfurt, in that even the printer, Wolfgang Schenck, who had just begun his work in the city, was challenged. Bauch observed that Schenck had a problem in getting Greek letters cut for this special occasion. Marschalk may have been helpful in this, for he had been a student of Konrad Muth, and this was to be a special *Lexicon* for his beloved humanist student, Georg Eberhard. Apparently Marschalk had already been offering courses in Greek. Bauch claims the Greek letters they prepared were large but nicely carved minuscules, but there were no breathing marks or accents in the Greek text. The work also appeared without a date of publication.[207]

Marschalk must have liked the reactions to his first book. Though only a small undertaking, it must be remembered that for the first time in Erfurt they had something printed in Greek. There seems to have been a streak in Marschalk, the *Stadtschreiber*, town secretary, and not a member of the Erfurt faculty, that wanted to bait some of the old-type scholastics on the academic staff. He immediately published a second book that declared war on scholasticism.[208] Marschalk really began a war with the schoolmen when he printed his *De Arte Grammatica Liber*, based on the third book of the fourth-century work by Martianus Capella with the title *De nuptiis Philologiae et Mercurii*, which has an amazing amount of material about liberal arts.[209] Although this work was available in manuscript form in the Middle Ages and known by many schoolmen, its first printing was in Vicenza, Italy, in 1499, which also reveals how well Marschalk followed the printed classical publication even in regions beyond the Alps.[210]

This printing by Wolfgang Schenck had some interesting features that antedate Luther's later method of printing his lecture notes for the students. Bauch adds that the text was so printed that it left ample space for notes and commentary between the lines; however, the author's commentary is smaller and contains many abbreviations.[211] The work was also introduced by two epigrams, the first being by his fellow humanist Maternus Pistoris, which was somewhat more restrained; while the other epigram was by Master Heinrich Aquilonipolensis, which was far bolder in its attack upon the medieval Latin used by the scholastic theologians. The second epigram praised the proposed new grammatical work at the expense of the centuries-old grammar of Alexander of Villedieu, or Alexander Gallus, also known as his *Doctrinale*. It was offensive to the schoolmen to read that now Cappella's way of teaching Latin was to replace their beloved Alexander Gallus.[212]

This Cappella grammar, says Bauch, had special significance for Erfurt because of its more extensive use of Greek; but of even deeper significance was its impact on the Alexander Gallus text. It meant that the more aggressive humanism of Nicholaus Marschalk pushed the bad Latin text off the market.[213] It also meant that now the Renaissance was removing the crude Latin from Erfurt, which had been somewhat treasured and useful for the scholastics.[214] But then Bauch, as an afterthought, wonders why Marschalk and Pistoris permitted this Master Henricus of Nordheim to prepare the second epigram, since he was scarcely understandable in his barbarous Latin, a treatise of which even Alexander Gallus himself would have been ashamed.[215]

Later, while at Wittenberg, Aquilonipolensis boasted that he had been the first to attack Alexander Gallus' *Doctrinale*.[216] After that Marschalk became too occupied as town secretary and stopped publishing, but his printer, Wolfgang Schenck, continued to publish humanistic publications of which the authors are unknown.[217]

Even though as the *Stadtschrieber* Marschalk was kept very busy, he still continued to further his humanistic endeavors to lead the young at Erfurt in the study of Latin and Greek. For that purpose new *Lehrbücher* were badly needed. His previous publications must have given him some standing among the faculty as a humanist, for, like Konrad Celtis, he now changed his name, as was customary in that day, calling himself Nicolaus Marscaleus Thurius, after his native Thuringia.[218] By September 14, 1500, Marschalk completed his first *Lehrbuch*, a text for instruction in Latin and Greek, which he entitled his *Orthographus N.T.M.* The book was printed by Schenck's press in 1501, which he dedicated to his friend, the learned Knight Johann Wolf von Hermansgrün.[219]

This *Lehrbuch* was designed to teach students both Latin and Greek; but, besides, it also had a characteristic making it suitable for a comparative study of the two languages. This is not just a treatise of words and rules, but also on historical, grammatical, and etymological aspects. The book contains many sections quoted from other authors, which indicates that Marschalk had done extensive reading in related sources, and also that he possessed quite a library of humanistic material procured in Italy.[220] However, the classical grammar, according to Gustav Bauch, lacked much for a proper instruction in Latin and Greek forms and syntax, as he treated the prepositions in more detail. He adds, however, that the *Orthographia* was not intended to be a grammar, especially when applied to Greek portions. Nor was the Greek section such an accomplishment, as he copied parts from a text of Aldus Manucius in 1495, and the introduction by Constantine Lascaris *Erotemata*, with its Latin interpretations.[221] Exactly how much of Lascaris' source material Marschalk possessed in his library remains unknown. Bauch has reproduced some of his explanations as to the material he drew from Lascaris' introduction of 1495.[222]

According to the previously cited Geanakopolos' volume, *Greek Scholars in Venice*, there were several editions of this *Erotemata* published prior to the one mentioned above and mentioned by Marschalk. Lascaris arrived in Italy in 1454 and published his first text entirely in Greek, at Milan in 1476, by the printer Demetrius Damilas.[223] Then a new edition of *Erotemata* or Questions, appeared in both Latin and Greek in 1494 by Crastoni.[224] This last edition, which Manutius reproduced in 1495, had the Lascaris introduction taken from the 1494 publications, which must have been in Marschalk's possession and used to produce this *Lesebuch*.

In 1501 Marschalk published another book, his *Grammatica Exegetica*, for which he used a new publisher Paul Hochenborg, which volume he also dedicated to his pupil, Peter Eberbach. In his dedication he defended the humanistic studies, which, in the development of true culture, required a study of both Latin and Greek. It may be with good judgment that the soft-treading friend, Maternus Pistoris, did not publish another of his epigrams, as the book was quite an attack on scholasticism.

Marschalk begins with his frontal attack on the scholastics, who had asserted that Plato also was hostile toward the poets, claiming that in his state the poets should be expelled from the city. Marschalk's reply was that according to Aristotle, that which divides humans from animals is the heavenly gift of speech; that poets had always been held in high esteem by mankind; and that those who had exposed their children to the *Studia humanitatis* were very wise. Thus, claimed the Stagirite, human speech is cleansed and the dirt of barbarism can be removed. The humanist added that many young people have a gift for development in oratory, but their style is furthered by the guidance of an able teacher, and also by the examples of great men. Had not Demosthenes, the great Greek orator, overcome troubles in speaking fluently by practicing on the beach? Did not Plato, who, according to Pliny, was the priest of wisdom, claim, in his work *Ion*, treating the origin of poetic art, that poets were the servants of God? Likewise, Cicero had praised the *Studia humanitatis*. Had he not also cited Aristotle, the prince among the peripatetics, as the teacher of Alexander the Great? He added that the great all praised poetry as being divine breath.[225]

After that, Marschalk enters upon a description of his *Grammatica Exegetica* with the observation that narrative grammar is very useful for lecturing, for orations and other literary activities. In part one he offers a detailed analysis of how rhetoric is useful for correspondence and letter writing, while in part two he gives students a treatment of poetry, metrik, and press composition.[226] Bauch also offers a detailed analysis of Marschalk's four volumes in which the *Grammatica Exegetica* is divided.[227]

Marschalk offered as his sources for support of the *Grammatica Exegetica* the works of Quintilian, Diomedes, Cicero, Gellius, and Varro, but, as in his *Orthographia*, he appears to be rather free in citing sources he may have used. Bauch remains rather dubious as to whether he actually used all of the sources he cites. At the close of the treatise Marschalk also gave a description of the theater and even the dress of the actors. In the Hachenborg publication, Erfurt witnessed use of a second type of Greek letters which were smaller but not always even minuscules. These appear to have been added after the printing of the Latin text.[228]

Another humanistic work appeared in 1502, which was to be a practical introduction to the study of the classics, called his *Enchiridion Poetarum Clarissimorum*. This was a small tome of eight quarto leaves, which offered students excerpts from Latin and Greek authors, making it an anthology of useful material. In this *Enchiridion* the Greek portions are given the prime position, accompanied by a Latin interlinear. Bauch has reproduced all of this material in a colophon, and pointed out that the work was taken from Priscian's grammar, books XII and XVIII. He doubts that Marschalk was the author, for several reasons. In the first place, the author knows little Greek, and why should he publish a small anthology on top of his previous lengthy publication? However, for that day, Erfurt students must have welcomed any material from the classics.[229]

In this Erfurt period of Marschalk's humanistic activities, he was not satisfied to limit his publications to Latin and Greek for study of the New Testament; he also began to teach Hebrew, in which he did some credible spade work. He published his *Introductio ad litteras hebraicas Veilissima*, in which he also offered an introduction to the Greek grammar. In this work Marschalk prepared the foundation for all Hebrew studies at Erfurt—in fact, for all of northern Germany.[230]

In this publication Marschalk practically copied the original Aldus text that he used in courses at Erfurt. Now scholars at Erfurt could begin the study of the Old Testament in the new Hebrew. There had been some study of Hebrew in the West for about a century or more. In fact, even Gratian, in his *Decretum*, had made some use of Hebrew, while Nicholaus von Lyra, at the Council of Vienna in 1311, had also stressed the need for the study of biblical languages. During the Reform Councils in the fifteenth century, theologians realized that the conversion of Jews demanded a future study of Hebrew in German universities. After the *Kaballa* began to be studied at Florence, and Reuchlin had become interested in its reported hidden meanings, the study of Hebrew widened into ever wider circles. However, in this Marschalk was a pioneer of Hebrew studies at Erfurt.[231]

Marschalk did not limit his publications to the fields of literature and languages; he also published a work prior to his arrival in Wittenberg, entitled *Laus Amusoris*, in which he also offered instruction in music. He did this by notes in descant, tenor, alto, and bass. This work reveals that Marschalk also possessed musical talent as well as literary ones. It is believed that his interest was aroused by the visit of Konrad Celtis, who had put odes to music. This study was supposed to result in Erfurt students composing music. Another Celtis student,

Conrad Mutian, was also favorably disposed to music; while Crotus Rubianus and Eoban Hessus were also musical. The Erfurt burghers also met the humanist at the Engelsburg to enjoy music. Justus Jonas had likewise developed an interest in music at Erfurt, which later he brought to Wittenberg's Castle Church. There can be little doubt that Marschalk's publication of his volume on music had quite an influence among his pupils, as well as the townspeople of Erfurt.[232]

Although Marschalk had many friends among the humanistically inclined students at Erfurt, and thus established a lasting foothold for humanism at that institution, his aggressive attacks on entrenched old scholasticism brought him many enemies. Prior to his departure for Wittenberg in 1502, he had already separated from Schenck and established his own printing press, which he then moved to the newly founded institution, where he was to wield a similar influence during the short time he remained, as he also left Wittenberg in 1505.[233] Marschalk's role at Wittenberg will be covered in the next section of this chapter.

HUMANISM AT THE UNIVERSITY OF WITTENBERG

In the previous sections an attempt was made to cover the various views of humanism among scholars today. Then at the close of the recent views, we saw how a lesser role was played by the Brethren of the Common Life. After that, the importance of humanism at Heidelberg under the leadership of Peter Luder and Stephan Hoest was presented. This had an impact there on Rudolf Agricola and Konrad Celtis, both of whom subsequently brought the *Studia humanitatis* to Leipzig and Erfurt. Finally it was also transported to the University of Wittenberg by a number of Italian humanists. Meanwhile, scholasticism had lost its former strength at the new school due to the inroads of the *Studia humanitatis* in the sixteenth century.

Before entering the role of humanism at the university on the Elbe, a few preliminary observations will help to clarify the subsequent coverage of the *Studia humanitatis*, as it first challenged the scholastic stronghold of the *Via Antiqua*, and also how later, through the final triumph of biblical humanism, it threw Aristotle from his throne during the second decade. It must be realized that Wittenberg, like Leipzig and Erfurt, had not just one type of humanism. It frequently depended on the discipline scholars were in and their past backgrounds. These distinctions must be kept in mind if one is to understand the roles they played in Wittenberg's early years.

First there were the traveling humanists, ardent students of the *Studia humanitatis*, like Peter Luder, Johann von Langen, Konrad Celtis, Marschalk, Hermann von Busche, and Petrus of Ravenna, who remained but relatively short periods at several schools. Yet they had a profound influence on the students, which resulted in a second generation of poets and humanistically minded members of the first Wittenberg faculty. There was a second type of Wittenberg scholar, like Sigismund Epp in the liberal arts, or Ludwig Henning in theology, who realized that humanistic claims were valid, that medieval Latin was in a sad state, and that the school needed new and better texts in languages and in philosophy, and who began to improve scholarship by publication of better sources in their disciplines. By questioning the very foundations of their offerings in the past, they tended to weaken the scholastically minded institution. Wittenberg had a third type of faculty member, like Johann von Staupitz and Polich von Mellerstadt, who were not hostile toward humanism. In fact they were friendly in their views, as they accepted in part the much-needed changes. Finally, the institution had a fourth type of scholar, men like Trebelius and Johann Lang, who wanted improved methods through the *Studia humanitatis* for biblical studies, through the original languages of the Holy Scriptures, Greek and Hebrew, and thus learned to use an effective exegesis to interpret the Greek New Testament and the Hebrew Old Testament. This last type, known as biblical humanism, came to Wittenberg through Martin Luther and Philip Melanchthon, which later served the media for the return to early Christianity during the German Reformation.

After the founding of the University of Wittenberg by Frederick the Wise, the role of the first type of humanism appears to have been quite influential. At the school's opening exercises, according to the *Liber Decanorum*, the Town Rat had arranged for a parade to the castle, where the opening session was to be held. Here they heard an oration that set the tone of the future institution. It is interesting that the welcoming address to the faculty and some select townsmen was delivered by the well-known humanist Hermann von Busche, rather than a theologian. The dean's book made the following record of the event:

> In accordance with the plans of the Town Council, the ceremonies were begun with a dignified procession to the Castle. Here a most eloquent oration was delivered by the Poet von Busche, which was filled with wise predictions.[234]

Hermann von Busche was of noble extraction from Westphalia, born in 1468. He had studied in the Netherlands under Alex Hegius, Rudolf Agricola, and Rudolf von Langen. Busche had also accompanied Langen on his trip to Italy, where he rounded out his humanistic background. After his return to Germany he became a traveling exponent of the *Studia humanitatis*, and helped plant classical humanism in a number of German universities. He happened to be at Leipzig during the Mellerstadt–Wimpina battle, in which he sided with the former. Thus when Mellerstadt left Leipzig for Wittenberg, he accompanied him there, where, no doubt through Polich's influence, Busche was offered a regular humanistic post. It may have been through Mellerstadt's influence, too, that he was chosen by the elector and the Town Council to deliver the opening address during the founding of the University of Wittenberg. This oration he delivered with much display of his humanistic learning. He selected Ovid to illustrate the role of learning at Wittenberg, to whom he pointed as the exalted guide to a better life. He claimed that to become truly learned and reach one's goal in eloquence, it was essential to acquire a humanistic attire.[235]

Busche was not blessed with the patience to await the results of his teachings in the classics at the *Leucuria*. How many young people at Wittenberg were influenced by Busche cannot be ascertained. But there must have been something in the next environment that he did not like. So in 1503 he packed up his bundle and left the institution. But the elector had favored poetry as part of the liberal arts offering, as seen in the previous chapter, so his courses were not dropped. Another humanistically trained instructor, Balthasar Fabricius, replaced him. He was also named Vache after his hometown, Vache, in Hessen. This student had come to Wittenberg in 1503 and took his M.A. degree in February of 1504 with the first graduating class. Fabricius was a much more reliable type of teacher. According to the *Rotulus of 1507*, he taught Virgil's *Aenead* and Valerius Maximus alternatively during the eleventh hour.[236] In the afternoon he also offered a course in Sallust on *The Jugurthian War*. He must have been quite successful, though never prominent. He remained at Wittenberg until 1541.[237]

A second humanist at Wittenberg, with a wonderful background in the classics from his mastery of the *Studia humanitatis*, was Petrus of Ravenna, named after his hometown. His real name was Petrus Tomais. He was a remarkably gifted professor, who held also a *utriusque iuris* title, a degree in both civil and canon law. The elector had learned of this man and invited him to Wittenberg. When he arrived he was met in Wittenberg by both the elector and his brother John. This out-and-out humanist was a very gifted orator who possessed a phenomenal memory; he was able to quote from Roman law books or their glosses at will without notes, to the amazement of the entire academic world. Petrus also had taught at a number of Italian universities, but mainly at Padua.[238]

Apparently the Saxon Court was anxious to hear a public lecture by this learned scholar, which was scheduled to be delivered in their presence. However, the entire audience seems to have been impressed by Petrus' learning in so many fields presented in such a polished oratory. Since he was also a lawyer, he chose for the title of his address, *De potestate summi pontificalis et Romani imperatoris*, or *Concerning the Power of the Supreme Pontiff of Rome and the Roman Emperor*. At the close he asked: Is papal approval essential for the founding of a university? Or is an approval of the emperor adequate? To this he replied that the approval of Emperor Maximilian I was entirely sufficient. Both pope and Kaiser had that power in a *Gottesstaat*, the divinely established state.[239]

The elector was so impressed and pleased with the oration that he asked the humanistic lawyer to remain at Wittenberg; but for some unknown reason, he never registered in the university *Matrikel* to become a regular member of the faculty. However, he did give lectures in the law school in civil and canon law and published *Kompendien* for his audiences. However, Petrus of Ravenna did not limit his activities to teaching. He delivered lectures to large crowds in public gatherings, covering the fields of theology and moral philosophy. The elector and John also attended one of these addresses and reported there were large crowds. The humanist's addresses were later printed in Cologne by the Saxon Court. Petrus' lectures covered a wide range of subjects, such as the Holy Scriptures, Immortality, the Final Judgment, Resurrection, God's Grace, and God's Wrath. He also attacked Mohammedanism and Judaism; however, he was always careful not to exceed the bound of the Catholic faith, which he praised for its lofty doctrines. As a thoroughly trained Italian humanist, his speeches were always chosen to please the prince. One can understand why conservative members of the faculty might be concerned about the impact of this learned professor in their respective disciplines and upon the student body. Thus some battles were inevitable, which made Petrus' longer stay undesirable. The humanist remained until the Pest in 1506, when he and his wife left for Cologne, where he met with a similar reception until he encouraged battles with their conservative theologians and he moved to Mainz. After that we lose track of him. His son, Vincentius, who was also a lawyer, remained at Wittenberg for a while, until he, too, left Wittenberg for Rome, in 1507.[240]

The third member of our classification, the out-and-out humanist who wielded considerable influence in the early University of Wittenberg, was Nicholaus Marschalk. It will be recalled that he attacked scholasticism rather sharply, causing friction with the scholastic faculty; whereupon he departed for a more welcome environment in the new institution of Frederick the Wise.

While at Erfurt, Marschalk had, like so many students in that day, not only published works to further the study of Greek and Hebrew, but had looked forward to his future profession. After the completion of his undergraduate studies in the philosophical faculty, he had begun to study law and had acquired a degree of *juris utriusque doctor*. He matriculated at Wittenberg during the first semester of the school in 1502, to continue his studies in law under the famous aforementioned professor, Petrus of Ravenna.[241] Petrus must have been impressed with Marschalk's maturity, for he suggested that he publish a *Lehrbuch* of his experiences for the benefit of the students. This came from Marschalk's own press under the title of *Methodus*. After that he entered the philosophical faculty, where he furthered the humanistic studies. On April 23, 1504, he was promoted to the doctorate, fully licensed to each everywhere, both civil and canon law.[242]

Meanwhile, Marschalk could hardly claim he had not been adequately recognized as a member of the Wittenberg faculty; for when the first bachelors were to be promoted at the new university, on January 18, 1503, the institution asked Nicholaus Marschalk to be the orator for the special occasion, which offered him an opportunity to demonstrate his learning as a humanist with distinction.[243]

At the time of the Marschalk address, even though the school had opened but for one semester, there must have been a number of students among the over four hundred registrants that came to Wittenberg from other schools, and were ready to take the baccalaureate degree. This must have been a special occasion for the whole academic community as the exercises of the first commencement of the *Leucuria*. Where this was held is no longer known, but it could not have been in the Castle Church, as it was not finished before 1509. Perhaps the affair took place in one of the larger rooms of the castle, where Hermann von Busche had delivered his address at the opening of the university.

Since the Valparaiso *Festschrift* of Marschalk's *Oratio* was translated by
Edgar Reinke, his rendition of its content is as follows:

> The theme of Marschalk's address is the laurel wreath, which, he says, the
> twenty-four candidates for the bachelor's degree are about to receive from
> his hands. After an introduction in which he describes the various kinds of
> wreaths and crowns worn by the ancient Romans, particularly those bestowed
> upon their miliary heroes, Marschalk extols the young graduates as worthy of
> the most highly prized garlands of all, the laurel wreath. They, like Hercules
> at the crossroads, Marschalk declares, have chosen virtue as the way of life;
> they have not emulated the young shepherd Paris, son of King Priam of Troy,
> who elected the life of voluptuous pleasure as his reward for having judged
> Venus the winner of the beauty contest on Mount Ida. Mention of Helen of
> Troy as the prize awarded to Paris by Venus leads Marschalk into a long
> digression in which he castigates women and disparages marriage, though he
> does soften somewhat his otherwise relentless criticism with a few interluded
> words of praise. At the conclusion of his oration Marschalk again lauds the
> candidates for adapting Pallas Athena, the virgin goddess of wisdom, as their
> model for the good life.[244]

The Marschalk *Oratio* was written in a Ciceronian style, as might be expected
from a linguist. The reader is struck by his frequent citations from Greek and
Latin literature and his acquaintance with Greek and Latin mythology. He seems
also to have known ancient history, from which he used illustrations. The translator of the *Oratio* points out that twenty-nine authors are represented, classical
and postclassical, of which fourteen are Greek and fifteen are Latin.[245] Without
doubt the address added to Marschalk's reputation as a classical scholar, especially among the younger members of the liberal arts faculty. Marschalk immediately printed the address on his own press, which he had moved from Erfurt.
The *Oratio* was printed in his own antique type, a text of 10 pages, with the
Greek still the former Schenck's *minuscules*. The *Oratio* was the first dated publication and the first printing with Greek characters in Wittenberg.[246]

However, in spite of all the advantages, Marschalk had offered to the Wittenberg student body in learning Latin and Greek in the study of the classics, he
seems to have been unhappy at the new school. Like Hermann von Busche and
Petrus of Ravenna, a real classical scholar was not well received by the scholastically minded members of the Wittenberg faculty. Bauch informs us that in 1503
he complained about their opposition to humanism, but that the elector
encouraged him to push ahead with much vigor and force.[247] Friedensburg says
Marschalk still had his *Schwierigkeiten* at Wittenberg and he complained to the
elector, but he left Wittenberg by 1505.[248]

But the departure of Nicholaus Marschalk was not without impact on the
younger students who had followed his previous attempts to improve the linguistic studies at the new school. A friend and fellow Thuringian, Hermann Trebelius, took up where Marschalk had left off. Trebelius prepared a number of
Greek *Lesestücke*, excerpts from the classics and the Fathers, that he accompanied with Latin translations. But his course aimed at a new objective beyond

that of the former Erfurt humanist. He aimed to teach students not only classical Greek, but also serve the theological students in their study of the Holy Scriptures.[249] Here was the beginning of biblical humanism, which was used so effectively by Martin Luther and Melanchthon, as well as in Martin Luther's translation of the Bible into German from 1521 to 1545, from the original Greek and Hebrew.

Another of the humanistic poets at Wittenberg was Georg Sibutus Darininus from Thuringia, who had studied the classics with Konrad Celtis at Vienna. He appears to have taught for a while at Cologne before his Wittenberg matriculation during the winter semester.[250] The *Rotulus of 1507*, by Christopher Scheurl, has this entry about the poet: *"poeta et orator laureatus, Sylium Italicum et silvulam de situ Albiorene urbis a se editam.*[251] In lectures he interpreted Silius Italicus' Heroic Poem, titled *Punica*. Sibutus also lectured on the poetic work *Silvula in Albiorum Illustratam*, which was a kind of dialogue praising Wittenberg, which he had recited in the presence of the elector and afterward had printed. In his lectures he attempted to interpret the poem to his students. Friedensburg tells us that for a number of years Sibutus and the poet Friulaner Ricardus Sbrulius stood at the very center of the humanistic movement in Wittenberg. The last was another crowned poet like Sibutus. Emperor Maximilian I had introduced Sbrulius to the Elector of Saxony, who later joined his company. The poets both looked forward to occasions where they might apply some of their poetry. This relationship continued until Sibutus decided to get married, and then he entered the field of medicine, which terminated the poetic relationship.[252]

Ricardus Sbrulius was a rather frivolous type of humanist, who continued his poetic activity even after he lived alone. Another humanist, Otto Beckmann, left us his observation about Sbrulius:

> Sbrulius himself is an author that publicly advances poetry and oratory in such a way that it is not without the greatest impact upon the students of our school.[253]

On another occasion, we gather from Beckmann's notes that the elector was fascinated by and loved to have him extol the learning found at the University of Wittenberg.

> In the Saxon lands, (in his travels) the Elector would always take him (Sbrulius) along, observing display of the learning at the University of Wittenberg.[254]

According to the Matrikel of the University of Wittenberg, Sbrulius came to Wittenberg in the summer of 1507, while Christopher Scheurl of Nürnberg was the rector, when he matriculated in the *Album* of the University. He acquired his baccalaureate degree in 1507; because of his "leaurea" he was promoted more rapidly. According to an address by Otto Beckmann, he called himself "An Italian knight from Prejus, a professor of human letters and philosophy at the University of Wittenberg."[255]

Because of Sbrulius' friendly relations with the elector as his poet, no doubt the university tolerated that he wanted to be placed as a current poet on a plane with those of antiquity. Perhaps it was by a desire on the part of members of the faculty to place him in the proper perspective as a poet, that Hermann von Busche was invited to Wittenberg in 1510 to challenge this young boaster: Friedensburg cites a section from Hamelmann *Vita Hermanni Buschi,* taken from Hamelmann's *Geschichtliche Werke,* II, 57:

> When Busche came to Wittenberg again in 1510, he entered into a competition with Sbrulius; and, because at the time he recited the poems of Baptista Mantus; while that one (Busche) recited verses from Virgil, Lucian, Propertius, Titulius and Ausenius. He also explained the Tragedies of Seneca. Thus it happened, both because of the magnificence with which Busche entertained them, delighted the audience, and because more frequently in the audience they favored that one (Busche) with applause than Sbrulius, that there arose a dissension between them.[256]

In the contest Sbrulius seems to have attempted to prove that present poets were on a par with the ancients, and in this Busche exposed his ignorance.[257]

But as a professor Sbrulius had other problems. He seems to have developed a bad reputation both with the faculty and with his students, because he was frequently seen with questionable women. Even though warned by friends, he appears to have continued, which caused his departure for Frankfurt in 1513. By 1516 we find him at Cologne. Contemporary humanists like von Hutten and Eobanus Rhegius did not regard him very highly as a poet. Hutten claimed that for a little bread he would dash off a poem praising or smearing someone, while Eobanus claimed he was arrogant and scornful of others.[258]

Another interesting figure among the humanists at early Wittenberg was the stormy poet from Braunschweig in Northern Germany, Thilemann Conradi of Göttingen, better known as Thiloninus Philymnus Syasticanus, who played quite a role in the introduction of the classical languages at Wittenberg. Before his conversion Philymnus was somewhat of a problem because of his frequent attacks on the scholastics in the faculty. Gustav Bauch, however, claims this man has been somewhat misrepresented, and gives a more detailed account of his labors as a Greek and Hebrew scholar.[259]

Philymnus began his undergraduate studies at Erfurt, where he studied some Greek, but he wrote his poems mainly in Latin. Among these was a poem of the Virgin Mary, which Mutianus Rufus criticized and he labeled it as "Spötterei" about the Mother of God. Next we find Philymnus in Italy, where he spent several months at Bologna, and also some time in Venice, no doubt attempting to improve his knowledge of Greek. He claimed to have studied with several Greek instructors.[260]

After that, Philymnus came to Wittenberg in 1509, where he completed his work toward a master of arts degree. He continued his poetic activity and wrote a prose treatise in 1509, which he dedicated to the vice chancellor of the school, Polich von Mellerstadt. This treatise, still extant in the Wolfenbüttel Library, is entitled *Comoedia Philymni Syasticani Cui Nomen Teratologia*.[261] It is a sharp attack on the theologians in the faculty and their scholasticism. He attempted to impress his readers with his mastery of Greek, in which field, says Bauch, at the time he was but a *Stümper*. In the *Comedy* he also remained anonymous about Ericius Cordus, a married poet. It closed with a Greek greeting to his *Schatz*. Bauch feels the section drawn in Hebrew from Marschalk's introduction is nothing but showing off on the part of the author.[262]

But it would be a false impression to claim that Philymnus was making no contributions to the advancement of humanism at Wittenberg. He continued his studies, so that by 1511 he was lecturing privately in the study of Greek and had even prepared an enlarged edition of the *Isagoge*, an introductory text published by Trebelius.[263] The introduction of Trebelius is virtually repeated literally by Philymnus, including the block print from Marschalk's *Eisagoge;* but, in the next paper, the new edition for Wittenberg students contains many more examples of quotations for student studies, and besides, students were supplied with a Latin interlinear. Bauch thinks the new additions may have been taken from Aldine publications. Among the readings were also some religious exercises, like Sedulius' "Mass to the Blessed Virgin," several psalms, and an oration to the "Most Holy Mother of God." The Greek was still the Marschalk-Schenck type without breathing marks or accents.[264]

In this publication by Philymnus we still do not possess a Greek grammar, but merely an enlarged *Lesefibel*, a Greek reader for the students. But in 1512 Georg Simler, a student of John Reuchlin and Philip Melanchthon's teacher at Tübingen, published a Latin and Greek grammar, which offered frequent exercises in Greek material, which was based on *Erotemata Guarani ex Chrysolorae libro maiusculo cum interpretatione latina*. It had Greek letters without an introduction. Hieronymus Gürtler of Wildenberg, the founder of the Special School in Goldberg, who happened to be in Wittenberg in 1512 as a medical student, put out a third new edition of this Greek grammar, which indicates that the original of Georg Simler became known in Wittenberg quite early.[265]

Thiloninus Philymnus must have advanced considerably as a teacher of Greek at Wittenberg by 1518. At the time he was a master in the New Friderici College, with a number of humanistic companions.[266] Philymnus read it through and knew enough Greek to find it a somewhat doubtful copy. Several years before he had been to Prague and spent some time with the famous Italian humanist Hieronymus Balbus, where he had seen the same Homer text and made a copy of it. His students asked him to publish the *Syntagma*. He agreed, translated the Homeric text into Latin Hexameter, and dedicated it to the Erfurt theologian Johann Werlich and Maternus Pistoris. The work was welcomed by Georgius Sibrutus and printed by Johann Grunenberg.[267]

The Erfurt reaction might have been expected. Cordus poked fun at Philymnus' seven feet of hexameter verse, while Mutianus Rufus and his pupils accused him of being a plagiarist. Gustav Bauch questions the ground for such claims, for the verses were not bad for the type of introduction it was. And his Greek text, written in minuscules, does not deserve any criticism.[268]

Philymnus attempted to return to Erfurt, but he met with sharp pulses, even though he offered lectures from Lucanus, Hesiod, and Juvenal. The sarcastic attacks were almost unbearable. Mutian and his whole following made life miserable. Even the leader of the Erfurt poets, Maternus Pistoris, joined in with Femilius Cordus and praised the talent of Cordus as being greater than that of Philymnus. This caused Philymnus to return to Wittenberg and attempt to start over again. After establishing a following among the students, he continued in 1516 to give, lectures in Latin, Greek, and even Hebrew.[269]

At this point, in Philymnus' life something happened about which we lack sufficient information. He seems to have undergone a conversion and changed the themes of his writings completely. Whether Martin Luther had anything to do with this remains unknown, but by now Luther was maturing as a professor in *Lectura in Biblia*, and becoming the later reformer. It seems that Philymnus began to apply his linguistic ability to biblical themes. In 1516 he published a book that he entitled *Triumphus Christi*. It covers the passion, death, and resurrection of Christ. It is really a poem directed against the relics that pious people gather. The true relics, he says, are the books of the Holy Scriptures, which should be faithfully read, especially the Holy Gospels. It is also interesting that Philymnus insisted that his students speak only Latin or Greek in his classes.

As will be seen in a later chapter, when biblical humanism began to take hold in the University of Wittenberg, in addition to Carlstadt and Amsdorf, the lawyers Schurff and Stähelin were won to the new linguistic approach of the Bible, followed by the two humanists, John Lang and Thiloninus Philymnus, both of whom were close to Luther. Gustav Bauch claims that Luther learned his first Hebrew from this now changed humanistic scholar.[270]

Another Wittenberg scholar, who was an able Greek student and no doubt wielded much influence in Wittenberg, was John Lang, who later became a very warm friend of Martin Luther. It was with John Lang that Luther began his serious study of Greek, since Lang possessed an excellent collection of Greek manuscripts. He entered Erfurt in the summer semester of 1511 and completed his A.B. degree in 1512. At Erfurt he was one of Nicholaus Marschalk's able students. Upon his arrival at Wittenberg, he taught Greek in liberal arts, where among his students were Eobanus Hessus and Justus Jonas.[271] He also began teaching Luther his first real Greek in 1514. In 1516 he became the prior of the Augustinian monastery at Erfurt, through Luther's influence, but remained in the inner circle, the triumvirate of Luther, Spalatin, and John Lang, which dethroned Aristotle in the University of Wittenberg.

From this review of the number of humanistic influences that were at work in the University of Wittenberg, which tended to question and undermine the authority of its scholastic stronghold, it should be of little surprise that in the subsequent period scholasticism was on the defensive. The scholastics imitated humanists by inserting classical quotations within their textual publications.

Where in its early period, such as in Heidelberg and Erfurt during the days of Stephan Hoest, Peter Luder, and Konrad Celtis, humanism existed on a rather friendly basis with scholasticism, now under Marschalk and his successors it tended to employ frontal attacks upon the whole methodology of the school-men. There also began an erosion from within, because so many of the professors in liberal arts, law, and medicine sympathized with the humanists in their insistence upon the *Studia humanitatis*, so as to broaden the base for students' education. Among the faculty members were those like Sigismund Epp, the first dean at Wittenberg in the philosophical faculty, who recognized that even the study of Aristotle was valuable only to the degree they used the most up-to-date texts as well as reliable grammars. We saw earlier that Dean Epp was an Augustinian whom Dean Staupitz had brought with him from Tübingen, a scholastically trained Scotist with a strong leaning toward humanism and its importance to liberal arts. Epp was not satisfied with the old texts used by past generations, but asked for the publication of new philosophical texts by Petrus Tartaretus, a late medieval scholastic who had taught at the Sorbonne in Paris between 1480 and 1490. The dean wanted his students to use this author's *Tractatus des Petrus Hispanus* to get a new interpretation of the famous Stagirite, who wrote his commentaries *Viam Scoti* in a more reliable light.[272]

Gustav Bauch makes an interesting observation about the *Tractatus* of Tartaretus, claiming that a new wind blows through this Paris professor's material. Not only was it a more reliable text on Aristotle but it was nicely interspersed with quotations from the classics, similar to that of Stephan Hoest at Heidelberg some fifty years prior. He also wanted to obtain a new text for the study of Lombard's *Sentences* by a printing of the *Eisegoge des Porphyrius*. This shows that Dean Epp was a sufficiently inclined humanist, even in philosophy, to ask the elector to have them printed at a cost of 500 Gulden.[273] He approached Dr. Frederick Kitscher, the prior of the Castle Church, about the undertaking, and also specified that he wanted Wolfgang Stöckel of Munich as the printer, rather than Marschalk, who had recently moved his press from Erfurt to Wittenberg.[274] What came of this undertaking remains unknown, for Dean Epp left Wittenberg shortly after that to go back to Tübingen in the winter semester of 1504–1505, where he was chosen as rector.[275]

Sigismund Epp was followed by Pater Ludwig Henning, a theologian, who also taught logic in liberal arts *Viam Scoti*.[276] He also, like Epp, insisted on the use of very modern texts for his courses, as he found that his students encountered difficulty in understanding the views of Scotus. Henning used a compendium by the Minarit master of theology Antonius Sirecti, who taught at the University of Paris from 1470 to 1475.[277] Another work that Henning used in his classes was a text by the master of theology, Mauritius Hibernicus, which he had written while Henning was his student.[278] Like Dean Epp, Henning also liked Tartaretus for his courses. This text remained in use until scholasticism was terminated at Wittenberg in 1518–1519.[279]

But not only had the pressure of humanism brought demands for more recent texts in philosophy; it had even attacked the very inner structure by criticizing the methodology employed. Henning was the type of progressive professor who not only realized that the reliability of a theologian depended upon the value of a translation being used, but also objected to the language employed to

expound on its meaning. He objected to the *Doctrinale* of Alexander of Villedieu, or Gallus for short, as it was 300 years old and taught students very bad
Latin. Instead, in all the schools of the university, and especially for beginners in
liberal arts, these professors wanted it to be replaced by Sulpius Verulanus,
which had been published in Perugia. Its second edition had spread rapidly
through the entire humanistic world and also to Wittenberg.[280]

Another faculty member was the aforementioned lawyer, Petrus of Ravenna,
or Petrus Tomais, who falls into the second classification, a professional man who
was also a well-trained humanist. On May 15, 1503, he ascended the *Kather,*
no doubt in the elector's own court auditorium of the Castle at Wittenberg,
where the law school then offered most of its courses. On this occasion he delivered a notable public address, discussed above. Later the Saxon Court had it
printed under the title *De potestate summi pontificis et Romanni imperators.*[281]
Frederick was so pleased with the able professor that he made special arrangements so he could give courses and deliver some public addresses. His lectures
were not without well-chosen words about the prince and his counselers.[282] In
1506 he left Wittenberg and did not return, in spite of pleadings from the elector,
but his influence for humanism must have lived on.[283]

Sad as the elector was at the departure of Petrus of Ravenna, he was replaced
by an extremely valuable lawyer, Hieronymus Schurff from Saint Gallen,
Switzerland. This Swiss lawyer was a very gifted, level-headed professor who was
not only valuable as a legal mind during the formative period, but later a close
friend of Martin Luther and the German Reformation. While he remained at
Wittenberg until 1545, Schurff's undergraduate training was at Basel and Tübingen, where his mind must have been directed toward the value of a humanistic
training. Hence he was of the second type, that looked favorably upon those
engaged in the *Studia humanitatis.* At Tübingen he studied under Konrad Summenhardt, who had also taught John Staupitz; it may have been Staupitz who
later brought him to Wittenberg. He came to the new university on the Elbe at
the very beginning, in 1502, where he began as the interpreter of Aristotle, *viam
Scoti,* in the philosophical faculty. He entered the law faculty in 1505, where he
took Petrus of Ravenna's place when the Italian left. He then became the ordinarius professor in Roman law, while Wolfgang Reisenpusch lectured on the
Institutes of Emperor Justinian.[284] The elector made good use of the able lawyer
Schurff; he likewise used him in his Saxon *Obergericht,* or Supreme Court, and
he also served as the elector's private legal advisor. As a professor he commanded
great respect, and no doubt influenced the rise of humanism in Wittenberg by
joining in with Martin Luther to introduce biblical humanism, which soon
dethroned Aristotle.

Another humanistically minded law professor at Wittenberg was Henning
Göde, who as the Probst at the Castle Church must have wielded quite an influence upon the school among the theologians as well as those in liberal arts.
Kleineidem speaks of him as the "king" among the jurists while at Erfurt, as in
fact he was highly regarded throughout all of Germany.[285] He matriculated
there in 1464, when the spirit of Peter Luder must have been very alive. He

served Erfurt in many capacities, including even a mission to Rome, on behalf of one of its cloisters. He also served both the university and the city in a number of ways.[286] He possessed a doctorate in both canon and civil law, and, Friedensburg says, became a "Saule" at Erfurt and acquired the nickname *Monarcha Juris*. He was known therefore as both "the wall" and "the monarch" of law at his alma mater. He served as their ordinarius professor in canon law.[287]

Later, difficulties arose in the Erfurt faculty, in which Henning Göde became involved. Frederick the Wise had used him on many occasions, and thus was anxious to bring this distinguished professor to Wittenberg. The elector offered Henning the post of prior of the Castle Church, as well as ordinarius professor of canon law at Wittenberg.[288] Thus Göde came to Wittenberg in 1510, where he served as Probst and as a professor until his death in 1521. The elector became attached to this able humanistic lawyer, whom he often took along on his trips, asking for *Rechtsgutachten*, legal advice in matters of government. What impact this distinguished head of the Wittenberg Castle Church and humanistic lawyer had on spreading humanism at Wittenberg can well be imagined.[289]

Finally, in our treatment of the second type of faculty member, who no doubt had great influence among the humanistic poets, and in his influence of the students, was the distinguished lawyer Christopher Scheurl of Wittenberg, about whom we have already heard much in the chapter on the founding of the university. This humanistic professor gave Wittenberg an Italian flavor by following the practice of Bologna, in listing the faculty in the *Rotulus of 1507*, and drafting the Wittenberg *Statutes of 1508*. Gustav Bauch regarded Scheurl as important enough to write a special treatise about this famous graduate from the University of Bologna.[290]

Christopher Scheurl was from a wealthy business family in Nürnberg, whose grandfather had become rich as a businessman in Breslau; while his father had later moved to Nürnberg, where he had married into the patrician family, the Tuchers, into which young Christopher was born in 1481. Naturally these leading Nürnbergers wished the very best for their son. After a good background in Nürnberg, the young lad spent a year at Heidelberg, where the traditions of Stephan Hoest, Agricola, and Konrad Celtis must have given him a humanistic start as a scholar. Since the family wished their son to become a lawyer, young Scheurl was sent to the University of Bologna, where he studied for eight years and not only took a doctorate in both canon and civil law, but was even honored by being chosen rector for a semester. It is interesting that Dr. Johann Staupitz, the vicar general of the Augustinian Hermits, and the former dean of theology at Wittenberg, attended his graduation.[291]

The above relationship between young Scheurl and Frederick the Wise makes it quite evident that the elector had an eye on the promising young lawyer, and that the Augustinian vicar was behind the acquisition of the professor; for when Christopher Scheurl arrived, at the Saxon Court to see the elector about a Wittenberg position, Staupitz was there to assist in the hiring of the future canonist.[292] But the hiring was not merely the activity of Johann Staupitz, but also much was due to the expressed wishes of the family. Bauch states that Scheurl's father had learned through Dogenhart Pfeffinger of Frederick's founding the University of Wittenberg in 1502, and the parents had thought of the possibility of a professorship there.[293] The elector offered Scheurl a position as ordinarius professor of canon law; in it he had to lecture on *sexto Decretalium* for 80 Gulden.[294] The elector delegated two monks to accompany Scheurl en route to Wittenberg, where the three arrived on April 8, 1507, and on April 13 Christopher began lecturing in canon law. So impressed were the faculty and students that they had acquired this young professor, that by May 1, 1507, they elected him rector of the university. The young patrician in turn invited 50 doctors, Bürger, and their wives to a dinner and dance.[295]

It would be repetitious to enter upon Scheurl's activity between 1507 and 1512, when he left Wittenberg to accept a post in Nürnberg as *Juroconsultant*, as it has been covered in a previous chapter. What concerns us here is his influence toward the triumph of humanism at Wittenberg, which without doubt was considerable. Gustav Bauch makes this observation about his attraction of friends:

> There he acquired a large circle of friends, such as Johann von Staupitz, with whom he became acquainted at Bologna, then there were Nicolaus von Amsdorf, Andreas Carlstadt, Otto Beckmann, Johann Doltz, Georg Spalatin, Wolfgang Stehelin, Hieronymous Schurff, Christian Beyer, Henning Goode, Lorenz Schlamau, Jodocus Trutfetter, Luther's teacher, and many others.[296]

After he returned to Nürnberg, Scheurl kept up a lively correspondence that has been preserved in *Scheurls Briefbuch*, so frequently cited before in other roles of this lawyer. Later he was also in friendly terms with Luther and Melanchthon.

As the rector of the university in the summer of 1507, Scheurl ruled the school's daily life with a stern hand. No one was permitted to appear in public armed during his entire rectorship. Since he was housed in Bitterfeld, four miles outside the city, he had to ride to school early in the mornings to deliver his lectures. Students flocked in large numbers to his classes. As a Bologna graduate he spoke a fluent Latin, the content of which must have been somewhat unusual, for the elector and John attended some of his lectures, which, no doubt, were delivered in the Castle Church, for the princes were in the back, hidden from the view of the students. The two Lords were so pleased with Scheurl's fine performance that they ordered them printed.[297]

While at Wittenberg, Christopher Scheurl introduced several innovations in the institution, until then unknown in German universities. The first was the *Rotulus of 1507*, a kind of small academic catalogue listing Wittenberg's staff and the courses which were being offered. A second innovation was the *Liber Decanorum Juris*, a dean's book, recording promotions of doctorates in jurisprudence. A third accomplishment was his drafting the *Statutes of 1508*, which the elector gave, covering first the institution as a whole, and then, the individual graduate schools and liberal arts. In his courses he lectured on the *Corpus*

Liber Sixtus, and its relationship to the *Corpus Juris canonici*, which course he appears to have rotated with a course in *Lehnrecht;* in the Liberal Arts College he also lectured on *Suetonius Transquillus.*[298]

But Scheurl appears to have been unhappy at Wittenberg. To this Bologna graduate, Wittenberg must have seemed quite primitive, with but a population of about 2100 natives. In comparison to the old Kaisertown of Nürnberg, he was not impressed with Wittenberg's environment.[299] The elector even tried to get him properly married, but Scheurl turned that offer down.[300] Scheurl never had any intention of spending the rest of his life in Wittenberg; thus when he was offered an excellent position as chief *Jurisconsult* in his hometown in 1512, he accepted it and continued in it for the remainder of his life.[301]

There was a third type of professor at Wittenberg, who, though not a humanistically minded professional, was friendly toward the humanists and thus favored their view in regard to modern texts in the different disciplines, less hair-splitting dialectics, and better Latin texts in the philosophical faculty. Into this category fall such men as Dr. Johann von Staupitz, Dr. Polich von Mellerstadt, Jodocus Trutfetter, Justus Jonas, and a number of lesser known faculty members. These types of professors did not further humanism with the same enthusiasm as Marschalk, Petrus of Ravenna, and Hermann von Busche, but by welcoming the proposed changes which the faculty wanted to make, they served as a force toward the final triumph of biblical humanism under Martin Luther in the subsequent period of the University of Wittenberg.[302]

Thus we see the original Wittenberg University was a typical medieval university, as it was founded by Frederick the Wise in 1502 with a strong scholastic orientation. All the degree requirements were built around this approach in the philosophical preparatory training for the baccalaureate and masters degrees. This continued in the graduate school of theology, where Aristotle also reigned supreme, whether interpreted by the *Via Moderna* or the *Via Antiqua.* However since its founding was late among German Universities, humanism had already made its inroads at Heidelberg, Tübingen, Leipzig, and Erfurt during the middle of the fifteenth century. This trend did not leave Wittenberg untouched, as it had Heidelberg and other schools. Frederick the Wise also loved poetry and saw to it that in liberal arts it was represented, which term really meant the *Studia humanitatis*, as it was a term taken over by Christopher Scheurl from the Tübingen Statutes when he drafted the new *Statutes of 1508* for the elector.

In this chapter we have traced the origin of the Italian Renaissance in its humanistic unfolding in Italy and later in the German universities. We have portrayed the unfolding of the *Studia humanitatis* under Peter Luder and Stephan Hoest, and its penetration of the scholastic stronghold of Aristotle and its continuance under Agricola and Konrad Celtis, and then its spread to Leipzig, Erfurt, and finally to Wittenberg. After that we treated the roles of various types of humanistic professors, and by the good will and support of lawyers and even some theologians we saw how humanism invaded the very fortress of Aristotelianism by the insistence on better textbooks in their scholastic lectures, more modern works in logic. We saw how this emphasized the need for better *Lehrbücher* to eliminate past false reasoning about scholasticism of the Middle Ages. One of the problems, as was shown, was the barbarous Latin that many scholastics used by holding onto the *Doctrinale* of Alexander of Villedieu, or *Gallus*, while humanistically inclined members wanted to supplant it by Sulpius Verulanus of Perugia, published in 1504. However, the Donatus remained for lower levels and was used side by side with the new grammar.

We also noted that Greek and even Hebrew was introduced by Nicholaus Marschalk and continued by his students of the next generation. Men like Hermann von Busche and Petrus of Ravenna showed the scholastics on the faculty how quotations from the classics could well be used in legal documents, addresses not to just embellish the textual material but as arguments to support their claims. Thus Bodenstein von Carlstadt began to embellish his scholastic texts with quotations to add color and display his knowledge of a little Greek and even more limited Hebrew, which some claim he took directly from the materials in the Aldus publications in Venice. We also saw how after Nicholaus Marschalk's departure, Georg Sbrulius became the center of the poetic humanistic circle, as they were on a friendly relationship with the elector.

There was also a new trend toward biblical humanism, which must have paved the way for Luther's development as the reformer. Even though Marschalk was gone, the instruction of Greek and Hebrew appears to have been continued. Hermann Trebelius, a Thuringian like Nicholaus Marschalk, continued where his teacher had left off. He prepared some Greek *Lesestücke*, a Greek primer, which gave students practice in the reading of excerpts from the classics and the Fathers, which prepared them for biblical humanism. Following Trebelius, Thiloninus Philymnus taught both Greek and Hebrew, giving his students a Greek *Isagoge*, which really continued what Trebelius had started in his Greek primer. It is believed that it was he who gave Luther his first instruction in Hebrew. But this contact with Luther appears to have been similar to that with other professors of the university who joined him in his biblical humanism reforms. Where Philymnus was aggressive against scholasticism and in his use of somewhat doubtful frivolity, he now had a change of heart. In fact, by 1516 he came out with a pious work which he named the *Triumphus Christi*, in which he attacked the relic gathering of the elector and pious Catholics, claiming the true relics of the Christian church were the Holy Scriptures. After that he became one of the members of Luther's team which introduced biblical humanism in Wittenberg and dethroned Aristotle, whose *Ethics* Luther had called the worst enemy of grace. Finally we must stress that it was John Lang, who taught Greek at the university and taught Luther his first Greek, who was without doubt one of the close friends and able pioneers in introducing Greek at the university on the Elbe. In a later chapter, the introduction of biblical humanism and its relationship to the German Reformation will be treated in detail.

20

The University's Endowment
and Finances

❖

Usually there is a close correlation between the financial endowment and sources of income and the standard of excellence of an institution of higher learning. In the previous chapters there have been references to this aspect of the university founded by the Elector Frederick the Wise. We have observed how Pope Julius II, in a detailed papal pronouncement, incorporated the institution with the fiscal resources of the endowed *Stift* of the Castle Church. He made some of its funds available to finance the school, insofar as it was possible in 1507.[1] But there has been no detailed analysis as to what degree the financial needs of Wittenberg were met from that and other private sources of the Saxon court. Here a more detailed explanation is provided of how the school was financed in the beginning, as well as later throughout the Reformation period. As will be observed, there were really three periods of incorporation by Frederick III and the subsequent electors, John and John Frederick, in 1507, 1526, and in 1536. As will become evident, the formation of an accurate picture of fiscal expenditures in terms of the Gulden and its present buying power, is a rather involved procedure, when evaluated against our present changing economy.[2] An attempt was made by the author in 1950, in terms of money values then, but that evaluation had to be completely recalculated for this study in order to arrive at an accurate contemporary evaluation of the purchasing value of the German Gulden or Florin.[3]

MONETARY VALUES OF THE PERIOD

In discussing sixteenth-century monetary values one encounters a wide range of differences as to how much money was worth in terms of salaries, properties, and the price of goods.[4] An attempt was made by Preserved Smith in a chapter entitled "Wealth and Prices" in his *The Age of the Reformation*.[5] He pointed out that the total wealth of Europe had increased 128 times between 1514 and 1914. Then he continued with this observation:

> It is impossible to say which is the harder task, to compare the total wealth of the world at two given periods, or to compare the value of money at different times. Even the mechanical difficulties in the comparison of prices are enormous. When we read that wheat at Wittenberg sold at one gulden a scheffel, it is necessary to determine in the first place how much a gulden and how much a scheffel represented in terms of dollars and bushels. When we discover that there were a half dozen different gulden, and half a dozen separate measures known as scheffels, varying from province to province and from time to time, and varying widely, it is evident that great caution is necessary in ascertaining exactly which gulden and exactly which scheffel is meant.[6]

But it is of little value to point out that the buying power of a Gulden in Luther's day is impossible to calculate with great accuracy and to everyone's satisfaction. Smith realized this, for after the above warning, and the presentation of many relative prices of that day, he ventured to conclude that some standard must be established. Smith decided to compare the date 1563 with that of one four centuries later, in 1913. Based on a variety of estimates, he concluded:

> If a comparison of the value of money is made, the final impression one gets is that an ounce of gold was in 1563, let us say, expected to do about ten times as much work as the same weight of precious metal in 1913.[7]

Now if one uses the buying power arrived at above in comparison to 1913, and then establishes some fair estimate of the Gulden's higher worth in relationship to the dollar today, one is better able to understand the institution's monetary transactions and future endowments. When one compares the buying power of the dollar in 1940 with its inflated value today, it becomes quite evident that there is a need for a complete reevaluation of the buying power of the Rhenish *Goldgulden* in relationship to prices today. For example, the annual salary of a full professor in American universities in 1940, like at Northwestern University, was $5,500. One could build a seven-room house in the Middle West for less than ten thousand dollars.[8] Luther, in his tax returns, as will be observed, evaluated his livestock in relationship to Gulden at an unbelievably low rate. A cow in those days was worth but three Gulden, while a full-grown pig was valued at one Gulden. Today the starting salary of a teacher with a bachelor's degree is $14,000, which is below the income of less well-educated blue collar workers. Inflation since 1940 has reduced the buying power of today's dollar by at least ten percent. Such inflationary values make it safe to assume that the 1913 buying power of the dollar was at least ten percent more than it was in 1940. This means that a recalculation of the buying power of sixteenth century Rhenish Gold Gulden requires an increase of at least twenty percent over its value in 1913 dollars.

Next one must determine what type of Gulden was used by the University. Preserved Smith spoke of a half-dozen kinds of Gulden in use throughout the German lands. Fortunately, Professor Johannes Friedensburg, in his preparation of the *Urkundenbuch I*, faced this very problem when he recorded Christopher Scheurl's *Rotulus of 1507*, listing the professors on a roll. He began with praise of conditions at the institution on the Elbe, and he added that a student could attend Wittenberg for a year at a living expense of eight Gulden.[9] Friedensburg became much interested in what value should be given to the gold content of the Gulden used to finance the University of Wittenberg. The present author was privileged, in his early days while studying in Germany, to visit Magdeburg in 1936, and to discuss conditions at the University with Friedensburg, including the value of the Rhenish Gold Gulden mentioned in the Scheurl observation cited above. He claimed that the Rhenish Gold Gulden was the standard Gulden used in Germany at the time.[10] The Gulden used was divided into 21 Groschen, and had a gold content of $1.34 in sixteenth century values. According to Smith, its buying power increased ten times by 1913, making its value in the early twentieth century $13.40. This meant that in the sixteenth century the Groschen was worth a little more than six cents, but in 1913 had about 64 cents in buying power.

When one turns to the later years of our own century, the buying power of the dollar has declined tremendously. Yet there would be a wide disagreement among modern economists and statisticians as to its exact value, due to its constant fluctuation. But we have to set some present value for the Gulden of Luther's day. It would be quite conservative I believe, to use a $75.00 value in our calculations in this chapter. By today's standards even a full professor's salary would then have been only 300 Gulden, which would make an annual salary of $22,500.[11] The reader may be familiar with the fact that in the 1940's the author calculated the Gulden at a very different rate of buying power.[12] Today an entirely new value needs to be calculated for the Gulden.

THE ENDOWMENT OF THE CASTLE CHURCH

The history of the Wittenberg *Stift*, the endowment of the Castle Church of All-Saints, dates far back into the Ascanier days of the dukes of Saxony. In fact, a castle and church must have stood there almost from the time of the founding of the New Saxony by Bernhard.[13] Fortunately, the German scholar Israel gathered the source data from the days of Duke Rudolf I, who for several reasons was not satisfied with the original castle and its church, and built a new castle with its All Saints Church.[14] The foundation date appears to have been April 18, 1343. They also appear to have dismantled the original *Schlosskapelle*, in which, as far back as September 10, 1342, 14 days of indulgences were available on certain holy and festival days from the bishop of the diocese of Brandenbrug.[15] When Duke Rudolf I founded the new All Saints Church, they offered mass, where humble and pious Christians believed they could trust in the grace of God and the intercessions of St. Peter and St. Paul. By April 18, 1348, came an extension of indulgences, when the Archbishop Baldwin of Trier, a bishop of the Holy Roman Empire, had sent Rudolf I some relics, which started the Ascanier relic gathering that resulted in the Wittenberg indulgence trade of Luther's day.[16]

When the new Castle Church was erected by Frederick the Wise, in 1490–1509, replacing the earlier one built by Rudolf I, the All Saints veneration of relics was already in full swing, for which the elector had the Wittenberg artist, Cranach, prepare an ornate guide. This book illustrated the different relics with their beautiful casements, giving the locations while on display each November 1, in the All Saints Church. The guide listed the number of days of indulgences that were available to pious worshipers.[17]

According to the earlier records, Cranach related how Duke Rudolf I of Saxony had valiantly fought in the French wars and so displayed his knightly valor that King Philip VI of France was extremely grateful; as an expression of gratitude, he sent Duke Rudolf the sacred relic of a "thorn" of Christ, which had wounded the sacred head of the Savior.[18] For the veneration of this relic the Elector Rudolf had his craftsmen prepare a casement with the golden image of a king, as demonstrated in the Cranach *Heiligsthumbuch* of All Saints Church relics.[19] Cranach added that Duke Rudolf erected a new Castle Church in honor of his Polish wife, Künigunde, dedicated to the Virgin Mary and in honor of All Saints.[20] What this second chapel, which stood there until 1490, looked like is no longer known.

After that the guide gives the history of the Wittenberg *Stift*, which grew into a well-endowed institution. On March 9, 1345, Bishop Ludwig, then presiding over the diocese of Brandenburg, including the Wittenberg region, widened the indulgences available from masses at the All Saints Church. Duke Rudolf I had asked Pope Clement VI for the right to honor the sacred relic around which the Castle Church had been erected. The pope in turn established the *Stift* as an endowed institution under a probst, and the pontiff granted him the further right to enlarge his staff for future religious services.[21] What happened meanwhile in Rome is no longer known, but something very unusual must have happened, for Pope Clement VI, in a proclamation of May 6, 1346, had placed the Wittenberg *Stift* directly under Rome, with its probst, its dean, and all of its endowed lands directly under the jurisdiction of the Holy See. This proclamation must have raised some questions about any future challenges. Thus he, as the Holy Father, removed the Wittenberg *Stift* from the possibility of being placed under an *Interdict*, and placed it beyond the authority of future papal legates to interfere with its indulgences.[22] After that, the bishop of Bamberg granted 40 days of indulgences to the *Stift*, thus offering also the approval of the bishop.[23]

Under the reign of Rudolf I, on February 24, 1353, the *Stift's* indulgences were extended to its staff for conducting masses for the dead, on behalf of members of the Ascanier family who had died or who would die in the future. Staff members were to say mass for Rudolf's wife Künigunde. *Gottesdienst*, or divine worship, was to be conducted in the chapel on religious holidays such as Christmas, Epiphany, Easter, Ascension Day, Pentecost, and the Virgin Mary days. On such holidays the *Stift* staff were to conduct mass for the dead of the Ducal family, in the presence of relics displayed on the altar during the service. In this document the sources of the *Stift* incomes were also cited.[24] Visitors' gifts were to be distributed from time to time. Half of the gift was to pass into the treasury of the *Stift*, to be used also for the maintenance of the altars; while the other half was distributed among the seven chaplains and the *Kuster*. Families also made land-grants, specific payments for masses of other dead, to preserve their *Seelenheil* while in purgatory.[25] Thus the *Stift* of All Saints Church under Duke Rudolf I was well established, with a sizable staff-receiving regular incomes.

When Rudolf II died in 1361, the new elector of the *Kurkreis,* which the *Golden Bull of 1356* had established, became the successor who, as future member of the Electoral College of the Holy Roman Empire, and also the *Erz-marschall* of the Reich and *Reichsvikar* in northern Germany during an *Inter-regnum,* continued the *Stift.* This elevation must have had quite an impact within the German nobility and the princes of the Reich. The elector's successor, Elector Rudolf II, began his reign by further strengthening the *Stift* of the All Saints Church at Wittenberg. In several of his early documents he emphasized how his father had founded the new Castle Church as part of the castle structure. In his first transaction he mentions how his father had supplied the church with funds, relics, treasures, properties, and incomes. He did, however, reserve the right to protect the chapel from harm by law.[26]

It would be too repetitious to relate the individual transactions of Rudolf II to strengthen the endowment of the *Allerheiligen Stift* at Wittenberg; suffice it to enumerate that by the end of the reign of Rudolf II, the Castle Church was endowed with incomes from 18 villages, 2 woods, and 3 priorities, while under his successor Wenceslaus, 18 more villages were added.[27] There are, however, some features of interest to be mentioned.

Under the reign of Wenceslaus, on March 12, 1375, that elector dedicated a new altar in honor of the martyr Wenceslaus, at which indulgences were to be offered for the *Seelenheil,* the soul's well-being in purgatory, of his parents and their descendants. Five *Dörfer* became the donors for the many masses to be read for this.[28] He also had the *Patronatsrecht*, the right to nominate a successor in case of a vacancy, over the *Pfarrkirche* St. Marien in Wittenberg, which brought the Castle Church and the Town Church rather close in some of their services. On July 13, 1379, Wenceslaus was given the right to sing the *Salve Regina* every Wednesday, and those who participated in the antiphony were given 100 days of indulgences.[29] No significant changes occurred under the last Ascanier, Duke Rudolf III, except that he merely continued to stress the *Seelen-heil* of his forefathers and a continuance of the masses for the dead on the Wenceslaus altar three times a year. Rudolf III's reign ended tragically in a tower crash in 1422.[30]

The tragic tower crash resulted in the death of the entire family of Rudolf III at Schweinitz in 1419, leaving only one survivor, a distant relative, Albert III. He also met an unfortunate death in a castle fire, while hunting at Lochau in 1422, thus ending the Ascanier line.[31] The Ascanier were succeeded, in 1425, by Frederick the Valiant of the Wettiner line of rulers. Nothing of real significance happened in regard to the *Stift* of the All Saints Church until the reign of Frederick the Wise, who in 1507 incorporated it with the University of Wittenberg, to serve as the main endowment source for the institution. The details of this will follow in a later part. Before entering upon that aspect of the role of the *Stift* of the Castle Church—Frederick's interest in creating religious masses and all types of services for the soul's welfare of his parents and their descendants[32] —some background is useful to the reader.

When Frederick the Wise founded the University of Wittenberg in 1502, the *Stift* of the All Saints Church was already a well-endowed institution with at least 30 villages as its sources of income, to which he added seven more parishes. These paid in Gulden, or in kind, with wheat, oats, barley, firewood, or vegetables. Many of the payments were made and then were converted into coinage at the weekly markets in their villages, and also at the marketplace in Wittenberg. Frederick the Wise must have had in mind earlier to convert funds from the Wittenberg *Stift* to help finance the school he was establishing; otherwise all of the funds would have had to have been paid out of his own pocket. In the formative years a number of faculty members were financed by *Stift* funds, including the prior, dean, and lesser staff of the *Stift*. But the main burden was borne by the elector's court. The incorporation of the *Stift* with the school occurred in 1507, when Pope Julius II united the Castle Church and the University of Wittenberg through a joint endowment.[33]

Prior to the incorporation of the All Saints Church with the university, the elector set up a whole new series of masses, religious services, and processions to be carried out by the probst, dean, and the clergymen of the Wittenberg *Stift*. This was drafted in Koburg on November 11, 1506, and stipulated in detail the services to be conducted throughout the church year, specifying before what altars they were to be carried out. Although such services for the dead were customary for many decades, as they observed, these appear to have been dedicated to the *Seelenheil* of the elector's parents and their descendants. The *Stiftung* called for services in honor of the Mother of God and to St. Anne on dedicated altars.[34] Such festival services were to be preceded by processions and followed by worship of relics displayed on her altar. Daily singing and reading of mass was to take place before the altar in the All Saints Church located behind the window on the west side in which Serotes' three priests and the organist were to participate, while four choir boys appointed by the probst or the dean of the *Stift* sang during mass. Special early masses, known as *Frühmessen*, were also to be conducted. The *Stift* was to conduct special services during Advent and Christmas, and special masses were to be held in honor of the Virgin during Lent, and from Easter until Trinity Sunday.[35]

The memory of St. Anne was also not forgotten by the elector in his arrangements for special religious processions in her honor. On the days of her ascension, there was to be a holy procession and worship before her altar. Holy relics were to adorn it during this festival. On Monday prior to the ascension of the Virgin, there was to be another procession to the altar of St. Anne, in which a priest brought her relics to her altar, while the choir boys sang and organ music

also accompanied the sacred act. After the services there was to be a reces-
sional, accompanied by antiphonal singing by the large choir of the *Stift*. Other
masses were to be read in honor of Mary, on the day of the *Annunciation* of the
incarnation of Christ by Gabriel, and again on the date of the birth of Jesus, on
Thursday and again on Friday in the Virgin's honor, because of Mary's compas-
sion for human beings.[36]

When the reader examines the detailed instructions of the many masses and
services, one realizes that this involved many clergymen and tremendous
expenses. During one period in the Middle Ages the *Stift* had been so well-
manned that 81 clergymen served as the staff. Even though some new services
were established by the elector, when they were contemplating uniting the *Stift*
with the newly founded university, the existing ones were continued and
required additional staff.

The elector realized that such a series of vigils and religious services in honor
of the Virgin Mary and St. Anne and in behalf of his deceased relatives, as well
as future generations of the families of Ernestine Saxony, would be very costly.
For the estimated sum due the *Stift*, Frederick dedicated the amount of 203
Rhenish Gulden, with a worth of $15,225 in today's money. In addition the *Stift*
was to receive 80 Scheffels of wheat for flour, while another source was to supply them with 76 Scheffels. In addition the *Stift* was to receive an ample supply
of wine.[37]

As in the case of the previous endowments of the Wittenberg *Stift* in the days
of the Ascanier, Frederick did not personally pay these sums out of the court
treasury. To meet this need, a series of Dörfer were obligated to raise this sum
of 203 Rhenish Gulden, either in money or in kind. In the source the first Dorf
cited was that of Axien, which had to pay 95 Gulden, about $7,125; but this
amount could be reduced, if certain services were rendered, to $4,775.[38] A sec-
ond Dorf, Pannigkau, was to pay 49 Gulden, or about $3,675, plus 21 Sheffels of
oats, 4 geese, and ¼ Mohn wine. A third Dorf, Dabrun, paid 21 Gulden and 9
Groschen, or about $1,575. The fifth Dorf, Pratau, annually paid 15 Gulden, or
about $1,125.[39] Furthermore, the electoral court likewise designated how the
funds were to be distributed among the *Stift's* staff after their service. The
procurator was to pay the chaplains involved in the many services throughout
the year, 25 Gulden each, or about $1,575; but they were also to receive 21
Sheffels of oats, 4 geese, and a ¼ Mohn wine. The organist was to be paid 10
Gulden, or $750, and free board; if he preferred cash his total salary would
increase to the same amount paid to the chaplain. Other members of the staff
were to be paid in a lump sum of 34 Gulden and 10 Groschen, or about $2,585,
which was to be divided between them. In addition the choir boys were to
receive 11 Gulden and 9 Groschen for singing at 60 masses (about $850 to be
divided among them.)[40]

At the end of the elector's directive for new services to be rendered to the
deceased Saxon families, he also provided wax candles costing 24 Gulden, or
about $1,800. The document also speaks of 8 Gulden for herring, 2 Gulden for
cheese, and 80 Scheffels of wheat. Thus all expenditures of the *Stift*, in connec-

tion with the newly assigned services of the All Saints Church clergy, were fully established. Now we must turn to the incorporation of the All Saints Church *Stift* itself with Wittenberg University, which made it the future institutional chapel for all its academic and festive services.

INCORPORATION OF THE *STIFT* AND UNIVERSITY

The Saxon court must have realized, even prior to the founding of the university, that it would require some kind of permanent financial endowment. But this appears not to have been made a matter of record. How early there were contacts with Pope Julius II, the pontiff in Rome, is not known. The pope must have received detailed instructions about the incomes of the Castle Church and what further funds could be made available by a papal bull. Grohmann in his *Annalen* offers us a good summary of what the elector faced:

> There can be no doubt that the funding of the University from its founding until 1507, came directly out of the treasury of the Elector Frederick III, for there existed not yet the necessary foundations from which the school could receive those incomes and payments. These sources of income did not exist until there was a permanent foundation in 1507, when the Stift of the Castle Church was incorporated with all its rich resources and villages with the University. In case one wishes to know how significant this gift was, or how the later flourishing of the school was dependent upon this incorporation, one has to be familiar with the past history of the Stift and how rich its resources really were that now passed into the hands of the University.[41]

Naturally the modern student of this period is interested in what the incomes of the Wittenberg *Stift* were, with its 30 Dörfer, lands, woods, and other sources of income. Here Grohmann again offers his readers some insight into the worth of the *Stift's* incomes from 1507 to 1536.[42] Recognizing the buying power of the Gulden at $75.00 dollars today and the *Stift's* income totaling 2,561 Gulden or $192,075, one must recognize that the *Stift's* income, before the incorporation, was already huge. This sum the elector increased, with 500 Gulden from several cloisters, and by obligation Thuringia was to pay 700 additional Gulden and his Meissen lands 700 Gulden, which equaled a total of 3,795 Gulden as future *Stift* income, or $214,625. However, not all this income could immediately be directed toward the university, as the *Stift* had its expenses of masses read and the needs of the Castle Church.[43]

As observed previously, the *Stift* of the Castle Church had been placed under the pontiff of Rome, so it was natural that Frederick as the ruler of the *Kurkreis* would appeal directly to Pope Julius II for the incorporation. Thus earlier the pontiff had been kept fully informed about the founding of the University of Wittenberg by the elector in 1502 and the subsequent legal confirmations by Roman legates prior to 1507, so he was fully aware of Frederick the Wise's needs about the endowment of his new institution. As is evident in the document, he was fully informed of the number of church vacancies existing in the dioceses of Magdeburg, Meiszen, Mainz, and Würzburg, as well as the *Probsteien* falling under the patronage of the elector of Saxony.[44] These *Probsteien* are enumerated in the document, being those of Kemberg, Klöden, Scheiben, and the *Pfarrkirche* at Orlamünde, and the vacancies that existed in Eisfeld, Schalcken, Schmiedeberg, Liebenwerde, Weide, Jessen, and the *Friedhofkapelle* of St. Marien in Wittenberg, which could augment the *Stift's* annual income.[45]

Pope Julius II's bull of 1507, incorporating the *Stift* of the Castle Church with the university, begins with the stipulation that the former Wittenberg *Probstei*, as it had existed in the past, was now to be reorganized and converted into a *Dekanat*, which would from now on be obligated to render religious services in the capital city of Electoral Saxony. This placed other churches under its care, which meant that the probst or prior of the Castle Church would also have a dean under him, who would be responsible for the religious services in Wittenberg. In place of the old, a new *Probstei* was to be established, combined with the *Probstei* in Kemberg, with the one in Kemberg paying 60 Gulden annually into its treasury; while the church in Orlamünde, being part of the *Archdiakonat* there, was to become part of the Castle Church *Stift*, obligated to pay 40 Gulden; a third, in Eisfeld, combined with the *Kantorie* there, was to pass under the new *Probstei*, paying 45 Gulden out of its annual income; a fourth church in Kloden, combined with the *Kustodie* there, was to contribute its 28 Gulden to the *Stift* of Wittenberg; a fifth church in Schlieben, a part of the *Scholastrie* in the village, was combined with the *Stift* of the Castle Church, offering its annual dues of 21 Gulden; and finally, the church in Schmiedeberg, combined with the *Syndikat*, was to pay annually 12 Gulden. All these places were new creations of the pope to serve the *Stift* and the university with additional incomes.[46] The little *Friedhofskapelle* next to St. Marien Church was also to come under the *Stift*.

The papal incorporation made provisions for the following principal officialdom of the new *Dekanat*:

> Probst
> Dekan
> Archdekan
> Cantor
> Custodian
> Scholasticus
> Syndic[47]

The *Bull of 1507* also specified the roles that were to be assigned to members of the new Dekanat staff. Their roles within the organization and that of the academic life of the institution were specified by the pontiff: They were (1) to participate in the election of new canons of the *Stift*; (2) to take part in the election of rectors of the university; (3) to be advanced academically to a master in theology, both regular and secular; (4) its members, with proper degrees, could teach in the university as doctors of law and medicine; (5) its members could also could serve as deans of the arts faculty; (6) serving in pairs, they could also engage in disputations.[48]

The papal *Bull of 1507* also stipulated the roles the staff of the new *Dekanat* were to play in the academic life of the university. It begins with the duties of the probst, stating he was to have a regular academic professorship in the institution and was to be a distinguished scholar, while the dekan was to preach on specified days. The *Scholaster* was to deliver lectures on the Sixth Book of the *Decretals*, or at other times, the Clementine *Decretals* in canon law. The *Syndicus* had to be a doctor of civil law, so he could give courses on the *Institutes* of the *Code of Justinian*. The archdeacon was to preach in the Castle Church on holidays, and three times a week he was to deliver theological lectures in the university, while the *Kantor* was to preach in the Town Church on holidays and also deliver theological lectures in the school. The *Kustus* was to participate in disputations with the masters of theology on Fridays, on theses from Holy Writ. The five *Präbeden*, who were from other places of the land, needed to possess a degree of bachelor of theology, the first of which had to supervise the disputations of students in the arts faculty, while the other four were to give lectures in philosophy in arts, which was to be determined by the elector. The selection of the above staff of the *Stift* would be made by the elector of Saxony; but once chosen, they were to be installed by the chancellor of the university.[49]

In the Middle Ages, academic rank was regarded as extremely important in the universities. This applied both to faculty rank and place in academic processions, and then where they were seated upon arrival in the Castle Church at Wittenberg. Thus the rector marched right behind his two beadles, bearing the symbols of the institution, while immediately behind him came the university chancellor, followed by the probst and then the Dekan of the Castle Church, followed by the respective deans of the faculties. These again were ranked in the order of theology, law, medicine, and liberal arts. Behind the faculty came the student body, also in the same prescribed order. In the bull these practices are again specified by the ranking of faculties and their officialdom, to be observed also by the university. The document also specified by what method vicars over the *Pfarrkirche* were to be chosen, and their roles. In the evaluation of the expenses that Frederick would be obligated to pay, the pope placed it at 2,000 Ducats.[50] Since a Ducat had a gold content of $2.00, the buying power of a Ducat in 1985 would be at least $125, which would make the amount due for the electoral treasury at least $250,000.[51]

The document continues with details of incorporation which are hardly germane to the significance of incorporation. Even Israel in his summary of the papal bull did not cover these.[52] Suffice it to point out that the papal bull of 1507 made the university and the *Stift* a corporate unit, so now the institution was placed on a solid foundation, which, as we shall see in the subsequent period, became ever more important in the days of John the Constant's reign, from 1525 to 1532, and his son John Frederick, from 1532 to 1547. Grohmann summarized the arrangement established by the elector, through a papal bull, as follows:

The incomes of the Stift of All Saints Church equaled, as one observes in the foundation of the Elector John Frederick in 1536, at this time 2561 Gulden and one Groschen. Thus all income came in the form of money and grains, chickens, also from geese, wood and other forms of income, they being, inherited or salable, as up to now it was in our Castle Church Stift, and calculated in terms of money amounted to an annual sum of 2561 Gulden and 1 Groschen, which was assigned to us and was incorporated thus, and was to remain without exception.[53]

Grohmann adds that one has to remember that this was but the basic income of the *Stift*, and that not all the sums were available to the members of the staff of the new university foundation, after Frederick had the *Stift* incorporated with the school. He adds that at the time they had a number of vicars, chaplains, and canons who were financed by outside revenues. When you consider this additional money, which later became available to the institution, it totaled 3,795 Gulden, or in modern money, about $284,725, which source remained until 1536.[54] Not even this sum was adequate for the later university budget, as we saw above, and the elector increased it by gifts from the other cloisters of his lands by having those of Thuringia pay 700, Meiszen 700, and Saxony 500 Gulden, which rounded out the picture.[55] But the elector appears also to have made certain that the original incomes, fixed in the *Bull of 1507*, would remain permanent for subsequent administrations, under his Ernestine Saxony descendants, and when conditions changed as staff died, less money was needed for their upkeep, for it increased the endowment. The record states it this way:

But when according to the will of God, the members of the endowed Castle Church die off and through that the additional needed sums of 610 Florins (or Gulden) and 6 Groschen become decreased and would pass on to the University; we therefore, want the sums from Thuringia and Mieszen cloisters, which now serve as part of the endowment, to be deducted and decreased. Should it happen that between us and our brother, during our lifetime, or after us, or between the heirs of both of us, there should be changes made within our lands, there, we wish it to be ordered and established, that those our heirs, who would obtain the control of the Electorate of Saxon (the *Kurkreis*), then would take over the entire income of the *Stift*, in the sum of 3795 Gulden, and that their descendants, as Electors of Saxony, would take over the entire obligation.[56]

The elector observed that, if the University of Wittenberg were to fall under the dominance of Albertine Saxony, the same endowments should continue, remaining 3,795 Gulden like the Wittenberg endowment, and that the obligations would then be assumed by the other house. It almost looks like Frederick III foresaw, in 1507, the *Schmalkaldic* war of 1547, for during that war Emperor Charles V, with his Saxon ally, defeated the Elector John Frederick in the battle of Mühlberg and the electorate was transferred to his cousin, Duke Moritz of Albertine Saxony, after which the university went over to the Albertine line and the finances became part of its problem.

Grohmann pointed out that in 1548, under the reign of Moritz of Albertine Saxony, the new surplus of the *Stift* was 2,740 Gulden and 9½ Groschen. Meanwhile a number of the *Stift* staff had passed away, and they no longer lived from the basic endowment. He also experienced that the Schmalkaldic War (1547–1555) had terminated some of the monastic sources of income, which required changes to compensate for the differences in the funds needed by the University of Wittenberg by the papal degree.[57]

In 1555 the new Elector August, the brother of Moritz, reconfirmed the endowment of the university. He made the 600 Gulden, added by Moritz to replace monastic losses, into a permanent source of income for the *Stift* of the Castle Church. The required sum was now to be paid by the cloister of Brehna, making the new total endowment 4,140 Gulden and 9½ Groschen, or about $309,855. However, this generous elector tried to increase the endowment, perhaps because of the rise in expenses, by 1569 to 5,054 Gulden, 14 Groschen and 7 Pfennige, which made a total endowment of about $378,800.[58] Thus if we designate Frederick the Wise as the far-sighted founder of the University of Wittenberg, the Elector August deserves to be called the *excellent conservator* of the institution, both in respect to finances and in many other respects, as will be observed in other connections.[59]

Not only was the Elector August generous in offering the increased endowment of the *Stift's* income, the elector was also very generous in thinking of the welfare of poor students, in which respect he went so far as to build them a special dwelling place. He placed upon the *Stift* in Meiszen the obligation of adding 1,020 Gulden to the school's income, which was to increase the salaries of its professors.[60] Here again Grohmann has offered us a better insight into this, when he wrote:

> Besides the actual money paid as foundation income of the University: (a) there was to be received 804 Scheffels of rye for the poor and the rest added to the economy: (b) 2000 Scheffels of rye to strengthen the economy, 'only for the support of poor students' so they will not be obligated to pay out more than 4 Groschen table expense per week; (c) 7 Scheffels of wheat from the Dorf Swiesigk and Bietegast; (d) 803 Scheffels of good quality oats; (e) 28 1/2 Scheffels of raw type oats; (f) 80 Scheffels of large or small barley: (g) also a large number of, for example, chickens, geese, Evern etc., which if described would exceed our bounds, which is not to include the smallest of items. (h) Besides the University received a lucrative income from fines of Dörfer in the case of inheritance settlements which are named in the Foundation.[61]

Among the school's number of privileges, the first named is that of hunting, which appears to have been important for the university, as it was no doubt both a sport and supplied game for the common table of poor students, about which we shall learn later. Grohmann feels these were important as shown by an action taken by the Elector George of Albertine Saxony in 1625, who arranged to restore rights of hunting to the school, under the condition that each of the licensed villages pay a sum of 16 good silver Groschen, without exception, which was to be paid into the game office. This appears to have involved sizable stretches where the university could hunt from the beginning to 1625:

> How extensive these lands of hunting were is evident from the repurchase of the territories in which the University had hunting rights. This stretch, as one observes from the decree of Johann Georg in 1625, included the University villages up to Euzsch, Melzwig, Reuden up the Pratawer Reisz and from the Lamsdorf, Panneck, and the fields of the Probst of Kemberg and Brauningen and other places and stretches of lands over the Elbe. Besides this Johann Georg gave the University, for the termination of hunting, the addition of the *Communitaetkorns*, which, as noted above, was considerable. This hunting right and other pasture rights the University possessed from the very beginning of its foundation. In a new foundation of the school by the Elector August in 1569, these rights were again confirmed, when he wrote: "As we confirm in all the previous articles, such as rabbit-hunting rights, fishing rights and others."[62]

Another right granted the university by the Elector Frederick III was to engage in fishing without permission. This extended up to one mile from Wittenberg, with the exception of two streams. There were a number of small streams where both the citizens and the university members could fish, with the exception of the rapidly flowing *Rische Bach* and the *Zahnischen Bach*, which Frederick the Wise had planted with hatchery trout.[63] There appears to have been some problem about the fishing rights under Elector John Frederick, concerning his Hauptmann, who no doubt was a kind of game warden. They registered a complaint with the elector, which reads as follows:

> As we also observed, who were here from the beginning of the University, that there was a certain custom, that the Burger and members of the University, were free to fish in the streams about the town for a mile or more, except in one stream, which is called the Rische Bach, as one writes the small amount seven, for it had been stocked with trout and therefore was placed off limits.[64]

The elector replied to this, implying that the same rights would continue for the town and the university, except for the *Rische Bach* and the *Zahnischen Bach*, as both were filled with Schwerlin and with *Krebse*. Thus in a decree by Elector John Frederick the same conditions were ordered to prevail as established by Elector August. In 1561 he again reconfirmed the earlier right. It appears that the university possessed fishing rights in its own villages, for this is definitely implied in the above complaint. It reads that the elector should continue to recognize the former freedoms to fish in the many streams of their villages.[65]

The university also had a privilege to trap game birds in the electoral forests, no doubt for the use of the common table for the students, for Elector August's 1561 directive to the game warden reads:

> As far as the catching of birds, we want the University and the townsmen to continue to have the right, as it has been the practice before, to trap birds in Starken, Meiszen, Zeusigken, Finken and what is involved in that, until our

descendants stop it by repurchases of the rights in our woods, and the lands of people which they used as pastures, that such practices may remain.[66]

From this it is evident that from the foundation of the university until the end of the reign of Elector August of Albertine Saxony, the rights to fish, hunt, and trap birds in the electoral lands were privileges of the institution and the townsmen.

THE INCOMES OF PROFESSORS

As stated earlier, until the incorporation of the University of Wittenberg with the *Stift* of the Castle Church by Pope Julius II in 1507, all expenses of the university staff, not connected with the *Stift* at Wittenberg or Prebends from its contributing Dörfer, had to be paid by the elector's own treasury.[67] But even after that, we possess no sources that state specifically what the academic staff was paid until the year 1516, when in a reorganization of the institution, there were some basic changes.[68]

However some documentary material, though very spotty and incomplete, offers good insight as to how the institution was financed, even though the amounts of their salaries are not given. Such payments were in many cases through monastic annual Prebends. In theology Martin Luther, during his lectures of *Lectura* in *Biblia*, appears to have been under the care of the Augustinian Hermits; Petrus Lupinus lived on a Prebend from Kloden; in Nicholas von Amsdorf's case, the sources of his living expenses are not even mentioned; the last professor in theology, Bodenstein von Carlstadt, received his support from a Prebend from Orlamünde.[69] Thus in Wittenberg's ranking school of theology, we know that its support was ecclesiastical but not in terms of Gulden as a regular salary.

In the field of civil and canon law, the probst of the *Stift* of the Castle Church, who lectured on the *Decretals*, Doctor Hennig Goede, was to be paid by a Prebend from Kemberg.[70] Another law professor, a Doctor Reuter, was to lecture for, in terms of today, an income of 1,500 dollars. At 8 A.M. in the summer and 9 A.M. in the winter, Hieronymous Schurff was to lecture on the *Code of Justinian*, for which he received the equivalent of 7,500 dollars annually. Mathäus Beckau was a third law professor giving lectures on the *Sexto*, who lived by a Prebend at Skieben.

In the afternoon, at 2 P.M., Professor Wolfgang Stähelin was to lecture on *Veteri*, with an annual income of 12,000 dollars. And finally, Doctor Christian Beyer, who had other income from the electoral court, for legal services, was to give some lectures in the new law, for which he was to receive 6,075 dollars.[71] In the field of medicine, they had a Doctor Swabe, who was paid a salary of 5,250 dollars annually.[72]

In liberal arts, Nicholas von Amsdorf lectured at 5 A.M. in the summer and 6 A.M. in the winter, but no source lists the subject matter taught, nor his livelihood, but rather states that he lectured in the *Kappelle zum Heiligen Leichnam* the Town Church. Another faculty member, Simon Heinz aus Brück, lectured on an unnamed subject, *viam Thome*, receiving an annual income of 1,500 dollars. Magister Feldkirchen, who gave lectures *viam Scoti* in Aristotle's physics, likewise had a Prebend of 1,500 dollars from the electoral treasury. During the same hour, Master Johannes Gunckele lectured on Physics *viam Thome*, receiving the equivalent salary. All these named were student instructors, obligated to teach a specified period shown in a previous chapter, as prescribed in the university *Statutes*. An unnamed master taught two courses, one at 8 A.M. in poetry and at 4 P.M. in rhetoric, for which he was paid a salary of 3,000 dollars.[73]

The record then gives coverage of several courses in canon law. Beginning at 12 noon, a licentiatus, Sebastianus, offered a course on Peter Hispanus *viam Scoti*, for which he received an income from a Prebend in Widera. At the same hour Master Staffelstern was to give a course on Peter Hispanus *viam Thome*, for which he was to be paid out of the university treasury—as his Prebend did not seem to be forthcoming— a sum of 1,500 dollars. In the afternoon, at 3 P.M., a Master Otto was to teach the students grammar and his income was an annual salary of 1,500 dollars. During this same hour, another Master Premsel from Torgau was to lecture, offering a course in Aristotle's *Metaphysics*, with the same annual salary; while early in the afternoon a master from the Augustinians was to lecture on Aristotle's *Ethics* and was paid out of cloister funds. Another master, Czorbig, was to offer a course in astronomy and rotated it with a course in mathematics, also for an annual salary of 1,500 dollars.[74]

This fragmentary account of faculty remuneration must be regarded as concluding the era of the original medieval university, prior to Wittenberg's transformation into a modern one during the German Reformation. In 1516 the *Stift* incomes of the Castle Church had not changed yet as they did in the twenties. At this early period Martin Luther was not fully developed as a biblical scholar, and the elector of Saxony was still too steeped in his boyhood medievalism to be ready to make the necessary curricula changes at Wittenberg.

THE ELECTOR JOHN INCREASES SALARIES

Between 1516 and the death of Frederick the Wise, as seen in a previous chapter,[75] the University of Wittenberg underwent many very profound changes. In time, as we saw, Frederick the Wise stopped his relic gatherings and under Luther's influence terminated the masses for the dead relatives, discontinued his relic worship, and by the time of his death in 1525, the *Stift* of All Saints Church became transformed into an endowment institution for the University of Wittenberg. Frederick was succeeded by his brother, John the Constant. By this time it seemed timely to reorganize the Wittenberg *Stift* and make it more fully the endowment source of the university. The details of this transaction belong more in the main theme of the Reformation, which is treated in a later chapter. Here it will be of interest to the reader to list Walter Friedens-burg's new salary schedule, given to the institution by the Elector John the Constant on October 11, 1525:

Martin Luther	not given
Prior Justus Jonas	not given
Town Pastor Bugenhagen	$4,500
Philip Melanchthon	$15,000
Jerome Schurff	$12,000
Christian Beyer	$7,500
Professor Apel	$5,250
Lit. Benedict Paulus	$3,000
Ulrich Bender	$2,250
Augustine Schurf	$6,000
Doctor Stackmann	$5,500
Joachim (Greek instructor Camerarius)	$4,500
Lecturer on Quintilian	$4,500
Master Vach	$3,000
Lecturer in Physics	$2,400
Aurogallus (Hebrew professor)	$4,505
Instructor in Mathematics	$3,000
Instructor in Pedagogy	$2,400
Premssel	$1,500
A Notary of the University	$1,500
The Beadles	$1,500
Doctor Eschausen	$2,400[76]

Hans von Dolzig, a member of the electoral court, wrote Georg Spalatin on October 25, 1525, that the arrangement of the university curricula had been set up in accordance with his recommendations, and the support of the Town Council, which offered the members of the institution some advance in salaries, but not much.[77] He added at the outset of his report the key professors who had participated in this settlement, namely, Martin Luther, Justus Jonas as the Probst, the town Pfarrer, Johannes Bugenhagen, and the humanist, Philip Melanchthon.

The background to this important document merits further elucidation as it was really a report on the first transformation of the funds of the endowed *Stift* of the Castle Church. Chancellor Brück observed that Pope Julius II had com-bined the *Stift* of All Saints Church with the university as a permanent endow-ment source. However, he observed that this transaction presented a number of problems that had to be resolved before the funds of the *Stift* could be entirely integrated with the university. The *Stift's* activities were rather complicated for many of its funds were dedicated to specific masses for the dead ancestors of Frederick the Wise and Duke John. Then there were also general incomes, made by Dörfer to the *Stift*, which had been made to the foundation since the time of Rudolf I of Ascania, the founder of the *Stift* in the fourteenth century. In

1507, Frederick the Wise had enlarged the funds of the *Stift* to cover more masses and religious services. Brück pointed out that such a complex system demands a large staff, managed by a Probst and Dekan, all of whom required funds as a livelihood. There was another aspect that complicated the proposed secularization of the *Stift*. Some of the *Stift's* incomes were made in Gulden, but a large part were also in kinds, which had to be sold in markets before they could be converted into salaries. This involved an additional management problem. As observed above in the early days, much of the needed money came out of the electoral treasury.

But by the middle twenties of the century, the University of Wittenberg had undergone a profound change under the leadership of Luther, Melanchthon, and the Saxon court. Meanwhile, Frederick the Wise, under the influence of his court preacher and father confessor, Georg Spalatin, as well as the reforms of Martin Luther, had become much more evangelical and was ready to support the German Reformation. He had agreed to make some basic curricula changes and go along with the evangelization of the *Pfarrkirche* by Martin Luther and the new pastor, Johannes Bugenhagen. In time, masses and relic worship had to be discontinued, as it contradicted the "Theology of the Cross" that had taken over the religious worship in the first Lutheran congregation in Wittenberg. After Luther's close friend and supporter, Justus Jonas, became the probst of the *Stift*, its conservative members in charge of the masses and religious services were fighting a lost cause.

By 1525 few of the old conservative Romanists were left. Frederick the Wise died earlier in the year, and his brother, John, who was much more evangelical and favored the Reformation openly, was ready now to move ahead with the endowment of the university. Now appeared to be the opportune time to reorganize the Wittenberg *Stift* and establish it as a regular source of endowment for the university. This makes Dolzig's report about the endowment transaction under Elector John so vital to the Reformation story. The previous salary report may be regarded as the elector's first step in the real endowment of the university on the Elbe.

THE CONDITIONS OF THE STIFT INCORPORATION

Up to October 25, 1525, the *Stift* of All Saints Church, although incorporated with the university since 1507, had remained an organization that functioned similarly to others in the Middle Ages. It offered only part of its funds and support of Prebends as a livelihood for the teaching staff, which contributed to the lessening of expenditures that fell upon the Electoral Court. In the Leucuria's second incorporation with the *Stift* under John the Constant, all funds were now to flow directly into the bursar's treasury, presided over by Treasurer Planck and his assistant, Paulus Koch, and now all the faculty of the school were to be paid by him. Thus the *Stift* had been incorporated with the university. In the new *Stift* relationship, the above amounts were to be paid by specific periods.[78]

Hans von Dolzig apparently realized, in the light of the now blossoming Reformation, the importance of this incorporation of the *Stift* on an entirely new financial basis. He closed his communication with Georg Spalatin with a *Summa Summarum*, in which he stated that this incorporation had been possible by God's grace, for which the university would offer its thanks, for the action conformed entirely with the wishes of the entire academic community. Even Martin Luther expressed his gratitude by offering his thanks for what had transpired in this settlement.[79]

As noted in the history of the closing days of the Elector Frederick the Wise,[80] in the middle twenties, the probst of the Castle Church, Justus Jonas, Pfarrer Johannes Bugenhagen of the *Stadtkirche*, the Wittenberg faculty, and also the town council, all regarded it to be blasphemous for the *Stift* of the Castle Church to continue with its *Seelenmessen*, established by the papal *Bull of 1507*, and then in the town church have people listen to a good gospel sermon, which stressed that man is saved solely by the grace of God, which pronounced masses as worthless. It is no wonder that Martin Luther rejoiced when the *Stift's* soul saving from purgatory was finally terminated.

These new salary scales, established by Elector John at the *Stift's* reincorporation with the university in 1525, continued throughout the reign of the elector until his death on August 21, 1532.[81] Two days later, his son John Frederick was made the successor as ruler of Electoral Saxony. This evangelically minded prince took a deep interest in the future of the University of Wittenberg, and decided to reorganize the entire institution by giving the seminary, law school, medical school, and liberal arts faculty new statutes.

The father, upon his death-bed, had given his son, John Frederick, a parting message about his concern for the future of the university. He observed that under the leadership of Martin Luther and Philip Melanchthon, the gospel had again blossomed in the schools, and that he wanted his son to support its cause at all costs. Accordingly, soon after that the new elector visited Wittenberg and discussed the status of the institution, at first in private with the Reformer, and later with the members of the theological faculty. Historical records do not offer all that transpired, as will be observed in a subsequent chapter, but the elector realized that the school of theology needed a complete reorganization, with an emphasis on the "New Theology" of Wittenberg that was being taught. In 1533, after the discussion between the elector and the staff, Philip Melanchthon was asked to draft new *Theological Statutes* for the university, which expressed the needs related to training candidates in theology and the type of examinations to be conducted at the various steps toward a doctorate in theology.[82]

Meanwhile the electoral court began to realize that there was a need for a complete reorganization of the university, including even an advancement in faculty salaries, which had not changed since 1525. Accordingly, the elector had his officials look into the current financial status of the school and what was needed for a proper financial and academic transformation of the institution that conformed to the education of students during the now-blossoming German Reformation. The elector then asked the faculty of the university to submit a complete report as to the current staff incomes. The reply is summarized in the following reply sent to him on April 14, 1535:

School of Theology

D. Martin Luther	$15,000
D. Justus Jonas as Probst of Castle Church's incomes	

D. Kaspar Kruciger, double income, $5,776 from lectures and from Aldenburg $2,250, totaling $8,025 and in addition 35 Scheffels of wheat.

D. Hieronimus Schurff has also a double income, $7,500 as a professor and $4,500 from the *Oberhofgericht*, the Hof Court membership, the Saxon Supreme Court, totaling $12,000.

D. Teuleben also had a double income, $7,500 for his professorship and $6,000 for his *Oberhofgericht* membership, the Saxon Supreme Court, totaling $13,500.

D. Sebalden Muenster, courses not mentioned	$6,000
D. Melchion Kling, courses not mentioned	$3,750
D. Benedictus Pauli, courses not mentioned	$3,000[83]

School of Medicine

D. Augustine Schurff	$7,500
D. Caspar Lindemann	$7,500

School of Liberal Arts

M. Philip Melanchthon as a professor	$15,000
M. Fach as professor of Poetry	$3,500
M. Aurogallus as professor of Hebrew	$4,500
D. Franciscus of Weimar, teacher of Greek	$3,000
M. Vitus Winsheim as teacher of Rhetoric	$4,500
M. Vitus Amerbach as lecturer of Physics	$4,500
M. Johannes Wolmar in Mathematics	$1,500
M. Johann Milichius in Mathematics	$3,750
L. Melchiar Fendt (Medic) in Physics instruction	$2,250
M. Ambrosius received for instruction in Grammar (offered some lectures)	$2,250[84]

After that the report lists 40 Gulden, or $3,000, paid the university notary, while the two university beadles received no more than $750 apiece. The elector also paid the *Lector mensae*, about which "common table" we shall elaborate later in this chapter in another connection.[85]

This first section in the university report about the financial status of the university, which the elector had requested, follows a list of four faculty members without a specific statement of what connection they had with the institution, whose salaries ranged from 20 to 40 Gulden. After that the report gives eight names without offering any definite data about their relationship to the university. These appear to have composed a part of the officialdom of the Castle Church. At the close, the reports adds, the *Chorales 4 und custos* received their incomes from treasurer Planck, but fails to mention an amount.

An analysis of the university's financial report, though not specifically stated, reveals that they regarded the university's situation to be far from satisfactory. Even though this is not the place to elaborate on the background for this fiscal status, some exposition of the reasons seems helpful to explain the cause of their complaints. No doubt the electoral officialdom was fully aware of why the re-founding of the university was the only solution.

There is an historic explanation of the sad status of financial affairs at Wittenberg, when the university reports upon the inquiry of the elector. The Diet of Worms in 1521 and the Kaiser's proclamation of the Edict of Worms had brought a devastating effect to the school on the Elbe. In 1520 the enrollment at Wittenberg was really high, with 552 matriculations in the University *Album*, which shows that about the same number of students enrolled from the North and South at Wittenberg. However, in the matter of one year, the enrollment had dropped to about half, because all conservative Catholic princes ordered their students to stay away from what now was regarded as a heretical center of learning.[86] When John the Constant, in 1525, reorganized the faculty salaries by its incorporation with the *Stift* of All Saints Church, the fear was that with such a small enrollment Wittenberg would go under; in fact, Martin Luther wrote his *Weckruf of 1524*[87] as an alarm signal that Germans should stress education. By 1528 to 1534 the enrollment had increased again to about 250 matriculations per year. But even that increase was hardly encouraging enough to the Elector John Frederick, and became the elector's real reason for becoming the second founder of the University of Wittenberg in 1536.[88]

If students remained at Wittenberg for five years, as some scholars believe, the annual matriculations would be about a fifth the total. Thus a decline in enrollment in the twenties in the number of students actually there at a given time might be even less than the matriculations reflect. The number in attendance also determined how many graduated. One of the faculty incomes was based on graduation fees. As they advanced, students paid fees not when they took courses but when they graduated with various degrees;[89] thus the fewer students there were, the less income in salaries. The elector remembered his father's parting admonition to look after the needs of the university, and he decided to make the following financial stipulations for the New Wittenberg after 1536, with the respective salary increases.[90]

THE SCHOOL OF THEOLOGY

This draft of payment to the University of Wittenberg was prepared, upon the request of the Elector John Frederick, by his Chancellor Gregorius Brück, on April 1, 1536. It was based on the above university report to the elector as to the status of the fiscal condition, but the place of origin was not given. Chancellor Brück's draft proposed that the following salaries be paid out of the university treasury:

Doctor Martin Luther[a]	$22,500
Philip Melanchthon[b]	$15,000
Probst Justus Jonas[c]	$8,500
Doctor Casper Cruciger[d]	$15,000
Pfarrer Johannes Bugenhagen[e]	$4,400

It is interesting that the electoral court now wanted to enlarge the theological faculty to five members. However, Chancellor Brück's breakdown of the individual professors leads to some misunderstanding, unless some additional information is advance.[91]

The School of Law

Doctor Hieronymous Schurff[a]	$18,750
Doctor Levin Emden of Magdeburg[b]	$22,500
A third position (unnamed)	$10,500
A fourth position (unnamed)	$7,500

a. Doctor Jerome Schurff was to receive 250 Gulden as a salary, divided as follows: 200 Gulden for his lectures in Civil Law and 50 addition Gulden for his services in the Oberhofgericht. Then Chancellor Brück wrote into the margin the word "cerung," which seems to imply supplementary income in kind, but not given in an amount. b. The Emden position is not quite clear, the larger sum of 300 Gulden appears to have been offered to attract him. Doctor Emden had matriculated at Wittenberg during the winter semester of 1503–1504 (Album I, 12). In a later period Emden was on the Frankfurt a.d.o. faculty and apparently did not attend. In case he turned it down, and it was to be filled by another with a lower salary of 180 Gulden. As will be shown in a later connection about the Wittenberg curriculum Luther and his fellow professors did not wish to continue the teaching of the pope's law, as they called it, which left a vacuum in the law department. Canon law as a profession had been lucrative in the Middle Ages in the Catholic Church; to drop it now meant a blow to the department. Later, in the thirties, as we shall see, there was the need for a *Landes-Kirchenrecht*, or Church Law in the Lutheran churches. Here now, as seen from Brück's draft, were three academic openings that needed to be filled.

The School of Medicine

Doctorine Augustus Schurpf[a]	$11,250
Doctor Kaspar Lindemann[b]	$7,500

a. The attendant note by Walter Friedensburg states that he was to serve as the ordinarius professor; if the aging Doctor Lindemann failed to give lectures, his income was to be added to that sum, making a total 250 Gulden.

b. Dr. Caspar Lindemann's pay was to be conditional; if he delivered medical lectures, he was to receive the full salary.

The School of Arts

In his proposal, Chancellor Brück failed to offer details as to the faculty members who filled the positions which were to receive the following annual salaries, in liberal arts:

Dialectics	$7,500
Hebrew	$7,500
Latin	$6,000
Mathematics I	$6,000
Mathematics II	$6,000
Physics	$6,000
Rhetoric I	$6,000
Rhetoric II	$6,000
Albert the Great	$6,000
Pedagogy I	$3,000
Pedagogy II	$3,000
Notary of the College	$3,750
Beadles each (2)	$1,500
Provider for Common Table	$3,000
Reader during Common Table Meals	$3,000
Famulus of the College	$4,500
Preacher of the Castle Church	$6,000
University Librarian	$3,000[93]

Now in the draft of salaries of Chancellor Brück he gives some miscellaneous entries of payments to individuals from the budget of the university. First he mentions four choir boys of the Castle Church who were paid $1,762 each, and were to be assisted by two poor students who were to receive $1,500 each. The organist in the Castle Church was to receive an annual salary of $4,800, which sum came from several sources. A cantor was to receive $525.00 for his services; but the custodian of the Castle Church was to be paid $4,885, of which $150.00 was to be used to purchase "presensbrot und semeln." The custodian of the lights and windows was given $1,500, and $9,000 was for the poor in the city.[94] The chancellor's draft of proposed university expenditures listed 3523 Gulden, 16 Groschen, and 10 Pf., which in modern calculations and by today's standards would total $264,225.[95]

After drafting the above salaries report of faculty incomes, Chancellor Brück had some afterthoughts; he added a second document by reporting what additional amounts would be accrued by the Wittenberg *Stift*, in case the expenditures were no longer made to the still living *Stift* staff, drawing annual incomes. He added that after their deaths, the money would pass into the treasury of the university.[96]

This detailed summary begins with Nicholas Amsdorf, who was paid 52 Gulden, 4 Groshen, and 5 Pfennige, but when his other incomes were added the total was 255 Gulden, or $21,200. Licentiatus Planck received a sum of $5,800. There were also five vicars in the local *Stift*, whom the university paid $8,475 in a combined sum. This is followed by a listing of incomes received from the Dörfer and endowed institutions paying dues into the *Stift*, totaling about $309,250.

In still a third draft, on April 2, 1536, Chancellor Brück also presented an *Entwurf* of future costs by conducting disputations at the university. He begins by pointing out that annual expeditures for *Disputations* and *Declamations* would amount to quite a sum. After that he broke it down as to costs of participants, and gave in detail what were its costs even in the liberal arts faculty, which would total $249,375. Besides this, he adds an "extraordinary supplement" of $25,759.[97]

As seen previously, *Disputations* and *Declamations* were regarded as vital to the education of students at the University of Wittenberg. Those who participated were thus rewarded from these as an additional source of income; faculty members were also fined in case they failed to give contributions to academic process.[98] In 1967 the author wrote a chapter entitled "Theses and Wittenberg" in *Luther for an Ecumenical Age*, from which we quote a pertinent section:

> The high value ascribed by the authorities to disputations as an educational tool is also evident in the amounts of money budgeted each year by the Saxon Court for payment of the faculty participants. As has been noted, such an undertaking required considerable effort by the professor in drafting the theses, securing their approval and a suitable date, selecting the necessary participants, posting the theses, and presiding over the debate. Senior faculty members were quite well rewarded for such labors. In the upper faculties the professor in charge was paid the equivalent of $100, the respondents $500, and bachelors playing a supporting role were given $20. As these sums were bonus amounts paid in addition to the regular salaries, the efforts would seem to have been appreciated and financially quite rewarding.[99]

Since this study will refer elsewhere to Luther's disputations, here it must suffice that he as dean often presided in disputations between 1536 and 1946, which added considerably to his income. In 1938–1939, a document from the electoral court offers us a little insight how much he was paid in one year. In this breakdown, Luther presided over 34 disputations, and later presided 20 times as dean of the theological faculty, for which the elector paid him $1,450.[100] In the law faculty a Doctor Melchior presided over 14 disputations, for which he was paid about $600; while a Dr. Sebaldus presided over 20 disputations, which gave him, in addition to his salary, about $550. In medicine, three faculty members rotated in presiding. Dr. Augustine Schurff presided over 14 disputations, for which he was paid about $540; while Melchior served as chairman over 24 disputations, for which he received around $635 in today's money. Then Dr. Curionus chaired more than 23 disputations, for which they rewarded him with about $650.[101]

In liberal arts the university had a different problem, which reduced the remunerations of the participants to a lower level than that of the three graduate schools. Some ranking professors, like Philip Melanchthon, were of course the exception, but most of the debtors were but masters of arts, without any advanced degrees. Besides, most of these disputations were conducted in the *Aula* of the New Friderici College and not in the more stately one of the Castle Church. Philip Melanchthon presided over 17 such disputations, for which he was paid but around $135, which was in addition to his rather high salary. All the rest were paid from $100 to $150 dollars for their labors.[102]

In liberal arts, professors in languages, literature, and oratory were not required to debate, but instead, they were to engage in declamations that Philip Melanchthon had instituted. Such speeches might be in Latin, Greek, and Hebrew, in which students were to become fluent. We possess the costs of Wittenberg's declamations for the academic year 1538–1539, for which the electoral court paid a sum totaling about $7,200.[103] Some of the declamations were written by advanced students and then recited from memory; others were those by classical authors, in Latin and Greek which they had memorized.[104]

PRIVILEGES OF THE UNIVERSITY

In calculating the incomes of the regular full professors of the university, or as the court listed them, *Lectures*, one must also consider the gifts and privileges that they enjoyed. The historian, Johann Grohmann, in his *Annalen* classified Wittenberg University professors as *potentia cives*, potential citizens.[105] They were not, in most respects, under the rule of the Town Council. The Elector John the Constant stated in 1525 that those members of the Wittenberg faculty known as *lectores* were already heavily loaded with their academic duties, and would not need to participate in town affairs; besides, their salaries were not paid by the *Stadtrat*, but came out of the university treasury. Therefore, the professors' houses were also to be exempted from the payment of city taxes. The same exemptions were likewise to apply to the university beadles, whose houses were also exempted from property taxes. However, even the ranking professors were not exempted from their national defense as citizens, table taxes, and the payment of a *Bachgeld* and a *Wachgeld* to maintain alert guards on the town walls day and night, which tax was three *Groschen* for every citizen. These same special taxes continued under the Ernestine dynasty, and they were renewed under the Albertine Elector August in 1563. But Elector August added a new feature by stating that the university faculty would also be exempt from paying the usual "building taxes," a tax used to finance internal city construction and improvements.[106]

The privileges also continued to relatives of tax-free professors. Wives of deceased, tax-free *lectores* were also to enjoy these privileges as their widows.[107] In case such a professor possessed more property than his house, he was obligated to pay taxes on the remainder like regular citizens. Other features of faculty exemptions are interesting. The Wittenberg faculty was permitted to brew beer for their home use, and they were permitted to keep a supply of wine on hand for home consumption and to entertain guests, provided it was not sweet wine, like Malvas and Rainfall. Supplies of beer and wine for the common table of the university students were also exempt from taxes. In later years there must have been some abuse of drinking privileges in homes, for in 1555 Elector August limited tax-free beer and wine to faculty homes, with the rector's approval. Professors like Philip Melanchthon, who had students rooming in his home, were also allowed to lay in a supply of tax-free drinks. But some faculty members also appear to have abused the privilege with renters, for in 1569 the Elector August withdrew this privilege.[108]

Permanent members of the university faculty, even though they paid the same taxes as Burghers, were exempted from taking the regular "Citizens' Oath." Faculty members were regarded as belonging to a special estate, which exempted them from all citizens' duties.[109] When professors paid certain special taxes, they were not paid to the Town Council but directly into the electoral treasury. A special tax was levied in 1523 for national defense, and the *Türkensteuer* in 1542, in which a later case Luther was obligated to make a complete listing of all his property, but the elector exempted him from making any payment. In such cases they were collected by the electoral officials.[110]

The sources list some interesting additional regulations. In the case of the death of a tax-free husband whose widow was then remarried to a man not on the university staff, they then had to pay regular taxes to the Town Council on the previously tax-free property. However, the sons and daughters of the deceased father had a tax-free home as long as they were not married.[111] This appears to have applied to children regardless of their ages, as long as they were single. If a faculty tax-free home was converted into a business, the owner became obligated to pay the regular taxes like other citizens. When such tax-free homes were sold to regular citizens, they also became taxable.[112]

This series of relations applied while Electoral Saxony was under the Ernestine line in 1547, but when the Albertine line of rulers took over the University of Wittenberg, during the Schmalkadic War (1547–55), under Moritz and August, a few changes were inaugurated with reference to university taxing privileges. They allowed relatives of tax-free professors to keep tax-free beer and wine in their homes, for the service of their guests, provided they did not engage in their sales. The university, which under August had many scholarship students, could keep an ample supply of beer and wine for the common table. The common table at that time seems to have been located in the New Friderici College.[113]

During the Ernestine period, the Saxon electors were especially gracious toward their favorite professors. As shown in previous chapters, they tried to make their living conditions more pleasant and comfortable. The first instance was that of Frederick the Wise's favoritism toward his court physician, Polich von Mellerstadt, who in that capacity had accompanied the elector on a trip to the Holy Land in 1493, and who had later been one of the two pillars in the founding of the university. Before the arrival of the Mellerstadts at the new university, the elector gave them a nice house near the *Markplatz*, a place which can no longer be identified. Another of the elector's favorites, as shown earlier, was the young reformer Martin Luther, to whom he willed the Black Cloister as wedding gift, at the time Martin Luther and Kathie were married in 1525. The elector had prepared seven rooms on the second floor, to serve as the future home of the Luther family. This was a very large and pretentious gift which the Luther children, after their parents' deaths, resold to the Elector August in 1564 for the sum of $267,500, an amount below Luther's estimate in the *Türkensteuer* of 1542.[114]

Another case of a well-blessed faculty member was the great sixteenth-century Greek scholar Philip Melanchthon, who was modest and desired no high salary. The Weimar archives of June 5, 1536, record that the Elector John Frederick did not forget the needs of Philip and his family. By now Philip had blossomed into a great scholar, both as a linguist and a theologian, who deserved better living quarters. Next to the street near the Friderici College stood an old building, which Elector Frederick ordered razed. In its place he erected a fine Renaissance dwelling which stands there today.[115] In the directive it states that Melanchthon was too busy a scholar to become involved, and the prince wanted the whole dwelling erected without Philip's participation. Perhaps to make matters still more pleasant and bring the reformer and Melanchthon even closer together, the elector gave Philip the garden in the back that bordered on the Luther Black Cloister property.[116]

Another faculty source of additional income accrued from special tasks performed by the rector, the chancellor, beadles, and other faculty members. The university rector received 5 Groschen, around $20, for every student that he matriculated; and he was also paid a fee in connection with the use of the university seal in the authentication of all official documents. When beadles performed in festive parades preceding student promotions, and other special occasions, they received extra fees.[117] When difficult academic problems arose, the rector called upon the four university reformers, who also were paid for their services. Another rather lucrative source of income for the deans, who were disputation participants in student promotions, came from the graduation fees. It will be recalled that Martin Luther, when he was promoted to his doctorate, had to walk to Leipzig to pick up the 50 Gulden that the elector had provided for his promotion, a nice sum of $3,750. As students in theology passed through the five degrees they were obligated to pay fees at every level. In the Graduate School of Law, a student coming up for a degree of *Utrius iuri*, a degree in both civil and canon law, paid a fee totaling $3,160. However, students taking a degree of a doctorate in civil law paid a smaller fee of $2,180. Students in the Graduate School of Medicine paid a fee of $2,775 to obtain their degrees which they needed to practice their profession or teach.[118] These funds were then distributed in the respective faculties in accordance with the elector's *Statutes of 1508*.

Obtaining a doctorate in those days was already an expensive matter requiring a well-to-do family or a rich uncle. The fees paid at the time of promotion did not end the candidate's expenses. Since medieval days the faculty had expected certain gratuities, as can be seen by the following quotation from the *Statutes*:

> Besides this, let the Masters and Doctors in theology keep for the Rector, the Masters and Doctors and the Deans of Arts, a *piretha* (a jar of ointment made from crushed flowers), to be presented to them, costing not more than 10 Groschen), or about $30, and a pair of gloves; however, in the case of the Masters of Arts and the Bachelors of the higher faculties, or the Poets, let the gift be a pair of gloves.[119]

Candidates with promotions toward bachelors and masters in liberal arts were required to pay much lower fees at promotion. The bachelors fee was but $160, while the masters was $610. Members of the mendicant orders were obligated to pay but a third of the other candidates, which applied to their whole education.[120] The method of distribution of funds collected from student promotions was extremely complicated. To cover all four schools of the university would become too involved and unrewarding. To illustrate this, this coverage will be limited to theology, showing how it was done in the principal graduate school. When a Wittenberg student entered the Graduate School of Theology, he faced a longstanding medieval line of procedure, which had developed at the University of Paris in the Middle Ages. The elector's new university followed that pattern of courses and degrees that a student needed to acquire toward a doctorate in theology. The first step a student needed to take to acquire a *Biblicus* in theology. When the dean approved his maturity, he was to pay a promotional fee of $450 into the bursar's office, which sum was then distributed to the participants. Out of the sum the bursar paid the rector $18, his presiding professor $75, and the two beadles in the parade $75, while the four reformers were given a lump sum of $75 to be distributed among them.[121] After becoming a *Biblicus* in theology, the student now set out the master Lombard's *Sentences*, taking courses and attending lectures in the Bible, until his dean and the faculty felt he was mature enough to obtain the second degree, known as *Sententiarius*, a teacher in the *Sentences* of Peter Lombard.[122] Before his promotion to that degree the student deposited $485 with the school treasurer, which funds were then distributed to the participants. Out of this sum, the bursar's office then paid $36 to the dean of theology, $75 to his teacher and professor who officiated during his promotion, and each beadle another $36 for leading the academic parade.[123] Now the young theologian faced a difficult task of proving to the faculty that he was qualified to become a doctor of theology by obtaining the *Formatus* degree, which was determined by an examination by the faculty and a public disputation. The candidate paid $75 into the treasury, but there was apparently no distribution.[124]

Once a theological student had acquired his *Formatus* degree, there came a long period for the student to mature, attending courses and lecturing on Lombard's *Sentences*, before the faculty regarded him as ready for the *Licentiatus* degree, which licensed him to teach theology in any European university. For that esteemed promotion, the candidate paid a sum of $845. This fee the bursar then distributed as follows: the rector received $36; the dean of theology $75; and the two beadles, for their part in the festivities, $75 divided between them. The remainder of the student fee of $500 was deposited into the university treasury.[125]

Finally there came the zenith of academic achievements, a doctorate in theology, attained only by students of ability and the necessary means. As observed above, a doctorate in theology in 1512 cost Luther a fee of 50 Gulden. Such a gala affair was preceded by a parade to the Aula in the Castle Church, and it opened with a vespering, a mass, and a colorful circular disputation. On such an occasion, $75 was set aside for the vespering and the remainder the treasurer distributed as follows: the professor in charge was paid $75; in such a debate, they had quite a display of argumentation, pro and con, by two *Gallis*, known then as the "fighting cocks," who were meant to confuse the candidate, who were paid $75; another $75 went to other participants. The beadles, who led the parade and were in charge of the affair, each were paid $75 for their part. After all had been reimbursed for their respective roles, the $750 that remained went into the university treasury.[126]

As one observes the various sources of income, which for the faculty were tax-free, including payments for registrations, disputations, and promotional exercises, which they received in addition to their regular salaries, it becomes evident that incomes were considerably enhanced from outside sources.

At this point the reader may be quite interested in Martin Luther's salary and the many privileges and gratuities given him by the electors of Saxony during the reformer's lifetime. Since this is quite an involved series of events, we need to treat it as a separate section of the fiscal story of Wittenberg, as it involves both Luther's period as a monk, and after 1525 the story of the Luther family and the variety of gifts that were made to them.

THE INCOME OF MARTIN LUTHER

In the early years of Martin Luther's professorship, after his promotion to the doctorate by Johann Staupitz in 1512, when he began to teach in the position of *Lectura in Biblia*, as a doctor of the Holy Scriptures, we possess no information as to his income. He was a simple Augustinian monk in the Augustinian Order, which was responsible for his livelihood. In those early days he was little known except to his fellow Augustinians. But after 1517, with his nailing of the Ninety-five Theses, which caused a great disturbance in the Roman Church, he soon became well-known throughout all Europe. Meanwhile between 1513 and 1520 Luther had developed as the budding reformer, attracting students from all parts of the continent. Meanwhile Wittenberg's matriculations had grown, so it had become a relatively large institution. By 1520 he was receiving gifts from people who agreed with his "New Theology" now being taught at the University of Wittenberg.

As shown elsewhere in previous chapters, by now the elector of Saxony had become very interested in Luther's "Theology of the Cross" and did everything possible, in the face of Rome's fury, to protect the university and promote its needs. It is well known that Frederick the Wise was quite a sportsman, who loved to hunt Hirsch and Ray at his hunting lodges at Schweinitz and Lochau. The former lodge was used by the elector until 1523, on which occasion he hosted a great deer hunt, having as guests King Christian of Denmark and many other distinguished persons. At this time Lochau was regarded by some as the finest hunting lodge in Europe, and Frederick retired here during his last illness, for there it was quiet and peaceful, with only his staff and a few doctors around. Because of Elector Frederick's frequent hunts, the lodges were well supplied with venison and Ray meat and whenever there was a marriage or festive occasion such as festive banquets at weddings and the university, his court preacher, Georg Spalatin, was in a good position to supply the necessary *Wildpret*.

Martin Luther, who was on the closest terms with Georg Spalatin, and knew of the elector's goodwill, used the occasions of weddings and promotions to obtain a good *Wildpret* for his friends and fellow professors by appealing to the electoral court on such occasions. The first instance was when Agricola, Luther's former *famulus*, who it was claimed had accompanied the reformer when he nailed his Ninety-five Theses, wanted to get married and they needed a *Wildpret* for the occasion. This the electoral court gladly provided. A second event occurred on May 26, 1522, when Wittenberg's Hebrew professor Mattäus Aurogallus, the faithful assistant to Luther in Old Testament translations of the Bible, was going to be married to Anna Doring. Luther wanted his friend to have a fine *Hochzeitsschauas*, and through Spalatin helped him to fulfill his wish by supplying them with a *Wildpret*. In a letter to the court preacher Luther asked him to thank the elector for the gift for his friend.[127] Then a little later, on October 10, 1522, the new pastor of the *Pfarrkirche* of Wittenberg, Johannes Bugenhagen, also entered holy wedlock, for which Luther served as the officiating clergyman. Once again the electoral court provided the *Wildpret*.[128] There were a number of other occasions where the electors graciously assisted to make the weddings gala affairs. We must now relate what a gracious gift was given to the reformer himself, after he had graciously assisted others. It is the account of a sympathetic lawyer, Heinrich Schmiedberg, a five-year Bologna student and a later *iuris utriusque* doctor of Leipzig, who then had risen to the chancellorship of the bishops of Freising and Naumburg.

Doctor Heinrich Schmiedberg had been at the Leipzig Debate between Luther and Eck in 1519, and as a result became very sympathetic toward the Reformation. He had developed deep mistrust of John Eck's methods in trying to condemn the Wittenberg professor. When Eck later appeared in Germany with the bull *Exsurge Domine* and asked the lawyer to assist him in spreading it in the region, he wanted to discuss the matter personally with Luther and the lawyers of the electoral court. On the way Schmiedberg became ill and feared death, so he made out his last testament and died before the proposed meetings. In his "Last Will" the doctor remembered the troubled Wittenberg professor with a nice sum of $7,500, indeed a kind remembrance in a moment when the reformer was being threatened by a papal excommunication.[129] The most significant illustration of the elector's benevolence is that associated with the wedding of Luther and Catherine von Bora in 1525, when they were blessed with a new home and their wedding expenses. The details of this gracious action on part of the elector have been treated in detail, so the reader is already familiar with what transpired. But no doubt the history behind the event needs some clarification at this point.

During the Reformation, the Black Cloister, once occupied by 41 monks, underwent quite a transformation.[130] It was almost empty after all the monks left. During those earlier days, when Luther was in charge as the *Studium regens*, he had a small office in the southwest tower, on the corner of the building, well illustrated by the etching by Wilber Seidel, as it still looked in 1588. After all the gospel-minded monks had departed, except Luther and Prior Brisger—and even the prior wanted to leave to enter the ministry—it made no sense for Luther to remain in the large building alone. He now wrote the elector for a small place near the city wall, so he would have somewhere to live.[131] This set the wheels in motion at the electoral court. We no longer know all that happened, but both the elector and his brother Duke John became involved. This was in the year 1524, and in 1525 Luther made it known he was going to marry Catherine von Bora. Meanwhile, when the elector died in 1525, John took over the problem after Frederick the Wise had already willed the reformer the Black Cloister as an outright gift. But now the matter had taken on a new dimension. Adequate facilities were needed in the large cloister. Elector John supplied the materials and asked the townsmen to renovate facilities on the main floor, providing the Luther family with seven rooms for adequate living quarters. They must have worked feverishly, for by the time of the wedding the quarters were ready for occupancy. Meanwhile Luther was very occupied with his Bible translations of the Old Testament, for he wrote to his friend Wenceslaus Link in Nürnberg, thanking him for supplying him with a pair of new glasses.[132]

According to the contemporary customs, a German marriage was an event consisting of two parts, the *Verlobung*, a small private wedding, which involved only the official participants, the pastor, and witnesses, and later the *Hochzeit*, the blessing of the couple in the Town Church, followed by an elaborate *Hochzeitsschmaus*, for relatives and the many guests. Such weddings were usually a costly affair.

Luther and Kathie's *Verlobung* took place on June 13, 1525, at their new quarters in the Black Cloister. The *Verlobung* was conducted by the pastor of the Town Church, Johannes Bugenhagen, in the presence of the probst of the Castle Church, Justus Jonas. The legal witness to certify the marriage was the professor of canon law at the university, Johannes Apel, and the parental witnesses were the Burgermeister Lucas Cranach and his wife, Barbara, in whose home Kathe had stayed as a maid. A part of the extreme privacy of this wedding was no doubt because both had been members of religious orders and tongues might wag, as they certainly did. After the *Verlobung* Luther and Kathe moved into their new quarters in the monastery, and now they had to prepare for the wedding and the banquet.

Since the *Hochzeit*, the public church celebration, was still two weeks away (on June 27, 1525), this allowed Luther some time to prepare properly for the event. On June 16, 1525, he wrote to Georg Spalatin at the electoral court, inviting him to the *Hochzeit* and to the banquet in the afternoon, and then asking him to use his influence to get a *Wildpret*, so they could have roasted deer.[133] A little later, on June 21, 1525, he also wrote the Saxon *marschall,* Hans von Dolzig, to provide them with the game for the banquet if possible. According to a report, it was dispatched by a messenger on horseback in due time.[134] The same day Luther sent a second letter to the Torgau Berger, Leonhard Koppe, the man who had assisted Kathe in her escape, along with eight other nuns, from Nimbschen in 1523. He invited him and his wife to the *Hochzeit* and asked him to deliver, at Luther's expense, a barrel of the best Torgauer beer so members at the banquet would be happy.[135]

Plans for the *Hochzeit* also involved the sending of invitations to many relatives. Among the Mansfeld relatives whom Luther invited were of course his parents, sisters, and their husbands. How many of Luther's fellow professors attended the *Hochzeit*, other than the Melanchthons, is not recorded. The wedding ceremony started at 10 A.M. in the Town Church, in which Pastor Bugenhagen began with a blessing of the wedding couple in the presence of the invited guests and the Wittenberg congregation. Then in the afternoon came the *Hochzeitsschmaus*, which must have been held in the monastery dining room on the first floor of the Black Cloister to accommodate all the guests. It is reported that in the evening they had an *Ehrentanz*, a gala folk-dancing party in the basement of the *Rathaus*.[136]

Since this section of the chapter deals principally with the incomes of Martin Luther, an evaluation of what it cost and the money expended in the form of funds and gifts may be of interest. As we have seen in the previous chapter,[137] the Elector John the Constant was already evangelical quite early, even while Luther was developing into the reformer. He must have been in favor of the marriage of Martin Luther and he must have realized what an expense was involved. It was he who ordered the preparations of the Luther dwellings in the Black Cloister, but when he learned of the marriage, he graciously sent Luther $7,500 as a gift to help the newly married couple get started.[138]

As might be expected, later the newly married couple received many gifts. The Town Council realized the cost of a large banquet and sent a sum of $1,500 to help defray the expenses.[139] They also supplied the newlyweds with additional drinks and a barrel of Einbeckish beer, which according to the town record cost the city a sum of six Gulden, or $420.[140] Nor was the university lacking in its appreciation, for it presented the Luthers with a large half-meter tall, beautiful and costly *Becher*, an ornamental cup trimmed with silver and gold and with an elaborately decorated lid. This gift was the product of an Augsburg artist, and had an estimated worth of 21 Gulden, or by today's standards about $1,575. A special wedding ring was worn by Luther, now a treasure in the

Braunschweig Museum.[141] It contained a small diamond and a ruby, under which was the inscription MLD, and inside it were inscribed the words of the Holy Scriptures: "What God has joined together, let no man put asunder."[142] Catherine also wore a beautiful ring, which is now the pride of the Leipzig museum. It was adorned with a ruby and a picture of the crucified Christ, and its inscription read: *D. Martinus Lutherus, Catherina u. Boren*, and underneath it had the date, 13 June, 1525.[143] On April 20, 1526, Luther wrote his brother-in-law, Johann Rühel, at Eisleben about a recent gift sent to his wife Catherine by the archbishop of Mainz, which was worth about $1,500. His wife no doubt treasured the gift. Apparently it was done secretly and Luther had just learned about it. Upon an investigation, the reformer learned it had been delivered by Philip Melanchthon to the Black Cloister. Luther felt a Christian should not accept a gift from a man with such false teachings as the archbishop of Mainz, and who lived in "wild wedlock."[144] Catherine's biographer, Kroker, claims Luther returned the gift, but his wife would really have liked to keep it.[145]

During Luther's married life they received many gifts, small and large, the details of which were never recorded. This is clearly evident from details of Luther's "Second Will," dated January 6, 1542, where he states that his "vases and trinkets, such as rings, coins of gold and silver, would total in worth about 1000 Gulden," or $75,000.[146]

The record is unclear why certain gifts were made to members of the Wittenberg faculty like Luther and Melanchthon. For example, Luther's former *Famulus*, Agricola, gave the Luthers an expensive *Tuchgeschenk*, a fine peace of cloth, for which Luther thanked him for his generosity, but then he added that it seemed hardly fitting to give such an expensive gift to paupers.[147] What seems even more strange, Agricola also gave a similar present to Melanchthon.[148] The answer to that we will perhaps never know.

In Luther's correspondence there is an interesting story that needs to be a part of this record. After the Luthers were living in the Black Cloister, in 1527, a small piece of property became available for purchase, which at the time Luther did not need, but which later, in 1541, he bought to serve as a small home for Catherine and her children after his death, should the large Black Cloister become too much of a burden to manage for her and the children. Luther also realized that under German law she would have practically no income. The details of what happened need to be related, as they shed light on a professor's income and on making ends meet in old age.

It will be recalled that when the elector gave Luther the Black Cloister as a wedding gift, the monastery was practically vacant and Luther had asked Frederick for a small piece of land next to the cloister, near the wall, where he might erect a small house for Prior Brisger and himself. According to Luther, Brisger built a small *Bude* and lived there for awhile, but soon entered the ministry at Altenburg. When the prior departed, he left the dwelling under the care of Bruno Brauer.[149]

At the time Luther saw no need for an additional dwelling, as he had sufficient worries keeping the large Black Cloister in repair, as we shall see later. In

1534 Luther suggested that Brisger sell his *Bude* to Brauer. However, on June 29, 1541, Luther decided to purchase the small house near the town wall for a household servant, Wolfgang Seberger. With his failing health, Luther must have realized that it would be wise to will the house to his wife and their children, which he did on June 6, 1542.[150]

Since here we are covering the income of the university professors and especially Luther's income and wealth, an excellent account of this is recorded in connection with Luther's "Second Will," drafted in 1542, where these facts are recorded in detail.[151] The purchase price of the small dwelling Luther had bought for Kathe was a total of $32,250, bought under these conditions. The down payment was to be $9,000, and there was to be an annual installment of $1,875 until it was paid.[152] This meant that Luther had to borrow money to meet these terms. The town record shows that payments were made while Luther lived, but his son Martin reported that three years after Luther's death there was still an indebtedness on the house of $12,000.[153]

As will be shown from data in the "second will," during that time, even though he still had a good salary and was blessed with many gifts, he had a difficult time making ends meet. He had a large household to feed and provide for, with purchases of additional gardens, cattle, and other livestock to provide for a large family of his own children and those of his sister. Fortunately, the electors realized this and gave him grain, firewood, and even clothing as they were needed. Elector John the Constant was very benevolent in his gifts of clothing, as we shall see from a letter in which Luther expressed his gratitude for the generosity. This letter was written toward the close of the elector's reign, August 17, 1531, and contains much insight on the attitude of the Saxon court and also the frugality of Luther in response to such frequent gifts.[154]

In the letter, Martin Luther begins with the statement that he has wanted to write this letter of appreciation for the elector's generosity for some time, but he now wants to express his humble and sincere thanks for the recent gifts of clothing and suits. Then he adds, in all humility, he wants to tell the elector that he is not that much in need of so many gifts, for he has more clothes now than he can wear with a good conscience. He feels that as a preacher he should not possess an overabundance of clothing, otherwise Christ's admonition to the rich might, also fall on him, that he had had his reward in this world. He does, however, wish to thank the elector for the fine "dark red cloth" and the nice "black coat," even though it is far too elegant and costly for him. He would never wear that fine coat except that it had been a present from his Electoral Grace. He closes by pleading with the prince to stop sending them such an abundance of clothes. Luther added that he would not mind it if the gifts were for others, who were more worthy to receive them, and he closed the letter with an amen.[155]

At the time when Martin Luther and Catherine von Bora were married, the Elector Frederick had most recently died, early in May 1525, and was buried May 10, 1525, but he had previously given Luther the Black Cloister as a gift. It appears that the whole transaction was done without an official record. Meanwhile, they had lived there for four years without questioning of local authorities. No doubt we no longer know all that transpired at the electoral court in 1529, but there must have been some discussion about the legality of Frederick's gift, and the electoral lawyers must have advised that for the sake of the Luthers and their children, and to avoid any future challenge, the transaction should be made a matter of record.

Thus on February 4, 1532, Elector John drafted a letter of confirmation of his brother's gift and added at the close that he certified it by his official seal which now officially confirmed Frederick the Wise's donation of the Black Cloister to Luther and his family.[156] He added that the Black Cloister was not only a gift to Luther and Catherine, but also applied to their heirs as an honest and free possession; and then he specified that the gift also included the garden in the back, as well as the courtyard in front of the monastery, to be their possessions without any restrictions. After this the Luthers could regard it as their outright home, for them or their heirs, to renovate and even sell. This implied that the Black Cloister, as in the case of other professors, would be tax-free, but their children were expected to pay 20 *Zinsgroschen*. The official confirmation also gave Luther and Käthie the right to brew beer, make malt, and serve drinks. They were also permitted to keep cattle and other animals like other citizens. However, the elector placed one condition on the donation, that in case they or their children after the parents' death wished to sell the Black Cloister, they were first to notify the city council and give the university the first opportunity to buy it, as did happen in 1564, when the Luther children sold the Black Cloister to the Elector August for $225,500, so he could convert the monastery into a home for 150 poor scholarship students. This certainly confirmed how important it was that the Elector John had made the gift to the Luthers official and legal.[157]

On August 7, 1535, Martin Luther informed the Elector John Frederick that two theological candidates at Wittenberg were coming up for their doctorates who were quite distinguished scholars. One was Johan Medler, chaplain to Elizabeth of Brandenburg, who had been expelled from her electorate, as she favored the Reformation; the other was Heinrich Weller.[158] The distinguished refugee had been offered a refuge by the Elector John Frederick in his Torgau Castle, then in Weimar, and eventually in Wittenberg, which made Chaplain Johan Medler's promotion a personal matter with the electoral court.[159] Luther therefore wanted to make the two promotions a very festive affair by ending it with an elaborate banquet. So Luther asked the elector to send them a *Wildpret* for the *prandium*[160] The two doctrinal promotions occurred on September 14, 1535.

Soon after that, on July 11, 1535, Joachim I died and was succeeded by the evangelically-minded Johann II of Brandenburg, who leagued himself with the northern reformers and introduced the Reformation into the Brandenburg lands. This made it possible for Elizabeth to return to her homeland, but Chaplain Dr. Medler decided to remain behind in the *Lutherstadt* for a few years. No doubt he enjoyed the environment of the University of Wittenberg, which had now been reorganized to a higher academic standard by Elector John Frederick's reorganization of the institution in 1535–1536, as we shall see in a later chapter.

Meanwhile the elector had not forgotten the Luther family, with its large household, and, like his father John, he showered them with many gifts. In 1536 Luther wrote the prince, again thanking him for his graciousness of offering them so many presents. The gifts now were six pails of wine, which the elector's custodian in Schweinitz had just delivered to Luther upon the elector's orders, and a wild boar. As in previous cases, Luther expressed the feeling that the elector's donations had exceeded all bounds in money, wine, bread, and other supplies, and just seemed too much for the gracious elector.[161] But John Frederick, who was so fond of the reformer, must have felt otherwise, as he was fully aware of Luther's needs with such a large family. On January 26, 1536, he ordered Wolf Schieferdecker, the electoral treasurer in Wittenberg, to supply Martin Luther annually with 200 Scheffels of wheat, two supplies of malt for brewing beer, and 100 cords of wood.[162] However, no doubt due to a misunderstanding, the officials delivered 40 cords of wood and Luther registered his complaint. When the elector learned of the mistake he immediately corrected the error. On April 1, 1536, he ordered the shortage of wood corrected. Then Luther received his full 100 cords of wood, two malts, and 200 bushels of wheat. He could comfortably feed the many in his household.[163]

As stated earlier, in 1535–1536, the elector gave the university of Wittenberg new *Statutes*, in which reorganization he raised the faculty salaries. Prior to 1536, Luther's salary had been but $16,500, and the elector now raised it to $22,500.[164] Then in 1541 it was increased to $26,450, and by the time of his death he was advanced in salary to $30,000.

LUTHER'S FIRST WILL IN 1537

In 1537 the Evangelical Princes of the Schmalkaldic League met, to which Martin Luther was invited to draft his Schmalkald Articles, which the Elector John Frederick wanted to use in case the papacy would hold a Church Council about Luther's heresy. On February 27, 1537, Luther arrived in Gotha and was quartered in the home of John Löwen as an overnight guest. During the night the reformer became seriously ill and thought he might die. It is no longer known whether Luther dictated "The First Will" to the town pastor, Johannes Bugenhagen, or whether Luther wrote it himself.[165]

The first will is more an insurance document for his faithful wife Catherine, to protect her against lawyers of the Saxon court. The reformer's opinion of lawyers was not very high, and he called upon his close friends, Melanchthon, Jonas, and Cruciger to protect her in case, as was then often the practice, lawyers attempted to take away her sons as minors. What seems to have been Luther's principal concern was that customary law in the *Saxonspiegel* relegated wives of even important historical figures to maids without any legal status. The reformer must have feared that Chancellor Brück of the electoral court would take advantage of her, using the customary law to remove them from her custody.[166] Luther had a strong feeling about this use of guardianship, even in princely courts. He felt that Käthie was a capable mother and manager of her family, and keeping the boys with her was his principal concern when he wrote his first will.[167] The Elector John Frederick, as Luther's close personal friend, went along with him even though the will was open to legal challenge.[168]

The will begins with Luther as the reformer of the church in opposition to Rome, in the restoration of the gospel within Christianity. Then he turned to the will, in which he names Melanchthon, Jonas, and Cruciger as the men to whom he entrusts the care of his faithful wife and her children. This is followed by a word of consolation to his honorable wife, who for twelve years had been his faithful helper, and he asks God that he may reward her for her loyalty and constant assistance. He states that he hopes the children will legally be permitted to remain under their mother's care; whereupon Luther greets members of the Wittenberg congregation, the pious Burghers of the town, and the Elector John Frederick, and asks them to place his family under their Christian treatment and those of the "household of faith." He concluded that his wife was in a better position to be the guardian of her children than others, and he prays that his family after his death will remain true to the faith. Then he closes with a prayer: "After this I commend my spirit into the hands of the Father and my Lord Jesus Christ, whom I have proclaimed and confessed here on earth.[169]

For a proper assessment of Luther and Catherine's wealth of worldly possessions, in property and treasures, toward the close of the reformer's life, two sources of information are available to scholars. There is the *Türkensteuer of 1542* and Luther's *Second Will of 1542*. Luther's *Second Will* was drafted January 9, 1542,[170] while the *Türkensteuer* was a tax the electoral court levied against citizens of Ernestine Saxony to stem the tide of war against the Turks in the West.[171] Since an account of the Turkish War tax is less complicated than Luther's *Second Will*, we shall first treat Luther's assessment of his possessions, as the elector had requested an itemized account of his property.

Previously we observed how Wittenberg professors were exempt from property taxes paid by regular citizens, with a few minor exceptions, but when it came to national defense they were obligated to pay their share. In Martin Luther's case, the elector asked him to likewise prepare a complete listing of all the property he owned and give his evaluation of its worth. This Luther did with all faithfulness, and it is known as the *Türkensteuer of 1542*. As Luther did this listing and evaluating, he did it with some reservations, some property he found was difficult to assess, and he granted his figures were but an estimate of what they might be worth on the current market. Here it must be added that the elector realized Luther was old and that this would be an added load, and he paid the tax out of the electoral treasury. But we are grateful that Luther did evaluate the worth of his possessions.

The Türkensteuer of 1542

The Black Cloister	$450, 000
Brauer House	31,500
Wolf's Garden	1, 500
Zarnischen St. Garden	37, 500
The Eichen Pfull Garden	6,700
Five Cows (3 Gulden each)	1,125
Nine Caves (2 Gulden each)	1,350
One Goat & two small ones	150
Eight pigs (1 Gulden each)	600
Two mother pigs (21 Gulden each)	375
Three small pigs	75
Total	$530, 925

The above amount seems excessive, but one must remember that most of the amount is the worth of the Black Cloister, which netted the Luthers no income unless it was sold. As a monastery it was a very large building, which later in 1564 the children were able to sell to the university for $277,500, when the Elector August wanted it for his scholarship students from poor families.[172] The gardens were absolutely essential to feed the twenty-five or so people Luther at times had in his household.

LUTHER'S SECOND WILL

Exactly why Luther drafted a Second Will, on January 6, 1542, is no longer known. German scholars believe a number of factors may have caused him to do this as he entered upon the preparation for his death. No doubt Chancellor Brück, one of the readers of the Augsburg Confession in 1530, and now the influential chancellor of the elector, was a factor, who had given him and his wife difficulties at times in the past.[173] Another factor may have been the reformer's health. He was plagued late in life with many illnesses and especially severe attacks of gallstones, and it was natural that he should fear death at any time. In the will, we see once again Luther's dislike for lawyers, as he wrote the will in his own hand so Käthie could clearly recognize it.[174] It seems strange that he did not even at first have it legally recorded; perhaps he felt his wife could handle it when it was in his own handwriting. But later, due to the influence of his friends, he decided to record it, on February 1, 1544, drafting a detailed account of the property and the Second Will. It was recorded in the town *Gerichtsbuch* by the *Stadtrichter*, the town judge, his very popular printer, Hans Lufft, who happened to hold that important office at that time.[175]

Luther wrote his Second Will assuming that it needed no further legal certification, as his Second Will was written in his own hand, which his wife Catherine would recognize. In this Will Luther begins with the property he wills to his wife Catherine: (1) the Zulsdorf farm, which he had purchased from her brother for her to keep her cattle and livestock, which he valued at $45,750, which included six buildings and some farm machinery; (2) the small Bruno house, which he had purchased for her and the children from Wolf, to serve as their dwelling, and also all his books and trinkets, such as rings, chains, gold and silver coins, which were valued at $75,000.[176] Strangely enough, Luther now failed to mention the previously listed family gardens or the Black Cloister. Perhaps he was fully aware that the Black Cloister had been an outright gift from the elector, and belonged both to him and Catherine and their descendants, and therefore, would not really now need to be willed to Käthie again. For the original gift had the one proviso that later it should be offered first to the university should it later be offered for sale by Luther or his descendants.

After the reformer had listed all his property, he gave his reasons for the type of will he had written. Catherine had been his loyal wife, had borne him five healthy children, and had constantly taken care of him, and he trusted her more than the lawyers to be their custodian. He knew that she would pay the obligations of his indebtedness, which he thought were about 450 Gulden or perhaps a little more.[177]

Luther's thoughts then turn to the time when Catherine and the young children would be living in the little Bruno house, and he grants that the children may present some problems, for the devil often gets into offspring and creates difficulties. He turns to the children and asks that they obey their mother, and he adds that he hopes she will always remain motherly to them. At the close he also addresses the Elector John Frederick, and asks him to control affairs so that the lawyers will not step in and disobey his wishes. He repeated again that he feels Catherine will be a better manager of the children's affairs than if the court lawyers placed the boys under appointed ones.[178] The principal reason why Luther drafted the Second Will at this time was doubtless that he wanted to make it a matter of the court records. Today the document Luther drafted appears in printed form in the *Weimar Ausgabe* of Luther's Works.[179]

At the time of the recording of the Second Will, Hans Lufft, as *Gerichtsherr*, identified himself as city judge and official recorder, and Martin Luther as a doctor of the Holy Scriptures, who in this document has bequeathed everything to his honorable wife, which he now makes a matter of official record. After these introductory statements by the *Gerichtsherr*, the judge made the following entries:

(1) The Brauer Haus, which Luther had purchased for Catherine as a dwelling for her and the children; (2) the Claus Hessener Garden and the land he had bought for her just beyond the *Elbthor*; (3) the Garden that he had purchased from Jacob Sedemann, which was now paid for in full; (4) the Hufe, known as the Kabelhaus; and (5) the garden on the Agelphal, purchased from Andresten Melbeste and also paid for in full. All these properties, directly under the jurisdiction of the Town Council, were henceforth to pass under Catherine's jurisdiction, without any jurisdiction of her children or interference. In the recorded will by the Judge, Catherine was now to be given power of

attorney over all these named properties. The power of the execution of the Second Will was given to Wolfgang Seberger, and the document was signed by the Court Judge Hans Lufft.[180]

In the coverage of Luther's Second Will, the Weimar Edition editors have given us several *Beilagen*, additional documents. They show how Luther had acquired the properties mentioned in the *Gerichtsbuch* cited above. These details are presented in the first *Beilagen*, while the second *Beilage* gives the history of how Luther purchased the Bruno Brauer Haus for Catherine, located near the Black Cloister. The third *Beilage* relates in full how on April 19, 1532, Martin Luther and Nicolaus Heffner had worked out the reformer's purchase of a small farm, under terms in which Claus Hildenhauer could dwell in its farmhouse until his death, which occurred on August 14, 1539. After this, according to the original contract, the entire property with its buildings became the property of Luther and Catherine and their heirs.[181]

Perhaps an enlargement upon this purchase, which with its gardens and buildings was very significant for the large Luther household, will be useful. This farm must have been quite large, as Luther assessed it at $49,000. The property had a house, barn, well, and fence, and the land extended some distance from the buildings. The location of this little farm was quite convenient, as it lay right outside of Elster Gate, where Catherine and her assistants could raise and use fresh vegetables and garden crops for the family table, in the dining hall of the monks in monastic days. In the town records Luther gives the terms of the purchase and also its estimated worth.[182] Finally, *Beilage* number four, which was pieced together by the Weimar editors from data found in the *Dresdner Hauptstadtarchiv*, may be of interest, as Luther wrote these notes in preparation for his Second Will. Since these notes are quite detailed and not all of equal importance, this account has been somewhat selective in its coverage.[183]

Luther began with an interesting observation about people. The reformer made this statement about people: "People are coarse; the world is thankless!" Apparently Luther referred to some of his experiences with the workers on the city fortifications, who were thoughtless and abusive while building the structure, which crowded the Black Cloister and their garden in the rear, and was destructive of property in front. He also had complained about them in the *Gerichtsbuch's* Second Will, that they demanded taxes on the Bruno Brauer Haus, which he had purchased for his wife, when prior to that it had been tax-free. Luther also spoke of the ungratefulness of members of the Wittenberg *Pfarrkirche* in one of his notes: "For thirty years I served as their preacher and received no salary; while they offered me so little in return, except several thousand shingles and a little plaster. I have often served them and stayed with them in pestilence years. Hence they may well guard themselves because of their unthankfulness, for they will not be blessed in this life.[184]

On another slip of paper Luther had written, "In case some should ask: "What happened to all the kitchen equipment and other household goods, the answer would be as follows: 'The tin kettles and other kitchen utensils, as also household goods, were donated to us by visitors, as was the practice at the beginning of the gospel. The remainder given us were hardly worth $1,500. Visitors would also steal a kitchen utensil of the former and our own, and thus it would disappear.'" In the long note Luther returned to the ungratefulness of the Wittenberg congregation, which he had served so many years, preaching, lecturing, and writing, but he said that it did not matter. Let it be such a lack of appreciation, for the elector, out of the goodness of his heart, had looked after them, even though he owed nothing to the church or the state. In another paragraph, Luther added that he believes people will even be less grateful for his services when he is gone. He observed that some were even jealous because God had so blessed the Luthers. For those he adds that the mouths of those foul individuals should be stuffed up until they became blood-red in their faces with shame. He concluded, however, that a number of the Burghers in Wittenberg had showered the university with praise, for which he was grateful and hoped the Lord would bless them.[185]

On another slip of notations the reformer relates what happened to the expensive vestments at Wittenberg of Roman Catholic days. He says that he realized there was considerable money involved, which had better be given to the needy; so he sold them. The money was then used to feed and help the needy monks and nuns. The record he made on the slip indicates that they brought 50 Gulden, or in today's value about $3,700, which did not quite meet the needs. So he increased the amount slightly by using part of the sum $7,500 the Elector John had given them in 1525 to set up housekeeping. He added that in the future they should not hold Catherine responsible, for all she possesses she had earned herself. No one will make charges against her except the knaves, who will criticize her. God will know how to take care of them.[186]

Among the notes that Luther and Catherine made of their expenditures, the following offers a little insight as to what was involved in keeping the Black Cloister household in expenses:

Brauhaus Haus (Käthie's beer brewery)	$8,750
Stall for horse, cows, and swine	$1,500
Bath (provided with a tub)	$375
Large basement (repair costs)	$8,750
New Cellar (excavation costs)	$3,750
Furnishing an upper room with closet	$7,500
Furnishing a lower room	$3,000
Repair of the stairs (twice)	$1,500
Muhm Lehn room (closet and chimney)	$375
Small chamber (chimney with draft)	$375
Small room furnishings for Johannes	$375
Small room for Georg Plato	$375
Garden near the house and well	$30,000
Boards for house (Gedielet)	$7,500

A wine cellar	$750
Roof repairs (for the period)	$9,850
Expenses on the new house	$30,000

This list of expenditures made on the Black Cloister—upkeep, improvements, and new quarters for guests—totals by calculating quite freely about $130,000 during the years from 1525 until 1542.[187]

THE UNIVERSITY COMMON TABLE

We now turn from the finances, salaries, and wills of Luther to another aspect of Wittenberg University. There is still one phase of the institution's fiscal program that remains untreated, namely, that of the "common table," for needy students and faculty members assigned to supervise students during meals. Unfortunately, the facts in the records are far too scanty to give us the details.[188] It appears as though the common table had its origin in connection with student prebends, which were extended to those in need, making it possible for able and worthy poor students to attend the university by a reduction of their living expenses.[189]

In his previously cited *Annalen*, Grohmann claims that Elector Frederick the Wise's idea of giving stipends for poor students predates even the founding of the University of Wittenberg. He claims that the elector had offered six scholarships to worthy poor students at the University of Leipzig, for which he had set aside 210 Rhenish Gulden. He stipulated that the original gift would be over a period of seven years, during which every student would receive 35 Rhenish Gulden, totaling about $2,535 per year.[190] In the original scholarships, the elector added that in case he founded his own university in the Ernestine Saxony lands, the scholarships would be continued in his own institution. There is evidence that Wittenberg received these scholarships after 1502.[191]

During the reign of the Elector John Frederick, in 1545, he planned to expand the scholarships for deserving students, who would otherwise be unable to attend *Leucuria*. The elector wanted scholarships to be extended to 150 deserving students, while 70 were immediately to be offered scholarships. It is also interesting how the student's status in society was a determining factor of the amount. According to the new plan, sons of impoverished nobles were to be given a scholarship for $3,000 per annum, minister's sons $2,000, while the sons in other classes of society were to receive but $1,875.[192] Since meanwhile the Schmalkaldic War broke out in 1547, and the elector was defeated and captured at Muhlberg near Wittenberg soon after that, the plan could not materialize.

The Kaiser took Electoral Saxony and gave it to Duke Moritz of the Albertine Saxon line. Meanwhile Moritz was too busy waging war to give his attention to scholarships, and the number never rose over twenty students during his electorship.[193]

When Elector Moritz died, after being mortally wounded in 1553, his brother August succeeded him as Elector, who was a far more magnanimous ruler and friend of the University of Wittenberg. He conceived a new plan for scholarships, or an expansion of John Frederick's 20 scholarships to the late 150 ones; but Elector August's plan was even more generous in helping scholarship students, by including free housing in addition to other financial assistance. He must have known about the special clause in Frederick the Wise's original donation of the Black Cloister, namely, that the university would have the first right to repurchase the building should Luther, or his heirs, wish sell the property. In 1564 Elector August bought the Black Cloister from Luther's heirs for $281,500, in order to convert it into a dwelling for 150 scholarship students. By 1577 this had been realized for 27 students, but soon afterward they increased it to 150, a number that could not all be housed in the Black Cloister. Accordingly, Elector August placed 27 students in the basement of the cloister, in newly furnished rooms. The students were even given a little pocket money along with their generous treatment.[194]

But the elector soon experienced that the housing of 150 students required considerably more space than was available. He then decided to erect an entirely new building, the *Augusteum* on the *Collegian Gasse*; and placed in between it and the *Brauhaus* of the Cloister, a recently purchased Toszen House.[195] Thus with the additional rooms in the *Augusteum*, the *Toszen Haus*, and the major rooms in the Black Cloister, there was now adequate room to house the 150 scholarship students.

Naturally the Reformation student is interested in how the common table came to be established and how it was managed. Even Grohmann, whose *Annalen* are so often cited, apparently was not able to learn much about its details. The only source we possess that offers some information about its origin and management is by Gottfried Suevus, who wrote his *Academia Wittenbergensis* in 1655.[196] He was a seventeenth-century Wittenberg professor who has given us much interesting information, as we saw in a previous chapter. This seems to deal with the early period of the university, and Suevus classified his source as being of the period of Frederick the Wise. Unfortunately we possess no information on the rest of the period of the Ernestine rule, nor of the short period when Moritz began as the elector of Saxony and the new prince of the University of Wittenberg. But the details begin when August became the elector and decided to create the 150 scholarships for students, who required a common table to keep their living expenses to a minimum. It may well be that August merely enlarged on the common table made available to scholarship students as started by Frederick the Wise.

The original document by Suevus begins with the original *Communis Monsae*, which was founded with rather rigorous regulations, that in the original document are called *Leges*, namely, Laws of Management. Frederick the Wise and his court lawyers must have realized that such a club, made up of nobles, clerics, and Burgher's sons, would present some management problems. Since students moved from one university to another quite frequently, some membership rules for those who belonged and dined at the common table were necessary. There was the rule that once a student had been accepted as a member, and left for another school and later returned to Wittenberg on a scholarship, he remained a member in good standing. Membership was, however, strictly regulated, and limited to able students with the proper credentials.

But in another paragraph of the document, one gains the impression that the original common table membership was a mixed group of well-to-do nobles, clergymen, and poor students supported by a rich donor. In another part it speaks of dues, that only those who pay their dues regularly can remain members of the common table. No doubt, in this group were Frederick's six scholarship students, or others who were poor students certified by rich donors outside the university. In the sixteenth century, indebtedness was regarded as an important matter and could have serious consequences. The rules of the organization state that if a member became delinquent in his membership fees in the club, he would first be warned by the officials in charge. But in case he failed to pay what he owed the club, he would be locked up until his obligations had been met. Anyone who lied about the member's delinquency was to meet with same consequences. Perjury in behalf of another's cause resulted into his expulsion from the club.[197]

Members of the common table ate two meals a day, namely, one in the morning and the other at five o'clock in the afternoon. The regulations required that there was relative silence at their meals, permitting devotional Bible reading, and at times, serious, confidential discussions between members of the club. The rules stress a fine companionship and an excellent *esprit de corps*. Both meals were opened with a blessing, at which time the membership was to be seated, heads bowed, with complete silence and a reverent composure. At breakfast time an ordinarius professor was to read a part of the Holy Scriptures, while in the afternoon at dinner he could read a part of Sleiden's Chronicle or read part of the Chronicle of Philip, in case the other was completed, and thus they were to alternate. At the end a clergyman would close the meal with a prayer and end with a plea for the well-being of the elector and his family; whereupon the members were to depart in silence to their quarters.[198]

The laws of the first common table also regulated the decorum of its members. Their conduct was to be agreeable, pious, modest, and peaceful at all times. The club seems to have been a semi-religious organization, in which filthiness, obscenity, levity, and even joking were out of place. Nor was there any disagreement and argumentation between the members while they were dining. Any shouting across the table was absolutely forbidden. In case any member raised objections to the club rules he was expelled from the common table for good.[199] Trustworthy advisors were to be in charge of the club, with a limited term of office. Those chosen were to regard themselves as the shepherds of their flock. The advisors were to serve as judges of their membership, and make improvements when possible. One of the regulations is related to possible thefts of beer and wine from the storage cellar. If such a case should arise, the supervisors consulted the rector, who with his inspectors worked out a solution. In case the offenders were found to be guilty of theft in property, food, and wine, they were to be forced to return the stolen goods or make proper reparations.[200] In the remainder of the Suevus document, various possible offenses are enumerated and relative degrees of fines imposed for such misconduct.[201]

It is not known where the common table was located in the days of the Ernestine rule, but it is believed it was in the New Friderici College building. In the reigns of the Electors John and John Frederick it is believed the same common table continued. In the beginning, it could not have been located in the Black Cloister, as it was occupied by monks and under the Electors John and John Frederick the Luthers lived in the building. But under the Albertine Line the situation for the Elector August had completely changed. He had purchased the Black Cloister, erected the *Augusteum,* moved in the Toszen House to accommodate 150 scholarship students. Under him the common table was only for poor scholars, who lived in the three houses at his expense and were to have a common table to reduce their academic costs. We also do not know where the common table was located, but without doubt such a large group could dine only in the former Augustinian monks' dining hall in the basement of the Black Cloister. We know they were well organized, with a regular provider, a kitchen chef, and other officials who supervised the care of housing and dining 150 students. However, the details of their dining rules and the supplying of a large body of men is not recorded.

21

The University Library

---------------- ❖ ----------------

The importance of the library of the University of Wittenberg in the history of the Lutheran Reformation can be illustrated by a remarkable incident. The books of the library of the University of Wittenberg were transported to Weimar during the Schmalkaldic War in 1547 and then, in 1558, became the nucleus of the newly established library of the University of Jena. In 1746, M. J. C. Mylius of Jena recorded the titles of these precious books, which had been used by the faculty and students of Wittenberg, a copy of the catalogue of which I possess.

Many German scholars have claimed that Melanchthon was the first to state that Luther had nailed his Ninety-five Theses at 2 P.M. on October 31, 1517. None of these scholars appears to have been familiar with Mylius's findings. In preparing his catalog, the *Memorabilia Bibliothecae*, Mylius must have become familiar with the contents of much of this material. As he picked up an old German Bible, a translation of 1540, which Luther must have used, he discovered that it had some of Luther's own marginal notes. At the end of the volume, Mylius made a tremendous discovery. Between the close of the *Register* and the words *Gedruckt zu Wittenberg durch Hans Lufft, M.D., 1540*, the Bible had an empty space, in which Luther had written the following:

> In the year of our Lord 1517, on the day prior to the festival of All Saints Day, at Wittenberg, Theses of Indulgences were posted on the doors of the churches by Martin Luther.
>
> Anno domini 1517, in profesto omnium sanctorum Wittenberge in valvis temporum propositae sunt de Indulgentis a D. Mart. Luthero.

This remarkable discovery by Mylius is no longer known to scholars today. Mylius's findings should remove all doubt about Luther's nailing of the Ninety-five Theses on the door of the Castle Church on October 31, 1517.

In the preceding chapters of this study, there is a description of the type of university Elector Frederick founded in 1502, in accordance with the *Stiftungs-*

brief of Emperor Maximilian I, which was executed by the elector in 1502. The confirmation documents from papal legates and the incorporation of the academic institution with the *Stift* of the Castle Church by Pope Julius II were in 1507.[1] Then, in sequence, we described the school's academic structure in accordance with the *Elector's Statutes of 1508;*[2] the early endowment of the institution by the elector with the *Stift* funds; and the scholastic courses and types of degrees offered in the first decade of the University of Wittenberg. After that there was a coverage of the early inroads of humanism into the original school and the later development of biblical humanism under the leadership of Martin Luther and Philip Melanchthon, with its return *ad fontem*, the biblical languages of Greek and Hebrew, which resulted in the transformation of the Christian church during the Reformation.[3]

The picture, however, is not complete without the student's acquaintance with the Wittenberg University library, founded by Frederick the Wise, continued and enlarged by his successors, John the Constant and his son John Frederick, until the Schmalkaldic War, when the last elector was captured and the entire library was transported to Weimar; then in 1558 it became the nucleus of the library of the University of Jena, founded by the sons of the previous Elector John Frederick. The description of the physical plant and the growth of the library through the purchase of rare manuscripts and recently printed books by its librarian and bibliophile, Georg Spalatin, will be the theme of this chapter.[4]

Several earlier publications by the author covered the nature and holdings of the Wittenberg library, but space did not permit going into any detail about its holdings.[5] In 1940 a descriptive article appeared in *The Library Quarterly*, of the University of Chicago Press, no. 3, under the title "Remnants of a Reformation Library," which was written by the author after research at the Jena University library in 1936, the present location of the once famous collection used by Luther, Melanchthon, and other professors while it was still in Wittenberg.[6] More limited coverage of this theme also appears in the author's book *Luther and His Times*.[7] At academic meetings scholars have often asked, "Why don't you tell us what was in the Wittenberg library? Since the library contained 3,132 volumes, exhaustive coverage of its 600-page catalogue, a copy of which the author possesses, is not possible even here, and we must limit ourselves to the most important works relative to the Reformation.

In 1936 while the author was doing research in various German universities, thanks to the assistance of the librarians at Jena, he had the delightful experience of handling and examining some of the very material that Georg Spalatin had assembled as librarian. Most importantly, he had the privilege of obtaining from the librarians a copy of the library catalogue prepared in 1740 by the Jena professor M. J. C. Mylius, a catalogue made while the original Reformation library was still intact.[8] This precious source and many other extant source materials of Spalatin's day formed the basis for the reconstruction of this colorful collection used by Wittenberg professors and students. How this library happened to come to Jena University will be taken up in a later part of this chapter.

THE FOUNDING OF THE LIBRARY

The University of Wittenberg was without a library for a decade prior to Elector Frederick's decision to establish a fine new library through his librarian Georg Spalatin. During this period there appears to have been a rather extensive collection of theological and legal works, kept somewhere in the Castle Church, dating back to 1504; this had been a monastic library of Thomas Loesser, a canon of Meiszen. These were no doubt some of the old pigskin tomes referred to in the Mylius account of the collection in the Wittenberg library in 1740.[9] Doubtless this was the original incentive for and nucleus around which the later library was to be built after 1512.[10] Since, as was observed above, the Thomists and Scotists, both in theology and law, dominated the academic life in the original university, these professors must have made ample use of this rich monastic collection.[11]

The exact reasons for Elector Frederick's resolution to found a new library in Wittenberg remain unknown. We may surmise that there were several factors. No doubt professors expressed the need for better tools in their academic research. The fact that the prince made Georg Spalatin the general superintendent of the building of the new library may indicate that he expressed a need for a real modern library. After all, Georg Spalatin had grown up in the humanistic atmosphere at Erfurt and passed under the influence of Conrad Rufus and Urbanus, of the Erfurt humanistic circle, saw the need for new Greek, Latin, and Hebrew books for the University of the Elbe, and may have urged the elector to found a library.[12]

As shown in earlier accounts by Sebastian Müller,[13] Mylius,[14] and Grohmann, there is some difference of opinion as to when the library was founded; but this may be due to different uses of the word *gestifted*, or founded, as it may have been planned in 1512 and did not materialize until 1514.

If we set the foundation date of the library on the basis of the first contacts made and book purchases, the most convincing evidence of its existence in 1512 may be found in an old pigskin-covered account reference book from Spalatin's personal library, which today is in the *Landesbibliothek* in Gotha, in the castle of Fredenstein. In this book the librarian kept a record of purchases made during the first year. According to this account book, between July 28, 1512, and Easter 1513, a total of 151 works of varying types were purchased for 202 Gulden, or $16,150.[15] The date of 1512 is also substantiated by a number of other contemporary records. In Spalatin's *Ephemerides*, the annual account of important events in his life, he made the following entry in 1512: "*Hoc anno Fredericus III Elector Saxoniae Bibliotheccam in Arce Wittenbergensi auspicatur, minostro et bibliothecario in hac, me, G. Spalatino usus.*"[16] Thus, Spalatin himself, the very participant in the event, confirms that the ducal library was founded in the castle at Wittenberg, with him in charge, as early as 1512. Frederick the Wise likewise confirms this date of founding in a letter to the famous Venetian printer and bookseller Aldus Manucius, in which he writes on December 1, 1512: "we are engaged in establishing a library in our castle at Wittenberg, Saxony."[17] In the same year, some months earlier, the new librarian had also written Aldus Manucius for available book lists from which he might order rare manuscripts and classical books for the new library. There is further confirmation for the date 1512 in the correspondence between Spalatin and Christopher Scheurl in Nürnberg, found in a Scheurl letter in his *Briefbuch*, in which he complains that Spalatin has not written, but excuses him on the grounds that he has learned through Pfeffinger that he has been made librarian of the new ducal library in Wittenberg, for which he is to be congratulated, and then adds that he learned "that you are so busy acquiring books from all over that you are scarcely able to breathe between sweatings."[18] In the correspondence of the famous Gotha humanist Conradus Mutianus, there is an interesting revelation of what lay behind Frederick the Wise's unusual purchases from the Aldus Press in Venice. In a letter to Urbanus himself, in 1513, he writes:

> Through my advice it was made possible for the Illustrious Frederick to purchase a Greek Library in Venice and he has opened it to the public, equipped in a most ornate fashion.[19]

We may conclude then, on the best contemporary evidence, that the ducal library came into existence during the summer of 1512, and was made available in an ornate way in the upper *Hofstube*, as shall be observed in a section below. At the time of Aldus' letter of 1513, it may have consisted of the Thomas Loesser scholastic works in theology and law and the new works added by that time from Venice as described by modern scholars.[20]

THE RELATIONSHIP OF LIBRARY AND SCHOOL

The question may be asked, What was the relationship between the library and the University of Wittenberg? Did Frederick the Wise regard it as his personal property or did he look upon it as belonging together with the remainder of the university? This question deserves an examination, in view of the fact that the third Elector John Frederick simply ordered it to be transported to Weimar during the Schmalkaldic War, leaving the university without a library. Or was there a change in the thinking in the later period, when John Frederick lost the Electorate of Saxony to Duke Moritz by the declaration of Emperor Charles V in 1547?

In order to view this problem in its broader perspective, we need to review the history of the institution. After the founding of the library the electors all took a keen interest in its growth and its use by able scholars and students in all fields, as will be noted in an analysis of the library's acquisitions. It was first housed on an upper floor of the castle in Wittenberg, and students passed through the doors of the Castle Church, entered the castle proper, and thus drew material from the library. As the Reformation emerged and the university underwent a transformation toward biblical humanism, the need for Greek, Hebrew, and Latin works increased; and, under Melanchthon's supervision, the classics again blossomed as tools of instruction. Then, in the magnanimous spirit of the young Elector John Frederick, Wittenberg University was refounded, given new statutes from 1533 to 1536; the library was moved to a large, more suitable court room, and a sum of $7,500 was spent annually on the enlargement of its rich holdings to meet the needs of the faculty and students.[21] Thus by 1547 the library, consisting of both manuscripts and an equal number of books, totaled:

Theological Works	1,040
Judicial Works	562
Medical Works	545
Philosophical Works	964
Summa omnium in bibliotheca	3,111
Electorali librorum	
et Musici	21[22]

This large collection of manuscripts and books, which according to the Mylius report, consisted of 1,746 folio-sized works, 626 of quarto size, and 22 of duodecimo size, was so heavy in the *alte Hofstube* that two special pillars had to be used as supports for the room, and even then it sagged considerably from the load.[23] Many of these pigskin-covered manuscripts were rare, as will be observed in another connection, and needed to be fastened by chains to bookcases, with benches below. Today this space is occupied by the *Pfarrhaus-archiv*.[24]

In the year 1547 the Schmalkaldic War broke out, in which Emperor Charles V and Duke Moritz of Albertine Saxony invaded the *Kurkreis*, while Elector John Frederick, attempting to retreat through the Lochauer Heide in a fog,[25] was surrounded by the Imperial forces near Mühlberg, and was captured. Charles V and his army then surrounded Wittenberg with his troops, and the citizens of the electoral town were in danger of being seized, and the city put on fire. The prince preferred to capitulate rather than endanger the citizens and his wife and family who were within. Thus with Elector John Frederick's capture, Electoral Saxony was lost, and with it the University of Wittenberg.[26] The Wittenberg capitulation followed on May 19, 1547,[27] in which the elector was forced to surrender the *Kurkeis* and his title of Elector to his treacherous and ambitious cousin, Duke Moritz.[28] During the settlement, however, John Frederick insisted that the Wittenberg Library was his own personal property, and he seems to have convinced Charles V of his claims.[29] On July 3, 1547, John Frederick wrote from the imperial camp in Bamberg to the librarian, Edenberger, to transport the whole library to the old cloister library in Weimar.[30] This seems to have been anticipated, for apparently it had already been done, for the court lawyers reported that Edenberger had already arrived in Weimar on June 28, 1547, with "7 Fudern Bucher."[31] Here they remained unopened in boxes according to John Frederick's instructions. Mentz adds that they were afraid to unload the books into the *Schlosz* because of the "large mice."[32] The elector wanted to keep the books boxed in the large containers until he could found his own new University of Jena.[33] The books appear to have been moved to Jena in the summer of 1549, where they were kept in all secrecy.[34] Thus later, in 1558, they became the original nucleus of the newly founded Jena library. Burderus later claimed the library might be more appropriately called the "John Frederick Library."[35]

On the basis of John Frederick's order to transport the library as his private property, some scholars have concluded that it was indeed his personal property; however, as will soon be evident this reasoning is not historical. Grohmann pointed out that the library may have appeared as private property in a special sense, but that this does not exclude the fact that he founded it for the use of the University of Wittenberg.[36] For a satisfactory conclusion the contemporary evidence must be further investigated.

In the aforementioned letter to Aldus, the elector wrote that he was engaged in establishing a library in the Castle at Wittenberg, which was to be "for the common good of all the professors and students of our University,"[37] While Spalatin, even though he commonly referred to the library in rather general terms,[38] in his early correspondence with Aldus, wrote: "The Prince is adorning his new University of Wittenberg with an excellent library, replete with books of all kinds, and all disciplines."[39] This leads us to conclude that the library from the very beginning was regarded as being a part of the new institution.

As observed in a previous chapter,[40] the University of Wittenberg was particularly well endowed by the funds the elector used from the *Stift* of the Castle Church; while in the beginning the remainder was paid out of his own private court funds. At one time this *Stift* had supported many Catholic clergymen, some of whom taught on the Wittenberg faculties, others who served the Castle Church and the elector in various religious services and masses. After the Reformation began to make its inroads on the university life, these services were no longer needed, and as clergy died, the funds used for their support were also directed toward funding the university. The relics in the Castle Church disappeared, and by 1526 few clergymen were left who needed the support of the Elector John. At this time there was an advance in the endowment funds of Wittenberg University in which the electoral *Rat*, Hans von Dolzig, served as the official in the undertaking. In Spalatin's correspondence with him at the time, he regarded the university library as a natural part of the institution. For example, in February 1526, Spalatin made this request:

> I beg again as in times past, that you graciously commit the care of the University of Wittenberg in all humility to my gracious Lord, the Elector of Saxony; and, that he keep in mind the Library with all faithfulness and the poor student.[41]

Certainly, here is no thought of the Wittenberg library being a separate entity from the rest of the institution.

The Elector John the Constant ruled in Ernestine Saxony from 1525 until his death in 1532, after which he was succeeded by his son John Frederick the

Magnanimous, the second founder of Wittenberg. John Frederick reorganized the School of Theology in 1533 and gave the University new status in 1536. In this 1536 document it is quite evident that at the time he regarded the library as an integral part of his university.[42]

This foundation document contains a special section pertaining to the ducal library. In a brief history of its origin it stated that the library was founded for "the benefit of the University and for poor students," after which it mentions that it will be moved to a more convenient place where it may be available to all.[43] And in addition, it also states that now 100 Gulden ($7,500) are available in the annual budget for the library's enlargement. The Statutes also provided for a librarian, with an annual salary of 40 Gulden ($3,900) a year, to be paid quarterly out of the endowed university funds. That he regarded the entire university, as well as the library, to be the property of the elector, is well illustrated in this document.[44] References, therefore, are found like those frequently made by Spalatin, such as "the Library of Your Electoral Grace in Wittenberg,"[45] and "the Library at Wittenberg in the Castle."[46]

If not prior to 1526, certainly from then on the relationship of the Wittenberg library and the university was regarded as being very close. Spalatin wrote the elector in October 1536, just after the new *Statutes of 1536* had gone into effect and the institution had been reformed after the pattern of Luther and his fellow reformers, and asked that the library should be continually enlarged from regular endowment funds.[47] Three days later Elector John Frederick replied from his Torgau Castle that from that time on, the 100 Gulden ($7,500) allowed in the *1536 Statutes* for the purchase of new books for the ducal library should be financed through "dem Gelde Fundation."[48]

In the year 1543, the librarian of the ducal library, Lukas Edenberger, wrote the prince that the university had been offered the opportunity to purchase a large globe of the world for the library, at a cost of forty Taler.[49] Unfortunately, the funds allowed from the budget had already been spent on books; but Philip Melanchthon was particularly anxious to use the globe in his astronomy classes.[50] To this request the elector replied on November 28, 1543, that it would be desirable that the "Himmelglobus" be purchased for the department of mathematics, where it could be used, while in the library it might remain unused or even be destroyed.[51]

There are other sources that support the claim of a close relationship between the Wittenberg library and the university. Mylius wrote:

> The Elector Frederick III, rightfully and deservedly called "The Wise;" laid the foundation for the Library. After the Elector had founded the University of Wittenberg in 1502 with great liberality of spirit and at great expense, having received expert advice and had put distinguished and excellent doctors on its faculty, he was further solicitous that still also a fine collection of books to be purchased, which could not only be of service to the Elector privately but, would also be useful to the scholars of the University whose private supply of books was curtailed or at any rate insufficient.[52]

The library may also be viewed from the angle of the Wittenberg faculty. That it played a role in the selection and the purchase of rare volumes is quite evident. This can be seen from the type of books that were purchased.[53] For example, Philip Melanchthon appears to have had much to do with the selection of books for the ducal library,[54] and he wrote Spalatin in 1533:

> Oh, that our plan of buying a variety of books would seem worthwhile to the Prince. For I have heard that the Prince wishes that only theological and native books be purchased; yet, I recall in discussing this matter in our correspondence with the Prince, to have read this remark, that a variety of all kinds of Latin and German works should be bought.[55]

Thus, when the problem is viewed from the angle of academic requirements, this can explain why and what was done; for only a university faculty would be interested in the many manuscripts and printed volumes published in Venice and other Italian cities. Not even the annual fairs at Leipzig[56] or Frankfurt am Main[57] could comply with the demands of the faculty. Accordingly, Spalatin was even asked to make frequent trips to Venice. This may have been especially true in the case of Luther and his collaborators, in refining his translations of his German Bible after the publication of his first edition of the *Deutsche Bibel* in 1534, in which Cruciger and Aurogallus used Hebrew and Chaldean texts for a more definitive translation. Apparently, the professors in the different faculties checked the book lists of available source material; and then Spalatin, when available, purchased whatever works were needed.[58] The above demand may have been the very reason why Spalatin, on February 11, 1533, wrote the prince, explaining that the books needed by the Wittenberg faculty could not be purchased in German lands:

> Eurer Churfurstlichen Gnaden wissen sich on Zweifel gnediglich zu erinnern meines vorigen untertenigen erbietens das ich umbetlich bucher Register gin Nurmberg und Leyptzick getrachtet. Zu furderung E.Chf. G. Librey zu Wittemberg. Nu sind sie mir kommen. Habs auch Magister Philip Melanchthon und Magister Lucasen Edemberger etc. zugeschickt. Darauf mir nechten von Inen schrifften zekommen, das sie zu bemelter Librey der bucher vermoge inligender Zceddeln disz Jars zuerkauffen am netigsten, wie es dann E.Chf. G. durch Nurmberger am bequemsten aus Venedig zu bestellen konnen verschaffen Dann in deutschen Landen werden sie schwerlich anzutreffen seyn.[59]

This statement implies that Spalatin had been in contact with Melanchthon and the Librarian Edenberger, after receiving booklists from Nürnberg, which could be ordered through its merchants from Venice and in this way comply with the Wittenberg faculty needs of rare books not available in German lands.

Trips to Venice in those days were difficult and expensive for a librarian to make; yet in 1539 the elector had Spalatin go to the great book center to purchase certain Hebrew and Greek works needed by the Wittenberg faculty. Mylius made this observation about the trip, "For, as is clear from the handwritten letter of Spalatin to the Elector, that the best Greek and Hebrew manuscripts were much missed by the venerable professors of Wittenberg, since copies could not be procured in Nürnberg or Leipzig."[60] The personal visit to Venice must have been more than satisfactory, for we learn from Mylius that Spalatin continued to make trips to Venice, in order to supply the faculty with the needed proper manuscripts.[61] This need must have been realized by the elector, for he knew that Luther and the *Sanhedrin* were busy preparing the reformer's 1539 and 1545 editions of the German Bible.[62] In addition to their use, the professor had the right to withdraw these rare works from the library, a practice that the elector granted rather reluctantly.[63]

From all this evidence, it is quite obvious that the ducal library stood in a very intimate relationship to the University of Wittenberg. It seems that since the elector owned the entire university, it was simply taken for granted that the ducal library was a part of the institution which he had founded. This close association of the university with the elector is shown further by the fact that the old *Friderici Collegium* and the *Neue Friderici* were named after the elector Frederick the Wise.[64] To have spoken of the library as the "University Library," which occurs only once,[65] would have implied that it was the property, in modern parlance, of a private corporation. The important thing is that the students and faculty looked upon the library as an integral part of the university. The leading professors assisted Spalatin in the purchase of its holdings, used the books and manuscripts freely, and regarded it as their own tool for their individual creative work.

It is significant that the library was founded in the very year that Martin Luther began his series of lectures on the *Psalms*, *Romans*, *Galatians*, and *Hebrews*, so it could supply him with original working material during his formative years. There can be little doubt that Spalatin's heavy purchases in Greek, Latin, and Hebrew works were closely related to his unfolding as the Wittenberg reformer, from 1513 to 1518. It became his workshop from then until his death in 1546. Luther's growth as the reformer and his winning of the Wittenberg faculty to his biblical humanism runs parallel with Spalatin's purchases of books for the new library; and this library, conversely, becomes the marrow for the development of the reformer and the growth of Lutheranism in the University of Wittenberg. Later the rich holdings of this library, as shown below, will offer new insight into the workshop of the German reformation. Let us now attempt to reconstruct this workshop of Luther and Melanchthon, in its outstanding physical appearance, growth, and contents.

THE PHYSICAL APPEARANCE OF THE LIBRARY

As is often so true, the contemporaries of an environment do not take the time to describe what is to them so self-evident, and taken for granted by everyone else. Thus even professors like Luther and Melanchthon make no reference to the physical environment in the wonderful library that was their reference center and no doubt often their workshop. Thus, in our reconstruction, we are forced to rely on other indirect references. We have seen how the *Dialogus of 1507* by Professor Meinhardt described the rooms of the castle as objects of beauty, with their Greek and Roman mythological scenes.[66] It hardly seems that the elector, who adorned his new library, according to Mutian of Gotha, with an environment worthy of mentioning by the famous printer Aldus Manucius in Venice, would have done less for the library. But we can use an indirect approach by asking, What was the environment in other libraries of the late Middle Ages like? How were they equipped with benches and library shelves and furniture customary at the time? Since so many of the rare volumes in this library were manuscripts of folio size, special bookshelves and chain arrangements were in keeping with similar practices elsewhere.

Since libraries, like individuals, vary greatly, some caution seems fitting in a reconstruction of what the ducal library may have looked like. No doubt a distinction must also be made between the first library in the upper room of the Schlosz and the more commodious and ornate one established on the second floor in the "alte Hofstube." Knowing the general library practice in Western Europe during the early part of the sixteenth century, we may assume that, as in fashions, they all had some characteristics in common.[67]

Antiquity had a wide variety of libraries, the most famous being those of Alexandria, Pergamum, and Rome. In addition, there were many private libraries. But before the existence of modern books, the form of scrolls necessitated a very different type building from those that were founded in the Middle Ages. With the development of the medieval *Scriptorium* and the copying of the scrolls of ancient culture in book form came an entire new world of learning. Had the monks not copied what was preserved from Greco-Roman works and the Jewish-Christian preservations, it would have been lost forever. Most of the old media became molded, crumbled into dust, or perished in the destructive fires of the centuries. There could have been no Carolingian, Ottoman 12th Century, or Italian renaissances without the Greco-Roman culture that monks had reproduced in modern book form.

The library as we know it today had its inception in the medieval monastery and grew out of a need for better use and preservation of precious medieval manuscripts.[68] In the exchange and copying of rare sources, the number of manuscripts became too large to be distributed among the members. Besides, such distribution exposed precious books to the rigorous climatic conditions of many parts of Northern Europe, or to theft, and the problems of their distribution became acute.[69] In 1396 the Cistercians at Meaux in Holderness conceived the idea of housing their books in a special room,[70] which innovation soon spread all over Western Europe. Then, during the renaissance, the funding of private and princely libraries became quite popular. It seems that the furnishing, handling, and chaining of valuable works became more or less universal throughout all the West. As most manuscripts were folio size, special bookcases and bars with chains became almost a necessity. This required large and sturdy bookshelves and, below, a working area.[71] But with the invention of the printing press, the practice of housing books changed somewhat; for cheaper printed books did not require the very elaborate protection of manuscripts.[72] It was then that the chaining of books was dropped for all but the precious volumes, and ordinary bookracks and bookcases came into use.

The details of the first library, located in a large upper room of the castle, remain unknown, except that Spalatin had a guest room next to it on the fourth floor while making his biannual inspections as superintendent.[73] This location is further confirmed in 1536 with a reference to it when it was moved from there to the "old Hofstube" on the second floor as being a more roomy and convenient place.[74] Some light as to the location of the two places of the library in 1512 and 1536 is shed in the publications of Professor Heubner, then the custodian of the town archives.[75] Unfortunately, Meinhardt's *Dialogus of 1507*, which described the inside of the castle, predated the founding of the library, and thus is of no value in this matter. It must also be remembered that in the early period the library was relatively small and could be housed in a smaller place. Perhaps it was housed on the north side of the upper floor, where it would be readily accessible from the stairway, the very room in which in 1936 Dr. Krüger housed the remaining Wittenberg relics preserved by the *Verein für Heimatskunde*.[76]

Although the location of the library after 1536 has become a little more definite, Dr. Heubner admits that it presents some problems when he writes:

> The question of the divisions of the rooms in the Castle is unusually difficult to determine. In the *Urbarium* III (town records of Wittenberg) part B6, there is a ground plan of the three stories in the Electoral Castle, dating to the time of the Silesian Wars, but before the time of 1740, with an identification of most of the rooms in accordance with their use at the time.[77]

In addition, Dr. Heubner cites two other inventories of the castle layout,[78] the one in 1539 and the other in 1611, both of which are used to locate the library of 1536. The 1539 one is by the then custodian Wolf Schieferdecker,[79] while the 1611 plan was reconstructed by Uszwald, Schwartz, and Volck, of the Magdeburger *Staatsarchiv*.[80]

According to these sources, Dr. Heubner concludes that the second library was located on the floor immediately above the large south room, referred to in the *Dialogus of 1507* as the *"Aesturium commune."*[81] This space now houses the Stadtarchiv and included the space now being occupied by the *Pfarrhausarchiv*.[82] Since its inception, the library grew tremendously and became so heavy they feared for its structural strength to bear the heavy load. In 1546 they placed two supporting pillars below, to help support the weight.[83] Thus the location of the second library must have been in what was known then as *die alte Hofstube*.[84]

The exact size of this room is of course impossible to determine today, but it must have been quite large to house the number and type of works it contained. We do not know how large the original Loeser collection of theological and legal manuscripts and books was, nor the sizes of many monastic libraries, which were acquired during the secularization of Saxon monasteries. The records show that the elector purchased 151 volumes of Greek and Latin works out of

Venice in the beginning, as stated above, many of which were dictionaries and reference tools for the study of Greek and Hebrew by Luther and his students during the formative years.[85] But it is not known how rapidly after that the library was enlarged. Spalatin spoke frequently about adding numerous books, but none of the references are definite enough to determine the exact size of the library at any given time.[86] But by the close of John Frederick's reign its size can definitely be determined. According to the historical records, the entire library was transported from Wittenberg to Weimar and later formed the original nucleus of the library of the University of Jena. According to Professor Mylius, the library still remained in a separate place until 1740, when he made a permanent recording of its contents. According to Mylius, the library contained 1,756 volumes in folio size, 626 in quarto, and only 22 in duodecimo size.[87] As will be observed later, about half of the volumes were manuscripts, bound in heavy pigskin bindings, which would increase the size and weight. Many of these works were rare and costly and could not be purchased in Germany.[88]

Perhaps a few comparisons with other libraries of the time will be of assistance in estimating the probable size of the room where the Wittenberg library was located after 1536:

> At Canterbury the library, built as I have said, over the Prior's Chapel, was 60 feet long, 22 feet broad; and we know, from some memoranda written in 1508, when a number of books were sent to be bound or repaired, that it contained sixteen bookcases, each of which had four shelves. I have calculated that this library could have contained about 2,000 volumes.[89]

The Queen of Sicily left the following description of the library at Clairvaux, dated July 13, 1517:

> The library is 189 feet long, by 17 feet wide. In it are 48 seats (bancs) and in each seat 4 shelves (poulpitres) furnished with books on all subjects, but chiefly theology: the greater number of the said books are of vellum, and written by hand, richly storied and illuminated. The building that contains the said library is magnificent, built of stone, and excellently lighted on both sides with fine large windows, well glazed, looking out on the said cloister. . . . The said library is paved throughout with small tiles adorned with various designs.[90]

Based on these estimates, we may conclude that a library of 3,132 volumes, 1,756 of which were large manuscripts, with pigskin coverbacks, would require a room of at least 60 feet by 35 feet. The reader may then picture the Wittenberg library being housed in a room about that size after 1536, conveniently located on the second floor of the south wing of the castle, well-lighted, with five large Gothic windows, which may be clearly seen in the Wittenberg woodcut of 1611, enlarged by Bossögel in 1744.[91] The windows probably had the same "bull's eye glass" as may still be seen today in *Lutherstube*[92] or the *Melanchthonhaus*,[93] both of which were built by the elector in that period of materials furnished by the court.

Even though we possess no descriptions of the inner appearance of the ducal library, there are, however, a number of indirect references, which assist us in

forming some mental picture of the appearance of its interior. The Wittenberg
Castle, prior to its bombardments in later years, was regarded as one of the most
beautiful in all Germany.[94] This has been covered previously, where there is a
detailed account of Frederick the Wise as a connoisseur of art, a rich prince who
built many fine churches and palaces. [95] This is certainly confirmed by the *Dialogus of 1507*, which describes its artistic interior in great detail.[96] It is hardly
likely that the proud prince, who employed so many leading artists of his day to
adorn the castle and the Castle Church, would be content with inferior adornment of his prized library, filled with thousands of precious books and manuscripts. Georg Spalatin, in his correspondence with the printer Aldus Manucius,
would hardly have used the verb *ornat*[97] to describe the elector's new library
had it not been attractive; and, claiming he was beautifying it, replete in all
fields. Nor would the Canon Mutian of Gotha have used the superlative to
describe the library to Aldus Manucius and the Venice Press, unless he thought
that the elector's library in Wittenberg was unusual in beauty, filled with manuscripts and rare Latin and Greek classics.[98] Certainly Mutian was both informed
and impressed, to laud Frederick the Wise's undertaking. This leads the reader
to conclude that even the first library environment, in the upper floor of the
ducal castle, was very attractive; while the second one, which replaced it on the
second floor, in 1536, must have been even more ornate and filled with up-to-
date bookcases and benches. The superintendent must have been anxious to
make it more commodious, for, in his correspondence, he speaks of adorning
the walls with portraits of important educators of the past.[99] Whether this was
done remains unknown, yet it confirms the superintendent's desire to beautify
the room with portraits in keeping with the rest of the building.[100] There is also
evidence that the library must have been spacious and not completely occupied
with benches and books, for there is a reference to the large "Globe of the
Heavens" that Melanchthon wanted to buy for his classes, that they planned to
keep in the library. [101] From all this evidence, we may safely conclude that the
ducal library of 1536 was housed in a well-planned, spacious, artistically decorated chamber equipped with contemporary-type furniture, in keeping with the
rest of the most attractive castle. Unfortunately, there is no contemporary
account or description of the library furniture or other equipment; yet the officials refer occasionally to *"Pulte und Bänke, sowie Ketten für die Kostbaren
Werke."*[102] In a letter of October 12, 1536, the elector informed Spalatin of the
changes he was making in the administration of the library by the employment
of a regular librarian, and then he added:

> When the Library has been brought into the *alte Hofstube*, see to it that there
> is a daily opening and closing made by him, but Spalatin is to have the respon-
> sibility and supervision that the designated books for the budgeted 100
> Gulden for their ordering and purchasing be made; and that at least semi-
> annually he make a visit to Wittenberg to look things over. Furthermore he is,
> when the rods and chains ordered from Nürnberg have arrived, to see to it
> that the Library then is properly equipped with these. Prior to this, however,
> he is to come to Torgau and talk things over with the Elector.[103]

From this brief communication of the elector to the superintendent of the library, in 1536 and later, it is quite clear that this implies a complete reequipment of the new library with bookcases, benches, and equipment to assure the safety of his precious works. But it also shows that Elector John Frederick was genuinely interested in equipping the library with the most modern furnishings, ordered from the great cultural center of Nürnberg; and besides, that he was concerned that the ducal library be opened and closed and managed in a most business-like manner. In a second communication, November 22, 1536, the elector ordered that the library officials keep a close watch on the "incomes and expenditures," so that the books not be "*verdert werden.*" This resulted in a yearly catalogue by the official Christopher Nocolas, under the direction of Georg Spalatin.[104]

Based on these descriptions, then, we can to some degree reconstruct the Wittenberg library in our minds, housed in luxurious quarters as already described. Since the furnishings came from Nürnberg, they were no doubt the latest Renaissance styles, to make this room harmonize with the rest of the castle.[105] The desks were designed and equipped to hold costly manuscripts, fastened securely with chains, as well as costly printed books from the Aldus Press and other Italian printers. Besides this Spalatin had to visit the fairs in Leipzig, Frankfurt am Main, and Nürnberg to purchase costly texts as they had become available in German lands.[106] Recently published tracts and works by Luther, Melanchthon, and Erasmus may have been placed on walled bookshelves now becoming customary in Northern Europe, which did not need to be chained.[107]

SUPERVISION AND MANAGEMENT OF THE LIBRARY

The preservation of medieval manuscripts became a serious concern for those in charge, which necessitated some kind of record keeping. And even the problem of use by monks, in case they took books to their cells, must have frequently caused mistreatment due to exposure and careless handling. This evolved systems of periodic checking, inspections, manuals of library rules, and whatever else appeared expedient to safeguard their precious holdings.[108]

Information on the early organization of the ducal library is very scanty. As noted above, Georg Spalatin, among his many other duties at the court of Frederick the Wise, served as general superintendent at the Wittenberg library from its inception, and made periodic visits to draft records of findings and suggested improvements.[109] There must have been a system of management for students and faculty members to use its rare volumes. On this we possess practically no information. The first rather indefinite reference to a regular librarian is in 1526,[110] but we do not know whether it was ever implemented. Rather, it appears from a letter of Spalatin to the elector written on December 26, 1534, that he informed him that the library still was without a regular salaried librarian.[111] Certainly he must have had some system of management, for he tells the elector he has drawn in most of the books which were loaned out.[112] Then Spalatin makes an unusual confession of the state of affairs with respect to the books of the ducal library, in the days of Elector John the Constant, although he has just spent 50 Gulden ($3,500) on the purchase of new books:

> The theological books lie in the Emporium of the Town Church behind the chancel, separated from the others. It would be a good idea for the library to be in proper place, and so arranged, that the books were fastened to chains, and a priest be designated to open and close the place, so that the library would be placed at the service of the entire university.[113]

This statement by the superintendent may have been exaggerated to create more orderly management of the library during a year when the university suffered a severe decline in student enrollment due to the fact that conservative Catholic princes turned against the University of Wittenberg after Luther's condemnation by the emperor at the Diet of Worms in 1521.[114] However, even in those hard times, there must have been some good system of organization through which books could be withdrawn from the library. Müller, in his Saxon *Annals*, spoke of the library as being located in the upper *Hofstube*, which had been opened "for public use." [115] Mylius became more specific by pointing out that the library was so organized that it might "be of advantage to the professors and students,"[116] while Mutian spoke of it as having been also "opened for the public."[117] Nor can we explain Spalatin's enthusiasm for enlarging the book collection with so many rare manuscripts, had there not been some form of management through which the books could be made available for those who had requested them. This is particularly true of Luther and Melanchthon's need for the classics and ancient manuscripts, used during their Bible translations. One wonders how they were catalogued and made ready for withdrawal as needed during the revisions of the university's curricula. But regardless of how this was managed, it appears evident that before 1534 the library did not have a regular librarian who was in charge during the absence of Spalatin. It is clear that faculty members and certain graduate students had access to the library when it was still housed in an upper room of the castle.

After the death of Elector John, the years 1533 to 1536 ushered in a new era for the University of Wittenberg. His successor, the young new Elector John Frederick, who had been tutored by Georg Spalatin at the court of Frederick the Wise, was an ardent supporter of the German Reformation. Meanwhile northern German Lands and Scandinavian countries had been won for the reforms instituted by the university, and a whole new generation of New Testament oriented students filled the classrooms of the university on the Elbe. Elector John Frederick became the founder of a new second university. He gave the theological faculty new Statutes in 1533, and new statutes to the whole university in 1536. As will be observed in subsequent chapters, the new Wittenberg now resembled more the humanistically oriented university of the eighteenth century than it did the universities of Paris and Bologna, after which the first university had been modeled. Such a changed atmosphere due to the German Reformation could hardly leave its library untouched.

Thus the year 1536 ushered in a new day for the Wittenberg library. A section of the *Statutes of 1536* was specifically devoted to the reorganization of the new library. The new room described above was ordered to be prepared in the castle and a regular librarian was to be in charge, paid semiannually from the endowed funds of the university. We have seen how the best bookcases and benches were to make the rare chained manuscripts available. There were to be regular hours for the opening and closing of the new library, as it was to be an integral part of the new educational program.[118] Although he is not mentioned in the official correspondence until 1539,[119] we assume that Lukas Edenberger was now the newly appointed librarian, and still under the supervision of Superintendent Georg Spalatin. The *Statutes* stated that 100 Gulden ($7,500) were to be available for the enlargement of the library holdings, and careful records were to be kept of the expenditures; lists were prepared for books as needed, on the basis of which of the superintendent would make his purchases. The librarian remained in touch with faculty, corresponded with scholars, and, together with Spalatin, also increased the library holdings from private sources.[120] One gathers from the correspondence with the electoral court that an invoice of all the titles of books and manuscripts was made,[121] of which two catalogue summaries have been preserved.[122] Books loaned out to the faculty were carefully recorded, and a time limit was placed on the period of withdrawal. These regulations of 1536 point to rather systematic library practices resembling those of today.

GROWTH OF THE WITTENBERG LIBRARY

Since previously in this study we aimed to explore the holdings of the Wittenberg library as recorded by Mylius in 1740, who contends they were then all in one collection at the University of Jena, the reader may also be interested in how the collection of books and manuscripts was acquired. When Professor Mylius speaks of an original nucleus of the library that was enlarged by the addition of theological and legal works from the Meissen Canon Thomas Loesser, he implies that there was an earlier nucleus dating back to 1504.[123] Whether this 1504 collection also consisted of some other old monastic libraries, a number of which were later incorporated into the ducal library,[124] or whether they were books that Frederick the Wise had acquired elsewhere, we are no longer able to determine. These were principally medieval books, but many may also have been valuable manuscripts. Some of the later listed works of St. Thomas, Albertus Magnus, and other scholastic works must have come from the original nucleus; for we know that the later works, purchased by Georg Spalatin, were those that were useful in the pursuit of biblical humanism, needed by Luther and Melanchthon for their new courses in Greek, Hebrew, and the Latin

Fathers. In the additions which Spalatin bought, we observe that they were books required for use in the new linguistic courses offered, after Luther and Melanchthon began to reform the University of Wittenberg.

The opening of the ducal library in 1512 was of fundamental assistance in ushering in the German Reformation, for it furnished the humanistic tools in Greek, Hebrew, and Latin needed for the transformation of classroom instruction in the reformed curricula. Both Spalatin and the elector, as stated above, wrote to Venice for catalogues of possible purchases from the press of Aldus Manucius, and other Italian houses, or from books acquired through German merchants. The new spirit is clearly evident from the works that were purchased the first year. Walter Friedensburg, who analyzed this list, made the following report about the acquisitions:

> What is more worthy of observation than the number (153 volumes) and cost of the acquired volumes (205 Gulden and 5 Grosche), is their contents. Here we look in vain for Aristotle and only now and then we encounter scholastic writings; they disappear almost entirely behind the number of writings by the Church Fathers, besides there is also a Bible with a "glossa ordinaria." Long is the list of a row of the classical authors of antiquity, among which many are written in the Greek language, and works of the first Christian century; there is also no lack of grammars and of dictionaries. Then come the works of Humanists, a Marsilio Ficino, an Aeneas Sylvius, Angelus Politianus, Leo Aretinus, a Pico della Mirandola, Laurentius Valla, Reuchlin and Erasmus which appear before us. Finally come the legal works, histories, medical astronomical works, an Itinerary of the Holy Land, all of which prepared a foundation upon which Spalatin supported by others could move ahead in the next few years.[125]

This emphasis on Latin, Greek, and Hebrew books, which reveals a definite Renaissance influence, became even more evident in future purchases. Spalatin, a member of the Gotha circle of humanists, received counsel and assistance from Mutian and his friends. Through these humanistic friends, young Spalatin could make his wants known in Italy. Christopher Scheurl, who had been at Wittenberg, congratulated the superintendent and also tried to be of assistance by informing him that he could obtain for him the works of the great astronomer John Regiomontanus, whose work at one time had been valued at more than a thousand Hungarian Gulden. Another friend of the elector, the aged professor Polich von Mellerstadt, told the librarian where to purchase a work of Ptolemy. A letter of Spalatin to Hans von Dolzig, on January 13, 1514, reveals the latter had visited the New Year's Leipzig Fair, where he looked for volumes to purchase, and inquired how he had fared. In 1515 Spalatin recorded in his diary: "In this same year Frederick III, Elector of Saxony wrote Aldus Manucius in Venice in behalf of Greek and Latin books for the Wittenberg Library, but as Aldus had died shortly before this, Andreas Asulanus, the father-in-law, sent the books."[126]

Meanwhile, Spalatin himself underwent a profound change. He had been a typical Erfurt graduate with a scholastic background in theology, but he had also passed under the influence of some humanistic friends in the Mutian circle of Gotha. Then during the early years of the library, Spalatin had come under the influence of Martin Luther and his "New Theology" at Wittenberg, which was transforming the university from a scholastic center into one of biblical humanism. In this new environment of the sacred languages, as they were known, Latin, Greek, and Hebrew began to be stressed in classrooms, Luther himself began a serious study of Greek and Hebrew, and began to use Erasmus' Greek *New Testament of 1516* and the writings of the Church Fathers. Courses in Hebrew and Greek were necessary to prepare the students for a proper understanding of Luther's biblical lectures. Between 1518 and 1520 Luther and Melanchthon had brought about a fundamental change in the academic curricula, which demanded new tools in Greek and Hebrew in their classrooms. This change in the university explains why the library purchased the new type of books to meet the needs of both faculty members and students. A brief analysis of what transpired that influenced the growth of the ducal library may offer valuable additional insight.

As we saw in previous chapters, humanism had also invaded the halls of the University of Wittenberg, as it did other institutions of Germany, but it was never used on the inside in the original university. Humanism was not required for promotions in the various academic disciplines and the three graduate schools. However it did not leave the scholastics untouched in style and ways of writing their texts for publication.

Wittenberg appointed its first real instructor in Greek and Hebrew, Thilonius Philymnus, who also became a convert to Luther's biblical humanism. Then in 1518, the elector appointed Philip Melanchthon at Wittenberg as the permanent Professor of Greek, whom his great uncle, John Reuchlin regarded as the ablest Greek scholar in Germany, outside of Erasmus. Several attempts were made to fill the post in Hebrew by converted Jews, but that did not work out too well until Aurogallus became the permanent professor in that discipline. All this change in the life of the University of Wittenberg between 1512 and 1518 lies in the background of the building of a properly equipped ducal library.

We saw in a previous section how Thomism and Scotism almost completely dominated the academic life of students at Wittenberg from 1502 to 1512, as it had done to its previous models, Paris and Bologna. Luther had traveled this same route toward his doctorate in theology, via the route of Lombard's *Sentences* and Aristotle as the supreme master of all western thought. But when Luther was appointed the successor of Johann Staupitz and began the series of lectures at Wittenberg on the *Psalms, Romans, Galatians,* and *Hebrews* between 1512 and 1518, he underwent a very fundamental change. No doubt here the new books in the ducal library were helpful. As a biblical scholar he began to explore the history of the early Christian church and the difference between the teachings of the apostolic age and the scholasticism he had been taught at Erfurt and Wittenberg. The reformer began to realize that in order to really understand the Bible, he had to learn Greek and Hebrew, to plumb the deeper meanings of theological texts in the Holy Scriptures. But he soon real-

ized that his students also needed to master these languages in order to understand his lectures.

Exactly where Luther learned his first Greek, whether already at Erfurt as a
student or at Wittenberg from John Lang, is difficult to determine. Later he
even attended Melanchthon's classes to deepen his grasp of the language.
Meanwhile he had also begun to study Hebrew, and began to use both of these
languages in his biblical exegesis as early as the lectures on *Romans, Galatians,*
and *Hebrews.* As a result of this new approach it became quite clear to him that
there was a fundamental difference between what he had learned in the two
universities and the teachings of the New Testament. He also learned how Aristotle had caused perversions in the teachings of the church Fathers. Out of this
new biblical exegesis grew Luther's realization that Aristotle would have to be
eliminated if the theology of the New Testament was to be taught at the university. But this meant a transformation of the whole academic curriculum of the
university in order to offer the students a series of courses in which Greek,
Latin, and Hebrew would be flourishing.

First Luther attacked Aristotle as the problem in his courses. He wrote John
Lang, who had now moved to Erfurt on February 8, 1517:

> Nothing burns in my soul as the desire to expose that imposter (Aristotle),
> who with his Greek mask has so completely deluded the church and to expose
> him in all his ignomy before the world.[128]

In the spring of 1516, Frederick the Wise had ordered an inspection of the
course offerings of the university, upon which occasion Luther suggested a
number of important reforms to Georg Spalatin. In a letter to the electoral
court, Luther implied it would certainly enhance the elector's reputation if
humanistic studies were started. Nor were the reformer's proposals left
unheeded, for on May 21, 1518, Luther again wrote the Erfurt Prior John Lang
that his suggestions were being realized:

> Our University is getting ahead. We expect before long to have lectures in
> two or three languages. New courses are to be given in Pliny, Quintilian,
> Mathematics and other subjects. The old courses in Petrus Hispanus,
> Tartaretus and Aristotle are to be dropped. The prince has already given his
> consent and the plans are before his council.[129]

A part of Luther's proposal to the prince had been that he create two professorships in Hebrew and Greek. Although it was not realized in Hebrew until
later, the regular professorship in Greek was soon started with the employment
and arrival of Philip Melanchthon on August 2, 1518.[130] Melanchthon delivered
his inaugural address soon after arrival, expressing the very theme Luther had
hoped he would, entitled: "How to Improve the Education of the Youth,"[131]
which certainly delighted Luther and the entire student body. Afterward
Luther wrote the librarian at the Saxon Court how pleased he was with the
choice, and in a letter to John Lang he wrote:

The very learned and perfect Grecian, Philip Melanchthon, is teaching here.
He is a mere boy in years (21), but he is not only a master of Greek and Latin,
but of all learning to which they are the keys.[132]

Melanchthon assumed the control of the process of bringing the new humanistic program to the university. For a while he taught both Hebrew and Greek.
He began the study of theology under Luther's tutelage and acquired a bachelor
of divinity in 1519. Soon he began to offer exegetical courses in books of the
New Testament, using his own special prepared texts which were equipped
with an added dictionary to simplify his instruction. Before long the university
also employed Aurogallus for the chair of professor of Hebrew, which rounded
out their linguistic requirements for the training of the students.[133]

Meanwhile Aristotle had also been replaced by courses in Augustine and others of the church Fathers, while Lombard's *Sentences* and canon law were terminated by 1520. This gave the Wittenberg School of Liberal Arts the capability
to train students in languages for the study of theology with an entirely new
approach.[134]

In light of the transformation of the University of Wittenberg from a scholastically oriented institution to the new humanistically oriented school, one can
understand why Spalatin made the type of purchases in the library's early years
after 1512. In the same year that Melanchthon arrived in Wittenberg, the
library was buying more Greek and Hebrew books in Venice. In his diary for
that year, he made the following entry: "In this year (1518) Frederick, the Elector of Saxony, enlarged the Library not only with other excellent selections but
also with the best works in Greek and Hebrew."[135]

Then came the stormy period of Worms and Luther's hiding in the Wartburg
from 1551 to 1522,[136] and Wittenberg's enrollment fell by two-thirds. Walter
Koehler, in his treatment of this period, claims the "Edict of Worms fell like a
white frost on all Germany."[137] Frederick the Wise died in 1525; after that his
successor, Elector John the Constant, became preoccupied with the Diets of
Speyer in 1526 and 1529, and in 1530, the Diet of Augsburg.

After that the sources about the library are practically silent, amid the confusion of the day in the university. The year 1526 brought a reorganization of the
endowment of the institution, as seen in a previous chapter,[138] in which the
funds of the university were placed on a more firm foundation by the complete
secularization of the *Stift* of the Castle Church. Spalatin took advantage of this
reorganization and asked that funds be set aside for the purchase of new books
for the university library based on the new endowment funds.[139] In this request,
Spalatin suggested that endowment money not needed for the school should be
used for the purchase of books at the yearly *Messe* in Leipzig, and he was then
"to buy good books for the library at Wittenberg in the castle and to improve it
from year to year."[140] Mylius is doubtful that this ever materialized, for John the
Constant had little time to devote to the library.[141] Mylius stated that we do not
know how many additions to the library were made; yet he added that the elector was a champion of true religion and must have added a number of volumes
to the library dealing with the religious conflict of the time.[142]

John the Constant lived through the stormy days of the drafting of the Augsburg Confession, which was read in the Kaiser's presence at the Diet of Augsburg in 1530. But before he died in 1532, he had his son John Frederick come to his bedside to commit the care of the university to him in his "Last Will." In this he asked that he take a special interest in preserving the University of Wittenberg, as in it the true light of the gospel had once more been brought forth. This commitment the young elector took very seriously, and he decided to once more place the university on a solid footing with the full support of the new generation of Lutherans.[143]

As stated before, John Frederick faced none of the problems that had confronted Frederick the Wise, who had been brought up as an orthodox, medieval type Roman Catholic.[144] He had been tutored by Spalatin as a young lad in the court of Frederick the Wise, and was a very devout follower of Luther, Melanchthon, and the Wittenberg faculty. Thus he was far more zealous in the cause of the Reformation than his uncle and father, both of whom had been brought up in a monastic atmosphere as children.[145] When he became elector in 1532, true to his boyhood vows,[146] he sought to improve the university to such an extent that he has often been called its second founder.[147] He immediately visited Wittenberg with his wife, discussed the problems of the school with Luther, Melanchthon, and Bugenhagen, and resolved to place the school on an entirely new footing. He gave the school a complete new set of university *Statutes* in 1536, which included ample provisions for the improvement of the ducal library. These provisions included the movement of the library to a more convenient location, into the *alte Hofstube*. The library was now to be properly manned by a full-time librarian and 100 Gulden ($7,500) spent out of the regular university funds for its improvement and planned growth.[148] In addition, private libraries, due to secularization, such as that of the Franciscans,[149] and that of the All Saints Church,[150] were to be added to the ducal library in its new location.

The reorganization of the University of Wittenberg in 1536, with Melanchthon as the central figure of the humanistic Liberal Arts College, as preparatory for the three graduate schools, created a whole new spirit within the institution. Philip placed a whole new emphasis on students mastering the classics and knowing the language of antiquity in which they were written. This placed new demands on the library. When the ducal library was established on the second floor in the castle, with a regular librarian in charge, a new activity was begun to make it more useful. On November 12, 1537, Spalatin wrote the elector that he had purchased many new books for the library in Wittenberg, including some Greek books which he had ordered in Nürnberg.[151] In another letter, without a date, doubtless written in the same year, Spalatin reported that he had just visited Wittenberg, where he had books bound, had placed a number of new volumes in the library, and that he also had placed an order for additional purchases, at "Frankford am Main during the next *Messe*."[152]

On March 3, the elector wrote Spalatin from Torgau, in reply to a former communication, and informed him that he had taken the necessary steps to have the desired books brought from the *Augustinerkloster* library in Grimma to Wittenberg.[153] It appears that Spalatin had selected this list on a previous visit, as the elector had written him on January 18, 1538, to go there to select the books that would be useful in Wittenberg.[154] Nor did Spalatin select only books for the Wittenberg library which represented the point of view of the electoral court. When Duke George, an arch enemy of the Reformation, died on April 17, 1539, Spalatin wrote the elector that he wished to acquire some of his books for the Wittenberg library, "that it might be an eternal witness and proof against the same writer, judge and smithy."[155] Since it was reported that Duke George had been engaged in acquiring many such hostile works, the elector was asked to talk things over with the new ruler, his brother Duke Henry, who was about to be installed as the head of Albertine Saxony, and that he might offer the occasion for the acquisition. He was asked whether the books might be brought into the Wittenberg library.[156] At the same time he also inquired whether the recent works of John Eck, directly against Luther's Ten Commandants, and his Catechism might be added.[157] From this letter we observe too that Dr. Brück and Philip Melanchthon had just been to the Frankfurt a.M. Messe and returned with a number of unbound volumes, while Spalatin now expected to visit Wittenberg in the near future to have the volumes bound and placed in the library.[158] According to Mylius, Spalatin also visited Venice in 1539 to make additional purchases for the ducal library.[159]

Apparently the Elector John Frederick thought that the hostile works of Duke George might be of value for the Wittenberg students, as they would be in a position to evaluate the many false charges that had been made against the Reformation of Luther and his followers. On May 26, 1536, the elector wrote Spalatin from Torgau, stating that books by Luther's enemies should be added to the ducal library. He did, however, hesitate to confront his cousin Duke Henry about the matter. Instead, he suggested having Master Eberhard Brisger contact Duke Henry's court preacher, Paulus, while he visited the Albertine lands in the near future. The elector felt Duke Henry would grant the request without any trouble.[160]

On April 25, 1541, the librarian, Lukas Edenberger, wrote Spalatin from Wittenberg that he had been unable to purchase old books dealing with "Human and Divine Law," which students needed. Apparently Christoph Schramm, a Wittenberg book dealer, had attempted to obtain them at the Messe of Frankfurt a.M., but without success. The librarian also added that they did not buy the *Talmud* in Venice, as prices had risen too high.[161] Nearly two years later, on November 13, 1543, Edenberger again contacted Spalatin concerning the possibility of purchasing the Hebrew books of the recently deceased brother of John Marschalk, Christof von Pappenheim,[162] and also that they buy the books from the library of King Mathias, which could be purchased through Markgraf Georg von Brandenburg. Edenberger suggested that the elector, when he was at the next Reichstag in Speyer, in 1544, should use his influence to bring this collection into the Wittenberg library.[163]

As mentioned earlier the final professor of Hebrew, Aurogallus, between the years 1520 and 1543, was related to the well-known Bohemian humanist

Bohuslaw von Hassenstein. Like Melanchthon in Greek, Aurogallus, or Gold-hahn, was an able Hebrew professor and was a close friend of Martin Luther, who often assisted him in refining his translations of difficult passages in the Old Testament. Later, after Aurogallus' death in 1543, Spalatin was able to add some of his valuable Hebrew books to the ducal library collections.[164] Spalatin was in the midst of a library inspection when the elector was contacted about the possibility of getting these manuscripts.[165] On November 28, 1543, the elector expressed his wholehearted approval, and suggested that they should select the useful material from the Hebrew professor's library and inform him of the estimated cost, whereupon he would make his decision.[166]

Thus far we have surveyed how the ducal library in the University of Wittenberg originated, from Thomas Loesser's books and the addition of other monastic libraries; and, after Spalatin became the librarian, how it grew by the systematic purchase of rare books at Leipzig and Frankfurt fairs, and the purchase of may rarer manuscripts from Venice, Rome, and other Italian libraries. Now the reader may rightly ask, What was in this Wittenberg University library to help ascertain what influence it may have yielded on the professor and students that frequented it?

GENERAL VIEW OF CONTENT

On a visit to Jena in 1936, the author made an attempt to locate some of the original books of the ducal library; but this proved to be futile even with the assistance of the library staff. It seems that in later centuries, as the institution grew, the old library became mixed with newer acquisitions. The reconstruction of the library holdings now presents a few problems. It appears that in 1547, when the librarian Edenberger was instructed to move the library to Weimar, he acted in great haste, putting books into seven large wooden boxes without any rhyme or reason. Then when the University of Jena was founded a new librarian placed them in bookcases, organizing them into two divisions. All of the manuscripts, from folio to duodecimo in size, were housed in one section, and the later printed books were placed in another. But such a grouping of books, with no regard to authorship, made it difficult to analyze the works and group them in some meaningful way, in order to describe the holdings. Then, in 1746, when Mylius decided to make a catalogue of the books in the former ducal library, he faced this same problem; but he claims that it was preserved in an original section and offered to give the reader a description of its holdings, writing:

> A special treatise of the Electoral Library of Wittenberg just as it was at the time of the original founding of the Jena University Library.[167]

Fortunately, Mylius has left us some impression of the external appearance of the 3,132 volumes on the library shelves, most of them neatly bound in pigskin bindings according to sizes, as described in section XI of the catalogue. Let us then turn to Mylius's own description in a little more detail:

With respect to the external features of this Library, practically every volume had a pigskin binding, and many of the bindings of these books give testimony of the antiquity of the age in which they were created. This Library, however, as we have already pointed out in the preceding paragraphs, consists of theological, legal, medical and philosophical works, in the so-called folio, quarto, octave and duodecimo forms.[168]

No doubt it becomes obvious that it would be impossible to list all the works found in the collection without exhausting your patience. Nor are students usually interested in books *per se*, but rather they want to know the books that might have been especially valuable to the university students and its leading professors as tools in their work. We shall therefore attempt to satisfy this quest at two levels: (1) in a general coverage by authors, and (2) describing the important works in some detail. And finally, (3) it may be of interest to know where the works were originally prepared or printed.

The catalogue begins with an introductory statement, covering the origin of the ducal library and its later removal from Wittenberg, as well as its nature and size at the time of arrival.[169] In the first section of the catalogue, Mylius lists the rare manuscripts in the ducal library, classifying them as follows: Hebrew, Greek, Latin manuscripts, Luther's German works, and those of Erasmus. Under the first classification, "Hebrew books," appear Old Testaments, Hebrew commentaries, Melanchthon's *Loci*, Chaldean grammars, the principal works of John Reuchlin, etc. Whereupon follow six pages of theological works in Greek; grammars, dictionaries, commentaries, and the writings of the Church Fathers, which material may have furnished the tools for Luther's biblical humanism.[170] In another section, entitled "Latin Books," appears a list almost three times the number in the Greek section, where he lists the writings of the church Fathers, the scholastic writings, and contemporary ones, which books may have come from the Loesser collections and other monasteries added later from time to time. In the last part of the theological section, Mylius records some of Luther's principal German works and most of those of Erasmus.[171]

In the next division of the catalogue, the author cites works which he titles as "Historical books," a sizable list covering around 140 volumes stemming from the Greek, Roman, and the contemporary world, the principal of which were by Homer, Herodotus, Josephus, Plutarch, Pliny, Tacitus, Polybius, Orosius, Eusebius, Petrarch, Poggio, Ausonius, and Reuchlin;[172] most of these works Melanchthon may have requested for students in his courses.

Then Mylius lists ten pages of titles covering the books in civil and canon law, which gives most of the accepted authors needed in courses of the scholastically minded original Wittenberg University. Most of these may be the very books given to the elector by Canon Loesser, for a number were marked: "Ex testamento eximii Thamonis Loesser, Canonici in Misnia 1504."[173]

Nor was philosophy neglected for the liberal arts people, for here the Jena professor recorded eight pages of books by Aristotle, Isocrates, Plato, Pythagoras, Cicero, Epictetus, Seneca, Plutarch, Boethius, Albertus Magnus, Lorenzo Valla, Ficino, Pico, Mellerstadt, and works by Melanchthon.[174] Much of this source material was very useful for Melanchthon and other professors after the university had been modernized under his direction in 1536.

The later Wittenberg was also much interested in mathematics as a tool for the expanding interest in astronomy and the age of discovery of Columbus and other explorers. Here Mylius lists 114 books available in the Liberal Arts faculty and its students, written by Albumasar, Boccaccio, Boethius, Regiomontanus, Platemaeus, Puerbach, Pomonius, Mela, and Thomas Aquinas.[175]

Nor was the library, especially after the twenties, short in many medical references, of which the work lists 150 titles, including the works of Hippocrates, Galen, Sernus, Cornelius Celsus, and Dryandrus, to mention a few.[176] Nor are the Arab works in the earlier literature missing. For good measure he also lists a number of the books on herbs, *Kräuterbücher*, used by the doctors of the day.

Melanchthon, the father of *Declamations* at Wittenberg, was much interested in poetry as an instructional tool. In Mylius' list of authors appears the following: Homer, Pindar, Plautus, Terence, Ausonius, Tibullus, Virgil, Catullus, Horace, Juvenal, Konrad Celtus, *varia*, and of Chlybis, *varia*, Pigres (Batrachomyomachia), Baptista Mantanus, Eobanus Hessus, and John Reuchlin.[177]

The reformers of Wittenberg, in the early twenties of the sixteenth century, believed that students should become well qualified in eloquence for effective preaching. Melanchthon placed a heavy emphasis on oratory, rhetoric, and grammar, for which he held the classical writers to offer the best examples for such training. The catalog reflects this by having a section on "Oratory, rhetoric, grammar *et mixti*." There are 120 titles, which are the following Renaissance authors: Cicero, Pliny, Lucian, Vives, Ficino, Pico, Poggio, Willchius, Camerarius, and Johannes Sturm.[178]

The library also possessed a list of maps, such as *Terra sancta, Italia* (large), *Italia* (small), *Rhetia superior, der Turcenzug, Peregrinatie Pauli, das Ungarland, Tabulae in officio Ciceronis, Anatomia viri*, and *Anatomia mulieris*.[179]

Even this brief review proves that the ducal library had many rare books and manuscripts, in which the classics, the church Fathers, the scholastics, and the humanists of the Renaissance were well represented. Mylius implies this in the closing section of his description of the Wittenberg collection:

> The most distinguished and rarest books in this Electoral Library, which we shall divide preferably into three classifications; and encourage a better acquaintance with these volumes among scholars we shall give their titles. The first classification shall be the books of unusual size, consisting of many volumes, and for this reason not so common but in general rather rare and precious, or at least worthy to remember for one reason or another.[180]

MYLIUS' PLAN FOR THE CATALOGUE

Any brief scrutiny of the catalogue of books cited by the Jena professor, or even as to the number and size, makes one aware of the task he faced. He might have used any other method, but he decided to use the above layout for the ducal library and then close the catalogue with books added since the original nucleus was brought there. He was fully aware that confusion might arise in the mind of the reader unless he began with a rather detailed introduction of reasons for a historical introduction.

Thus Mylius begins with a rather detailed coverage of the origin and growth of the ducal library while it was still in Wittenberg, and then follows with the Schmalkadic War in 1547, the defeat and captivity of the Elector John Frederick, the transfer of the ducal library to Weimar, and how the rich collection formed the original nucleus of the Jena Library in 1558. To avoid confusion, the author then points out that this nucleus remained as a separate unit until his day in 1746, making it possible for him to describe its nature, type of books, and offering us this historical account. Then the historical introduction closes with a summary of the number of theological, legal, medical, and philosophical books he had found in the Wittenberg library of the German Reformation.[181]

The rest of the catalogue is divided into chapters, beginning with part two, in which Mylius attempts to convey to the reader how rich this library really was in pigskin-covered manuscripts, which totaled about half the library holdings. He records the number of folios, quartos, and octavos in this chapter two of rare old manuscripts, which he classifies as the most valuable in the whole library collection.[182] After a detailed coverage of the manuscripts regarded as most rare, he turns to the printed books dating from 1440 to 1520.[183] At the close of this third chapter, Mylius has prepared an index, in chronological order, of the number of publications and the places in Europe where these printed works originated.[184]

In chapter four Mylius has a very descriptive list of old manuscripts, not in a class with those of chapter two, in some cases parts of old Latin Bibles and theological commentaries that no doubt came from monastic libraries referred to above. Many may even be out of the original Loesser collection cited at the beginning of this chapter.[185]

Finally, in chapter five follows a description of old codices and old Latin Bibles, noted for their illuminations and colored initials in gold and silver, which are said to have been the pride of the Saxon electors. He even goes into detail as to which were written on parchment and those on paper resembling parchment. Many of Augustine's works are described here, the works of St. Paul with *Glossen* (commentary), tools of the Wittenberg faculty like Lombard's *Sentences*, those of Albertus Magnus' *Summa*, etc., making this one of the most instructive books for students of the university. Then follows the legal, medical, and philosophical books, which will be covered in more detail below. This chapter embraces a very detailed account of these types of works in the library.[186]

At the close Mylius has prepared a very detailed *Index Auctorum* in theology, law, medicine, and philosophy, citing the location of the works and writings of the contributors.[187] This *Index* is detailed, and in it the reader can at a glance see how many of an author's works were in the library, which in turn is broken down into the disciplines, according to the organization of the academic world at the time. It begins with an index of the theologians cited, then the legal authors, the medical writers, and the philosophical authors of the respective books.

THE APPEARANCE OF THE RARE BOOKS

In chapter two, the catalogue of the ducal library offers statistical insight as to the appearance of the rare book section in the form of manuscripts. He has told us that all these old volumes were bound in pigskin, which appears to have been their original bindings, as many were quite old when they were acquired. He begins with the folio-sized works that Mylius cites as 69 in number and there were none in the quarto or octavo sizes.[188]

At the beginning of the catalogue listing, in chapter two, Mylius has given the reader a numerical listing of how many volumes the ducal library contained in its various disciplines. It is sometimes somewhat confusing how he counted, no doubt because many of these large volumes contained several different books, which was self-evident to him but hardly to the reader. In the early pages he lists 69 large tomes, mainly in the theological fields, but none in quarto or octavo, no doubt as they did not lend themselves to smaller sizes in the *scriptoria* of monasteries.[189]

After that comes the law library books, in which 32 are of folio size, 5 in quarto size, and 9 in octavo sizes, which meant that 46 books were rated by the author as quite precious.[190] The medical volumes were numerous, with 37 in folio size, 15 in quarto, and 15 in octavo sizes, making their rare books total 67 in the three types of bindings.[191] This covered the three schools of theology, law, and medicine in what he regarded as the rare book section.

Since the liberal arts college was much larger, its rare book section was more diversified. Mylius points out that in folio sizes there were 27 in philology and grammar, 10 in logic, physics, and metaphysics, 34 in mathematics, 34 in philology and philosophy, and 23 poetical books. This totaled 128 books in folio size that were regarded as belonging to the most precious category.[192] Then he lists in quarto size 11 in grammar, 3 in history, as well as 4 in poetry, 1 in philosophy, 14 in mathematics, 3 in grammar and philosophy, 2 in orations and rhetoric, 1 in history, 2 in mathematics, 15 in poetry and philosophy and philology,[193] totaling 44 volumes in quarto.

Total of Manuscripts

Folio Volumes	278
Quarto Volumes	49
Octavo Volumes	48
Total	375

As the reader turns to chapter three of the catalogue, he finds the author has given a detailed enumeration of printed books purchased for the library, cover-

ing all of the years from 1440 to 1520. Here he used the same order of presentation, beginning with those in theology of folio size and continuing with the
smaller ones. Then, in turn, he has also given titles of those in civil and canon
law. He also used the same order in medicine and the various departments of
the liberal arts.[194] Since these were not manuscripts, Mylius has regarded them
as of less importance than those of the previous chapter, or even those in chapter four; but because we are much interested in how these library holdings
reflect the German Reformation, this may be the most precious part of the
entire library, especially for today's students, and we plan to bring this out in
subsequent parts of this present chapter. Prior to coverage of the books in this
chapter, a summary of the number of volumes, sizes, and physical aspects of the
library will be made.[195]

The books in theology of folio size, among the printed works, totaled 132;
those of quarto size, 1558; while there were but 17 printed volumes of octavo
size. The large folio-sized lawbooks, in civil and canon law, were quite impressive, as they totaled 129 of the pigskin-covered volumes; but only 11 of the
leather volumes were in quarto size, and but 5 in the smaller octavo types. Most
of the medical books in the folio size were imported from Italy, and were in
Latin and Greek. The library had 46 large tomes of this size; while 18 were of
quarto size and only 7 in the octavo size.

After the completion of chapter two, in the next one the author offers us a
record of the library's printed books, which he dates from 1440 to 1520.[196] Some
of these must have resembled manuscripts, prepared before the invention of
movable type of Johann Gutenberg.[197] In many respects, in this study, these
printed books are just as interesting as the rare old manuscripts; for their purchase serves as a mirror reflecting how the German Reformation changed the
institution during this period. A profound change in the later years, due to the
reforms of the Wittenberg faculty, ran exactly parallel to Spalatin's acquisition of
printed books for the library.[198]

The liberal arts library holdings in printed books were much more extensive,
for its programs were much more diversified and demanded books that were in
demand for many departments. The chapter on the arts college begins with a
citation of books in grammar and lexicography, where Mylius gives the titles of
26 books; then in rhetoric with 21 titles; logic, physics, and metaphysics of 31
books; mathematics with 10 books; and astronomy with 22 works.

In the next series of library books, the coverage is in ethics, politics, and economics, where 36 titles are given; which is followed by 52 volumes which he
classified as histories. There are also a substantial number of books which he
listed in poetry, that total no less than 42 volumes. The author closes his account
with the number of books in folio size, by giving titles of 20 volumes in various
types of books in philology.[199]

By the author's own count, the liberal arts library possessed 360 printed
books dating from 1440 to 1547, the period the library was housed in Wittenberg. The publication date, of course, does not always indicate where the book
was purchased, but from other references we know that these types of books

frequently were not printed prior to Spalatin's service as the librarian and superintendent. All of these first cited books of quarto size.

The titles listed in quarto size are the type Melanchthon and teachers in grammar and rhetoric needed in their humanistic instruction, beginning with 1518 and blossoming greatly in the twenties. Here he lists 38 grammars in Greek and Hebrew and other tools for the study of those languages. This is followed by a list of 20 rhetoric and oratory, 27 in physics and metaphysics, and 4 books in logic. After that follow 27 books in ethics, politics, and economics, 32 in history, and 24 in philosophy, which are all in quarto sizes.

After that come four rare in grammar in octavo size, 9 in physics, three in history, and he closes with 13 that he classified as ancient poetry, with the plays of Aeschylus, Euripides, Sophocles, and Ovid's treatises, his *Metamorphoses* and other works which octavo volumes Melanchthon must have used in the Greek courses.

OBSERVATIONS ABOUT THE PRINTED BOOKS

There can be no doubt that early printing with movable type faced many technical and financial problems. The predecessor of the printing press was the medieval *Scriptorium*, where many valuable manuscripts originated, which were later copied and printed into books, which were made similar in appearance to the predecessors. This involved discovering manuscripts worthy of publication, whether their content was to be used in toto or in part, as it reflected the thinking of an earlier age, and might express viewpoints that were no longer acceptable in the century of the printer. This did not, of course, apply to the classics, as their writings did not affect the teachings of the Roman church. Nor did the production of manuscripts of new authors cease, while block printing actually attempted to compete with the new method of rapid reproduction.

At the close of the Mylius chapter three of printed books dating from 1440 to 1520, he adds a criticism of his own about the way printers often abused texts in manuscripts when they reproduced old works by use of the printing press. He even charges some of the printers with duplicity, reproducing an original that looked like a manuscript and then selling it as an original.[200] He ascribed this to printers in monasteries, living under the critical eye of the Roman Church, who caused corruptions due to carelessness. He cites Erasmus's *Jerome*, Eusebius's *History of the Christian Church*, and the Greek and Latin Fathers, in which original manuscript contents were perverted by omissions or even additions, and thus misrepresented the views of the original authors.[201] Sometimes they even changed the whole text to make it conform to the teachings of the age in which it was reprinted.[202] The printer's caution may have been due to the condemnation of some earlier teaching by a church council, or a papal decree about the church's later position about past views expressed in very ancient manuscripts.[203]

On the other hand, the Aldus Press, from where Spalatin procured so many of his classics to be used by Melanchthon and Greek students at Wittenberg, did not fall into this category of printer abuse. It was more the special concern of Greek scholars at Venice, that they were printing the most reliable manuscript from the angle of the original copying by monks in a *scriptorium*.[204] As shown by modern writers,[205] Aldus was in constant search for the best manuscripts of the Greek and Latin classics which he might reproduce, and a humanist like Spalatin was very careful in his purchases by going in person to the Venice, Frankfurt, and Leipzig fairs. Mylius realized that it was due to Spalatin's zeal and thoroughness that the classics collections were selected, and that in his day they were in the ducal library.[206] He closes his evaluation with a citation of the principal printers, from whose presses in their library books were originally purchased.[207] In the same section follows a valuable index of how many books came from various places in the printing world at that time.[208]

INDEX OF PLACES OF ORIGIN

The author closes the section on printed books with a useful list of the places of origin of the books in the Wittenberg library and the dates of the printed books. We have added a numerical count of how many came from a specific place. Since he has put these towns in chronological order, the same method will be followed. For the reader's convenience, Mylius has also added the page number where it is enumerated.[209] The listing is as follows:

Altenberg	1503	1
Antwerp	1511	1
Ascensianum	1511	1
Strassburg	1486–1518	101
Astensis	1518	1
Augsburg	1487–1519	14
Basel	1478–1521	99
Bologna	1487–1517	13
Brescia	1504	1
Cologne	1475–1520	24
Alcala	1514 Ximines, Bible	1
Krakow	1504	1
Cremona	1592	2
Erfurt	1500–1504	4
Fano	1507	1
Ferrara	1509	1
Florence	1488–1518	6
Frankfurt a.M.	1508	1
Goerlitz	1481	1
Hagenau	1500–1518	23
Heidelberg	1485	1

Wurzburg	1502	1
Leipzig	1493–1520	45
Louvain	1515–1517	2
Lyon	1489–1518	79
Magdeburg	1507	1
Milan	1507–1518	22
Nemmingen	1499	1
Metz	1517	1
Mainz	1459–1520	7
Modina	1500	1
Neapoli	1517	1
Nürnberg	1474–1521	48
Olmütz	1501	1
Oppenheim	1510–1518	5
Orthona	1518	1
Padua	1487	1
Pavia	1483	1
Pavia Ticini	1483–1516	21
Paris	1496–1521	114
Parma	1514	1
Parugia	1501	1
Pfortzheim	1503	1
Pfortzheim	1505–1508	5
Pisaro (Urbino)	1512	4
Regii	1481–1499	2
Reutlingen	1485	1
Rome	1469–1517	17
Rostock	1515	1
Rouen	1513	1
Speyer	1482–1485	2
Stecklberg	1519	1
Treviso	1477	2
Zurich	1492	1
Torino	1518	1
Zurich	1501	1
Trient	1499	1
Trino	1512–1516	8
Tubingen	1498–1516	9
Venice	1469–1519	307
Vicenza	1480–1491	4
Ulm	1475–1499	3
Wittenberg	1504–1521	6

According to Mylius' calculations, it is simply amazing how many had come out of Venice by 1520. Of the manuscripts dated before 1490 there were 34 reproduced in the form of books, 159 by the year 1500, 219 by 1505; there were 249 by 1510, 285 by 1515, and 22 were added after Aldus' death, making the grand total of classics and reproduced rare books by 1519 equal 307 volumes.[210] In the preceding parts, we have discussed the ducal library books and manuscripts from the angle of their numbers and their sizes. Now we must consider the actual holdings of various types. It will be impossible to name the titles of each section. Nor would that be useful for the student of this period. Instead we shall single out those regarded as precious and useful to the Wittenberg professors in the cause of the German Reformation.

THE RARE MANUSCRIPTS IN THE LIBRARY

The Italian Renaissance, linguistically considered, underwent three stages of development of printing. First there was a development of Latin type and the printing of treatises in that language; then came the Greek, with its special problems of type cutting and setting; and finally, the Hebrew, with even more complicated problems of printing in the languages of Hebrew, Aramaic, and Chaldean.[211] Mylius began his chapter on rare manuscripts with books of folio size in theology with a description of works related to a translation and proper interpretation of the Holy Scriptures. In our story this becomes very informative when related to Luther's translation of the German Bible between 1522 and 1545.[212] Luther began his translation of the New Bible in 1521 at the Wartburg and completed the New Testament by 1522.[213] Almost immediately he began to translate the Old Testament piecemeal with the assistance of Amsdorf and Aurogallus and completed a rough draft by 1529.[214] After that he wanted to draw upon expert advice by creating a committee of specialists of the Wittenberg faculty to check the entire Bible verse by verse, with a secretary taking notes.[215] By a careful review of the previous translation, the *Sanhedrin* was able to complete the first entire German Bible in 1534.[216] This refining was continued by the use of better Aramaic, Chaldean, and Hebrew texts, which Caspar Cruciger and Aurogallus used in their better rendition from the Hebrew original, in different places such as Job, and also the parts difficult to render into good readable German. Meanwhile, Melanchthon had a similar task in improving the New Testament; he and Luther must have made their needs known to Spalatin, who purchased rare manuscripts to assist them in this important undertaking.[217] By using improved texts they came out with the 1539, the 1541, and finally the 1545 Bibles, which were quite different from the earlier translations.[218] This is the real explanation of why nine rare folio texts in manuscript form were cited by Mylius as being in the ducal library.[219] Although Hebrew O.T. parts appeared earlier, according to the Hebrew scholar Berkowitz,[220] The *Editio Princeps* of the Hebrew Bible had appeared in 1488,[221] and Spalatin had purchased it from Bomberg; also the *Biblia Rabbinica*, which Mylius cites in the chapter on rare manuscripts.[222] Daniel

Bomberg was a native of Amsterdam who had gone to Venice to start a press equal in quality to that of Aldus in Greek.[223] Bomberg was a Christian who employed a monk, Felix Pratensis, who helped him in creating an excellent manuscript in the large folio size.

There is an aspect of the history of the Hebrew language that needs consideration in view of the type of work done on the *Biblia Rabbinica*. When the Hebrews were led into the 70 years of captivity in Babylon, the older generations had already died, and the children living in Babylon learned Chaldean, but then forgot the Hebrew of their fathers. This presented a problem upon their return to Palestine. This caused a fundamental change in Hebrew. Prior to this period, there were no vowel points, as the earlier Hebrews supplied the vowels. But after 325 B.C., capable rabbinical experts had to not only supply the vowels in the subsequent Hebrew text, but also the accents and divisions. The Chaldean word *Targum* really means interpretation; thus scholars like Onkelos, Jonathan, and others furnished a Chaldean commentary on the Hebrew text, to deepen the young students' understanding of the less known Hebrew of the post-exilic period.[236] This is the type of Hebrew text that Bomberg created in his *Biblia Rabbinica* in 1516–1517.[225] It was a large work in folio size, with 667 leaves divided in four parts.

Mylius cites as his initial work the *Bibliorum Hebraea* with Chaldean parts and a *Targum* of Onkelos, as well as a commentary by R. Salomon and others, the same one as cited by Berkowitz,[226] who says this rare work was done with the Targum of Onkelos, Jonathan, and Rabbi Joseph of Jerusalem; that it also had a *Targum* II with a commentary of Rashi Kimchi and edited by Felix Pratensis, under the printer Daniel Bomberg.[227]

But our surprise does not end here. Spalatin had also procured for Luther and the Sanhedrin an improved publication of Bomberg's *Biblia Rabbinica*, which had appeared in 1524–1525.[228] Mylius writes, *Bibliorum Hebraeo-Chaldicorum partes 4, cum comment. R. Salomon et Aben Esrae. Venet. a Dan. Bambergio. 1525.*[229]

The second *Biblia Rabbinica* contained quite a few changes from the previous one, which would be useful to scholars like Cruciger and Aurogallus, for it had the *mesora magna* and the *mesora parva*,[230] the *Targum* of Onkolos, the *Targum* of Jonathan, and the Commentary of Rashi Kimchi and ibn Ezra, Jacob ben Chayyim.[231] The text used three different fonts. It had the Aramaic one in the center, and two different ones on the sides. The commentary is in small, unpointed form, while the *masora* is often squeezed into openings in the margins. Thus it really has a four-column format.[232] Just when Spalatin purchased this is not clear, but he lists its publication date as 1525.[233]

Next Mylius lists a second valuable exegetical tool for the reformers, namely, the publication of Cardinal Ximenes' Polyglot Bible, which Spalatin had also procured from Spain.[234] After 1502 Ximenes had assembled capable scholars to Alcalá, among whom was the Greek scholar Demetrius Ducas.[235] They conceived the idea of publishing a Bible in Greek, Hebrew, and Latin. The scholars had formed a kind of Biblical Academy, but it seems difficult to define the exact roles of each member.[236] The New Testament was completed in 1514, and had both the Greek and Latin texts in parallel columns. The next three years had been devoted to a preparation of the Old Testament text. But meanwhile Cardinal Ximenes died, and Erasmus had priorities in Rome with his Greek New Testament printed by Froben in Basel in 1516, so the Polyglot Bible did not reach the public market until the early twenties. In quality the Ximenes New Testament was superior to the Erasmian text of 1516.[237] Luther used the Erasmian Greek New Testament and the improved 1519 and 1522 new editions, but the Polyglot Ximenes Bible must certainly have been welcome for his translation of the Old Testament.[238]

The next folio volume in theology, cited by Mylius as being in this ducal collection, is a four-volume work by Erasmus, the *Opera Heironymi* printed at Basel in 1516.[239] They had a similar set of *Chrysostom*, printed in Basel in 1539.[240] Also, among the collection were Chrysostom's Epistles of St. Paul in Greek.[241] The library possessed the entire works of St. Augustine. Among the works was also the *Opus Talmudicum* in six parts, published in Venice in 1529.[242] These ended the rare folio sizes in the theology, as there seems to have been no smaller books.

In law the first folio volume cited in *Panddectae* was based on an edition of Gregory Haloandrus, printed in Basel in 1541; after the Greek and Latin *Noveliae* drawn from the *Institutes*, printed in Basel in 1541; then the *Codices* in twelve books taken from the *Institutes*, printed in Basel in 1541; and twelve books of the Codices from the Justinian Code, printed in Nürnberg in 1530, which first edition they had procured through Haloandrus.[243] They also had the *Institutes* done by Theophilus in Greek, printed in Basel in 1534; a *Summa* of nine books of *Codices* by Placentinus, from Mainz in 1536; and the Theolosian Code in sixteen books, from Basel in 1528, as well as four volumes of *Tractatas Tractorum Tractatrium Doctorum iuris*, 4 volumes from Lyon, France, in 1535.[249]

Next Mylius turns our interest to the conciliar movement of the fifteenth century prior to the Reformation, in which he cites a number of folio volumes. He cites Peter Corneus' four-volume work on Councils, printed in Lyon in 1531; then Angelus of Peruvius' historical account of the Councils, also printed in Lyon in 1532, which appears to have been in the *Sammelband* about Hippolytus of Marseilles, done in Lyon in 1531.[245] Then in 1534 they added Jason, a four-volume work on Councils by the same Lyon press. They also had a folio copy of Abbot Siculus' two volumes on Councils, printed in Lyon in 1512; in addition, the four-volume work of Peter Paulus of Paris on Councils, printed in Venice in 1543. They also had the anonymous work *Cravettse Consilia* from Lyon in 1543, and one by Francis Ozerius, printed in Venice in the same year.[246] In the library was also Henning Göde's treatise on Councils, printed in Wittenberg in 1544, and one by Vladricus at Basel in 1538.

Mylius then cites the works of the school of law at Wittenberg of quarto size in the ducal library, *De origine iurisdictiorum, item de legibus*, and John of Paris' *De potestate papapi et regali* (Paris, 1506), which appears to have been a *Sammelband* of the two works. The quarto size does not seem to have been used much.

The author listed several volumes in octavo size, beginning with the *Institutes* of the *Code of Justinian*, from Nürnberg, 1529; continuing with the *Institutes* in Greek and Latin and his added *Glossen*, by Theophilus, printed in Antwerp in 1536. This was bound with another volume by Albert Totius, *De vero et perfecto Clerico* (Lyon, 1535), and Johann Nicholaus Arelatanus, *De Secundis Nuptiis*, in 1536, *sine loco*. They also had a copy of Aimaris Rivalius, *History of Law*, printed in Mainz in 1533. There was a second small *Sammelband* of two works, by Antonius Nebrissensus, a *Legal Lexicon*, printed in 1537, and Balbus' *Decisiones*, also published at Mainz in 1535. The list of small legal volumes ends with Capellas of Toulouse, *Decisiones*, printed in Mainz in 1531.[247]

In the early years of the Wittenberg University, the school of medicine was inferior to those of theology and jurisprudence, manned by but a small staff, but by the twenties of the sixteenth century it began to take on a new depth and interest in the dissection of bodies and an extension to health in the Wittenberg community. This is also reflected in the library additions by sources of antiquity.

Mylius cites Hippocrates' *Opera omnia graece*, printed in Venice in 1526, and the seven volumes of Paulus Aegineta, all in Greek, printed in Basel in 1538.[248] Then they purchased Hippocrates' *Libri omnes graece*, printed in 1538, which books must have been bound in a *Sammelband* with the work of Paulus Aegineta.[249] They also possessed Jac. Hullerius' *De materia chirugica*, which was three volumes printed in Paris in 1544.

During that period Galen's medical treatises were rated very high, as shown by five sets of his writings in this collection of rare works. The series begins with *Galeni librorum graecorum*, 5 volumes printed at Basel in 1538; followed by Galen's works in Latin, 7 vols., *cura Bapt. Montani*, printed at Basel in 1542; Galen's *Operum libri Isagogici*, also printed at Basel in 1542; *Opera Latina*, with interpretations by Thomas Linacer, Guil, Copo and others, printed at Basel in 1529; and finally certain works in Galen's *Opera Latina*, with various interpretations, printed at Basel in 1536.[250] This was followed by Mylius examining another *Sammelband*, which contained the *Chiromantia* by Job. De Indagine, printed at Strassburg in 1534; Oclauii Horatiani, *Rerum Medicinalium* in 4 vols., printed at Strassburg in 1532; and the third on Palm reading, *Albucasis chirugicorum*. This volume was also printed in Strassburg in that year.[251] Nor were Arabic sources left unexplored, for Mylius recorded that they had Avicenna, *Opera cum castigationibus Andr, Alpagi*, from Venice in 1544.[252] Then in another *Sammelband* were *Actii Amideni primi libri*, VIII, printed in Greek at Venice in 1534; and, in part two, the works of Alexander Trallianus in Greek, in twelve books.[253]

Next he cites several books of interpretations by Janus Cornarius which were in the ducal collection, including his *Aetii Tetrabiblos* interpretations, printed at Basel in 1542. The second work by Cornarius was in another *Sammelband*, titled *De cognoscendis et curandis morbis sermones*, interpreted by Janus Cornarius, printed at Basel in 1533; while in the same multi-volume work was the *Opuscula* of Nicolus Leenanius, prepared by Andreas Leenanius at Basel in 1532; and finally, in it was Julius Hyginus' *Fabularum liber, Accedunt Palae-*

phati; *Fulgentii, Procli et aliorum Mythologiae*, printed at Basel in 1535. Here follows more folio *Sammelbände*. In the first volume he records the interpretations by John Baptistus Mantanus and Jano Cornarius of *Aetii Libri* XVI, printed at Basel in 1535; while it had in part two, *Clementii Clementini Medicinales Lucubrationes*, also printed in Basel in 1535. In another multi-volume folio volume were the *Traleiani libri* V, interpreted by Albanus Torinus, printed at Basel in 1533; while the second part has the *Opera medica* by Oribasius of Sardinia, printed at Basel in 1529.[254] Constantinus of Africa's work, *Medici, Opera reliqua*, was another Basel work printed in 1539, which was followed by the famous work of Andreas Vesalius, *De humani corporis, fabrica, libri* VIII, printed in Basel in 1541.[255]

Also included was Johann Ruellius' *De materia medici libri* V, with a commentary on the work by the Florentine secretary, from Cologne, 1529.[256] Vitalis de Furnus, *Salutarium remediorum liber*, printed at Mainz in 1531, introduces his books on herbs. Next comes a *Kräuterbuch*, which was purchased from Augsburg in 1534.[257] They also had a *Sammelband* of folio size with Eucharius Rosslein's *Kräuterbuch* from Strassburg in 1539, and a Hieronymous *Kräuterbuch* procured also from Strassburg. Next he lists Leonhardt Fuchsius' commentary, *De natura stirpium*, from Basel in 1542.[258]

After that Mylius cites a multi-volume folio work in practical medicine, which contained Johann Gatenariae's *Practica*, from Basel, in 1537; bound with Johann Manardius' *Epistolarum Medicinalium libri* XXII, also from Basel, and then Manardius' *Annotationes in simplicia*, as the last part of the folios. Another two-volume folio of Ionus Damascenus, *Therapeutica methodus*, paraphrased in part by Albanus Torinus, and also by Iatrus, from Basel in 1543; and part two of Johann Tagaultus' *Chirugiae libri* from Paris in 1543.[259]

In the next section, Mylius reports on what he found in quartos of rare books in the Wittenberg library. In the first part of a smaller quarto *Sammelband* of two parts he cites: Cornelius Crisus, *Medicinae libri XII* and Quserenus, *Liber de Medicine*, both from Venice, 1528; and in part two, Gutbeberus Tonstallus, *Libri IV, de arte supputandi*, from Paris, in 1529.[260] The library had Johannes Dryandrus' volume on *Anatomia*, from Marburg, 1537.[261] They also had another two volumes in quarto size with the first part, a *Feld-Buch der Wund-Artzeney*, from Strassburg in 1535; and in part two, Otto Brunfels, *Kräuterbuch*, from Strassburg in 1534.[262] In another multi-volume binding were again two parts; the first by Caelus Apitius, *De re culinaria libri X*; then Platinae on the same subject; and Paulus Aeginetae, *De facultatibus alimentorum*, all from Basel, 1541; while in part II were the Arab Averroes' *Collectiones de re medica*, sectiones, from Lyon in 1537.[263] In another two-volume tome, they had Averroes' *Apitius*, with notes by Gabr. Hummelbergus, from Zürich in 1542; while in the second part was Cour Gesner, *Catalogus plantarum*, also from Zürich in the same year.[264] Next Mylius lists a three-volume *Sammelband*, in which the first part is by Leonhard Fuchsius, *Medicin, libri* from Basel, in 1539; while in part two, Fuchsius' *Libri IV controuersiar.*, also from Basel; in the third part was Laurentius Bonicontrus' *De rebus coelestibus*, 3 vols.; it also came from Basel in 1546.[265]

In another two volumes, bound together, part 1 has the work by Nicol Leonicus, *De varia historia libri III*, from Basel in 1531; while part II has Gariopontus, *Liber febriun*, Basel, 1531.[266] They also had Aloysius Mundallae, *Epistolae Medicinalles*, from Basel in 1543.[267] This ends his rare volumes of quartos. After this he lists the octavo-sized books in medicine, which he regards as quite rare, among which are four *Sammelbände* and one single volume, which we now list. The first *Sammelband* has four books. It begins with Averroes, *Colliget.*, from Lyon in 1531; another volume by Abhomeron et Averroes, quaedam, from Lyon in the same year; another by them, *Campus Elysius Galliae*, from Lyon in 1531; and finally their work *Periarebon sive de principiis*, also from Lyon in 1531.[268] Another *Sammelband* had five books of octavo size, beginning with Hieronymous Montus, *Ferniones VI. de Medicis*, from Lyon in 1534; a second volume by Hippocrates, *Epistolae*, interpreted by Cornarius, from Cologne in 1542; a third by Jodocus Willichus, *Commentarius anatomicus, item dialogus de locutis*, from Lyon in 1544; Leonelius Faventtinus, *De aegritudinibus insantium*, from Ingolstadt in 1544.[269] Part two of this work by Guiliemus Budaeus, *De philosophia libri 2, de studio litterarum recte instituemdoi*, came from Paris in 1536. They also had a second, separate volume of Aristotle's *Operum omnium*, as in the previous *Sammelband*, Tomi 3, done in Basel in 1542.[270] Among the books Mylius recorded was one by Joach. Camerarius, *Theophrasti opera*, edited by him and published in Basel, in 1541. They also had Caius Pliny's *Naturalis historiae libri XXXVII*, with notes by Beatus Rhenanus, printed in Basel, in 1514. Then they also had Pliny's *Epistolarum libri X*, which had a commentary by Joh. Catanarius from Paris, printed in 1533.[271]

In this same category, Mylius has a work by Francis George Venatus, *De harmonia mundi totius cantica tria*, purchased from Paris, in 1546, a reproduction of a Venice publication of 1525, which he classified as rare. The library also had a work by Vitelinus, *Peri optikus*, more commonly known as *Perspectiuam*, out of Nürnberg, in 1535.[272] In the next section he cites an interesting *Sammelband*, treating principally the discoveries of the "New World," which is too detailed for our coverage, covering the ones of Christopher Columbus, Vespucius America, and Vespucianis navigations, and the strange new lands and their customs, done at Basel in 1532. Then he lists another *Sammelband*, about Ferdinand Cortes' narrations about the new Spanish Kingdom of Charles V, with its seas and oceans as well as the mores and the conditions in the "New World," from Cologne, in 1532.[273] This is followed by Shaft Münster, *Beschreibung aller Länder*, published in Basel, 1544, and Petrus Apianus, *Mathematici Ingolstadiensis, Astronomicum Caesarium*, done in Ingolstadt, in 1540.[274]

The next division of books in liberal arts, in folio size, covers ethics, politics, and economics, rated by the author as being important. It starts with *Platonis opera in latinus versa a Marsilius Ficinus*, from Basel in 1539. After that he cites a copy of Plutarch's *Opuscula moralia*, printed in 1542 at Basel.[275] He closed this section with a *Sammelband* of three volumes, beginning with Vegedius et al., titled *Picturae bellicae*, from Paris in 1535; (2) Albrecht Dürer's

De urbibus, arcibus et castellis condendia ac muniendis, from Paris in 1535; and (3) Francis Patricius, *De institutione republicae*, from Paris in 1535.[276]

At this point Mylius dealt with some bulky, large-sized books, covering the field of liberal arts in philosophy and philology. Here he begins with Flavius Josephus, *Opera Omnia, graece impressa*, published in Basel in 1544. He cites a second Josephus *Opera omnia*, done with Erasmus' Latin interpretations, also done in Basel, in 1540. Then he found a Eusebius ecclesiastical-historical work, treating Socrates, Theodoritus, Sozomenus, and Evagrius by Stephanus Luti-tiae, from Paris in 1544. Among the works was also a Latin translation by Joachim Camerarius of *Theodoriti rerum ecclesiasticarum libri V*, from Basel in 1536.[277] The next entry is Eusebius' *Chronicon*, which the library purchased from Basel in 1536; it is the first part of a two-volume work, Valerius Anselm's *RYD Catalogus annorum et principum genius* the first, the other part covering the years up to the present, from Berne, in 1536. Next came a work by Constantinus Phrygionis, *Chronicon* from Basel, 1534. It is followed by another *Sammelband*, beginning with Herodotus, in Greek, and a preface by Joachim Camerarius, from Basel in 1541; and (2) another by Gemistius, *Gesta*, in two volumes, came from Basel in 1541; while part (3) has *Thucydidis graece tantum, et recensione eiusdem*, by Joachim Camerarius, printed in Basel in 1540.[278] Next comes a large *Sammelband* of three parts, beginning (1) with a work done by Lorenzo Valla, *Thucydides latine versus*, from Cologne, in 1527; (2) while another part is the same, but without place or date; and (3) is listed as *Beati Rhenani rerum germanicarum*, in three parts, from Basel, in 1531.[279] Another folio volume had *Xenophontis opera omnia, quae graeco extant*, done in Venice in 1521; while another folio had *Xenophontis historica Asperi et philosophica opera latine interpretibus variis*, Basel, 1534. The library also had Plutarch's *Vitae*, in Latin, printed in Basel in 1535.[280] The collection also possessed *Titi Livii opera*, with notes by Beatus Rhenanus, et al., from Basel in 1535. Mylius cites also a *Historiae romanae*, by Valleius Paterculus, from Basel, in 1520; they also had a copy of Joh. Cuspinianus' *De Caesaribus romanis* out of Strassburg in 1540.[281] There was also a Henr. Mutius work, *De Gamanorum prima origine, moribus, institutis, legibus*, out of Basel, in 1539; and part (2) Freculphus *Chronicorum Tomi II*, out of Cologne in 1539. The library also had Poggius of Florence's *Opera*, purchased from Basel in 1538.[282] Among the purchases was also Polydoe Virgil's *Anglicae historiae*, XXVI books, printed at Basel in 1534; and Blondus' *Pii Pontificis epitome in Decades Blondi, ab inclinatione imperii*, from Basel in 1533.[283]

In the next section Mylius lists the library's folio volumes in philosophy and in philology, beginning with Homer's *Iliad* and *Odyssey*, which has the text in Greek and the interpretations in Latin, purchased from Basel in 1535. This is followed in the listing by a volume by Eustathius, *Commentarius in Homerum*, from Rome, in 1542, which Mylius says was elegantly printed. The library also had a copy of *30 Eclogae, graece tantum* of Theocritus, *Theognidis, Pythagorae, Phocyllidis carmen*, Venice, by the Aldus Press, in 1495; Part II had another volume in the *Sammelband* by Philostratus, *De Vita Apollonii Thyanaci*, in both

Greek and Latin, from Venice, in 1501; and Part III had Eusebius' *In Hiero-clem, latine tantum*, which was also from the Aldus Press at Venice, in 1502.[284] This multivolume work is followed by a work by Terence, *Cum scholis Donati et Commentariis*, by Johann Calphurnius, from Basel, in 1532. Then there was another work by Micyllus, *Luciani opera omnia*, in Latin, from Francof, 1538.[285] Subsequently there follows a listing of *Erasmi Roterodammi omnia*, done in 9 folio tomes (7 Bände), from Basel, in 1541.[286] In the library collection was also Polydore Vergil *Adagiorum liber*, as well as his *De que inventoribus rerum libri VIII*, a folio size from Basel, in 1521; also Ludov. Caelii Rhodigini, *Lectionum antiquarum partes* 2, Basel, in 1542; and the *Caelii calcagnini opera*, from Basel, in 1544.[287] Among these books in the stacks, Mylius found two volumes by Philip Melanchthon, which were bound together in *Operum Tomi V*, from Basel, in 1541.[288] This is the end of Mylius' folio-sized volumes, and he now turned to the quarto-sized books in the Wittenberg library. He claims there was one of that size listed in the university library, a work by Julius Pollucus, *Onomasticon*, with a commentary by Gualterus, printed in Basel in 1541.[289]

Among the tomes of this quarto size in the library were very many excellent works. Mylius begins with Giovanni Boccaccio, I, *Decamerone, sive Cente Novella*, imported from Venice in 1542; then also Pindar's *Odae*, accompanied by a commentary in Greek, from Frankfurt a.M. in 1542, Homer's *Ilias, latino carmine reddita ab Elio Eobano Hesso*, printed at Basel in 1540.[290] Then, at the end, he lists the works he regards as very rare, a quarto in four-part *Sammel-band*: in this he found (1) Stephan Doletus' *Carminum, libri IV*, printed in Lyon in 1538; then (2) Doletus' *Liber de re navali*, from Lyon in 1537; while in (3) is Joachim Mynsingerus' *Dentaria Frundeck* Neccharides *et alia eiusdem*, from Basel in 1540; and finally (4) his *Elegiarum liber unus: Epigrammatum*, out of Basel in 1540; and *Austriados libri 2* from Basel, in 1540.[291]

He then reported on the quatro volumes in philosophy and philology, where he found a copy of Lorenzo Valla's *Lucubrationes*, Lyon, in 1532.[292] But in mathematics he now cited nine quarto volumes, which he listed. He begins with *Nicandri Theriaca* with Latin interpretations and a Greek commentary from Cologne, in 1530; then he found another work, *Veterinaria Medicinae libri 2*, in Greek, from Basel in 1537, which he says does not pertain to mathematics but to medicine. Next he cites Georgius Pylandrius, *Annulus sphaericus, in membranna impressus*, from Milan in 1544.[293]

After this Mylius recorded quarto-sized books in astronomy for the former ducal library. He begins with a four-volume *Sammelband*, by Alphonsius' *Regis astronomicae tabulae*, from Venice in 1524; in Part (2) *Elisabethae reginae tabulae astronomicae cum additionibus Gaurici*, done in Venice, in 1524; the part (3) *Alphabitii ad magisterium indiciorum astrorum Isagoge cum commentaririis Saxonii*, from Paris, in 1521; and (4) *Joh. Dryandri trium diversorum instrumentorum astronomicorum componendi ratio atque usus*, from Marburg, in 1537.[294] They also had another *Sammelband* with two books: (1) Nicholas Copernicus' *Tabulae revolutionum*, purchased from Nürnberg in 1543; and (2) Sebastian Munster's *Künstliche Beschreibung der Horologien*, out of Basel, in 1537. In another quarto-sized *Sammelband* were two books bound together in a cover: (1) was Gavricas Gavrici, *Tractatus Astrologiae iudiciarae*, from Nürnberg, in 1540; and (2) *Anton. de Montulmo de iudiciis Natiuitatum*, from Nürnberg, in 1540, with illustrations by Joh. de Monte regio.[295] He ends the quarto list on astrology with a volume titled *Astrologica quaedam, e graeco versa a Canerario*, from Nürnberg in 1532.[296]

Next he turns to the quarto-sized volumes on rhetoric of the library's rare books, beginning with Procopius' *Rhetoris orationes, 6, de Instiniani caesaris aedificiis, interprete Arnoldo Wesaliense*, out of Mainz, in 1538; followed by Petrus Bembus, *Epistolae*, from Basel, in 1539. Next he cites Geoponoca, *De re rustica selectorum libri 20, graece*, purchased also from Basel in 1539, as well as his *A Jano cornario in latinum versa*, bought in the same year.[297] From here Mylius shifts to the historical works, by citing Leonardus Aretinus' *Epistolarum libri VIII*, from Basel in 1535, and Leonus Baptista, *De Albertis tractat de picturis*, Basel, 1540. Among the books was also Johann Dryandrus' *De chirondis libri III*, out of Marburg, in 1538.

At the close of Part II, Mylius also covers the octavo volumes related to poetry, which was of special interest to Melanchthon and his liberal arts students. He cites a two-volume *Sammelband*, which has the *Florilegium diversorum epigramarum libri IV*, with annotations by Vincentius Obsopaeus, from Basel, in 1540; (2) it had the *Epigrammarum graeca veterum poetarum cum epitaphiis et epigrammatibus* by Joachim Camerarius and Iac. Micyllus, from Basel, in 1538. They also had the *Commentaria graeca in VII Euripidis tragoedias, collecta ab Absenio, archiepiscope Monenhasiae*, imported from Venice, in 1534; also *Historia rei numariae*, by Joachim Camerarius, from Tübingen, in 1539. This is followed by another *Sammelband* in three volumes, (1) by Eobanus Hessus, *Aliquot carmina et Psalmi*, from Leipzig in 1535; another work by him (2) *Aliquot carmina et Psalmi*, printed in Leipzig in 1530; and (3) *Sylvarum libri 6* from Hagenau, in 1536, all of which are in a small octavo binding.[298] Another three-volume work, in an octavo binding, contains: (1) Aonius Palearius' treatise *De animorum immortalitate, libri 3*, from Lyon, in 1536; (2) Stephanus Doletus' *Varia*, from Lyon, in 1536; and (3) Nicol. Borsonius' *Acramina*, also from Lyon, in 1536.[299] Mylius found another octavo-sized volume, in three parts: (1) by Iac. Sannazararius, an *Opera omnia*, from Lyon, in 1536; (2) Gilbertius Ducherius' *Epigrammatum libri 2*, from Lyon, in 1538; and (3) Nicol. Borsonius' *Nugarium, libri 8*, which was also from Lyon, in 1538. Finally, Mylius also found, in this class, an Ulrich von Hutten *Opera poetica*, sine loco published in 1538; as well as Guil. Philandrus' *Castigationes Quintilianum*, from Basel, in 1536.[300] This terminates Mylius' recording from Part II of the Wittenberg library.

THE PRINTED BOOKS IN THE LIBRARY

In Section III of the ducal library books, one is surprised at the number of printed books in the collection, which, to enumerate in some be detail would not only be impossible, but would also be boring to the reader. Yet the readers need to gain some feel of what type books were available to the Wittenberg faculty and its students. This demands a selection and a summation of the institution's goals. Some have claimed had Luther attended Leipzig instead of Erfurt University, he would have become a Thomist and the Reformation would not have occurred. It may prove of interest to the reader to observe the range of scholastic works in the university library during the reformer's formative period, and also the number of humanistic works that were available to him and Melanchthon in the later decades.

As in the previous section, Mylius begins this part with the large folio-sized printed books. As stated above, the range of the printed books extends from 1440 to 1520, which last date he regards as the beginning of the Reformation. Mylius's book enumeration begins with the citation of Anton Koburger's *Die teutsche Bibel*, two parts in two vols., from Nürnberg, in 1483.[301] After this he enumerates a whole series of works of the great churchmen, beginning with Athanasius' *Opera*, against heresy in Latin, from Vincenettae, in 1482; Basil's *Opera*, from Rome, in 1515. This Mylius follows with Lorenzo Valla's interpretations of the *Latin New Testament*, done in Greek at Paris, in 1505; and also St. Hilary's *Opera complura*, from Paris, in 1510. After this, he cites St. Boniface's Christian persecutions, VI vols., from Basel, in 1509; and the works of St. Jerome Parts 1 and 2, out of Venice, in 1498; also John Chrysostom's *Opera latina*, 2 vols., from Venice in 1503; Augustine's *Primo quinquagena in Psalmos*, from Basel, in 1497; and Augustine's *De civitate Dei commento*, from Venice, 1489; as well as the bishop of Hippo's interpretations of St. Paul's Epistles, done from the codices of the Venerable Bede, printed in Paris in 1499. Among these books Mylius also found Gregory the Great's *Papae epistolae*, from Venice, in 1504.[302]

In the next section Mylius cites a whole series of sermons, beginning with Thomas Hasselbach on the Epistles of St. Paul, printed in 1478, but s.l.; St. Bonaventura's *De tempora et sanctis*, from Reutlingen, in 1485; Petrus of Ravenna, Italy, I.V.D. *et equitis aurati*, sermones extraordinarii, printed in Wittenberg, in 1505, and delivered at the initial opening of the university in 1502, while was on the university faculty.[303] Here Mylius cited a folio-sized tome by St. Thomas, *De arte et vero modo praedicandi tractatus*, s.l., in 1483.[304] Among these books on preaching was also a Concordantae Biblicae, from Speyer, in 1485.

In the next section, Mylius records a number of works on *Lombard's Sentences*, no doubt used in courses in theology in the early period of the university. This begins with Joh. Scotus' super 3. *Liberos Sententiae*, done in Venice, in 1490; and Part 2, *Quodlibeta cum eius tabula*, in two volumes. Next he cites Thomas Aquinas' *Super 4 Libros Sententiae*, purchased from Venice in 1486, 1487, 1490, and 1498, and they also had his *Quodlibetales Questiones*, from Venice, in 1498. Among Wittenberg's scholastic tomes Mylius also found *Thomas de Aquino Summa Theologiae*, par. 1, 2 et 3. cum *Matthaci annotationibus*, Venice, in 1509 and 1512. They also had Paulus Cortesius' *Sententias*, and Bernard of Clairveaux's *Opus, complectens sermones de tempore et sanctis* etc., out of Paris in 1508; Bonaventura's *Opuscula*, from Venice, in 1504; Nicolas von Lyra, *Operum partes IV*, bound in four folio Tomes, from Venice, in 1489; Thomas Aquinas' super 4, *Evangelia aureum opus*, from Venice in 1506, and his *Super epistolas Paulli commentarius*, from Venice, in 1510.[305]

Next Mylius covered a number of sermons, beginning with Joh. Geilerus of Kaiserberg's *Sermones*, out of Strassburg, in 1515; Pomerius' *Sermones de tempore*, from Strassburg, in 1509, as well as his *Sanctis* that same year; Guilhelm of Paris, *Sermones de tempore et sanctis*, from Tübingen, in 1498; Nicholas of Blonius, *Sermones de tempore et sanctis*, out of Strassburg, in 1495; M. Paulus Wan, *Sermones Dominicales*, from Hagenau, in 1512, and Johann von Promyard, *Ordin, predicat, Summa Praedicantium*, from Nürnberg, in 1518.[306]

Then Mylius recorded a whole body of material on Peter Lombard's *Sentences* in the library collection, which was the official textbook of theological students. He begins with Luther's bitter opponent at Augsburg in 1518, Cardinal Thomas Cajetan, who had published *Partem summae commentaria*, printed in Venice, 1508; then follows St. Thomas' *Opuscula tabulae*, with his conclusions, statements, and Scriptural proof, printed in Venice, in 1497; also, there was Bonaventura's treatise on the *Sentences*, in 4 books from Lyon, in 1510, printed in 2 volumes. After that comes Joh. Capreolus' *Defenseonum Thomae de Aquino libri 4*, from Venice, in 1514–1515, 2 vols.; Guil. Ockam's treatise *Super 4 libros Sententiarum Centilogium theologicum*, from Lyon, in 1495; a.b. Richardus de Media Villa in libros 4. *Sententiae*, out of Venice, in 1509; a.b.c. Albertus M., Bishop of Ratisbon, *Super 4. Libros. Sententiarum*, from Basel, in 1506, 3 vols.; Albertus, *Prima et seconda pars summae, alias dictae, de mirabili scietia Dei*, from Basel, in 1507; *Durandi de S.Portiano in 4 libros sententiarum, quaestionum resolutiones et decissiones*, from Paris, in 1508. They also had (in NB. 70) Marsilius Inghen super 1,2. 3. et 4. *Librum sententiarum*, out of Strassburg, in 1501, 2 vols; Carolus Bouillus' *Quaestionum theologicarum*, from Paris, in 1513; Petrus de Palude, *Super 4 libros sententiarum*, from Paris, 1514; Thomas of Strassburg, Lombard's *Sentences*, from Strassburg, in 1490, in two Tomes; Dionysius, *Cistertiensis super libros 4 sententiar*, from Paris, in 1515; Adam Goddam, *Super libros 4. sententiar*, from Paris in 1512; Thomas Aquinas, *Quodlibeta* from Nürnberg, printed in 1474.[307] Mylius does not indicate when these various works were purchased but gives only the printing date.

At this point Mylius' tone changes somewhat, concerning the books which treat different aspects of medieval theology, produced during the early years of printing. Among these, he cited Peter of Bergamus, *Super omnia Thomae opera tabulae*, printed in Basel, 1478; and then in the *Via Moderna* philosophy, he names Gabriel Biel's *Super 4 libros sententiae*, printed in Lyon, in 1514. He found also the *Opus moralium* of Pope Gregory the Great, which was printed in Venice, in 1480; then also, Guilermus of Paris' operum, in two parts, from Nürnberg, written in 1440, but not printed, by Joh. Rosenbach, in 2 vols, at Nürnberg in 1496.[308] Next he cites a work by Brother Hieronymus of Ferrara, *Triumphus crucis de veritate 8 libri, Sine loco et anno*; and the library also had

Gabriel Biel's *Canonis Missae tam mystica quae litteralis expositio*, printed in Basel, in 1510; among the books was also a rare old volume (N.B. 90) titled, *Rituum ecclesiasticorum sive sacrarum cerimoniarum romanae Ecclesiae libri 3. non ante impressi* (b) *per Gregorios de Gregoriis*, printed in Venice, in 1516; there was also a similar work, *Elucidatorium Ecclesiasticum, ad officia Ecclesiae pertinentia 4. libris planius exponens, Iodoco Clichroveo explanatore*, done in Basel, in 1517. They also had Cardinal Nicolaus von Cusa's *operum*, in two tomes, done in Paris in 1514.[309]

In the books recorded by Mylius were also Wilhelm Durandus' *Rationale divinorum officiorum*, from Venice, in 1509, as Part (1); and (2) M. Paulus Venetus' treatise *Quadratura*, also from Venice, in 1493, and (3) Venetus' *50 Sophismata*, from Venice, in 1493, as the volumes of a *Sammelband*. They also had Thomas à Kempis, *Opera*, printed in Nürnberg, 1494; and also Petrus Montius' *De unius legis Vertate et sectarum falsirare*, from Milan in 1509; M. Petrus Comestorius, *Historia scholastica et evangelica, S. Scriptorae seriem brevem nimis et expositam exponens.*, from Strassburg, in 1500.[310]

After this he recorded a *Sammelband* with books of folio size, beginning with Joh. Picus Mirandulanus' *Heptaplud de opere sex dierum Geneseos*; and (2) *Disputationum adversus Astrologos libri XII*, from Bologna, in 1496; it has also *Pici de rerum* Praenotione, 9 books, containing religious truth as opposed to superstition, from Strassburg, in 1507; and (3) a 2-volume work, *Der Beschlossene Garten des Rosencrantzes Maria*, from Nürnberg, in 1505, with many colorful illustrations.[311]

Next Mylius recorded the printed theological books, in quarto size, in which he cited the following for the readers. As the library had many quarto-sized volumes, we can only highlight the most important ones. He begins with Cyprian's *Opera*, printed in Paris, in 1512; after that, Gregory of Nazianzus' *Carmina graeca, cum latina interpretatione*, printed in Venice, in 1504. Then comes *Lionis Papae epistolae, prelo Ascensiano*, in 1511, in part (1) of a *Sammelband;* and in (2) Anton. Mancinellus' *Veliterni Sermonum decus*, from Strassburg, in 1510; and the (3) part, John Reuchlin's *Liber congestorum, de arte praedicandi*, done in Pfortzheim, in 1508; and (4) Picus Mirandolanus, *Staurostichon*, from Tübingen in 1512. Next Mylius described another *Sammelband* set, with (1) Anselm's *Apuscula, Sine loco et anno*; H. Schenck, *De sumave honestissimae semperque Venerandae virginis nobilitatis descriptio*, printed in Würzburg, in 1502; and (3) Raymundus' *Quomodo principes et praelati facinora publica punire debeant*, s.d. et s.l.; and (4) *Quae sit vera mens legati Germaniae;* D. Christopher Scheurl's *Oratio attingens literarum et laudem ecclesiae collegiate Wittenburgen*, which he printed in Leipzig, in 1508; and (6) Hieronymus Emser, *Dialogus de origine propinandi, et an fit toleranda compotation in republica bene instituta, nec ne?*[312]

Among the library books were also many on the Psalms, which Mylius recorded next, beginning with a multivolume *Sammelband* by B. Bruno, *Psalterium*, printed in Nürnberg, in 1497; and (2) *Psalterium cum apparatu vulgari* (i.e. *germanico*) firmiter appresso, in Latin, with a German text, from

Basel, in 1503; and (3) Pope Gregory's 7 *Psalmos poenitentiales explanatio* from Mainz, in 1495. Another exegetical work was by Conrad Herespachius, *Icti simplex et dilucida explicatio Psalmorum Davidicorum*, also from Basel, in 1478, then Beseromus Rudingerus, *In Psalterium paraphrasis latina*, rendered in the coarse language of the Bohemian Brethren, 5 vols., from Görlitz, in 1481. In another *Sammelband* of writers was a work by Albertus Magnus, *De Muliere forti*, based on Solomon's Proverbs, from Cologne, in 1499; (2) Alanus de Maximis' Theologie, s.l. et s.a., (3) Cassiodorus, *De anima*, from Pfortzheim in 1507. He also spoke of another multi-volume work with Joachim von Florence's works, such as *Scriptum super Iesaiam*, from Venice, in 1512; (2) also his *Expositio libri CYRILLI, de magnis tribulationibus et statu ecclesiae, cum multis figuris ligneis;* (3) *Tractatus de Antichristo, IOH., Parisiensis;* (4) *Quaedam prophetiae, ut et SIBYLLAE Erithee;* (5) and other tracts. In another *Sammelband* Mylius records another series of works, beginning with Pope Gregory VII's *Psalmos poenitentiales*, done in Paris in 1512; (2) his *Liber pastoralis curae*, 1512; then (3) *Super Cantica Canticorum*, printed in Paris, in 1509; (4) *40 Homiliae* super Evangelia, also done in Paris, in 1509; (5) his *Homiliae 22 super Ezechielem*, from Paris, in 1512; and (6) his *Dialogorum libri 4.* from Paris, in 1500. Then Mylius recorded another *Sammelband* of books by Nicholas von Lyra, *Postilla seu expositio litteralis moralis super epistolas et evangelia quadragesimalia* Anton. Betontini, printed in Venice, in 1492; (2) a treatise by D. Peter Reginaldetus, of the Minor Orders, *Speculum naalis retributionis operum, tam bonorum, tam malorum*, from Basel, in 1499; this is followed by Peter Avreolis' *Tractatus de conceptione Marae virginis, quem scripsit anno 1338*. Then among many less important treatises in the tome, there is the treatise by Thomas Aquinas, *Libelli de occultis naturae et motu cordis*, which appeared in print at Leipzig in 1499.[313]

Next Mylius recorded the sermons of Gabriel Biel, in a quarto-sized, two-volume, bound tome, starting with (1) *Sermones Dominicales de tempore*, from Hagenau, in 1516; and (2) his *Passionis dominicae sermo historialis*, sine loco et anno. They also had, in another binding, Biel's *Sermones de festis Christi* and *De festis Mariae et sanctis*, from Hagenau, in 1510; and in another *Sammelband*, part three, Marsilius Ficinus' *De triplici vita, sana longa, coelitus comparanda*, printed in 1489, sine loco.[314] In another multivolume binding was *Acta Concilii Constantiensis*, printed in Hagenau, in 1500; (2) Saint Augustine's *Sermones 59 ad Heremitas*, sine loco et anno; and (3) Joh. de Lapide, *Resolutorium dubiorum, circa canonem missae occurrentium*, done in Cologne, in 1500; (4) *Vita Christi, edita a Bonaventura per capita 95*, sine loco et anno; and (5) *Expositio misteriorum missae, Christi passionem figurantium, metrice et prosaice proposita*, from Leipzig, 1501; (6) Senecas, *Liber de gubernatione,* from Leipzig, 1498.[315]

In the library was also Augustine's *Liber de Trinitate*, printed in Venice, in 1489; then, Ricardus' *De sancta Trinitate, libri VI*, done in Paris, in 1510. In another *Sammelband*, among others, there was Nicol Clemangis' *De corrupto ecclesiae statu*, sine loco et anno; and Johann Huss, *De ecclesia et causa*

Boemica capp. 25, also, s.l. et s.a. In another multivolume work was S. Athanasius' *In libro Psalmorum*, translated by John Reuchlin, from Tübingen, in 1515.[316] Mylius cites several important works in another *Sammelband, Opusculum Joh. Clichtovaei de mystica numerorum significatione*, done in Paris, in 1513; and (2) Athanasius' *Opusculum in Psalmos* and (3) Basil, *Oratio de invidia* and (4) Cardinal Bessarius' *De sacramento Eucharistiae*, from Strassburg, in 1513.[317] In another many-volume binding was (1) Marsilius Ficinus' *Opusculum de religionis christiana*, done in Paris in 1510; then (2) Paul Riccius' *In apostolicum symbolum, a priori demonstratiuus dialogus*, from Augsburg, 1514; (3) Raymundus' *LVIII ars magna generalis et ultima*, Ludg., in 1517. There was another three-volume tome, beginning with Erasmus, *Lucubrationes theologicae variae*, from Strassburg, in 1515; his *Cato* from Cologne, in 1515.[318] Mylius also cited Thomas Aquinas' *Opuscula*, printed in Venice, in 1497, and Bonaventura's *Compendium S.S. Theologae*, and Thomas Aquinas' *De vitio et virtutibus*.

Mylius also cited a few volumes in octavo size, but most are not worthy of our recording, except a few. He cites Dionysius the Areopagite's *Opuscula graece tantum*, s.l., in 1516; Lactantius, *Firmiani, divinarum institutionum libri* 7 in the first volume, and (2) *De ira Dei liber unus*, done in Venice in 1516; and (3) Tertullian's *Apologeticus adversus gentes*, printed at Venice, in 1515.[319] Among the rest is Pope Gregory I's, *Homiliae 40, de deversis lectionibus Evangelii* from Lyon, in 1516; and (2) his *Dialogi super Cantica Canticorum;* (3) his *Pastorale*, from Lyon in 1516; (4) his *Homiliae 22 super Ezechielem;* and (5) *Explanatio in VII Psalmos poenitentiales*, all from Lyons, in 1516.[320]

THE PRINTED BOOKS IN LAW

Since the books in law are very numerous, only a representative picture of the library's holdings can be given. As previously, Mylius again Starts with the folio-sized volumes. Thus here he begins with the *Code of Justinian*. He starts with the *Digestum Vetus cum glossis*, printed in Venice in 1488; then the *Infortiatum cum glossis*, done in Venice in 1491; the *Digestum novum cum glossis* from Venice, in 1493; the *Codicis libri IX, cum glossis*, from Venice in 1491; the *Institutiones et Novellae cum glossis*, done in Venice, in 1489.[321] This certainly offered the Wittenberg School of Law ample source material in Roman Law of the Code of Justinian.

Since the law school, as in other German universities, taught both civil and canon law,[322] the latter was also well supplied with printed volumes. Gratian's *Decretum*, the work of the famous canon law professor at Bologna, was regarded as the standard work for canon law; it was also used by the early Wittenberg Law School.[323] Mylius found Gratian's *Distinctionum*, which was printed in Venice in 1490; his *Decretalium* libri, from Venice in 1492, was also there; also, they had *Sextus Decretalium*, printed in Venice in 1491; and they had the *Rosarium Decretalium et Distinctionum*, from Rome, done in 1475; there was also the *Summa Azonis super codicem*, printed in Speyer in 1482.

They also prided themselves on having the work of the famous humanist, Petrus of Ravenna, entitled *Compendium iuris canonici*, printed at Wittenberg in 1504–1506, in three parts, bound in two volumes.[324] The library possessed also the *Summa* of Alexander of Hales, 4 vols., from Nürnberg, done in 1481–1482. In another multivolume bound tome was the folio-sized *Summa* of Baptista de Salis, done in Nürnberg in 1488; also, they had the *Summa* of Antonius of Florence, printed in Venice in 1480–1487, in 4 volumes. Among the books was also the *Lectura abbatis super V. libros Decretalis*, from Strassburg printed in 1510; as well as a *Summa* of Joh. de Vanckel, *Super Sextum Decretalium et Clementinas*, printed in Cologne in 1488. There was also a *Summa* by Pisanus, *in ius canonicum*, but s.d. et s.l. Then he cites a work by Sifridus, *Declarationes titulorum utriusque iuris*, done in Cologne in 1491, also Bartolus' *Super Degestum vetus*, printed in Venice, in 1491, and his *Super Informiatum*, from Venice, done in 1489; also his work *Super Digestum novum*, done also in 1489; and also his *1. and 2. partem codices*, in 1491. Then comes Baldus' *Super 9. libros codicis*, done in Venice in 1485, in a *Sammelband*, part one, (2) his *Singularia*, and (3) his *Repertoria cum singularibus* Angeli., from Lyon, done in 1502. The library also had a tome by Paulus de Castro *utriusque iuris famosissimus monarcha*, super 1. et 2. *veteris*, from Lyon, done in 1510, which had some additions by Francis Curtius; and later he did some additions on 1. et 2. *Infortiati* in 1511; and he did two *Codic.* and the *novi*, both printed in same year. In another volume Alexander Imola also treated 1. et. 2. of the veter., done in Venice, in 1491; and he did the same *Super 1. et 2. Infortiati*, and also *1. et 2. Codic.* and *1. et. 2. of novi*, all done in Venice, in 1491. They had another similar series in folio size by Albericus de Rosale, *Super ff. Veter*, out of Lyon, in 1518, who then also did *Super ff. Nova Novimom* there, in 1517; then on the *Codices*, in 1518; *Super Dictionarium*, done there in 1505 and in 1506 respectively. Next Mylius cited the work, a.b.c. Bartholomaeus de Salyceto, *Super 9 libros codicis*, printed in Venice as a 3 vol. tome, in 1502–1503. And they had another study by a.b. Odofredus, *Super 9 libros codices.*, done in Tridini, in 1514, a tome of 2 vols.[325]

These library holdings in civil and canon law continue with many works in Mylius' recordings. Joc. Butrigarius wrote a tome *Super 9 libros codicis*, printed in Paris in 1516; while in the same *Sammelband* was (2) Iacob. Rebuffius' *Lecturae super tribus ultimis libris codicis*, from Lyon, done in 1513. Then they had Nicasius de Voerds' *Super institutiones*, printed in Cologne, in 1493, and also Christopher Porcius, *Super 1.2.3. institutes*, from Lyon, done in 1514, which was bound with Job. de Platea's *Super 3 ultimos libros codicis*, from Lyon, in 1516.[326]

THE LIBRARY'S BOOKS IN FEUDAL LAW

The next books Mylius examined were in feudal law, of folio size. The first was a *Sammelband*, which contained Baldus' treatise *Super Feuda*, done in Pavia, in 1490; the (2) Jac. de Alvarottis, *Super feuda*, from Venice, in 1477.

Here follows a work by Francis Curtius, *Tractatus feudalis*, from Pavia, done in 1506 as part one; then (2) a work by Martin de Caratis, *Super feuda*, from Tridini in 1516; and (3) Andr. de Isernia, *Super feuda*, done in Venice, in 1514.[327]

Now Mylius records the works in canon law, in which the ducal library was amply supplied. This begins with Johannes Andreas' *Novellae super libros Decretal*, printed in Venice in 1505. Prior to this Andreas had published his earlier *Lectura super 6tum librum Decretalium*, in Venice, in 1491, which was in this collection. There were a number of books of folio size by Panormitanus in a *Sammelband*: (1) the *Sive abbas Siculus super 1. et 2. Decretal*, done in Venice, in 1492; (2) his *Repertorium*, from Venice, sine a.d., his *Super 3. 4. et 5. Decretals*, from Venice, in 1492. In the library was also Hostiensus' *Super 1. et 2. Decretals*, out of Strassburg, in 1512; also Guido Papa's *Super decretales*, from Lyon, in 1516, as part (1) of a *Sammelband;* (2) *Super nonnullos titulos* ff.; and (3) *Singularia* and (4) *Tractatus*, all from Lyon, printed in 1517. They also had the archdeacon of Bologna Guido de Bayso's treatise *Super Decretales, cura Petri Albignani Trecii*, from Venice, printed in 1480; then in another volume, his *Super 6tum Decretal*, done in Venice, in 1504. The library also had a three-volume work in a *Sammelband*, beginning (1) with Felinus Sandaeus, *Super 1. 2. 3. 4. et 5. Decretal.*, printed in Lyon, in 1505–1506, 3 vols. They had Ludow de Bologninis' *Consilia*, done in Bologna, in 1499. In four large folio volumes the library had Antonius Buirius' *Super 1. 2. 3. 4. et 5. Decretal*, done in Venice, in 1500–1503. Another work was that of Franciscus Zabarellis, *Super Clementinas*, in Torino, in 1492. Andreas Barbata also wrote *Super Clementinas*, printed in Venice, in 1516, as the (1) part in a *Sammelband;* and (2) Alberici de Rosale et Baldi de Perusio printed a volume, *Singularis tractatus de materia Statutorum*, done in Milan in 1511 and (3) was a volume by the Benedictines, by Benedicti de Benedictis *Consilia ultim, volunt*, printed in Milan, in 1515. They had a two-volume folio, in which part (1) was by Barthol. Brixiens., entitled *Casus Decretorum*, from Basel in 1489; and in (2) was a work *Repetitiones Lanfranci super Decretal,* done in Cologne in 1488.

In the next part Mylius found a number of books in the ducal library of Wittenberg dealing with the German law codes of the past. Even though civil law had become popular in the universities, the imperial court, and at territorial levels, throughout the lands, the former medieval law codes were still practiced. In the northern German lands, the former *Saxonspiegel* affected the rules of the princes; while in the southern German lands, the former *Swabenspiegel* still played a role. Both these old law codes were taught at Wittenberg University and in other German universities. One of the first Mylius recorded was the *Saxonspiegel*, out of Augsburg, entitled, *Sachsen-Spiegel samt den Cautelen und Additionen*, by Bocktorffs, printed in Augsburg, in 1496. Another folio volume was entitled *Klag-Antwort ausgesprochene Urteil aus geistlichen und weltlichen Rechten*, published in Augsburg, in 1497. The library also had another Lehn-Recht book, of the above work, *Sachsen-Spiegel mit Additionen, samt Land-Rechts und Lehn-Rechts Richtsteige*, done in Augsburg, in 1517.

There was also a book with the title, *Weichbilde und Lehn-Rechts*, done in Augsburg in 1499. Another book was called *Remissorium*, done the same year in Augsburg. Mylius also found a folio entitled *Lehnrecht, Münchs-Schrift*, s.l. et s.a. The book collection also included Wilhelm Durandus' *Speculum*, printed in Milan in 1502. There was also a work entitled *Processus iuris* by Urbachius, printed in Strassburg, in 1499, as part one of a two-volume work, with the second part treating the *Vocabularius iuris*, out of Hagenau, in 1508. There was also work by Panormitanus, *Concilia abbatis*, printed in Venice, in 1474; and they had also his *Disputationes*, done in Venice in 1487; also his *Decretals* out of Venice, 1490, as well as his *Consiliorum volumen* from there in 1491.[328]

Next Mylius informs us of books dealing with Councils. He began with a 5-volume set by Alexander Tartagnus, in folio size, the *Conciliorum volumina 5.*, printed in 1492; next comes Frederici de Petruciis, *De Senis decretor Doct, Quaestiones*, done in Milan in 1518. Then he reports on a three-volume *Sammelband, Quaestiones variae et tractatus super Concilio Basilcenci*, done in Lyon, in 1512; in part (2) Joh. de Imola, *Consilia*, from Milan, printed in 1514; and (3) Oldradi de Ponte, *De Laude Consilia*, done in Venice, in 1515. Another find for Mylius was Francisi de Aretio, *Consilia*, done in Milan, in 1496. They also had in a *Sammelband*, (1) *Decisiones dominorum de Rota*, done in Venice in 1491; and Alexander Tartagnus in (2) *Consiliorum* volumen I, done at Venice in 1492. Next came Philippi Decii, *Consilio* vol. I out of Lyon, in 1512, and part (2) of the set, Petri de Anchorano, *Consilia*, done in Pavia, in 1510. Next come Philippus Decimus' *Consilia*, from Pavia, in 1509; and as part (1) in a binding, (2) Dominici de sancto Germiniano, *Consilia*, printed in Pavia, in 1509, and (3) Andreas Novelia, *Super 6 Decretales*, done in Venice in 1499; and by the same author, *Mercuriale i.e. de regulis Iuris*, also done in Pavia, in 1508. Then comes another two-volume work, with part (1) by Bartholomew Socinus, *Consiliorum*, 3 vols., done at Pavia in 1516; (2) by Bartholowmaw Morilanus' *Socinorum Consil. I*, from Trino, in 1516. Also represented was Paulus de Castro, with his *Consilia Volumina 2*, from Pavia, bound in two volumes, in 1513. They also had a work by Joan. Andreae, *Commentarius super sexto Decretalium*, printed at Venice in 1491; and Cardinal Henrici de Hostiensis, *Summae Iuris*, 5 vols., published at Lyon, in 1512.[329]

After this Mylius records several quarto volumes in law, of which some deserve mentioning. He cites Johann Fabri, who published a *Breviarium in codicem*, that came out at Paris, in 1516; and Paulus of Florence, who printed his *Breviarium in ius canonicum*, at Memmingen in 1499; while Lupoldus published a work *De iuribus imperii*, at Strassburg in 1508. The library also had a few important books of law in octavo size, among which was an *Introductorium in utriusque iuris libros*, appearing at Basel in 1517. There was also Peter Pertica's *Questiones*, from Lyon, in 1517, and Cosmae Guymier, *Pragmatica sancto*, printed in Paris, in 1514.[330] This concludes our selection of the most important books of the Wittenberg library in the three kinds of law.

PRINTED BOOKS IN MEDICINE

In his recording of books in medicine, Mylius again begins with the folio-sized printed books. The first tome is a *Sammelband*, with (1) *Foroliviensis in aphor. Hippocratis*, published in Venice, in 1490; and (2) *Idem super I. librum Galeni*, called by Galen, at Venice, in 1490. Next came Galen's *Therapeutica graece*, also from Venice, in 1500: a.b. *eiusdem. Latin. Tomi 2*, Venice, in 1502; *cura Hieron. Suriani.*, 2 vols. He also found on the shelf, *Aisaravii, sive Albucasae, Medici arabis, liber Theoreticae et Practicae, August 1519*. They also had Galen's *Methodus medendi, Thoma Linacro interprete*, printed in Paris, in 1519. They also had Trusianus' *Monachi Carthusiensis, in lib. Galeni*, from Bologna, in 1489. There was also a two-volume work, with Part I, *Avicennae opera*, from Venice in 1490; and (2) Averroes, *Comment, Avicennae, cantica*, from Venice in 1484. Here follows a recording a.b.c.d. *Avicennae cum expositione Gentilis Canon I et II*, done in Pavia, in 1510, which was bound with his *Canon III, Part I*, from Pavia, in 1511; also by him was *Canon III, part I, part 2, ibid. 1511*; also *Canon IV* from Pavia, in 1511, and *Canon V* from Pavia, in 1512, which are in four volumes. They had Joh. Mesue, *Opera*, from Venice, done in 1478, and a later edition in 1508. The library also had Arnold of Villa's *Nova Opera* from Lyon, published in 1509. Among the medical folios was also Gabriel of Zerbis' *Anatomia*, done in 1502 at Venice, which was bound with another folio, Versalius' *Anatomia*, in German from Nürnberg, printed in 1508. Practical medicine was also represented, in Arculanus' *Practica*, done in Venice in 1504; also, they had Dioscorides' *De meteria medica*, bound with Nicander's *De Theoriaca*, also from Venice in 1499. Among the medical folio volumes there was another *Sammelband* with three volumes, which began with (1) *Dioscoridis de meteria medica libri V versi ab Hermolao Barbaro*, at Venice, in 1516; then (2) *Hermolai Barbarii Corolarii Libri V*, Venice, in 1516; and (3) an *Introductorium Astronomicum* done in Paris, in 1517. Then there was Michael Scott's *Pysiognomia Aristotelis Coclitis, eiuscumque Chiromantia*, from Pavia, done in 1515. Among the works was Dioscoridius' *De materia medica, Libri VI*, interpreted by Marcellus Vergilius of Florence, in 1518, and (2) Alexander Aphrodisaeus, *In libros de anima commentarius*, interpreted by Hieronymus Donatus, printed at Venice, in 1500. The Jena professor found another two-volume folio, with part (1) John Michaelis Savanarolae, *Practica*, done in Venice, in 1487; and (2) *Idem de Febribus*, from Bologna, in 1487. They also had Joh. M. de Gradi, *Practica*, out of Venice, in 1502. Next he cites a three-volume *Sammelband*, in which (1) was by Bartholomaeus Moniagnanane, *Consilia, cum tribus tractatibus de Balneis Pataninis, et de compositione, et dosi medicinarum ac Antidotario*; (2) *Consilia Anton. Cermisoni*, of Pavia; and (3) *Tractatus de animali Theria, domini Francisci Caballi*, from Venice in 1514. Then his final three-volume work among the folio medical works begins with (1) Ugonis, *Senensis, artium et medicinae doctoris, consilia medica*, Venice, in 1510; (2) *Chirurgia Petri de Largelata*, done in Venice, in 1513; and (3) Joh. Almanar's *De Morbo gallico*, out of Pavia, in 1516.[331]

MEDICAL BOOKS IN QUARTO SIZE

There were some books in quarto size worthy of being cited. Mylius begins with a *Sammelband*, in which (1) is of Galen's *Differentiis morborum libri 2;* (2) his *De inaequali intemperatura liber 1. de artecuratiua ad Glauconem libri 2; idem de Crisibus libri 3. Leoniceno interprete*, printed in Paris, in 1514; and in part (3) Alexander Benedicius, *Anatomice et Aphormi medecinales*, done in Paris, in 1514. Another two-volume work, bound together, had as part (1) Galen's *De effectorum morborum notitia*, which was interpreted by Guil Copo, in Paris, in 1513; (2) Nicol Leonicus, *De Plinii et aliorum Medicorum erroribus*, done in Ferrara, in 1509. Another tome of two volumes begins with Dioscorides, *De simplici medicina*, from Lyon in 1512; and part (2) had Anton. Gazius, *Florida corona*, from Lyon, in 1514. Another large *Sammelband*, containing five volumes, began with Marsilius Ficinus, *De triplici vita, cum regimine Salernitano*, from Strassburg, in 1511; (2) Albertus Magnus, *De virtutibus herbarum, lapidum etc.*; (3) Joh. Vochs' *Tractatus de pestilentia anni 1507*, done in Cologne, in 1507, and then in Magdeburg, in 1507; (4) Marcer, *De virtutibus herbarum;* and (5) Mundinus' *Anatomia*, out of Strassburg in 1513. Next came another two-volume work, in which (1) was by Udalricus Pinder, *Epiphanie Medicorum I, Speculum videndi urinas hominum;* (2) *Clauis aperiendi portas pulsum*; (3) Berilius, *Discernendi causas et differentias febrium* s.l., in 1506. Here follows a four-volume *Sammelband*, beginning with (1) Magninus, *Medici Mediolanens, regimen sanitatis*, from Strassburg, in 1503; (2) Simon Pistoris, *Regiment wieder die Peste*, out of Leipzig, in 1506; (3) Marsilius Ficinus, *De triplici vita;* and (4) Petrus Ravennas, *De memoria artificiosa*, from Erfurt, in 1500. They also had a two-volume work, beginning with (1) Bertrucius of Bologna, *Collectorium totius medicinae*, out of Lyon, in 1509; and (2) Joh. Ganivellius, *Amicus Medicor.*, from Lyon, in 1508.[332]

SOME OCTOVO-SIZED MEDICAL WORKS

The library also had a few medical works in small octavo size which need to be cited. In a small *Sammelband* there was (1) a work by Abuletrus, son of Zacharias, *Sivi Rasis divisiones et constantini monarchi viaticum*, from Lyon, in 1510. Another two-volume *Sammelband* began (1) with *Simphoriani Champerii (Campegius) Lugdunensis, Antoni ducis Lotharingiae et Barri primarii physici, Symphonia Platonis cum Aristotele et Galeni cum Hippocrate*, done in Paris, in 1516; (2) *Eiusdem Medicinale bellum inter Aristotelem et Galenum*, s.d. Here follows another two-volume tome, beginning with (1) *Rosa gallica, contenens praecepta, auctoritates atque sententias ex praecipius medicae artis autoribus*, done at Paris in 1514; and, (2) *Eiusdem Practica Nova in Medicina*, but s.l. et s.d. Mylius says these octavo books were found in the rare book catalogues of that day.[333]

ANCIENT FOLIO-SIZE BOOKS IN THE ARTS

He points out that these books in liberal arts will stress philosophy and philology, and also grammar and lexicography. It begins with Theodor Gaza's *Intro-
ductionis Grammaticae graecae*, Libri IV, by the famous Greek scholar in
Venice. In the same work was the *Opusculum de mensibus*, namely, Apollonius'
De constructione libri IV, and that of Herodianus' *De numeria*, all written in
Greek, printed at Venice in 1495. As the liberal arts college at Wittenberg was
much larger that the graduate schools, its needs in books were much greater in
the variety of disciplines. Since oratory and rhetoric were basic to the reorganization of Wittenberg into a humanistic institution, it is not strange that Spalatin
made these purchases from the Aldus Press in Venice, as portrayed in another
chapter of this volume.[334] Among the many other works cited was *Thesaurus
graecae lingue*, which is called *Cornu copiae et Horti Adonidos*, printed in
Venice, in 1496. There Mylius also found a dictionary in Greek, *Cum Cyrilli
opusculo de vocibus*, with the various accents, from Venice in 1497. There was
also *Suidas graece*, from Venice, in 1514.

Next Mylius turned to oratory, citing Aristotle's *Orations* in Greek, which
were printed in Florence, in 1517. Next he took off the Jena Library shelf a
Sammelband, beginning with Isocrates' *Orationes: Alcidamantes contra
dicendi magistros*; *Gorgias de laudibus Helenae*; *Aristides de laudibus
Athenarum et de Romae*, all in Greek, done in Venice in 1513. Mylius added
various Greek works in oratory from the Aldus Press in Venice in 1513. They
had Demosthenes' *Orationes, graece, cum Libanii argumentis*, printed in
Venice, in 1504. There was also Ulpianus' *Commenterieli in quasdam Demos-
thenis orationes*, done in Venice, in 1503. Among the folios they also had a series
of works on rhetoric, by Aphthonius, Hermogenes, Aristoteles, Sopater, etc.,
authors in the art of rhetoric, in Greek, from Venice, in 1508. Then comes *M.T.
Cisceronis opera rhetorica, oratoria et Forensia*, done from Paris in 1511. The
library also had Cicero's *Opera philosophica*, out of Paris, in 1511. In another
folio *Sammelband* was Mariius Fabrii Victorini, *Comment. in Rhetoricam
Cisceronis*, printed in Venice, in 1493; and (2) Alexandri Aphrodisei, *Aristotelis
et Plutarchi Problemata latine*, from Venice, in 1488. He also cites Omnibanus
Leonicus' *Commentaria in oratorem Ciceronis*, from Venice, a 4-volume set, in
1488. Then Mylius cites another two volume set, beginning (1) with *Quincti-
lianus cum commentario* by R. Regius, done at Venice, in 1473; (2) Job. Tartellii
Orthographia, also from Venice, in 1491. In another volume of the library was
an *Epistolas Ciceronis variorum Commenta*, from Venice, in 1492; and part
(2) had Cicero's *orationem, de fato, de Topica et de universitate commentarii*,
from Venice in 1492. Another work was that by Caius Pliny, *Secundi Epistolae*,
with a commentary by Job. Mariae Cantanaei, printed at Milan in 1506.
Another work was by Marcus A. Sabellcus, *Epistolas, orationes et poemata*,
from Venice, in 1507. This classification ends with *Francise Philelphi epistolarum Libri XXXVII*, also completed in Venice, in 1507.[335]

BOOKS IN LOGIC, PHYSICS, AND METAPHYSICS

In this important listing, Mylius begins with Aristotle's *Organum*, in Greek, done in Venice, in 1495. Next comes a *Sammelband* from the Aldus Press in Venice, with part (1) *Aristotelis et Alexandri Aphrodisci problemata graece, it.*; and (2) *Aristotelis et Theophrasti libri metaphysici*, from Venice, in 1497, *apud Aldum Manutium*. Another large-bound tome of several parts, beginning with (1) is Aristotle's *Libri physici graece*, from Venice, in 1497, *it*; (2) *Accessere Aristotelis' vita per Job. Philoponum, Laertium et Galenum, it*; *Theophrasti de igne, ventis, signis aquarum et lapidibus libri ibid*. Among the books was also *Aristotelis libri de animalibus, anima etc.*, printed in Venice in 1497. Another *Sammelband* begins with (1) *Aristotelis opera fere omnia, latine reddita ab Hermolas Barbaro et aliis*, from Venice, in 1507. The library also had Simplicius, *In 10. Categorias Aristotelis. graece*, from Venice, in 1499. There was also the often-cited Petrus Tararetus, *Commentaria in libros Physicorum Aristoteli*, on the work *De caelo et de mundo, in libros metacroologicos de caussa de sensu et sensato*; *Metaphysicacorum super libros logicos Aristotelis et in summulas Hispani*, printed at Wittenberg in 1504. In the ducal library was also a folio-sized final work of Polich von Mellerstadt, published posthumously in his honor, entitled in the first part *Martini Polichi Millerstadii, cursus logici et commentaria in omnes libros logicos Aristotelis*, which they had printed at Leipzig in 1512; while the next part was named *Cursus physici in 8 libros Physic. de coelo et mundo, de generatione et corruptione, de anima*, done at Leipzig in 1514, shortly after the professor's death. Another two-volume work was (1) *Iac. Stapulensie, praedicabilia Logica*, from Paris, in 1510; and part (2), Laurentius Vala's *Dialecticae libri III*, from Paris, printed in 1509.[336]

The library had another *Sammelband* with books dealing mainly with Plato. It begins with *Iamblichus, de mysteriis Aegyptiorum, Chaldaeorum, Assyriorum: Proclus in Platonicum Alcibiadem de anima atque daemone, dequa sacrificio et magia: Porphyrius de devinis atque daemonibus: Synesius, Platonicus, de somniis*; *Psellus de daemonibus*; *Expositio Prisciani et Marsillii in Theophrasti libros de sensu phatasia intellectu: Alcinous de doctrina Platonis: Pseupsippua de Platonis definitionibus*; *Pathagorae aurea verba et symbola*; *Xenocratus liber de morte*; and *Marsillii Facini*. All these were done in Latin at Venice, in 1497.[337]

The works on Aristotle continue in another *Sammelband*, beginning with Albertus Magnus, *Aristotele libros Physicorum, 19 vols. Commentar., in libros de coelo et munde*, done at Venice, in 1490. In another folio of two volumes the library had *Aristotelis de natura partibus et generatione animalium libri, latine rediti a Theodore Gaza*, done at Venice in 1492; and part (2) has Albertus Magnus' *Comment. in libros Meteororum Aristotelis*, printed in Venice, in 1488. The library also had Augustinus Niphus, *In IV Libros Aristotelis de coelo et mundo*, from Naples, in 1517. The collection also had Caius Pliny the Elder's *Naturalis Historiae libri XXXVII*, from Venice, in 1491.[338] They had another Pliny the Elder work, which Mylius rated as quite rare, his *Naturalis Historiae libri*

XXXVII, done in Venice in 1469. In the collection was another two-volume
tome, beginning (1) with *Hermolai Barbari, castigationes Plinianae*, from
Rome, in 1492; (2) *Eiusd. editio in Plenium secunda: Emendatio in Pomponium
Melam: Obscurae voces in Plinio cum expositione*, from Rome, in 1493. The
library also had another volume by Albertus Magnus, *De animalibus eoruadem
propretatibus*, from Rome, in 1478.[339]

ANCIENT BOOKS IN MATHEMATICS

Mylius begins this recording with a folio-sized *Sammelband* in mathematics,
beginning (1) with Jordanus Nemorarius, *Elementa arithmetica*, with demon-
strations by Jac. Fabri Stapulensis, 10 vols., and 4 in music; also the *Epitome in
libros arithmeticos Boetii*; *Rithmimachiae ludus, qui et pugna numerorum
appellatur*, from Paris, in 1496; (2) *Eiusd. Fabri in totam Physicam Commentarii*, from Paris, in 1510. Another work was by *Guilielm Nudaei de esse et partibus eius libri V*, from Paris, in 1514. *Euclidis Elementa Geometriae, latine*,
from Vicenza, in 1491. Another folio in two parts, had (1) Euclid's *Megarensis
Geometricorum elementorum* with a *commentary* by Campanius of Gaul,
Thomas of Alexandria, and others adding their interpretations, libros XV
printed at Paris, in 1516; and (2) *Burbachius Mathematici, Quadratum geo-
metricum*, from Nürnberg, in 1516. Another folio of two books, Epitome Joh.
de Monte-regio, *In Almagestum Ptolemari*, printed in Venice, in 1516. Part 2
had *Summa Astrologiae iudicialia, quae vulgo noncupater Anglicana*, printed at
Venice, in 1489. Among the books was also Ptolemy's *Almagestum*, from Venice,
in 1515; and (2) was bound with Thomas Aquinas' *In libros Aristotelis in coelo et
mundo*, from Venice in 1506. Another folio contained Julius Firmicus' *Astronomicorum libri* 19 and Marcus Manilius' *Astronomicorum libri V*; *Arati
Phaenomina graece et latina*; *Theonis Commentaria graeca In Aratum*; Procli
Sphaera graece et latine, from Venice in 1499. Another four-part volume begins
(1) with *Petrus Cirvellus uberrimum sphere mundi commentum, intersertis
quaestionibus Petri de Aliaco*, from Paris, in 1503; (2) *Job. Boccacius Certoldus,
libri IX de cassibus illustrium virorum*, done in Paris, s.d.; and (3) Rudolf Agricola, *Phrisii, Libri 3. de inventione dialectica*, from Louvain, in 1515; and
(4) Michael Coccinius, *De rebus gestia in Italia a mense Maio*, Tübingen, in
1511. *Ad Kalendas Maii anno 1512, sequentis, sine loco et anno*. Here follows
another four-volume *Sammelband*, beginning with (1) Albubather, *De Astrolo-
gia*, from Venice, in 1492; (2) *Hermetis Centiloquium*; (3) Halius, *De iudiciis
Astrorum*, from Venice, in 1485; and (4) *Summa Astrologiae, quae vocaturs
Anglicana*, from Venice, in 1489. They also had Strabo, *De situ orbis, ex editione
Aldina graece*, from Venice, in 1510. The library also had Ptolemy's *Geography*
in Latin, from Rome, in 1490, and another edition of Ptolemy's *Georgraphia*,
printed in Strassburg, in 1513.[340]

POLITICS AND ECONOMICS OF ANTIQUITY

In the next section, Mylius begins with Plato's *Operum Tomi 2* in Greek from Venice, done in 1513. Then follows another folio-sized treatise, Plato's *Opera* done in verse form by Marsilius Ficinus, printed in Venice, in 1517. Then comes *Aristotelis opera Ethica, Politica et Oeconomica*, all in Greek, done in Venice, in 1498. Among the library books, Mylius found a large *Sammelband* with seven books, which begins with (1) the *Ethica Aristotelis*, interpreted by *Ioan. Argyropylo libri 10, Romae 1492*; (2) Avicennae, *De anima qui est sextus naturalium eiusdem*, from Pavia, s.d.; (3) Albertus Magnus, *De Mineralibus*, from Pavia, in 1491; (4) Johannis Archbishop of Canterbury, *Perspectua*, s.l. et s.d.; (5) Albertus Magnus, *De praedicabilibus et praedicamentis*; (6) *Eiusd. Alberti M., Commentum super 6 libros principiorum Gilberti Porretani*, from Pavia, s.l. et anno; and (7) *Ausonii opera* printed in Milan, in 1490.[341] Mylius found another volume done by *Jac. Fab. Staupulensis Mathematica*, done at Pais, in 1503, as the first of a four-volume *Sammelband*; (2) *Sphaera Sacrorosci et Euclidis Geometr, Libri IV*, from Paris, in 1507; (3) *Iac. Fabri Stapulensis, introductio in X libros Ethicos Aristotelis*, done at Paris, in 1506; and (4) was *Staupulensis in libros politicos et oeconom. Aristotelis*, also from Paris, in 1506.[342] Another *Sammelband* offered a concord of some questions and criticism of St. Thomas and Albert the Great. This began with (1) Master Johann Versoris, *Questiones super libros Ethicorum Aristotelis*, from Cologne in 1491; (2) *Tractatus, ostendens Concordiam Thome et Alberti in multis, in quibus dictantur esse contrarii*, s.l. et s.d.; (3) *Versoris questiones super 4. libros de coelo et mundo*; (4) *Idem super libros 2 de generatione et corruptione, cum textu Aristotelis*, published at Colone, in 1489; and (5) *Eiusd. questiones super 4. libros Meteororum*. s.l. et s.d.[343]

Where in the above much emphasis is placed on Aristotle, as was true in the pre-Luther Wittenberg, now Mylius tells us of other authors of antiquity. He begins with Lucius Seneca, *Opera omnia*, which were done in Venice, in 1492; (2) Francis Petrarch, *De remediis utriusque fortunae*, done at Cremonia, in 1492. The library also had Seneca's *Opera omnia*, edited by Erasmus, printed at Basel, in 1515.[344] Next Mylius cites *Plutarchi operum moralium*, parts 1 and 2, done in Venice, 1509. They had another two-volume folio tome, beginning with Maximus Tyrius, *Philosophi Platonici, sermones, e graeco versi a* Casino, from Pavia, in 1517; while (2) had Felicis Malleoli, *Vulgo Hemmerlein, vel Hemmerlin, varie oblectationis opuscula et tractarum*, at Basel, in 1494. *Liber rareissimus et lepidisaimus.* Another folio was Plotinus, *Opera*, edited and illustrated by Marsilius Ficinus, from Florence, in 1492. Two volumes had Boethius, *De consolatione Philosophias, cum comment*, by Thomas Aquinas; and (2) Thomas Aquinas, *Quodlibeta*, printed in Nürnberg in 1474.[345]

HISTORICAL BOOKS OF ANTIQUITY

This section begins with a two-volume folio work, (1) with the historian Josephus, *Opera omnia latine*; and (2) Egesippuus, *De bello Judaico*, from Milan, in

1513. Mylius found another folio, Bede's *Et Historia Ecclesiastica Anglorum et Ecclesiastica. Eusebis Ruffino interprete*, printed in Hagenau, in 1506. Among the books was also M. Petri Commestoris, *Historia Scholastica*, from Strassburg, in 1515, and Eusebius, *Historia Ecclesiastica* as part of a two-volume set; and (2) Bede's *Historia Ecclesiastica gentis Anglicorum*, done in Strassburg, in 1514. There was also a work by Jacobus, *Lombardica Historia*, from Nürnberg, in 1501. Next follows Petri de Natalibus, *Catalogus Sanctorum et gestorum eorum*, out of Venice, in 1506. Later in 1514 this catalogue of the saints was printed in Strassburg; while three years later, Strassburg also printed this work in a folio-sized edition in Wittenberg, under the title *Heiligen Leben*. The library also had a *Martyrilogium ordinis Benedicti*, in red and black letters, but s.d. et s.l. Another folio was by Leondrus Albertus, 6 vols. *De viris illustribus ordinis Praedicatorum*, done at Bologna, in 1517. Among the books was also the famous chronicle of Hartmann Schedel, *Liber chronicorum*, with its many illustrations, from Nürnberg in 1493. The library also possessed a *Sammelband* out of the Aldus Press in Venice, with part (1) by *Herodoti Historiarum libri IX quibis Musarum indita sunt nomina, graece impressi, Venice, ex officina Aldina 1502*; (2) *Bessarionis, Cardinalis Niceni, et Patriarchae Constantinopol* was titled *Calumniatorem Platonis libri IV*; (3) *eiusdem, correctio librorum de legibus trapezuntio interprete, eius tractae de natura et arte adversus Trapezuntium.* Venice, 1503. *ap. Aldum omnia 3 posteriora scripta sunt impressa.*[346] There was another multi-volume folio tome, with part (1) *Thucydides graece tantum, Venice, ex officina Aldina*, in 1502; (2) *Xenophontis omissa*, (3) Georgius Gemistius, *De iis, quae post pugnam ad Martiniam gesta sunt*, and (4) *Herodiani libri IIX Anar.*, 1505. In another *Sammelband*, a tome of four parts begins with (1) *Velleii Paterculi Historia romanae volumina*, 2 vols. printed at Basel in 1520, and in part (2) it had Francisci Petrarchae, *Opera*, from Venice in 1501; in (3) *Marcianus Cappella de nuptiis Mercurii et Philologae cum annotationibus Joh. Dubrauii*, done at Vienna, in 1516. In another folio they had Philippus Beroaldus' *Cornelii Taciti opera*, from Rome in 1515. They also had Jornandes, *De rebus Gothorum*; while in part (2) they had *Othonis Frisingensis rerum, ab origine mundi gestarum, libri IIX*, from Vienna, in 1514; (3) *Pavei, Diaconi, de origine et rebus gestis Longobardorum Libri VI*, from Paris, in 1514; (4) *Luitprandi rerum, per Europam suo tempore gestarum, libri VI*, from Paris in 1514; and Annonius, *De regnum Francorum origine et gestis*, from Paris in 1514. In another folio *Sammelband*, part (1) had Procopius' *De rebus Gothorum*, done at Rome, in 1506; part (2) had Agathias, *De bello Gothorum*, Rome, in 1516; and (3) had two parts, Jornandes, *De rebus Gothorum*, and a Deacon Paulus, *De gestis longobardorum* Aagusti, Vindelicor. 1515. Another four-volume work in a bound tome (1) begins with Joh. Trittenhemius, *Compendium primi Voluminis annalium, de origine regum et gestis Francorum*, from Mainz, in 1515; part (2) *Petri Montii Exercitiorum et artis militaris collectanea*, from Milan, in 1509; (3) *Eiusd. de singulari certamine libri 3*, from Milan, in 1509; and (4) Poggius *Florentini opera*, from Strassburg, in 1510. In another three-volume work was (1) Franciscus Irenius *Germaniae Exegeseos volumina XII*, Hagenau, in 1518:

(2) Quintus Curtius, *De rebus gestis Alexandri*, M. from Strassburg, in 1518; and (3) Conrad Celtis, *Descriptio Noribergae*, from Hagenau, in 1518. The library also had Johann Kalhoff's *Cölner Chronic*, by a Cologne Bürger, s.d.[347] Among the folios there was another work, in German, *Chronicke der löblichen Erd-genossenschafft*, out of Basel, done in 1507. Next came Campanus' *Opera*, completed in 1495, which was followed by Platina's *De vitis Pontificium*, completed in Venice, in 1504. Then comes Valerius Maximus' *Dictorum ac factorum memorabilium libri cum nova interpretationes Oliverii*, also done in Venice, by 1491. He also found an interesting work by Baptistae Fulgosi, *De dictis factisque memorabilibus collectanea*, printed in Milan, in 1509.[348]

POETICAL BOOKS OF ANTIQUITY

In this section Mylius begins with Homer, *Ilias et Odyssea, Barrachomy-onuchia et hymni*, done in Florence in 1488, by the industry of Demetrius of Crete, which Mylius rates as the first and rarest of all editions. In a two-volume *Sammelband*, in part (1) Lorenzo Valla translated Homer's *Illias*, which was printed at Leipzig in 1512; while part (2) had Apuleius' *De asino aureo cum comment.* by *Philipp. Beroaldi*, printed in Paris in 1512. The library also had a four-volume *Sammelband*, in which part (1) has the *Odyssea Homeri, per Raphaelem Valaterraanum conversa*, printed at Rome, in 1510; while part (2) was Blondus Flavius, *De Rome triumphane, libri X*, from Venice, in 1511, and part (3) had Julius Solinus' *De situ orbis terrarum*, from Pias in 1512; and (4) had Vibius Sequester, *De fluminibus, montibus, lacubus, et gentibus*, from Pisa, in 1512. Another two-volume tome had (1) *Homeri Odyssea, latine*, out of Strassburg, in 1510; and (2) *Matialis Epigrammata, cum Comment. Calderini et Merulae*, printed in Venice, 1510. Mylius cited another four-volume *Sammelband*, beginning (1) with *Theocriti Eclogae: Theognidis, Pythagorae, Phocyllidis carmina*, done in Venice, in 1495; (2) *Hesiodi opera omnia, graece tantum. ibid.*, 1495; (3) Philostratus, *De vita Apollonii Tyanei, graece et latine*, Venit., 1502, *ap. Aldus*; and (4) *Eusebius contra Hieroclem, itidem graece et latine*, by the Aldus Press, at Venice, in 1502. They also had a volume in Greek with a *Scholia*, of *Aristophanis Comoediae IX*, done at Venice, in 1498. There was another folio-sized work, *Plauti Commoesiae, cum comment. Petri Vallae et Bernhardi Saraceni*, also from Venice, in 1499. Among the books found by Mylius was a work by Terence, the *Terentii quinque Commoediae*, printed at Milan in 1509; while another Terence was in a *Sammelband, Terentii Comoediae Directorio glossa interlineari et Commentariis*, published at Strassburg in 1496. Another two-folio volume had *Lucretius cum commentariis Joh. Baptistae PII*, done at Bologna in 1511; while (2) had *Claudianus de raptu Proserpinae, cum Comment. Iani Parrasii*, from Milan done in 1500.[349]

At this point Mylius recorded a number of works about Ovid, beginning with a three-volume *Sammelband*, starting with Ovid's *Metamorphoses*, with a *comm.* by Raphael Regius, from Venice, in 1493; while in part (2) it had Ovid's

Epistolae, also from Venice, in 1492; and in part (3) the set had Ovid's *Factorum libri*, also done in Venice in 1492. In another volume the library had Ovid's *Opera omnia, emendata a Barneba Celsano*, Vicent., in 1492. In another two-volume, folio-sized tome from Paris, the library had a work titled, *Annotationes doctorum virorum in Grammaticos, Oratores, Poetas, Philosophos, Theologos, et Leges*, in 1511; and (2) *Silii Italici Carminum libri XVII, cum Comment. Petri Marst*, done at Paris in 1512.[350]

ANCIENT PHILOLOGICAL BOOKS

This part begins with a two-volume folio set, with part (1) *Athenaeus graece*, printed at Venice in 1514; and part (2) *Hesychii Lexicon*, from Venice in the same year. Then Mylius reports on a large *Sammelband*, a tome of six works, all in Greek, by the Aldus Press, beginning with (1) as he recorded the parts. *Aesopi ut et Gabriae fabulae*; (2) *Phurnutus* vel *curnutus de natura Deorum*; (3) Palaephatus, *De non credendis historiis*; (4) Herachlides, *De Allegoriis apud Homerum*: (5) *Ori Hieroglyphica etc.*, out of Venice, in 1505; and (6) *Progymnasmata Aphionii Commentarii anonymi, it, Syriani, Sopatri et Marcellini Comm. in Hermogenis, Rhetorica*, all done in Venice, in 1509; *ap. Aldum, pleraque tantum graeca sunt.*[351] Among the books recorded, Mylius found another folio with *Aesopi, Apologi, cum carminum et fabularum additionibus*, done by Sabast. Brand., printed at Basel, in 1501. Another had Lucian's *Opera* in a two-part folio set, with part (1) *Callistrati descriptiones*, entirely in Greek, from the Aldus Press at Venice, in 1503. Next Mylius records a two-volume folio set, in part (1) Auli Gellius, *Noctes Atticae*, from Venice, in 1509; while in part (2) was Cornelius Tacitus' *Historici fragmenta, ex recensione Joh. Riuii*, from Venice, done in 1512. Mylius next recorded another *Sammelband*, the large folio type, with five works, beginning with (1) *Macrobius, in somnium Scipionis, et libri eiusd. Saturnalium*, done in Venice, in 1492; part (2) Celsus, *De re medica libri*, printed at Venice, in 1493; part (3) *Quint. Curtius de rebus gestis Alexandri M.*, also from Venice, in 1491, and (4) had *Crispi Sallustii opera omnia, a Pomponio emendata*, printed at Venice, in 1493; (5) was *Lactantii, Firmiani opera*, also completed in Venice in 1493. Next Mylius cites another folio set of several volumes, with (1) Lucius Apuleius' *Opera*, from Venice, in 1493; while part (2) had Philadelphius' *Orationes, ac alia quaedam opuscula*, from Venice, in 1492; and (3) *Aulii Gellii opera omnia* from Venice, in 1493. Another two-volume set was by the Italian humanist Boccatius, which work in (1) is *Boccatii opus de genealogiis Deorum gentilium, Regii*, 1481; and (2) his *libes de montibus sylvis* etc. Another Renaissance author follows here, as Mylius found *Poggii Florentini operum pars 1 et 2*, published at Strassburg, in 1513. Next comes Georg Valla, *De expetendis et fugiendis rebus, Tomi II*, from Venice in 1501. They also had *Raphaelis Volaterrani Commentarior libri XXXIIX, et Xenophontis Oeconomicus, ab eodem versus*, from Basel, in 1511. In the library were also the works of Erasmus, his *Adagia,* printed in Basel in 1515, and his *Adagiorum Chiliades 3. totidemque Centuriae,* from Venice, in 1508.[352]

Ancient Grammatical Volumes

Since Mylius had concluded the important folio-sized volumes, he now has turned to the books of quarto size, the Hebrew and Greek texts used by the Wittenberg faculty of theology. This begins with *Wolffgangi Fabritii Capitonis Hebraicar. Institutionum libri* II, Basel, 1518. Another work was by the professor of Hebrew, Jab. Böschenstein, titled *Introductorium in Hebraeas litteras,* printed in Augsburg in 1514.[353] The work had the Hebrew and German texts for the Ten Commandants, the Lord's Prayer, the Apostle's Creed, and similar teaching materials in both languages. The Jena professor also found here John Reuchlin's work, *De accentibus et orthographia linguae hebraeicae,* printed in Hagenau, in 1518. Mylius also found a huge *Sammelband,* a bound tome with seven works, which began (1) with *Theodori Gazai Grammaticae graecae Institutiones, libri II, interprete Erasmo Roterodamo,* done in Basel in 1516; (2) *Eiusd. Gasae Grammatica graeca.* from Basel done the same year;[354] (3) *Oecolampadii epistola apologitica, de risu paschali,* out of Basel, in 1518: (4) *Marcelli Vergilii oratio, de militiae laudibus,* from Basel in 1518; (5) *Gutherberti Tonstalli oratio in laudem matrimonii,* out of Basel, in 1519; (6) *Ex Luciano quaedam traducta,* printed in Strassburg in 1517, and (7) *Udalrici Zasii, defensio* contra *Eckium, super eo, quod fides non esset seruanda hosti,* also printed at Basel, in 1517. Among the library's works, according to Mylius, was that in another *Sammelband,* the work of the Greek scholars in Venice, was (1) that of *Constantini Lascaris de nomine et verbo liber tertius, gr. et lat. latina interpretatio per Aldum Manutium, Venet. 1517.* In with it was another *Lascaris,* liber I. de *8 partibus orationis; et liber 2. de constructione;* (2) *Erotemata Chrysolorae, graece tantum,* printed at Paris in 1507.[355]

In the next part of Wittenberg's purchases of humanistic works, it clearly reveals Melanchthon's influence.[356] They bought Urban Bellunensus *Institutiones graece Grammatices,* printed at Venice in 1497. They even obtained a work by Aldus Manucius himself, his *Grammaticae graece institutio,* from Venice, in 1515. Another work was by the Englishman Master Richard Crocer, his *Tabulae in linguam graecae,* printed in Leipzig, in 1516. They also had Nicolas Porottus' *Rudimenta Grammatices et regulae Grammatices Guarini,* done at Venice, in 1493. Next Mylius cites Pyladis, Brixiani, *Grammatica latina. Annotationes in Alexandrum de villa Dei carmen scholasticum de nominum declinationibus et coniugationibus, genealogia et vocabularium. Venit. 1508.* There was also an Aldus Manucius work, *Institut. Grammat. Latinar,* printed in Basel in 1508. Another five-volume *Sammelband* is worth recording, beginning with (1) Georgius Simlarus, *Vuimpinensis, observationes de arte grammatica, de litteris graecis ac diphtongis;* (2) *Erotemata Guarini ex Chrysolorae libello mainseulo,* done at Tübingen, in 1512; (3) Valerius Probus, *De litteris antiquis;*

(4) Pomponius Laetus, *De Romanorum magistratibus et sacerdotiis*, printed at Oppenheim, in 1510; and (5) *Bellum Grammaticale nominis et verbi, Regum de principolitate orationis contendentum*, done in Strassburg, in 1512. Another six-volume work began with (1) Job. Aventinus, *Grammatica latina*, from Leipzig, in 1515; (2) Jacob. *Purliliarum comes, De liberorum educatione*, from Strassburg, in 1510; (3) Baptista Guarinus' *De mode docendi et discendi*, from Strassburg, 1514; (4) *Ludov. Heliani oratio de bello adversus Veneros et Tureas, habita*, Augsburg, 1510; (5) Erasmus Roterodamus, *De constructione 8. partium orationis*, Cologne, 1514; and (6) *eiusd. copia rerum et verborum etc similia* etc., Strassburg, 1515.[357]

Among the grammatical works, Mylius found another four-volume *Sammelband* of quarto size, starting with (1) Diomedus' *Grammaticae libri III*, done in Cologne, in 1518; part (2) contained a copy of Philip Melanchthon's *Grammatica graeca*, printed in Hagenau in 1518.[358] In the same binding (3) *Eiusd. oratio, de Arribus liberalibus, Tubingae habita, et sine anno impressa*: (4) Lucianus' *Oration ad calumniam. a Philippo Melanchtone latine facta*. from Leipzig, in 1518. In the listing of library books, there was also a work by Cardinal Hadrianius, *De sermo latino, et modis latine loquendi*, Basel, 1518. In another three-volume quarto were (1) Erasmus' *De copia rerum etc.*, from Strassburg, in 1513; (2) his *Moria*, from there, in 1511; and (3) Jodocus Clichtoveus, *De vera nobilitate*, from Paris, in 1512.[359]

ANCIENT BOOKS IN RHETORIC AND ORATORY

In this section Mylius continues to cover the quarto-sized books in rhetoric and grammar. It starts with a famous collection of Cicero's works, which Aldus Manucius had printed. Among these was *Marci Tulli Ciceronis, Rhetoricorum ad Herennium libri IV, de inventione libri II, de oratore libri III, de claris oratoribus: Orator ad Brutum, Partit., Topica ad Trebatium, Partit. Oratoriae*, printed at Venice in 1514, *ap. Aldus Manutium*. The next work recorded is that of Petrus Mosellanus, *Oratio de variarum linguarum cognitione paranda*, printed on parchment, at Leipzig, in 1518. Then Mylius recorded another *Sammelband*, with part (1) a work by Francis Petrarch, *Epistolae familiares*, from Venice in 1492; part (2) Pliny, *Secundi epistolae, eiusd. Panegyricus in imperatorum Trajanum et de viris illustribus exemplaria duo*, from Venice, in 1485; (3) Mercurius Trismegistus, *De potestate et sapientia Dei a Marsilio Ficino*, from Venice, in 1493; (4) Petr. Paulus Vergerius (a) *De ingenuis moribus*, s.d. et s.l. There was a one-volume quarto by Marsilius Ficinus of Florence, *Epistolae*, done at Nürnberg in 1497. Next Mylius recorded another three-volume *Sammelband* of the works of Erasmus of Rotterdam, beginning (1) with his *Enchiridion militis christiani*, from Basel in 1518; (2) *Acutarium selectarum aliquot epistolarum Erasmi, Roterodami ad eroditos et horum ad illum*, done in Basel, in 1518; (3) *Encomium Matrimonii et artis medicae*, also from Basel, in 1518. Next came another work by Philippi Beroaldi, *Orationes*, *epigrammata et alia*, Basel, 1513 [360] In the library Mylius also found a number of volumes of Ulrich von Hutten, the first being in a quarto-sized *Sammelband* of five volumes, which he recorded next, beginning with his *Orationes et Dialogi*, from Steckelberg, in 1519, as part (1) and (2) his *Invectiuae et epistolae*; (3) *Dialogi Huttenici*; (4) *Bulla Leonis X. contra Lutherum*; and (5) his *Defensio Lutheranorum*, s.d. et s.l. In a long note Mylius explains that Hutten's works are rare and hard to find.[361]

BOOKS OF ANTIQUITY IN LOGIC

Among the books in logic of quarto size, Mylius began with one from the Aldus Press in Venice, *Epiphyllides in Dialecticis*, Venice, in 1497. There was also a three-volume *Sammelband*, which had (1) Gregorii Nazianzeni, *Apologeticus de epiphanis, de fide, de grandinis vastatione, latine*, from Strassburg, in 1508; (2) Thomas Murner's *Chartiludium, sive Logica memoratiua* from Strassburg, published in 1509; Jac. Hochstraten, *Ordin. Predicator, Iustificatorium, principum Alamannie, adversus Petrum Ravennatem*, s.l. et s.a.[362]

BOOKS IN PHYSICS AND METAPHYSICS

Under this classification, in quarto size, Mylius recorded but three titles of books in the ducal library, which were six volumes in a single *Sammelband*, which contained (1) M. Conrad Wimpina, *Tractatus quidam Physici*, but is s.l. et s.a,; part (2) *Aegidii de Roma tractatus Philosophiae essentialibus, de doctrina Rhetoricae, Politicae et Ethicae et de gradibus formarum* 1493; (3) *Tractatulus de inventione medii et de propositionibus. modalibus*, from Leipzig, printed in 1500; (4) Joh. Fabri, *Tractatus de modo decendi alios*, from Leipzig, s.d.; (5) Thomas Aquinas' *De occultis naturae effectibus*, printed at Leipzig in 1499; and in (6) was Conrad Wimpina's *De parvis Logicalibus*, done also at Leipzig, in 1499. There was also a quarto book by Joh. Cameritus, *Index Plinianus*, from Vienna in 1514.[363]

BOOKS IN ETHICS, POLITICS, AND ECONOMICS

In this section, Mylius reported on a *Sammelband*, beginning (1) with Lorenzo Valla in his *De voluptate ac vero beno*, from Paris, done in 1512; part (2) had Bede's *De sex aetatibus huius seculi* etc.; part (3) Victor, *De regionibus urbis Rome, ambo libri*, done at Venice in 1505; and in (4) *Confutatio Alcorani*, s.l. et s.a.; (5) *Margarita Facetiarum, Arragon, regis Vastedicta*, s.l. et s.d. In another quarto collection were some of Thomas More, beginning with (1) Thomas More, *De optimo reipublicae atatu eoque nova insula Utopiae libellus, it.*; (2) *Epigrammata eiusd. a Bernhard Trebatio latinrate donata*, from Basel in 1518; (3) *Orus Apollo de Hierglyphicis notis*, from Basel, 1518; and (4) *Epistolae aliquot Roterodami et aliorum ad eundem*, also from Basel, in 1518. In another three-volume quarto he recorded for us, we have (1) Erasmus of Rotterdam, *Institutio principis christiani*, from Basel, in 1516; (2) *Eiusd. Panegyricus Philippum, Caroli. V. filium.* from Basel, in 1516; (3) *Plutarchi scriptum. quo pacto possit adulator dignosci ab amioo itemque de utilitate capienda ab inimicis*, also from Basel in 1516. Another three-volume *Sammelband* that Mylius recorded began with (1) Sebastian Branrt, *Navis stultifera*, from Basel, in 1497; (2) *Michaelis Lochmaieri Parochiale*, from Leipzig, in 1497; and (3) Conrad Wimpina, *In Rectoratu suo Lipsiensis studii orationes.* 3 vols., Leipzig, s.a. Next came another three-volume quarto set, with (1) Matthaeus Bassus' *De re militari*, out of Strassburg, in 1515; (2) Erasmus' *Bellum*, printed in Louvain in 1517; and (3) Erasmus' *Stella de interpretamentis gemmarum*, out of Nürnberg, printed in 1517. There was another one from the Aldus Press, *Catonis, Varronis, Columeldae, Palladii libri de re rustica cum Giorgia Alexandrini enarratione*, printed at Venice in 1514.[364]

HISTORICAL BOOKS OF ANTIQUITY

Mylius' recordings of a set of historical books in a *Sammelband* begins with (1) Eusebius' *Chronicon*, with additions from Mathew Palmer, at Paris in 1512; and (2) continues with Sigebertus' *Chronicon ab anno 381–1113*, done at Paris in 1513. Another work was the *Vitae Patrum*, by Hieronymus, printed at Lyon, in 1509. In another three-volume set was: part (1) Joh. Trittenheimius, *De scriptoribus ecclesiasticis*, printed at Paris in 1512; (2) Carolus Bovillus' *Comment. in primordiale Evangelium Johannis*; in (3) *Vita Remundi Eremitae*: and (4) *Bovilli Philo Philosophorum aliquot Epistolae*, completed in 1511. Another *Sammelband* began with *Diogenis Laertii libri X. de vitis Philosophorum*, from Paris, s.a.; (2) *Herodoti 9 Musae, Valla interprete, it.* (3) *Oratio Isocratis de laudibus Helenae, interprete Jon. Petre Lucense*, printed in Paris in 1510. We now have a three-volume bound quarto, beginning with (1) Diodorus Siculus, *Poggio Florentine interprete*, done at Paris, s.a.; (2) *Pomponii Laeti opera*, from Strassburg, done in 1510; and part (3) Leonardus Aretinus' *De bello Italico adversus Gothos, libri IV*, from Paris, done in 1507. Next Mylius reports on another three-volume bound set, beginning (1) with Constantinus M. Emperator, interpreted by John Reuchlin, done at Tübingen, in 1513; (2) Hippocrates, *De praeparatione hominis, eodem interprete*, from Tübingen, done in 1512; and (3) Rabbi Joseph Hyssopaeus, *Poeta, eodem interprete*, from Tübingen in 1512. In a similar quarto-sized set, we have (1) Nicholae Ritius, *De regibus Francorum, Hispaniae, Hierosolymorum, Neapolis, et Siciliae, Ungariae*, from Basel, done in 1517. (3) Joh. Comertis, *Annotationes in lucium Florum*, printed in Vienna, in 1511; and (3) *Galeotti, de homine libri II, et Georg. Merulae in annotationes*, printed in Basel, in 1517. They also had Christopher Scheurl's work *De laudibus Germaniae et ducum Saxoniae*, printed at Bologna, in 1506. Among other works was also Philip Melanchthon's *Declamatiuncula in D. Pauli doctrinam*, printed in 1520, but s.l.[365]

POETICAL BOOKS OF ANTIQUITY

In the smaller books on poetry, Mylius begins with (1) in a two-volume set, Joach. Vadianus, *De poetica et carminis ratione*, from Vienna, done in 1518; and part (2) Henr. Clareanus, *De rationale syllabarum eiusd. quaedam Elegiae*, from Basel, in 1516. The library also had *Orphei Argonautica, graece*, from Florence, in 1500. Next Mylius found a four-volume tome, with (1) *Horatii, Epistolae*, from Leipzig, 1504; (2) Sedulius' *Historia Evangelica*, from Leipzig, 1504; (3) *Regulae Grammaticales antiquorum*, from Nürnberg, in 1501; and (4) *Expositio Donati secundum Doctorem sanctum*, from Leipzig, 1505. Another four-volume *Sammelband* begins with (1) Valerius Flaccus's *Argonautica*, from Venice, in 1500; part (2) Carolus Bovillus' *Physicorum elementorum libri X*, out of Paris, done in 1512; and part (3) *Hippocratis, Coi, praesagiorum libri III, et de ratione victus in morbis acutis*, libri IV, *Guilielma Copo Basileensi, interprete, s.l. et s.d.*; and (4) *Francisci Barbari de re uxoria libri II* from Paris, printed in 1513.[366] In another quarto *Sammelband* of five quarto volumes, part (1) begins with Horatius' *Epistolae*, from Leipzig in 1504; Sedulius, *Iuvenci et Aratobis poemata*, from the Aldus Press, at Venice, in 1501; (3) Sulpitius Severus' *De vita et miraculis S. Martini Dialogor. libri. 3, s.l. et s.a.*; (4) *Vita S. Nicolae Myrens episcopi, e graeco in latinum per Leonard. Justinianum, Patricium, Venetum, s.l. et s.a.* and (5) *Petri Candidi Homero-Centra, vel Centrones. gr. et latin*, without location or year mentioned. Another two-volume quarto has (1) *Prudentii Opera* from Venice, in 1501; and (2) *Prosperi Epigrammata super quasdam Augustini sententias: Joh. Damasceni hymni gr. et lat.*, Venice, 1501. Another quarto volume had Claudinaus' *Opera, emendata per Thadacum Vgoletum, Parmensem*, out of Venice, done in 1495. Next Mylius reports on a seven-volume *Sammelband*, with poet (1) Janus Pannonius' *Sylva panegyrica et epigrammata*, done at Basel, in 1518; (2) Pictorius' *Sacra et saryrica epigrammata; (3) Michael Verini quaedam*; (4) *B. Dardani epigrammata*; (5) *Jovii, Lippii, Favsti, Andrelini disticha*, (6) *Ludou. Lazarelli Bombyx*, from Basel, 1518; and (7) *Henric. Glareani Elegiarum, libri II*, also from Basel in 1516. Another recorded *Sammelband* had four volumes, with part (1) *Publii Fausti Andrelini, Buccolica*, printed at Paris, in 1510; (2) *Eiusdem IX epistolae adagiales de Neapolitana Fornouiensique victoria*, from Paris, printed in 1496; (3) *Eiusdem Elegiae de virtutibus*, printed at Strassburg, in 1509; and (4) Pamphilus, *De amore*, also from Paris in 1510. Next follows another quarto set of four volumes, with (1) Michael Marvullus' *Hymni Epigrammato*, done in Florence, in 1497; (2) Conrad Celtis' *Poemata*, done at Strassburg, in 1513; (3) *Cantalycii, episcopi, de Parthenopebis recepta, libri IV*, from Strassburg, in 1513; and (4) *Elisii Calentii Croacus, sive de bello ranarum*, also from Strassburg, in 1511. Next comes a two-volume work from Conrad Celtis, then the poet laureate, which begins with (1) *4 libri amorum secundum 4 latera Germaniae: de urbe Noriberga: de vira S. Sebaldi*; and (2) *Panegyricus ad Maximilianum, Omnia*, Nürnberg, in 1502. The library also possessed a single work by *Bapt. Mantuani Fastorum Libri XII*, from Strassburg, in 1518. Then Mylius also found John Reuchlin's *Scenica progymnasmata*, printed at Tübingen, in 1513. Also in the collection was *Nicol. Marsselalci, Thurii, Enchiridion Poetarum clariasimorum*, from Erfurt, in 1502.[367]

SMALLER PHILOSOPHICAL WORKS

Where earlier Mylius reported on the larger folio volumes in philosophy, he now reported on philosophy printed in quarto-sized works. No doubt these smaller books were more easily accessible to students. Mylius begins with Lucianus' *De ratione scribendae historiae, e graece traductus in latinum a Bilibalde Birckheymero*, Nürnberg, 1515; while (2) was *Luciani Deorum Dialogi 70*, in Greek and Latin, from Strassburg, in 1515; (3) Seneca, *Ludus de morte Claudii Caesaris*; *Synesius de laudibus caluitii*: Erasmus, *De encomiis Moriae*, done at Basel, in 1515. They also had Lucian's *Dialogi et alia quaedem, versa ab Erasmo Roterod. et Thoma Moro* (a) from Paris, in 1514. (2) Pliny's *De viris illustribus in republ. et re militari et administranda republ.*; (3) Suetonius, *De claris Grammatica et Rhetoribus, omnia haec scripta*, from Strassbrug, 1514 *exclusa*; and (5) *Francise, de educatione liberorum et eorum moribus*, out of Tübingen, 1513. In another six-volume binding we have (1) Polydorus Vergilius, *De inventoribus rerum libri III*, from Strassburg in 1512; (2) *eiusdem Proverbiorum liber*, out of Strassburg in 1511; (3) Anton. Mancinellus, *De parentum cura in libros* etc., from Strassburg in 1512; *eiusdem, epigrammatum libellus, ibid.*; (5) *Hieroclis, Stoici Philosophi, in aurea Pythagorae carmina Commentarius*, from Strassburg, in 1511; and (6) Lorenzo Valla, *De vero falsoque bono*, out of Cologne, in 1509.[368]

As observed above, the ducal library was rather rich in manuscripts and folio-sized printed materials, written by Desiderus Erasmus, but it also had a number of quarto-sized works. In a two-part *Sammelband* (1) it had *Erasmi querela pacis ac multa, ex Luciano versa*, printed at Basel, in 1517; and (2) *Erasmus Paraphrasis in epistolam ad Romanos*, from Basel, in 1518. Then Mylius reports on a six-volume set, starting with Erasmus' *Enchiridion militis christiani*; while part (2) was Erasmus' *Disputatio de tedio in pauore christi: Exortatio ad virtutem: oratio in laudem puere Jesu*; *Enarratio Allegoria in Psalm I, et varia Erasmi carmina*, from Strassburg, in 1517; (3) Erasmus, *compendium varae Theologiae*, from Basel, in 1519; and (4) *Joh. Francise Picus Mirandulan, de appetina primae materiae et de Elementis, ut et libri II, Rhetorici, de imitatione Petr. Bembum itamque, et Petri Bembi Veneti, liber unus ad Picum de imitatione*, from Basel in 1518. They also had Andreas Meinharti, Dialogus illustratae Witebergae, Leipzig, in 1508.[369]

There were also some books with maps and mathematics. In a *Sammelband* of three volumes, part (1) offers *Instructio in cartem itineram Martini Hila-comili cum luculdentiori ipsius Europae enarratione, a Ringoanno Philesio con-scripta*; out of Strassburg, 1511; (2) Job. Martini Silicei, *Ars arithmetica, in Theoricen et Praxim scissa*, Tübingen, 1514; and (3) Augustinus Ritius, *De motu octave sphaera*, from Trino, in 1513; *Cum eiusd. epistola de astronomie aucto-ribus*. They also had Hyginus, *De sphaera coelrdti, eiusdemque usriis signis ac planetis*, from Venice, in 1502; and part (2) *Bartholomaei Coloniensis, epistola Mythologica*, from Venice, in 1503; (3) *Philippi Beroaldi opusculum de felici-tate*, from Bologna, in 1502. Another four-volume quarto began (1) Alchabitius, *De iudicis astrorum*, out of Venice, 1491; (2) *Sphaera mundi*, done at Venice, in 1491; (3) *Flores Flores Albumasaris*, Augsburg, in 1488; and (4) Alfonsus' *tabu-lae astronomicae*, also from Venice, in 1492. Here follows another three-volume work, with (1) Albumasar, *De magnis conjunctionibus annorum revolutionibus, ac eorum profectionibus, Tractatus, IIX*, Augsburg, 1489; *Eiusd. Introducto-rium in Astronomiam*, from Augsburg, 1489; (3) *Leupoldi compilatio de astro-rum scientia*, from Augsburg, in 1489. They also had Guidonnis Bonati, *Tractatus Astronomiae*, also from Augsburg, 1491. Next came a three-volume *Sammelband*, starting with (1) Elisabethe's *Regine Hispanie et Sicilie tabule astronomice*, Venice, 1503; (2) *Liber 9 iuducum in iuducus astrorum*, Venice, in 1509; and (3) Abrahe Avenaris, *Iudici, astrologi peritiffimi de re iudiciali opera, a Petre de Abano, philosopho excellentissimo, post accuratam castigationem, in latinum traducta*, out of Venice, in 1507. Another two-volume tome treats the discovery of America. It begins with (1) *Cosmographie Introductio, Naviga-tiones 4. Americi Vespuci*, printed at Strassburg, in 1509; in (2) Alcabitius' *Ad magisterium iudiciorum astronorum isagoge, cum commentario Joan Saxonii*, from Paris, in 1511. In another two-volume quarto tome, part (1) has Regio-montanus' *Tabulae astronomicae*, from Augsburg, in 1490; part (2) Abraham, *Iudaci, liber de nativitatibus*, Venice, 1485. In another four-volume tome, part (1) begins with Pomponius' *Melae geographae libri 3, Viennae Pannon cum cas-tigationibus integris* Harmolai, Barbari (2) *Clarorum virorum epistolae latinae, graecae et hebraicae ad Joh. Reuchlinum, Phorcensem*, Tübingen, 1514; (3) Eobonus Hessus' *Heroidum christianarum epistolae*, out of Leipzig, in 1514; and (4) *eiusd. sylvae duae nuper editae, Prussia et amor, ibid.* 1514.[370]

ANCIENT BOOKS IN OCTAVO SIZE

In the library, books of this size were not numerous. Mylius found a small book that begins with (1) *Erotemata graecae grammaticae Chrysolorae, de ver-bis anomalis, de formatione temperum, ex libro Chalcondilae: Quartus liber Gazae de constructione de Encliticis: sententiae monostishi ex varia poetis*, all from Venice, 1512, by the Aldus Press; and (2) *Quinti calabri, Derelictorum ab Homero libri XIV*, from Venice, and (3) Tryphiodori, *grammatici Troiae captio it, Coluthus de raptu Helenae*, from Venice, s.a., ap Aldus.[371]

In another section Mylius cited a number of literary works, which were used by the liberal arts students in the twenties and thirties, when the German Reformation began to bloom, with Melanchthon's emphasis on biblical humanism in the university on the Elbe. The first of the octavo-size volumes was entitled *Florilegium diversorum epigrammatum*, in 7 books, done by the Aldus Press at Venice, in Greek, in 1503. Next comes a two-volume set, with (1) *Pindari opera: Callimachi hymni*: Dionysius, *De situ orbis Lycophronis Alexandra*, from Venice, in 1513; while (2) *Agapeti scheda regia, sive de officio regis gr. et lat.*, from Venice, in 1509. Another single work cited is *Oppiani opera* gr. et lat., from Venice, in 1517. There was also a work, *Aeschyli tragoediae* 6, graece, from Venice in 1518. Another fine work was *Euripidis Tragoediae*, XVII, all in Greek, from Venice, the Aldus Press, with commentaries, s.a. Another tome by the Aldus Press was a three-volume *Sammelband*, which began (1) with *Euripidis Ephigenia in tauris, Rhesus, Troades, Bacchae, Cyclops, Heraclidae, Helena, Ion, Hercules furens, graece tantum*, from Venice in 1503, ap. Aldus; (2) *Eiusd. Hecuba et Iphigenia in Aulide, in latinum translatae ab Erasmo Roterdame, latine tantum*; and (3) is an ode by Erasmus, *De laudibus Britanniae, regisque Henrici VII*, acegiorum liberorum eius. *Eiusd. Ode, de senectute incommodis, omnia*, from Venice, in 1507, ap. Aldum. Mylius also found a *Sophoclis tragoediae*, 7 from Venice, in 1502. Next came Ovid's *Metamorphseon libri XV*, from Venice, in 1516. There was also Ovid's *epistolae Heroidum: Amores: de arte amandi: de remedio amoris; medicamene faciei*, printed at Venice in 1515. In another octavo-sized binding with two works, (1) had Jovianus Pontanus, *Opera poetica*, from Venice, in 1505; while in (2) was Joh. aurel. Augvrelli, *Varia poemata*, from the Aldus Press, at Venice, in 1505. And finally there was Auli Gellius, *Noctium Atticarum*, libri XIX, also from Venice, in 1515.[372]

Mylius closes this recording of the Wittenberg library with a series of observations of the printed books in Part III of his records. These include the works he regarded as rare, unusual, and worth recording in chapters II and III. But the Jena professor continues to list books and manuscripts, in chapters IV and V, some of which are important or at least relevant to the German Reformation; but to include these would no doubt burden the reader with additional material that is not too important for the Reformation or the university's history.

22

Luther's Transformation
of the University

❖

Before launching upon a detailed account of the beginning of the German Reformation under the leadership of Martin Luther and the faculty of the University of Wittenberg, a description of the larger movement seems essential. Let us ask the question: What was the German Reformation? To this question many answers have been given in the last four centuries. Often the mistake has been made in our time, even by scholars, of trying to understand the Reformation from a twentieth century perspective. Many Lutherans have identified Luther's nailing of his Ninety-Five Theses on the door of the Castle Church as the beginning of the German Reformation, and said that he aimed to found the Lutheran church of today. In fact, the religious movement known as the Reformation can be properly understood only when viewed in light of a contemporary perspective, and that is possible only after intimate acquaintance with the sources of that day. Let us begin with an analysis of some assumptions that a historian needs to make to properly understand the German Reformation.

There are at least five assumptions the scholar needs to make in order to understand the Reformation, for without them no satisfactory approach is possible. The first is that the Reformation was a much broader movement than is frequently realized. Its roots extend far back into the Middle Ages. The famous Dominican professor of Mainz, Germany, Joseph Lortz, in his fine book of 1964, *How the Reformation Came*, claims that the Reformation dates much farther back than scholars once believed. In his book he stresses that many voices shouted to heaven for reforms as far back as 1200.[1] Thus he stressed that the reforms initiated at Wittenberg, were but the fruition of the previous work of many others. The Obermann school at Tübingen has also produced many publications that have enriched our background knowledge of the Reformation, proving that the Wittenberg movement can only be understood in the light of its medieval background.[2] A second assumption needs to be made, that prior to the Council of Trent (1545–1563) there was no doctrinal unity in the Roman

425

Church. As the Yale professor, Jaroslav Pelikan, has shown in his recent fourth volume of *The Christian Tradition*, in a chapter titled "Doctrinal Pluralism in the Later Middle Ages," the lack of unity in doctrine prepared the way for the reforms of Martin Luther.[3] As observed earlier, in the graduate school of theology at Wittenberg, the basic text was *Lombard's Sentences*, in four volumes, but the Wittenberg *Statutes* specify that it was to be interpreted *viam Thome* and *viam Scoti*, and later it was also taught in the *Via Moderna* of Occam and Biel. The *Statutes* state that all three ways were to "be taught without prejudice."[4] Thus in many German universities three different interpretations of Peter Lombard's doctrinal teachings were taught. The fact that this diversity of philosophies was being taught in Luther's day was bound to lead to doctrinal confusion. Thus Heiko Obermann was able to write an excellent book on this problem, *The Harvest of Medieval Theology*, in which he shows that scholasticism, at the close of the Middle Ages, was like an orchard with many ripe fruit trees ready to be harvested,[5] from which Occam and Biel could pluck what proved useful for the *Via Moderna* philosophy. Since Luther was an ardent student of the teachings of Occam and Biel among the schoolmen, it is not difficult to assess what Luther's basic approach was when he accepted Johann Staupitz's post of *Lectura in Biblia*, in 1513, and began his course on the *Dictata super Psalterium* and Occam's *Pactum* theology.

    A third assumption made by many Reformation scholars is that there was but one Luther, and thus they could quote from him regardless of the period in his life involved. This assumes that any statement that he made in his formative period, as a scholastic, can be quoted along with the later views of the mature reformer.[6] This approach can lead to real confusion for the reader, when he attempts to assess what Luther taught in doctrinal matters. There was not just one Luther but three, and these dare not be confused. Martin Luther began as a staunch Roman Catholic who really believed the teachings of the Roman Church, but as interpreted by his *Via Moderna* professors, à la Occam and Biel, at Erfurt and Wittenberg. Luther claims he was still an ardent papalist when he nailed his Ninety-Five Theses on the door of the Castle Church. Then there is the second Luther, the emerging young reformer, who while he gave his courses on the *Psalms, Romans, Galatians,* and *Hebrews*, between 1513 and 1518, studied the past of the Roman church, the Greek and Latin Fathers, learned Greek and Hebrew as a biblical humanist, and by 1520 developed his "Theology of the Cross," which was then known as Wittenberg's "New Theology." Thus Luther constantly changed while he matured into the reformer, as we will see later in this chapter. The scholarship expended on this phase of Luther's development throughout the last century has been tremendous, and the results have at times been bewildering. This theme has recently again been discussed by the German specialist in the field, Walter von Löwenich, in his 1983 book *Martin Luther*, in which he describes this period as *Luthers Werdezeit* as the Reformer.[7] We must also realize that later there was the doctrinally mature Luther, who developed into the real reformer from 1520 to 1535, whose theological depth resulted from years of study of the Holy Scriptures and the history of early Christianity, whose Ecumenical Creeds he regarded as normative for the Reformation.[8] He did not wish to found a new church but to cleanse and reform Christianity by a return to its original standards of doctrinal teachings.

Finally the research scholar must also be aware of the fact that even though the German Reformation was a university movement that began in the University of Wittenberg and there was a polemical warfare between academic institutions and between scholars, it took a decade before the people in a rural society learned of the Reformation, after which it became a "ground swell" movement, in which people became hungry for the gospel of the Holy Scriptures and tired of the financial exploitation of Rome, with its many innovations to enrich the treasury of the Curia. Rome's indulgence trade had really drained German lands of their funds. The Albert of Mainz scandal with the activities of his many agents, well illustrated by the wild claims of John Tetzel, well substantiates this. Both Saxon rulers, Frederick the Wise and Duke George, refused to permit him to enter their lands and drain off their gold.[9]

Joseph Lortz, the great postwar German Dominican scholar, expressed very well the feelings of the people about the abuses of Rome, when he wrote these findings about conditions before the Reformation:

> At any rate, whatever complaints against the Curia existed at the beginning of the fourteenth century, they continued to swell in mounting surge. At the end of the fifteenth century the world was literally filled with cries, impatient, angry, sad, revolutionary, defiant cries against the domination by Rome and the clergy, against Rome's oppression and extortion, against its despotism and against its all too hedonistic way of life.[10]

A sixth assumption of a proper understanding of the Reformation is that Luther never, like later Lutherans, regarded himself as the founder of a new church. The name "Lutheran" was first used by Luther's enemies and had a derogatory meaning. Luther was once asked about the name and he replied, like St. Paul to the Corinthians, they should not name themselves after him but simply call themselves Christians. In his view and in that of other contemporaries, Luther was simply restoring the gospel and reforming the church founded by Jesus Christ. In this study, therefore, we have designated the members of the Roman Church with its many innovations as *Altgläubigen*, the old believers, staunch supporters of Rome, in a theology developed by medieval scholasticism; while the followers of Luther and reformers of the church are known as the *Neuglaubigen*, the new believers, wanting a return to the Christian church of the Ecumenical Creeds of apostolic times and a theology based on the Holy Scriptures. This return is remarkably well illustrated by a tract that Luther wrote to Emperor Charles V and his close supporters in Insbruck on the way to the Diet of Augsburg in 1530. Luther could not attend the Diet because of his excommunication by the Edict of Worms, and he remained at the Coburg during the Diet in 1530; yet prior to it he mailed a powerful *Flugschrift* to the

Kaiser. In this extant message he stressed that he was not an enemy of the Christian church founded by Jesus Christ and his apostles, which Rome claimed for itself. In fact, he asserted, the *Neuglaubigen* had returned to simple, gospel-oriented, apostolic Christianity, which the Roman Church had altered with 120 innovations of human origin that were contrary to the gospel and the teachings of early Christianity. At the close of this tract Luther added a list of the 120 abuses that Rome had introduced for worldly gain.[11]

The last assumption that a scholar needs to make in order to really understand the Reformation, as viewed by contemporaries, is to realize that it was a very complex historical period of half a century, involving Luther, the entire Wittenberg faculty, and 16,292 students who attended Wittenberg between 1520 and 1560 and most of whom later returned to their native lands and spread the "New Theology" of Wittenberg throughout Europe. Besides, Luther's reforms were opposed by four universities and also supported by an equal number. The schools that opposed the Reformation were Louvain, Cologne, Paris, and Ingolstadt, while Erfurt, Tübingen, and, in time, Leipzig and Frankfurt a.d.O. joined in the restoration of the gospel and evangelical reforms.

These previously cited assumptions need to be kept in mind, as they underlie the present coverage of the German Reformation, especially in the subsequent chapters. The Reformation can be understood only when approached from this perspective, for it remained an upper strata movement for a decade and became a reality at the people's level only later, when the evangelical movement became crystallized in hundreds of Church Ordinances, as will be seen in the final chapter of this book.

Before taking up the main theme of this chapter, Luther's transformation of Wittenberg, the reader needs to become better acquainted with Luther as a human being, for this was no doubt a factor in why he became the father of the Reformation. In the author's graduate school days, he wrote a Masters Thesis for Dean Siebert at Ohio State University, entitled *Martin Luther as a Preacher*. In that research it became quite evident that the human side of the reformer played a vital role for decades in his life as a preacher and pastor in the Wittenberg *Pfarrkirche*. There can be no doubt that he, like Bernard of Clairveaux and George Whitefield, was one of the great preachers of history, both as an orator and as an actor.

MARTIN LUTHER THE MAN

There is very little known about Luther's ancestors, except that they were *Erbzinsleute*, whose five Höfe were located in the Thuringian forest not far removed from Eisenach and the Wartburg Castle where the reformer was hidden by the elector in 1521–1522.[12] There is little left of the region or the original *Stammhaus* of Heine Luder, Luther's grandfather, and his grandmother, Margaretha Ziegler. The *Stammhaus* shown tourists today in Möhre is not original, as it was not erected until 1618 by the descendants of the family.[13]

The grandfather, Heine Luder, and Margaretha Ziegler, had four sons, named Groszhans, Klein Hans, Veit, and Heinz. As *Erbzinsleute*, they were in a direct princely relationship, and paid taxes directly to his court. The law of primogeniture did not apply to them, as the properties of Luther's grandparents would pass directly to the youngest son, Heinz. Since this was the feudal law of *Erbzinsleute*, Groszhans and his wife, Margaretha Lindemann,[14] realized they would have to enter another profession. They decided to enter the then booming copper mining business near the Harz Mountains,[15] and settled in Eisleben, where Martin Luther was born and baptized. For some reason Groszhans decided to move to nearby Mansfeld within a year, as he must have regarded it to be a more promising region.[16] Like many young married couples, they found the first years to be a hard beginning; but Luther's father was not the type to remain a simple mine laborer. He soon became a productive owner of mines, with laborers working several shafts. In fact, by the time young Martin was eight years old, his parents were ranked among the most influential citizens of Mansfeld, and his father was in charge of a quarter of the town and an official in the governing town council.[17] Meanwhile, Luther's father must have become quite prosperous, for when Martin became an Augustinian Hermit and was holding his *Primice*, Groszhans appeared, accompanied by 20 horsemen, and offered the Augustinians in Erfurt a "goodwill gift" of 20 Gulden, which totaled about $1,500.[18]

This is not the place to expand on Martin Luther's education while in Mansfeld, Magdeburg, and Eisenach. Suffice it to observe that Luther had received a good background for his later entry into Erfurt University; where, under gifted professors like Trutfetter and Usingen, he received an excellent introduction to medieval scholasticism as taught by the *Via Moderna*. After Luther's entry into the Augustinian Order, his superiors soon realized his unusual gifts as a scholar and encouraged him to continue his studies toward a doctorate in theology. This meant that he would have to travel the difficult road of becoming a *Biblicus*, *Sententiarius*, *Formatus*, and *Licentiarius* by the *Via Moderna* interpretation of the *Sentences* of Peter Lombard and a study of the Holy Scriptures in its four senses of interpretation. Since Lombard's *Sentences*, a massive four-volume text in dogmatics, lent itself to several ways of interpretation, Luther was taught according to its interpretation by the modern way of Occam and Biel, which the *Via Moderna* school regarded as better than that of the *Via Antiqua* of St. Thomas and Duns Scotus.[19] The young Luther also attracted the attention Johann v. Staupitz, vicar of the German Congregation of the Augustinian Hermits, who brought the Augustinian monk to Wittenberg in 1508–1509 to fill a temporary vacancy in its course in *Nichomachean Ethics*, concerning how to live a good life, in which the Augustinian monk was made ready for his *Biblicus* degree by 1509. But he could not take it, as we saw above, because he lacked the funds necessary for his promotion, so he had to return to Erfurt, where they were willing to pay his fees.[20]

After being promoted at Erfurt to the *Biblicus* degree, Luther seems to have advanced rather rapidly to the next step of being made a *Sententiarius*, for already in 1509 he was lecturing in the Erfurt cloister on Lombard's *Sentences*, which he completed by 1510. Fortunately, we still possess Luther's lecture notes. Herbert Rommel analyzed these notes very thoroughly, based on the actual text in the WA, IX, 10 ff.[21] Though we lack recorded details, after that Luther was promoted at Erfurt to the *Formatus* and *Licentiatus* degrees at Erfurt, before his second return to Wittenberg, and Dean Johann von Staupitz wanted to groom him as his successor upon his retirement from his *Lectura in Biblia* post, for which Luther needed to be promoted to his doctorate. The *Liber Decanorum*, the University of Wittenberg Deans' Book, contains the entry that Luther was "already in possession of a *Licentiatus* degree in theology and thus was ready for the promotion."[22] Since Luther's promotion to the doctorate was already covered in detail in an earlier chapter,[23] that event needs no further coverage at this point.

Even though Luther's promotion to the doctorate in theology has been covered in detail, we would still have a *lacuna* here without a brief response to the question, "Why did Martin Luther return to Wittenberg a second time?" Even though there is no complete explanation, some scholars believe there was a connection between the monastic struggle between the vicar of the Augustinian Hermits of the German Congregation and a number of its chapters. If Luther had obtained his doctorate at Erfurt, his whole life might have been different, for he would not have been given the *Lectura in Biblia* post and in it grown into the reformer. Walter von Löwenich has offered us some explanation as to what caused this change in his life.[24] Let us examine this transitional period.

In 1506 Editio von Viterbo became the vicar general of the Augustinian Hermits. The vicar general was quite reform-minded, and attempted to strengthen the Augustinian Order by a union of the reformed and the more lax chapters; whereupon it became Johann von Staupitz's obligation as the vicar general to introduce these reforms in the German lands. After that a real conflict broke out within the 31 chapters, by 22 chapters agreeing to form such a union and 7 opposing it. Among the opponents were the two powerful chapters of Erfurt and Nürnberg. Thus the young Luther was chosen as the *socius itenererius*, the travel companion for an older, unknown monk, who was to be chief negotiator with the Italian General of the Order. These two monks were sent to Italy to plead the cause of the chapters opposed to the union. But General Viterbo refused to listen to their cause. As a result there developed friction between Staupitz and Erfurt over the proposed reforms, and the young Luther was caught in between the hostility. Both Luther and John Lang pleaded with the Erfurt chapter to make their peace with Vicar Staupitz. As a result, John Lang was expelled from the Erfurt chapter and Luther must also have been a *persona non grata* in their midst. Some scholars believe that Vicar Johann von Staupitz, who dropped the whole unification matter in May 1512, had meanwhile begun to admire Martin, so that he began to see in him a possible successor to the post of *Lectura in Biblia* when he retired.[25] Meanwhile, the busy Vicar General, who was often of business trips, returned for a while to Wittenberg in 1512, on which occasion he promoted Martin Luther to the doctorate, even paying the promotion fee of 50 Gulden, which Frederick the Wise had agreed to advance.[26]

It is quite difficult today to form an accurate visual image of Martin Luther. In 1936, while engaged in research in Germany, the author visited Weimar, and asked whether he might obtain their pictures of Luther, whereupon the custodian, after some delay, appeared with a large pile of Luther etchings and paintings. Here was the Luther of the past four centuries, ranging from emaciated saint to a modern pugilist of the Nazi period. Most individuals today have an image of the more corpulent reformer of the later Reformation period. Let us see what problems the historian faces in attempting form an accurate image of the Martin Luther as known by his contemporaries.

Unfortunately, neither of Germany's two greatest contemporary artists, Albrecht Dürer of Nürnberg and Hans Holbein the Younger, the fine portrait painter of Henry VIII, Erasmus, and Philip Melanchthon, ever met Luther.[27] The best portraits we possess today were done by the local Wittenberg artist, Lucas Cranach d.Ä., whose zeal in painting the reformer outstripped his talents. Any comparison of portraits of Melanchthon done by Cranach and Holbein the Younger will reveal the difference. Yet we know that Luther's likeness was reproduced perhaps more often than that of any other German, so that it was well-known by every school child; for hundreds of copies were made in the forms of paintings, etchings, and woodcuts, and even done on china, leather, and other media.[28] In the Halle exhibition of 1931, all such material was on display, which Johannes Ficker had grouped by periods.[29] Today we possess only one rather small, indistinct picture of Luther as a monk, now in the *Lutherhalle* at Wittenberg.[30] The artist who arranged the Ficker exposition at Halle in 1931 placed the Luther pictures into several groups: in the first grouping we see Luther as a monk and professor of theology; these were done from 1520 to 1524. Many copies were made of Lucas Cranach d.Ä.'s originals, among which were Luther the monk, now in Munich, done in 1520; another as a monk, now in Vienna; and Luther as a professor of theology, now in the Feste Coburg. For a proper study, these copies need to be compared with the Cranach originals.[31] In another display they had Luther as "Junker Jörg," painted by Cranach at the time of his brief visit to Wittenberg from the Wartburg in 1521, when Luther came to get material for his translation of the New Testament. This was the first attempt by the Wittenberg artist to do a portrait of Luther in oil.[32] Ficker's third classification of Luther paintings deals with the period of Luther and Catherine's marriage in 1525, for which Cranach did the attractive round painting of Luther.[33] Cranach also did the two companion paintings of Luther and Catherine in 1526, which were part of two sets of oil paintings of the newly married couple.[34] The two paintings of Luther and Käthe best portray the newly married couple at the beginning of their family life. In an excellent publication by Oskar Thulin, in 1958, we have additional paintings reproduced that belong to this same time period. Cranach the Elder also did a fine portrait of the reformer in a professor's attire, which now hangs in the National Gallery in Stockholm, Sweden, which Ficker placed into the third classification in the exhibit. The best portrait of Catherine, belonging to the same year, is now in the State Museum in Berlin.[35] In part four of the Ficker exhibit, they displayed Luther as the preacher, which portraits were classified as being of the year 1528; and, finally, there was another picture of Luther as a professor, fully robed in an academic gown, which is perhaps to be regarded as the finest reproduction of the reformer by the Elder Cranach.[36] This completes the list of Luther portraits and etchings done in his lifetime. Those numerous altar portrayals of later years, mostly of corpulent Luther, were done by Lucas Cranach d.J., and painted from imagination and not from life. These are not worthy of serious consideration by historians. The last Luther painting by Lucas Cranach d.Ä. was that in the *Flügelaltar* in the Town Church at Wittenberg, in which Luther is delivering a sermon, with Catherine and little Hans in the audience. In this altar painting we do not have a real likeness of Luther and have an imaginary pulpit.[37]

Our coverage of Luther portaits and etchings would not be complete without a few additions. It is interesting that the University of Wittenberg, it its *Matrikel* of 1531, contains two nice pictures of Luther and Melanchthon, both attired as professors of that day. The painting of Luther resembles the above cited Luther as the professor, while the young Melanchthon has a very attractive face. No doubt both were done by the Elder Cranach in the time span when he did Luther as the professor in 1532.[38] Finally, it must be added that some attempts were made to make a death mask of Luther in Eisleben, before he was transported to his final burial place in the Castle Church at Wittenberg. The artist from Halle, Lukas Furtennagel, did a death mask of Luther in Eisleben, which is the only authentic one we possess.[39] In Halle, on the way to Wittenberg, they also made a reproduction of Luther's hands. Thulin observed that the right hand still appeared like it could hold a pen, as it had done so often in the past.[40]

Although the quality of Cranach's paintings, when compared with the quality of those of Holbein and Dürer, falls very far short of the two masters, yet they are useful in forming an image of the reformer's actual appearance. Even though Dürer expressed the desire some day to produce a living likeness of Luther, he never found an occasion to even meet him and paint the reformer. Lucas Cranach d.Ä. had trouble with tactile values, the creation of flesh colors, and simply was unable to paint Luther's sparkling, penetrating eyes, as referred to by contemporaries. Cranach's painting of Melanchthon is even worse, as he failed to portray any of the humanist's brilliance, so well captured by Holbein d.J., or in the etching of Melanchthon with the bulging forehead by Dürer. Yet we are thankful for the Cranach wedding pictures of Luther and Catherine and the excellent painting of Luther the professor in 1532.

As the historian turns to the contemporary descriptions of Luther, the problem is multiplied. Most of Luther's friends took him for granted, as they felt he was known by everyone; while Luther's enemies left us nothing but biased character defamations, far removed from historical reality. For practical purposes these descriptions of Luther by his contemporaries may be divided into two categories: (1) accounts of those that are descriptive of the man, and (2) those that were attempting to defame him, or those who wished to stress the spiritual attributes of him as the reformer. A description of Luther's physical features may be useful. His contemporaries who knew him as a monk described him as thin and frail in appearance, practically skin and bones.[41] But the Luther in the early twenties, when he began to eat more normally after rejecting the necessity of fasting as a monk, took on what Heinrich Boehmer called a "befitting plumpness."[42] Thus during his wedding pictures Luther is already quite normal in appearance; while in Cranach's of 1528 and 1532, Luther is already a little more corpulent, though he was never as heavy as portrayed in Lucas Cranach d.J.'s altar paintings.[43] Besides, it must be remembered that a man dressed in clerical robes does always look heavier.

At the outset let us begin with the Luther whom friends and enemies tried to describe. Added to his physical characteristics in his early years, there is a fine description of Luther as he participated in the Leipzig Debate in 1519 by the humanist Petrus Mosellanus of Leipzig.[44] There is also a description of the reformer by the papal *Nuncius* Vergerio, who noted Luther's heavy bone structure and his heavy shoulders, a fact not discernible in the 1520 Cranach portraits referred to above.[45] A third contemporary in the early period was the Swiss student Johannes Kessler, who accidentally encountered Luther in Jena on the way to Wittenberg, with Luther dressed as "Junker Jörg," in knight's attire and with a beard. Luther just happened to stay there while en route to Wittenberg, on his secret visit to acquire the necessary source material for his translation of the New Testament at the Wartburg in 1521–1522. This Swiss scholar from St. Gallen later wrote his *Sabbata*, in which he described the accidental encounter with the reformer. In this he observed that Luther walked "very erect, bending backwards rather than forwards, with his face raised towards heaven."[46] Another source worth our attention is that of a Wittenberg student, who in two letters to his brother Ambrosius at Constance in 1521 tells us about Luther's fame on the Wittenberg campus.[47] There is also a description of the reformer by his table companion, Erasmus Alber, who stressed Luther's soul and spiritual qualities. In this account he also quoted the Humanist D. Urbanus Rhegius, who had spent a day with Luther at the Feste Coburg in 1530.[48]

There are also a number of defamatory descriptions of Luther by his bitterest enemies, Pope Leo X and Adrian VI.[49] One cannot but be grateful that Philip Melanchthon, who lived next door to Luther for years, at least stated that the reformer's eyes were brown with "dark, golden rings."[50] Most of the contemporary references to Luther's eyes, as we will see from the quotations that follow, compared their penetrating sparkle to the eyes of falcons, hawks, or basilisks. This quality seems to have been quite a factor in Luther's influence in the classroom, in the pulpit, and in front of large audiences. Members of the congregation and students in the classroom felt quite uneasy, as the reformer seemed to look right through them and could see what they had done during the past week; while hostile Catholics credited his eyes with animal-like qualities that hypnotized his audiences so that they became Lutheran. Their views can best be illustrated by examples, which will follow later. Therefore, a section of contemporary descriptions of Martin Luther will illustrate the above claims in greater detail.

Perhaps the best description of Luther's appearance and physical features is the following by Peter Mosellanus at Leipzig, made in 1519 during the Leipzig Debate:

> Martin is a medium-sized individual, with a haggard appearance, which has been drained through undue worry and academic studies, so much so that one could practically count the bones in his body even through his skin. He has a manly type of appearance, is fresh and young looking. He possesses a high, clear voice and is very learned, having a phenomenal knowledge of the Holy Scriptures, so that he can practically cite anywhere from it at will. Greek and Hebrew he has learned to a degree that he is able to pass judgment on any interpretation based on his use of the original. Nor does he lack in a resourcefulness of material and has a large vocabulary and a wide acquaintance with matters in general. In life he is very polite and friendly with people, nor is there any sternness or stiffness in his conduct. He is able to adjust himself to all situations. Socially in a crowd he is jolly, full of life and engages in a little kidding. He remains friendly and composed even though he is pushed by his enemies threatening him from all sides. It is quite evident that God's strength is with him in all his difficult undertakings. People point out that Luther has one fault, in that he is inclined to become too loud and biting, certainly more so than appears becoming for a man in theology, who wishes to find new paths, certainly more than what is proper for a learned man in God's Word. But this weakness, they say, is common to all who have studied quite recently.[51]

Erasmus Alber, one of Luther's household members and one of his Table Talk companions, who had much occasion to observe Luther's character, has left us this account:

> He wrote all his books with his own hand, for which God gave him such a fine memory, the like of which one finds few. He also possessed an excellent eyesight, so that even late in life he did not need to use glasses. Luther was such a fine, versatile, friendly and pious man who was well satisfied with all his labors. He exercised moderation in all his actions; and he never engaged in superfluous words. To the obstinate he could be fierce, while towards the weak minded comforting. When he was asked about the meaning of passages in the Holy Scriptures, he was always ready with an answer. Luther was not a head-strong man; he was never boorish in attacking anyone. In his answers he was always friendly and offered good reports. He never complained in a situation and was compassionate and even with the stupid and the feeble, always glad to be of assistance towards the needy and gave good advice. In his Table Talks you could learn as much as a sermon, a fact to which Urbanus Rhegius testified in a letter.[52]

In 1530, during the Diet of Augsburg, Luther was not permitted to attend because of his excommunication by Rome and the Edict of Worms in 1521, and stayed within the Ernestine lands, at the *Feste Coburg*, to which he had accompanied the Elector John and the Wittenberg delegation. While there awaiting the outcome and the drafting of the Augsburg Confession without him, he had a prominent visitor, the humanist Urbanus Rhegius, who has left us this impression of an unusual day he spent with the reformer:

> At the Coburg I spent a whole day with the man of God. This turned out for me to be the happiest day of my whole life. He is such a great theologian that in the whole world there is no one like Luther. For me now Martin is the most important person in my life, for I personally have seen him, heard him speak, which cannot be expressed in written form or even the use of endless diction.[53]

In the same year Urbanus Rhegius wrote another letter in which he made some additional observations about Luther during his Coburg experience:

> I claim no one can hate Luther who knows him personally. One detects some of his spirit in his books; but it is far more true when one hears him speak in person about divine things. Then one has to admit, he is a far greater man than one can observe in his writings. I have now personally observed how great is the Grace of God in this man. Many of us write books, but what are we when compared with this man. Pupils we are but he remains the Master. I know him better now than before since I have seen him. He is a special instrument of the Holy Spirit.[54]

Details of such descriptions of Martin Luther, by friends and by foes, could be multiplied far beyond the present purpose. The aim here is to acquaint the reader with the man whom Vicar Johann von Staupitz chose to become his successor in *Lectura in Biblia*, and explain why he became the reformer of the German Reformation. To balance the picture of him, however, it may be of interest to see how he was viewed by the popes and all the extreme *Altgläubigen* in the West. As would be expected, Pope Leo X had a strong view of Luther, while his successor, Pope Adrian VI, was vehement in the extreme. Let us reserve their reactions for later and begin with the reactions to an interview with Luther by Bishop Dandiscus of Ermland. This bishop had been on a trip to Spain, and on the way back, he stopped in Wittenberg. When he visited the Black Cloister, it was empty, with only Luther and Prior Brisger as its occupants. Apparently he first looked up Philip Melanchthon, whom he praised as a fine scholar and linguist. Philip took him to Luther, with whom he seems to have engaged in a discussion about the current activities in Rome and the Kaiser, the *Neuglaubigen*, and the "New Theology" of Wittenberg. Luther, who was not in his monk's attire, shook his hand and invited him to sit down. During the conversation he accused Luther of being too critical of the pope and the papacy, and also of the Kaiser and the Catholic princes. He stated later that he had found Luther a man of understanding and knowledge and fluent in his speech. He failed to describe Luther's appearance, but observed that he looked like he does in his pictures. Like so many others, the bishop noted that Luther had "piercing, penetrating eyes, unusually sparkling, like one often finds in the possessed."[55]

Both Popes Leo X and his successor, Adrian VI, were very vindictive and spiteful in their judgment of Luther's reforms at Wittenberg. In his Bull *Exsurge Domine*, which John Eck helped draft, Pope Leo X compared the reformer to a "wild boar" who had invaded and was devastating "the vineyard of the Lord." The language of Pope Adrian VI, the tutor of Charles V, was most vehement and devastating. Being quite a scholar from the Netherlands, his judgment carried weight among the *Altglaubigen*. After being made Leo X's successor, Adrian VI started Catholic reforms to counteract the Reformation. Nor did he spare the *Altglaubigen* for creating the conditions that made Luther possible; but he had also decided to build fire under the Elector Frederick the Wise, who at the time was attending the Diet of Nürnberg (1523–1524); he regarded him as the real culprit for protecting Luther and allowing the reforms in his lands. He called the reformer the Son of Perdition, who had come to Frederick in sheep's clothing but inwardly was a ravening wolf destroying the kingdom of God. He accused the elector of being too blind to see it. In a bold *Breve* that he dispatched to the Saxon Prince and the Council of Regency meeting at Nürnberg, he called Martin Luther a *Kirchendieb*, a church thief, who was robbing the true Christian church. He accused Luther of taking holy pictures of God and the cross of Christ, crushing them with his hands and stepping on them with his ulcerated feet. Why did Frederick not become wise to this apostate to his monk's vow? He said Luther emptied monasteries and nunneries and the ex-priest had the finest whores. He charged that Luther belittled the Holy Fathers, opposed the church's Holy Councils, and burned the sacred church canons. For him Luther was really the devil clad as an angel of light. Was the elector so blind as not to realize all that was happening?[56]

Fortunately, the sick and aging elector had advanced far enough in his understanding of Luther's restoration of the gospel and Wittenberg's "New Theology" not to be influenced by Adrian's charges. This question of Frederick the Wise protecting Luther has been rather thoroughly discussed in a chapter of *The Setting of the Reformation*, and needs no further elaboration here. Members of the Council of Regency also felt it unwise to attempt to enforce the Edict of Worms of 1521.[57]

Before turning to Luther's activity in the classroom and the pulpit, the reader may welcome a more detailed impression about the physical characteristics of the Wittenberg professor and preacher. Let us then briefly review Luther's physical features. He was about five feet ten inches tall, but as previously indicated, his weight varied throughout his lifetime. We saw that at the Leipzig Debate in 1519, Luther was extremely thin because of fasting, but after a more normal life he added some weight. Yet it is doubtful that he ever weighed over 175 pounds. Both Luther's friends and enemies felt the Wittenberg professor had very unusual eyes. Nicolaus Selnecker pointed out that Luther had fiery, sparkling eyes, like those of a hawk, falcon, eagle, or fox.[58] Melanchthon, as we saw above, added that Luther's eyes were brown and strong, like those of a lion, and then added that they had golden rings like those of an eagle or men of genius.[59] There can be no doubt that Luther's eyes had quite an influence upon his effectiveness in his life's work at Wittenberg.

It is also interesting to read what the *Altglaubigen*, the old-style believers, recorded about Luther's appearance. When Luther was summoned to Augsburg in 1518, during the Diet of Augsburg, he was asked to appear before the Roman *Nuncius*, Cardinal Cajetan, an expert in the philosophy of Thomas Aquinas. The Thomist met with a real surprise by being confronted with Wittenberg's "New Theology" based on the Holy Scriptures. After much argumentation the cardinal was disgusted and would discuss no more with that strange "beast with the deepseated eyes," and gave his reason that "strange thoughts flit through his head."[60] Another interesting observation of the Wittenberg monk was made by a second papal *Nuncius*, Cardinal Aleander, in his *Depeschen* from Worms to Rome in 1521, after a fleeting impression when the reformer and his companions arrived at Worms. In his excitement Aleander wrote: "This Luther, as he stepped down from the carriage, looked around in all directions with his demonic eyes and said, "God will be with me."[61] After that Luther disappeared in the crowd.

Another attribute that greatly enhanced Luther's physical qualifications as a public figure was his pleasant voice. It was clear and penetrating, with enough timber to add, with its sonorous qualities, a musical ring to lectures and sermons. Students stated it was pleasant to hear him lecture. The carrying qualities added much to his effectiveness as a public speaker.[62] In a day when amplification was unknown, such a carrying quality in a large church, cathedral, and open marketplace was a decided asset. It is claimed that the musical quality in Luther's voice gave it a pleasant resonance. Erasmus Alber, the table companion, observed that the reformer seldom raised his voice; yet it was clear, ringing, and easily understood as he lectured from his Katheder in the *Grosse Hörsaal* in the Black Cloister.[63]

Another element that contributed much to Luther's greatness as a historical figure was his productivity, which made him the most voluminous writer of tracts and books in Western Civilization. There can be no doubt that Luther's *Streitschriften*, his polemical replies to hostile *Altglaubigen* attacks, did play a powerful role in the spread of the German Reformation. The *Flugschriften* of that day served as the newspapers in the public marketplace, and Luther defended his reforms through this media in a most effective way. Melanchthon, in his funeral oration at Luther's grave in the Castle Church, eulogized the departed reformer as one of the great men of history, in which he compared him with Isaiah, John the Baptist, and Augustine; in his message he called their departed leader the Honorable Lord D. Martin Luther, our Dear Father and Preceptor and High Servant in Christ.[64] His contemporaries realized what a great historical figure had departed from their midst.

Luther's tremendous productivity of more than 350 tracts, books, and other Reformation publications, was in part due to his phenomenal memory, which made it possible for him to recall at will an ocean of material that he had published in his lifetime. Luther worked very rapidly and did not made second drafts as the material flowed from his goose quill pen and was rushed to the publishers. It is claimed that in 1527, in which he replied to Erasmus's attack in the tract *The Freedom of the Will*, after some weighing of a reply, he finally wrote his reply in a record time of three days. The reformer knew his Latin Vulgate practically by heart, and could quote it freely in his lectures without verification, and even cite the Bible passages, in which reference, scholars claim he seldom made a mistake. Equally well he could quote from the classics what he had learned in his Eisenach days in the academy. In his courses of *Lectura in Biblia* covering the *Psalms, Romans, Galatians*, and *Hebrews* (1513–1518), it is amazing how familiar he was with the Fathers on which he drew for his lectures. This versatility in many fields is well illustrated in the Leipzig Debate.[65] His student Erasmus Alber well expressed what most *Neuglaubigen* thought, that God knew what he was doing when he chose Luther to attack the Antichrist in Rome, in order once more to reveal the gospel to the world; for, in the case of the reformer, God chose a man after his own heart and assigned to him a great task, the life of which had not been seen since the apostles, by a man with such wonderful gifts.[66]

Admirable as was Luther's storehouse of knowledge, still more unusual were the originality and penetrating quality of his creative mind. As will be seen later in more detail, Luther had been educated along traditional Roman Catholic lines in the *Via Moderna*; yet, after his *Turmerlebnis* about the *Iustitia Dei* as viewed by the Holy Scriptures, in a relatively short time he came up with an entirely new interpretation based on the Bible and his rediscovery of teachings of the early Christian church.[67] Much recent research by scholars has confirmed how mature Luther was by the time he lectured on *Hebrews* in 1518, using the Chrysostom *Homilies on Hebrews*, as well as the works of Ambrose, Jerome, and Augustine among the Fathers, and the glosses of Lyra, Burgos, Valla, Faber, and Erasmus, but which views he also viewed, analyzed, weighed, and judged in the light of the Holy Scriptures.[68] Later in life the mature reformer stated that Chrysostom's *Homilies on Hebrews* had been the main source for his interpretation of that book. Luther wrote a tract in 1539, in which he wrote:

> Let us take a book of the Bible and look at the interpretations of the Fathers and the same thing will happen to them that happened to me when I took up the Epistle to the Hebrews with the Gloss of St. Chrysostom, Titus, Galatians with the help of St. Augustine, the Psalter with all the exegetes that I could find and so on.[69]

In theology, Luther asserted that the exegete should drink directly from the fountainhead of truth, the Holy Scriptures. As Kenneth Hagen has shown, Luther quoted from the above sources, but he also criticized them when they failed to measure up to the Holy Scriptures as theology's divine standard.[70] As we shall observe, in time St. Paul's new theology appeared in his lectures, based on the New Testament and breathing an atmosphere unknown to the West in a thousand years.[71]

In the pulpit Martin Luther also exhibited unusual dramatic ability, acting roles of the devil and evildoers, and the next minute assuming the role of Christ as our Savior, similar to other great preachers of the Christian church. It is recorded that during the Crusades, Bernard of Clairveaux charmed German audiences by his acting in a pulpit, even though they could not understand a word he said; while George Whitefield, the great Methodist preacher, even charmed his audience with the clever withdrawal and use of his handkerchief during a sermon. In my Master's thesis research on "Martin Luther as a Preacher," at Ohio State University, I found that Luther displayed a similar charm during his sermons.[72] Luther's musical ability also played quite a role in his popularity.

Important as all these attributes cited were, they still do not explain his leadership and success as the reformer of Germany. To this must be added his personality and spiritual qualities with which he was endowed in an unusual degree. Combined with the genius of Luther as a man went the simple and childlike faith and trust in God. This faith impressed Urbanus Rhegius at the Coburg in 1530. As Rhegius walked past Luther's room, he overheard him speaking with someone, who he thought was in there with him. But as he listened at the door, he found Luther was earnestly engaged in a prayer with God, pleading for the strengthening of Philip Melanchthon and his supporters at the Diet of Augsburg, to encourage poor Philip amid all the pressure he faced from the emperor and the Catholic opposition. Later the humanist wrote: "No one could more energetically and earnestly pray than he, no one could genuinely console the afflicted."[73] Luther appears to have had no fear for the future, for he implicitly trusted in God's providential protection. During his stormy days at Worms in 1521, he was even disappointed that God did not consider him worthy of martyrdom.[74] He did not want the elector to hide him in the Wartburg, and when the Wittenberg disturbances in 1522 got out of control, he returned and wrote Frederick that he did not need the elector's protection, for he had a higher power to protect him than the prince of the Saxon Lands. In fact, he added that the elector was far more in need of God's protection than Luther.[75] Melanchthon once related that when he was very sick and near death, Luther stood by the window and pleaded with God to save him, and Philip added that Luther had prayed him back to life. This spiritual quality was also well illustrated at Worms in the face of the Kaiser and the German electors, when he refused to recant his "Wittenberg theology," for his conscience was "bound by the Word of God" and he could not do otherwise.[76]

Thus it is clear that during Luther's lifetime, friend and foe had a very different impression of the reformer. After Luther died in his native town of Eisleben, on February 18, 1546, three great funeral sermons were preached in commemoration of his departure. The first by Doctor Justus Jonas, who had accompanied the reformer there to settle a dispute between the princes of the region, at a service in Saint Andrew Church, the next day; [77] the next one, more an oration delivered by Philip Melanchthon, next to Luther's grave and the coffin, a farewell message by the University of Wittenberg delivered to the students and faculty;[78] and finally, the actual funeral sermon was given by the Town Church pastor, Dr.

Johannes Bugenhagen, delivered in a service held at the Castle Church. In all these farewell messages, Luther was honored as their father who had departed from this world and one of the greatest of the men of history.

In his lifetime Luther had the bitterest of enemies. In the early years, he had been opposed by the universities of Cologne and Louvain, who had furnished John Eck the 41 Articles of Luther's condemnation in the papal bull *Exsurge Domine*, which led to his excommunication in the final bull *Decet* in 1521; and the same year he had been condemned in 104 theses drafted by the University of Paris, and also by the Kaiser in his *Edict of Worms*, which could not be enforced. He had been bitterly attacked by hostile scholars from the Court of Duke George and even by Henry VIII of England and his supporters. After his death the Council of Trent (1545–1563) had completely rejected all reforms Luther had proposed to return the Christian church to the original purity of its Apostolic Age and the day of the great creeds of Christendom. The centuries that followed resulted in the great division of Christendom. It is of interest to note that the leaders of the opposition to the Reformation were Dominicans and Jesuits, who relied in their verdict on Luther's bitterest enemies, and with little or no knowledge of Luther's writings, which they did not regard as worthy of examination. They did, however, establish external reforms, but no changes in doctrine.

Meanwhile in the nineteenth century something happened to counter the propaganda that Catholics had so successfully directed against Lutheranism and Protestantism as a whole. This came from an entirely new and nonreligious quarter—the rise of the Leopold von Ranke school of historical criticism and writing based on actual historical sources. Von Ranke and his pupils began to unearth all types of new historical material hitherto unknown in the academic world. For the first time, the actual facts of original sources concerning the German Reformation began to appear in print, revealing the events that had occurred in Luther's lifetime. New, larger collections of Luther's writings began to circulate in the academic world. The *Erlangen Edition* of Luther's Works and the *Enders Edition* of Luther's correspondence appeared in the nineteenth century. Then, in 1883, the German government began to publish the *Weimar Edition* of Luther's works, which in time has grown into around 100 volumes of definitive, rare source material. Both Catholic and Protestant scholars thus began to discover historical data which had not previously been known, and a new perspective of the Reformation began to emerge as a result of publications by able scholars.

Then in the 1930s came the Nazi regime, and Hitler attempted to unify Christianity by making all Germans into *Deutsche Christen*. By the end of World War II, most of the ranking German clergy, both Catholic and Evangelical, were in prison. The church went underground to survive, and the *Una Sancta* movement was born, in which joint religious services were conducted between Lutherans and Catholics. The chief clergymen of the two faiths were incarcerated in the same cells, awaiting the gas chamber. This created a closer tie between the former religious enemies. A good example was the Dominican Joseph Lortz, who later recalled how he and his Lutheran cellmates had knelt down at night, both turning to the same Christ for God's mercy, forgiveness, and grace. Lortz said he learned to know his cellmate much better and felt there could not be too much wrong with the man of the opposite faith.

After World War II, the ecumenical movement emerged in Germany. This author participated in the occupation of Germany after the war, and gained insight into what was happening through a joint assignment as Gast Professor of the University of Erlangen and University Advisor in the State Department of the U.S. government. All the documentary sources of the university were made available to our Counter Intelligence to avoid the danger of the return of any former Nazis into the faculties of the University of Erlangen. At that time the author visited some Una Sancta services in Nürnberg. Out of this climate a Catholic ecumenical movement began, like that of the Joseph Lortz school in Mainz. Where formerly, in the sixteenth century, the Dominicans and Jesuits had been the leaders in getting Luther excommunicated, they have now become the leaders in healing the harm inflicted in the opposition to reforms of Martin Luther within the Christian church. Scholars such as Peter Lang and Karl Meissinger also played a significant role within the ecumenical movement, correcting the false picture of Luther. There has also been the influence of the meetings every five years of seven International Luther Congresses, in which scholars from all over the world, both Protestant and Catholic, have read papers, discussed them in seminars, and exchanged their viewpoints and findings. Another influence in the changed Reformation perspective has come from the Tübingen School, under the leadership of Professor Heiko Obermann, which has gone into the medieval background of the German Reformation.

The postwar ecumenical movement is far too involved and includes too many participants for elaboration here.[79] Three Catholic leaders stand out among many who deserve elaboration, as through their influence the academic world has now a very different view from that held several decades ago. These scholars were Joseph Lortz, Adolf Herte, and Herbert Jedin, who gave the ecumenical movement new insight as to what actually transpired during the sixteenth century. These great Luther scholars whose writings they studied, made them examine and weigh the views held by the Catholic Church in the last four centuries. Men like Lortz and Herte had wondered how accurate a picture of Martin Luther they had been given by Denifle and Grisar, and they began to investigate the facts for themselves. Let us begin with Adolf Herte of Paderborn and examine the role he played in the movement.

Those familiar with the Reformation know that among Luther's most bitter enemies was Cochlaeus, writing many *Flugschriften* against the reformer. His propaganda furnished a useful arsenal for the Council of Trent and, in subsequent centuries, even for Denifle and Grisar in the twentieth century. In fact, it gave Catholics such a dark picture of the Wittenberg professor that Heinrich Boehmer decided to reply to Rome's charges in his 1914 volume *Luther in the Light of Recent Research*, which served as a Herte catalyst to investigate damnable lies in Cochlaeus's *Flugschriften* and in his final 1549 Luther biography.[80]

Professor Adolf Herte, the former Dominican historian at Paderborn, did his doctoral thesis on Johannes Cochlaeus, entitled *Die Luther Biographie des Johannes Cochlaeus, eine Quellenkritische Untersuchung.*[81] This thesis was but the beginning of Herte's definitive studies, which were to deeply influence both his fellow Dominicans and also the Jesuits. He really wanted to discover the truth about the lies told about Luther and Catherine, which had been the standard weapons of the Catholic world for the last 400 years.[82] He found them to be pure fabrications on the part of Cochlaeus, with the purpose of destroying the reformer's character. Herte also checked another lie which he had spread about Catherine, who he claimed had carried out sexual relations with Wittenberg students. Herte learned that all these tales were fabricated by him and passed into the post-Reformation arsenal.[83]

After he had discovered that Cochlaeus' tales were fabrications, Herte wanted to know what influence these lies had had in the Council of Trent, and likewise what role they had played in the Catholic propaganda of later centuries. His investigation spread to France and the Netherlands, and he also dug deeply into Luther's writings, church histories, and polemical writings. In this new research, Herte learned that the members of the Council of Trent made good use of Cochlaeus' fairy tales and that Catholic authors from all parts of Europe used the same lies to condemn Luther and the Reformation. He also learned that Denifle and Griser had drawn freely from Cochlaeus' fabrications. All this material Herte then worked into his three-volume masterpiece titled *Das Katholische Lutherbild in Bann der Lutherkommentare des Cochlaeus*, published as a set by the Paderborn professor.[84]

This publication fell like a bombshell into the Catholic camp, and it stimulated further studies in the already ecumenically-minded world of Reformation historians and theologians on both sides. Among those who were deeply moved was Joseph Lortz and some of his able students. This resulted in a Catholic–Lutheran dialogue which has been widely publicized elsewhere. The conservative Roman *Lehramt* was not pleased to find its arsenal destroyed, and it made Herte pay heavily for his bold publication. Rome had Herte moved from his professorship in Paderborn to an obscure place.

This brings us to the actual ecumenical movement in Germany under the leadership of Professor Joseph Lortz of Mainz, who was another Dominican with an interesting background. We have already touched upon his war record under Hitler, who tried to make all Germans *Deutsche Christen*, leaving both Protestants and Catholics in the same dilemma. Ranking clergyman like the Lutheran Bishop Meiser of Munich, Bishop Wurm of Württenburg-Baden, Bishop Lilje of Hannover, Bishop Dibelius of Berlin, and Niemöller were all in prison and facing death, while among the Catholics, Joseph Lortz of Mainz, Bishop Neuhausler, Cardinal Faulhaber of Munich, and many others were threatened with the same fate, as the police record after the war revealed.[85] Had not Patton's army liberated the high-ranking clergymen, no one knows what their fate might have been.

Professor Joseph Lortz began his Reformation studies in 1915, like Adolf Herte, but was more interested in the broader movement than was his fellow Dominican in Paderborn. Lortz's first major publication was his *Die Reformation in Deutschland* (1939–1940), 2 vols. This wonderful study of the Dominican, who had not yet come under Herte's influence, really made the Catholic world take notice. Yet, as he admitted later, Herte had not yet opened his eyes. He did, however, already present the contemporary abuses in Rome during the Reformation, and even stated that Catholics should stop panning Luther, for the reformer had been a real, creative, and profound thinker. He already wondered: Why was the Reformation possible? As he admitted later, he was not yet ready to express views about Luther, as he had not really studied the sources but relied on the publications of others. Thus he was still too much under the influence of the Council of Trent, in which he believed the theology of St. Thomas was untouchable, in the light of which he felt Luther was subjective in his views. However, some of his able students began to research different aspects of the Reformation in the original sources, and Lortz began to be less sure of himself. He decided to study the actual evidence in *Luthers Werke*, his works in *Flugschriften*, Sermons, and his spiritual treatises. The result was, as will be seen, that the honest Catholic scholar came to realize he had really never known Luther the man nor the spiritual depths of his pastoral treatises.

Between 1940 and 1964, a different Lortz began to emerge, as is so ably expressed in his little book *How the Reformation Came* (New York, 1964), from which a few quotations will illustrate how the Dominican professor had grown. He had the Jesuit Daniel J. O'Hanlen write the introduction, who expressed Lortz's views in these lines:

> The biased and unreliable character of Cochlaeus' work is thoroughly exposed by Herte's three-volume study. Up to now, the English-speaking readers have not been able to correct the unfair picture of Luther, which is found in what Father Sartory calls the pansexual interpretation of Denifle or the pathological interpretation of Grisar.[86]

Then he admits there is a real need for the adjustment of modern Catholic thinking about Martin Luther, as they had a false picture of the reformer, and Lortz asked the Catholics to change:

> We have to learn afresh, adjust our view. Metanoia means first of all to think anew: not so much the gaining of new knowledge, rather a new way of thinking. And nothing is more difficult to achieve than this: to see with new eyes that which we have seen before.[87]

In the text proper of Lortz's book in 1964, he offers a detailed account of conditions in German lands and in Rome, where many voices were calling for reforms. He had also become convinced that it was Rome and its supporters who had brought about the split in the Catholic Church in Luther's day, rather than the reverse view held by many staunch *Altgläubigen*. Thus he expressed his concern and need for rectification of previous claims. On this the Preface adds:

We must now honestly confess that there was much Catholic guilt for the split. "The guilt we share calls for an unconditional mea culpa as the precondition for the solution of the task we called to mind in the beginning of this book. If we do not make this confession, then it will be impossible to arrive at an understanding at the human level or at a settlement in the Christian sphere."[88]

But it was not just Joseph Lortz who felt that something had gone wrong during the German Reformation. When the Second Vatican Council was about to meet in Rome, the Catholic bishops of Germany had the following pastoral letter read from all the pulpits in West Germany:

> In our Confiteor before the Council we should include the centuries-old scandal of divided Christianity. In Germany especially, where the Western Schism was born, do we suffer with particular anguish from this deep wound in the mystical body of Christ. We cannot simply accept this situation as an unalterable fact; instead, we feel ourselves involved in a thousand ways in the great tragedy of the Church in our country. The straightforward objectivity of historical research, conducted by Catholic scholars as well as others, shows that there were many great abuses and serious scandals in the life of the Church at the end of the Middle Ages. Consequently we feel compelled openly to confess the guilt we share through solidarity with our forefathers.[89]

In this excellent little book of Joseph Lortz, filled with interesting observations of conditions in the Roman Church, there is an emphasis about the abuses in indulgences by John Tetzel, the role of the Fuggers in Augsburg, and the laxness and immorality in Rome. But Heinrich Bornkamm, the author of many Reformation studies, criticized Lortz's position as not going far enough; Lortz stressed the immoral abuses in the Roman Church, but failed to attack the doctrinal departures from the Holy Scriptures, due to his acceptance of medieval scholasticism. The Dominican Pater still believed had Luther attended another university, he would have received a better Thomistic education, and then his soul struggle due to the doctrines of the *Via Moderna* might not have occurred. At this point in Lortz's doctrinal views, due to Trent and the *Lehramt* in Rome, his doctrinal position of St. Thomas still remained untouchable in this fine little book.

Meanwhile, in the next five years, the great Dominican ecumenical leader did not stand still, but made a more thorough study of Luther's teachings. There was also the influence of his pupils, like Irwin Iserloh, Stephan Pfuertner, and the Lutheran scholars who debated with him at conferences, all of which made him reexamine his former claims. During this period a number of Catholic scholars were preparing their massive *Festschrift, Reformata Reformanda* in 1965, done in honor of Herbert Jedin, an authority on the Council of Trent. For this Joseph Lortz wrote an extended study on *Martin Luther*, in which a mature evaluation of the reformer was expressed.[90] Here Lortz revealed, with amazing frankness for a Catholic of his stature, what he had learned from years of Luther research in the sources. In this study Lortz showed that he now grasped the reformer's desire for the restoration of the gospel in the Christian Church, and that he had plumbed the depths of Luther's exegesis in the "Theology of the Cross" and his paradoxical ways of expressing divine truths of the Holy Scriptures, such as the status of believers redeemed by the cross of Christ as that of *Simul Justus et Peccator*, in the period of the believer's sanctification when "the just shall live by faith."[91] Lortz says that Luther tried to harmonize contradictory concepts by the use of paradox. The amazing thing about the essay on Luther by Lortz is the fairness and appreciation of Luther as a theologian and for his greatness in the history of the Christian church. This can best be illustrated by a few examples of how Lortz felt late in life about the reformer of Germany:

> Luther is a spiritual giant, or, in case we were to quote Althaus, "An Ocean," and the danger lies in getting drowned in its waters; the danger is that one does not master Luther sufficiently, both because of the massiveness of the material and its uniqueness.[92]

Later he attests even more to Luther's greatness by placing him into the gallery of the greatest theologians since antiquity:

> It is almost a commonplace, yet it should be repeated. Luther belongs in the highest gallery of men that have been unusually creative in power; he is a genius in the highest sense and possesses originality both in the religious realm and in the field of theological expression.[93]

Then in his evaluation of Luther he adds: in a sense he determined the religious situation in the world today, for Martin Luther was the Reformation.[94] That stated that the Wittenberg theologian has been exonerated today, for he stated that Cochlaeus, Denifle, and Grisar are no longer accepted in the Catholic world today, not even in Italy, Spain, and Latin America.[95] In the same connection, Lortz also admitted that Luther did not cause the schism in the Roman Church, but stated that the Catholics literally threw him out:

> We must recognize how large the Catholic guilt really was in forcing Luther out of the Roman Church and that the Schism occurred, which now weighs so heavily on us Catholics. Hence we are strongly motivated by the desire to bring the Luther-richness (*Reichtum*) back into the Catholic Church.[96]

The Lortz essay continues with an unusual admission for a Dominican about the life and work of Martin Luther. He admitted that when he published his first book, he did not agree with the reformer that *Sola Scriptura* was the teaching on which the Christian church stands and falls; but he admitted now that Luther was right, for through that method he had rediscovered the doctrines and teachings of the early church; in fact, Lortz claimed he found the reformer far more Catholic than he had believed, and Catholics now could penetrate Luther's thought better than Lutherans today. It is simply amazing, says Lortz, what questions Luther asked and the tirelessness of spiritual inquiry.[97]

The Dominican Father regarded Luther as a *Willensmensch*, a strong-willed, explosive type of person, whose temperament created his spiritual accomplishments; while Luther's "Tower Experience" was not just a breakthrough but a creative experience, for later it became a part of his spiritual message of "Justifi-

cation by Faith." It was the culmination of a "blessed soul struggle." At the end
the reformer said, "then I broke through," in his discovery of *Iustitia Dei* as
revealed in the Holy Scriptures.[98] But Lortz observed in passing that it was not
so much the young Luther that interested him, but the views of the more reflec-
tive, pious theologian of his later years, no doubt because that was the mature
Luther of the Reformation. Lortz liked the mysteries in divine revelation that
Luther had plumbed, and discussed in his theology, without any boasting about
his spiritual growth. For example, in a 1529 sermon to the Wittenberg congregation, Luther had confessed that it was difficult for him now to believe that we
are saved solely by God's grace, that in this he had come to the "A" in the ABCs,
but the "B" and "C" have not yet been mastered. The Dominican also stated
that he had come to a place later in his life where he admitted that he still did
not understand Romans 1:17 too well; for humans to believe in work-righteous-
ness was so easy and natural, that we cannot grasp why God chose to redeem us
without the works of the law. Lortz felt that to really understand and know the
reformer you have to get away from his polemical *Flugschriften*, in which there
is always an enemy to be convinced, and in which Luther often exaggerated just
for emphasis. Then Lortz said that if you really want to know Luther, visit him in
the quiet of his study, discuss spiritual problems with him, or read his Small Catechism and some of his soul-saving sermons.[99]

Joseph Lortz also thought that great men of history must be judged in terms
of their peculiarities and characteristics; otherwise, he claimed, it resulted in
misunderstanding. He felt Luther could not be judged like other men, like
Occam, Scotus, or even St. Thomas. The Dominican theologian agreed with
Rudolf Herman, that Luther was an intellect of a special type, which comes out
of his eruptive and explosive reactions due to his unusual and unique temperament.[100] After extolling the Wittenberg professor for his various attributes and
noting the continued attacks and criticisms of his enemies, whose views he
brushes off as being by the uninformed, who lack a real understanding of
Luther, he advanced this statement, which reveals his final estimate of the
reformer:

> If the article of "Justification by Faith" by Luther, on which the Church
> stands or falls, is no longer divisive, and we Catholics are one with Luther on
> this main point; may we not also be in agreement with him on others? Per-
> haps even a definition of the Church could be drafted—of course in complete
> agreement with the Scriptures—which could be acceptable to both sides. Is
> there for Luther no instructional post? Does he not deserve a church position
> by divine right? We recall how deeply Luther's formulations of doctrine are
> tied into the historical situation. Can anyone really claim that Luther would
> have rejected an Apostolic Hierarchy, which lived and taught in accordance
> with the faith in the living Christ?[101]

The Dominican leader was of course fully aware that the papacy and the traditions of the Roman Church stood in the way, but as an afterthought Lortz
cited Luther's commentary on *Galatians* of 1535, from which he quoted this

passage: "If the Pope were to grant that, on Justification by Faith and the Grace of God, we were right, we would not only carry him in our hands, but even kiss his feet."[102] This statement, he added, was worthy of serious thought by Catholics. After all, had Luther not replied as he did at Worms, would he have been honest?[103]

Nor is this change in Lortz so surprising, as the ecumenical movement has brought about some surprising changes in the Catholic world. Since the fifties there have been seven Luther Congresses, and scholars of both traditions even commemorated the 450th Anniversary of Luther's nailing of his Ninety-five Theses. Then at a "Luther Jubilee" in 1983, in Washington, D.C., hundreds celebrated Luther's birth for a whole week and engaged in lively discussions. Those who have gone to these meetings know how typical Joseph Lortz's views are among many able scholars of both traditions. Besides, there have been many meetings of theologians from both camps engaged in attempts to unify Christianity and heal the schism that so disturbed Joseph Lortz.

LUTHER TRANSFORMS THE UNIVERSITY

In the previous section an attempt was made to better acquaint students with Martin Luther, the historic figure who became the reformer during the German Reformation. In this introductory part, the views of leaders among both the *Altglaubigen* and the *Neuglaubigen* have been treated. Now we need to examine Luther's role as the lecturer in *Lectura in Biblia*, through which he transformed the University of Wittenberg into a new institution. Perhaps our best study of this subject is still Walter Friedensburg's history of the *Leucuria* in 1917.[104] This began in the quiet of Luther's study, before his nailing of the *Ninety-five Theses*, after which the battle with Rome broke out.[105] The study of Luther's formative years has been an intriguing subject for scholars in the last 400 years.[106]

Since the theme of this book is concerned with the Reformation from a specific viewpoint, not all the material here is relevant to our theme. Since we wish to show Luther's role as the reformer in the context of a whole academic institution, its faculty, and 16,292 students, many works lie outside the scope of this approach. Some eighty scholars, however, have contributed in source material relative to Luther's formative years and the development of the "New Theology" of Wittenberg, which involves the *Turmerlebnis* and his discovery of "Justification by Faith" by 1514, and his later development of his "Theology of the Cross."

In an earlier part of this chapter we saw how under the deanship of Professor Trutfetter, in the winter semester of 1508–1509, at the University of Wittenberg, the theological student Wolfgang Ostermeyer took time off to prepare for his promotion to the *Licentiatus* degree. He had been teaching a course in Aristotle's *Ethics*, and Martin Luther was brought to Wittenberg to take his place.[107] It is possible that Luther's former professor at Erfurt, Jodocus Trutfetter, had a

hand in this. But Luther soon returned to Erfurt, where apparently the Augustinians wanted him to complete his doctorate with them.[108] The steps in
between that period, Luther's progress in his studies at Erfurt, his trip with a
travel companion to Rome in 1510–1511, and Luther's subsequent recall to
Wittenberg by Dean Staupitz are familiar to the reader from previous coverage.
The events associated with Luther's promotion to the doctorate in theology
have also been treated in a previous account in some detail.

The fact that Johann von Staupitz had promoted Luther to the doctorate in
theology in order to accept his post of *Lectura in Biblia*, the young professor
took very seriously. Luther felt all through his life that as a doctor of the Holy
Scriptures he had a real responsibility, not only to interpret God's Holy Word,
but also to speak up against any false interpretations in which the Roman
Church had engaged in the Middle Ages, and during his day by the papacy and
the Roman Curia itself.[109]

The members of the Wittenberg faculty must have been fully aware of the
fact that the young Luther was a man of great promise. The joint founder of the
university, Dr. Polich von Mellerstadt, who frequently served as dean of theology, in the early period, was always on the lookout for the elector for promising
talent in the school; he seems to have been impressed with the ability of the
Augustinian monk, for he observed:

> He possesses a striking, sharp intellect, which the like I have failed to
> encounter in my whole life.[110] This monk will confuse all the doctors and
> advance a new teaching which will reform the whole of the Roman Church;
> for, he relies in them upon the Prophets and the writings of the Apostles, and
> he stands on the Word of Christ. No one can oppose this with philosophy nor
> sophistry, be it that of the Scotists, Alberts, Thomists and the whole of Tar-
> tarist, nor overthrow it.[111]

Some more evidence of others realizing Luther's unusual qualifications came
from Dean Staupitz, shortly before his promotion to the doctorate, we learn
that there had been an encounter between him and the Augustinian monk
under a pear tree in front of the Black Cloister, in which the vicar general
wanted to promote Luther to the doctorate and the Augustinian monk felt he
was not ready. But the dean must have known Luther's abilities far better than a
Wittenberg theological student.[112] To this account, Walter Friedensburg adds
that thus Wittenberg promoted its greatest Bürger to the doctorate for all time.
And with the dean's assignment to his own post of *Lectura in Biblia*, he was
offered the opportunity to prove his abilities to his promoters. This the Christian world was soon to experience. But before he could realize his ultimate goal,
Luther had to first reform the faculty of the University of Wittenberg.[113]

For an understanding of what Luther was up against in transforming the
institution itself, we need to briefly review some of the preceding academic history treated in previous chapters in detail. We saw there that the University, at
its foundation in 1502, was modeled after Paris and Bologna, like other German
universities with a scholastic academic structure. Although humanism was

allowed as an elective, its student were obligated to travel by the road of medieval scholasticism, like other German schools, to graduate or enter one of the three graduate schools of theology, law, or medicine. We also saw how humanism was earlier introduced by Peter Luder and Stephan Hoest into the University of Heidelberg, and how it began to make inroads into the curricula and undermine scholasticism, which occurred two decades before Agricola and Celtis arrived on the scene; then how humanism spread to Leipzig and Erfurt before it invaded the new university on the Elbe. In this spread, traveling humanists planted the seeds during their visits at Leipzig, Erfurt, and Wittenberg, and later Nicholas Marschalk and his pupils completed the work. The first charges on the scholastic fortress were on the fringes of academic life. The two sacred languages, Greek and Hebrew, were taught on an elective basis. But even some of the leading professors began to be attracted to the new humanism for an embellishment of their style of scholastic writing. Then, as at Heidelberg under Stephan Hoest, leading professors in liberal arts began to wonder how sound their scholastic background for an education really was. Men like Dean Sigismund Epp of the philosophical faculty of liberal arts, with humanistic leanings from Tübingen, was dissatisfied with the old scholastic textbooks being used and wanted to have them replaced with more recent publications. He wanted more recent commentaries on Lombard's *Sentences*. Dean Epp was also dissatisfied with the 300-year-old textbook used to teach Latin, by Alexander of Villedieu, which had reduced disputations to the use of "hog Latin," as the humanists called it in derision, and wanted teachers to use the more recent textbook of Sulpius Verulanus, to teach students better, Ciceronian Latin.

Then came the more aggressive humanist Marschalk, who with his pupils began to attack scholasticism itself, as they were teaching the very languages of Greek and Latin in which the original Bible was written. Professors in philosophy and theology became embarrassed and tried to make themselves more attractive to students by embellishing their writings with quotations from the classics. By that time a new type of biblical humanism had emerged, which advocated the use of Greek and Hebrew, which the students needed to understand the Holy Scriptures in its basic meanings. So by the time Martin Luther assumed the post of *Lectura in Biblia*, professors in liberal arts were already using biblical humanism in their course offerings, from whom Luther learned Greek and Hebrew for his interpretations of the Holy Scriptures.[114] In such a humanistic climate of biblical humanism, Luther emerged as the reformer.

Most scholars who have studied Luther's beginnings as a biblical exegete from 1513 to 1518 have concentrated on the changes that took place in his lectures and his monastic struggle, finally ending with him as the German reformer; but few have studied all this change in his classroom lectures without realizing that all this transpired as part of a whole university movement, during which he made his discoveries as a biblical exegete and student of early Christianity. Since this study has attempted to weigh all this in the light of the Reformation as a university movement, it becomes advantageous to examine the internal growth of the university itself, as it underwent very fundamental changes, dropping its scholastic offerings and introducing courses in biblical languages for deeper study of the Holy Scriptures. It also gave courses in the Fathers in an attempt to return to the teachings of the early Christian church. This university transformation demands some further elaboration, as it is vital to Luther's role in the German Reformation story, in the later creation of a new university in the twenties and thirties, from which the German Reformation emerged.

It was quite clear to Martin Luther and Philip Melanchthon that Aristotle and Plato would have to go before the badly needed linguistic changes could be made in the University of Wittenberg curricula, for the pagan philosophy of Aristotle and Plato ran directly contrary to the teachings of the Holy Scriptures. Thus a study of the Bible in its original languages required that students would have to be offered instruction in Greek and Hebrew to understand Luther's lectures. In the details of such a growth and basic change in the university's academic curricula one gains a better understanding of Luther's unfolding and the development of his "Theology of the Cross."

When Martin Luther assumed his new professorship of *Lectura in Biblia* to offer courses in the Bible, he was relatively unknown except in his own academic circle. This is quite evident from a kind of Sixteenth Century "Who's Who," issued by Trittenheim's *Schriftstellerlexikon* in 1514, of famous people in German universities, even including promising *vir luster*, those perhaps famous some day. He failed to include Luther, who was then giving his lectures, the *Dicta super Psalterium*, and no one seems to have called his attention to the future reformer.[115] Yet it must be remembered that these were the quiet years, from 1512 to 1517, for the young Luther before the storm broke out with Rome. During the period when Luther lectured on the *Psalms, Romans, Galatians*, and *Hebrews*, he could quietly analyze what he had been taught by his professors at Erfurt and Wittenberg in the medieval scholastic theology of the *Via Moderna*, compare it with St. Paul's Epistles, and widen his knowledge of the Fathers and the Early Christian church. Walter von Löwenich of Erlangen, in his new biography *Martin Luther*, has pointed out that this was really the time when Luther found himself and matured into his later theology as the reformer.[116] Walter Friedensburg points out that the range of Luther's knowledge by this time was quite extensive. He says that in the scholastic world he was familiar with St. Thomas, Duns Scotus, William Occam, Gregor of Rimini, Pierre d'Ailly, Gerson, and Biel, and he knew them well; and that among the recent theologians he knew the works of Lefevre, Pico della Mirandola, and Erasmus, while among the classical writers he knew Virgil, Ovid, Horace, Quintilian, Pliny, and Varro, and he had also begun a serious study of Greek and Hebrew.[117] Besides, he says, he was familiar with Aristotle's teachings, as can be observed in his *The Address to the German Nobility* in 1520, where he condemned the great authority of medieval scholasticism:

> I know very well what I am talking about; Aristotle is as well known to me as your kind; and, I have read him with more understanding than St. Thomas

and Duns Scotus, so that I am not boasting about myself; in case it is necessary I can prove it.[118]

In the medieval institutions of higher learning, such as Paris and Bologna, covered in previous chapters, students did not have printed textbooks like today. As we saw earlier in Bologna, students were forced to take elaborate notes, which they wrote between the lines and on the margins of notebooks. This method of preparing *Glossen* and *Scholien* dated as far back as the early church Fathers. In the classroom the professor read and analyzed the text and commented on the more difficult parts, known in German as *Glossen*, which the students copied almost verbatim. Later the teacher would enlarge the text of his *Handexemplar*, which students copied, and were known as *Scholien*. When Luther used this method, in the *Scholien* he often departed far from the notes he had previously prepared. Luther used the Vulgate text printed with wide margins and spaces between the lines for student notes. This Luther methodology, customary in his day, he used when he gave his early lectures in the *Grosse Hörsaal* in the Black Cloister between 1512 and 1518.[119]

As the reader will detect, there was a close connection between Martin Luther's own theological development into the reformer and his transformation of the university into an institution in which his "New Theology" became the dominant note transforming it into a new school. We of course possess no record of how his students reacted to the changes that were introduced into their classrooms. We possess but glimpses of what did transpire behind the scenes. But Walter Friedensburg, in his history of the university, has singled out two examples of what was happening in the institution by 1516 and 1517. We saw earlier in a chapter on the humanism how Luther studied Greek and Hebrew under the guidance of John Lang and Hebrew under Thiloninus Philymnus, which had contributed to his development as a biblical exegete and his philological maturity.[120] This was bound to run into conflict with what was being taught elsewhere in courses at the University of Wittenberg.

As has been previously shown, in the beginning the university on the Elbe was little different from other institutions of higher learning, for as elsewhere scholasticism was deeply entrenched in liberal arts and the graduate schools of theology in Germany. At first they had four Thomists under their chairman, Bodenstein von Carlstadt, with Wolf Reuter and Beckau in liberal arts, teaching courses *viam Thome*; and there were another four Scholasts under Nicholas von Amsdorf, with Kannegieszer, Küchenmeister, and Koenig interpreting Aristotle in courses *Viam Scoti*.[121] Then, after the arrival of Jodocus Trutfetter in 1507, the university also began to offer courses in the *Via Moderna*, which were continued after his return to Erfurt in 1510. By 1516 Luther already had his *Turmerlebnis* behind him, the discovery of the biblical meaning of *Iustitia Dei* as found in Romans 1:17, "The Just shall live by faith," and not by the works of the law, and realized that Wittenberg's scholastic education was contrary to the Holy Scriptures and the Fathers. He must have felt it was time for him to attack Wittenberg's scholastic stronghold by means of an academic disputation.

In the dean's records of the *Liber Decanorum*, it is quite clear that disputations were a regular way of testing a student's maturity for an advancement in degrees in the school of theology at the University of Wittenberg. Since a mastery of Lombard's *Sentences* of Roman Catholic doctrine, in four volumes, was required for advancement in degrees that led to a doctorate of theology, students were required to demonstrate their skill and maturity in the Castle Church before the entire assembled body of faculty and students in a public disputation, for the *Biblicus, Sententiarius, Formatus*, and *Licentiatus* degrees, for which occasion the student's professor drafted the theses. Since the scholastic professors would participate in the debate, here was a fine chance for him to challenge Thomists and Scotists in an attack on their philosophical stronghold with his "New Theology," which his students had learned in his lectures based on the Holy Scriptures and the Fathers.

On December 25, 1516, one of Luther's able students, Master Bartholomaeus Bernhardi of Feldkirchen, came up for a disputation seeking to be promoted to the *Sententiarius* degree, qualifying him to teach Lombard's *Sentences*. He had already qualified by examination before the theological faculty, and this was now to test his mettle as a debater. It so happened that the dean of the theological faculty at the time was the Thomist Bodenstein von Carlstadt, who would naturally participate in the disputation, supported by Peter Lupinus, a fellow Thomist, and they would challenge his interpretations of the proposed theses, or even attempt to confuse Bernhardi.[122] Since Martin Luther had drafted the theses and served as the chairman, he had complete control over the procedure. As it turned out, the disputation became quite an explosive affair, which could become embarrassing to the faculty opposition if their ground was not too supportive of their claims. Bernhardi had been well trained by Doctor Luther in his scriptural teachings on "Sin and Grace," so his attacks on scholasticism based on God's Holy Word created quite an impression on the rest of the faculty and the student body. Bernhardi argued that according to the Holy Scriptures the natural man cannot fulfill God's commandments without having God's saving grace.[123] Naturally the proud Dean Carlstadt and his assistant were embarrassed, for Bernhardi's mastery of Scripture and Augustine were just too much for the Thomistic masters and their philosophy.

The German historian Karl Bauer and others have claimed that Carlstadt was full of *Ehrgeisz*, filled with an ambition far beyond his actual ability. Since he was dean, his later entry in the *Liber Decanorum*, page 19, is most revealing of his self-praise:

> Under the Deanship of the most Venerable Man, Master Andreas Carlstadt, a Master of Arts and a Doctor of Laws and Theology, being exempt from his Holy Duties as Archdeacon and Canon of the Collegiate Church, these events occurred in Wittenberg in the year 1516, which here follow.[124]

The *Liber Decanorum* kept by the respective deans of the theological faculty are to be an accurate account of what happened. Since the author possesses the C. E. Förstemann printed copy of the deans' entries and also a photocopy of the original handwritten account, he has found Carlstadt's recording of this vital event in Wittenberg's history most revealing. After a laudatory self-praise, much of it falsely acquired, or even a degree purchased in Italy,[125] he does not even relate how he and Lupinus fared in the doctrinal debate and were defeated by young Bernhardi. There is not even a reference in his record as to what had transpired.[126]

Later, in a *Tischreden* of Luther, he claimed the disputation made Carlstadt ill, for this was Luther's student, and these two Thomists were his strongest scholastic opponents at the time. It had been just too much for the proud dean to have Bernhardi quote Lombard, Gratian, and Augustine, and to bring before the whole school Luther's new views of justification by faith and sin and grace, which were directly contrary to those of the Schoolmen.[127] In this connection, Barge, in his biography of Carlstadt, made the observation that both Carlstadt and Lupinus were taken by surprise, for in the debate, for the first time, they were made the opponents of the gospel, based on the writings of Augustine, the Fathers, and the Holy Scriptures.[128] No doubt Luther's familiarity with Augustine overwhelmed Carlstadt, as did Bernhardi's citation of the weak points in St. Thomas, whose philosophy he dared to question. Carlstadt was far from convinced, and wanted to make a study of Augustine for himself.[129] On January 13, 1517, he made a special trip to Leipzig, purchased a whole set of Augustine's writings, and began reading Augustine's treatise on *The Letter and the Spirit*.[130] After reading this book and having some further discussions with Luther, Carlstadt became convinced that Thomism misrepresented the Scriptures on sin and grace, and he became an ardent champion of the "New Theology" of Wittenberg. The other participant in the debate, Lupinus, needed no further proof, joined Luther in his reforms of the university, and supported his "Theology of the Cross" and the Reformation. But Carlstadt could not stand Luther's growing popularity in the institution, and tried to draw more attention to himself. In April 1517, while still under the deanship, Carlstadt nailed 151 Theses on the door of the Castle Church, to draw attention by public disputation with fellow faculty members to the cause of the gospel, which Luther was already restoring by his lectures.[131]

In the fall of 1517, Francis Gunther of Nordhausen, an able student of Luther's, was ready to be promoted to a *Biblicus*, and he needed to engage in a disputation in the Castle Church. Naturally the chairman of this debate was again his professor, Martin Luther, who drafted the theses for the occasion.[132] The theses were so framed that Francis Gunther had to engage in an attack upon the Schoolmen, namely, the teachings of Scotus, Occam, Biel, and d'Ailly by means of Augustine and the Holy Scriptures. In this frontal attack, the student presented the viewpoint that the *Via Moderna* teachers held a philosophy quite similar to Pelagius in Augustine's day, which was a charge quite difficult for Amsdorf and his fellow Occamist professor in the disputation to take. Thus Martin Luther had made an attack on the Stagirite in order to dethrone him at Wittenberg. For Gunther's disputation, the reformer had prepared 97 Theses, which he entitled, *A Disputation Against Scholastic Theology*, which was later published at Wittenberg in 1520. The Latin text used is now available in WA I, 221–228.[133] Since Luther at this time was the dean of theology, he could set the tone of the disputation. The reformer's feelings about Aristotle had by now become very intense, for he wrote John Lang in Erfurt on February 8, 1517:

> No one inflames my feelings as that actor Aristotle, who with his Greek mask mimics the Church. If there were but the time, I would like to expose him and show his ignominy to the entire world.[134]

It seems that the Bernhardi Disputation and Carlstadt's subsequent investigation of Augustine had left quite an impression on the Thomists in the Wittenberg faculty, for Luther wrote in another letter to Lang how pleased he was with the progress his reforms were making:

> Our Theology and Augustine are continuing to prosper and reign in our University through the hand of God, Aristotle is declining and is heading for a fall, which will end him forever. It is remarkable how much Lombard's *Sentences* are despised. No one can command an audience unless he proposes to lecture on this (new) theology; namely, unless he lectures on the Bible, St. Augustine or some Doctor of ecclesiastical authority.[135]

From this it is quite evident that the Bernhardi disputation had left quite an impression in the university, certainly enough to cause the Thomists to give up their former stand after reading Augustine's *De Littera et Spiritu* and join the reform movement.[136] Friedensburg points out that Carlstadt was red-faced with shame and respect at the same time.[137] Barge offers us even a stronger reaction given by the leader of the Thomists: "I recognized that I was deceived in a thousand scholastic writings, I was like a mule in the mill, like a blind stone, that in the past I had up to now talked without making any sense."[138]

Meanwhile Martin Luther had, as we saw, prepared another student, Francis Gunther, for his promotion as *Biblicus* in theology. Once more this public debate was held in the *Aula* of the Castle Church. It must have been of great interest to faculty and students, as it turned out to be the turning point of the institution. By now Luther had completed his lectures on *Romans*, in which Gunther must have been a student. Since the topics discussed were relevant to the *Via Moderna*, the participants must have been Amsdorf and his fellow Scotists, but we no longer know all who participated. This debate has been analyzed and discussed by a number of scholars, but we are deeply indebted to Leif Grane's *Contra Gabrielem*, published in Denmark during 1962.[139]

At Wittenberg they had three types of disputations: (a) the student training type held in the dorms, especially the New Friderici *Aula*; (b) the student promotional type; and (c) the annual professional type given by professors for instructional purposes. Both the second and third types were held in the *Aula* of the Castle Church, as stated previously. The Gunther disputation on September 4, 1517, was thus a promotional one.[140]

Since this debate proved to be the turning point in the history of the university, a further discussion of the topics for the debate will be of interest. As the presiding official, Luther had drawn up 97 theses, of which the first served as a kind of introductory challenge. It charged that Scotus and Biel were making claims that Augustine had been too severe in his criticisms of the heretic Pelagius. This also was true of the scholastics Gregor von Remini and Bonaventura, which made the debate a direct attack on scholasticism itself.[141] Later theses then claim, based on Augustine, that the human will is not free, but that it leans more toward evil, and in that, they say, the *Via Moderna* is misleading. Theses 6–19 form a unit. In these Luther attacked the "Freedom of the Will," in which the theses claimed the scholastics had misrepresented Augustine's teaching. According to later ones, man cannot love God without God's grace, and will love the creation more than its creator. Luther stated that all the *Via Moderna* on "Free Will" are heretical according to the teachings of the Fathers.[142]

Theses 20–30 then formed another natural unit for debate, which gave Gunther another theme by which he could attack the *Via Moderna* and scholasticism on their teachings about natural concupiscence in humans, claiming that the natural man is unable to perform "Good Works" pleasing to God. In the theses Luther made a direct attack on Gabriel Biel, by claiming that an *Actus Amicitiae*, or an act of love without God's grace, is impossible for the natural man. In these sets of theses he was also charged with false statements about *Verdienst*, or acquired merits. Here Luther naturally attacked in a thesis Biel's claim that when the natural man does, *facere quod in se est*, or does all within his powers, he then acquires from God the *Meritum de congruo*; after which God begins to bestow upon him his "saving grace." This offered an opportunity for a lively discussion against Scotus, Lombard, Occam, and Biel, for it implied that natural man could prepare himself for God's saving grace by his own efforts and natural powers.[143] It was really a contradiction of St. Paul's *Romans* 1:17 that "the just shall live by faith," in direct contradiction to his discovery of *Iustitia Dei*, as revealed in the Bible during his *Turmerlebnis* a few years earlier.

In theses 37–42, there was another natural grouping of topics around Aristotle's teachings on morality according to Gabriel Biel's writings on *Ethics* of the pagan philosopher.[144] This series begins with the thesis that mankind does not acquire any righteousness before God by performing "good works," as is claimed by Aristotle's *Ethics*, for it is almost in its entirety opposed to biblical teaching and directly contradicts all the teachings in the Christian doctrine of the early church. Furthermore, according to these theses, Aristotle's teaching about happiness is also in direct contradiction to Catholic doctrine. Nor is it true that one cannot become a theologian without Aristotle, as scholastics claim, but just the opposite is true, one cannot become a theologian unless it be without Aristotle. In fact one becomes a heretic by relying too much upon the philosophy of the Stagirite.[145] Luther really summarized this body of theses as follows:

> It is false to say that without Aristotle one cannot become a theologian. The opposite is true, no one becomes a theologian unless it be without Aristotle; for the whole of Aristotle is related as darkness is to light and his *Ethics* is the worst enemy of Grace.[146]

Later in the theses, Luther attacks both Aristotle and Porphyry, even stating
that the world would have been better off if the latter had never been born. In a
latter part Luther also attacks Gabriel Biel's teachings about man's meritorious
preparation for God's grace, for he pointed out that no human act can be
regarded as meritorious before God's throne of Grace, as the reformer
expressed it in thesis fifty-five:

> For the Grace of God is never present in an inactive way, but it is a living,
> active, and operative spirit; nor can it through the absolute power of God act,
> so that an act of love may be present without the presence of the Grace of
> God. This is in direct opposition to Gabriel.[147]

Grane claims the whole disputation really centered around the real Augustinian theology and its perversion through scholasticism, due to the introduction of
Aristotelian philosophy in the writings of Scotus, Occam, Biel, and others. The
debate centered about the very themes that Luther had stressed in his lectures,
namely, those of the natural man, law, grace, and love. Luther realized that Aristotle was behind the teaching of Occam and Biel. Grane asserts that when the
teachings of the *Via Moderna* were weighed in the light of Augustine and the
Holy Scriptures, he discovered that they were Aristotelian rather than Christian, and a far departure from Early Catholicism.[148]

This disputation must have left quite an impression on the entire university
assembled in the *Aula* of the Castle Church. Carlstadt and Lupinus had already
joined and supported Luther's "New Theology"; while Nicholas von Amsdorf,
who had been somewhat dubious, and his staff now enthusiastically embraced
the new Wittenberg reforms.[149] Earlier in this volume we have encountered
Amsdorf, who was a Scotist of noble extraction, and related to Vicar Johann von
Staupitz on his mother's side.[150] He had first studied at Leipzig and was drawn
to the *Leucuria* quite early, completed his liberal arts there, and rose in theology to a *Licentiatus* degree by 1508. Amsdorf was a conservative, a member of
the Stift of the Castle Church, and later a very ardent supporter of Luther.[151]

It is not strange that this debate, aimed at the overthrow of Aristotle in theological instruction at Wittenberg, also had a tremendous effect in other faculties. In the law school, Doctor Hieronymous Schurff and Dr. Wolfgang Stähelin
joined the reform movement.[152] Dr. Schurff proved to be very useful in the trying days of Worms in 1521, where he served the Elector Frederick as his chief
lawyer; but Stähelin proved to be less stable, and left Wittenberg; while later he
was chancellor of Duke Henry of Saxony.[153] The school of medicine was still too
feeble at this date to play any role.

But all this change in the curricula of Wittenberg would not have been possible, had meanwhile a similar transformation not also been under way in the
Saxon Court, as described in the author's book *The Setting of the Reformation*.
We say there how Frederick the Wise had been reared as a typical *Altglaubigen*,
but how he gradually changed under the influence of his Father confessor and
court chaplain, Georg Spalatin, who was a very prolific correspondent and
friend of Martin Luther. Under Spalatin's spiritual guidance he had now

reached the point where he favored the proposed Wittenberg reforms of Luther and Melanchthon.[154] Walter Friedensburg says Georg Spalatin, in his role as the salesman of the transformation of the University of Wittenberg, "wrote his name into the Reformation history in Golden letters."[155] Then he adds, it was Spalatin who helped give the university greater significance. At this point there needs to be an enlargement of the many contributions Spalatin made in the reforms of the University of Wittenberg, for without the elector's approval, curricula changes in the school could not be made even by Spalatin, as the prince regarded Wittenberg as his own institution.

The Setting of the Reformation described Spalatin from the angle of his important role as Father confessor and intimate advisor of Elector Frederick the Wise in his battle with Rome. In that volume the reader sees how Spalatin, a former Erfurt humanist, became a close friend of Martin Luther, and how through frequent correspondence he followed the progress of the German Reformation; and then, by much discussion with the elector, had convinced him that Luther's cause in the restoration of the gospel was just, and that the reformer should be supported in his attempts to reorganize the University of Wittenberg, unless actually proven to be in error by a neutral Church Council based entirely on the Holy Scriptures. The prince followed Luther's role as the reformer of his school very closely, and Spalatin, as his guide and interpreter, convinced him that scholasticism should be replaced by biblical humanism. This caused the development of an entirely new school, in which the restoration of Latin, Greek, and Hebrew and the teachings of the church Fathers were to be studied in the original languages in which they were written. Thus the elector was in full agreement with Spalatin, who wanted to make the curricula changes proposed by Luther and the Wittenberg faculty. In the execution of the desired reorganization Spalatin was eminently qualified to carry out the elector's orders. To realize this one must look a little more closely at his educational background and other qualifications to supervise the desired changes in the university on the Elbe.

Spalatin's humanistic schooling began at St. Lorenz Academy in Nürnberg, where his promising gifts as a linguist were evident quite early. When he later attended the University of Erfurt, he was fortunate enough to become a devoted student of Nicholas Marschalk, and moved in the "Erfurt Circle," where he associated with humanists Konrad Muth, Johann Lang, and Urbanus Rhegius, all of whom played important roles in his future. After his departure from Erfurt, Spalatin's first appointment came through the assistance of the great Gotha humanist Konrad Muth, to a position in the Cistercian Monastery of Georgenthal. It was also through his former Erfurt associate that Spalatin was able to make his first contacts with the famous Venetian Aldus Press, which later became so important in building a good Wittenberg library.[156] It was also through Muth that he entered the court of Frederick the Wise, to become the tutor to young Prince John Frederick, his brother's son. Because of his likable personality and his gifts, young Spalatin soon rose in the court of the elector, by being made his "Court Preacher" and "Father Confessor." He also drafted his secret correspondence with Rome and other courts of Europe, as much of it was in Latin, in which Frederick was not too versed. Such a relationship offered him an excellent opportunity for guidance and interpretations of Luther's writings and his development of the "Theology of the Cross," which was known as Wittenberg's "New Theology." But it also made him an excellent salesman of the humanistic needs of the University of Wittenberg. This explains why it has been claimed that Luther, Lang, and Spalatin formed the triumvirate of the German Reformation.

But when Georg Spalatin became the "Court Preacher" of Frederick the Wise he needed to study theology. In 1515 he began to ask himself what type a real theologian should be. He wrote to his mentor Conrad Muth and asked him for guidance. The Gotha humanist replied that his friend regarded Luther as an "Apollo" to whom he was to turn for guidance.[157] When he contacted him in October 1516, Luther had completed his lectures on *Romans* and had made use of Erasmus' Greek New Testament of that year. Luther's reply, like his above-described Wittenberg disputations, revealed that his discovery of the biblical meaning of *Iustitia Dei* during the *Turmerlebnis* was by then behind him. In his reply Luther warned the court preacher that if he wished to become a true theologian and understand the Holy Scriptures, he must not follow Erasmus, with his emphasis on St. Jerome's methods of interpretation, but rely instead on Augustine, Ambrose, and Cyprian as more reliable biblical exegetes. He told Spalatin that man needs to be made righteous by God before he can perform "good works" which are pleasing to him. He stressed that the Holy Gospel is most important in our salvation. By this letter it became clear to Spalatin that Luther had arrived as the reformer, and he was anxious to know how he should approach and interpret the Bible as God's Holy Word.[158] Thus Spalatin learned from Luther to preach good gospel sermons to the elector and became an able interpreter of the new humanistic trends in Luther's "New Theology" and helped him in the much-needed university reforms.

By March 21, 1518, Luther could write an optimistic letter to John Lang at Erfurt, about the progress they had made with the elector in the curricula reforms by the introduction of courses in the biblical languages, so the students could understand God's Word in the originals:

> Our University is moving ahead. We expect before long to offer lectures in two or three languages. New courses are to be given in Pliny, Quintilian, mathematics and other subjects. The other courses of Petrus Hispanus, Tataretus and Aristotle are to be dropped.[159]

Wittenberg's curricula changes, even though they had the elector's approval, were not as easily realized as Luther had hoped. The schools' introduction of courses in Greek, so students could follow Luther's interpretation of the New Testament, as will be seen, met with no difficulty; but to find a satisfactory professor in the Hebrew was not as easy and simple an undertaking. New courses in Greek were realized by the employment of Philip Melanchthon, who turned out to be a gifted fellow reformer with Luther; but in Hebrew, after a few unfortunate attempts under Böschenstein and others, Luther finally found the right man in Mattäus Goldhahn, known as *Aurogallus* among the students, who became an able Hebrew professor, and remained in the university until 1541. He was of great assistance to both Luther and Melanchthon, helping Luther in his Bible translations and assisting Melanchthon by lightening his teaching load in the 1520s.

BASIC CHANGES IN THE UNIVERSITY

The reader observed in an earlier chapter, relative to the founding of University of Wittenberg, how the Elector Frederick the Wise asked a faculty member, Christopher Scheurl of Nürnberg, to draft the *Statutes of 1508*, to govern the new institution in its four schools, liberal arts and the three graduate schools. He must have been aware of the need for future changes, for he also set up a system of four reformers, who were to watch the institution and propose changes when needed. Liberal arts already needed reform in the winter semester of 1509–1510.[160] Some problems arose about the election of a rector, the pay of the Syndicus. In the beginning the school was to hold several university banquets, known *prandia ducalia*, which were stopped in 1513, and there was also an increase of school discipline, pertaining to students' conduct and their carrying weapons, which no doubt was due to an attack on a rector.[161]

There were, however, few *curricula* changes in the early years. Gustav Bauch, in his ZDVGAS XXVI, relates that a professor from Silesia, a master from Krakau, Batholomäus Stein, had joined Wittenberg's faculty due to Christopher Scheurl, and began to offer the first course in geography, based on Pompanius Mela's *Orbis pictus*. No doubt he made quite an impression in the *Leucuria*, by giving his *Antrittsrede* in honor of Holy Catherine on November 25, 1512, Wittenberg's patron saint of the arts. But like Christopher Scheurl, Stein did not remain long, and returned to Breslau, where he became well known for his geography of Breslau and Silesia.[162] Unfortunately there was no immediate replacement for the departed Stein.

In the year 1514, the school of liberal arts witnessed a widening of the arts curriculum by the creation of a department of mathematics. This was something new, as until then mathematics was taught as a part of Aristotle's *Metaphysics*. The new position had been created with the elector's approval and his financial support. However, the conservative scholastics in the faculty had their misgivings about mathematics being an academic discipline apart from Aristotle, as he was the sole source of that field of learning. Thus it was offered only as summer course for bachelors, based on the *Computus Ecclesiasticus* and the treatment of the *Spheres* by Johannes de Sacrobusio in winter courses for students in Euclid. A general course in mathematics was based on the writings of Jean de Meurs, a fourteenth-century mathematician. The first mathematics professor was Bonifazius Erasmi, or known as De Rode of Zöbig. Shortly after his appointment as mathematics instructor, he was chosen dean of the philosophical faculty, which must have added to his standing in his new position.[163]

There were also complaints in the school of law, that their professors often failed to meet their regular classes. Accordingly, the rector sent two representatives of the university to make an investigation of the charges. The problem seemed to apply to both civil and canon law professors. A record in the Weimar Archives states that a report was made on April 9, 1516,[164] in which they found the difficulty was related to the faculty income. It seems the professors in canon law were better paid, but those in civil law had difficulty making ends meet. The two investigators recommended that six members be added to the university staff, who would be regularly funded. These were to consist of two in medicine, two in civil law, and five in liberal arts.[165]

In all the changes, the university historian Walter Friedensburg claims to detect a change in the past thinking of the electoral Court toward privately endowed incomes for all faculty in the secular fields. But its realization was somewhat slow in being carried out, as the elector no doubt had difficulty in knowing how he could bring it into reality by the Stift, especially for faculty whose fields were purely secular through ecclesiastic funds.[166] The highest paid professor in the theological faculty at the time was Martin Luther.[167] Among the ranking civil law professors were Hieronymous Schurff, Stähelin, and Bayer, while the medical faculty had Dr. Schwabe, who seemed to be ailing due to sickness and often could not lecture. In the arts faculty Carlstadt was away in 1516 and Amsdorf took his place, but the *Via Moderna* was not being taught. Professor Vach and Otto Beckmann taught humanistic courses in rhetoric and grammar, while Master Zöbig was teaching courses in mathematics and astronomy.[168]

After the elector's lawyers had presented their findings on faculty finances, the prince asked questions about details of university incomes. He asked: How many students were promoted? What income did that yield? What incomes did they have through wine and beer? How many books had the university purchased and by means of what funds?[169] To this series of questions the faculty made a complete reply, which was treated in a chapter on the financing of the University.[170]

By the spring of 1518 it was quite evident that the disputations of 1516 and 1517 had offered much fruit. Dramatic changes had taken place in the philosophical faculty with reference to Aristotle's writings. Instead of interpreting them *viam Thome* or *viam Scoti*, the Stagirite was now permitted to speak for himself. The faculty insisted on the best texts and recent translations. Meanwhile courses in Pliny and Quintilian were given to improve students' linguistic ability, and a course in grammar was given based on Priscian. There the students were also offered courses in Greek and Hebrew.[171]

Walter Freidensburg, in his *Urkundenburg*, I, 85–86, offers an enlarged account of Wittenberg's curriculum changes in its philosophical faculty. From Spalatin's Weimar records one can ascertain what changes occurred in liberal arts. At this time Johannes Ferreus of Hesse gave lectures on Aristotle's *De Ani-*

malibus, based on the most recent texts available; and the following year he rotated it with a course in Quintilian. Bartholomaeus Bernhardi gave courses in Aristotle's *Physics* and *Metaphysics*, interpreting him without theological implications, based on the most recent original sources. Augustin Schurff, brother of the distinguished lawyer in Roman law, offered courses in Aristotle's *Logic*.[172] In this record Spalatin already speaks of starting a *Pedagogium* for the training of the young students in the *Studia humanitatis*, especially in the three sacred languages, Latin, Greek, and Hebrew, about which we will learn much later after the arrival of Philip Melanchthon.

After Luther began his lectures on *Galatians* and *Hebrews*, he started to base his lectures more and more on the original text of Erasmus' *Greek New Testament*, and a knowledge of Greek and Hebrew seemed almost essential for his hearers. By now Spalatin was in complete support of Luther's needs in his lecture series. Frederick the Wise also seemed to be fully in agreement with the Wittenberg changes to be made in course offerings, and Spalatin proposed the establishment of a *Pedagogium*, in which young and more mature students were to be taught an introductory knowledge of Latin, Greek, and Hebrew, and authorized the school to establish a staff under two masters, Johannes Bockenheim and Jodocus Morlyn, who were to teach students the basic languages needed to understand Luther's "Theology of the Cross," which he was expounding in his lectures.[173] As will be seen later in Wittenberg's history, Philip Melanchthon took good advantage of this new possibility, to place the *Pedagogium* on a much higher plane in the curriculum, offering specific courses as background training for the future graduate students. This new emphasis on a mastery of languages was no doubt related to the practice from now on in the Wittenberg *Bursen*, where the dorm students could converse only in Latin instead of their native tongues.

Martin Luther was very pleased with the progress the university was making in the study of languages and that Quintilian and Pliny were now being taught, as reported to Spalatin:

> I prefer Quintilian above all other authors, as his writings are not only very instructive; but that they also relate the history of the discipline of eloquence; so that in word and in action, we in a fortunate way enrich our knowledge. He is therefore usually well suited, not only to instruct the youth but also to enrich the lives of mature men.[174]

NEW PROFESSORSHIPS IN GREEK AND HEBREW

Luther was very pleased with the academic progress by moving away from a scholastically oriented institution to one in which biblical humanism had made the study of the Holy Scriptures possible, based on their original languages, and that a *Pedagogium* was to be established to begin training youth in a linguistic background for advanced study.[175] But for Luther this was not enough. There was a great need for future scholars who used these disciplines in their theological studies. He realized that an able clergy was possible only by the establishment of two regular professorships, one in Greek and another in Hebrew. After his Heidelberg meeting of the Augustinians, Luther wrote Georg Spalatin, on May 18, 1518: "I hope and implore you, not to forget the Gymnasium with the introduction of Greek and Hebrew.[176]

Luther was, however, soon to learn that the Electoral Court had given Georg Spalatin permission to establish chairs in Greek and Hebrew. Then Luther interviewed the Leipzig humanist Peter Schade, generally called Peter Mosellanus, whose birthplace was on the Mosel River, for a possible professor to fill the professorship in Greek. As it turned out, this choice was not according to the elector's wishes, even though he was an able Greek scholar. Mosellanus, a man of Luther's age, had studied at Cologne, Erfurt, and Leipzig. He had also worked for a while with Aesticampanian at Freiburg in Brisgau on the Rhine. He had begun his professorship at Leipzig in 1517.[177] But he was not happy there, as the Thomists on the Leipzig faculty did not offer him, as a humanist, a favorable academic climate for promoting Greek and the *Studia humanitatis*; so he was seeking a more friendly environment as the *Leucuria* on the Elbe.

Meanwhile, the Electoral Court, no doubt through Spalatin's suggestion, had contacted the great Hebrew scholar John Reuchlin, asking him for guidance in filling the Wittenberg Greek professorship.[178] They may even have hoped that the Hebrew scholar in Stuttgart could be drawn to come to Wittenberg in person and accept the new position; for Reuchlin had said, though laughingly, that he was too old to accept a move clear to the *Leucuria* in Frederick's native Saxony. In his reply, Reuchlin offered some names the elector might consider for the post in Hebrew, if he wished to establish that position; but for a chair in Greek, he had a definite preference. Being the young Philip's great uncle, the famous Hebrew scholar no doubt was somewhat biased. He had guided this prodigy in his schooling from the beginning, and he had observed what a flair for languages he possessed, which had made a deep impression on his teachers and the elderly Hebraists. In fact, he was so pleased with the boy's progress that he decided to rename Philip Schwarzerd, as was customary among humanists, Philip Melanchthon. In fact, Reuchlin wrote the elector that in his opinion, young Philip was the greatest Greek scholar in all Europe, with the exception of Erasmus of Rotterdam.[179] Then, no doubt to impress Frederick, he added that other schools were already trying to employ Philip. For example, he added, Ingolstadt had attempted to draw him into its ranks. In fact, they had tried hard to finalize the matter, but he had declined their offer. However, as to Frederick's new university, young Philip had expressed a desire to go there, for there was blossoming a very favorable climate for him to assist the elector in his attempts to introduce a trilingual humanistic curricula for teaching Latin, Greek, and Hebrew.[180]

As any historian of the German Reformation knows, John Reuchlin's evaluation of his great nephew was certainly not an exaggeration, as Philip Melanchthon became one of the greatest scholars in the sixteenth century and the close coworker of Martin Luther. For without Philip's academic role in the transformation of the University of Wittenberg, in the twenties and thirties, its success would have been far less. By creating a liberal arts program in which languages and the *Studia humanitatis* flourished, he prepared the theological students for that discipline. If Luther was the reformer of the Christian church in German lands, Philip was the creator of the academic climate in which the Reformation could emerge as it did in a university movement. So important were Philip's contributions that he was called the *Praeceptor Germaniae* by his fellow countrymen in later centuries. Although Melanchthon had a *Biblicus* degree in theology, he was never ordained, nor did he preach. He preferred to remain in the liberal arts faculty, and a professor of Greek and Hebrew, where he could properly supervise the training of students for graduate courses in theology, law, and medicine, so they could do their work in the original sacred languages, or become better trained lawyers and doctors. The Reformation was made possible through a well-educated clergy, initiated in Melanchthon's *Pedagogium*, with its prescribed courses in 1526, that was enlarged into a well-balanced program in 1535–1536 by the Elector John Frederick, which prepared an able gospel-oriented ministry, that flourished throughout the lands where the Reformation spread, under the supervision of the University of Wittenberg. How wise the elector's choice of Philip Melanchthon was is evident.[181]

Melanchthon was born in Bretten, in the Schwarzwald and Odenwald, in the Rhine valley, an old cultural region of the *Kaiserzeit*. His great uncle John Reuchlin was from Pfortzheim; while Philip's grandmother Elizabeth was married to a businessman, Johann Reuter, who later was a lawyer in Bretten. Their daughter Barbara, Philip's mother, was married to a skilled armament craftsman, a *Rüstmeister*, in the service of the Reich, named Georg Schwarzerd. The father was from Heidelberg and had entered into the service of the Pfalzgraf of Heidelberg. As a *Rüstmeister* in metallurgy, he had studied under Peter Vischer and Albrecht Dürer in Nürnberg, and later was in the service of the elector and his armies, producing the most useful armor. Even the elector of the land had a role in the marriage. Thus when Philip Schwarzerd was born on February 16, 1497, they named him Philip after the Elector Philip of the Palatinate. As long as young Philip could recall, his father was always weak and sickly. This malady he had acquired during the Bavarian War of 1504, and he seems never to have recovered from it. Five children were born in the marriage; Philip had one brother and three sisters. The year 1508 was tragic for the family, for within a few days both their father and grandfather Reuter died, which for them was a shock. Philip's mother was financially unable to raise the family, so she remarried; after this both Philip and George moved to live with the grandmother, which caused Philip to be closer to her than his mother.[182]

Grandfather Reuter of Pforzheim played an important role in the early education of young Philip, by bringing in an able Latin tutor, Johann Unger, an able linguist who later followed Georg Simler as the rector of the Pforzheim Latin School. Unger not only taught Philip Latin grammar, but also prepared him for the study of the Greek language. Then in 1508–1509, an able humanist, Georg

Simler, from the Reuchlin circle, took over young Philip and continued the instruction in Latin and Greek, building on the foundation laid by Johann Unger. Simler taught the young humanist to converse in Latin and acquainted him with the principal parts in classical plays.[183] In these years the foundation was laid, which later ripened into the very famous humanist. When Simler left Pforzheim in 1510 to study law at the University of Tübingen, to become a doctor of laws, he and Philip were to cross paths again, only now he was already a very mature scholar in his own right.[104]

Philip Melanchthon was a very precocious young man, who in 1509 could already matriculate as a youth of twelve, at the distinguished University of Heidelberg. This pleased his great uncle, John Reuchlin, for whom Philip had great respect and listened to his instructions with care. The older Hebrew scholar had quite a reputation in Germany, and must have prepared his way in housing and means of living. Thus Philip did not need to be quartered in one of the *Bursen*, but roomed with a theological professor, Pallas Spangel, a conservative Thomist who also much influenced the young man in his student days.[185]

As previously observed in the chapter on humanism,[186] in the period of Peter Luder and Stephan Hoest, Heidelberg was a school where the *Studia humanitatis* flourished, paving the way for Rudolf Agricola and Konrad Celtis, who continued in the cause of the new learning. Thus a rather favorable relationship had developed there between humanism and scholasticism. In the years 1496–1498, Johann Reuchlin had found the atmosphere there quite favorable for humanistic studies, but during the Bavarian War of Succession, the Palatinate had been left in a rather sad state, in which its elector, Ludwig, had to move slowly in its territorial restorations. Academically, scholasticism still dominated the university curricula, but poetry and eloquence were regarded as acceptable tools of speech adornment.[187]

Anyone familiar with Melanchthon's *Briefwechsel* in the *Corpus Reformatorum* will have noticed that many of the letters, during his early years at Wittenberg, were directed toward old friends in the Upper Rhine region. These friendships date back to his academic days at Heidelberg and Tübingen. In Heidelberg these were made through contacts in the home of Professor Spangel and through his great uncle John Reuchlin.[188] Where in the days of Peter Luder and Stephan Hoest and their successors, the *Studia humanitatis* had had rather free reign, by now the *Via Antiqua* and the humanism of Wimpfeling had created a circle more in keeping with Spangel and Reuchlin, which had deeply influenced the young Melanchthon.[189]

The Wimpfeling type of humanism was quite acceptable to both the *Via Antiqua* and the *Via Moderna* in German universities. It was a pedagogical type deeply permeated by the spirit of the doctrines of the medieval Roman church, in which the real spirit in the ancient writers never came into conflict with scholastic doctrine. Wimpfeling, being a very conservative humanist, restricted his teaching material for students mainly to the prose writers of antiquity, but avoided poetic writings with a worldly spirit. In his basic approach he did not run into any conflict with the basic philosophy of scholasticism.[190] Like Gersen,

Wimpfeling aimed at a synthesis of humanism with the theology of the Roman church. At the time the young Melanchthon, according to Maurer, was deeply influenced by the pedagogical humanism of the Wimpfeling circle, but later, as he matured, he completely outgrew the Heidelberg days.[191]

The Heidelberg days, however, had resulted in a number of friendships, some close and others more remote, like Nikolaus Grebel, and the later Baden chancellor Vehus, all of whom he learned to know; but he was in close relationship with Caspar Hedio, Johannes Schwebel, and Irenius, who later became a Lutheran. Two lasting friendships were formed with two former Heidelberg friends, Theobald Billican, later one of his best friends, and Johannes Brenz, the later reformer of the southwest from Schwabish-Hal.

At Heidelberg the students' curriculum was scholastically oriented for all who wished to meet degree requirements. Students could not pass through the philosophical faculty for the bachelor and masters degrees without taking the basic courses in the *Via Antiqua*, while the liberal arts courses were elective. Thus Melanchthon's Heidelberg education also centered around the natural science and dialectics of Aristotle, presented according to Thomist and Scotist schools of Greek philosophy of the medieval *Via Antiqua*. It would be false and misleading to think that young Philip, who had been such a brilliant student in humanistic studies of Latin and Greek at the Pforzheim School, under Simler, had at Heidelberg failed to continue his humanistic courses in liberal arts as electives. According to Hartfelder, the extensive investigator of the life of Philip Melanchthon, young Melanchthon had received his bachelor of arts degree on June 10, 1511; but, according to his pupil Camerarius' biography, when he wanted to take his master of arts degree, the professors thought he was still too young and childish-looking to become a master of arts graduate.[192] In a more recent biography of Philip, however, Wilhelm Maurer rejects the Camerarius claim, citing a number of scholars who were given that highly honored degree at an early age. In this instance Maurer's explanation is that the death of Professor Pallas Spangel brought about a change in the family circle. Melanchthon's family, and especially his great uncle, may have advised Philip to move to Tübingen, where he now was housed in one of their *Bursen*.[193]

A few months after Professor Spangel's death, Philip matriculated in Tübingen University, where on 17 September 1512 he signed the *Matrikel*, entering his name as *Philip Schwarzerd ex Bretten*.[194] In this school scholasticism and humanism lived closely together. Professor Summenhardt was a friend of Wimpfeling, and the university had a *Lehrstuhl*, a professorship in poetry and eloquence, which was under Heinrich Bebel, who as the friend of Philip influenced him in *bonne Litterae*.[195] Tübingen, like most German universities, had *Bursen*, in which the *Via Antiqua* and the *Via Moderna* students lived under the same roof, with but a wall in between them. These *Bursen* were supervised by six masters. Here young bachelors received their instruction in the writings of Aristotle, to prepare them for the masters degree. Most of the teachers were graduate students. Philip was asked to teach Greek Grammar and Literature.[196]

Among his teachers, Melanchthon placed his great uncle John Reuchlin at

the top of the list at Tübingen. After the great uncle later resigned as judge of
the Swabian League, he was free to see young Philip more frequently. Historically, John Reuchlin is usually known as the great Hebrew scholar of the day,
but he was far more than a Hebraist. Reuchlin had a wide range of academic
background, for he had attended the University of Paris and studied in Italy and
become a master of Latin prose, as well as Greek and Hebrew, which really
made him a trilinguist. This able scholar was also equally at home in the classics,
and could guide young Philip in reading the most important works of antiquity.
In his earlier years he had also taught Greek and Hebrew, through which he
developed into a fine teacher. This became of tremendous assistance in the
early maturing of his great nephew. Thus young Philip turned into a Gräzist and
a Hebraist during the six years he was both a student and an instructor at Tübingen.[197] The two earlier Melanchthon instructors at Pforzheim, Georg Simler
and Johann Hildebrand, were now graduate students at the university, while
Simler was even a conservator in the *Via Antiqua Burse*, and became a warm
friend of Philip while there.[198]

Philip in those years must already have been an excellent Greek instructor,
for a number of his students already became polished Gräcists. Among these
were Kurrer and Maurus from Scharndorf, while Kasper Kurrer was already
translating authors from Greek. When in 1518 Melanchthon delivered his
Antrittsrede at Wittenberg, it was Kurrer who translated it for publication.[199]
Later Kurrer became a professor of Greek at Tübingen and also served as the
notary of the institution. A second student for whom Melanchthon had a high
regard was the aforementioned Bernhardus Maurus. When in 1517 Philip published a new Latin translation of Plutarch's *Nota Pythagorica*, he dedicated it to
his former student Maurus, for whose abilities he had great respect.[200] Then
when Melanchthon published his first and lasting masterpiece, the *Institutiones
graecae grammaticae*, published at Hagenau in 1518, he again dedicated it to
Maurus.[201] A third Melanchthon student at Tübingen was Paul Altmann of
Salzburg, known among Greek scholars as Geräander, and also a good friend of
Philip's great uncle. When Melanchthon published his translation of *Terence*,
he dedicated it to Altmann, who at the time was editor of the Anselm Press,
where it was published.[202] A fourth Melanchthon friend who needs mention
was Ambrosiua Blarer (Blaurer), the brother of the Luther and Melanchthon
student at Wittenberg in 1520, about whom we shall learn more later, as he
became active in the Reformation in Southwestern Germany.[203] Besides these,
young Philip also became a close friend of Johannes Hausschein, later known as
Oecolampadius, the Basel reformer, who became a kind of second father to
Philip.[204] At the time a new edition of Rudolph Agricola's *Dialectics* appeared,
and the older man presented Philip with an edition. The two scholars read *Hesiod* together, and Philip regarded him as an intelligent, pious man, whom he
treated like a father.[205] When Melanchthon expressed his desire to publish a
new edition of Aristotle's works, Oecolampadius encouraged the young man in
the ambitious undertaking.[206]

Wilhelm Maurer, in his recent biography of Philip, asked: What did Tübingen have to offer the young Gräcist that he did no already know? Prior to the acquisition of his masters degree in the *Via Moderna*, he no doubt received many new insights. At Tübingen the famous Gabriel Biel had left a scholastic tradition after his death, which Wendelin Steinbach had continued in the *Via Moderna*, who no doubt influenced Philip with a pious way of life. Late Steinbach became the Father confessor of Duke Eberhard of Württemburg. Steinbach was a dedicated medievalist, a devoted pupil of Occam, Gerson, and Peter d'Ailly. The philosophy of Gerson seems to have been popular in the theological faculty of Tübingen, but its influence on Philip appears to have been but transitory.[207] Like other students at Tübingen, Melanchthon learned how the *Via Moderna* interpreted Aristotle's philosophy, and, no doubt, to what degree it differed from that of the interpretations of the *Via Antiqua* at Heidelberg. But there can be little doubt that young Philip was much absorbed in the *Studia humanitatis*, which he did largely on his own under the guidance of his great uncle and the classes he taught in Greek.

In liberal arts, Heinrich Bebel, the occupant of the chair in humanism, was now at the peak of his fame. But Wilhelm Maurer the biographer pointed out that he never was Melanchthon's teacher in the strict sense. Bebel had a number of devoted followers, who were really the cause of his fame. However, he was not really a Gräcist, but a teacher of Latin style. What he taught his pupils, Philip had already learned from Simler in the Pforzheim Latin School and in Heidelberg. No doubt Bebel's range in his use of classical sources was wider than that of the Wimpfeling circle, which attempted to keep within the bounds of Catholicism. But what could Melanchthon learn in Greek from Bebel, as he had already gone far beyond him in his Greek studies? Bebel was friendly toward the gifted young Philip, while John Reuchlin was the judge of the elector, and he cooled considerably afterwards, but he had great respect for the young Gräcist.[208]

With such a wonderful background, it is of little wonder John Reuchlin would recommend his great nephew to the elector of Saxony for the Greek professorship at Wittenberg. Since Frederick the Wise had asked Reuchlin for his advice, it was now a matter of waiting for the reply from the Saxon court. There appear to have been other reasons for young Philip to leave Tübingen. He wrote Reuchlin on July 12, 1518, that he had outgrown the childish atmosphere of his Tübingen *Burse*. No doubt he felt ready to accept the more responsible Wittenberg professorship in Greek and Hebrew. Now he awaited word from his great uncle that the elector had expressed his willingness to employ him as the reformer's coworker. If a message arrived, he would follow Reuchlin's advice in detail.[209]

The elector and Spalatin were at the time attending the Imperial Diet of Augsburg, from which Frederick sent a favorable reply. On July 24, 1518, the great uncle announced the good news to Philip that the elector had approved his appointment, and he advised him to depart immediately, as the elector might soon leave Augsburg. There they were to meet and complete the appointment.[210] Reuchlin advised Philip to visit his sister Elizabeth Reuter before leaving, and then also bid his mother, Barbara Kalb, farewell; whereupon he was to travel by way of Stuttgart to Augsburg as fast as possible.[211] In order to be certain that there was no misunderstanding, the great uncle also dispatched a reply, on July 25, 1518, informing the Saxon prince that he had informed Philip of the elector's message, that his great nephew was ready to accept the Greek professorship, and that young Philip would serve the elector with honor and meet his needs. He informed the elector that Philip would arrive in Augsburg with his personal library and await the elector's reception, He added that he would have liked to come along, but that at the time he was so preoccupied with other matters that he could not come.[212]

Philip lost no time after the arrival of the great uncle's message. He bade farewell to his grandmother and mother and then hurried on to Augsburg to meet the elector and announce his acceptance of Wittenberg's Greek professorship. After Philip's transaction with Frederick the Wise, he moved on to the university on the Elbe, where he arrived on August 25, 1518, and he was no doubt well received. Friedensburg points out that because of Philip's young and childlike appearance, there may have been some doubts about the elector's appointment.[213] All this was soon to turn into admiration when the faculty and students were to realize what a great Gräcist and humanistic scholar he really was.

As was then customary in German universities, new professors delivered an *Antrittsrede*, announcing their plans for the future. Such an introductory lecture was usually delivered in the *Aula* from a Katheder, in the presence of the rector and the whole institution, just like the professorial lectures in the Castle Church. Such events began with a university procession, an event of great significance, which the entire student body was obligated to attend. After four days Melanchthon was ready to deliver his first public address in his new alma mater. After meeting Frederick in Augsburg, Philip must have given much thought to his historic *Antrittsrede*. In fact, he may have made some early drafts of the speech on the way. Historians in the texts on the history of education have cited this famous address, which really announced his whole academic career at Wittenberg for four decades. Even the title must have intrigued Luther, *Concerning the Improvement of the Studies of the Youth*, as it fitted in so nicely with his own biblical humanism which he had initiated at the *Leucuria* with the assistance of the Electoral Court. But the address took the entire faculty and student body by surprise, as it contained so many epoch-making promises. The message fitted so well into what the Electoral Court had already initiated and what the reformer and his fellow-minded professors were attempting, and it placed the elector in a fine light for making such an excellent appointment. The Wittenberg students must also have been elated to learn they could now pursue their new studies in the *Studia humanitatis* at the *Leucuria* already in progress, which Philip had promised to bring to fruition. In his address, Melanchthon had delivered some powerful blows against scholasticism, which he now wanted to replace with new humanistic studies. Philip praised the theological faculty and the Electoral Court for having introduced Greek and Hebrew in the study of theology.[214] In his message Philip pointed out what fine linguistic learning existed in the early Christian church, which meanwhile had been perverted by the scholastics in the Middle Ages. They created a false Aristotle and a dialectics that really was no system but a perversion of logic, and was of no service to true learning. At this point he deplored how this whole system of false learning had enveloped the whole European world for many centuries with its perverse method of instruction. He stressed that the pulpits of the Roman Church had been filled with a clergy who extolled this false system of learning and misled their parishes. He praised the Wittenberg students, for now they could drink from the sources in the original languages; and now Aristotle was allowed to speak directly to readers in his own original Greek language, without some professor interpreting him in lecture halls. Lectures could now be delivered on Quintilian and Pliny, and also the poets and oratory, while mathematics had now become a discipline of its own. In the study of the Holy Scriptures, students no longer needed glosses and the commentaries of others, but could now enter the true sources of our faith and really understand the Holy Scriptures. After the discovery of divine revelation in the original, reforms are possible, with the elevation of the church to its former status at the time of the Fathers.[215] It was the true message of the future of the German Reformation.

On the same day Martin Luther dashed off a letter full of enthusiasm to Georg Spalatin in the court, expressing his pleasure concerning the new Greek professor, and offering this reaction: "As long as we have Melanchthon, I care for no other Greek instructor."[216] Later he wrote another letter to John Lang at Erfurt about young Philip: "He seems like a boy when one considers his age, but a man of our age (35), when one considers the versatility of the man and his knowledge of books.[217]

Melanchthon had never met Luther, whom he now learned to know for the first time. No doubt they had some interesting conversations after they first met. Philip seems to have been deeply impressed, and liked Luther as much as the reformer liked Philip, for he wrote John Lang at Erfurt, their mutual friend, "If there is anything on earth I love, it is Martin and his pious writings; but above anything else, I love Martin himself."[218] He spoke of Luther as the *Streiter Gottes*, the battler for God. After a little longer acquaintance, he praised Luther even more, making the claim: "Never was there a greater man on the face of the earth, I would rather die than sever myself from that man."[219]

Philip Melanchthon's first address to the University of Wittenberg was not just an empty expression to please an audience; he was ready to back up his convictions with the support of the Reformation for the next forty-two years. Friedensburg points out that Philip now joined Luther in his battle with Rome. During the debate with John Eck in 1519, he got into the battle supporting the reformer, even though he was aware of his own possible fate. During the Reformation, Luther had no closer friend and warmer supporter of his cause than Philip. He and Luther were such close friends that they had even had an underground passageway between the Black Cloister and the Melanchthon house, and he and Luther spent many pleasant hours at a stone table in Philip's backyard over a Stein of beer. As will be seen later, Luther even became one of the students in Philip's Greek classes, to improve his mastery of the language; while Luther persuaded Philip to study theology; he took a *Biblicus* degree in 1519 and began offering courses in the Holy Scriptures. Melanchthon played a leading role in the reorganization of the university, serving with Luther in advising Spalatin and the elector in the school's curricula changes by the introduction of the *Studia humanitatis* of the institution and introducing trilingual course offerings in Latin, Greek, and Hebrew.[220] While Luther was tied up with Bible translations and controlling the course of the Reformation, Melanchthon became the chief pedagogical advisor and academic reformer of the university for the next four decades.[221]

Melanchthon's key role in the academic program at Wittenberg was the improvement of the linguistic instruction, especially in the mastery of Greek for their future theologians in the study of the New Testament in the school of theology. But as the institution had some difficulty in the establishment of a professorship in Hebrew, that load also fell upon Melanchthon as well. In the early years, Philip taught Greek grammar and exegesis and lectured on Homer; then, upon Luther's request, he delivered exegetical lectures on the New Testament. This fitted in well with his training of students in Greek, for there he could make use of the original texts which he had printed for his courses. As he was the leading spirit in the liberal arts school, he also supplied his students with an edition of Plutarch to improve their mastery of the classics. He also published a new translation of Lucian's *Calumnia*, as well as a Latin edition of Aristophanes' *Clouds*, all done from the Greek, to acquaint his student with a classical background, as well as offering courses in the exegesis of the New Testament. Then, in 1520, when the professor Aesticampanius died, Philip was ready to teach his course in Pliny and temporarily drop his lectures on *Romans*, as the court had requested. This Luther did not exactly regard as a satisfactory solution.[222]

The introduction of Greek and Hebrew courses in the Wittenberg curricula was not sufficient for the needs of the student body. As the *Leucuria* was scholastically oriented, it forced students to master the philosophy of Aristotle in order to advance academically towards degrees. The study of scholastic philosophy occupied practically all of a student's time, which left little for the study of Greek and Hebrew as electives. Both Luther and Melanchthon realized that this could not continue, and some fundamental curricula changes seemed imperative. Now that Luther had dethroned Aristotle, students were tired of the Stagirite's *Ethics*, as it was hostile to future biblical studies. Naturally Luther took this matter to the Saxon Court. Already on September 2, 1518, the reformer wrote Georg Spalatin about these necessary changes:

> We are offering the most useful courses, and the young people are very enthusiastic in regard to the Holy Scriptures and real Theology; but they cannot follow their real inclinations without interruption because the old courses are still required for their examinations. We beg you, therefore, that Aristotle's *Ethics*, which is as hostile towards theology as the wolf to the lamb, be taken from the list of required courses.[223]

Accordingly a plan was initiated to reorganize the university's curricula in 1520, in which Aristotle's *Physics, Metaphysics,* and *Ethics* were all dropped, while his courses in *Logic, Rhetoric,* and *Poetry* were to be continued, which the faculty regarded as useful for the development of eloquence for future clergy. Canon law was also to be discontinued, which limited instruction in the school of law to feudal law, based on the *Saxonspiegel,* and *Swabenspiegel,* the medieval customary feudal law codes of Northern and Southern Germany; and the civil law, the *Corpus iuris* of the *Code of Justinian.* The dropping of canon law created a vacuum which could not immediately be corrected, as we shall see, until in the thirties a new *Landeskirchenrecht* began to replace the laws dealing with family life and human relations in society, formerly controlled by the Roman Church. Now Latin, Greek, and Hebrew were to be stressed in liberal arts, in order that students might understand the lectures of Luther and Melanchthon in courses on the Holy Scriptures. Such planning was quite ambitious, and its fruition could not be fully realized until Melanchthon's deanship in 1523.[224]

The arrival of Philip Melanchthon in 1518 seems to have inspired a large number in the student body and strengthened the school's cause in introducing courses in Greek into the institution. Georg Spalatin, who visited Wittenberg in the cause of its library, came there on December 3–7. He visited Melanchthon's classroom and found that around 500 to 600 students were in attendance, which number required the *Aula* in the *New Friderici Collegium;* while Martin Luther had around 400 students in the crowded *Grosse Hörsaal* of the Black Cloister in his theological lectures.[225] Spalatin had also observed that the Town Church was filled to overflowing on Sundays by students eager to hear the gospel sermons.

As seen previously, the following dramatic series of events in the reformer's life in his battle with Rome brought much difficulty for Melanchthon.[226] First came the Leipzig Debate, then the papal bull *Exsurge Domine,* the Edict of Worms, the final bull *Decet,* the Articles of Condemnation by the University of Paris, and then Luther's abduction and protection at the Wartburg by the elector. As though this were not enough, Carlstadt and the Wittenberg disturbances tended to undo the Reformation. All this was too much for young Melanchthon, who amid the wild destruction was not ready to enter the pulpit and stop the confusion. Yet Philip tried to carry on the reforms instituted. Upon receiving his *Biblicus* degree in 1519, he offered 28 lecture courses on the Bible between 1519 and 1529.[227] In this, as a Greek scholar, the young exegete did it very methodically by the use of printed texts with dictionaries at the end, thus using the original Greek texts as a basis for his New Testament exegesis. This even impressed Luther, as Philip was such an expert in the original Greek of the Bible.

Thomas Blarer, then a student there observing the new trends at Wittenberg, has left us an interesting description of how Luther and Philip worked together, not just in exegetical activities but also in religious guidance of their students:

Recently I confessed to Luther, who has warned us to attend communion. Formerly we confessed to Melanchthon, who has given himself entirely to the study of the Holy Scriptures, to which he is attempting to lead the students. The result is there are practically no students, who do not go around with a Bible in hand, which is a fact that has even impressed myself. Luther is lecturing on the Psalter, while Melanchthon is lecturing on St. Paul. Melanchthon is, so to say, Luther's traveling companion in Christ. The same enthusiasm unites the two, the same reliability as scholars, the same working together in all undertakings and teaching.[228]

On another occasion, Thomas Blaurer seems to have been in a particularly joyful mood, in which he expressed his happiness about coming to the university on the Elbe to study the Holy Scriptures, and to be now privileged to hear Luther expounding the Bible:

I consider myself fortunate, that under God's guidance, I have come to the place, where, it seems to me, one learns the Christian religion right; and where the only man is living who really understands the Bible, a fact which I daily witness here.[229]

During this same period, another student from Rothenburg ob der Tauber, Johann Hornburg, wrote to a Leipzig student named Althamer, that at the *Leucuria* he was beginning to learn all over again and that he wished he had come there earlier.[230] And a third student, Felix Ulscenius, who was a friend of Capito in Strassburg, expressed himself rather freely about the Wittenberg environment and the university. He pointed out that in the city on the Elbe, the center of things was Martin Luther, whom he regarded as the powerful interpreter of the Word of God. He added that he had the same high regard for Luther's exegesis in the classroom as his eloquent, polished sermons in the pulpit. Hence, he observed, no fellow Augustinian missed an opportunity of crowding into the little chapel near the Black Cloister to hear him. Therefore his fellow travelers regarded themselves fortunate to be his contemporaries, who was really leading the world back to the gospel.[231]

As students had a very high regard for Luther, they likewise loved Philip Melanchthon and his lectures, who interpreted the classics with much learning and interpreted the Holy Bible from Greek texts. As an aside he also expressed himself on Wittenberg's environment. The regions around the Luther town are unattractive and the citizens are mostly uneducated persons with a lack of real culture; yet their tables are not lacking in food, which is really abundant, but they appear to have no knowledge of different German wines.[232]

From the above evidence of student observation, the University of Wittenberg had undergone quite a transformation by 1520–1521 under the two capable leaders who had transformed the *Leucuria* from a scholastically oriented institution into one in which biblical humanism had triumphed. But there was still one aspect that needed the attention of the Electoral Court. Melanchthon so far had met the needs of instruction in Greek and Hebrew, but what Wittenberg still needed was a permanent chair in Hebrew to prepare students to study the Old Testament in the original texts. Upon the thorough investigations of Gustav Bauch, we are able to explore the early attempts and difficulties that the Saxon Court encountered to introduce Hebrew on a firm, permanent basis at Wittenberg. Luther and Melanchthon believed Hebrew professors should not just teach it as a language, but that Hebrew should also be taught as a medium of unlocking the deeper, hidden, divine revelations of the Holy Scriptures.

INTRODUCTION OF A PROFESSORSHIP IN HEBREW

As previously observed in earlier chapters of the *Leucorea*, in the coverage of humanism, there had been some Hebrew instruction there from the very beginning by Professor Marschalk and his students as an elective, but the university had no regular professorship in Hebrew. Nor is it correct to hold that no Hebrew was taught as a language at other German universities. The great linguistic scholar Gustav Bauch, at the beginning of this century, has still not been surpassed in his humanistic studies of Greek and Hebrew in European Universities. Bauch makes the observation that Wittenberg was the first institution of higher learning in Germany to establish Hebrew on a permanent and lasting foundation.[233]

Gustav Bauch's research about the study of Hebrew in German universities dates far back to the days of the Reform Councils at the close of the Middle Ages; yet this study must be limited to a few observations.[234] In the fifteenth century the study of Hebrew had a different orientation from that of Luther's day. Nicholas von Lyra wanted Hebrew taught in the universities to train clergymen who could preach to Jews in their own language and convert them to Christianity; while, later at Wittenberg, Luther and Melanchthon wanted Hebrew taught as a language per se, but as a medium for better exegesis of the Old Testament.[235]

Spain was a promising field for Jewish conversions long before the Spanish Inquisition. The order of the Dominican Vincente Ferrer battled against Judaism, while King Ferdinand of Aragon arranged for a disputation in 1413 between Jews and the Catholic clergy at Tortosa. The fascinating Vincente preached to masses of Jews under an open sky. After their conversion, some Jews even attempted to convince their countrymen that the Talmud supported messianic claims of Christianity.[236] This reference to the Talmud backfired when, on May 11, 1415, Pope Benedict XIII forbade Christian reading of the Talmud. He ordered that henceforth Jews in Spain were to listen to Catholic sermons three times yearly.[237]

The issue of Jewish conversions was also a topic of discussion at the Council of Basel, in 1434, perhaps upon the request of converted Jews in attendance. According to the opinion of the Council's members, Catholic universities in the West were to offer instruction in Greek, Arabic, Hebrew, and Chaldean, so they would graduate priests who could address Jewish congregations in their own language.[238] A good illustration is the case Petrus Nigri, or Peter Schwarz, who was an enthusiastic Thomist from Knaaden in Bohemia; he associated with learned Bohemian nobles like Bohuslav von Loblowitz and Hassenstein, and was a friendly neighbor.[239] Peter Nigri had studied at Montpilier, Salamanca, and Freiburg im Breisgau, and was well-versed in Hebrew and Chaldean. He challenged Jewish rabbis to engage in a public debate, in Regensburg, Frankfurt am Main, Worms, and Nürnberg, in 1478, but no Jews were willing to debate with him. After that Prince Ludwig of Bavaria became involved, as well as Bishop Heinrich III, and they placed a Catholic parish in the middle of a Jewish settlement in Regensburg. They placed Petrus Nigri in charge of converting the Jewish section, but to their surprise, not a Jew came to be baptized.[240] Peter Schwarz now published a book in Hebrew, which later was studied by John Reuchlin, Konrad Pellican, and Bartholomeus Kaiser, all later Hebrew scholars. The latter Hebrew scholar later applied for the position in Wittenberg. Thus the study of Hebrew and related languages had quite a long history before Wittenberg was attempting to establish a professorship in the Hebrew language, so students could understand lectures on the Old Testament.

While Luther and the Electoral Court were very successful in the establishment of a professorship in Greek and filling it with very able Philip Melanchthon in 1518, the filling of a new post in Hebrew proved to be another matter and offered a number of difficulties. But the *Leucuria* kept pressing for such an appointment, when Luther wrote Georg Spalatin the following letter:

> I also ask that before leaving, you sound out the opinion of the Most Illustrious Sovereign concerning a professor of Hebrew and let me know what he thinks. John Keller from Burgkundstadt (Cellarius Gnostopolitanus) has been with us; he plans to leave shortly. He taught Hebrew at Heidelberg and is the author of a small grammar (Introduction to Hebrew), in which I believe he has excelled. He has promised to do everything in his power to be a reliable teacher, in case he could be certain that he would receive an adequate salary from the Most Illustrious Sovereign. At the moment he is in Leipzig awaiting our answer. Therefore, please reply promptly.[241]

Luther's request from the court came at the most inopportune time, as Frederick the Wise was just departing for the *Kaiserwahl*, in 1519, at Frankfurt am Main, for the election of a new German Kaiser, and an immediate reply could hardly be expected.

The proposed Hebrew professor was the humanist John Keller, a man but moderately qualified in comparison with others. Keller had moved around considerably during his career, having taught at Louvain, Mainz, Tübingen, and Heidelberg for short periods. Luther apparently was not too enthusiastic about his appointment in his statement, "He does know something in his field." While Melanchthon, who knew him from his Tübingen days, was even less impressed.[242] The affair with Keller dragged on and on, until finally he was offered a salary of $3,750, which was less money than he received in Leipzig, where he was already employed.[243]

Meanwhile Melanchthon remained overloaded with teaching both Greek and Hebrew, along with his publications and other activities. On September 16, 1518, Luther wrote John Lang in Erfurt that Philip was a most erudite man in being able to teach both Greek and Hebrew, but that he was not as versed in Hebrew literature as in the Greek.[244] One can realize how relieved Philip was when he learned that now Johann Böschenstein would soon assume the position of Professor of Hebrew. Luther had received word from Böschenstein, and informed Philip that help was on the way. At the time, Luther happened to be away from Wittenberg for his interview with Cardinal Cajetan in Augsburg, where he had learned about the Böschenstein appointment through Carlstadt in Wittenberg.[245]

Johann Böschenstein was the second trial-run professor in Hebrew at the university to fill the new professorship. He was born in Ezzlingen, Germany, in 1472, and by now was 47 years old and 11 years Luther's senior. The elector had contacted John Reuchlin for possible candidates to fill the Wittenberg vacancy, but Böschenstein was not among those he had recommended. This Jewish scholar had taught for a while at Ingolstadt and had given private Hebrew instruction in Augsburg. Among his students were Dr. Kaspar Ammon, Sebastian Speranticus of Denkelsbühl, Johann Eck, and Andreas Osiander. He had also published an elementary book in Hebrew by 1514, upon the recommendation of John Reuchlin.[246]

While Martin Luther was in Augsburg for the Cajetan hearing, in 1518, he finalized the Böschenstein appointment while in the city, in which contract the elector agreed to pay him an annual salary of $4,500.[247] Soon after that, on October 11, Luther wrote Melanchthon about the appointment and said that he could learn the details from Carlstadt.[248] Upon receiving the good news Melanchthon was looking forward to working with the new Hebrew scholar. He even purchased some Hebrew Bibles and planned on a joint publication of the Proverbs of Solomon, with necessary *Scholien*, as he did in his New Testament lectures.[249] Luther had also hoped the new professor would prove to be very helpful in Bible interpretations.

The new Hebrew professor did not turn out to be very useful, but rather a real disappointment to the faculty. He did not last long, for already early in 1519, Böschenstein requested a leave of absence and never returned. He proved to be a kind of misfit. For students who were just beginning to learn Hebrew, he did not seem to come down to their level. Therefore as an introductory teacher in Hebrew he proved to be a disappointment. Nor did he seem to fit into the new Wittenberg program of biblical humanism, and could not engage the faculty in private discussions about university goals. He was a quiet, aloof type, and was difficult to reach. But Friedensburg added that he privately worked hard on a new Hebrew grammar, which he dedicated to the elector.[250] Luther was disappointed, because Hebrew instruction as Böschenstein wanted to teach it was limited to Hebrew as a language, and not its use in biblical exegesis; while Greek was taught by Melanchthon as it applied to New Testament interpretation.[251] Luther apparently discussed the matter with the Hebrew professor, for he observed that everything that he and Philip regarded as being important in the use of the Hebrew for Old Testament interpretation, the Jewish professor regarded as being unimportant to him, in fact even worthless.[252] The Weimar Edition editors state that the differences between the Hebrew professor and the reformer were due to the fact that Luther wanted to use Hebrew to interpret the Holy Scriptures in the original, while Böschenstein wanted to teach Hebrew as a Semitic language and teach students to converse in the language.[253]

The Wittenberg faculty seemed relieved to have Böschenstein depart, as Luther hoped to employ one of his students, Bartholomäus Kaiser, but that also failed to materialize. The institution really would have been retarded in Hebrew studies, had Melanchthon not stepped in to serve as an interim substitute. The atmosphere in Wittenberg must have had its impact on Böschenstein, for he later joined the Reformation and married, even though he was a clergyman. He died in 1540.[254]

After that the Electoral Court attempted again to hire another baptized Jew as a Hebrew instructor, Johannes Callerius, of Kundstadt from Upper Franconia, who had good credentials, but at the last minute he decided to join the Leipzig faculty, their first establishment of a chair in Hebrew. After that Wittenberg had to use a man named Bernard von Göppingen, as a Hebrew instructor, between the summer of 1519 and Easter in 1520, a good reliable person, but not very strong in academic background.[255]

The last Jewish professor whom the university employed from among the traveling Hebraists was Matthaus Adrianus from Spain. According to Gustav Bauch, Adrian was a native of Spain, but whether he was expelled from there during the Inquisition in 1492 remains unknown.[256] John Reuchlin claimed he was baptized a Christian, which is supported with much other evidence. He had learned enough Hebrew as a young man to qualify as a good teacher of the language, but like so many of his fellow Jews, he decided to study medicine and become a doctor. The evidence of Adrian's earlier years is very fragmentary.[257] According to Conrad Pellikan, who studied under him, Adrian appeared first in Basel, and instructed the sons of the famous Basel printer Amerbach in Hebrew; he became very intimate with the family and the printer took him into his own home. Pellikan claims the Spanish Jew was an excellent Hebrew tutor; from whom he had learned much about the language.[258] His stay in Basel did last several years, when in 1513 he moved on to Strassburg, where he became Pellikan's teacher for a while; then he went to Heidelberg, where he tutored several students until 1516, two of whom we will encounter later as well-known reformers, Johannes Brenz of Swabish-Hal, and Johann Oecolampadius, the later reformer in Basel of the Swiss camp.[259] History reveals little about this period of Adrian's life, his reasons for going to Heidelberg, and his later departure.

Later he went to Luttich, teaching Berselius in Hebrew, who happened to be a friend of Erasmus, through whom Adrian then obtained a letter of introduction to Erasmus of Rotterdam, then at Louvain. This message on September 17, 1517, must have come just at the opportune time. A rich friend of Erasmus, Hironymus Buslidius, had endowed a new chair at Louvain University with

20,000 Franken, to establish a trilingual college at the institution, and Erasmus was to select the proper professor to head the *collegium trilingue*, and he now naturally recommended Matthäus Adrianus to become the professor in Hebrew.[260]

At the beginning, matters in the trilingual college seem to have moved quite smoothly. Erasmus was full of praise of Adrian's learning and his importance. He spoke of him as a friend of John Reuchlin and the friendly Capito in Strassburg. But on March 21, 1519, when Adrian delivered his *Antrittsrede*, he emphasized the importance of Greek and Hebrew for a good theologian, which offended some of the scholastics in the theological faculty. As it turned out, the conservative theologians at Louvain did not even favor the new movement of Erasmus. What made matters worse, Adrian was the type who loved to needle conservative theologians. The humanist stated that St. Jerome was just an ordinary man, which the later Luther enemy, Latomus, and his kind could not tolerate. As a result, Latomus published a *Schmähschrift*, a tract in which he attacked Adrian.[261] Nor was this Erasmus' only problem, who had previously praised Adrian shortly before with Oecolampadius, when he learned the Hebrew professor was in financial difficulties with Capito. Gustav Bauch claims that men like Adrian faced monetary problems, often leaving without paying their debts, a fact which even offended Dorpius, the leader of his supporters. Erasmus now soured on Adrian as rapidly as their previous friendship had begun.[262] Thus after the attack by Latomus, Adrian was through at Louvain, and had to look elsewhere for a new position to teach Hebrew.

Meanwhile, at Wittenberg, Luther and Melanchthon were looking around for a good Hebrew professor. They had learned from Gregory Kopp, a house physician of Cardinal Albert of Mainz, to consider the employment of the Jewish convert, Werner Einhorn, who might be available.[263] Thus when Adrian contacted Luther, it meant they had now two possibilities, without any certainty of getting either. Since the Einhorn investigation was already under way, no answer could be given to Adrian until the former possible employment of the previous candidate was settled. Thus Luther had written Adrian to wait eight days, so he could in the meantime contact the Electoral Court.[264] Luther pressed Spalatin for an immediate answer about the possible employment of Werner Einhorn, the possible candidate for their professorship in Hebrew, which he expressed in a humorous vein:

> In the whole affair we must be extremely careful that, as the saying goes, in trying to sit on two chairs, we do not fall between them. This could be a case in which, if we turn down one, the other one might by chance go somewhere else, either of his own accord, or, because he was employed by Mainz. Many friends have strongly urged me to hire Mathew, at least for a period of one year.[265]

Philip Melanchthon also appears to have preferred Adrian as their future Hebrew professor.[266] Negotiations continued, so that by April 30, 1520, Luther was able to write Capito that the elector had hired Adrian as their Hebrew professor for a salary of $7,500 per annum.[267] The new Hebrew professor arrived in Wittenberg when the student peak enrollment had occurred prior to the Diet of Worms, in 1521. By that time the city was overcrowded with students and also the *Vorstätter*, the neighboring little villages. Not a satisfactory room was to be found anywhere for the Hebrew professor. Luther even wrote to the Saxon Court that the overcrowded little Wittenberg could offer no satisfactory facilities for the Hebraist.[268] Adrian still did not have a place to stay by May 5, 1520.[269] Luther and Melanchthon attempted to accommodate the Hebrew professor by inviting him into their homes and to eat at their tables, but even then he proved difficult to please. Luther found him to be impolite, and inconsiderate of others; he would have liked to move out some students to accommodate him. But to have Adrian as a regular boarder meant quite an additional expense for Luther and Melanchthon, whose salaries at the time were quite modest. On May 1, 1520, Luther wrote Spalatin, asking whether the court might not supply them with two or three extra Gulden to defray their additional expenses for a cost of living.[270] Adrian must also have been unhappy living under such conditions, for he spent much of his time at the Lucas Cranach *Apoteke*, at the north corner of the town marketplace.[271]

The Hebrew professor was pleased with the zeal to learn Hebrew of the Wittenberg students. In contrast at Louvain, he had found students needed to be spurred on to study the biblical language of the Old Testament, while at Wittenberg he had to control their enthusiasm. Now he could publish his Louvain *Antrittsrede*, in which high praise was extended to Spalatin and the elector. In it he praised the court preacher, comparing him to Erasmus in his zeal to further linguistic studies, as opposed to the ones of the Sophists, while the elector was portrayed as the patron of true learning.[272]

Adrian was anxious to continue his private research, for which he needed the necessary Hebrew source material, about which he approached Luther,[273] and later, also Spalatin.[274] He wanted them to contact a Probst Busso von Alversleben in Brandenburg, who must have been in a position to offer him the desired literature. Before the research material arrived, the impatient Adrian went in person to Brandenburg to get the sources.[275] Whether the housing shortage was a reason remains unknown, but by June 1520, the Hebrew professor became married, to the great surprise of his friends. They all, however, wished the couple well for the future.[276]

Soon after that, however, the good relationship between the Hebrew professor and the faculty became estranged, and especially between Luther and Adrian. Why the change took place was not made a matter of record. The Hebrew professor had quite a high opinion of himself and was too free in his criticism of others. His most serious mistake was that he began to criticize the reformer's sermons, which, in the face of Luther's reputation as a preacher among citizens, was certainly not the expression of much wisdom. Adrian, though a baptized Jew, had never outgrown the Mosaic law, for he criticized Luther's theology of the cross, namely, that "The Just shall live by faith." In a report to the Saxon Court, Luther related the situation in a humorous vein, when he observed that the Jew wanted to instruct him on the gospel, when he did not even understand his Old Testament, nor the termination of the law of Moses.[277] In his complaint about the turn of events to Spalatin, he added: "I have done nothing to the man."[278] Gustav Bauch believes Adrian's intentions may even have been deeper:

> Adrian attacked the doctrine of justification, and in case he would not have been held back, would also have the evil desire to attack Luther publicly. He had a sharp encounter with Luther, so that Luther explained to Spalatin that this 'most uninformed man in matters of theology' was no longer of any use to them and to remove him at once.[279]

Adrian must have been aware which way the wind was blowing, for the Weimar editors added that the Hebrew professor asked for his release, which was immediately granted.[280] What happened to Adrian and his new wife is no longer known. Even Bauch, in all his exhaustive research, failed to discover where he went, whether to Leipzig, or to Freiburg im Breisgau on the Rhine.[281] Luther and Melanchthon were no doubt relieved by the departure of this trouble-maker.

Luther and Melanchthon by now must have been somewhat disillusioned about hiring converted Jews to teach students Hebrew and a proper exegesis of the Holy Scriptures. Luther immediately recommended a fellow Wittenberger, Mathäus Goldhahn, more commonly known by his humanistic name Aurogallus, to replace Adrian as the Hebrew professor.[282] Melanchthon's reaction was that they had relied long enough on travelling converted Jews to fill the professorship in Hebrew. Philip said he regarded Adrian to be a pseudo-Christian, who had done nothing but create trouble in the little republic.[283] Melanchthon agreed with Luther that it would be better for the university to not depend on Jewish teachers unknown to them, and he also favored hiring Aurogallus; they had known him for a long time and had observed his abilities in Latin, Greek, and Hebrew. Philip added that he had personally witnessed Matthäus' interpretations of Hebrew texts and observed his writings in that language.[284]

All this had just occurred at the time when Martin Luther was summoned to the Diet of Worms in 1521, to appear before Kaiser Charles V and German Estates of the Empire. The elector was already there, awaiting Luther's arrival and the outcome. Thus to expect an immediate appointment of Aurogallus was out of the question. However, on June 17, 1521, Graf Wolfgang, then the rector of the university, and Melanchthon came to the support of the appointment of the Hebraist, and Matthäus Goldhahn was appointed as the new Hebrew Professor of *Leucuria*.[285]

Wittenberg could not have made a better choice in its appointment of Aurogallus. Even though young, with a lack of academic experience, the new Hebraist was soon to prove himself; for by 1523 he published his first book, *Compendium Hebräae Grammaticus*, and he enlarged it with Aramaic additions in 1525. After that he also published a *Hebrew Lexicon* by 1526. Upon Luther's return from his captivity in the Wartburg, where he had translated the

New Testament into German by 1522, he continued to translate the Old Testament in sections, and Aurogallus was of great assistance in some of the difficult Hebrew parts until 1531. Then, when Luther felt the need for further refinement, he called upon a number of the school's faculty specialists to prepare even better editions of the German Bible between 1534 and 1545. Aurogallus served as the Hebrew professor, along with Cruciger in Aramaic. Melanchthon in Greek, and Bugenhagen in Latin. In all these sessions, held in the *Luther-zimmer* of the reformer, Aurogallus served as a capable Hebraist in Luther's translations of the Old Testament.

Now Wittenberg had achieved what Luther and Melanchthon had hoped could happen; namely, the institution now had permanent chairs in Greek and Hebrew by two able scholars, so that in the future the students could learn the two sacred languages of the Bible at the college level and be properly prepared for graduate study in theology, law, and medicine.

23

The New
Reformation University

❖

The original University of Wittenberg, founded by Frederick the Wise in 1502, was modeled after the Universities of Paris and Bologna. This typical medieval university, like its predecessors, was scholastically oriented and quite similar to other German institutions of higher learning; this pattern continued until the second decade of the sixteenth century. But the university began to undergo very radical changes when Martin Luther was given the position of *Lectura in Biblia* by the Dean of Theology, Johann von Staupitz, the Vicar of the Order of the Augustinian Hermits. Luther began the series of lectures on the *Psalms, Romans, Galatians* and *Hebrews* in 1513–1518, during which he had his *Turmerlebnis,* in which he discovered the true meaning of *Iustitia Dei* and then developed into the reformer, who through biblical humanism transformed the university curricula, dethroning Aristotle by winning the assistance of the whole Wittenberg faculty to the support of his "Theology of the Cross." In this changed curricula, Greek and Hebrew were introduced with the assistance of Philip Melanchthon after 1518. Thus the Reformation, which was born in the heart of Martin Luther, spread to the entire Wittenberg faculty. In the twenties, Luther and Melanchthon began to transform the academic side of the institution, paving the way for what transpired in the thirties under Elector John Frederick in 1533–1536. Thus the Reformation caused a gradual change in the original institution, making it into a new University of Wittenberg that created a whole new atmosphere throughout Europe by the spreading of the gospel and the creation of Evangelical churches oriented around the early Christian church with its ecumenical creeds. Thus the new University of Wittenberg became the very center of the German Reformation out of which streamed thousands of students and reformers to spread Wittenberg's "New Theology" through German lands and all over the European continent.

The young Prince John Frederick was extremely well qualified to take over the reign of Electoral Saxony and the furtherance of the University of Witten-

481

berg when his father died in 1532, since from his youth he had been a faithful follower of Martin Luther and a strong champion of the spread of the gospel throughout Europe. When his father was on his deathbed, he impressed upon his son in his last will the solemn wish that he assist the University of Wittenberg in whatever way possible, as in it there had arisen in recent times the powerful Word of God, through the reformer Martin Luther and Philip Melanchthon. John Frederick then could not foresee the generosity he would expend in its future. Thus John Frederick decided that he would, with the assistance of the Wittenberg faculty, establish what needed to be done to make Wittenberg University the kind of institution he wanted it to be. Thus with the assistance of the court lawyers and university reports, his new *Fundungsbrief*, Foundation Document, which we must examine and describe in some detail.[1]

The foundation of the University of Wittenberg, in which the German Reformation could mature and spread into all parts of Europe, was no small undertaking. First it required an analysis of the school's entire faculty and students. Besides, this enlarged university called for an increased endowment which would furnish the institution a stable income in the future. To have a good faculty meant there would have to be an increased salary scale, desirable course offerings, and a better managed, enlarged University Library.[2]

After John Frederick became the Elector he visited Wittenberg to discuss the status of the University with leading faculty members, after the devastation wrought by radical reformers such as Carlstadt and the Zwickau Prophets, by stopping theological promotions, disputations, and declamations. Moreover, after a discussion with Luther and other seminary professors, the Elector directed that they draft the *Statutes of 1533* for a new theological school that would educate theologians in accordance with the standards of the German Reformation. On that same visit, Elector John Frederick ordered the restoration of degrees in theology leading to the doctorate; the new practice was initiated by promoting three doctoral candidates in the Castle Church in which the Elector and his wife participated. This new school of theology was then later incorporated in the *Statutes of 1536.*

Before reorganizing the whole University of Wittenberg, some preparatory work was necessary, which was assigned to Chancellor Brück. Before he could draft the *Fundationsurkunde of 1536,* Chancellor Brück had to gather the necessary data for the proper founding of the New University. This material he started to gather in 1535 by writing the Wittenberg faculty as to the present faculty salaries, the personnel then in the Liberal Arts College, and the Graduate Schools of Theology, Law, and Medicine, so as to arrive at what was really involved in the undertaking.[3] Once all this preliminary investigation and codification had been done, the Elector was ready to found a new University of Wittenberg in 1536.

In a communication of April 30, 1536, from Torgau, the Elector John Frederick informed Spalatin that he planned to come to Wittenberg the next week for the Foundation of the University of Wittenberg and that he wished Spalatin to appear and others he wished to bring, which foundation exercises would occur on Thursday and Friday, May 4 and 5, 1536.[4] The Spalatin delegation must have arrived as scheduled, for the Elector issued his *Fundationsurkunde of 1536* on May 5, 1536.[5]

The Foundation document opens with an introduction, in which the Elector John Frederick begins with praise of his uncle Frederick the Wise, who with the assistance of Almighty God, "founded the original University to His honor and praise in the Electoral Town of Wittenberg in 1502, during the reign of Emperor Maximilian I, now held in thankful memory by us all." He also expressed his gratitude that he staffed the school with a courageous and able faculty, trained in all the disciplines, learned and experienced, which the Elector supported with all enthusiasm and energy to his end. After that he turned to Martin Luther and Philip Melanchthon for having created the background for his now gracious founding of the new University of Wittenberg:

> Because the Gracious God, under praiseworthy conditions and circumstances, has restored His divine saving Word through the teachings of the honorable highly educated man, our dear, worthy of remembrance, Doctor of the Holy Scriptures, Martin Luther; which teachings, in these last times of the world, he has brought forth, and with really Christian understanding, which has become the blessing to all people, of which in all eternity, we must offer him praise and thanks. Likewise God has allowed to appear in all richness and graciousness the languages of Latin, Greek and Hebrew, among other Liberal Arts, through the special, outstanding ability and energy, of our highly educated and dear Master, Philip Melanchthon, which languages serve for the furthering of Law and Christian understanding of the Holy Scriptures.[6]

Then in his *Foundation of 1536,* the Elector once more returns to his father's "Last Will," who was no less moved through the grace of God when he wanted to preserve the spread of the saving Word of God of the Holy Gospel. John Frederick therefore asked Spalatin to support the Institution of Higher Learning at Wittenberg and its faculty and wished for this to continue with future Electors of Saxony. He then stated that he and his brother Johann Ernst feel deeply obligated to support his father's "Last Testament" and to obey his will for the spreading of the Gospel and also to develop a liberal Christian education through the Liberal Arts, and of Christian living, for in this respect the new university could be of real service in the Christian secular society. The Elector then stated that therefore he had resolved, in the name of Almighty God, to further the above causes by his reforming the university and establishing praiseworthy ordinances for its future. Thus there would be no problems about its future endowment. The Elector closed his introductory statement by placing the same obligations upon his successors—that they must protect the University of Wittenberg against all future enemies of the Word of God.[7]

By 1533 the Elector had already visited the University, to determine the institution's needs for a complete reorientation of the University; after a discussion with the Reformer and then the seminary faculty, the doctoral promotions were restored and the School of Theology was given the *Statutes of 1533,* which changes were now bodily incorporated as part of the new foundation of the university.

After the Elector's introduction, the *Fundationsurkunde* begins with the new regulations relative to the School of Theology. The new Graduate School of Theology was now to consist of six faculty members—where in the *Statutes of 1536* there had been but four. The roles of Luther and Melanchthon were not clearly defined because of their other duties and the Elector did not wish to overburden them. The new Seminary staff was to consist of the full-time professors, while the fourth, Bugenhagen as the Town Pastor, was to carry only a part-time load as he would be busy with the regular ministry. The three regular professors were to be obligated to lecture regularly on Monday, Tuesday, Thursday, and Friday. But the full schedule of courses offered was limited in the case of the third, as he was also to be the regular *Schloszpredige* who had to preach twice a week, on Wednesdays and Sundays. And finally, the pastor of the *Stadtkirche*, who was a member of the university theological faculty in only a limited sense, was regarded as too busy for a full load of lecturing because of his many other duties. According to the *Statutes of 1533*, the qualifications of a faculty member were acquaintance with the "doctrines of the Church," the testimony of the Church Fathers in their interpretations of the Bible in their courses. Here the doctrinal guide of all participants was the *Augsburg Confession* in accordance with the seminary *Statutes of 1533*.

All three regular professors of the seminary were to offer courses on the Holy Scriptures, interpreted on the basis of the original languages of Greek and Hebrew, but the third one was also to offer a course now and then based on Augustine's *De Spiritu et littera*, so that students might not lose the correct understanding of "Grace" as taught by St. Paul.[8]

The foundation document also prescribed what Luther and Melanchthon and the rest of the seminary staff had agreed upon with the Saxon Court, as to the course offering which future theological students could attend.[9] The ranking New Testament professor was to offer courses in the biblical books of *Romans, Galatians,* and the *Gospel of St. John;* while a second, an Old Testament professor, would give lectures on *Genesis,* the *Psalms,* and the *Book of Isaiah;* Bugenhagen, the Preacher of the Castle Church, would give lectures on the Epistles of *St. Peter* and *St. John.* The town pastor, when he taught, was to interpret the *Gospel of St. Matthew* and *Deuteronomy,* and sometimes the *Minor Prophets.* These selected books of the Bible, required of theological students on the way to the doctorate, Luther regarded as the richest in Gospel messages and formed the complete picture of the doctrines with which a theologian needed to become familiar.

Since Luther and Melanchthon were also occupied with so many outside requirements, the Elector wanted them to remain free to give courses in the Seminary whenever they desired. Melanchthon, the leader of the Liberal Arts College, was too busy translating the Classics to be bound by exact additional theological duties. The aging Luther, often plagued with poor health, was also extremely busy. His translation of the Holy Scriptures into German, had appeared first in 1534, but he was now busy in revising a second edition with the assistance of his *Sanhedrin* of Wittenberg professors, trying to polish its style and improve its accuracy from the Greek and Hebrew original texts. At the same time, he was Dean of the School of Religion and engaged in many doctoral Disputations, in which he served as the Chairman. Then the Elector frequently used him in his struggle with the papacy. For example, in 1537 the Elector had him write the *Schmalkald Articles*. Thus the Elector loved the reformer and wanted him to give courses in the seminary whenever he felt so inclined and able. The Elector also had Melanchthon go on many missions after the Diet of Augsburg with Roman Catholic theologians. Thus the foundation document of John Frederick did not require a definite assignment as to Luther and Melanchthon's in offering courses in the field of Theology and left it a matter of free choice.[10] In the actual new University of Wittenberg, the following conditions have prevailed during the rest of Luther's lifetime:

> Doctor Martin Luther, no assignment of courses. Philip Melanchthon, voluntary course offerings in Bible Probst of the Castle Church. Justus Jonas regular. Dr. Kasper Cruciger, regular, and Preacher of Castle Church Pfarrer Johannes Bugenhagen, additional courses in Bible.[11]

THE SCHOOL OF LIBERAL ARTS

Since the Liberal Arts faculty served as the foundation of all advanced studies at the University of Wittenberg and was responsible for a proper education of the larger part of the *Leucuria's* student body, its future program was regarded as extremely important. The foundation document pointed out that here the students of the languages and other arts so essential to theologians, lawyers and medical doctors for a background, thus dare not be neglected. In the future, as had been the practice since 1526, when Philip Melanchthon had created this Liberal Arts background, it was now to come into full bloom at the newly founded University of Wittenberg of the future.

According to the Foundation Document, in the future, professors in the various disciplines were to teach four times a week, on Mondays, Tuesdays, Thursdays and Fridays in *Greek, Hebrew, Terence* and *Latin Grammar.* Two professors were to offer courses in elementary and advanced *Mathematics.* They were also to offer courses in *Dialectics* and *Rhetoric.* There were also to be courses in *Physics* and in *Natural Philosophy.*

As stressed earlier, Melanchthon believed that instruction in the biblical languages, Latin, Greek, and Hebrew, should begin early in the *Paedegogium*, for which instruction the new university was to employ a full-time properly trained professor. This then totals eleven regular professors, who were engaged in these preparatory disciplines. Besides this, as Luther and Melanchthon had impressed on the Elector and the Saxon Court that *Disputations* were absolutely essential for the proper training of students in the three Graduate Schools, the Foundation Document stressed that disputations were to be restored in all the faculties of the new institution. The professors of the three

486   *The Reformation as a University Movement*

Graduate Schools were to engage in professorial disputations every quarter, in a system of rotation where every professor engaged in a Disputation once a year.[12] Disputations in the Liberal Arts faculty were usually between students and were more of a practice type, held usually in the *Aula* of the New Friderici College. Professors in languages, teaching Terence and courses in rhetoric, were excused from Disputations but were obligated to engage in public *Declamations* in Latin and Greek.

It would have been interesting to have had more details on faculty course offerings, but we do get a concise presentation in Chancellor Brück's preparatory report for the Elector's *Foundation Document,* which may prove of interest:

Lectures in Liberal Arts

Master Philip Melanchthon	Dialectics
Master Fach	Poetry
Hebrew Scholar Aurogallus	Hebrew
Master Franciscus von Weimar	Greek
Master Vitus Winsheim	Rhetoric
Master Vitus Amerbach	Physics
Master Johann Volmar	Mathematics I
Master Jabod Milichius	Mathematics II
Master Ambrosius	Grammar
Licentiatus Melchior	Physics
No name given	Notary
No name given	Two Beadles
No name given	Lecturer at Meals

Lower Officialdom Given

Doctor Eschan	No data on work
Doctor Pindero	No data
Licentiatus	No data
Gifts to poor students	40 Gulden

Living Canonists of Castle Church

Gangolff Becker	No data given
Master Herman Kipp	No data given
Er. Georg Donat	
Er. Peter Juterbock	
Er. Levin Starck	
Er. Erhart Hagen	
Er. Johan Quadelaburgk, Pfarrer at Utzsch	
Er. Johann, the Organist	
Four Chorales[13]	

THEOLOGICAL EDUCATION AFTER 1536

After a description of the *Fundationsurkunde* of 1536, a brief summary of what happened to Wittenberg in its training of students for the gospel ministry in the new Evangelical churches of the Reformation may prove to be of interest. Already in the twenties Luther and Melanchthon had realized that students without a proper classical background would not become good theologians and interpreters of the Holy Scriptures as they lacked the proper linguistic tools. Now there had returned an emphasis of a proper background to really understand the Holy Scriptures.[14]

We have noted above how the Elector John Frederick and his wife came to Wittenberg to establish the real status of the school as an institution of higher learning and determine what needed to be done to create a new university that could function as the center of the now spreading German Reformation. He began by a restoration of seminary degrees, and giving the School of Theology new statutes which conformed to wishes of Luther and Melanchthon of the establishment of doctoral promotions and later the specifications of the *Statutes of 1533* became a part of the new founding of the University of Wittenberg, as its contents were then incorporated in the Foundation Document of 1536. Thus the clauses of that document became the norm for training the future ministry.

The Melanchthon *Statutes of 1533*, which were incorporated in the *Liber Decanorum* of the Theological Faculty, were published as a directive by the Elector John Frederick and reveal how far the Reformation had penetrated Wittenberg's theological education, and that the Elector was a strong supporter of Luther's "Theology of the Cross." Walter Friedensburg in his university history points out that the new courses in the seminary were no longer philosophical but philological, and were based on exegetical interpretations through use of the original Greek and Hebrew texts of the Holy Scriptures, which were made possible by professors and students with humanistic training in the Liberal Arts. Melanchthon was so pleased with the new Wittenberg *Statutes of 1533*, that he copied them into the *Liber Decanorum*.[15]

The theological Graduate School was placed under the control of the University Rector as it was originally. In the revision of the degrees, they kept most of the former degree titles except that the contents of the methodology that were given now were very different. The degrees towards the doctorate were still the same except *Licentiatus* was dropped:

> Biblicus
> Sententiarius
> Formatus
> Doctor of Theologie[16]

The first four degrees were no longer regarded as training steps toward the final goal of a Doctor of Theology, as the students had to attend four years of exegetical courses in the above prescribed courses in the Elector's *Fundationsurkunde of 1536*.[17] Thus when he was regarded as a mature exegete of the prescribed most important books of the Bible and able to defend his interpretations of Holy Scripture before the faculty, he was advanced to the doctorate by the way described in the *Statutes of 1533*, which needs no further elaboration. The Elector also made the faculty of the School of Theology the guardians of pure doctrine as expressed in *Augsburg Confession of 1530*, and the teachings of the German Reformation. In accordance with the *Statutes of 1533*, the future clergy graduating from the new School of Religion were going to enter the ministry with a very different background from that of Roman *Altglaubigen* in dogmatics, as was the case of the original Wittenberg of Frederick the Wise. They no longer needed to quote Lombard's *Sentences* but could use the original Greek and Hebrew texts of Holy Scripture to defend their religious beliefs through their own biblical exegesis.[18] Now the University of Wittenberg could become the very core and center of the German Reformation, with the Reformer at the head as the Dean of the theological faculty.

The *Foundation of 1536* specifically states what courses were to be taught by the four regular faculty members; yet it specifies that Luther and Melanchthon are not obliged to offer any required courses. The reader may be interested in a description of their future contributions and a description of the actual teaching staff of the School of Religion. Let us begin with a review of the *Weimar Ausgabe* account of the courses Luther taught during the whole period of his professorship:

> Early Lectures on the Psalms, Romans, Galatians and Hebrews (1513–1518); in 1526, the 13 Minor Prophets and Ecclesiastes; in 1527 the Epistle of John, of Titus and Philemon; in 1527, the Epistle of John, of Titus and Philemon; in 1527–1529, the Prophet Isaiah; from 1531–1535, Galatians; and 1535–1545, Genesis, no doubt 9-10 in the morning.[19]

Luther's activities in his battles with Rome and the whole *Altglaubigen* world kept him busy not only in refuting many bitter attacks but also creating the positive tools to further the cause of the Reformation, like the *German Bible*, the two *Cathechisms*, the revision of the *Deutsche Messe* in the Town Church, the *Ordination Formula*, and so on. Luther's activities as Dean of Theology were themselves enough to keep him from doing much lecturing.

Philip Melanchthon, though not obligated to give specific courses in the theological department of the new school, had been very helpful in delivering exegetical lectures in the New Testament ever since 1519, after which he gave 28 courses in the twenties. Luther had nothing but the highest respect for Philip as a biblical exegete, because of his mastery of Greek and Hebrew. He did, however, prefer to lecture in the New Testament and had a great fondness for the Epistle of St. Paul to the Romans. Friedensburg says that Melanchthon worked tirelessly for the building up and maintenance of Luther's "New Theology" of Wittenberg.[20] In the new School of Theology there were many disputations, in which Luther as Dean presided and others on the faculty participated and Luther was very pleased with Philip's role in that. The German Reformation had no better teacher than Melanchthon, who took Luther's basic ideas and used them in learned treatises to further the German Reformation.[21] In 1532, he published his Commentary on Romans, entitled *Commentarius in epistolam Pauli ad Romanus,* an Epistle on which he lectured so frequently since he was promoted to a *Biblicus* under Luther in 1519.[22] Philip also gave lectures on *Colossians* and the *Proverbs of Solomon.* In 1542, he even gave lectures on his *Loci communes.* However, Melanchthon's contribution to the German Reformation, raising it to a higher level, was his role as *Praeceptor Germaniae* in his leadership in the development of Arts as a background to Theology, Law, and Medicine, as we saw above. Here he stressed instruction in Latin, Greek, and Hebrew as tools for higher Graduate Studies. To further the *Studia humanitatis,* he translated almost all the essential classics of Greece and Rome into Latin to benefit the students in their study of the Classics.[23]

A third ranking member of the staff of the School of Theology was the Prior of the Castle Church, Doctor Justus Jonas. He was gifted in languages and especially in translating many of Luther's works. In 1529, Johannes Mathesius, one of Luther's *Tischreden* companions, heard Professor Jonas preach on Martin Luther's *Catechism.* He was the Rector of the university three times and served as Dean of the theological faculty during the trying years of 1523–1535, when they had no theological promotions. He also liked to lecture on *Romans,* the *Acts of the Apostles,* and the *Psalms.* The Probst of the Castle Church remained at his post in Wittenberg until 1541, when he became the Reformer of Halle, Germany, and then was made Pfarrer of *St. Marien Kirche* and was finally elevated to be the Superintendent of the Reformation in that whole Halle region. Thus Justus Jonas was not only an *Ordinarius* Professor of the New Seminary but also a very close friend and co-worker of Luther, who did much to spread the German Reformation.[24]

Another very able pastor and reformer in Northern Germany was Johannes Bugenhagen, or Dr. Pomeranus, as he was commonly known, named after his native land, Pomerania. In 1533 he was promoted to the doctorate with two others, when the Elector reinstated theological degrees in the new School of Theology. Bugenhagen served not only as an able Pfarrer of the *Stadtkirche* and later the Superintendent of the *Consistorium* at Wittenberg, but also as one of the great church organizers in the Northern German lands, Denmark, and Sweden, whom the reformer entrusted with this task of reformer and church organizer, while Luther served as his substitute Pfarrer of the Town Church for many years.

Finally, the fifth member of the new theological faculty of the School of Religion in the new Wittenberg University was Dr. Caspar Cruciger, who was one of the three promoted to the doctorate in the presence of the Elector and his wife in 1533.[25] Cruciger, a great specialist in Hebrew and Aramaic, had received his earlier education at the University of Leipzig, where he was a student among the humanistic circles of Liberal Arts. He later studied Hebrew at Wittenberg and became both a gifted linguist and Old Testament scholar. Cruciger had also been most helpful as a member of Luther's Sanhedrin, in his refinement of the later editions of the *Deutsche Bibel* through his knowledge of Hebrew and Aramaic. Students also benefited from his research in the history of early Christianity during the period of the great ecumenical creeds.[26]

Immediately after the Diet of Worms in 1521, when Luther was condemned by both the church and state and five of the *Altglaubigen* universities, the support of all the *Altglaubigen* regions of the University of Wittenberg was withdrawn. This caused a tremendous drop in enrollment during the twenties. Meanwhile, Dean Carlstadt and the Zwickau Prophets had practically undone all the creative reforms of Luther and Melanchthon by trying to introduce their wild reforms by force, while Martin Luther was at the Wartburg under the Elector's protection. Yet Luther and Melanchthon, with heroic efforts and the Elector's reforms, did not allow the school to go under, but prepared it for the day of Elector John Frederick's creation of the new University of Wittenberg of 1533–1536, which caused the triumph of the German Reformation.

Our title for this volume, "The Reformation as a University Movement," does not apply to the university of Frederick the Wise, which was a typical medieval university in which Aristotle reigned supreme. Luther and Melanchthon's changes to an institution of biblical humanism were impressive; but it was the new University of Wittenberg created by Elector John Frederick in 1533–1536 in which Luther's "Theology of the Cross" could reign supreme. This is what brought the German Reformation to its fruition and guided it in its spread.

Conclusion

❖

The University of Wittenberg was the very core and center of the reforms instituted by Martin Luther. The Reformation was born in his heart while he was a young professor at Wittenberg, as he emerged from scholasticism in the development of his "theology of the cross." He would not rest until he had won the Wittenberg faculty to his support and, with the Wittenberg faculty, transformed the university and gained a following in a large student body, 16,292 students, who started later reforms of the Christian church. The reformer accomplished this in spite of the bitter opposition of Rome and the empire and the hostile attacks of the universities of Louvain, Cologne, and Ingolstadt, which culminated in the condemnation of Luther's writings by the Sorbonne of the University of Paris in 1521.

Thus, in spite of all the bitter opposition, by 1536 the University of Wittenberg had risen to become the model of reforms of Christianity within the Roman church.

Church historians have often approached the German Reformation with a false set of assumptions. The common approach often has been to assume that Martin Luther, by his *Flugschriften* and tracts on the teachings of the Holy Scripture, had won whole communities of believers for gospel reforms within the Catholic church. What such an approach fails to realize is that the average believer was not reached by Luther's writings, for the Reformation was really an upper-strata movement in which professors, the clergy, and an educated laity were involved. The Reformation began in Wittenberg and from there spread to the outside world among educated classes everywhere who, by a variety of ways, started local reforms in various communities. It often started with university students who had studied with Luther and Melanchthon or with converted clergy who urged a reform in the Roman church.

As the reforms of Luther and his followers and Luther's "new theology" spread among the intellectual classes, they enraged professors at several univer-

491

sities, and *Streitschriften* broke out for and against the Reformation by theologians, to which Luther and Melanchthon replied. Once the battle was on, however, other universities, like Erfurt, Tübingen, and, in time, Leipzig and Frankfurt an der Oder, became certain that Catholic reforms were necessary, and they joined in a battle for reform and the restoration of the gospel. This academic battle was but the beginning of the Reformation. It was not until the Church Visitations and the work of reformers active in the field that the Reformation began, after a decade, to reach the parish and congregational level. When the common laypersons became aware of Luther's reforms and when the reformers began to establish church urdinances, the Reformation became a reality and expressed itself in *Landeskirchen*. Thus, the first period of the Reformation was created by tracts read by scholars who became *Neuglaubigen* followers of Luther. In the second period, the 1530s, the Reformation became a reform movement on the local congregational level under the leadership of gospel-minded Pfarrer and other clergymen.

In this volume I have tried to correct a false view of the actual nature of Luther's reforms. Luther did not regard his life's calling as founding the Lutheran church. If this had been the case, his call for reforms would not have taken the path it did. He believed the *Altglaubigen* had gone far from the early Christian church, as shown in his two powerful tracts of 1530 and 1538, that the Roman church required reform of abuses, and that it needed to return to God's Holy Scripture and the ministry of the gospel of Jesus Christ. The Reformation thus was a movement of return to the early days of the great ecumenical creeds, as set forth in Luther's tract of 1538.

Rome and its hierarchy, by its indulgences and masses, had become one of the greatest fiscal organizations in western Europe and was not about to allow radical change. Had not Pope Leo X once remarked, "Since God has given us the papacy, let us enjoy it"? The Renaissance popes had no desire to restore apostolic standards in place of marble palaces. Through the Council of Trent they drafted their teachings and beliefs in codified form and excluded Luther's new Evangelical *Landeskirchen* which, in subsequent centuries became known as the Lutheran church in Europe. But Luther never believed that by belonging to an outward church body you were saved and thereby became a member of the Christian church founded by Jesus Christ; for him, membership in that body was possible only for individual Christians who believed in justification by faith and in the redemption wrought at Golgotha for the forgiveness of sins, which resulted in a life in conformity to the will of our Lord and Savior.

The Setting of the Reformation: Notes

(See the list of abbreviations of this volume.)

Chapter 2
The Decline of Rome
and the German Invasions

1. Russell, "Celts," 232–65.
2. Russell, "Celts," 233.
3. Thompson, *Middle*, 1:86. Only part of the Ulfalas Bible remains in Sweden and is known as the *Codex Argentius*, as it is in silver letters. I was privileged to examine this treasure in Uppsala, while serving as the executive director of the Foundation for Reformation Research.
4. Lissner. See also Thompson, *Early*, for new insight on tribal locations.
5. Thompson, *Early*, 1–2.
6. Thompson, 3–7.
7. Thompson, 8–12.
8. Thompson, 12–15.
9. Thompson, 17–28.
10. Goodyear, 5–12, 16–46.
11. Thompson, 14–15, and 73.
12. Lissner, 250; Thompson, 73–74; and Thompson, *Middle*, 1:5, on Caesar's protective policy against Gaul.
13. Thompson, 17.
14. Thompson, 72–80, offers a new approach on Roman strategy.
15. Thompson, *Middle*, 1:5.
16. Lissner, 258–59.
17. Lissner, 262–64.
18. Macmullen, 119–52.
19. Macmullen, 152–53.

20. Haywood, 97–99.
21. Haywood, 97–99.
22. Cary, 101–4.
23. Haywood, 99–101.
24. Cary, 104.
25. Cary, 104.
26. Thompson, *Middle*, 1:88–89.
27. Musset, 29–33. See also Thompson, *Middle*, 1:88–89.
28. Thompson, *Middle*, 1:59.
29. Lissner, 273.

Chapter 3
The Sorben in Electoral Saxony

1. See Lamprecht. In 3:369, the following statement appears: "Weit mehr als die Eroberung der Slavenlander im zwölften und dreizehnten Jahrhundert erscheint deren Germanization als ein wahrhaft erstaunlicher Vorgang: es ist die Grosstat unseres Volkes während des Mittelalters." He must have thought largely of the northern Slavs, where it no doubt applied much more than in the Wittenberg region, where Herrmann claims the Slavs made up nine-tenths of the population. Cf. Thompson, *Feudal*, 2:451–528. In the chronicles cited the writer calls attention to Widukind; Thietmar; Adam; and Helmold. See also Giesebrecht.
2. See Widukind, 2:48–50. Thietmar, 1:18–24, repeats the *Bergen* story of Henry I and tells how he built Meissen in 929. Thompson, *Feudal*, 2:480–83, tells of the *Burgward* system in Sorben lands and gives a map of their locations. But all of this was still built on the

older views. Schlesinger, *Burgen*, 3:158ff., has
a much more recent view of the construction
of *Burgen* from Frankish times on; he shows
that *Burgen* already existed in Boniface's day.
See 163–65 on Slavic castles. Schlesinger,
Burgen, 3:168–69, has a very fine chart of
these *Burgen*, especially useful for the Electoral Saxony region. Schuchhart tried to locate
some of these Sorben castles in 1931, but
found it to be impossible. Herrmann, 149–75,
has an excellent section on Slavic *Burgen*. He
claims that the Slavs had several types of
Burgen in the beginning: (a) those for princes;
(b) those for nobles; and (c) the *Landburg*, or
Rundwalle type. But conditions changed after
A.D. 900, when the Germans controlled the
land. Their castles were made into a suburb
type like those of the Slavs in the Meissen
castle.

3. Herrmann, 14, tells of the extent of the
excavations. On the excavations in the Dessau-
Mosikau region see Gimbutas, 125–26; for
extensive research and excavations in the
"Great Moravian Empire," see 147–50. Portal,
22, shows a map of greater Moravia around
A.D. 900, and also the excavation sites at Staré-
Mesto and Mikulcice. See Schuchhart, 7ff., for
excavations in the north.

4. Cf. Thompson, *Feudal*, 2:490–520.

5. Herrmann, 127–28, tells us that the
Sorben in the Dessau region, who were the
same Prague-type Sorben as around Wittenberg, preferred to build their villages in semi-
circles and that this type of village continued
throughout the Middle Ages. Wittenberg is
laid out that way, with the flat side facing the
Elbe.

6. Stocki, vii, claims that these influences
occurred around A.D. 600–700.

7. Stocki, 1–4.

8. Stocki, 25.

9. Stocki, 4.

10. Stocki, 36–48.

11. Stocki, 49–73.

12. Gimbutas, 106. Herrmann shows that
their burial urns, which were found under
excavated houses in the Sorben region, were
the Prague type.

13. Stocki, 9, tells how he used Sanskrit,
Greek, Latin, and Germanic sources for his
establishment of Indo-European race studies.

14. Stocki, vii.

15. Portal, 21.

16. Portal, 22.

17. Portal, 22.

18. Gimbutas, 98. See 102 on the spread to
the north through the "Moravian Gate." The
Romans had the Avars attack the Slavs and
then drove them on their northward migrations.

19. See Herrmann, 22ff.; Schlesinger,
Burgen, 3:12–14, 22; Widukind, 2:82–83.

20. Herrmann, 26.

21. Herrmann, 9–11.

22. Herrmann, 9. Cf. Gimbutas, 127. This
is based on a statement by Einhard.

23. Herrmann, 18. Schlesinger, *Burgen*,
3:67ff., tells how the Sorben were but one
branch of many Slavs living between the Saale
and the Elbe. Einhard claimed that the Saale
was the limit of their westward movement by
782. He stated that the word "Sorben" came
from the Slavic word *Zurba* in use around
1040. But Cosmas of Prague used the word
Zribia, and it may mean "those living in the
lowlands." In 631 Frediger already referred to
the Sorben as a gens and stated they may have
had a number of subdivisions. S&A contains a
chart with the *Burgwälle* the Sorben erected
in the Saale region.

24. Schlesinger's studies on the Sorben are
invaluable on what the spade unearthed of
Slavic origins, invasions, culture, and government. See Schlesinger, *Burgen*.

25. Herrmann (see abbreviations) is a gold-
mine of information, based on an excellent
combination of the older chronicles and
sources that he has interpreted in light of
twentieth-century excavations.

26. See Schlesinger, *Burgen*, 3:7–8, 163–
69, on *Burgwälle*, rounded-out fortresses made
of dirt (removed during the construction of
moats) and elevated for defense. The matter of
Burgen and the various types used by the Slavs,
Franks, and Saxons has been thoroughly
explored in the research of Schmid, Grimm,
and Schlesinger.

27. Herrmann, 49ff., treats in detail the
nature of Slavic *Rodung* of the newly occupied
regions.

28. Herrmann, 81–87, treats iron production in detail. See Schlesinger, *Burgen*, 3:19,
on Torgau being an early marketplace on the
Elbe, where, he says, "dasz der Name Torgau
'Markort' bedeutet," and that by 1119 there
was already a *locus mercatus* in Torgau.

29. Herrmann, 4–56.

30. Herrmann, 54–57, ills. 20–24.

31. See Herrmann, 57–66.

32. Herrmann, 57–59, 66–69.

33. Herrmann, 62.

34. Herrmann, 62–63.

35. Herrmann, 62.

36. Herrmann, 63–65.

37. Herrmann, 69–72

38. Herrmann, 72–73.

39. Herrmann, 73.

40. Gimbutas, 134.

41. Gimbutas, 134. Cf. Herrmann, 126–36, in which he gives a number of illustrations of *Siedlungsformen,* esp. 127, ill. 51.

42. Gimbutas, 134–35.

43. Gimbutas, 141.

44. Schlesinger, *Burgen,* 3:26.

45. Schlesinger, *Burgen,* 3:12–14.

46. Schlesinger, *Burgen,* 3:12. See also Gimbutas, 141–42.

47. Herrmann, 21–23, which was based on Thietmar, 2:38. Cf. Schlesinger, *Burgen,* 3:20.

48. Gimbutas, 141. Cf. 145–46.

49. Gimbutas, 141–42.

50. Widukind, 2:82–83; Herrmann, 275–76; and Schlesinger, *Burgen,* 3:22.

51. Schlesinger, *Burgen,* 3:22. Cf. Herrmann, 309–13.

52. Herrmann, 139–47.

53. Schlesinger, *Burgen,* 3:163.

54. Schlesinger, *Burgen,* 3:16. See n. 72, for special studies.

55. Schlesinger, *Burgen,* 3:164.

56. Gimbutas, 147.

57. Gimbutas, 147.

58. Gimbutas, 147–49.

59. Schlesinger, *Burgen,* 3:163–65.

60. Schlesinger, *Burgen,* 3:164–65.

61. Schlesinger, *Burgen,* 3:160. Cf. n. 15 for the excavator's publications and especially his "Atlas."

62. Schlesinger, *Burgen,* 3:160–61.

63. Schlesinger, *Burgen,* 3:161.

64. Schlesinger, *Burgen,* 3:165.

65. Herrmann, 168, contains his chart of Slavic *Burgen* and German *Burgwarden.* See 168–74 for a discussion of this. See Thompson, *Feudal* 2:482 ff., for an older, now slightly dated, view. Cf. 482, for his chart of *Burgward* systems.

66. See Schlesinger, *Burgen,* 3:21ff.

67. Schlesinger, *Burgen,* 3:164–65. Cf. Herrmann, 277, 304–6.

68. Herrmann, 148.

69. Herrmann, 147–48.

70. Herrmann, 308–9.

71. Herrmann, 309–10.

72. Herrmann, 309–10.

73. Schlesinger, *Burgen,* 3:213–14.

74. See Herrmann, 198–208. Cf. Schlesinger, *Burgen,* 3:214–16.

75. Schlesinger, *Burgen,* 3:216–17.

76. Schlesinger, *Burgen,* 3:218–19.

77. Schlesinger, *Burgen,* 3:218–19.

78. Schlesinger, *Burgen,* 3:219–20.

79. Schwiebert, *Luther,* 257ff. Grohmann includes a detailed account of how Wittenberg was financed.

80. Schlesinger, *Burgen,* 3:220. Cf. Schwiebert, *Luther,* 210.

81. Schlesinger, *Burgen,* 3:29. Cf. Herrmann, 208.

82. Schlesinger, *Burgen,* 3:29–30. An old source dated 1181 reads: "As seniors of the village, which in their own language are known as *Supanos.*"

83. Schlesinger, *Burgen,* 3:29–30.

84. Schlesinger, *Burgen,* 3:30–31.

85. Herrmann, 198ff.

86. Herrmann, 304–6.

87. Schlesinger, *Burgen,* 3:31–32.

88. Schlesinger, *Burgen,* 3:31–32.

89. Herrmann, 307–8.

90. See "Dutch and Flemish Colonization in Medieval Germany," Thompson, *Feudal,* 2:545–79.

91. Herrmann, 307.

92. Herrmann, 307.

93. Thompson, *Feudal,* 2:508–9.

94. Herrmann, 307.

95. Herrmann, 308.

96. Herrmann, 308.

97. Schlesinger, *Burgen,* 3:33, n. 183, gives a rather lengthy bibliography of treatises on this class by K&K[2], Scheltz, Lehmenn, Oelmann, Schultze, and Krünitz. The recent studies by W. Haupt & J. Huth and Dr. Lehmann were very significant for his findings.

98. Schlesinger, *Burgen,* 3:34.

99. Schlesinger, *Burgen,* 3:34, esp. n. 188b.

100. Schlesinger, *Burgen,* 3:36.

101. Schlesinger, *Burgen,* 3:37.

102. Schlesinger, *Burgen,* 3:37.

103. Schlesinger, *Burgen,* 3:45–46.

104. Herrmann, 209–10.

105. See Hensel.

106. Herrmann, 229–62.

107. Schlesinger has no special section on

the civilization and culture of the Slavs, but in his treatment of the many aspects of their institutions it is very clear that the Sorben in Electoral Saxony were as advanced as other Slavic tribes, and no doubt equal to the culture of the contemporary Germans of the older west.

108. See chap. 4 below.

109. See Herrmann, 14ff., under "Einwanderung und Herkunft der Stammesgruppen."

110. See Hensel.

111. See n. 106 above for Herrmann's analysis of their culture and n. 109 for the identification of Sorben pottery as belonging to the same *Stämme* as the Moravian, Slovakian, and Bohemian civilizations.

112. Herrmann, 229–30.

Chapter 4
The Origins of Electoral Saxony

1. See Baron. Cf. Strauss.

2. See "Frederick the Wise in the Hour of Decision," in Schwiebert, *Luther*.

3. A good study of this historic document is Haller, *Sturz*. A very thorough analysis and reconstruction of the actual text is Güterbock, *Gelnhauser*.

4. Güterbock, *Gelnhauser*, 1–2.

5. See Thompson, *Feudal*, 1:167ff.; Adam, 3; and Helmold, 1:7, for a good discussion of "Old Saxony."

6. Haller, *Sturz*, 443.

7. Haller, *Sturz*, 443. Güterbock, *Gelnhauser*, 2–3, doubts that the poison in the ink caused the document to become so defective; he believes that dampness caused the document to fade.

8. See Güterbock, *Gelnhauser*, 11, n. 4.

9. See Güterbock, *Gelnhauser*, 10–12.

10. See Barraclough, "The Problem of the Duchies," 1:32–45; and "The Monarchy and Its Resources," 1:47–73, for a good introduction to the problem.

11. See "The Rebellion of Saxony," Thompson, *Feudal*, 1:185–216, for a good example of the Franconian period of the *Kaiserzeit*.

12. These six were Saxony, Lotharingia, Franconia, Swabia, Bavaria, and Carinthia. Henry III was both duke and king in Franconia, Swabia, Bavaria, and Carinthia.

13. Barraclough, 1:29ff.

14. Barraclough, 1:45. See also Boedler, 3–9.

15. Thompson, *Feudal*, 1:125–66.

16. Thompson, *Feudal*, 1:157–58.

17. Barraclough, "The Hohenstaufen State," 1:113–18. Cf. Thompson, *Feudal*, 1:351ff., for a more negative view of the Franconians and Hohenstaufen on crown lands.

18. Thompson, *Feudal*, 1:272–74, 356–57.

19. Thompson, *Feudal*, 1:356–57.

20. See Giesebrecht, 5:3ff.

21. Thompson, *Feudal*, 439.

22. Hahn, 4.

23. Hahn, 4.

24. Heinemann, 4.

25. Berendt, 5–6. Cf. Helmold, 1:10.

26. Heinemann, 4.

27. Heinemann, 4.

28. Heinemann, 316–19.

29. Thompson, *Feudal*, 2:517ff.

30. Heinemann, 4.

31. It seems that for a while before 1173 the Ascanier were in conflict with the Kaiser over the *Grafschaft* Aschersleben, between the Saale and the Wipper rivers and over the *Erbgut* Plötzgau.

32. Hahn, 7.

33. Hahn, 6.

34. Herrmann, 317–18.

35. This region grew in 1290 by the addition of Brehna.

36. Cf. n. 18 above.

37. Thompson, *Feudal*, 1:273–75.

38. Fay, 1:173–76.

39. Frederick I was born in 1115. Henry the Lion was born in 1129, making a difference of fourteen years in their ages.

40. See Giesebrecht, 5:3–39.

41. *Encyclopedia Britannica*, s.v., "Henry the Lion."

42. Haller, *Sturz*, 342–45; Güterbock, *Gelnhauser*, 141–45.

43. Haller, *Sturz*, 342–45; Güterbock, *Gelnhauser*, 141–45.

44. Munz, *Frederick*, 347.

45. Gronen, 49, 71, believes that Henry II of England may have been behind the Lombard League, in which Henry the Lion was involved. This could have enraged the Staufer even more.

46. Gronen, 71.

47. See Haskins for a good account of Henry II.

48. Helmold, 1:258ff. Cf. Herrmann, 328ff.

49. Munz, *Frederick*, 340, based on Helmold, 2:102.

50. Thompson, *Feudal*, is not very kindly disposed toward Frederick's "Grand Design" of medieval imperialism trying to govern both Germany and Italy. Munz, *Frederick*, 315ff., has what seems to be a more balanced approach to Frederick's reign.

51. See Widukind, 2:64ff. Cf. Heer, 68ff.

52. Haller, *Sturz*, 297–99.

53. Schuchhart, 7, and esp. 31ff.

54. Haller, *Sturz*, 297–99.

55. Munz, *Frederick*, 341.

56. Gronen, 49.

57. Haller, *Sturz*, 326–30, 343–45.

58. See Thompson, *Feudal*, 1:348.

59. Güterbock, *Schisma*, 395–96.

60. See Haller, *Sturz*, 302–6.

61. Haller, *Sturz*, 306; cf. 313–16.

62. See Munz, *Frederick*, 347.

63. See Munz, *Frederick*, 346–47.

64. Munz, *Frederick*, 315–16, analyzes Frederick's state of mind after the Legnano defeat; 317–24 describes how he turned to a new decision to ride the wave of the new territorial feudalism.

65. In May 1177, Frederick decided to change his mind and forge more constructive plans for the future.

66. Munz, *Frederick*, 325, claims that Christian's troops also terrorized regions around Bologna, Ravenna, and Ferrara. Yet the bishops of those areas remained loyal to Pope Alexander III.

67. See Munz, *Frederick*, 326–29.

68. Munz, *Frederick*, 329–31.

69. Munz, *Frederick*, 331–32.

70. Dungern, 4.

71. See Giesebrecht, 5:897. See also Mariotte, 49; Munz, *Frederick*, 333–35.

72. Munz, *Frederick*, 348–49.

73. Munz, *Frederick*, 349.

74. See Hahn, 5. Erdmann, 337ff., believes that the "Swabian Conspiracy" was Henry's act of treason.

75. Erdmann, 323–24.

76. Munz, *Frederick*, 353. Cf. Gronen, 86–87.

77. Munz, *Frederick*, 348.

78. Munz, *Frederick*, 335ff.

79. See Erdmann, 412; Dungern, 4.

80. Munz, *Frederick*, 350–51, based on Arnold von Lübeck, *Chronica Slavorum*, 2:10.

81. Erdmann, 333–39.

82. Haller, *Sturz*, 412ff. Cf. Güterbock, *Gelnhauser*, 45–46.

83. Güterbock, *Gelnhauser*, 46.

84. Haller, *Sturz*, 412ff.; also 418.

85. Güterbock, *Gelnhauser*, 141–43.

86. Güterbock, *Gelnhauser*, 147. Cf. Boedler, 1–2.

87. Boedler, 14–16.

88. Güterbock, *Gelnhauser*, 147.

89. Boedler, 1–2.

90. Munz, *Frederick*, 353. Cf. Erdmann, 348.

91. Munz, *Frederick*, 358.

92. Giesebrecht, 5:925ff. Cf. Gronen, 92ff.

93. Gronen, 92–93.

94. Giesebrecht, 5:941.

95. Munz, *Frederick*, 358.

96. Giesebrecht, 5:944. Cf. Gronen, 94.

97. Gronen, 94. Cf. Boedler, 7–10.

98. Gronen, 94.

99. See Giesebrecht, 5:944.

100. Giesebrecht, 5:944, calls it the "kiss of peace."

101. See Giesebrecht, 5:944–45.

102. See Giesebrecht, 5:945–46.

103. Gronen, 96.

Chapter 5
The Emergence of the New Saxony

1. Boedler, 9–21.

2. Hahn, 23ff.

3. Boedler, 2–7.

4. Thompson, *Feudal*, 1:125–66, tells about the impact of the "Investiture Struggle" in German lands; 158–59 show its impact on the territorial princes.

5. Boedler, 2–6.

6. Boedler, 26–32.

7. Boedler, 28–32.

8. Hahn, 41–44.

9. Hahn, 23–24. This author based his conclusion on a source collection by Stumpf, nos. 4111, 12, in which the signature "Dux Saxoniae" appears.

10. Hahn, 23–24.

11. Fritz Hasenritter, "Beiträge zum Urkunden-und-Kanzleiwesen Heinrich des Löwen," *Greifwalder Abhandlungen zur Geschichte des Mittelalters* (Greifwald: 1936), 72–74.

12. Hahn, 24.

13. Hahn, 41. He quoted Arnold of Lübeck, 3:1, as his source.

14. Hahn, 45–46.

15. Heinemann, 288–89; cf. Berendt, 8.

16. Schwiebert, *Luther*, 199ff.

17. E. Weise, *Geschichte der kursächsischen Staaten*, 2 vols. (Leipzig, 1803), 2:211. Cited by Berendt. Not available to this author.

18. Schalscheleth, 3ff. This author (P. Heynig) was rather critical in his views about Wittenberg and no doubt feared reprisals by fellow Wittenberg professors.

19. Schalscheleth, 3ff.

20. Heinemann, 287.

21. See Thompson, *Feudal*, 2:545ff., esp. 553–55.

22. Boedler, 25.

23. Boedler, 26.

24. Berendt, 8.

25. Boedler, 25.

26. Boedler, 27.

27. Boedler, 32.

28. Berendt, 77.

29. Berendt, 8.

30. Hahn, 41–42. Cf. n. 18 above.

31. Berendt, 8–9.

32. Berendt, 8–9.

33. Berendt, 8–9. The conclusion is based on *Annales Stadenser Hon. Ser. His.*, 16:155.

34. Berendt, 9–10.

35. Berendt, 9–10.

36. Weise, *Geschichte der kursächsischen Staaten*, 2:211.

37. Berendt, 10–11.

38. Berendt, 13.

39. Berendt, 14.

40. Berendt, 14.

41. Berendt, 18.

42. Berendt, 29–30.

43. Charitius, 144. With the assistance of Johannes Ficker in Halle, I was able to decipher Charitius' rather strange handwriting.

44. While working in Wittenberg during 1936, I became well acquainted with Professor Heubner and the castle staff. I participated in a tour of the lower rooms of the castle tower and viewed the twenty-seven oaken caskets containing the mortal remains of the Ascanier family.

45. Berendt, 17–18.

46. Berendt, 17–18.

47. Berendt, 42.

48. Cf. Schalscheleth, 25–41.

49. For a history of the castle church, see Schwiebert, *Luther*, 235–43.

50. Boedler, 66.

51. Boedler, 66–67. See also Harnack, 65ff.

52. Boedler, 67.

53. Cf. Boedler, 67 n. 10.

54. Fay, 1:213–15.

55. Fay, 1:247–50.

56. Zeumer, 1:61–63.

57. Fay, 1:248. See also Zeumer, 1:16–18

58. Fay, 1:247–48.

59. Zeumer, 1:10–12.

60. Zeumer, 1:178–81.

61. Zeumer, 1:110–11. Cf. 2:66–69 (10 December). He has only the Latin text from Prague, dated 6 October 1355.

62. Zeumer, 1:239–44.

63. Zeumer, 1:110. No copy of the German document seems to be extant, but for the Latin text see 2:66–69. This original is in Dresden, but the ribbon and seal are no longer attached.

64. Zeumer, 1:111–13.

65. Zeumer, 1:123ff.

66. Zeumer, 1:144ff.

67. Zeumer, 1:170.

68. Zeumer, 1:181–83.

69. Zeumer, 1:152.

70. Zeumer, 1:152–53.

71. Zeumer, 1:153–54.

72. Zeumer, 1:110–11.

73. Historians have referred to documents ten and eighteen in the Golden Bull as the "Saxon Clauses," as they deal separately with Electoral Saxony and are therefore separate from the text of the German constitution. But they are cited in the text.

74. Zeumer, 2:66–69.

75. Zeumer, 2:66–69.

76. Zeumer, 2:66–69.

77. Zeumer, 2:70.

78. Zeumer, 2:79–82. This is now in the Haupt Staatsarchiv in Dresden.

79. Zeumer, 2:79–82.

80. Zeumer, 2:118–23. This contains the text of the Metz investiture agreement, 27 December 1356.

81. Zeumer, 1:43. Cf. Schalscheleth, 21–22. See also Schwiebert, *Luther*, 78, concerning the Hussite invasions.

82. Zeumer, 2:82–85.

83. Zeumer, 1:14–18.

84. Zeumer, 1:30.

85. Zeumer, 1:181–82.
86. Zeumer, 2:239. See his "Exkurs."
87. Zeumer, 2:240, in the "Exkurs."
88. Zeumer, 2:241 and n. 1.
89. Zeumer, 2:24, in "Exkurs," n. 1.
90. Zeumer, 2:242.
91. Zeumer, 2:242.
92. Zeumer, 2:124–25.
93. Zeumer, 2:128. See Doc. 34.
94. Zeumer, 2:244.
95. Boedler, 77.
96. Boedler, 71–72.
97. Zeumer, 1:33–34; Boedler, 72.
98. Boedler, 72–77.
99. Zeumer, 1:236.
100. Boedler, 72–77.
101. Zeumer, 1:62.
102. Zeumer, 1:64.
103. Zeumer, 1:233.
104. Zeumer, 1:233.
105. Böttiger, 2:307.
106. Böttiger, 2:309.
107. Böttiger, 2:309.
108. Böttiger, 2:309.
109. Böttiger, 2:309.
110. Fay, 1:251.
111. Schalscheleth, 16–18; Böttiger, 2:309.
112. Böttiger, 2:310.
113. Böttiger, 2:310.
114. Böttiger, 2:310.
115. Böttiger, 2:311.
116. Böttiger, 2:311.
117. Böttiger, 2:311.
118. Böttiger, 2:311.
119. Böttiger, 2:312.

Chapter 6
Sources for Constructing a History
of Thuringia and Meissen

1. AR; Patze, *Geschichte* 1:2–3, contains an excellent discussion of the historical sources of Thuringia.
2. Patze, *Geschichte*, 1:3–4.
3. K&K[1], 66–67.
4. Patze, *Geschichte*, 1:3. Cf. notes on 382.
5. Patze, *Geschichte*, 1:4. Cf. notes on 382. In his introduction to AR, Wegele relates how the present text, located in Hannover, came into existence and was compiled out of many elements, among them an older, original AR, which has since disappeared (xiii ff.).

6. See AR, Introduction, 1:xv–xvii, for a thorough discussion of the interrelationship between AR and the Erfurt chronicle of Saint Peters and others. Cf. Patze, *Geschichte*, 1:4.
7. S. Petri. See AR, Introduction, 1:xv–xvi, for a discussion of the original S. Petri chronicle. Cf. Patze, *Geschichte*, 1:5.
8. Patze, *Geschichte*, 1:5. Cf. notes on 382.
9. Patze, *Geschichte*, 1:5.
10. Patze, *Geschichte*, 1:16, still offered a reproduction of the autograph of this text as preserved by Goethe, in the *Archiv der Gesellschaft für deutsche Geschichtskunde*.
11. Patze, *Geschichte*, 1:7. Cf. notes on 382.
12. Thiele. Cf. Michelson, 219ff.
13. Patze, *Geschichte*, 1:7. For the Johann Rothe chronicle, see Rothe.
14. Patze, *Geschichte*, 1:8.
15. Patze, *Geschichte*, 1:9.
16. Patze, *Geschichte*, 1:9. See also, "Die Chronik des Hartung Cammermeisters," *Geschichtsquellen der Provinz Sachsen*, vol. 35, R. Reiche, ed. (1896).
17. AR, xi. See Patze, *Entstehung* 1:153–55, for a good, recent introduction.
18. Patze, *Geschichte*, 1:10. Cf. Patze, *Entstehung*, 1:23.
19. Patze, *Entstehung*, 1:210–11. Cf. Karl Wenck, Wartburg, 1:37.
20. Patze, *Geschichte*, 1:10.
21. Patze, *Geschichte*, 1:10.
22. According to Karl Wenck, Wartburg, 1:40, in the early days the Ludowinger had no specific dwelling that they called their home. When the rulers traveled, they were accompanied by their *Kanzlei*, or office staff. They seemed to move most frequently between the Eckardsberge, Neuenburg, Weiszenses, and Wartburg castles. Beginning with Ludwig III, the Wartburg became their favorite place. Cf. Ernst Martin, "The Wartburg Blossoming in Knightly Poetry," Wartburg. See also Siegfried Asche, Wartburg, 1:21–26.
23. Patze, *Geschichte*, 1:11.
24. Böttiger, 2:229–30. Cf. Patze, *Geschichte*, 1:11.
25. Patze, *Geschichte*, 1:11. Cf. Patze, *Entstehung*, 1:153.
26. Patze, *Geschichte*, 1:12. See also notes on 383.
27. Patze, *Geschichte*, 1:12.
28. Patze, *Geschichte*, 1:13–14. Cf. notes on 384.

29. For the *Eccardiana* in print, see J. G. Eccard, *Historia genealogica pricium Saxoniae superioris* (Leipzig, 1722), esp. 351–468. For a comparison with Johann Rothe's account, see H. Helmhold, "Johannes Rothe, der thüringische Chronist," *Thüringen Fähnlein* 3 (1934): 388–91.

30. Patze, *Geschichte*, 1:15. See also notes on 384.

31. Patze, *Geschichte*, 1:15–16.

32. Patze, *Geschichte*, 1:16. The chronicle is really part of a *Sammelwerk* on Thuringian history written for Rothe by Urban Schlorff, the *Schösser* of Yenneberg.

33. *Adami Ursini Molygergensis Chronicon Thuringiae*, 1547, in *Scriptores Rerum Germanicarum Praecipue Saxonicarum*, Io. Menckenius, ed., vol. 3 (1730), 1239–1359).

34. Patze, *Geschichte*, 1:16–17. Cf. notes on 385.

35. Patze, *Geschichte*, 1:17–18.

36. Patze, *Geschichte*, 1:18.

Chapter 7
Early Thuringian and Meissen History

1. Schlesinger, *Beiträge* 9, 13.

2. Patze, *Entstehung*, 1:109–11, 123–41.

3. Thietmar, 6:50. Cf. also 69 and 86. Cf. Patze, *Geschichte*, 1:55.

4. Patze, *Entstehung*, 1:64–66.

5. Patze, *Entstehung*, 1:107.

6. K&K[1], 47–48. See also Thietmar, 3:83–85; Patze, *Geschichte*, 1:108.

7. Thompson, *Feudal*, 2:482–83.

8. Patze, *Entstehung*, 1:108–9; K&K[1], 49, claims there were five children, three boys and two girls, Liutgard and Oda.

9. K&K[1], 49. Cf. Helbig, 55.

10. K&K[1], 49.

11. Thietmar, 5:154; Böttiger, 2:76.

12. Helbig, 55, holds that it must have been the "Groszen des Landes" for the guarantee of their east flank, hat the boundaries might be further extended into the marks.

13. Helbig, 55.

14. O. Dobenecker, "Über Ursprung und Bedeutung der Thüringischen Landgrafschaft," *Zeitschrift des Vereins für Thüringische Geschichte*, new series, 15 (1891):305. Cf. Helbig, 55, for more extended literature.

15. Patze, *Entstehung*, 1:115–17. Cf. Thietmar, 8:361–64, part 20.

16. Thietmar, 4:127–29, treats the story in detail.

17. Thietmar, 4:151.

18. Thietmar, 4:152.

19. Thietmar, 4:152–53.

20. Thietmar, 4:153.

21. Thietmar, 4:154.

22. K&K[1], 49–50. Cf. Patze, *Geschichte*, 1:123. See Thietmar, 6:235–36, on the accusation of selling Slavs to the Jews. Cf. 6:211, part 28, where slave trade seems to have been practiced.

23. Thietmar, 7:294–95. Cf. K&K[1], 51.

24. K&K[1], 51.

25. K&K[1], 51.

26. K&K[1], 52. Cf. Patze, *Geschichte*, 1:123–24.

27. See Widukind, 2:112.

28. Cf. Otto Posse, *Die Markgrafen von Meiszen und das Haus Wettin bis zu Konrad des Groszen* (Leipzig: 1881), 124ff.

29. Patze, *Entstehung*, 1:101.

30. Patze, *Entstehung*, 1:101. Cf. Ruth Schönkopf, *Die Sächsischen Grafen, 919–1024*, Studien und Vorarbeiten zum Historischen Atlas Niedersachsens (Göttingen: 1957), 56.

31. Patze, *Entstehung*, 1:105.

32. Patze, *Entstehung*, 1:103, n. 57.

33. See Giesebrecht, 1:206. Cf. Lamprecht, 2:121; Barraclough, 1:33.

34. See Widukind, 2:69–70, 72, 89–90. Cf. Thietmar, 2:29.

35. See Widukind, 2:72, 74. Cf. Thietmar, 1:8.

36. Widukind, 2:74–76. Cf. Thietmar, 2:30.

37. See Widukind, 2:76–93. Cf. Patze, *Geschichte*, 1:103–4.

38. See Patze, *Entstehung*, 1:104; Robert Holtzmann, *Geschichte der sächsischen Kaiserzeit*, 3rd ed. (Munich: 1955), 161; Patze, *Geschichte*, 1:104, n. 64 (quoting Saxo, 6:618).

39. K&K[1], 61; Patze, *Geschichte*, 1:105–106.

40. K&K[1], 61.

41. K&K[1], 61.

42. K&K[1], 61–62.

43. Barraclough, 2:131–71; see also 2:95–129; Thompson, *Feudal*, 2:68–124, 125–166.

44. K&K[1], 62.

45. K&K[1], 62.

46. K&K[1], 62–63.

47. K&K[1], 63–64. See also Patze, *Geschichte*, 1:185–86.

48. Böttiger, 2:86. Cf. notes 1 and 2.

49. K&K[1], 65–67. See also Böttiger, 2:95.

50. See Thietmar, 6:232, n. 2.

51. Thietmar, 6:232. See also K&K[1], 72.

52. K&K[1], 72.

53. K&K[1], 72. Cf. Böttiger, 2:88.

54. Böttiger, 2:87.

55. Böttiger, 2:89.

56. K&K[1], 73.

57. K&K[1], 73.

Chapter 8
The Rise of the Ludowinger

1. See chapter 6 in this volume and its notes.

2. See the Introduction to AR, 1:xv.

3. AR, 1:25ff. See also Patze, *Entstehung*, 1:153–66.

4. Patze, *Entstehung*, 1:143.

5. Patze, *Entstehung*, 1:143.

6. Patze, *Entstehung*, 1:143, n. 1, cites A. Grosz, *Die Anfänge des ersten thüringischen Landgrafengeschlechts*, phil. diss. (Göttingen: 1880), 37ff., in support of the claim that this is the oldest attempt to trace their ancestry.

7. Knochenhauer, 23ff.

8. Knochenhauer, 24.

9. Knochenhauer, 23, n. 1.

10. Knochenhauer, 30.

11. AR, 1:1–2. Since we no longer possess the original of the AR, but only a reworked text from later centuries, it is possible that the *Urtext* was not nearly as elaborate in giving details.

12. Knochenhauer, 26–31.

13. Knochenhauer, 26–27. Cf. AR, 1:2, for more details.

14. AR, 1:2–3.

15. AR, 1:3.

16. Knochenhauer, 30–32.

17. *Magnum Chronicum Belgicum*, Pistorius, ed., in *Rerum Germanicarum Scriptores*, 6:83.

18. Patze, *Entstehung*, 1:147-49.

19. Böttiger, 2:104-6.

20. Robert Folz, *Le Souvenir et la Légende de Charlamagne dans l'Empire germanique médiéval* (Dijon: 1950), 7:xi.

21. Claus Cramer, "Die Anfänge der Ludowinger," *Zeitschrift für Historische Geschichte* 68 (1957): 89.

22. Patze, *Entstehung*, 1:165–66.

23. Patze, *Entstehung*, 1:166.

24. AR, 1:4, n. 3.

25. AR, 1:4. Cf. Patze, *Entstehung*, 1:166.

26. Patze, *Entstehung*, 1:167.

27. AR, 1:4.

28. AR, 1:4.

29. Böttiger, 2:105-6.

30. AR, 1:4. Knochenhauer, 39–40, claims that this document about Henry III granting the right to build it was also forged. But evidence shows that Ludwig owned the land free of any control.

31. Patze, *Entstehung*, 1:173.

32. Theodor Mayer, "Friederich I. und Heinrich der Loewe," *Kaisertum und Herzogsgewalt im Zeitalter Friedrichs I.* (Leipzig: 1944), 372.

33. AR, 1:3.

34. Böttiger, 2:106.

35. Knochenhauer, 42–43, esp. notes 1 & 2 on 42.

36. AR, 1:5.

37. AR, 1:8.

38. Knochenhauer, 45.

39. AR, 1:5–7.

40. AR, 1:7–8.

41. AR, 1:7–8.

42. Patze, *Entstehung*, 1:180–85. Cf. Thompson, *Feudal*, 1:125ff.

43. Knochenhauer, 46-47. Cf. AR, 1:9.

44. AR, 1:9.

45. Rothe, 261.

46. AR, 1:9, implies that Adelheid planned the murder.

47. Rothe, 261–62; AR, 1:10.

48. AR, 1:10. Cf. Rothe, 262.

49. AR, 1:10. Cf. Rothe, 262.

50. Böttiger, 2:9–10, relates this as a simple story of how Frederick was out hunting near his castle with two other nobleman and was killed.

51. AR, 1:10–11.

52. Rothe, 265.

53. Patze, *Entstehung*, 1:180–88.

54. Fay, 1:146–49.

55. AR, 1:11. The editor adds in n. 6 that based on the Widukind research, any date set before 1075 would be incorrect.

56. See AR, 1:11. Cf. Patze, *Entstehung*, 1:192–93.

57. AR, 1:11.

58. AR, 1:12; Rothe, 263–64.
59. AR, 1:12; Rothe, 264.
60. AR, 1:12. See also Patze, *Entstehung*, 1:188–90.
61. Thompson, *Feudal*, 1:187ff.
62. Thompson, *Feudal*, 1:191ff.
63. Siegfried Asche, Wartburg, 1:12–20.
64. Karl Wenck, Wartburg, 1:32–33.
65. Karl Wenck, Wartburg, 1:32–33.
66. AR, 1:8–9.
67. Rothe, 265–66.
68. Rothe, 265. This is a rather strange tale that anyone who has visited the Wartburg would find impossible to believe.
69. Rothe, 266.
70. Rothe, 266.
71. Rothe, 266–67.
72. Rothe, 267.
73. Knochenhauer, 47, accepted the AR account. See also Karl Wenck, Wartburg, 1:29.
74. Karl Wenck, Wartburg, 1:31. Cf. Siegfried Asche, Wartburg, 1:11.
75. Karl Wenck, Wartburg, 1:32.
76. Karl Wenck, Wartburg, 1:32.
77. Karl Wenck, Wartburg, 1:32. Cf. Paul Weber, Wartburg, 1:52–55.
78. AR, 1:11.
79. Rothe, 264–65. It also states that Ludwig had permission to erect the castle from both the *Reich* and the neighboring nobility.
80. Karl Wenck, Wartburg, 1:34.
81. Karl Wenck, Wartburg, 1:34.
82. Siegfried Asche, Wartburg, 1:12 & 20.
83. Knochenhauer, 55.
84. AR, 1:12–13. On 12, n. 9, the editor added his belief that it was much more likely that Ludwig's captivity was tied into the Saxon nobles rebellion against Henry IV, in and around 1073. He cites a critical study by Widukind in support of that view.
85. Rothe, 268–69. Cf. AR, 1:13.
86. AR, 1:14.
87. AR, 1:14–15; Rothe, 171–72.
88. Rothe, 271–72. Cf. AR, 1:15–16.
89. AR, 1:17–18.
90. AR, 1:16.
91. Rothe, 272.
92. AR, 1:17.
93. Patze, *Entstehung*, 1:153–55.
94. Knochenhauer, 53.
95. Rothe, 273–74.
96. Patze, *Entstehung*, 1:190.
97. AR, 1:20. Cf. Knochenhauer, 64.

98. S. Petri, 207.
99. Knochenhauer, 67.
100. Patze, *Entstehung*, 1:189.
101. Knochenhauer, 67.
102. AR, 1:20–21. Cf. Patze, *Entstehung*, 1:188–90. See also Knochenhauer, 67–68.
103. AR, 1:20. Cf. Knochenhauer, 68–69.
104. Patze, *Entstehung*, 1:190, n. 81; Giesebrecht, 3:1239.
105. Knochenhauer, 69, n. 2. The Pfalzgraf died from his wounds on 9 March 1113.
106. AR, 1:20. See also S. Petri, 207.
107. See S. Petri, 207. Cf. Karl Wenck, Wartburg, 1:34.
108. Knochenhauer, 70.
109. See S. Petri, 207.
110. Knochenhauer, 70, esp. n. 4.
111. S. Petri, 208.
112. Knochenhauer, 71.
113. Knochenhauer, 74.
114. Knochenhauer, 75.
115. Patze, *Entstehung*, 1:192.
116. Patze, *Entstehung*, 1:192.
117. Böttiger, 2:110.
118. Böttiger, 2:110, states that Ludwig was 83 years old when he died. According to Knochenhauer, 76, n. 2, he was born on 6 May 1040 and baptized on 29 August of that year. This would make him 16 years old by November 1056 and 74 when he was released from his last captivity.
119. AR, 1:20.
120. See S. Petri, 210.
121. Knochenhauer, 80.
122. Patze, *Entstehung*, 1:199ff.; Knochenhauer, 80–81.
123. Knochenhauer, 80.
124. Patze, *Entstehung*, 1:202.
125. Knochenhauer, 81.
126. Patze, *Entstehung*, 1:204.
127. Patze, *Entstehung*, 1:204-5.
128. Patze, *Entstehung*, 1:208.
129. Knochenhauer, 83–84.
130. Thompson, *Feudal*, 1:235–36.
131. Thompson, *Feudal*, 1:236.
132. For a study of the Billung family, see H. J. Freytag, "Die Herrschaft der Billunger in Sachsen," *Studien und Vorarbeiten zum Historischen Atlas Niedersachsens*, vol. 20 (Göttingen: 1951).
133. Thompson, *Feudal*, 1:236.
134. Thompson, *Feudal*, 1:270.
135. Thompson, *Feudal*, 1:235.
136. Fay, 1:170.

137. Thompson, *Feudal*, 1:238.
138. Fay, 1:170.
139. Thompson, *Feudal*, 1:238.
140. Fay, 1:170. Cf. Thompson, *Feudal,* 1:238.
141. Thompson, *Feudal*, 1:238.
142. Fay, 1:171.
143. Thompson, *Feudal*, 1:239.
144. Fay, 1:171.
145. Thompson, *Feudal*, 1:262.
146. Patze, *Entstehung*, 1:208.
147. Thompson, *Feudal*, 1:236.
148. Saxo, 6:141–42.
149. Knochenhauer, 87; Patze, *Entstehung*, 1:209.
150. Knochenhauer, 87–88.
151. See AR, 1:23. Cf. Saxo, 6:146–47.
152. See Saxo, 6:147. Cf. Hildesheim, 97.
153. AR, 1:24; Saxo, 6:147; S. Petri, 211; Pagaviensis, 132.
154. See AR, 1:24.
155. AR, 1:24.
156. Pagaviensis, 132.
157. Saxo, 6:147.
158. Knochenhauer, 89.
159. Patze, *Entstehung*, 1:208.
160. Patze, *Entstehung*, 1:99.
161. Knochenhauer, 112. Cf., however, Siegfried Asche, Wartburg, 1:13, who gives evidence of a change in the social status of the Ludowinger.
162. S. Petri, 212.
163. Patze, *Entstehung*, 1:209. See also Knochenhauer, 115.
164. Rothe, 283.
165. Pagaviensis, 134–36; AR, 1:29; Rothe, 283.
166. AR, 1:29–30.
167. Patze, *Entstehung*, 1:209.
168. Fay, 1:173–74.
169. Saxo, 6:175. Cf. Rothe, 285.
170. Saxo, 6:175.
171. Thompson, *Feudal*, 1:274.
172. Patze, *Entstehung*, 1:210. Cf. Knochenhauer, 121. Saxo, 6:178, claims he was poisoned.
173. Patze, *Entstehung*, 1:210. Cf. Saxo, 6:178.
174. G. Waitz, ed., *Ottonis et Rahowini Gosta Friderici I, Imperatoris* (Hannover: 1884), 31:29.
175. Patze, *Entstehung*, 1:210–211. Cf. AR, 1:30, n. 8.
176. Patze, *Entstehung*, 1:211.

177. Knochenhauer, 125; Rothe, 290.
178. Knochenhauer, 129.
179. AR, 1:32ff.; S. Petri, 216ff.; Pagaviensis, 137ff.; Knochenhauer, 133-34.
180. Knochenhauer, 130.
181. S. Petri, 217. See also Pagaviensis, 137; Knochenhauer, 130.
182. Knochenhauer, 131.
183. S. Petri, 217. Cf. Knochenhauer, 132.
184. S. Petri, 217.
185. Knochenhauer, 133–34.
186. Knochenhauer, 134–34.
187. S. Petri, 217; Pagaviensis, 138. Cf. Fay, 1:176.
188. Knochenhauer, 141–42.
189. See Knochenhauer, 144. Cf. Patze, *Entstehung*, 1:205, n. 36.
190. Knochenhauer, 143.
191. Knochenhauer, 147–50.
192. Patze, *Entstehung*, 1:216.
193. Knochenhauer, 151.
194. Knochenhauer, 151.
195. Knochenhauer, 151–52.
196. Grandaur, 4:32, n. 8; Patze, *Entstehung*, 1:216–17.
197. Patze, *Entstehung*, 1:217.
198. Pagaviensis, 140; S. Petri, 219. Cf. Patze, *Entstehung*, 1:217.
199. Grandaur, 4:34–35. See also S. Petri, 34, n. 3. Cf. Knochenhauer, 155.
200. Knochenhauer, 158–59.
201. Knochenhauer, 159.
202. Knochenhauer, 160.
203. Knochenhauer, 160–61.
204. Helmold, 2:92; Knochenhauer, 168–69.
205. Knochenhauer, 169–70.
206. See S. Petri for the year 1166.
207. Knochenhauer, 170.
208. Knochenhauer, 171.
209. AR, 1:35.
210. See also AR, 1:35, n. 9.
211. Knochenhauer, 171–72.
212. See also Grandaur, 4:41, n. 4.
213. AR, 1:35–36.
214. Knochenhauer, 179–80. Cf. the family tree chart in the supplement to Patze. It shows that Hermann I was made Pfalzgraf of Saxony for a period, but when Ludwig died on a crusade in 1190, Hermann I became the Landgraf from 1190–1217. The other younger brother, Heinrich Raspe III, had died in 1180, while Ludwig the Pious was still the ruler of Thuringia and Hesse.

Chapter 9
The Reigns of Ludwig IV and Hermann I

1. Rothe, 300–301.
2. Knochenhauer, 172.
3. AR, 1:17.
4. Knochenhauer, 182.
5. Knochenhauer, 183.
6. AR, 1:42; S. Petri, 224.
7. See AR, 1:42; Pagaviensis, 147.
8. S. Petri, 224; AR, 1:42 and n. 6.
9. Patze, *Entstehung*, 1:231–32. Cf. n. 153. See also Knochenhauer, 186.
10. Patze, *Entstehung*, 1:232.
11. Patze, *Entstehung*, 1:232 and n. 160.
12. AR, 1:46 and n. 3.
13. Patze, *Entstehung*, 1:232.
14. Patze, *Entstehung*, 1:233.
15. S. Petri, 226; Grandaur, 4:46; Knochenhauer, 187–88.
16. Patze, *Entstehung*, 1:233; Knochenhauer, 188.
17. Patze, *Entstehung*, 1:233, based on Holder-Eggers, ed., *Annales S. Petri Erph. Maiores*, 63.
18. Knochenhauer, 191–92.
19. S. Petri, 227; Pagaviensis, 147. Cf. Knochenhauer, 192; Patze, *Entstehung*, 1:227.
20. Pagaviensis, 147. Cf. Knochenhauer, 191–95; Patze, *Entstehung*, 1:234.
21. See Starke.
22. Starke, 68 n. 15.
23. Starke, 69.
24. Starke, 69.
25. Starke, 50 and n. 50. Cf. Knochenhauer, 195.
26. Patze, *Entstehung*, 1:235.
27. Patze, *Entstehung*, 1:235.
28. Patze, *Entstehung*, 1:235.
29. Starke, 50 and n. 50.
30. Patze, *Entstehung*, 1:235–36.
31. Patze, *Entstehung*, 1:236.
32. Patze, *Entstehung*, 1:238.
33. Patze, *Entstehung*, 1:238.
34. Knochenhauer, 198.
35. Knochenhauer, 198.
36. Patze, *Entstehung*, 1:342–43.
37. Knochenhauer, 198–99.
38. Grandaur, 4:51. Cf. Knochenhauer, 201.
39. Grandaur, 4:52.
40. Grandaur, 4:52. See also 52, n. 53. Cf. Knochenhauer, 204.
41. Grandaur, 4:52–53.

42. Knochenhauer, 205–9.
43. Grandaur, 4:53.
44. Grandaur, 4:53–54; AR, 1:43.
45. AR, 1:43–44; Grandaur, 4:54, and n. 5.
46. Knochenhauer, 222.
47. Grandaur, 4:54–55; AR,1:44–45; Knochenhauer, 211.
48. See AR, 1:46ff. Cf. Knochenhauer, 215 and n. 2.
49. AR, 1:37. Here the chronicler erred by claiming that Ludwig married an Austrian woman. See n. 5; Knochenhauer, 221, n. 4. See also Patze, *Entstehung*, 1:249, on Jutta's marriage to Dietrich, the Count von Groitzsch.
50. Böttiger, 2:185. Cf. Siegfried Asche, Wartburg, 1:24.
51. Siegfried Asche, Wartburg, 1:24.
52. Ernst Martin, Wartburg, 170ff.
53. Patze, *Entstehung*, 1:249–50.
54. Patze, *Entstehung*, 1:249–50.
55. See Rothe, 314.
56. Rothe, 315. Cf. Knochenhauer, 227–28.
57. AR, 1:65; Rothe, 315; Knochenhauer, 227–28.
58. AR, 1:65.
59. Knochenhauer, 227.
60. Rothe, 316.
61. S. Petri, 231; Grandaur, 4:56–57.
62. S. Petri, 232; Grandaur, 4:56.
63. Grandaur, 4:56, n. 4.
64. S. Petri, 232; Grandaur, 4:7 & 55.
65. AR, 1:65. Cf. Knochenhauer, 228.
66. Knochenhauer, 229.
67. Knochenhauer, 229.
68. Knochenhauer, 229.
69. Rothe, 309 & 316.
70. Knochenhauer, 230.
71. Knochenhauer, 230.
72. S. Petri, 232; Grandaur, 4:57–58.
73. Rothe, 316–17.
74. Rothe, 316–17; Knochenhauer, 230–31.
75. AR, 1:66; Knochenhauer, 231.
76. AR, 1:66ff.; S. Petri, 232.
77. AR, 1:67.
78. Rothe, 316–17; Knochenhauer, 232. See also AR, 1:67.
79. Knochenhauer, 232.
80. Knochenhauer, 232.
81. AR, 1:68–69. See also Knochenhauer, 233.
82. Knochenhauer, 233.
83. S. Petri, 232.

84. Patze, *Entstehung*, 1:251–52.

85. S. Petri, 232.

86. Thompson, *Feudal*, 1:397.

87. S. Petri, 232–33. See also Patze, *Entstehung*, 1:252–53.

88. Knochenhauer, 235.

89. Knochenhauer, 236.

90. S. Petri, 233; Grandaur, 4:59–61, also 59, n. 7.

91. Knochenhauer, 241.

92. S. Petri, 233–34.

93. S. Petri, 233–34.

94. S. Petri, 233; Grandaur, 4:59–60.

95. Grandaur, 4:60, n. 4.

96. Patze, *Entstehung*, 1:253.

97. Knochenhauer, 241.

98. AR, 1:82ff.

99. AR, 1:83.

100. AR, 1:83.

101. AR, 1:83. Cf. S. Petri, 233.

102. Knochenhauer, 242.

103. Grandaur, 4:60, n. 7.

104. S. Petri, 233; Knochenhauer, 243.

105. AR, 1:84ff. See also S. Petri, 233.

106. See S. Petri, 233–34; Rothe, 318; Grandaur, 4:61. Cf. Knochenhauer, 245, n. 1.

107. S. Petri, 234. See also Knochenhauer, 245.

108. S. Petri, 233; Grandaur, 4:61; Knochenhauer, 247; Rothe, 318–19.

109. Knochenhauer, 247.

110. S. Petri, 234; Rothe, 319; Grandaur, 4:61. See also Knochenhauer, 248, n. 1.

111. Knochenhauer, 248, n. 1.

112. Knochenhauer, 248–49.

113. Knochenhauer, 249–50.

114. AR, 1:93–94.

115. AR, 1:94.

116. Knochenhauer, 250–51.

117. See AR, 1:96–98. Cf. S. Petri, 234–35; Grandaur, 4:62; Knochenhauer, 252, n. 1.

118. Patze, *Entstehung*, 1:256–57; Knochenhauer, 253–54.

119. AR, 1:96–98; S. Petri, 234–35. See also Grandaur, 4:63.

120. Rothe, 320; Patze, *Entstehung*; 1:257–58; Knochenhauer, 254.

121. S. Petri, 235; Rothe, 321; Grandaur, 4:63.

122. Knochenhauer, 261.

123. S. Petri, 235; Rothe, 322; Grandaur, 4:63–64.

124. S. Petri, 235; Grandaur, 4:64.

125. S. Petri, 235; Grandaur, 4:64–65, esp. n. 3 on 64.

126. Patze, *Entstehung*, 1:258.

127. Knochenhauer, 261.

128. S. Petri, 235–36; Grandaur, 4:65; Rothe, 322.

129. Grandaur, 4:65, n. 8; Knochenhauer, 262.

130. Patze, *Entstehung*, 1:258.

131. AR, 1:114–15; S. Petri, 236–37; Rothe, 322; Grandaur, 4:66–68. See also S. Petri, 237.

132. AR, 1:114–15; S. Petri, 236–37. Cf. Grandaur, 4:66, n. 4.

133. Grandaur, 4:66, n. 4.

134. S. Petri, 237; Rothe, 323; Grandaur, 4:68, n. 2.

135. Knochenhauer, 267.

136. Knochenhauer, 265.

137. S. Petri, 236–37; Grandaur, 4:67.

138. S. Petri, 236–37.

139. Rothe, 322; S. Petri, 236–37; Grandaur, 4:67–68; Knochenhauer, 265–66.

140. S. Petri, 236–37.

141. Knochenhauer, 265.

142. Knochenhauer, 266.

143. Knochenhauer, 266–67.

144. Knochenhauer, 267–68.

145. S. Petri, 237–38; Grandaur, 4:68–69.

146. AR, 1:123. Cf. Knochenhauer, 270.

147. Knochenhauer, 270–71.

148. See AR, 1:123; Knochenhauer, 273.

149. S. Petri, 293; Grandaur, 4:71.

150. AR, 1:124.

151. Knochenhauer, 274.

152. S. Petri, 239; AR, 1:125.

153. AR, 1:125.

154. Knochenhauer, 276.

155. S. Petri, 240; Knochenhauer, 276.

156. S. Petri, 240.

157. S. Petri, 240; Knochenhauer, 276–77.

158. See S. Petri, 240.

159. Grandaur, 4:74, n. 2.

160. Grandaur, 4:74, n. 2.

161. Knochenhauer, 278.

162. Grandaur, 4:74, n. 2.

163. Knochenhauer, 279, n. 1.

164. S. Petri, 240; AR, 1:129.

165. S. Petri, 241; AR, 1:130. See also Grandaur, 4:75. Cf. Knochenhauer, 279–80.

166. Knochenhauer, 280.

167. S. Petri, 241; Grandaur, 4:75, n. 4.

168. Knochenhauer, 281.

169. Knochenhauer, n. 2.

170. Winckelmann, 1:44, n. 2.
171. Winckelmann, 1:44ff.
172. Knochenhauer, 282.
173. S. Petri, 241; Grandaur, 4:75; Knochenhauer, 282–83.
174. Knochenhauer, 283.
175. S. Petri, 241; Grandaur, 4:76.
176. AR, 1:142–43.
177. See AR, 1:142–43.
178. Knochenhauer, 284–85.
179. Knochenhauer, 284–85.
180. AR, 1:155.
181. Rothe, 339.
182. See S. Petri, 242. See also Rothe, 340.
183. Karl Wenck, Wartburg, 1:213.

Chapter 10
The Reign of Ludwig V and Holy Elizabeth

1. AR, 1:90.
2. Karl Wenck, Wartburg, 1:183.
3. AR, 1:111–227, passim.
4. Rothe, 356–58.
5. AR, 1:111.
6. AR, 1:122ff.
7. AR, 1:126.
8. AR, 1:126.
9. Rothe, 358.
10. Knochenhauer, 297.
11. Patze, *Entstehung*, 1:262.
12. Patze, *Entstehung*, 1:262–63.
13. AR, 1:146–47.
14. AR, 1:146–47.
15. AR, 1:146–47, and n. 4.
16. AR, 1:147.
17. Rothe, 343–44.
18. AR, 1:147–48.
19. AR, 1:148–50.
20. AR, 1:155.
21. Knochenhauer, 299–300.
22. AR, 1:155.
23. Patze, *Entstehung*, 1:263.
24. AR, 1:155.
25. AR, 1:155.
26. Patze, *Entstehung*, 1:263.
27. Patze, *Entstehung*, 1:263; Knochenhauer, 302–3.
28. AR, 1:170, and n. 1; Cf. Patze, 1:263; Knochenhauer, 304.
29. AR, 1:170–71 (here the chronicler's account hardly agrees with what we know of events at the time); Knochenhauer, 304; Patze, *Entstehung*, 1:263–64.

30. Patze, *Entstehung*, 1:263–64.
31. Knochenhauer, 305.
32. Patze, *Entstehung*, 1:263–64; Knochenhauer, 305.
33. Patze, *Entstehung*, 1:264.
34. Knochenhauer, 304–5.
35. AR, 1:171. Cf. Knochenhauer, 305.
36. Patze, *Entstehung*, 1:264.
37. AR, 1:173; Knochenhauer, 306.
38. See Knochenhauer, 284ff.; 306, n. 3.
39. See Knochenhauer, 306, n. 4.
40. Knochenhauer, 307, n. 2.
41. Knochenhauer, 307, n. 2.
42. Patze, *Entstehung*, 1:264–65.
43. The original account is in AR, 1:173–77 and repeated in Berthold, 32–35; but it is already somewhat confused in Rothe, 349–50.
44. Knochenhauer, 308.
45. Knochenhauer, 308–9.
46. AR, 1:174–75.
47. AR, 1:175.
48. Knochenhauer, 309–10.
49. Knochenhauer, 309–10.
50. Knochenhauer, 309–10.
51. Knochenhauer, 310.
52. AR, 1:174ff.
53. See Knochenhauer, 311, n. 1.
54. Knochenhauer, 311, n. 3.
55. Knochenhauer, 311–12.
56. AR, 1:176ff.
57. AR, 1:178. Cf Berthold, 36–40.
58. AR, 1:178, n. 2. Cf. Knochenhauer, 312, n. 1.
59. AR, 1:178, notes 4–6; Knochenhauer, 313.
60. Rothe, 360.
61. Berthold, 36ff.; Knochenhauer, 313.
62. Berthold, 36–40.
63. AR, 1:179–80.
64. AR, 1:180.
65. AR, 1:180; Knochenhauer, 313.
66. AR, 1:181; Knochenhauer, 313–14.
67. Knochenhauer, 314.
68. AR, 1:182; Berthold, 40. Cf. Knochenhauer, 314, n. 1.
69. Knochenhauer, 315.
70. Knochenhauer, 315.
71. Knochenhauer, 315.
72. AR, 1:183, 193; Berthold, 40 and 47ff. Cf. Patze, *Entstehung*, 1:269.
73. Knochenhauer, 316–17.
74. Patze, *Entstehung*, 1:269. Cf. Knochenhauer, 317, n. 1.
75. Knochenhauer, 317.

76. See Patze, *Entstehung*, 1:270, n. 30.
77. Cf. Patze, *Entstehung*, 1:270, n. 1.
78. AR, 1:184–86; Berthold, 40ff.
79. AR, 1:184.
80. AR, 1:180ff. See also Knochenhauer, 318, n. 2.
81. AR, 1:184–85.
82. Cf. Knochenhauer, 318. See also AR, 1:188ff.
83. AR, 1:318–19.
84. AR, 1:187–88; Berthold, 43. Cf. Knochenhauer, 323, n. 2; see also 320, n. 2.
85. AR, 1:188ff. Cf. Knochenhauer, 319.
86. AR, 1:189. Cf. Knochenhauer, 319–20.
87. AR, 1:190; Berthold, 45.
88. AR, 1:190.
89. Karl Wenck, Wartburg, 1:191–92.
90. Karl Wenck, Wartburg, 1:192.
91. Karl Wenck, Wartburg, 1:193.
92. Karl Wenck, Wartburg, 1:194.
93. Karl Wenck, Wartburg, 1:195.
94. Karl Wenck, Wartburg, 1:195.
95. Karl Wenck, Wartburg, 1:195.
96. Karl Wenck, Wartburg, 1:195.
97. AR, 1:190–91.
98. Karl Wenck, Wartburg, 1:196–97; AR, 1:197–98.
99. AR, 1:198–99.
100. AR, 1:199–200.
101. Knochenhauer, 325.
102. AR, 1:203–5. Cf. Knochenhauer's evaluation, 325–26.
103. AR, 1:203.
104. AR, 1:205–6.
105. AR, 1:205–6.
106. AR, 1:205–7.
107. AR, 1:205, n. 5. Cf. Rothe, 369, and Knochenhauer, 326.
108. Knochenhauer, 326. See also AR, 1:206, n. 1.
109. AR, 1:206–7; Rothe, 369–70. Cf. Knochenhauer, 326–27.
110. Rothe, 170.
111. AR, 1:207.
112. AR, 1:207–8; Rothe, 370–71; Berthold, 61.
113. Knochenhauer, 327.
114. AR, 1:208.
115. Rothe, 371–72.
116. AR, 1:209–11; Rothe, 374; Knochenhauer, 328.
117. Knochenhauer, 328.
118. Rothe, 375.
119. AR, 1:211.

120. Rothe, 376.
121. Rothe, 377.
122. Rothe, 378.
123. Rothe, 378.
124. Rothe, 379.
125. Rothe, 379.
126. Rothe, 380. Cf. Karl Wenck, Wartburg, 1:215–16.
127. Rothe, 381.
128. Karl Wenck, Wartburg, 1:193–200. Cf. Böttiger, 2:207–10.
129. Rothe, 382–83.
130. Karl Wenck, Wartburg, 1:215–16.
131. Rothe, 384–85.
132. Rothe, 386.

Chapter 11
The Reign of Heinrich Raspe

1. Knochenhauer, 333. See also Patze, *Entstehung*, 1:271, and Böttiger, 2:209.
2. Karl Wenck, Wartburg, 1:215.
3. Böttiger, 2:211–12; Karl Wenck, Wartburg, 1:215.
4. Karl Wenck, Wartburg, 1:215.
5. Karl Wenck, Wartburg, 1:215–16.
6. Knochenhauer, 334.
7. Knochenhauer, 336, and n. 2.
8. Knochenhauer, 336, n. 4.
9. Knochenhauer, 336, n. 5.
10. Knochenhauer, 337.
11. AR, 1:213. Rothe embellished the story considerably, but may have possessed additional sources. Cf. Böttiger, 2:212.
12. AR, 1:214.
13. Böttiger, 2:212.
14. Rothe, 396.
15. Knochenhauer, 338.
16. Patze, *Entstehung*, 1:274ff.
17. Patze, *Entstehung*, 1:274–75.
18. Knochenhauer, 339.
19. Knochenhauer, 339.
20. Patze, *Entstehung*, 1:275.
21. AR, 1:215.
22. Knochenhauer, 339, n. 3.
23. AR, 1:215; Knochenhauer, 339, n. 4.
24. AR, 1:215.
25. Böttiger, 2:212.
26. Böttiger, 2:212.
27. Patze, *Entstehung*, 1:286.
28. Knochenhauer, 341, and n. 1.
29. S. Petri, for the year 1232.

30. AR, 1:215; S. Petri, for the year 1233.
31. AR, 1:215.
32. Rothe, 389–90.
33. S. Petri, for the year 1233.
34. Winckelmann, 1:405.
35. Knochenhauer, 342, n. 4.
36. Heinrich Raspe served as one of Frederick II's witnesses on a document from Venice dated March 1232. Knochenhauer, 343, n. 3.
37. Karl Wenck, Wartburg, 1:216.
38. Karl Wenck, Wartburg, 1:216–17.
39. Karl Wenck, Wartburg, 1:216–17.
40. Karl Wenck, Wartburg, 1:217.
41. Karl Wenck, Wartburg, 1:217.
42. Patze, Entstehung, 1:287–88.
43. Knochenhauer, 343.
44. Knochenhauer, 344.
45. S. Petri, 255.
46. Knochenhauer, 344.
47. Knochenhauer, 344–45.
48. S. Petri, 255. Cf. Knochenhauer, 345.
49. AR, 1:220; S. Petri, 255.
50. Knochenhauer, 346.
51. Böttiger, 2:212.
52. Rothe, 398ff. Cf. AR, 1:223.
53. Böttiger, 2:213.
54. Rothe, 258.
55. Karl Wenck, Wartburg, 1:218.
56. Patze, Entstehung, 1:289.
57. Patze, Entstehung, 1:289, claims that the Landfürst of Silesia, a cousin of Holy Elizabeth, blunted the Tarter advance and thus saved the West.
58. AR, 1:223. See also S. Petri, 259. Cf. Knochenhauer, 256–57.
59. Patze, Entstehung, 1:290.
60. Knochenhauer, 356–57.
61. Rothe, 400–1. Cf. S. Petri, for the year 1242.
62. Patze, Entstehung, 1:290, no. 97; Knochenhauer, 357; Karl Wenck, Wartburg, 1:218.
63. See Knochenhauer, 357–58.
64. Karl Wenck, Wartburg, 1:218.
65. Knochenhauer, 358, n. 2.
66. See Knochenhauer, 359.
67. In a source pertaining to the cloister in Georgenthal, in the year 1242, Heinrich Raspe called himself, "sacri imperii per Germaniam procurator." Cited by Knochenhauer, 360.
68. Karl Wenck, Wartburg, 1:218.
69. Knochenhauer, 360.
70. Patze, Entstehung, 1:289–90.
71. Haller, Johannes, Das Papstum (Stuttgart: 1952), 4:164ff.
72. Patze, Entstehung, 1:291.
73. Rothe, 401.
74. Patze, Entstehung, 1:290.
75. Patze, Entstehung, 1:290, n. 97.
76. Patze, Entstehung, 1:291.
77. Patze, Entstehung, 1:292.
78. Patze, Entstehung, 1:292.
79. Patze, Entstehung, 1:292.
80. Patze, Entstehung, 1:292.
81. Knochenhauer, 361.
82. See S. Petri, 261. Cf. AR, 1:224.
83. S. Petri, 261.
84. Knochenhauer, 362.
85. Rothe, 403.
86. S. Petri, 261. See also Knochenhauer, 362, n. 4.
87. Patze, Entstehung, 1:293; Karl Wenck, Wartburg, 1:220–21.
88. Karl Wenck, Wartburg, 1:219–21.
89. Rothe, 404.
90. Karl Wenck, Wartburg, 1:219–21.
91. Karl Wenck, Wartburg, 1:220.
92. Knochenhauer, 363–64.
93. Karl Wenck, Wartburg, 1:220.
94. Patze, Entstehung, 1:294.
95. Karl Wenck, Wartburg, 1:294.
96. See Patze, Entstehung, 1:294.
97. Cf. Patze, Entstehung, 1:294, n. 115.
98. Patze, Entstehung, 1:294.
99. Knochenhauer, 362–63; Böttiger, 2:215.
100. Patze, Entstehung, 1:294, cites as his source a thesis by Rübesamen, "Landgraf Heinrich Raspe von Thüringen, der Gegenkönig Friedrich II" (Halle: 1885).
101. Patze, Entstehung, 1:295, n. 123, cites the evidence of additional sums spent by Rome.
102. Patze, Entstehung, 1:295.
103. Karl Wenck, Wartburg, 1:120–21.
104. Karl Wenck, Wartburg, 1:120–21.
105. Knochenhauer, 364; Karl Wenck, Wartburg, 1:120. Cf. Patze, Entstehung, 1:265.
106. Schirmacher, 4:429; Böttiger, 2:215.
107. Karl Wenck, Wartburg, 1:120–21. Cf. Knochenhauer, 264; Patze, Entstehung, 1:295.
108. Patze, Entstehung, 1:295.
109. Patze, Entstehung, 1:295–96.
110. Patze, Entstehung, 1:296.
111. Rübesamen, "Landgraf Heinrich Raspe . . . ," 50.
112. Karl Wenck, Wartburg, 1:221.

113. Karl Wenck, Wartburg, 1:221; Patze, *Entstehung*, 1:296. Both based their views on AR, 1:225.

114. AR, 1:225.

115. AR, 1:225.

116. Patze, *Entstehung*, 1:298.

117. Patze, *Entstehung*, 1:298–99.

118. Patze, *Entstehung*, 1:298–99.

Chapter 12
Thuringia under the House of Wettin

1. Böttiger, 2:226–27.

2. AR, 1:234. Cf. Rommel, 2:32.

3. Rommel, 2:32, and n. 28.

4. Böttiger, 2:227, and n. 1.

5. Böttiger, 2:228.

6. See Patze, *Geschichte*, 2:48–49. Cf. Karl Wenck, Wartburg, 1:228.

7. Böttiger, 2:236.

8. Böttiger, 2:238–40.

9. Böttiger, 2:240.

10. Patze, *Geschichte*, 2:55–56; Böttiger, 2:240–42.

11. Böttiger, 2:241.

12. See Böttiger, 2:241, and Karl Wenck, Wartburg, 1:233, for details.

13. AR, 1:261; Rothe, 463.

14. AR, 1:261–65.

15. Karl Wenck, Wartburg, 1:133–34. Cf. Böttiger, 2:243, n. 3.

16. Böttiger, 2:244, and n. 1.

17. Böttiger, 2:244–45.

18. AR, 1:270–74. Cf. Patze, *Geschichte*, 2:59–61; Karl Wenck, Wartburg, 1:234; Rothe, 472–79.

19. Rothe, 472–73; Karl Wenck, Wartburg, 1:233–34; Patze, *Geschichte*, 2:59ff.

20. Rothe, 472–73.

21. Rothe, 472–73.

22. Rothe, 473.

23. AR, 1:272; Rothe, 476.

24. AR, 1:273–74; Patze, *Geschichte*, 2:57–58.

25. See Patze, *Geschichte*, 2:59–61. See also Karl Wenck, Wartburg, 1:234–35.

26. Böttiger, 2:242; Karl Wenck, Wartburg, 1:236.

27. Rothe, 484–87.

28. Patze, *Geschichte*, 2:61ff.; Böttiger, 2:247.

29. AR, 1:276; Rothe, 489.

30. AR, 1:276; Rothe, 489–90.

31. AR, 1:276; Rothe, 489–90.

32. AR, 1:276–77; Rothe, 490.

33. Böttiger, 2:247; Karl Wenck, Wartburg, 1:235; Patze, *Geschichte*, 2:63–64.

34. AR, 1:278; Rothe, 493–94.

35. AR, 1:278–79; Rothe, 495.

36. Rothe, 495.

37. Rothe, 495; AR, 1:278–79.

38. Rothe, 495.

39. Böttiger, 2:248.

40. Böttiger, 2:248.

41. Rothe, 496–97.

42. AR, 1:497.

43. AR, 1:284–85; Böttiger, 2:249; Karl Wenck, Wartburg, 1:236.

44. See AR, 1:240; Böttiger, 2:249; Karl Wenck, Wartburg, 1:236.

45. AR, 1:288–89; Rothe, 506.

46. AR, 1:289.

47. See AR, 1:289; Rothe, 505–6; Böttiger, 2:250.

48. AR, 1:289; Rothe, 505; Patze, *Geschichte*, 2:65.

49. AR, 1:289.

50. Rothe, 508–10; Karl Wenck, Wartburg, 1:237.

51. AR, 1:290; Rothe, 210–12; Karl Wenck, Wartburg, 1:237–38, has much detail about the siege.

52. Rothe, 513; Böttiger, 2:250.

53. Rothe, 513–14. Cf. Böttiger, 2:250.

54. Böttiger, 2:251; Karl Wenck, Wartburg, 1:238–39.

55. AR, 1:290; Rothe, 514–15. Cf. Böttiger, 2:252.

56. See Patze, *Geschichte*, 2:67; Karl Wenck, Wartburg, 1:239.

57. AR, 1:293; Rothe, 515–16.

58. AR, 1:294; Rothe, 520, says the queen had the assassin beheaded.

59. AR, 1:294–95; Rothe, 520.

60. Rothe, 521–22; Böttiger, 2:252; Patze, *Geschichte*, 2:67; Karl Wenck, Wartburg, 1:239–40.

61. Böttiger, 2:262; Patze, *Geschichte*, 2:67–68; Karl Wenck, Wartburg, 1:260; Rothe, 522–23.

62. AR, 1:295; Rothe, 525.

63. AR, 1:295–96; Rothe, 524–27.

64. AR, 1:296; Rothe, 227–28.

65. AR, 1:296–97; Rothe, 528–29.

66. AR, 1:297–98; Rothe, 529–30.

67. AR, 1:298.

68. Patze, *Geschichte*, 2:298.
69. AR, 1:298.
70. Böttiger, 2:252–53.
71. AR, 1:299–300; Rothe, 532–33.
72. Patze, *Geschichte*, 2:72; Karl Wenck, Wartburg, 1:240.
73. Karl Wenck, Wartburg, 1:240; Rothe, 534–35.
74. Karl Wenck, Wartburg, 1:240; Rothe, 536.
75. Rothe, 536–37; Karl Wenck, Wartburg, 1:240; Patze, *Geschichte*, 2:72.
76. Patze, *Geschichte*, 2:72–73.
77. Karl Wenck, Wartburg, 1:240.
78. Karl Wenck, Wartburg, 1:240.
79. Rothe, 547ff.; Böttiger, 2:262; Karl Wenck, Wartburg, 1:241.
80. Patze, *Geschichte*, 2:74.
81. AR, 1:303; Patze, *Geschichte*, 2:74; Böttiger, 2:288.
82. Patze, *Geschichte*, 2:74.
83. See Zeumer, 2:51–52.
84. AR, 1:303.
85. Patze, *Geschichte*, 2:75–76.
86. Patze, *Geschichte*, 2:75–76.
87. AR, 1:305.
88. Patze, *Geschichte*, 2:76.
89. AR, 1:305; Rothe, 558–59; Böttiger, 2:288.
90. Rothe, 558; Patze, *Geschichte*, 2:76; Böttiger, 2:288.
91. Böttiger, 2:288–91; Patze, *Geschichte*, 2:77.
92. Böttiger, 2:288–89.
93. Patze, *Geschichte*, 2:98ff.
94. Patze, *Geschichte*, 2:77.
95. Patze, *Geschichte*, 2:77–78.
96. Patze, *Geschichte*, 2:77.
97. Patze, *Geschichte*, 2:78.
98. AR, 1:306; Rothe, 559–60; and Patze, *Geschichte*, 2:78.
99. Patze, *Geschichte*, 2:78.
100. Patze, *Geschichte*, 2:79–80.
101. Patze, *Geschichte*, 2:79.
102. AR, 1:307.
103. Rothe, 365–66.
104. Böttiger, 2:290–91.
105. Böttiger, 2:291.
106. AR, 1:307.
107. Rothe, 562.
108. Rothe, 562.
109. Rothe, 567.
110. Rothe, 567–68.
111. Patze, *Geschichte*, 2:80–81.

112. Patze, *Geschichte*, 2:81.
113. Patze, *Geschichte*, 2:81.
114. Patze, *Geschichte*, 2:82.
115. Rothe, 563–64; Böttiger, 2:291–92; Patze, *Geschichte*, 2:82.
116. Rothe, 563–64; Böttiger, 2:291–92; and Patze, *Geschichte*, 2:82.
117. Patze, *Geschichte*, 2:82. Cf. Böttiger, 2:292–93.
118. Patze, *Geschichte*, 2:82–83.
119. Böttiger, 2:292.
120. Rothe, 575; Böttiger, 2:293–95.
121. See Patze, *Geschichte*, 2:84.
122. Patze, *Geschichte*, 2:84.
123. Rothe, 575–76.
124. See Rothe, 575–76.
125. Rothe, 576–77; Patze, *Geschichte*, 2:84–85; Böttiger, 2:293–94.
126. Patze, *Geschichte*, 2:87; Böttiger, 2:293–94.
127. Patze, *Geschichte*, 2:87.
128. Patze, *Geschichte*, 2:87–88; Böttiger, 2:293–94.
129. Patze, *Geschichte*, 2:87–88; Böttiger, 2:293–94.
130. Rothe, 587.
131. Rothe, 589.
132. Böttiger, 2:295–96.
133. Böttiger, 2:296.
134. Rothe, 584; Böttiger, 2:294–95.
135. See Rothe, 583–86, and Böttiger, 2:294–96.
136. Rothe, 583–84.
137. Rothe, 585.
138. Rothe, 585–86.
139. Rothe, 586.
140. Rothe, 589ff.
141. Böttiger, 2:295–97; Patze, *Geschichte*, 2:89.
142. Rothe, 587ff.
143. Patze, *Geschichte*, 2:89; Böttiger, 2:297–98.
144. Patze, *Geschichte*, 2:89; Böttiger, 2:297–98.
145. Böttiger, 2:297–98.
146. Patze, *Geschichte*, 2:89.
147. Patze, *Geschichte*, 2:89–90.
148. Patze, *Geschichte*, 2:90.
149. Patze, *Geschichte*, 2:90–91.
150. Rothe, 592–93; Patze, *Geschichte*, 2:91.
151. Patze, *Geschichte*, 2:93.
152. Patze, *Geschichte*, 2:93–94.
153. Patze, *Geschichte*, 2:94–95; Böttiger, 2:298–99.

154. Patze, *Geschichte*, 2:94.
155. Patze, *Geschichte*, 2:94.
156. S. Petri, for the year 1349; Rothe, 598; Patze, *Geschichte*, 2:94–95.
157. Patze, *Geschichte*, 2:95.
158. Patze, *Geschichte*, 2:95.
159. Patze, *Geschichte*, 2:97.
160. Patze, *Geschichte*, 2:97.
161. K&K^2, 1:140.
162. Böttiger, 2:299–300.
163. Böttiger, 2:300–301.
164. Patze, *Geschichte*, 2:100.
165. Patze, *Geschichte*, 2:100.
166. Böttiger, 2:300.
167. Patze, *Geschichte*, 2:102; Rothe, 311.
168. Patze, *Geschichte*, 2:103.
169. Rothe, 609.
170. Rothe, 611–12; Patze, *Geschichte*, 2:104.
171. Patze, *Geschichte*, 2:104.
172. Rothe, 612–16; Patze, *Geschichte*, 2:104.
173. Rothe, 616–17. Cf. 618.
174. Rothe, 620; Patze, *Geschichte*, 2:106.
175. Rothe, 620–21.
176. Rothe, 621–24.
177. Rothe, 224–25.
178. Patze, *Geschichte*, 2:106; Böttiger, 2:299–300.
179. Rothe, 616; Patze, *Geschichte*, 2:107ff.
180. Patze, *Geschichte*, 2:107ff.
181. Patze, *Geschichte*, 2:107.
182. Patze, *Geschichte*, 2:108.
183. Patze, *Geschichte*, 2:108–9.
184. Patze, *Geschichte*, 2:108–9.
185. Patze, *Geschichte*, 2:109.
186. Böttiger, 2:303–4.
187. Patze, *Geschichte*, 2:111.
188. Patze, *Geschichte*, 2:111.
189. Patze, *Geschichte*, 2:111.
190. Patze, *Geschichte*, 2:112–13.
191. Rothe, 625–28.
192. Rothe, 628–29.
193. Rothe, 628–29.
194. Patze, *Geschichte*, 2:114–15; Rothe, 629.
195. Patze, *Geschichte*, 2:114–15.
196. Patze, *Geschichte*, 2:115.
197. Patze, *Geschichte*, 2:115. Cf. Rothe, 630–31.
198. Rothe, 361.
199. Patze, *Geschichte*, 2:226; K&K^2, 1:141–42; Böttiger, 2:304–5.
200. K&K^2, 1:141–42.

201. K&K^2, 1:142; Patze, *Geschichte*, 2:227–28.
202. Patze, *Geschichte*, 2:227–28; Böttiger, 2:304–5.
203. Patze, *Geschichte*, 2:228; K&K^2, 1:142.
204. Patze, *Geschichte*, 2:123–24.
205. K&K^2, 1:141.
206. K&K^2, 1:141–42.
207. Patze, *Geschichte*, 2:229.
208. Patze, *Geschichte*, 2:229; K&K^2, 1:141–43.
209. Patze, *Geschichte*, 2:229.
210. Patze, *Geschichte*, 2:230.
211. Patze, *Geschichte*, 2:230–31.
212. Patze, *Geschichte*, 2:231–32; K&K^2, 1:142–43.
213. Patze, *Geschichte*, 2:232–33.
214. Patze, *Geschichte*, 2:232–33.
215. Patze, *Geschichte*, 2:245–46.
216. Patze, *Geschichte*, 2:245–47.

Chapter 13
Frederick the Valiant and His Successors

1. K&K^1, 128–29.
2. K&K^1, 129.
3. K&K^2, 1:131.
4. Patze, *Geschichte*, 2:122.
5. Patze, *Geschichte*, 2:123–24.
6. Rothe, 650.
7. Patze, *Geschichte*, 2:125ff.
8. Patze, *Geschichte*, 2:125ff.
9. Patze, *Geschichte*, 2:125ff.
10. Patze, *Geschichte*, 2:125ff.
11. K&K^2, 1:132.
12. K&K^2, 1:132.
13. Patze, *Geschichte*, 2:124.
14. K&K^2, 1:133.
15. K&K^2, 1:133.
16. Patze, *Geschichte*, 2:128.
17. Patze, *Geschichte*, 2:128.
18. Patze, *Geschichte*, 2:129.
19. Patze, *Geschichte*, 2:126.
20. Patze, *Geschichte*, 2:127–28.
21. Patze, *Geschichte*, 2:126–27.
22. Patze, *Geschichte*, 2:128–29.
23. Rothe, 655. Cf. Thompson, *Medieval*, 983–85.
24. Thompson, *Medieval*, 983–84.
25. K&K^2, 1:134; Thompson, *Medieval*, 984.
26. K&K^2, 1:134. The messengers pre-

sented the four "Prager Articles" that stressed: (1) free teaching of the word of God; (2) communion in both kinds; (3) the dissolution of church property; and (4) the applicability of the death penalty to the clergy.

27. K&K², 1:134.
28. K&K², 1:134.
29. K&K¹, 129ff. Thompson, *Medieval*, 983–85.
30. K&K¹, 155.
31. Patze, *Geschichte*, 2:129.
32. Patze, *Geschichte*, 2:130.
33. Böttiger, 2:2:315.
34. K&K¹, 155.
35. K&K², 1:134–35.
36. K&K², 1:135.
37. Thompson, *Medieval*, 985.
38. Cf. Böttiger, 2:315.
39. Rothe, 658–61. Cf. Böttiger, 2:315–16; K&K¹, 155–56.
40. See Böttiger, 2:315. Cf. Rothe, 658; K&K¹, 155.
41. Rothe, 658–59. Cf. K&K¹, 155; Böttiger, 2:315.
42. Rothe, 659–60. All the later writers based their accounts on the work of this Eisenach chronicler.
43. Böttiger, 2:315.
44. K&K¹, 155; Böttiger, 2:316–17; K&K², 1:136.
45. Böttiger, 2:317–18.
46. Böttiger, 2:317.
47. Böttiger, 2:318–19.
48. Böttiger, 2:319–20.
49. K&K¹, 156.
50. Rothe, 665. See also Patze, *Geschichte*, 2:130–31.
51. Rothe, 664; Patze, *Geschichte*, 2:130–31.
52. K&K¹, 156.
53. Rothe, 665; Patze, *Geschichte*, 2:130–31. Cf. Böttiger, 2:320–21.
54. See Böttiger, 2:320–21; K&K¹, 156.
55. Böttiger, 2:321–22.
56. Thompson, *Medieval*, 985–86. See also K&K¹, 156.
57. Patze, *Geschichte*, 2:131–32.
58. Böttiger, 2:322–23.
59. Böttiger, 2:131–32. Another son, Henry, died at age fourteen.
60. Patze, *Geschichte*, 2:131–32. See also Böttiger, 2:322–23.
61. Böttiger, 2:323–24.

62. K&K¹, 157–58.
63. K&K¹, 156–57.
64. K&K¹, 157.
65. K&K¹, 157.
66. Böttiger, 2:324–25; Patze, *Geschichte*, 2:133; K&K¹, 158.
67. Böttiger, 2:324–25.
68. Patze, *Geschichte*, 2:132.
69. Patze, *Geschichte*, 2:132.
70. Patze, *Geschichte*, 2:131–34.
71. Patze, *Geschichte*, 2:134.
72. Patze, *Geschichte*, 2:134. Cf. Böttiger, 2:324–25.
73. Patze, *Geschichte*, 2:134. See also Böttiger, 2:325.
74. Patze, *Geschichte*, 2:134–35. See also Böttiger, 2:324–25.
75. Böttiger, 2:325; Patze, *Geschichte*, 2:135.
76. Patze, *Geschichte*, 2:135.
77. Patze, *Geschichte*, 2:135.
78. Patze, *Geschichte*, 2:135.
79. Böttiger, 2:325–26. See also Patze, *Geschichte*, 2:135.
80. Patze, *Geschichte*, 2:136.
81. Patze, *Geschichte*, 2:137.
82. See Patze, *Geschichte*, 2:137.
83. Patze, *Geschichte*, 2:137.
84. K&K¹, 157–58.
85. Patze, *Geschichte*, 2:137–38.
86. Patze, *Geschichte*, 2:137–38.
87. Patze, *Geschichte*, 2:138–39.
88. Patze, *Geschichte*, 2:138–39.
89. K&K¹, 158; K&K² 2:138.
90. K&K² 1:138–39. Cf. Patze, *Geschichte*, 2:139. See also Böttiger, 2:327–28.
91. See Böttiger, 2:327–30; Patze, *Geschichte*, 2:158–59.
92. Patze, *Geschichte*, 2:140–41.
93. Patze, *Geschichte*, 2:141–42.
94. Patze, *Geschichte*, 2:142.
95. K&K¹, 159.
96. Böttiger, 2:331–32.
97. Patze, *Geschichte*, 2:143–44. See also Böttiger, 2:325–26.
98. Patze, *Geschichte*, 2:144–45.
99. Patze, *Geschichte*, 2:145.
100. Patze, *Geschichte*, 2:145.
101. Patze, *Geschichte*, 2:144–45. Blaschke, 13ff.
102. Patze, *Geschichte*, 2:144–46.
103. Patze, *Geschichte*, 2:146.
104. Schwiebert, *Luther*, 82.

Chapter 14
The Prosperous Reign of Frederick the Wise

1. Blaschke.
2. Blaschke, 13–14.
3. Blaschke, 14.
4. Blaschke, 15.
5. K&K^1, 141.
6. K&K^1, 141.
7. K&K^1, 141.
8. K&K^2, 2:191.
9. K&K^2, 2:192.
10. K&K^1, 141.
11. Ingetraut Ludolphy, "Die Ursachen der Gegnerschaft zwischen Luther und Herzog Georg von Sachsen," *Luther Jahrbuch* (1965), 34–35.
12. See Spalatin, *Friedrich*; Spalatin, *Chronik*; G. Berbig, *Georgii Spalatini, Ephemerides inchoatae anno MCCCLXXX*, Quellen und Darstellungen aus der Geschichte des Reformationsjahrhunderts, vol. 5 (Leipzig: 1908).
13. Kolde, 12.
14. Kirn, 8–9.
15. See Spalatin, *Friedrich*, 45–46. See also Kolde, 12.
16. Kirn, 9; see also Haller, *Politik*, p. 6.
17. K&K^2, 2:193ff.; Kirn, 8–10, 12–13.
18. See Kolde, 25–28. See also K&K^2, 2:192–93; Spalatin, *Friedrich*, 61; and the elector's letters to John in Karl E. Förstemann, *Neues Urkundenbuch zur Geschichte der Evangelischen Kirchenordnung* (Hamburg: 1842).
19. See Kirn, 15–16.
20. Haller, 64. See also Kirn, 10.
21. Kirn, 10–12.
22. Kirn, 11.
23. Spalatin, *Friedrich*, 24–25, 56. Cf. WA, 19:646; Enders, 14:230; WA Tr, 2:5256; Kirn, 12–14.
24. K&K^2, 2:193–94.
25. K&K^2, 2:193–94.
26. K&K^1, 144.
27. K&K^1, 144.
28. K&K^1, 144–45.
29. K&K^1, 145–46.
30. K&K^1, 145–46.
31. K&K^1, 146.
32. Kirn, 24, cites the case of a Pastor Zwilling, who had participated with Carlstadt and his "Zwickau prophets" in the Wittenberg

disturbances of 1521–22. When Luther returned from the Wartburg and quieted Wittenberg, he felt sorry for this young man and tried to get him placed in Altenburg as the town pastor. But since Zwilling had participated in revolutionary acts, the elector would not accept this. The elector also refused to cooperate with Luther in 1523 in a matter involving the city of Leisnig.

33. See Spalatin, *Friedrich*, 27–29; 63–67.
34. Schwiebert, "Library." See also Schwiebert, *Luther*, 244ff.
35. Kirn, 26–28; K&K^2 2:194; Blaschke, 22.
36. Kirn, 26–27.
37. Kirn, 27.
38. Paul Kalkoff, *Ablasz und Reliquienverehrung an der Schlosskirche zu Wittenberg unter Friederich dem Weisen* (Gotha: Perthes, 1907).
39. Kirn, 27.
40. Kirn, 27–28.
41. K&K^2, 2:194.
42. Blaschke, 21–22; Kirn, 27–28.
43. K&K^2, 2:194.
44. Kirn, 27–28.
45. Blaschke, 33–42; K&K^2, 2:197–99; K&K^1, 151–53.
46. See Blaschke, 41; 79–86. See also Schwiebert, *Luther*, 235–44.
47. K&K^1, 151; K&K^2 2:197–98.
48. K&K^1, 151.
49. Blaschke, 39.
50. Blaschke, 39.
51. K&K^2, 2:197–98.
52. K&K^1, 151. Cf. Schwiebert, *Luther*, 107–8.
53. Blaschke, 39–40.
54. K&K^2, 2:198–99.
55. Blaschke, 40–41.
56. Blaschke, 42.
57. K&K^1, 152–53.
58. Blaschke, 38–39.
59. Blaschke, 84.
60. Charitius. See Matthaeus Faber, *Kurzgefaszte Historische Nachricht von der Schlosz und Akademischen Stiftskirche zu Aller-Heiligen* (Wittenberg: 1717).
61. Spalatin, *Friedrich*. See also Schwiebert, *Luther*, 357–68.
62. Schwiebert, *Luther*, 235. Cf. Gottfried Krüger, *Die Lutherstadt Wittenberg der Jahrhunderte* (Wittenberg: 1938), 28. For a

detailed history of the founding of the
University of Wittenberg, see vol. 2 of the present work.

63. Oskar Thulin, *Die Lutherstadt Wittenberg und Thorgau* (Berlin: 1932), 14.

64. Spalatin, *Friedrich*, 42.

65. Lucas Cranach d.Ä., *Wittenberger
Heiligtumsbuch* (Wittenberg: 1509). Today we
possess a facsimile reproduction in the
Liebhaber-Bibliothek alter Illustrationen, by
Georg Hirsch (Munich: 1884).

66. Johannes Hausleiter, *Die Universität
Wittenberg vor dem Eintritt Luthers* (Leipzig:
1903), 20.

67. Kolde, 19; 28ff.; 33; Julius Köstlin,
*Friedrich der Weise und die Schloszkirche zu
Wittenberg* (Wittenberg: 1892), 57ff; Paul
Kalkoff, *Ablaasz und Reliqienverehrung an
der Schloszkirche zu Wittenberg* (Gotha:
1907), 12–24; 66–84.

68. Irmgard Höss, *Georg Spalatin (1484–
1545): Ein Leben in der Zeit des Humanismus
und der Reformation* (Weimar: 1956).

69. Anni Koch, "Die Kontroverse über die
Stellung Friedrich des Weisen zur Reformation," *Archiv für Reformationsgeschichte* 23
(1926):213ff.

70. Kolde.

71. See the following works by Paul
Kalkoff: *Die Depeschen des Nuncius Aleander
vom Wormser Reichstagen 1521* (ed. and
trans.), vol. 17 of *Schriften des Vereins von
Reformationsgeschichte* (1886); *Der Wormser
Reichstag von 1521* (Munich and Berlin:
1921); "Friedrich der Weise, der Beschützer
Luthers und das Reformationswerkes," *Archiv
für Reformationsgeschichte* 13 (1916); "Die
Stellung Friederich des Weisen zur
Kaiserwahl von 1519 und die Hildesheimer
Stiftsfehde," *Archiv für Reformationsgeschichte* 24 (1927); *Luther und die Ent-
scheidungsjahre der Reformation* (Munich
and Leipzig: 1917).

72. Kirn.

73. Spalatin, *Friedrich*, and Spalatin,
Chronik.

74. Spalatin, *Friedrich*, 28.

75. Spalatin, *Friedrich*, 28–29.

76. Spalatin, *Friedrich*, 30.

77. Spalatin, *Friedrich*, 30.

78. Spalatin, *Friedrich*, 30.

79. Spalatin, *Friedrich*, 29.

80. Spalatin, *Chronik*, 49–50. He ended
with "Er ist mir wil zu kune."

The Reformation
as a University Movement:
Notes

❖

Chapter 15
The Models for the University of Wittenberg

1. The original of Kaiser Maximilian's *Stiftungsbrief,* issued in Ulm, July 6, 1502, is on parchment, well preserved in Halle, Germany, WUA. Tit. 3, no. 1. It still retains the original seal. It was first printed by G. Suevus, *Academia Wittebergensis ad anno fundationis 1502 ... usque ad annum 1655* (Wittebergae, 1655). Bl. A.-Ag, a publication that is now quite rare. A more accessible copy can be found in Friedensburg, *Urkundenbuch,* 1:1–3; also in F. Israël, *Das Wittenberger Universitätsarchiv, seine Geschichte und Bestände,* published in *Forschungen zur Thüringisch-Sächsischen Geschichte,* Heft 4, 96–99. See also Grohmann, 1:10ff., incomplete. The document states twice that Wittenberg is to be modeled after older Italian, German, and French universities and to enjoy all the rights and privileges "quibus universitates Bononiensis, Senensis, Patavina, Papiensis, Perusina, Parisiensis et Lipsensis" have enjoyed.

2. Kristeller, 4–7.

3. Schachner, 4–5; Kibre, 3–6.

4. Kaufmann, 1:47.

5. Haskins, *Rise of Universities,* 8. Above we have dealt in some detail with Haskins's *Renaissance of the Twelfth Century* and *Medieval Science.*

6. Schachner, 37–40.

7. Thorndike, *University Records,* 3.

8. Among a number of excellent studies on the origin of the universities, a fine brief introduction is Charles H. Haskins, *The Rise of the Universities* (New York, 1940); the most exhaustive and thorough study is the revised edition of the late Hastings Rashdall, *The Universities of Europe in the Middle Ages* (Oxford, 1936), 3 vols.; new rev. ed., 1951, ed. F. M. Powicke, A. B. Emden. The first volume covers Salerno, Bologna, and Paris. Another excellent study is Schachner, *Medieval Universities,* cited above. O. P. Kristeller, *Die italienischen Universitäten der Renaissance* (Köln, s.d.), has a good treatment of the University of Bologna. Kibre, *Scholarly Privileges,* states that its aim is to update the student privileges since the famous work of Rashdall.

9. Rashdall, 1:292–93. He thinks it had all the characteristics of a later university by the end of 1175.

10. Haskins, *Renaissance,* 368–69. He claims Paris started out with a much wider curricula but that later liberal arts were crowded out by the "New Logic" and a craze for disputations.

11. Leff, 16. Cf. Kibre, *Scholarly Privileges,* 85. She claims the city of Paris under Philip I, Louis VI, Louis VII, prior to Philip Augustus, was already known as the city of letters.

12. Leff, 16.

13. Rashdall, 1:275–80. He points out that the shift from the education of regular clergy to that of secular clerics was a great revolution in education during the eleventh century; he sees, in this, already the germ of the Cathedral School of Paris becoming a university. He does not agree with Remegius that the University of Paris grew out of the work of William of Champeaux. At that time it did not rival or

surpass others until Abelard came and drew students from all over Europe. But, like Leff, he holds that it was not just Abelard, but the intellectual movement of which he became a part, that explains soon after the growth of the Cathedral School into a university.

14. Rashdall, 1:280–82. Haskins, *Rise of Universities,* 20–21, claims the chancellor controlled teaching certificates for teachers and the whole diocese. This explains why Abelard had to move out of town to teach after being opposed by William of Champeaux. But the action of the pope in 1179 indicated that he was already aware of some kind of an organization of Masters at Paris at that time, even though they still did not have organized status from the king and Rome.

15. Schachner, 40ff.

16. Schachner, 40–43.

17. Schachner, 40–43. Cf. Rait, 11.

18. Haskins, *Renaissance,* 369.

19. Kibre, *Scholarly Privileges,* 85.

20. Schachner, 43–44.

21. Schachner, 44; Haskins, *Rise of Universities,* 14, points out how native citizens controlled rents, sale of books, and did real profiteering at the expense of helpless students. The only solution was for them to band together. Cf. Schachner, 157.

22. Rashdall, 1:294.

23. Schachner, 62. Rashdall, 1:296–97, points out a reference in the charter that states that there will be no student arrested by secular justice of the *capitale Parisiensium scholarum,* over which there has been much academic debate. Rashdall does not agree with Denifle that it refers to the existence of a rector at this date. Kaufmann agrees with Rashdall that at this date the body of Masters was still without official organization.

24. Kibre, *Scholarly Privileges,* 87.

25. Rashdall, 1:303.

26. Rashdall, 1:303–4.

27. Schachner, 63.

28. Schachner, 64. Licensing was not to be combined with faculty recommendations. The Masters of the superior faculties and six from the Arts faculty recommended who should be licensed. Members of the Arts panel were to be selected as follows: three were to be chosen by the superior faculty and three by the chancellor. Now the chancellor could no longer imprison members of the university for trifle

offenses. Nor could he exact fees and pocket the money.

29. Schachner, 62–63.

30. Rashdall, 1:309–12. The author also points out that by now Paris had its four nations represented by their officials. By 1237 Paris also definitely had rectors.

31. Kibre, *Scholarly Privileges,* 91. Cf. Schachner, 66; Rashdall, 1:317.

32. Schachner, 66; Rashdall, 1:317.

33. Kibre, *Scholarly Privileges,* 99. The pope renewed the privilege of exempting its Masters and scholars from excommunication without special license from the Holy See. He stated that academic life needed to be quiet and without disturbances.

34. Rashdall, 1:318–19. For a good discussion on the English Nation, see G. C. Boyce, *The English-German Nation in the University of Paris* (Bruges, 1927).

35. Kibre, *Scholarly Privileges,* 92. She relates that a similar quarrel broke out between students and townsmen on February 26–27, 1229, in Rue Saint Marchel, where the authorities blamed the students and one member was executed. Several others were imprisoned by the provost and the guards. She claims that the Masters, the next day, drew up a protest and voted to leave Paris. They stopped their lectures and drew up twenty-one conditions that would have to be met. They demanded full satisfaction or leave for six years.

36. Schachner, 67–69.

37. Schachner, 69.

38. Tierney, *Sources,* 1:264–67. This has a translation of the *Statutes* of Pope Gregory IX for the University of Paris in 1231. Cf. Schachner, 68–72; also Kibre, *Scholarly Privileges,* 92–95, for a good summary of the contents of the pope's bull, *Parens scientiarum,* in 1231.

39. Rashdall, 1:337–38.

40. Rashdall, 1:338–40.

41. Kibre, *Scholarly Privileges,* 96–103.

42. Kibre, *Scholarly Privileges,* 93–103.

43. Rashdall, 1:340–41.

44. Rashdall, 1:342–43. Rashdall claims the "Court of Conservators" in time became so powerful that the university had to seek protection from Rome against the conservators.

45. Kaufmann, 1:270–71.

46. Rashdall, 1:312–15.

47. Rashdall, 1:315.

48. Rashdall, 1:315–17. It seems in 1266 each nation still had its rector.

49. Schachner, 119.

50. Rashdall, 1:321–24. For quite some time Medicine was rated even below Arts.

51. Schachner, 119–20.

52. Schachner, 120–21. Such turbulence was not limited to faculty meetings with the students. Similar fist fights often occurred after a disputation in which views were expressed, especially in theology, that went against the convictions of the opposition.

53. Rashdall, 1:324–25; Schachner, 120.

54. Rashdall, 1:324–26.

55. Rashdall, 1:326.

56. Rashdall, 1:327.

57. Rashdall, 1:327.

58. Rashdall, 1:327–28. Denifle holds a slightly different view of the emergence of the Paris rectorship. He claims that even the Arts faculty with its four nations did not fully recognize the rector as their head until 1274 and the entire faculties of Theology, Law, and Medicine until the middle of the fourteenth century. This may apply somewhat to its Franciscans and Dominicans in Theology.

59. Leff, 34.

60. Kaufmann, 1:275–76.

61. Kaufmann, 1:275–78.

62. Schachner, 95–96.

63. Schachner, 95–96. Not all translations, according to Haskins, were that badly done. This would be true more for the translations in Spain. The philosophy of Cordova, which involved Jews with unusual intellectual acuteness working with Arabs gave translations a special flavor. They used their own philosophical and cultural idioms.

64. Rashdall, 1:353. Alexander of Aphrodisias, in his interpretation of Avicenna and especially Averroes developed especially the most anti-Christian elements in the Arabic philosophy. This seems to have intrigued many of the bolder clerics to lively disputation on the Arabic denials of basic doctrines of the Catholic Church. Schachner, 97.

65. Rashdall, 1:354.

66. Schachner, 95–96.

67. Schachner, 98.

68. Schachner, 98.

69. Rashdall, 1:354. Tradition says that he had a stroke, became speechless, and lost his memory and that later in life he had to relearn

the *Credo* and the *Paternoster* from his own child.

70. Schachner, 99.

71. Rashdall, 1:355–56, and especially n. 2. The works of Aristotle probably were *De Anima,* his *Physics,* and *Metaphysics.*

72. Rashdall, 1:357.

73. Rashdall, 1:358.

74. Schachner, 100–101. The papacy realized that by twisting the teachings of Aristotle to fit the dogmas of the church, the works of the great Greek philosopher could become extremely useful to the church. As we shall see, during the Reformation, Luther attacked the views of Aristotle and called his *Ethics* the worst enemy of grace. The University of Wittenberg between 1517 and 1521 purged itself of all scholastic teachings as the new theology became entirely New Testament oriented. So the Reformation undid what was being fostered by the Dominican friars Albert and Thomas.

75. Leff, 35–37. Cf. Kaufmann, 1:278–79.

76. Kaufmann, 1:278–79.

77. Leff, 37.

78. Kaufmann, 1:280.

79. Kaufmann, 1:281. Leff, 39–40, gives a little different version of the course of events in the fifties. Up to 1250 the Friars had asked for no *licentia docendi,* and when the Masters attempted to stop the swelling of their numbers, Pope Innocent IV first supported the Mendicants. On July 1, 1253, he lifted the Medicants' excommunication and forced their admission into the *consortium.* The Friars now wanted their chairs to be made permanent. Then they were excommunicated for their action. When two beadles were sent to them, it caused an affray. In the battle with the Friars the university had incurred considerable expenses, and the pope favored that they be reimbursed. The pope also supported the inviolability of the university statutes and supported William of St. Amour, their proctor in Rome. This restricted the Friars' preaching, holding mass, and officiating at burials. Just when all the Friar activity seemed to have ended, Innocent IV died and his successor, Alexander VI, reversed everything.

80. Kaufmann, 1:283–84.

81. Kaufmann, 1:284–91. Before long the grounds changed. The Masters found that Dominicans were but men with feet of clay.

They were no longer feared in the faculty. The Dominican general Johann von Parma and others pulled away the veil. The secular clergy became milder in their opposition. Paris began to believe that great men like Albert the Great and St. Thomas brought color to the institution. Paris now turned into a wonderful Dominican institution.

82. Leff, 36–37. Rashdall, 1:363, points out that the great Franciscan Alexander of Hales developed a whole system of orthodox Aristotelianism. Cf. Schwiebert, *Luther*, 304–5, for his claim that in heaven there was a *Thesaurus Meritorium*, or a treasury of good works filled with the merits of Christ and the saints upon which indulgences could draw to lessen the sinner's stay in purgatory after death.

83. Leff, 37–38.

84. Rashdall, 1:365–66.

85. Taylor, *Medieval Mind*, 2:450–57. In this undertaking he aimed to eliminate the problems in Aristotle's writings, and especially Averroës and Avicenna were to be refuted. He also eliminated from his text any evidence of contradictions between Aristotle's Latin text and church dogma. But this spadework proved to be very useful to St. Thomas when he prepared his masterful treatises such as the *Sum of Theology*.

86. Taylor, *Medieval Mind*, 2:450–57.

87. Weisheipl, 3. This author feels Thomas laid out the main plan for his monumental *Sum of Theology* while still in Rome; but it was not until he was a professor at Paris that he decided to meet Averroës head-on, for he there realized the plight of young Masters exposed to this pagan philosophy so harmful to Christian believers. But he needed the Greek scholar Moerbecke for an accurate statement of what the original Aristotle had actually written rendered in good Latin. In fact, while in the papal employ he and Moerbecke could talk it over, the latter being a Greek scholar who often worked in Greece.

88. Schachner, 102–3.

89. Schachner, 103. Of course, St. Thomas, who lived so long ago, could hardly know how completely wrong Aristotle was in regard to nature when viewed in the light of modern science. In science when you mix chemicals, you no longer have that with which you started but an alloy. So also in Christian dogma the doctrine of transubstantiation was no longer tenable in the case of bread and wine in the

Eucharist. Thus he believed in the "real presence" of Christ who did not become a part of the bread and wine but an invisible glorified diety not limited to physical space.

90. Schachner, 119.

91. Rashdall, 1:439–40.

92. Rait, 133–35. He adds that this was not foolproof, as there were ways of getting around even this test. Poor students undergoing Latin training were placed on matriculation lists. By then some students also learned French, which was needed to complete charters and conduct courts, but such training had to be on the side.

93. Rashdall, 1:440.

94. Rashdall, 1:440–41. Of the three books available in translation, they called Book I *Ethica vetus* and Books II and III *Ethica nova*. This seems to have been true of Paris in the beginning.

95. Rashdall, 1:440–41. Rait, 137, mentions also, with regard to grammar, Alexander de Villa Dei.

96. Rait, 137–38.

97. Rashdall, 1:442–43.

98. Rashdall, 1:443. The papal legates were Giles of Montaigu, cardinal of Saint Martin, and John de Blandy, cardinal of Saint Mark. They still were to study the Old and New logic, also the *Topics* of Boethius and part or all of Aristotle's *De Anima*.

99. Rait, 139–40.

100. Kaufmann, 1:214; Rait, 140; Haskins, *Rise of Universities*, 61–82.

101. Kaufman, 1:215–16.

102. For a description of the Katheder in Wittenberg, "The Theses and Wittenberg," *Luther for an Ecumenical Age*, ed. Carl S. Meyer (St. Louis: Concordia, 1967), 121. That one was about nine feet tall and almost reached to the ceiling in the *Grosze Hörsaal* of the Black Cloister in Wittenberg. For a good picture of it, see Paul Schreckenbach and Franz Neubert, *Martin Luther* (Leipzig, 1921), 57.

103. Rashdall, 1:472–73. Schachner, 134–35, points out that the acquisition of a doctorate in theology was a tedious, profitless business, while the study of canon law offered a lucrative future. In fact, only the rich, or those from families of means, could afford to become theologians. Thus the buying and selling of degrees became quite a lucrative business.

104. Rashdall, 1:474–75. Later at Paris the

distinction between the ordinary and extra-ordinary lectures does not seem to have been too pronounced. In fact, theology as a profession deteriorated. Statutory action indicates that the Masters were too lazy to deliver lectures and turned the training of theologians over to graduate students, while they merely presided over disputations and participated in graduation exercises.

105. Rashdall, 1:474–75.
106. Schachner, 136; Rashdall, 1:477.
107. Rashdall, 1:477.
108. Rashdall, 1:477–78.
109. Schachner, 117.
110. Schachner, 147.
111. Schachner, 148.
112. Rashdall, 1:89–92.
113. Kristeller, 7.
114. Schachner, 48–49.
115. Rashdall, 1:93–94.
116. Rashdall, 1:150–51.
117. Schachner, 150–51. Cf. Rashdall, 1:97–98.
118. Schachner, 153–55.
119. In 1507 Christopher Scheurl prepared a *Rotulus* for the faculty at Wittenberg, modeled after the pattern of Bologna, in which he listed the members of the first teaching staff. He lists seven in Papal Law, and of these, five have doctorates in both civil and canon law. For details see Friedensburg, 1:14–16.
120. Kaufmann, 1:162–66. The origin of this imperial proclamation, as it related to Bologna and other Italian and Spanish universities, was treated previously in chapter 2 in considerable detail. The word *Habita,* as the proclamation of privileges came to be known, is from the initial word in the document, just as in papal bulls. It protected both the professors and law students at Bologna. It stipulated that the city officials could not lock up students arbitrarily but that they had the right of trial before their professor or the bishop. It also controlled student life economically by a board determining how much a townsman could charge for quarters and living.
121. Kaufmann, 1:164–65. This *Habita* was officially released by the Kaiser at the Reichstag "auf den Roncalischen Feldern November 1158." In n. 2 the author adds, "Die Authentica Habita wurde eingefügt in den Kodex, welcher die kaiserlichen Konstitutionen, Erlasse mit Gesetzkraft, in 12 Büchern vereinigte." At the close it states "Ne lilius pro

patre." It stressed that a son could not be arrested for a father's debts and also the opposite. Protection of Bologna students was no doubt what the Kaiser aimed to accomplish, student rights against native abuse. He then quotes the official text of the *Habita,* found in the *Corpus juris civilis,* ed. Krüger and Hommsen (1877), 2:511.
122. Kaufmann, 1:164–65. According to the official proclamation of the *Habita,* any city burgher who overcharged students, after his case was not brought to his professor, would be forced to pay four times that amount, in case he was found guilty, for such an offense.
123. Kaufmann, 1:164–65. This *Habita* seems to have been used by other institutions, as the Kaiser used no names, but seems to have meant it to be a general document applicable to any academic institution. But in northern Europe its influence was pronounced.
124. Kaufmann, 1:157–58.
125. Rashdall, 1:217, n. 4. This account came from Odofredus.
126. Rashdall, 1:217, n. 4.
127. Rait, 17. He claims that the professors were a closed corporation long before the origin of the university. Kaufmann, 1:161–66, claims that the emperor's *Habita* protected both foreign students and professors.
128. Rashdall, 1:146–47, n. 1.
129. Rait, 13–15. Cf. Rashdall, 1:155–57. He thinks that originally there may have been four universities, student associations or guilds, namely, the Ultramontane, Lombards, Tuscans, and Romans. These were all guilds of foreign students.
130. Kibre, *Nations,* 6. Rashdall, 1:148, points out that the fact that university guilds were called a *Universitas* while the doctors' organizations were referred to as colleges was due to a pure historical accident. Kibre has done an excellent study of the *Nations* in Bologna and Paris. It gives much more detailed information as to their origin and nature than any previous study. This is due, in part, to the use of much Italian research since the days of Rashdall.
131. Kibre, *Nations,* 3–4.
132. Kibre, *Nations,* 9–10. The original German Nation was represented by students from the original stem duchies, Swabia, Bavaria, Saxony, and Franconia; but, by 1497,

Bohemia, Moravia, Lithuania, and Denmark were included.

133. Kibre, *Nations*. The author has examined this aspect in great detail. Among the officers were the proctors, syndics, statutarii, notaries, and beadles.

134. Kibre, *Nations*, 31–35. Among the duties of the proctors were to collect the five to fifty *solidi* registration fee, according to wealth, to keep books on the Nations' property and resources, enter names of new registrants into the *Matrikel*, and at the end of the year turn over records of expenditures and assets. In matriculation they recorded the student's full name, any titles, and homeland place. They also recorded the religious services held, officiating clergymen, singers; moneys expended for wax, candles, palms, wine, spices, a new chalice, and an altar piece. They even recorded what was spent on broken windows and church repairs, as well as what they paid to syndics and notaries, beadle salaries, alms, and care for the poor.

135. Kibre, *Nations*, 38–41.

136. Kibre, *Nations*, 38–41.

137. Rashdall, 1:186–87.

138. Kibre, *Nations*, 60.

139. Kibre, *Nations*, 51–53.

140. Kibre, *Nations*, 53–55.

141. Rashdall, 1:191–92; Kibre, *Nations*, 55–56.

142. Kristeller, 21.

143. Kibre, *Nations*, 50–52.

144. Kristeller, 21–24.

145. Kristeller, 24–25.

146. Kristeller, 25.

147. Kristeller, 51.

148. Rashdall, 1:219–21.

149. Rashdall, 1:221–24.

Chapter 16
The Electoral Town of Wittenberg

1. An insert in Eschenhagen, 16–17. This is, however, much more embellished than the original.

2. In Schwiebert, *Luther*, 192–93, as an insert. The original is a colored study of the Lutherstadt, the only kind in existence. After my return from Germany, it seemed desirable to have an enlarged copy of the original for

classroom lectures. One of my Reformation students, Renada Ludwig, an art major, did an excellent colored rendition of the Heubner original. Since in the original I had failed to give O. H. Heubner a sketch of the little chapel of the Augustinian Monastery, we added that and made a few minor changes. Unfortunately, the publisher felt it too costly to reproduce that fine classroom colored Wittenberg into print. Thus it appeared in black and white, losing much of the real luster.

3. The Northwestern artist who did the second picture, an etching of Wittenberg in 1580, was Wilbert Seidel. See Schwiebert, *Luther*, 222, and its identifications of the buildings. Electoral Saxony was lost to the elector John Frederick in the Schmalkaldic War in 1547 and given to his cousin Duke Moritz of Meiszen. Later, in 1553, the duke was mortally wounded in a battle, and his brother August became the elector from 1553 to 1586. August was a very benevolent patron of the university and decided to offer scholarships to poor students. To carry out the plan he built a new building along the Collegien Gasse, in front of the Lutherhaus. He purchased the Luther home from the surviving Luther children. Then he moved a building purchased from the Toszen family to join the Augusteum and the Luther House as a unit, to provide ample space for the scholarship students. This is well portrayed in the excellent Seidel picture, in which no. 6 is the Toszen House. My son, Ernest G. Schwiebert, Jr., did a nice aerial sketch of the three buildings as viewed from the north. This was redrawn from north of the Dilich Federzeichnungen and other sources, showing (a) the Luther House on the left, the Augusteum College on the right, joined at the center in the rear by the Toszen House. For this sketch see Schwiebert, *Luther*, 231. For the purchase and joining of the Toszen House, see Grohmann, 1:78.

4. Schwiebert, E.T.W., 104–5; *Luther*, 192–93; 202.

5. Boehmer, *Luther*, 59.

6. Krüger, *V.d.L.*, 13–14; Boehmer, *Luther*, 59.

7. Schalscheleth, 47.

8. WA Tr 2:669, no. 2800.

9. Schwiebert, *Luther*, 486–87.

10. Schalscheleth, 47.

11. The author of the *Dialogus of 1507*

gives an abbreviated title on the title page along with the university seal and on the second page gives its full title. The frontispiece abbreviated title reads: *Dialogus illustrate ac Augustissime urbis Albiorene vulgo Vittenberg dicte Situm Amenitatem ac Illustrationem docens Tirocinia nobilium artium iacentibus Editus.* That there be no confusion, the work was written in 1507 and was published the next year, but we prefer to use the year of its drafting.

12. Sennertus, 56–57; Schwiebert, *Luther,* 256.

13. Eschenhagen, "Das Stadtbild," 14–27, passim.

14. Hausleiter, 5ff. He pointed out that the *Dialogus* was not entirely unknown at the time of his discovery. Walther Schulze and Gustav Bauch had apparently seen copies.

15. Hausleiter, 5ff.

16. Hausleiter, 16, Map of the Town.

17. Krüger, *V.d.L.,* 15:15.

18. Eschenhagen, 14.

19. Eschenhagen, 15–16.

20. Charitius, 159. He relates how in the North Church tower there was a room for a watchman, who rang a small bell each hour and who was on guard against town fires and announced the danger of an approaching enemy outside the city. Thus he signaled the watchmen at the city gates when to close the gates. Then he also tells of the three bells in the south tower. The large one was too heavy to be rung and had to be pushed by men with their feet or hit with a hammer. This large bell tolled when students, like Luther in 1512, received their doctorates. I was curious, after reading this in Charitius, so I made arrangements with churchmen to go up to the room in the North Town tower and also see the impressive bells. He went up in a lift that supplied the keeper with food and water. Here was an old lady who had been in the upper room for forty years and had never been on the ground. Then I read to her the part from Charitius, and she said that it was still like that today.

21. Charitius, 80–82. He based some of his material on Professor Kirchmaier's Dissertation on Wittenberg, 132.

22. Schalscheleth, 51–52.

23. Sennertus, *Athenae,* 11.

24. Charitius, 81. Cf. WA Tr, 2, no. 2540.

25. Charitius, 81, who quotes Hortleder, 3:218.

26. Charitius, 84. See Krüger, *Lutherstadt,* for a woodcut of Charles V's siege period after he had taken his position in the *Feldlager;* also a Kupferstich out of Hortleder, 1645, 13, 17.

27. Eschenhagen, 16.

28. *Dialogus of 1507,* 125.

29. Eschenhagen, 20.

30. Eschenhagen, 20. In 1510 Balthazar Heyns was brought before the town court and fined two Groschen for failure to regularly sweep the street. The Markplatz was cleaned by day laborers employed by the city.

31. Schwiebert, E.T.W., 101, and n. 14.

32. Krüger, *V.d.L.,* 17.

33. Eschenhagen, 41.

34. Eschenhagen, 41.

35. Eschenhagen, 40.

36. Eschenhagen, 31.

37. Eschenhagen, 31–34.

38. For a good introduction to the *Dialogus of 1507,* see D. R. Hausleiter, *Die Universität Wittenberg vor dem Eintritt Luthers* (Leipzig, 1903), 5ff. Dr. Polich von Mellerstadt was the court physician of Elector Frederick the Wise and a professor at the University of Leipzig, where he regarded himself as an authority on the newly discovered "French Disease." He also regarded himself as somewhat of a humanist even though he remained a scholastic as we shall show later in a chapter on humanism. A bitter rivalry broke out between him and another Leipzig professor, Wimpina. Both left Leipzig to found new universities. Wimpina founded the University of Frankfurt a.d.O., and Mellerstadt became one of the elector founders of the University of Wittenberg and its first rector. Wimpina engaged in heavy recruiting for his new school, and this caused Mellerstadt to request that a young instructor in liberal arts write the *Dialogus of 1507* to draw students to Wittenberg. Even though the work gets a little carried away in its descriptions, it does give us a good picture of the Lutherstadt before the reformer. It is really the only detailed account of a tour of the city in 1507 that we possess.

39. This excellent Oak Bridge had been built by Frederick the Wise to cross the Elbe from the old river road from Torgau to Magdeburg. A good picture is in the famous Large Woodcut of 1611. Let us say they

started from the Toll House and walked toward the Elbe Gate. See also Krüger, *Lutherstadt,* 26–27. Meinhard says it was named after the River Elbe.

40. This building was later converted into the Cranach Art Studio and a school, and some forty students studied there.

41. The Mellerstadt property has never been definitely located. Dr. Krüger told me on our town tour in 1936 that he had searched everywhere but failed to find definite evidence but that he thought it was on lot no. 4 on the town plan.

42. As we shall notice later, in the chapter on the founding of the University of Wittenberg, the aged professor was quite a figure in the new institution and highly respected by the elector.

43. *Dialogus of 1507,* 124. Eschenhagen, 23, claims this building was at the corner of the Coszwiger and Elbe streets. This building was in later years the property of Lucas Cranach, who purchased it in 1521. It was built between 1502 and 1507, the same time Konrad Pflueger built the Old Friderici College. The New Friderici College on Collegien Gasse was not done until four years later. The drugstore sold herbs, wax candles, paints, wine, and paper. It was here, in the *Dialogus,* that Meinhard purchased the large wax candles they used on the morning they visited the Castle Church on All Saints Day, to pray in front of the various relics.

44. Eschenhagen, 24, points out that Wittenberg had three such bath houses, and this one is called "Belleum Jovis" because it was right near the castle "arces Jovis." This one had a basin hanging on the front door to indicate it was open that day (*Dialogus of 1507,* 124).

45. *Dialogus of 1507,* 124.

46. Eschenhagen, 14–15. The wall was repaired again in 1509, 1510, 1512, and 1522 before it was rebuilt.

47. *Dialogus of 1507,* 124.

48. *Dialogus of 1507.* The remains of the chapel were still there, and you can see by the vaulting that it had been a church. By then it was converted into a blacksmith shop. No doubt the little chapel then was very ornate and attractive.

49. *Dialogus of 1507,* 124–25. Meinhard was right, as later this became the dwelling for the Wittenberg Law School. Earlier arrange-

ments involved divided classes. Some were in the castle and some in the college buildings. Later the electoral consistory was also housed here, whose function it was to supervise the religious life in electoral Saxony. The castle rooms, with their excellent paintings on the walls, always were the principal place of law course instruction. See Schwiebert, *Luther,* 219.

50. *Dialogus of 1507,* 125.

51. *Dialogus of 1507.* Since we will cover the Jewish question in some detail later, no details here are necessary.

52. *Dialogus of 1507.*

53. *Dialogus of 1507.*

54. *Dialogus of 1507,* 126.

55. *Dialogus of 1507.*

56. Schwiebert, *Luther,* 192–93, and n. 2 above. The numbering in the text is the same as in the picture to simplify identification; the number is also the same in the *Town Plan of 1623,* see p. 203; and for the changed Wittenberg of 1586, drawn for me by Wilbert Seidel, under my direction at Northwestern University, see p. 223, which also identifies the later buildings.

57. Schwiebert, *Luther,* 231.

58. See *Dialogus of 1507,* 126. For rooms in the castle, to be treated in more detail in the chapter on the University of Wittenberg, see *Dialogus of 1507,* 69ff. Luther's lectures on the Psalms, Romans, Galatians, and Hebrews were delivered in the *Grosse Hörsaal* of the monastery.

59. Stein, 4–5. This rare old study is the best, most detailed account we possess today. Another valuable study is by J. Jordan, "Aus der Lutherhalle Geschichte des Lutherhauses nach 1564," *Luther Jahrbuch,* 1921–1922.

60. Stein, 12. He adds that Luther was *regens studii,* while John Lang was *professor secundus;* Carlstadt also lectured for a while there on canon law.

61. Stein, 13–14.

62. Such a reconstruction was far from simple, as we shall see from the changes that were made after Luther's death, when the later Elector August purchased the Lutherhaus and converted it into a Stependiaten Haus for the quartering of 150 scholarship students who were too poor to go to school but very capable. In this connection, Jordan, 110ff., is most useful. Even though the *Lutherzimmer* was not changed through the rebuilding for scholarship

students, most of the rest was. The *Luther-zimmer* is not to be confused with the little square tower room in which the reformer lived as *regens studii* while a monk. By the nineteenth century, the university had moved to Halle and the old Lutherhaus was badly neglected. Now the government, in 1842, employed a Berlin architect, F. A. Stüler, to renovate and restore the Lutherhalle into its original form of Luther's day. The *Luther-zimmer* was not changed, but all the tourist names on the walls were removed except that of Peter the Great written above the door leading to the next room.

63. Sennertus, *Athenae*, 34ff., records this about the sale of the Luther home by his children in 1564: "Cum ruinossa esset et vasta, ab heredibus empta domus florennis ter mille et septingentis, refecta florennis pluribus ter mille cessit Academiae." He was a philologist and critic on the Wittenberg faculty (1606–1689). See also Grohmann, 1:74. This originally appeared in two volumes and now is available in a new edition by the Biblio Verlag, Osnabrück, 1969, with the two volumes combined.

64. Thulin, *Martin Luther*, 59, has an excellent reproduction of the *Katherinen-portal*. This was done in Gothic style. It has two lower seats of sandstone with Luther's stone image and his coat of arms. Her message to Luther read, "In silence and in hope shall your strength be."

65. See n. 61 above.

66. In 1936 the author tried to estimate the size of this room today, which the staff in Lutherhalle today regard as unchanged, and found it twenty-seven steps long and ten steps wide. Allowing that a step is nearly three feet, the room was more than seventy-five by thirty feet, which is a fair-sized lecture room even by today's standards. This would have permitted around 350 to 400 students to attend his lectures. Cf. Friedensburg, *Urkundenbuch*, 1:108, where Georg Spalatin in 1520 had just attended Melanchthon and Luther's classrooms and reported that Melanchthon had five hundred to six hundred auditors, no doubt in the large auditorium in the New Friderici College, and Luther "unter vierhundert auditors," among whom were many nice theological students.

67. Friedensburg, *G.U.W.*, 81. On the Common Table, see Gottfridus Suevus, *Aca-demia Wittebergensis*, "Leges Communis Mensae in Academia Wittbergensi," 157.

68. Friedensburg, *Urkundenbuch*, 1:165–66, no. 185.

69. Friedensburg, *Urkundenbuch*, 1:165–66. The elector asked that the Landvogt Hans Metsch advance the new supervisors with 100 Gulden so the project could be under way by the period of Lent in 1536. The writer cites Nik. Müller Z f. KG. der Prov. Sachsen, 8 (1911), 111, n. 3, for more data on Hieronymous Krapp. Augustin Schurff was a brother of Christopher Schurff, the distinguished Wittenberg law professor who represented Luther at Worms in 1521.

70. Matthaeus Merian, *Topographia Superioris Saxoniae, Thuringiae, Misniae, etc.* (Frankfurt, 1650). Dean Kronke of Valparaiso University was in possession of such a fine set, which he permitted me to use. Some are even colored. Wilhelm Dilichs, *Federzeichnungen Kursächsischer und Meisnischer Ortschaften aus dem Jahren 1626–1629* (Dresden, 1907), ed. Paul E. Richter and Christian Krollmann. There is a copy in Harper Memorial Library, the University of Chicago, of which I possess photostatic copies.

71. Schwiebert, *Luther*, 87ff. It has a Dilich from the east side. See also Krüger, *Lutherstadt*, 30ff., which has pictures from the west, north, and east sides.

72. Krüger, *Lutherstadt*, 34–35.

73. Eschenhagen, 42ff.

74. Eschenhagen, 42ff.

75. Eschenhagen, 43–44.

76. Eschenhagen, 43, based this on the *Kammereirechnungen* of 1530, where it is listed as an annual payment to the chancellory accompanied by a *Geleitbrief.*

77. Eschenhagen, 49.

78. Eschenhagen, 49.

79. Eschenhagen, 45ff.

80. On Luther's views, see "Ordinance of a Common Chest," trans. Albert T. W. Steinhauser, *Luther's Works*, from the original, Cranach und Döring, *Ordnung eyns gemeynen kastens, Ratschlag wie die geystlichen gutter zu handeln sind*, 45, 169ff., which presents Luther's views. On the rat's duties, see Eschenhagen, 47; Mentzius, *Syntagma*, 1:24–25.

81. E. G. Schwiebert, *The University of Wittenberg and Some Other Universities in Their Relation to the German Reformation* (doctoral dissertation written under the direc-

tion of Preserved Smith, Cornell University, 1929) 114, n. 75; Charitius, 108–9. There seems to be some contradiction in past accounts. I am inclined to agree with Charitius that the transfer took place in Luther's day, but Dr. Krüger claimed they were not excavated until 1883 and then transferred. The author says the mortal remains and a row of twenty-seven coffins in the lower vault of the castle tower joined to the Castle Church on the west end. Charitius, 110, relates that the elector John Frederick really converted the monastery into a relief center for the poor and a hospital.

82. Eschenhagen, 50ff., shows how complex the city government really was and that the Rat really just represented the Wittenberger Gemeinde, whose views had to be considered in difficult situations. No doubt Wittenberg's capitulation to Charles V in 1547 was just such a situation that might even demand an assembly of the Gemeinde in the town Marktplatz.

83. Eschenhagen, 46.

84. Eschenhagen, 46. But all the town burghers were subject to the *Stadtgericht,* namely, the town council sitting as a court of law.

85. Eschenhagen, 59, n. 225. This offense was that he did not appear in time for guard duty in one of the towers.

86. Eschenhagen, 58ff. See especially p. 61.

87. Eschenhagen, 58ff. During such inspections the citizens were also informed on what caused possible fire hazards. It seems that in case some buildings had to be demolished, the permission of the Rat was first required.

88. Eschenhagen, 61. Control of street sanitation lay under the jurisdiction of the *Straszenpolizei* of the town council.

89. Thulin, *Martin Luther,* picture no. 52, has a good front view of the Melanchthon house. This was treated in some detail in the previous chapter. For the penetration of the new Renaissance style, see Merian, *Topographia.* He gives an excellent reproduction of German towns, many even in color.

90. Eschenhagen, 62–63. The elector was also much interested in its supervision and management. The professors of medicine at the university were also drawn upon for guidance.

91. Eschenhagen, 63–64.

92. Eschenhagen, 63–64.

93. Eschenhagen, 65–66.

94. Eschenhagen, 71.

95. Eschenhagen, 74.

96. Eschenhagen, 55–56. Burghers generally were obligated to military service, but there were cases when the man's office in the town council or elsewhere in the government of the town made him exempt. The 99 Schock or 300 Gulden amounted to about $25,000 in present buying power.

97. Friedensburg, *Urkundenbuch,* 1:101–3, when Hans von Dolzig moved in with troops to quell the student riot, July 16, 1520. Document 16 explains the causes.

98. Friedensburg, G.U.W., 1ff., states that the elector regarded Wittenberg as his own private property. Even the university library was removed in 1547 when Emperor Charles V transferred the electorate of Saxony to the Albertine line of Saxony. He had it taken to Weimar, and it was later used as the nucleus of the University of Jena when he established it in 1558.

99. Eschenhagen, 109–10. Even though the transition in electoral succession was hereditary in the Wettiner line, the *Huldigung* ultimately of this succession was given by the Wittenberg *Gemeinde,* of which the town Rat and other officials were the representatives.

Chapter 17
The Founding of the University

1. Kaufmann, 2:44. This is still the best detailed account of the German universities in the Middle Ages. Rashdall, 2:212ff., has an excellent summary of the sixteen institutions that preceded Wittenberg.

2. Kaufmann, 2:xiii–xvii.

3. Rashdall, 2:212–80, for a good summary.

4. Kaufmann, 2:158.

5. Rashdall, 2:253–56; Kaufmann, 2:158.

6. Kaufmann, 2:158–59.

7. Walter Friedensburg, *Geschichte der Universität Wittenberg,* is the standard account of the early history in Teil I, while his *Urkundenbuch der Universität Wittenberg,* vol. 1, contains most of the essential documents including the *Statutes of 1508. Das Wittenberger Universitätsarchiv, seine Ge-*

schichte und Bestände, ed. Friedrich Israël, 62ff., has valuable material. J. C. A. Grohmann, *Annalen der Universität Wittenberg*, 1:1ff., tells of the founding. See also Karl Bauer, *Die Wittenberger Universitätstheologie und die Anfänge der Deutschen Reformation*, 1ff. *Liber Decanorum Facultatis Theologicae Acadamiae Vitebergensis*, Ex autographio, ed. C. D. Förstemann, is a good introduction and contains dean's records; and the fine sources in Gottfried Suevus, *Academia Wittebergensis ad Anno Fundationis 1502 ...*, 15ff.

8. For the strange partition of 1485, see vol. 1, chap. 16, pp. 63–68. Prior to this, Frederick the Wise had already expressed his interest in higher education by sponsoring six students at the University of Leipzig.

9. Bauch, *Leipziger Frühhumanismus*, 7. For a very detailed account used by Bauch, see Fuchs, 1ff., especially p. 127. His investigation, though wide, was limited to accounts of contemporaries in Germany up to 1510. For his conclusions, see pp. 382ff. and those of Mellerstadt, 401.

10. Fuchs, 401.

11. Grohmann, 3; Fuchs, 401; Bauch, *Leipziger Frühhumanismus*, 9–10.

12. Bauch, *Leipziger Frühhumanismus*, 7; Prantl, *Geschichte der Logic*, 4:273.

13. Friedensburg, *G.U.W.*, 10; Fuchs, 401.

14. Bauch, *Leipziger Frühhumanismus*, 9–10.

15. Fuchs, 416ff., gives us the summary of many contemporary eyewitnesses of the terrible disease, for which they had no understanding nor a cure. On p. 16 he gives the many designations used, and on p. 417 he tells how terrible the disease was, "eine erschrockenliche, stinkende, pfynnige und onleidenliche kranckheit," which was worse than leprosy. He says Erasmus objected to the disease as it had spread all over and was common to all lands.

16. Friedensburg, *G.U.W.*, 11.

17. Bauch, *Leipziger Frühhumanismus*, 11.

18. Bauch, *Leipziger Frühhumanismus*, 114–32. Wimpina even turned to Bohuslaus von Hassenstein, the chairman of the "sodalitas" of the humanists, to serve as a judge in this matter, but he refused to get involved and urged peace between the two great Leipzig "Lights." He urged them to make a peaceful close to their strife.

19. Bauch, *Leipziger Frühhumanismus*, 140–47. He really put Mellerstadt in his place, which no doubt explains why at Wittenberg the ambitious Polich wanted to obtain a doctorate in theology, which he acquired in an unbelievably short time, as we shall see.

20. Friedensburg, *G.U.W.*, 12–13.

21. Otto Clemen, "Aus den Anfänge der Universität Wittenberg," *Neue Jahreberichtung für Paedagogik* 9 (1906), 132–35.

22. Friedensburg, *G.U.W.*, 13–14.

23. Much of the material known comes from Theodore Kolde, *Die deutsche Augustiner Congregation und Johann Staupitz* (Gotha, 1879); another source is Paul Kirn, *Friederich der Weise und die Kirche* (Leipzig und Berlin, 1928). Both Kolde and Kirn have been cited frequently in this study (vol. 1, 13ff.). An excellent recent study is that of David Steinmetz, *Misericordia Dei: The Theology of Johannes von Staupitz in Its Late Medieval Setting* (Leiden, 1968), 1–38. The first part is an introduction that confirms most of the standard material known earlier with a few new points of view. Not much research can alter the findings in Spalatin, Boehmer, and the Luther correspondence between Luther and Staupitz.

24. Steinmetz, 2.

25. Friedensburg, *G.U.W.*, 14; Steinmetz, 4–5.

26. Steinmetz, 4–5.

27. Friedensburg, *G.U.W.*, 15.

28. Friedensburg, *G.U.W.*, 15–16.

29. Friedensburg, *Urkundenbuch*, 1:1–3, as Friedensburg reproduced the text in 1926 in clearer Latin than is found in some subsequent printings by Gottfried Suevus, *Academia Wittebergensis* (Wittenberg, 1655), 15–18. See also Grohmann, 1:10–14; Israël, 96–99.

30. Kaufmann, "Die Universitätsprivilegien," 1:118–65.

31. Friedensburg, *G.U.W.*, 16.

32. Suevus, 16–17.

33. Friedensburg, *G.U.W.*, 16.

34. Friedensburg, *G.U.W.*, 17.

35. Friedensburg, *Urkundenbuch*, 1:3–4. The author adds that the three years' free tuition was extended to 1509.

36. Israël, 100–102; see also Suevus, 29–33, for a 1655 copy. This repeats some of the charter but contains nothing new.

37. Grohmann, 1:46.

38. Friedensburg, *G.U.W.*, 21–22.

39. Friedensburg, *G.U.W.*, 25. This was based on old sources, such as Th. Muther, "Die ersten Statuten der Wittenberger Artistenfakultät von Jahre 1504," *Neue Mitteilungen aus den Gebiet historischer antiquaren Forschungen* 13 (1874): 177–208. Muther drew it from the Arts faculty dean's book. See also Roth, *Urkunden zur Geschichte der Universität Tübingen aus de Jahren 1476–1550*. In the Vorwort, Rudolf Roth admits that due to a fire in 1534 and other reasons, the record of Tübingen remains incomplete.

40. Friedensburg, *Urkundenbuch*, 1:18–58. The author translated these *Statutes* for the first time. These are written in Latin and divided into several parts: General Statutes, October 1, 1508, Doc. No. 22; Statutes to the Theological Faculty, November 15, Doc. No. 23; Statutes for the Law Faculty, November 15, Doc. No. 24; Statutes to the Medical Faculty, November 15, Doc. No. 25; Statutes to the Arts Faculty, November 25, Doc. No. 26. (All these will be cited by documents and pages below.)

41. Friedensburg, *G.U.W.*, 25–26.

42. The original draft is in the *Germanische Museum* in Nürnberg in the Cod. Scheurl, alte Nr. 281, neue Nr. klein folio 71, IR, 405a–515b. We will cite the printed text in Freidensburg, *Urkundenbuch*, 1:18ff.

43. Friedensburg, *G.U.W.*, 27.

44. Friedensburg, *Urkundenbuch*, 1:19, in Doc. No. 22.

45. Scheurl, *Briefbuch*, 1:55; Friedensburg, *G.U.W.*, 28.

46. Friedensburg, *G.U.W.*, 27–29. The Reformers could also put suitable supervisors in the university *Bursen*, or dorms, regulate the assignment of courses, and watch over the student promotions. They could place fines on examination offenses, and they were given part of the income from the dorms.

47. Friedensburg, *G.U.W.*, 29–30.

48. Israël, 103.

49. Friedensburg, *Urkundenbuch*, 1:20, Doc. No. 22.

50. Friedensburg, *Urkundenbuch*, 1:20–21, Doc. No. 22.

51. Friedensburg, *Urkundenbuch*, 1:20–21, Doc. No. 22.

52. Friedensburg, *Urkundenbuch*, 1:21–22, Doc. No. 22. The registration of students was not simple, as it involved verification of student claims of studies from other institutions and the records of one's past academic performance and conduct. Students did not pay tuition until they wanted to be promoted, at which time they had to pay a prescribed amount.

53. In all minor offenses, conflicts between students and townspeople, student rowdiness, and students breaking into homes were beyond the jurisdiction of the town council. In cases of grave offenses involving bloodshed and crimes against the state, student offenders were turned over to the elector's court. Problems of lasting consequences might even be turned over to the reformers.

54. Friedensburg, *Urkundenbuch*, 1:21–22, Doc. No. 22; Friedensburg, *G.U.W.*, 31–32.

55. In 1936 the author was privileged to go with one of the guides to see the place where the university kept its funds and other treasures.

56. Friedensburg, *Urkundenbuch*, 1:22, Doc. No. 22. For the bull of incorporation of the *Stift* of the Castle Church with the university, by Julius II, in 1507, see Suevus, 20–28.

57. Friedensburg, *G.U.W.*, 34.

58. Ernest G. Schwiebert, "The Theses and Wittenberg," *Luther for an Ecumenical Age* (St. Louis, 1967), 120–48, gives a detailed discussion on how disputations were methods of university instruction supplementing the lectures. Failure for professors to debate carried a heavy fine. Only those in the classics were exempted and later were to give declamations.

59. Friedensburg, *G.U.W.*, 33–34.

60. Friedensburg, *Urkundenbuch*, 1:23–24, Doc. No. 22.

61. Friedensburg, *Urkundenbuch*, 1:23–24, Doc. No. 22. The author participated in such *Rectoratfeiers* while he was Gast Professor at the University of Erlangen in 1948–1950. Offenders of rank were punished with a fine of about $75.

62. Friedensburg, *G.U.W.*, 39.

63. The *Biblicus* paid 5 Gulden, 20 Groschen for his promotion; the *Sententiarius*, 6 Gulden, 9 Groschen; the *Formatus*, 1 Gulden; the *Licentiatus*, 11 Gulden, 20 Groschen; and a doctor 16 Gulden. It was distributed like other degrees, but the details are hardly important.

64. Friedensburg, *Urkundenbuch*, 1:25, Doc. No. 22.

65. Friedensburg, *Urkundenbuch*, 1:26–27. In this the rector was to contribute five

Groschen ($3.60 worth of a Groschen), each doctor two Groschen, bachelors one Groschen, in Higher Faculties, Liberal Arts A.B., one-half a Groschen, students three Denarii. It seemed though, at least in the School of Theology, the banquet was often given.

66. *Matrikel,* the year 1644–1645, plate 31.

67. Friedensburg, *G.U.W.,* 35–36.

68. Friedensburg, *G.U.W.,* 38–39.

69. Friedensburg, *G.U.W.,* 38–39; *Aristotle.*

70. Friedensburg, *Urkundenbuch,* 1:56–58, Doc. No. 26.

71. Friedensburg, *Urkundenbuch,* 1:14–17. The "Rotulus" of 1507 was an innovation in German universities. Christopher Scheurl had attended Bologna University, where they had a listing of the faculty and courses taught in such a form. See also Grohmann, 1:79–84; and Kaufmann, 2:574–77.

72. *Liber Decanorum,* 3.

73. Friedensburg, *Urkundenbuch,* 1:56. According to the *Rotulus of 1507* (see Friedensburg, *Urkundenbuch,* 1:15), Andreas von Carlstadt gave the course "in via sancti Thome," Nicolaus Amsdorff "in via Scoti"; and after 1508 Jodocus Trutfetter gave the same course by way of Occam.

74. Aristotle wrote seven books on nature in which he treated the basic principles of object, the conditions of change, and the role of motion in nature in relation to space and time. Knowledge was to be acquired not by induction but by posterior analytics. He discussed the role of the Prime Mover in everything, including the universe. Nature, as treated, is never static; there is constant change and continuity. For him the basic elements in nature are earth, fire, water, and air. Time for Aristotle was also basic to investigations. See *Aristotle,* 71–74.

75. Friedensburg, *Urkundenbuch,* 1:15. This is in the *Rotulus of 1507,* where it indicated who taught these courses in Scheurl's day as rector.

76. Friedensburg, *Urkundenbuch,* 1:16.

77. *Aristotle,* 76–82; Friedensburg, *Urkundenbuch,* 1:16. The *Rotulus* has the names of the lecturers at that noon hour.

78. *Aristotle,* 91–103. According to the *Liber Decanorum,* 4, Ostermeyer was preparing himself to be promoted to the *Licentiatus* degree in 1509 and took time off. His replacement was Martin Luther of Erfurt, whom

Dean John Staupitz brought there to teach the course. According to Walther von Loewenich, *Martin Luther, Der Mann und das Werk* (Munich, 1982), 62–63, Luther had to spend four hours, at 12:00 and at 2:00 give lectures on the *Nikomachische Ethik* and lead students in practice disputations, which he did not like but would rather have lectured on theology, he wrote Vicar Braun in Eisenach.

79. Friedensburg, *Urkundenbuch,* 1:16.

80. Friedensburg, *Urkundenbuch,* 1:16–17, and n. 10.

81. *Aristotle,* 110–12. The details of metaphysics as taught by the Roman Church of Thomas Aquinas are far too complicated and involved to explore in this study. At bottom this philosophy undergirds the doctrine of transubstantiation and the Roman Mass. Martin Luther regarded Aristotle's *Ethics* and *Metaphysics* as untenable in the light of the New Testament and God's revelation in the Bible.

82. Friedensburg, *Urkundenbuch,* 1:16. "Syium Italicum et Silvulam de situ Albiorene urbis a se editum." On this see also Friedensburg, *G.U.W.,* 71.

83. Friedensburg, *Urkundenbuch,* 1:53–54. The Arts college also had a system of conventors who checked on student conduct, attendance of classes, living in the dorms, etc. This, no doubt, lightened the work of the dean somewhat, as he could not be everywhere to comply with the statutes.

84. On promotions for bachelors who were trying for the A.B. degree, it states that students should be honest with their examiners, "asserting that they have heard the material of Petrus Hispanus on the new and old Logic of Aristotle, *Analytics* from the first to the last, of the Four Topics, Aristotle's *Sophistic Confutation,* and no less of the subject of grammar." Friedensburg, *Urkundenbuch,* 1:54.

85. Friedensburg, *Urkundenbuch,* 1:54, on Disputations attended the Statutes read, "from the beginning to the end let him be present at thirty disputations," and he must have engaged in disputations for the lecture courses at least four times.

86. Friedensburg, *Urkundenbuch,* 1:54–55.

87. Friedensburg, *Urkundenbuch,* 1:54–55.

88. Friedensburg, *Urkundenbuch,* 1:54–55.

89. Friedensburg, *Urkundenbuch,* 1:55.

90. Friedensburg, *Urkundenbuch,* 1:56–57.

As will be seen below, there is considerable evidence of this on the part of Polich von Mellerstadt and the *Via Moderna* professor, Trutfetter, and his favoritism toward the ambitious Carlstadt. At Paris, Pierre D'Aillie, a *Via Moderna* professor already questioned the Catholic view of transubstantiation in the Roman Mass because of the new view of substance and accidents.

91. For a discussion of Wittenberg's different types of such disputations, see Schwiebert, *Theses*, 126ff., also above, n. 58; and see also Friedensburg, *Urkundenbuch*, 1:55–56.

92. Friedensburg, *Urkundenbuch*, 1:56.

93. Friedensburg, *Urkundenbuch*, 1:56.

94. Friedensburg, *Urkundenbuch*, 1:56.

95. Friedensburg, *Urkundenbuch*, 1:56.

96. Friedensburg, *Urkundenbuch*, 1:15–16.

97. Friedensburg, *G.U.W.*, 68. This is not the place to enlarge on the type of professors they were, as it can be treated better in a later section.

98. This theme will be further explored below in our treatment of the discussion of scholasticism at Wittenberg. Two studies by Gustav Bauch, "Wittenberg und die Scholastik," and *Carlstadt als Scholastiker.*

99. Friedensburg, *Urkundenbuch*, 1:56–58.

100. Friedensburg, *Urkundenbuch*, 1:15. The *Statutes of 1508* and the *Rotulus of 1507* had the following listing of the Law faculty: D. Fredericus de Kitsch, iuris utriusque doctor Senensis, prepositus Vittembergensis (probst of the Castle Church and professor in pontifical law, both ordinary and extraordinary); D. Johannes Monhofer, juris utriusque (Doctor) Perusinus, Decanus Vittembergensis of Castle Church; D. Wolfgangus Stähelin, artius et juris utriusque doctor Tübingensis, ordinarius Vittembergensis; D. Laurentius Schlamaw, decretorum doctor, custus et pastor Vittembergensis; D. Christopherus Scheurl Nurembergensis, juris utriusque doctor Bononiensis, novorum jurium ordinarius; D. Uldalricus Denstadt, pastor in Eysfelt et Cantor Vittembergensis of the Castle Church; and D. Christophorus Grosz, iuris utriusque baccalaureus Vittembergensis, which made the total seven in Canon Law.

In Roman Law there were D. Jheronymus Schurff, artium et juris utriusque doctor et ordinarius Vittembergensis, in Codice (Code of Justinian); D. Wolfgangus Reisempusch, juris utrius baccalaureus Vittembergensis, in

institutionibus. In jure extraordinarie, D. Christophorus Scheurl … usus feudorum.

101. Friedensburg, *Urkundenbuch*, 1:44.

102. Edith Eschenhagen, "Wittenberger Studien," *Luther Jahrbuch* 9 (1927) 18; see *Dialogus of 1507*, 126. For a detailed treatment of the interior of the Wittenberg castle, see Schwiebert, *Luther and the Universities*, 1:17:67ff.; also vols. 2, 4:38.

103. Friedensburg, *Urkundenbuch*, 1:42–44. The books were first known as *Liber Extra* (c. 1234) and were given full status as *Liber Sextus* in 1298 by Pope Boniface VIII.

104. Friedensburg, *Urkundenbuch*, 1:42–44, and n. 5.

105. The *Liber Decanorum*, 8ff.

106. Friedensburg, *Urkundenbuch*, 1:34.

107. Schwiebert, *Theses*, 130.

108. Friedensburg, *Urkundenbuch*, 1:34.

109. Friedensburg, *Urkundenbuch*, 1:34.

110. Friedensburg, *Urkundenbuch*, 1:34.

111. Friedensburg, *Urkundenbuch*, 1:35.

112. Friedensburg, *Urkundenbuch*, 1:36.

Chapter 18
The University's Staff and Students

1. Schwiebert, *Luther*, 262–68; Grohmann, 1:43–53.

2. Suevus, 63–75, has an excellent record of the rectors and many details of their roles.

3. See above, chapter 6.

4. The position of vice-chancellor gave Polich real power within the university academic life, often in case the chancellor could not participate in the promotion of students and the granting of degrees, the vice-chancellor took over that colorful role in the presence of the whole assembled university, where they met in the Aula of the Castle Church.

5. Friedensburg, *Urkundenbuch*, 1:22–23. The personnel of this body changed during this period. Stauptiz left after 1503 when he became the vicar general of the Augustinian Hermits as he had to go on trips; the priors of the Castle Church changed, as some left, in 1507 it was Jodocus Trutfetter, and after that Bodenstein von Carlstadt; the rectors, of course, changed every semester. The only permanent member of the reformers was Polich von Mellerstadt, who was on this until his death in 1513.

6. Friedensburg, *G.U.W.*, 28.

7. Friedensburg, *G.U.W.*, 28.

8. Scheurl, *Briefbuch*, 1:55.

9. Friedensburg, *Urkundenbuch*, 1:13–14; Israël, 103.

10. Grohmann, 1:19. According to the record, none of these officials needed to act as none of the privileges were threatened.

11. Sennertus, *Athenae*, 80–82, gives the deans in philosophy for the whole period from 1502 to 1655; for the period from 1502 to 1517 the above is covered. He also lists the number of promotions that were made under each dean. There were nineteen deanships in the original institutions in Liberal Arts.

12. Suevus, 181-99, has a detailed breakdown of the deans between 1502 and 1517 in Theology. It does the same with respect to the other schools.

13. Suevus, 181–202. In this section the author has combined in different sections deans and their promotions, grouped under the various steps in theology toward the doctorate, listing them under Biblicus, Sententiarius, Formatus, Licentiatus, and Doctorates. In this study we have in this chapter only those of the years 1502–1517. Suevus continues them to 1655. This material will be utilized in later chapters.

14. Suevus, 181–202.

15. Friedensburg, *Urkundenbuch*, 1:14–15.

16. Friedensburg, *Urkundenbuch*, 1:14–15.

17. On the course offerings see chapter 6, where they are defined by the *Statutes of 1508*.

18. Suevus, 211, Catalogus Lincentiatorum in Utroq; Jure in Academia Wittebergensis, Qui gradum Doctoris deinceps assumpsisse, ex Judicibus Antecessorum non reperiuntur.

19. Friedensburg, *Urkundenbuch*, 1:15.

20. Friedensburg, *Urkundenbuch*, 1:15.

21. Friedensburg, *Urkundenbuch*, 1:15.

22. At the time of the *Rotulus of 1507*, Scheurl lists the dean at the time as D. Johannes Monhofer of Perugia who was a doctor of both Canon and Civil Law.

23. Friedensburg, *G.U.W.*, 62.

24. Friedensburg, *G.U.W.*, 63–64.

25. Sennertus, *Athenae*, 80–82. Here he lists the deans of Philosophy by their terms and the number of students that were promoted under them.

26. *Album, Academiae Vitebergensis*, ed.

C. E. Förstemann (Leipzig, 1841ff.), 3 vols. This offers a rector-by-rector entry, mostly in his own hand in the original. See also Suevus, 63ff., based on the Förstemann printed edition of the *Album*. The original has been kept in Halle, but it was on display in Leipzig when our microfilm copy was made, which was made in a large usable copy.

27. Langer, *Einzugsbereich*. See chart for the period 1472–1555, vol. 2. For the years 1520–1560, see Schwiebert, *Thesis*, 73–74.

28. For a more detailed discussion of the origin and role of *Dialogus of 1508*, see chapter 4.

29. The accompanying chart offers a graphic view of the rise and fall of the early enrollments of the University of Wittenberg until 1517, by which time the impact of the German Reformation began to transform the institution.

30. Langer, *Einzugbereich*, vol. 2, chart 1, where the schools are plotted on a comparative basis.

31. Langer, *Einzugbereich*, vol. 2, chart 1. Cf. Schwiebert, *Thesis*, 69.

32. Friedensburg, *Urkundenbuch*, 1:56. The *Statutes of 1508* stipulate: "Let each professor teach freely his course, in the way of St. Thomas, that of Duns Scotus, or that of Gregory, and present his views without prejudice." In n. 1 Friedensburg pointed out that another hand later had struck out Gregory and added Occam (p. 58).

33. Friedensburg, *G.U.W.*, 80–81; Bauch, WudS, 314–19, for an excellent review.

34. Bauch, WudS, 288. Since the next chapter will be devoted to German humanism and its impact on the early university, this aspect does not need any treatment here.

35. Friedensburg, *G.U.W.*, 39. For an analysis of Aristotle's writings see earlier chapters of vol. 2; also *Aristotle*, 8ff.

36. Friedensburg, *G.U.W.*, 68; Friedensburg, *Urkundenbuch*, 1:15–16. The *Rotulus of 1507* offers some detail on what courses in the three ways were offered in the forenoon and the afternoons.

37. Friedensburg, *G.U.W.*, 46.

38. Bauer, 6.

39. Bauch, WudS, 293–97.

40. Stier, 30.

41. Bauch, WudS, 293.

42. As will be shown in the next chapter, modern scholarly studies are still challenging

older and more accepted views about German humanism. More recent studies have offered some valuable points of view: R. R. Post, *The Modern Devotion: Confrontation with Reformation and Humanism* (Leiden, 1968); Frank Baron, trans. and ed., *Stephan Hoest, Reden und Briefe, Quellen zur Geschichte der Scholastik und des Humanismus* (München, 1971). These studies claim that the *Studia humanitatis* contributed to breaking down the authority of Aristotle, which in Heidelberg began with Peter Luder, the teacher of Stephan Hoest, and then continued through Wimpfeling, Agricola, Erasmus, Reuchlin, and the German Reformation in which Aristotle was dethroned. In this movement the Scholastics at Heidelberg and Leipzig and later Wittenberg were forced to recognize that humanism had something to offer in style and poetic beauty that tended to attempt, like Mellerstadt and Carlstadt to work out a union between the two, in which Hoest appears to have been more successful than the Wittenberg scholastics.

43. This theme will be pursued in the subsequent chapter and in connection with other Wittenberg professors.

44. *Liber Decanorum*, 2, relates how Mellerstadt asked to be made a doctor of Theology and was advanced so rapidly that in a matter of months he was made a doctor in an impressive ceremony, and an impressive banquet was offered with all expenses paid by the elector and his brother, Duke John. It is not difficult to understand how this would create resentment.

45. Friedensburg, *G.U.W.*, 46.
46. Friedensburg, *G.U.W.*, 46.
47. Friedensburg, *G.U.W.*, 46–47.
48. Prantl, 4:273.
49. Prantl, 4:217–29.
50. Friedensburg, *G.U.W.*, 46–47.
51. Friedensburg, *G.U.W.*, 47–48. This second volume was entitled *Martini Polichii Mellerstadii exquisite cursus physici collectanea* (Leipzig by Melchior Lotter, 1514).
52. See chapter 6 for details.
53. An excellent study of Johannes Staupitz's theology was done by the Duke University professor David Steinmetz, *Misericordia Dei: The Theology of Johannes von Staupitz in Its Late Medieval Setting* (Leiden, 1968), 1–34. It is largely biographical, and he points out that Staupitz was a noble and an

early companion of Frederick the Wise. For further details, see also Theodore Kolde, *Die deutsche Augustinerkongregation und Johannes Staupitz* (Gotha, 1870).

54. *Liber Decanorum*, 1.
55. Friedensburg, *G.U.W.*, 48.
56. *Liber Decanorum*, 13; Suevus, 72.
57. Boehmer, *Der Junge Luther*, 110.
58. Friedensburg, *G.U.W.*, 48.
59. *Liber Decanorum*, 4; Boehmer, *Luther*, 63.
60. *Liber Decanorum*, 13, relates the story of Luther's promotion to the doctorate and his advancement to regular *Lectura in Biblia*, which Staupitz had just vacated. See also Boehmer, *Luther*, 88–92.
61. Staupitz's role as Luther's protector continued at least through the Heidelberg Disputation and Luther's appearance before Cajetan at Augsburg.
62. Friedensburg, *G.U.W.*, 80.
63. Friedensburg, *G.U.W.*, 80. As will be observed, this was especially true of Polich von Mellerstadt and the head of the Thomists, Bodenstein von Carlstadt, who resented the appointment.
64. Boehmer, *Luther*, 25.
65. Boehmer, *Luther*, 26.
66. Boehmer, *Luther*, 40.
67. Friedensburg, *G.U.W.*, 80–81. Most of his material was taken from G. Plitt, *Jodocus Trutfetter von Eisenach, der Lehre Luthers* (Erlangen, 1876). Karl Bauer, p. 10, claims Trutfetter told him as a student to take the Holy Scriptures as his sole authority; Enders 1:188, relates that Luther wrote how much Trutfetter had influenced him when he wrote: "cui debeo omne bonum."
68. Bauer, 12; Friedensburg, *G.U.W.*, 81. On Trutfetter's relationship with the Poets, see Bauch, WudS, 14-15; Plitt, 10, 12, 33. The text he used was called *Breviarum dialecticum.*
69. Friedensburg, *G.U.W.*, 81.
70. Friedensburg, *G.U.W.*, 81. See also the chart of Deans of Theology above on p. 234 of this chapter.
71. Bauch, WudS, 314–15.
72. Bauer, 9.
73. Christoph Scheurl, *Briefbuch*, 1:142: "Viam Modernam instituens sine intermissione, legebat, studebat, docebat, praedicabit, orabat."
74. Bauch, WudS, 314–15.

75. Friedensburg, *G.U.W.*, 81–82.

76. Friedensburg, *G.U.W.*, 81–82.

77. Bauer, WudS, 9. The elector hated to see Trutfetter go but could not prevent what had transpired, in case he knew it.

78. Bauer, 9.

79. Bauch, WudS, 284ff. On Sigismund Epp, the first dean of Liberal Arts, see 301–6. The second study is a searching study of Andreas cited as Bauch, *Andreas Carlstadt als Scholastiker*, 37ff.

80. Bauch, WudS, 302.

81. Petrus of Ravenna, *Compendium pulcherimum Juris canonici clarissimi Juris utraque Doctoris et Equitis Petris Ravennatis*. This printing delayed Epp's project.

82. Bauch, WudS, 304–5.

83. For confirmation of this trend in the second half of the fifteenth century, see R. R. Post, *The Modern Devotion: Confrontation with Reformation and Humanism* (Leiden, 1968); and especially Frank Baron, trans. and ed., *Stephan Hoest, Reden und Briefe, Quellen zur Geschichte der Scholastik und des Humanismus* (München, 1971). This study claims the *Studia humanitas* caused the breakdown of the authority of Aristotle in Heidelberg in the second half of the fifteenth century, which began with Peter Luder, the teacher of Stephan Hoest, and then continued through Wimpheling, Agricola, Erasmus, and Reuchlin, and culminated in the German Reformation in which Aristotle was dethroned. Similar trends can be detected in Tübingen, Leipzig, Erfurt, and finally now in Wittenberg. For details of this theme see chapter 8.

84. Hoest, 40–42, as an illustration.

85. Bauch, WudS, 305–6.

86. Friedensburg, *G.U.W.*, 65–66; *Urkundenbuch*, 1:15–16.

87. *Rotulus of 1507*, 15–16.

88. *Rotulus of 1507*, 16.

89. *Liber Decanorum*, 3.

90. *Liber Decanorum*, 11.

91. W.A., Br. 1:64–69; for Luther's letter to John Lang about the disputation see n. 5, p. 68; also *Liber Decanorum*, 19; Bernhardi was later the probst of Kemberg, Enders, 1:58, n. 3; also 17, n. 1.

92. On September 4, 1517, another Luther student, Francis Gunther of Nordhausen, engaged in a disputation for his Biblicus degree, *Liber Decanorum*, 20; Luther's letter

to John Lang, Sept. 4, 1517, WA Br, 1:103–4, also n. 2.

93. Friedensburg, *G.U.W.*, 100.

94. Schwiebert, *Luther*, 295.

95. Bauer, 38.

96. Gustav Bauch did the two best studies of Bodenstein von Carlstadt in 1897–1898, which, though now old, are the best in print. Most of Bauer and Friedensburg, in their views are based on his. In the first study, "Wittenberg und die Scholastik," cited above as WudS, was done for an overall description, in which pp. 313ff. are devoted to Carlstadt; his second more comprehensive treatment, *Andreas Carlstadt als Scholastiker*, 38–57, gives us a very searching yet fair picture by this able scholar.

97. Friedensburg, *G.U.W.*, 66–68.

98. Bauer, 7.

99. M. Anton Lauterbach's *Diaconi zu Wittenberg, Tagebuch auf das Jahr 1538, die Hauptquelle der Tischreden Luthers*, ed. Johann Karl Seidemann (Dresden, 1872), 190.

100. Bauer, 7.

101. Barge, *Andreas Bodenstein von Karlstadt*, 2:534, Anlage 5, puts his birth in 1480.

102. Bauer, 7.

103. Friedensburg, *G.U.W.*, 66.

104. WA Br 2:423 and n. 12. He became engaged to her on Dec. 26, 1521, and the marriage was on Jan. 19, 1522; see also Barge, 1:364f.

105. Bauch, *CaS*, 37; Bauer, 7; Bauch, WudS, 317. Friedensburg, *G.U.W.*, 66, added that Carlstadt was a native of Erfurt, which explains his entry of Erfurt University there.

106. Bauch, *CaS*, 38.

107. Bauer, 7.

108. Bauch, *CaS*, 38.

109. Bauch, *CaS*, 38.

110. Prantl, 4:273.

111. Bauch, *CaS*, 38, points out that he entered into the record his name as Andreas Bodenstayn alias Rudolffus Carlstadius ingenuarum artium magister atque sacrae theologiae baccalaureae.

112. Bauch, *CaS*, 39.

113. *Liber Decanorum*, 3, 4, 9, 11, 15, 17, 18, 21, 23, 25, 27. As will be shown in a later chapter, at the end while Luther was gone, he as dean terminated all the academic degrees, claiming they could not be supported the Holy Scriptures. See also Bauch, *CaS*, 39–40.

114. Bauer, 8; Bauch, *CaS*, 40.
115. *Rotulus of 1507*, 16, in Friedensburg's *Urkundenbuch*, 1:16, lists *Magister Andreas Carlstadt metaphisicam Aristotilis;* Grohmann, 2:83.
116. Bauch, *CaS*, 40-41.
117. Bauch, *CaS*, 40.
118. Bauch, *CaS*, 40–41.
119. Bauch, *CaS*, 40–41.
120. Bauer, 8.
121. Bauch, WudS, 318–19. The title of the work is *De intentionibus Opusculum Magistri Andree Bodenstein Carlstadii Compilatum ad Sancti emularum Thome Commoditatem* (Leipzig, 1507). The library of the University of Tübingen was kind enough to make the author a copy of the original. For more details, see Bauch, *CaS*, 42.
122. Prantl, 4:306.
123. Bauch, *CaS*, 42.
124. Bauch, WudS, 319-20.
125. Bauch, *CaS*, 45.
126. Bauch, *CaS*, 45. How sincere this public praise was is a little difficult to determine. Carlstadt was a good friend of Polich von Mellerstadt. They both hated Jodocus Trutfetter and the *Via Moderna*. Later Scheurl seems to have cooled off and often wrote to Trutfetter.
127. Scheurl, *Briefbuch*, 1:142; Bauer, 9.
128. Bauch, *CaS*, 45.
129. Bauch, *CaS*, 46.
130. Prantl, 3:220.
131. Prantl, 3:288.
132. Prantl, 3:245.
133. Bauch, *CaS*, 46–47. It seems that Carlstadt felt he was coming up with a real key to the fact that Duns Scotus and St. Thomas had never been as far apart as other scholars had presented them. Bauch says the fact that Carlstadt did not bodily incorporate the Scotists' material was due to a weakening trend at Wittenberg in Scholasticism. Carlstadt never did penetrate any of the Scholastic writers very deeply; such thoroughness was not within his capabilities.
134. Prantl, 4:5.
135. Bauch, *CaS*, 48. Carlstadt combines the *distinctio ratio rei* with the Scotist one and then cites a whole battery of scholastic writers in support. But the book does not penetrate any of the views very deeply. The book is more a *Disputation* than his *Intentiones*. This material was not thoroughly handled until Cajetan wrote on St. Thomas.

136. Bauch, *CaS*, 49.
137. Bauch, *CaS*, 50.
138. Bauch, *CaS*, 53–54. For those who wish to see what Carlstadt used in these publications, Bauch, *CaS*, 53–54, gives some illustrations.
139. Bauch, *CaS*, 53–54.
140. Bauer, 8. We know that degrees were for sale in some Italian universities. It seems impossible for Carlstadt, who had no previous training in the Code of Justinian and related Roman law, nor a regular background in Canon law, that he could have done this on a level. But how he did acquire the degree is a mystery. One wonders what the Wittenberg law faculty thought of this undertaking.
141. Bauer, 7. For a more detailed account, see Schwiebert, *Luther*, 294–95. On September 25, 1516, Bartholomaeus Bernhardi engaged in a disputation with Luther presiding and Carlstadt and Lupinus furnishing the opposition in the Castle Church. The theme was sin and grace as taught by the church father Augustine versus Scholastic teaching and Aristotle. Lupinus won, but the arrogant Carlstadt was humiliated. On January 13, 1517, he went to Leipzig to purchase the works of St. Augustine (cf. Friedensburg, *G.U.W.*, 160). Later he became such an Augustinian that he drafted 151 Theses before the Wittenberg faculty to prove that Augustine was right.
142. This part of Carlstadt's life takes us beyond the period of the original university, but his later life proves all the more historians' claims about the type of man he was even in the earlier days.
143. Friedensburg, *G.U.W.*, 58.
144. Friedensburg, *G.U.W.*, 58–61.
145. Friedensburg, *G.U.W.*, 58–61. The title of this work was *Libellus der laudibus Germanic et ducem Saxonie editus a Christophoro Scheurlo Nürembergensi iuris utriusque doctore*, 1506 et 1508.
146. Friedensburg, *Urkundenbuch*, 1:15– 16.
147. Friedensburg, *Urkundenbuch*, 1:18– 57; those of 1533–1536, 54–84. These were treated in some detail in chapter 6; as was shown, they were modeled after the *Statutes of 1504*, but the style and wording are definitely those of the able jurist from Bologna as is evident from his Latin.
148. Scheurl, *Briefbuch*, 1:11.
149. Scheurl, *Briefbuch*, 1:57, which entry was made March 17, 1509.

150. Friedensburg, *G.U.W.*, 61.

151. Friedensburg, *G.U.W.*, 67.

152. *Liber Decanorum*, 2–3; Friedensburg, *G.U.W.*, 68.

153. Friedensburg, *G.U.W.*, 67. This position as custodian continued throughout his life until his death in 1521.

154. *Liber Decanorum*, 9.

155. *Liber Decanorum*, 3–21.

156. *Liber Decanorum*, 20.

157. This theme will be explored in some detail in a later chapter on how Luther won the Wittenberg faculty to his support.

158. Friedensburg, *G.U.W.*, 54–56. Petrua Tomais, better known as Petrus of Ravenna, was an able lawyer, scholar, and humanist. Since he stayed but a short time, his role was important only in the beginning. He will be treated in more detail in the next chapter on humanism at Wittenberg.

159. Friedensburg, *G.U.W.*, 56. He based this on Hermelink, *Die theologische Fakultät in Tübingen von der Reformation*, 156ff.

160. Friedensburg, *G.U.W.*, 56–58.

161. Friedensburg, *G.U.W.*, 56–58. The fact that a Gulden in those days had the value of about $75, made it now about $7,500 a year. In 1517 he complained to the elector that the agreement of also getting a "freien Tisch" and less wine and the beer did not taste bad. But this must be added to his income.

162. Friedensburg, *Urkundenbuch*, 1:15, has this entry: "D. Iheronymus Schurff, artium et juris utriusque doctor et ordinarius Vittembergensis, in Codice." Apparently Wolfgang Reisenousch was just a beginner in *juris utriusque*, or Civil and Canon Law as he is listed as a bachelor.

163. Friedensburg, *G.U.W.*, 57.

164. Friedensburg, *G.U.W.*, 58.

165. Friedensburg, *G.U.W.*, 58.

166. Friedensburg, *G.U.W.*, 62.

Chapter 19
Humanism and Wittenberg

1. There are a number of fine studies on the Renaissance that give us depth of insight into the problems raised by the best scholars in the last hundred years. An excellent study of the period is by J. Huizinga, "Das Problem der Rennaissance," *Wege der Kulturgeschichte* (München, 1930), 89ff. Another excellent study is that of Ernst Walser, *Studien zur Geistesgeschichte der Renaissance* (Basel, 1932). A more recent American scholar with a good summary is William J. Bouwsma, *The Interpretation of Renaissance Humanism* (Washington, D.C., 1959), 1ff. The other studies are more specialized. The two early studies were by Georg Voigt, *The Revival of Classical Antiquity* (Berlin, 1859), and Jacob Burckhardt, *The Civilization of the Renaissance in Italy* (Basel, 1860), which appeared in numerous editions.

2. Bouwsma, 3.

3. Bouwsma, 3. This was due to an exact checking in subsequent scholars in the claims of Burckhardt's thesis in particular, by asking: What was the Renaissance? Did it actually happen?

4. Huizinga, 93–94. Later some tried to trace the origin of the term as far back as St. Jerome, as will be shown.

5. Huizinga, 92.

6. Huizinga, 108–9; Bouwsma, 6.

7. Huizinga, 109.

8. Emile Gebhardt, *Des Origines de la Renaissance in Etalie* (1879).

9. Emile Gebhardt, *Histoire de la Renaissance Religieuse au Moyen Age* (1892), which tied the movement into the return to nature of St. Francis and the religious views of Joachim von Flora.

10. H. Thodes, *Franz von Assisi und die Anfänge der Kunst der Renaissance in Italien* (Berlin, 1885). This work claimed that the original impulses for the Renaissance were already there in the days of St. Francis, such as the love of nature, man's attitude toward the world, and individual emotional experience. Now came both an attack of Burckhardt and much renewed study of the Middle Ages. Now scholars denied that the humanism of the Renaissance was hostile toward Christianity nor was it particularly modern in its approach.

11. Huizinga, 111.

12. Huizinga, 113–14. These are the questions asked by scholars like Huizinga, Bouwsma, Courejod, and many others.

13. Huizinga, 113–14.

14. Huizinga, 116–17.

15. Charles Homer Haskins, *The Renaissance of the Twelfth Century* (Cambridge, 1928), after a detailed introduction treating the twelfth-century culture in detail, covering

the themes: "Intellectual Centers," "Books and Libraries," "The Latin Language," "Latin Poetry," "The Revival of Jurisprudence," "Historical Writing," "The Translations," "The Revival of Science," "The Revival of Philosophy," and "The Beginnings of Universities." In my doctoral examination at Cornell University in 1929, under my mentor, Preserved Smith, as a university fellow, Carl Becker, one of the examiners, began with the following observation: "Recently, I read a book on the myth of the Italian Renaissance. What do you think this book was all about?" Fortunately Preserved Smith had earlier asked me to read this work by Haskins, and I was able to use it in my reply. Even though I did not know the author and title of the book that Becker had reference to, it offered a very acceptable reply.

16. Haskins, *Renaissance*, vii–viii.

17. Konrad Burdach, *Reformation, Renaissance, Humanismus* (Berlin, 1918). This original work was reviewed by Alfred V. Martin, *Historische Zeitschrift*, 126 (Frankfurt a.M., 1922). See also Burdach's "Sinn und Ursprung der Worte 'Renaissance und Reformation,'" *Sitzungsberichte der preussischen Akademie der Wissenschaften*, 32 (1910): 594–646.

18. Burdach, 111–12.

19. Burdach, 112–14.

20. Burdach, 112–14. Martin in his review felt Burdach went too far in his claims of the Renaissance's influence in the modern world.

21. Ernst Troeltsch, *Historische Zeitschrift* (1906), 97, in which he expressed this thesis, but it did not receive too wide an acclaim. See also Huizinga, 108ff., for a summation and criticism of Troeltsch. That much of medievalism among the masses in both the periods of the Renaissance can hardly be disputed, but much of what he claimed is based on lack of information, especially about the German Reformation, as we shall note in details below.

22. Huizinga, 119–20.

23. The material used for this Walser section is based in the main on the excellent work of Ernst Walser, *Studien zur Geistesgeschichte der Renaissance* (Basel, 1932) (cited below as Walser). However, in this coverage of the large study, only his "Cultural-Plurality Thesis" and "The stream" idea can be stressed.

24. Werner Kaegi, *The Renaissance Investigations of Ernst Walser*, xiii.

25. Kaegi, xiii.

26. Kaegi, 17–18. Walser wrote his mother

that this offered him greater freedom for his study of the Renaissance, which offered an entirely new life. Among his Roman companions were the poet Carducci and the scholars Pascoli and D'Annuzio.

27. Kaegi, xv. Irwin Panofsky of Princeton University has more recently shown that Leonardo was quite a thinker and a methodical worker and deserved more credit than Roth had claimed.

28. Kaegi, xx–xxi.

29. Kaegi, xxii–xxiii.

30. Kaegi, xxvii. He now traced the history from the decline of antiquity to modern times in his lectures as a mature scholar. He explored such themes as the sovereignty of the individual, the discovery and mastery of the earth, and man's place in the universe, human anatomy, the development of the exact sciences in modern times, and the cultural, philosophical method, and historical criticism.

31. Kaegi, xxvii.

32. Kaegi, xxix.

33. Walser, quoted by Kaegi, 33; and Huizinga made a similar observation about the same time.

34. Kaegi, xxxv.

35. Kaegi, xxxvii. In his peculiar brogue Burckhardt said to Walser, "Weise Sie, mit däm Individualismus—i glaub ganz nimmi dra; aber i sag nit, ai hän gar e Fraid."

36. Huizinga, 120.

37. Kaegi, 10.

38. Kaegi enlarges on Walser's stream idea (p. 39) but points out that in some cases the flow remained unchanged, while in others, like art, there was a *Neugestaltung*, new formations in Cimabue and Giotto, which then flows on to the *Quatrocento* of Leonardo, Raphael, Titian, and Michelangelo. He also points out that it was natural for different nations to have other ancestors to return to than the Romans. For Italy the Ancients were their forefathers, and it was natural for them to look back to them for inspiration.

39. Kaegi, 39.

40. Paul Joachimsen, "Der Humanismus und die Entwicklung des deutschen Geistes," *Deutsche Vierteljahrschrift für Literaturwissenschaft und Geistesgeschichte* (Halle, 1930), 8:419.

41. Joachimsen, 8:420.

42. Knapton, 67.

43. Thomson, *Renaissance*, 76-77.

44. Thomson, *Renaissance*, 78.

45. Thomson, *Renaissance*, 79.

46. Thomson, *Renaissance*, 80.

47. He is even so highly regarded as a scholar that Folger Shakespeare Library commemorated his death in 1974 by a whole week of scholarly programs in which scholars from all over the modern world participated. For us guests this honor and recognition were very impressive.

48. Joachimsen, 8:421–24. See also Thomson, *Renaissance*, 80.

49. Thomson, *Renaissance*, 81.

50. Thomson, *Renaissance*, 82.

51. Thomson, *Renaissance*, 82.

52. For Petrarch as a historian, with his praise of Rome and his rejection of the translatium imperii to Charlemagne and the subsequent history of the Holy Roman Empire, combined with his contempt for the barbarians, see Wallace K. Ferguson, *The Renaissance in Historical Thought* (Cambridge, 1948), 8–9. See also Thomson, *Renaissance*, 82.

53. Thomson, *Renaissance*, 82–84.

54. Thomson, *Renaissance*, 86–90.

55. Knapton, 68.

56. Thomson, *Renaissance*, 90. His father, Boccacio di'Chellinoa, had an estate at Certaldo, some twenty miles out of Florence, but he was really a Florentine, while we know less about his mother.

57. Knapton, 68.

58. Thomson, *Renaissance*, 90–91; Knapton, 68.

59. Thomson, *Renaissance*, 90.

60. Thomson, *Renaissance*, 90ff.

61. Thomson, *Renaissance*, 90ff.

62. Knapton, 68.

63. Thomson, *Renaissance*, 93–95. For a slightly more favorable view, see J. W. Thompson and E. N. Johnson, *An Introduction to Medieval Europe* (New York, 1937), 1009, who claim that Boccaccio taught Greek and influenced younger humanists to take up the study of that language.

64. Thomson, *Renaissance*, 93. Thomson feels that among these works Boccaccio's *De Genealogies* is perhaps the most scholarly and had the most lasting effect, as it stimulated other scholars to become interested in ancient mythology. His *De Montibus* attempted to acquaint students with the geography of Antiquity.

65. Knapton, 68–69.

66. Thomson, *Renaissance*, 95.

67. Thomson, *Renaissance*, 95.

68. Ferguson, 10, 26.

69. By the middle of 1516 the University of Wittenberg began to undergo curriculum changes under Luther's and Melanchthon's leadership with an emphasis on Latin, Greek, and Hebrew to introduce biblical humanism into the university. By the twenties it was in full swing. This will be treated in detail in a later chapter.

70. Knapton, 69.

71. For an excellent recent account of the Greek scholars that came to Venice and worked in the famous Aldus Press and taught and lectured elsewhere in Italy, see D. J. Geanakopolos, *Greek Scholars in Venice* (Cambridge, 1962). Northern Humanism really through their influence in Greek received its real start. It was here that Erasmus learned most of his Greek and Wittenberg University added tremendously to its holdings, as can be observed in chapter 10 of this volume.

72. Knapton, 70.

73. Johnson, 101.

74. James W. Thompson, *The Medieval Library* (New York, 1957), 559.

75. Thompson, *Medieval Library*, 559.

76. Thompson, *Medieval Library*, 562–63.

77. Thompson, *Medieval Library*, 562–63. Pope Pius II, Aeneas Silvius Piccolomini was more interested in a private collection of his own than in the Vatican Library.

78. Thompson, *Medieval Library*, 563.

79. Thompson, *Medieval Library*, 563.

80. Thompson, *Medieval Library*, 566.

81. Thompson, *Medieval Library*, 566.

82. Geanakopolos, 1–8.

83. Geanakopolos, 279.

84. Geanakopolos, 283.

85. Geanakopolos, 283.

86. Geanakopolos, 285.

87. For the purchases of the Ducal Library of the University of Wittenberg, see chapter 10.

88. Thompson, *Medieval Library*, 581.

89. Thompson, *Medieval Library*, 585.

90. Thompson, *Medieval Library*, 585.

91. Thompson, *Medieval Library*, 585.

92. Knapton, 73.

93. Joachimsen, 8:432. When one considers that in 1500 modern cities in German

lands like Leipzig had a population of only six thousand, Erfurt thirty-two thousand, and Nürnberg perhaps seventy-five thousand, one must conclude that most Germans still lived in villages and engaged in farming.

94. Rashdall, 2:212–22.

95. Spitz, 5-6.

96. Joachimsen, 8:438.

97. Joachimsen, 8:435–37. Some of these ideas are those of Joachimsen, while others are those of the author, which will become more evident when the University of Hiedelberg is reviewed during the period of Peter Luder and Stephan Hoest, from 1450 to 1475.

98. To the modern world such reasoning appears fantastic, but in the sixteenth century it seemed very real. Even in the election of Emperor Charles V in 1519 there were three candidates aspiring to become emperor, Francis I of France, King Henry VIII of England, and Charles V of Spain.

99. Joachimsen, 8:438–41.

100. Post, *The Modern Devotion*. This author, after a detailed study, questions the ideas set forth by Meswerdt and repeated by Hyma, Spitz, and others that the Brethren of the Common Life had a very deep influence on humanism, giving it a Christian flavor, and that men like Agicola, Erasmus, Wimpfeling, and even Luther were influenced by them and turned to the Biblical Humanism of the German Reformation.

101. *Hoest.* See author's review in *Renaissance Quarterly*, vol. 26, no. 3.

102. Spitz, 6–7.

103. See chapter 21.

104. Joachimsen, 8:442.

105. Joachimsen, 8:442–45.

106. Post, 1.

107. Post, 8–11.

108. Albert Hyma published two books on the Brethren: *The Christian Renaissance* and *A History of the Devotio Moderna* (Grand Rapids, 1924); a new edition appeared under the title *The Brethren of the Common Life* (Grand Rapids, 1950). Even though one of his doctoral candidates wrote a thesis on this subject, questioning his former views, Hyma did not change his views.

109. Post, 12–16.

110. Post, 16–17.

111. *Hoest*, Vorwort, 7–10.

112. Rashdall, 2:212–51.

113. *Hoest*, 13–15. See above, n. 90.

114. *Hoest*, 15.

115. *Hoest*, 15.

116. *Hoest*, 15–26.

117. *Hoest*, 32.

118. *Hoest*, 32.

119. *Hoest*, 35–36.

120. *Hoest*, 35–38.

121. *Hoest*, 38–40. The original text of Marsilius von Inghen had been reworked and enlarged, and it covered the *Summulae* of Pope John XXII, commonly known as Petrus Hispanus. Here was the basic complaint of the *Via Antiqua* faculty. They wanted the Parva logica dropped. The old school wanted the *Summulae* of Petrus Hispanus. Here in this speech Hoest does not touch on universals as he does for the graduation of the *Via Moderna*.

122. *Hoest*, 41.

123. *Hoest*, 41.

124. *Hoest*, 42. For the complete text, see pp. 65–79.

125. *Hoest*, 43.

126. *Hoest*, 44.

127. Baron claims that Hoest had some mistaken notions about the founders of the *Via Moderna;* but he feels that perhaps Hoest mixed up his own later views with those of the men he cited.

128. *Hoest*, 48.

129. *Hoest*, 48–49.

130. *Hoest*, 50–52.

131. *Hoest*, 55.

132. *Hoest*, 56.

133. *Hoest*, 59–60.

134. *Hoest*, 62–64.

135. Frank Baron, in this study of the Hoest material, speaks of his *Zusammenfassung*, a putting together of his impressions as to the significance of the Early Humanism of Heidelberg. The interesting aspect is that a specialist in scholasticism and humanism was able to break the stranglehold of scholasticism, at least to a degree, and to prepare the way for its impact on the University of Wittenberg in the early days and for Luther's triumph of Biblical Humanism, which practically eliminated Aristotle from the university's curriculum (*Hoest*, 70ff.).

136. *Hoest*, 70–71.

137. *Hoest*, 71–72.

138. *Hoest*, 72ff.

139. This theme will be developed in a later chapter on the introduction of the Refor-

mation at the University of Wittenberg. When John Reuchlin recommended his great nephew to the elector of Saxony, he spoke of him as the greatest Greek scholar next to Erasmus. So his humanistic training at Heidelberg must have been excellent.

140. See below, chapter 22.

141. Bauch, *Leipziger Frühhumanismus*, 1.

142. Bauch, *Leipziger Frühhumanismus*, 1.

143. Bauch, *Leipziger Frühhumanismus*, 1–2.

144. Kaufmann, 2:44–45.

145. Rashdall, 2:212. In this original founding, the emperor had received the approval of Pope Clement VI in 1347.

146. Rothe, 655; see also Johnson, 983–85.

147. R. R. Post states at the outset that the more recent findings based on detailed study of evidence do not bear out the claims of Mestwerdt, repeated somewhat by Hyma, Spitz, and others, namely, that the Brethren of the Common Life had a very deep influence on Humanism, giving it a Christian flavor and that men like Agricola, Erasmus, and Wimpfeling, and later Luther, were under their influence, which resulted in Biblical Humanism and the Reformation. The Lewis Spitz chapter on Agricola is excellent, especially the part showing the Italian influences on this Humanist. Unfortunately, he did not have the advantage of the recent Post and Stephan Hoest studies; otherwise he might have increased the influence of Peter Luder, who was twenty years in Italy and taught at Heidelberg introducing the *Studia humanitatis* for four years from 1456 to 1560. Agricola was really the successor of Stephan Hoest like Wimpfeling and others.

148. Bauch, WudS, 287.

149. Bauch, WudS, 288.

150. Bauch, WudS, 288.

151. Bauch, *Leipziger Frühhumanismus*, 4–6. Wattenbach shows how Peter Luder taught at Leipzig in the winter semester of 1462–1463 and the summer of 1463. There was also Johann Tolkopf of the Oberpfalz.

152. Gess, 16, 43–93.

153. Gess, 44.

154. Schwiebert, *Theses,* 98.

155. Prantl, 4:273; Bauch, *Leipziger Frühhumanismus*, 7–9.

156. Joachimsen, 442–45.

157. The full title of the chapter is "Celtis, the Arch-Humanist."

158. Spitz, 81, claims Celtis studied at Cologne, Heidelberg, Rostock, and Leipzig.

159. Bauch, *Leipziger Frühhumanismus*, 18.

160. Spitz, 81–82.

161. Joachimsen, 442.

162. Bauch, *Leipziger Frühhumanismus*, 18.

163. Spitz, 86–87.

164. Bauch, *Leipziger Frühhumanismus*, 20–22. Part of it is based on other parts of Bauch's many humanistic studies.

165. Bauch, *Leipziger Frühhumanismus*, 20–22.

166. Bauch, *Leipziger Frühhumanismus*, 22–23.

167. Bauch, *Leipziger Frühhumanismus*, 22–23.

168. Bauch, *Leipziger Frühhumanismus*, 23–25.

169. Bauch, *Leipziger Frühhumanismus*, 25–27.

170. Bauch, *Leipziger Frühhumanismus*, 25–27.

171. Bauch, *Leipziger Frühhumanismus*, 27–32.

172. Bauch, *Leipziger Frühhumanismus*, 34.

173. Bauch, *Leipziger Frühhumanismus*, 34–35.

174. Bauch, *Leipziger Frühhumanismus*, 38.

175. Bauch, *Leipziger Frühhumanismus*, 39–45.

176. Bauch, *Leipziger Frühhumanismus*, 53–54. Bauch shows how the battle continued, but since it did not add anything, the details are really not relevant to our theme.

177. Gustav Bauch, "Die Vertreibung des Johannes Rhegius Aesticampianus aus Leipzig," *Archiv für Literaturgeschichte* (Leipzig, 1885), 1ff.

178. Bauch, Rhegius, 1.

179. Bauch, Rhegius, 2–3.

180. Bauch, Rhegius, 6–11.

181. Bauch, Rhegius, 11–18.

182. Bauch, Rhegius, 18–33. For a discussion of Wittenberg's curricula reorganization, see Schwiebert, *Luther,* 275–302. See also a later chapter in this study.

183. See chaps. 4-10, in which Erfurt's role in the Middle Ages is treated in detail. Its rich merchants were quite independent, and there were frequent conflicts between the city of

Erfurt and its own archbishops and in which
the ruling houses also became involved a number of times.

184. This size was large in comparison to
Leipzig, which had but six thousand inhabitants a century later.

185. Rashdall, 1:246–48.

186. Rashdall, 1:248. Kaufmann, 2:158–
59, claims that Prague used the Statutes of
Bologna, while Leipzig and Erfurt used those
of Prague.

187. Kleineidem, 1:142–44.

188. Kleineidem, 1:144–45.

189. Junghans, 63.

190. Schwiebert, *Luther,* 125.

191. Schwiebert, *Luther,* 132.

192. Gustav Bauch, *Erfurt Frühhumanismus,* 71ff.; Kleineidem, 146.

193. Kleineidem, 146–47.

194. Kleineidem, 147.

195. Kleineidem, 147.

196. Schwiebert, *Luther,* 135, and n. 103.

197. Schwiebert, *Luther,* 135.

198. WA, 9, 31, 35, 37; Paulus, *Usingen,* 8.

199. Rommel, *Randbemerkungen,* 4–10;
Schubert, *Luther-Jahrbuch,* 8:11 ; cf. Plitt, 14,
29.

200. Junghans, 65.

201. Bauch, *Erfurt Frühhumanismus,* 190.

202. Junghans, 66, and n. 130.

203. Bauch, "Anfänge des griechischen
Sprache," 6:47ff. Bauch thinks some of the
source material used by Marschalk was
Emanuel Chrysolarus' *Greek Grammar,* which
had been critically reworked by Theodorus
Gaza, and the *Investigations* of Constantine
Lascaris. Geanakopolos, 57, credits Lascaris
with the authorship of the first complete publication written entirely in Greek in Europe,
his *Erotemata* published in Milan in 1476 by
the printer Demetrius Damiles. Then a new
edition of the *Erotemata,* or *Questions,* in
1494 with a Latin translation by Crastoni.

204. This publication, based on Valparaiso
University's rich Reformation collection of
sources from Europe, built up by a previous
specialist several decades before, was entitled
*Nicoli Marscalei Thurii oratio habita albiori
akademia in alemania iam nuperrima ad pro-
motionem primorum baccalauriorum numero
quattuor et viginti anno domini mcccccciii.* The
festschrift was published in an attractive red
binding. It began with an elaborate historical

introduction about Marschalk's role as a classical scholar in Latin and Greek and his publications. The introduction closes with a critical
review of the oration, which follows.

205. See the acknowledgments in front.

206. Kleineidem, 171; Reinke, *Oratio,*
3–4.

207. Bauch, *Anfänge der Griechischen
Sprache,* 50–51. The title of the Venetian publication was *Pselli Ad Imperatorium Constan-
tinum De Victus Ratione Georgio Valla
Interprete.*

208. Bauch, *Anfänge der Griechischen
Sprache,* 52.

209. Junghans, 66.

210. Junghans, 66.

211. Bauch, *Anfänge der Griechischen
Sprache,* 51.

212. Bauch, *Anfänge der Griechischen
Sprache,* 52; cf. Junghans, 67. For the Latin
text of this second epigram, see Bauch,
Anfänge der Griechischen Sprache, 53.

213. Bauch, *Anfänge der Griechischen
Sprache,* 52.

214. Bauch, *Anfänge der Griechischen
Sprache,* 52, n. 2.

215. Bauch, *Anfänge der Griechischen
Sprache,* 52.

216. Junghans, 67. Later he published a
work by a Florentine *Cathaloqua Platonicus,*
which attempted to harmonize Plato and
Christianity.

217. Bauch, *Anfänge der Griechischen
Sprache,* 52.

218. Bauch, *Anfänge der Griechischen
Sprache,* 54.

219. Bauch, *Anfänge der Griechischen
Sprache,* 54.

220. Bauch, *Anfänge der Griechischen
Sprache,* 54–56, offers us quite an illustration
of what the *Lehrbuch* actually contained in
richness of instructive material.

221. Bauch, *Anfänge der Griechischen
Sprache,* 56.

222. Bauch, *Anfänge der Griechischen
Sprache,* 57. He begins with the statement,
"In hoc libro haec Continentur. Constantini
Lascari Erotemata cum interpretatione la-
tina." Then he states in some detail what he
used from Lascaris' introduction.

223. Geanakopolos, 57.

224. Geanakopolos, 138.

225. Junghans, 67–70, based on Bauch's

detailed defense in *Anfänge der Griechischen Sprache,* 59–60. Bauch also cites the Church Fathers and even the scholastic writer Gratian in defense of the study of the humanities.

226. Bauch, *Anfänge der Griechischen Sprache,* 62.

227. Bauch, *Anfänge der Griechischen Sprache,* 62–63. In part one he enlarges on oratory and its nature and importance. In part two he deals with poetry and its divisions. What is comedy and tragedy? How does one write satire? He treats iambic song writing, epigrams, elegies, narrative poems, lyrics, and military songs. In part three the importance of parts of speech, concerning letters, vowels, consonants, syllables, diphthongs, in Latin and Greek. In part four he treats prose and accents, tone, rhythm, numbers, harmony, symmetry, modulations, and types of writing. He treats both Latin and Greek, but the emphasis is on Latin.

228. Bauch, *Anfänge der Griechischen Sprache,* 64.

229. Bauch, *Anfänge der Griechischen Sprache,* 65.

230. Junghans, 70–71.

231. Junghans, 71.

232. Junghans, 71–73, and n. 163.

233. Friedensburg, *G.U.W.,* 75. Marschalk had written a letter to the elector of Saxony about having encountered Schwierigkeiten at Erfurt and invited him to come to Wittenberg. His influence at Wittenberg was not lost as it traces its Greek studies to him at the new university.

234. *Liber Decanorum,* 1.

235. Friedensburg, *G.U.W.,* 68–69.

236. Friedensburg, *Urkundenbuch,* 1:16.

237. Friedensburg, *G.U.W.,* 70–71.

238. Friedensburg, *G.U.W.,* 54.

239. Friedensburg, *G.U.W.,* 54–55.

240. Friedensburg, *G.U.W.,* 56.

241. Bauch, *Anfänge der Griechischen Sprache,* 77.

242. Bauch, *Anfänge der Griechischen Sprache,* 77.

243. Bauch, *Anfänge der Griechischen Sprache,* 77. The author is grateful that Valparaiso asked its faculty to procure a copy of Marschalk's oration and the translation of the address by Professor Reinke from the original text. President O. P. Kretzmann had it published as a special festschrift to commem-

orate the 450th anniversary of Martin Luther's nailing of his Ninety-five Theses (cited below as *Festschrift*).

244. *Festschrift,* 16–17.

245. *Festschrift,* 17.

246. *Festschrift,* 17; cf. Friedensburg, *G.U.W.,* 76, who says that Marschalk's *Oratio* brought Homer to Wittenberg.

247. Bauch, *Anfänge der Griechischen Sprache,* 76–77.

248. Friedensburg, *G.U.W.,* 75–76; cf. Reinke, *Oratio,* 20ff., for the later fate of Marschalk.

249. Friedensburg, *G.U.W.,* 76.

250. Friedensburg, *G.U.W.,* 70.

251. Friedensburg, *Urkundenbuch,* 1:16 and n. 11.

252. Friedensburg, *G.U.W.,* 71.

253. Friedensburg, *G.U.W.,* 71.

254. *Album,* 1:23.

255. Friedensburg, *G.U.W.,* 71.

256. Friedensburg, *G.U.W.,* 72, n. 1.

257. Friedensburg, *G.U.W.,* 72.

258. Friedensburg, *G.U.W.,* 72.

259. Bauch, *Anfänge der Griechischen Sprache,* 82–92.

260. Bauch cites the following, which he claimed to have had as instructors in Greek: Jacobus a Cruce, Johannes Baptista Pius, Philippus Beroaldus, Jr., Johannes Baptista Egnatius, and even Marcus Musurus. How much actual contact he had with the men is no longer known, for in his hurried flight it would have been impossible.

261. Bauch, *Anfänge der Griechischen Sprache,* 83–84.

262. Bauch, *Anfänge der Griechischen Sprache,* 84.

263. Friedensburg, *G.U.W.,* 77.

264. Bauch, *Anfänge der Griechischen Sprache,* 85.

265. Bauch, *Anfänge der Griechischen Sprache,* 86.

266. Bauch, *Anfänge der Griechischen Sprache,* 86. The head of the *Neue Collegium,* the *Praepositus,* at the time, was M. Johann Räuber of Bockenheim. With him were M. Balthasar Fabricius Phachus and M. Konrad Salmünster. These were his fellow humanists, who brought him a text of Homer's *Batrachomyomachia* to be considered for printing.

267. Bauch, *Anfänge der Griechischen Sprache,* 87.

268. Bauch, *Anfänge der Griechischen Sprache,* 88–89.

269. Gustav Bauch, "Die Einführung des Hebraischen in Wittenberg," *Monatschrift für Geschichte und Wissenschaft des Judentums,* Neue Floge, 48 (1904): 147. Cf. Schwiebert, *Luther,* 296.

270. Bauch, *Anfänge der Griechischen Sprache,* 90. It is interesting that the year before Luther nailed his Ninety-five Theses in 1517, that Philymnus should have raised the same objections to John Tetzer's indulgence sales and praise of relic worship.

271. Friedensburg, *G.U.W.,* 144–45.

272. Bauch, WudS, 304–6.

273. For the complete account, see above, chapter 7.

274. Bauch, WudS, 304–6.

275. Bauch, WudS, 305–6.

276. *Liber Decanorum,* 2, tells us that Father Paul Carnificis served as dean of Theology in 1504 but was recalled by the Minor Orders. But upon his departure he was replaced by another of the regular clergy, Father Ludwig Henning, a Master in theology from Padua, who was chosen for the position and afterwards was also made dean of the theological faculty. But like many others educated in Italy, he also taught Logic viam Scoti in the philosophical faculty.

277. Bauch, WudS, 306. See also Prantl, 4:196.

278. Prantl, 4:269.

279. Bauch, WudS, 307.

280. Bauch, WudS, 309.

281. Friedensburg, *G.U.W.,* 54–55.

282. Friedensburg, *G.U.W.,* 55.

283. Friedensburg, *G.U.W.,* 55–56.

284. Friedensburg, *G.U.W.,* 56–58. For his role with Luther, see Schwiebert, *Luther,* 296.

285. Kleineidem, 167.

286. Kleineidem, 167.

287. Friedensburg, *G.U.W.,* 61.

288. Friedensburg, *G.U.W.,* 62.

289. Friedensburg, *G.U.W.,* 68.

290. Bauch, Scheurl, 33ff.

291. Bauch, Scheurl, 33; Friedensburg, *G.U.W.,* 58ff.

292. Bauch, Scheurl, 35.

293. Bauch, Scheurl, 34-35. Bauch relates how young Christopher rode on horseback to the Saxon Court and met Frederick and Staupitz.

294. Bauch, Scheurl, 36. The eighty must be multiplied by about $75 a Gulden in mod-

ern buying power. See next chapter for the finances of the shcool.

295. Bauch, Scheurl, 36. Gustav Bauch had access to Scheurl's Nürnberg sources, even using much of the sixteenth-century wording, added the dinner and dance cost him 14 Gulden and 10 Groschen, which totals over a thousand dollars.

296. Bauch, Scheurl, 33.

297. Bauch, Scheurl, 37. Bauch quotes Scheurl's notes: Frederich and John were "auf der obersten Porkirchen verborgen" that they hear it "mit grossen Wolgefallen anherten." Afterward he told Pfeffinger, his official, that he would finance to have those printed in book format, an expense of 600 to 800 Gulden.

298. Friedensburg, *G.U.W.,* 60.

299. Friedensburg, *G.U.W.,* 60.

300. Scheurl, *Briefbuch,* 1:57.

301. Friedensburg, *G.U.W.,* 61. See also Harold J. Grimm, *Lazarus Spengler: A Law Leader of the Reformation* (Columbus, 1978), 27. This offers a good insight into Old Nürnberg and the environment in which Christopher Scheurl grew up and later served as rechtskonsul, the legal advisor of the city council.

302. In a subsequent chapter the author has treated the period of the middle of the next decade at the university, when Martin Luther became the reformer who, through a return to the original Greek and Hebrew texts of the Holy Scriptures, won the Wittenberg faculty to a revision of the university curriculum and dethroned Aristotle with the assistance of Philip Melanchthon and made Wittenberg the center of Biblical Humanism.

Chapter 20
The University's Endowment and Finances

1. Suevus, 20–28. Cf. Israël, 66–68.

2. Schwiebert, *Luther,* 257–68, has an evaluation of the problem as of that date, when the dollar's buying power was about ten times that of today.

3. Schwiebert, *Luther,* 257.

4. This has to be done on the basis of sixteenth-century sources and those compared with 1914, 1940, and 1985.

5. Smith, *Reformation,* 458–76.

6. Smith, *Reformation,* 458–76.

7. Smith, *Reformation,* 472.

8. For the author's evaluation of the Gulden in 1950, see Schwiebert, *Luther,* 257–72. The author is most familiar with prices in our universities around 1945, when a full professor at Northwestern University and Ohio State University was not paid above $6,000 a year. We built a seven-room, Elizabethan-style house with oak floors and a full basement in that region for $9,600. That house today could not be erected for less than $85,000. We purchased an Oldsmobile 88 for $2,200.

9. Friedensburg, *Urkundenbuch,* 1:14. Scheurl writes: "ubi annuus victus octo-saureis." For Friedensburg's note on the value of the Gulden, see n. 10.

10. Friedensburg, *Urkundenbuch,* 1:16, n. 2. Friedensburg adds, "Der in 21 Groschen eingeteilte Goldgulden oder rhenische Gulden war die maszgebende Münze in Mittel-deutschland. Vgl. Kius, "Die Preis und Lohn-verhältnisse des 16. Jahrhunderts in Thüringen," *Hildebrands Jahrbuch f. National-ökonomie und Statistik,* 1 (1863) 65ff.

11. Below we will deal with the Witten-berg budget and professors' income, which could be left in Gulden, but then they would not have much meaning. Luther had a salary later in life of three hundred Gulden and a number of exemptions, but out of that he had to maintain a household of around twenty-five people. Of course he had an efficient manager in his wife Kathie that no doubt saved much by her cattle and livestock.

12. Schwiebert, *Luther,* 257–68.

13. See chap. 4.

14. Israël, 24–66.

15. Israël, 24–25.

16. Israël, 24–25.

17. Israël, 25.

18. Lucas Cranach, *Wittemberger Heilig-thumsbuch,* 1–2, tells all about the original "thorn" out of the "Crown of Thorns, which wounded the heart of Christ," and why he acquired the sacred relic from King Philip of France.

19. Cranach, 3, no. 80. Cf. Israël, 26.

20. Cranach, 1. He claims the new church was erected within the castle grounds and was finished in 1353.

21. Israël, 26.

22. Israël, 27.

23. Israël, 27.

24. Israël, 27-29. The sources of income

were to be from Trebichau, Dorf Eutzsch, the Rathaus in Kemberg one schock, the Dorf Wep one schock, and from Krewe not stated how much. Each of the lower clergy was to receive five mark silver; the prokaplan was to get ten mark silver, while the kuster was to get two mark silver.

25. Israël, 30–31.

26. Israël, 31. Here he also on Feb. 2, 1361, restates what amounts were paid by places according to previous agreements.

27. Israël, 31–35.

28. Israël, 34.

29. Israël, 34.

30. Israël, 41.

31. Schwiebert, *Luther,* 78, n. 14.

32. Israël, 62–66.

33. Israël, 66–69, has a summary of the Bull of 1507, which incorporated the Stift with the school as a source of its future endow-ment. For the text, see Suevus, 29–31.

34. Israël, 62–66.

35. Israël, 62–63.

36. Israël, 63.

37. Israël, 65.

38. Israël, 65.

39. Israël, 65.

40. Israël, 66.

41. Grohmann, 1:45–46.

42. Grohmann, 1:51, is not quite as clear in his explanation as we would have liked, but he seems to have assumed that the incomes in kind and funds remained constant since the incorporation in 1507 up to the reorganization of the university in 1536. He thinks the total was 2,561 Gulden, 1 Groschen, and with Frederick's addition of cloisters of Saxony, 500 Gulden; Thuringia, 700 Gulden; and Meiszen, 700 Gulden annually so that the total at the time of the incorporation was 3,795 Gulden.

43. Grohmann, 1:51. This must not be confused with the masses for Frederick's ancestors. This was a private establishment made by him in 1506. Outside of that a sizable staff was supported by the endowment. Later, however, as the staff died and was not replaced, more funds became available for the finances of the university.

44. Suevus, 20, for the text; Israël, 66–67, for a summary.

45. Suevus, 20.

46. Suevus, 21. The bull stipulated how five Ducal canons were to be paid in place of former vicars. The first canon was to receive

ten Gulden from the chapel next to the Pfarrkirche; the second canon was to receive also
ten from Schalcken; the third canon was to get
the same amount Liebenswerde; the fourth in
Weida was likewise to get ten Gulden; while
the fifth in the five canons was to get nine
Gulden from Jessen.

47. Suevus, 21.
48. Suevus, 23.
49. Suevus, 23.
50. Suevus, 24.
51. Fortunately the elector was a rich man,
as was shown in chap. 14.
52. Israël, 68.
53. Grohmann, 1:51.
54. Grohmann, 1:51.
55. Grohmann, 1:51.
56. Grohmann, 1:52.
57. Grohmann, 1:52–53. Duke Moritz was
so ambitious about his private advances that
he turned traitor twice, first by joining Emperor Charles V in attacking electoral Saxony.
Once he had attained his goal and was made
the elector of Saxony in place of John Frederick, he turned again against the emperor and
was killed in 1553 in the Battle of Sievers-
hausen and was succeeded by his brother
August, who then was over the electorate and
the university until 1586. He was a much
milder and generous prince who took such
good care of the University of Wittenberg that
he has been called its second founder.
58. Grohmann, 53.
59. Grohmann, 53.
60. Grohmann, 54.
61. Grohmann, 54–55. Here he gives a
long list of Pfarrlehen who had to render services to the university.
62. Grohmann, 55–56.
63. Grohmann, 56.
64. Grohmann, 56-57.
65. Grohmann, 57.
66. Grohmann, 45-48.
67. Friedensburg, *Urkundenbuch,* 1:77ff.
68. Friedensburg, *Urkundenbuch,* 1:77.
69. Friedensburg, *Urkundenbuch,* 1:77.
70. Friedensburg, *Urkundenbuch,* 1:77.
71. Friedensburg, *Urkundenbuch,* 1:77.
72. Friedensburg, *Urkundenbuch,* 1:77.
73. Friedensburg, *Urkundenbuch,* 1:78.
74. Friedensburg, *Urkundenbuch,* 1:78.
Friedensburg added in a note: "Bonifazius
Erasmi oder De Rode aus Zörbig."

75. See chap. 14.
76. Friedensburg, *Urkundenbuch,* 1:142–
43. The source adds, "Summa 1300 gl. exclusis
Doctor Martinus under der Probst."
77. Friedensburg, *Urkundenbuch,* 1:144.
78. Friedensburg, *Urkundenbuch,* 1:144–45.
79. Friedensburg, *Urkundenbuch,* 145.
80. This story is covered in some detail in
chap. 14, from the angle of Frederick the
Wise, who was torn between his new gospel
belief of "justification by faith" and his masses
for his parents and ancestors.
81. Friedensburg, *Urkundenbuch,* 153.
82. For the text of the new Statutes of 1533,
see Friedensburg, *Urkundenbuch,* 1:154–58.
The statutes will be discussed in a later chapter
in connection with the history of the University
of Wittenberg.
83. Friedensburg, *Urkundenbuch,* 1:162–65.
84. Friedensburg, *Urkundenbuch,* 1:163.
85. Friedensburg, *Urkundenbuch,* 1:163.
86. See the chart on student matriculations
in Schwiebert, *Wittenberg and Other Universities,* 72–73. The author, in his doctoral work,
plotted these students, as stated above, elsewhere, and its effect on the institution will be
treated in detail in a chapter on the spread of
the German Reformation.
87. WA 30:508–88. The effect was not
immediately evident, but it was the seed for
enrollments from 1540 to 1550 of six hundred
to seven hundred students. See University
Album 3:806–807.
88. Friedensburg, *Urkundenbuch,* 1:167–
69. This document has a breakdown of the
salaries and expenditures, while a later one
contains the actual academic aspects.
89. Friedensburg, *Urkundenbuch,* 1:25–
27. For advanced degrees this became a sizable sum.
90. Friedensburg, *Urkundenbuch,* 1:167–69.
91. The following entries were made by
Chancellor Brück and his court officials: a.
Doctor Martinus is to receive 300 Gulden, but
he is not to be bound to any specific courses.
Martin Luther was married in 1525 and maintained a large household by then of five living
children, twelve orphans of relatives, tutors of
the children, sisters, and an aunt of Catherine
von Bora, some retired ministers, totaling
sometimes at evening devotions some twenty-
five members. This demanded additional
money to provide for such a large group. b.

Philip Melanchthon was to receive but 200 Gulden, but he was far from being neglected, for the elector built him at this time the fine Renaissance-style home next to the New Friderici College and gave him a fine garden, which is still there today. Philip also was not to be bound to any specific courses, the draft states. c. Probst Justus Jonas of the Castle Church's Stift, was to lecture four times a week, with a salary of 36 Gulden, while his income as probst was to net him 78 Gulden, 3 Groschen, and 9 Pfennige. In kind he was to receive 16½ Scheffel of rye, 650 Scheffel of oats, 31 geese, 10 lambs, 5 colts, and 2 calves. d. The Hebrew and Aramaic professor was to receive 200 Gulden for lecturing twice a week and then additional pay for preaching. The town pastor, Johannes Bugenhagen, was to have his regular pastor's salary from the Pfarrkirche, and for his two lectures per week in the seminary he was to receive 60 Gulden.

92. Friedensburg, *Urkundenbuch*, 1:168.

93. Friedensburg, *Urkundenbuch*, 1:168–69.

94. Friedensburg, *Urkundenbuch*, 171. Here Brück adds that the above advance in the salaries of Luther, Lindemann, Jerome Schurpf and Philip Melanchthon advanced the budget by $35,250, which if it were omitted that sum would be less.

95. Friedensburg, *Urkundenbuch*, 1:169–70.

96. Friedensburg, *Urkundenbuch*, 1:170–71.

97. Friedensburg, *Urkundenbuch*, 1:171–72.

98. Friedensburg, *Urkundenbuch*, 1:171–72. For a detailed analysis of the place of Disputations in the Wittenberg academic life, see Schwiebert, *Theses*, 120–43. The calculations in this study are somewhat misleading, as they are based on the Gulden value in relation to 1967 rather than those of 1985. For faculty incomes and fines, see pp. 125–26. In that 1967 calculation the Gulden was evaluated at $50, so another fourth must be added to get the 1985 worth of Gulden.

99. Schwiebert, *Theses*, 125.

100. Friedensburg, *Urkundenbuch*, 1:177–78, from the Elector John Frederick's *Statutes of 1536*. According to this, each regular professor was obligated to take his turn at holding a disputation, which were held four times a year by different members in the Upper Faculties. In case one ignores the 1967 figures of the value of the Gulden and uses our 1985 calculations, each professor was paid $150 while

the professors who were the respondents received $75 and the students arguing pro and con were paid $18. At such rates even one professorial disputation was about $375. The payments in Law and Medicine were about the same, but in Liberal Arts they were much less as many participants had not even completed their degress in any higher faculties.

101. Friedensburg, *Urkundenbuch*, 1:202–5.

102. Friedensburg, *Urkundenbuch*, 1:202–3.

103. Friedensburg, *Urkundenbuch*, 1:202–3.

104. Friedensburg, *Urkundenbuch*, 1:203.

105. Grohmann, 1:27.

106. Friedensburg, *Urkundenbuch*, 1:35.

107. Friedensburg, *Urkundenbuch*, 1:36.

108. Friedensburg, *Urkundenbuch*, 1:37.

109. Friedensburg, *Urkundenbuch*, 1:38.

110. Friedensburg, *Urkundenbuch*, 1:39.

111. Friedensburg, *Urkundenbuch*, 1:39–40.

112. Friedensburg, *Urkundenbuch*, 1:41.

113. Friedensburg, *Urkundenbuch*, 1:42.

114. Enders, 14:217. It was sold for 3,700 Gulden in 1564 by the Luther children, where Luther had evaluated it as being worth 6,000 Gulden. The Elector August bought it as part of his plan to house 150 scholarship students. As we shall see, the reformer and his family were blessed with many gifts and well provided for when he and his large household needed it.

115. The author spent considerable time in this interesting museum, so well preserved today with Melanchthon's fine study, and made many sketches of its attractions.

116. Friedensburg, *Urkundenbuch*, 1:165–66. According to the record, Dr. Augustine Schurff and Hieronymus Krapp were responsible for the project, and the Landgraff Metsch was to advance $75,000 for the construction.

117. Friedensburg, *Urkundenbuch*, 1, doc. 22, chap. 5, has these entries of the fees charged.

118. Friedensburg, *Urkundenbuch*, 1, doc. 22, chap. 18.

119. Friedensburg, *Urkundenbuch*, 1, doc. 22, chap. 18.

120. Friedensburg, *Urkundenbuch*, 1, doc. 22, chap. 18.

121. Friedensburg, *Urkundenbuch*, 1, doc. 22, chap. 18.

122. Friedensburg, *Urkundenbuch*, 1, doc. 22, chap. 18.

123. Friedensburg, *Urkundenbuch*, 1, doc. 22, chap. 18.

124. Friedensburg, *Urkundenbuch*, 1, doc. 22, chap. 18.

125. Friedensburg, *Urkundenbuch*, 1, doc. 22, chap. 18. When Martin Luther came up for his doctorate in 1512 and as a monk had no funds, the elector advanced the necessary fifty Gulden, which covered the expenses and the additional expenses of gifts cited above. At the time, it was also customary to offer the faculty and a few friends an evening with a "Doctors' Schmausz," a nice doctoral banquet.

126. WA Br, 2:180–81.

127. WA Br, 2:537: Enders, 3:370.

128. WA Br, 2:606.

129. WA Br, 2:213–16.

130. The history of this building and of the rebuilding of the place into a *Lutherhaus* are treated in some detail in the previous chapter.

131. WA Br, 3:196-97. As we shall see in a *Türkensteuer* of 1542, Luther evaluated this dwelling at 6,000 Gulden and the university bought it from Luther's children in 1564 for a sum of $277,500.

132. WA, 3:437–38.

133. WA, 3:533; Enders, 4:197.

134. WA, 3:537–38.

135. WA, 3:538–39.

136. Luther was opposed to the wild dances in which partners were swung around until the dresses came over them and exposed their bodies.

137. See the section in chapter 19 when the Elector Frederick the Wise was at Worms in 1521 and John was always pushing for Luther's support.

138. Kroker, 68. As the court learned of Luther's marriage, "Kurfürst Johann sante 100 Gulden zur Wirtschaft und die erste Einrichtung." This according to modern money values was abou $7,500.

139. Kroker, 70.

140. Kroker, 70.

141. Kroker, 71.

142. Kroker, 71. The ring was so constructed that it could be opened and the above information could be observed.

143. Kroker, 71–72.

144. WA, 4:56–57.

145. Kroker, 72.

146. WA Br, 9:572; Enders, 14, 149[2]; EA, 56, 2.

147. WA Br, 4:148-49.

148. CR, 1:853ff.

149. WA Br, 4:56-57.

150. WA Br, 4:56-57; Enders, 10:99.

151. WA Br, 9:576–77, "Beilage II."

152. WA Br, 9:576–77, "Beliage II."

153. WA Br, 9:576–77, "Beliage II." At the close there is a town record written in a hand similar to Melanchthon that has this information.

154. WA Br, 5:133-34; Enders, 7:148; EA, 54, 95-96.

155. WA Br, 5:134.

156. WA, 6:257–58; Enders, 9:148. This transaction was very important, as we shall observe in 1542 when Luther wrote his "Second Will."

157. For the sale of this property in 1564, see Grohmann, 74.

158. WA Br, 7:222–24.

159. WA Br, 7:224, n. 8.

160. WA Br, 7:222–24.

161. WA Br, 7:335; Enders, 10:295.

162. Enders, letter 2357.

163. Enders, letter 2357, n. 2.

164. Friedensburg, *Urkundenbuch*, 1:167.

165. Enders, 9:2502, n. 1. This was really not a will like his Sendon Will on 6, 1542, as it is not specific about any of his possessions, while the second is very detailed.

166. WA Tr, 4:4139. The Weimar editor points out that Luther really was not sufficiently informed about the law (WA Br, 9:571). According to the Customary Law, a husband could will a definite income to his wife, and even the children under a guardian could be given a definite income.

167. WA Tr, 4:5041.

168. WA Br, 9:571; Kroker, 232.

169. Enders, 11, no. 2509.

170. WA Br 9:571, 171. WA Br, 10:22.

171. WA Br 10:22.

172. Friedensburg, *Urkundenbuch*, 1:348–49. The three sons were Johannes, a lawyer; Martin, a theologian; and Paul, an able doctor of medicine, who served in the Courts of Gotha, Brandenburg, and that of Elector August of Saxony and the sister Margaret who had married Georg von Kuhnhaim. All were involved in the sale. The contract stated that the downpayment would be 1,700 Gulden

while the second payment was to be in 1567 of an additional 1,000 Gulden and the final 1,000 in 1572. Meanwhile, the 2,000 Gulden that remained were to be mortgaged at 5 percent, and the Gulden were to be the old type with 21 Groschen in a gulden. The original document was fully legalized by the lawyers of the Albertine Saxon Court. See also Grohmann, 1:70–78. He errs on the amount of the sale.

173. Kroker, 232ff., explains the previous difficulty with the chancellor and how he later attempted to influence the elector on the custodianship of Catherine's sons just as Luther had feared, even though the elector wished to comply with the wishes of Luther's second will in 1542.

174. WA Tr, 4:5041; WA Br, 9:571ff.; Enders, 14:149; EA, 3:2; and Kroker, 232.

175. Kroker, 230.
176. WA Br, 9:571ff.
177. WA Br, 9:572.
178. WA Br, 9:573.
179. WA Br, 9:574–76.
180. WA Br, 9:574–76.
181. WA Br, 9:578–79.
182. WA Br, 9:578–79.
183. WA Br, 9:579–87.
184. WA Br, 9:57–80.
185. WA Br, 9:580.
186. WA Br, 9:581.
187. WA Br, 9:582.
188. WA Br, 9:582–83.
189. WA Br, 9:85.
190. Grohmann, 1:63.
191. Grohmann, 1:64–66.
192. Grohmann, 1:66.
193. Grohmann, 1:66–78.
194. Grohmann, 1:66–78.
195. Gottfried Suevus, a former Wittenberg professor in the seventeenth century, gathered a source collection, in which is an undated document entitled *Leges Communeis Mensae in Academia Wittebergensi, Witterbergae, 1655.* The document refers to the electoral court; Frederick the Wise; John, his brother; and his wife, which places the document into the period of the university, and Suevus placed it with foundation documents, which is further evidence for the date.

196. Grohmann, 1:57.
197. Grohmann, 1:57.
198. Grohmann, 1:57.
299. Grohmann, 1:57.
200. Grohmann, 1:58-59.

201. These minor offenses appear to have been improper conduct, such as taking a bite of bread before the clergyman had given the blessing, entering the dining hall in an improper way, and similar offenses. These ranged from 2 Pfennige to 2 Groschen. Eschenhagen, 73, gives us the money values around 1500: 12 Pfennige made a Groschen, 21 Groschen made a Gulden. In case one evaluates the Gulden at $75, as we have done, 2 Pfennige would equal a small fine of 62 cents, while the 2 Groschen would equal about $7 in buying power today.

Chapter 21
The University Library

1. Friedensburg, *Urkundenbuch*, 1:1–3.
2. The original parchment text is in Halle, Germany, no. 84. Friedensburg, *Urkundenbuch*, 1:17, does not reproduce the text but cites several printed texts. The author used the text in Suevus, *Academia Wittebergensis* (1655).
3. See chapter 20 above.
4. For an analysis of the inner appearance of the castle, with which the library room and its interior decorations must be harmonized, see the descriptions in the *Dialogus of 1507* of paintings in the castle found in chap. 16.
5. After reading this article, Roland Bainton of Yale University wrote me that he wished I would write another longer treatise on what the library contained as my brief account had but whetted his appetite. This study aims to meet that need.
6. Schwiebert, *Wittenberg Library*, 494–531.
7. Schwiebert, *Luther,* 144–53.
8. Mylius.
9. Mylius, 2, n. a, concluded that these Loesser books are the ones he listed in sec. 6, *Vide infra dicta sub finem sec. VI.*
10. Hildebrandt, 40.
11. See above, chap. 16.
12. The relationship of Spalatin with Wittenberg University has been rather thoroughly explored in chaps. 13 and 14. He was a close friend of Martin Luther and Philip Melanchthon, both of whom must have deeply influenced him in future purchases.
13. Müller, 68.
14. Mylius, 2.

15. Hildebrandt, 40, disagrees with the Friedensburg account claiming there were 163 volumes; while Freidensburg, *G.U.W.*, 154, makes the above 151 works as the total. The buying power of a Gulden in 1913 values was ten to one, but modern inflation has raised it to about $75 for a florin or a Rhenish gold Gulden, used in Wittenberg's financial records.

16. Spalatin, *Ephemerides*, 5:53.

17. Friedensburg, *G.U.W.*, 153–54; Buchwald, *Archiv für die Geschichte des deutschen Buchhandels* (1896), 18:10.

18. Friedensburg, *G.U.W.*, 68. Cf. Hildebrandt, 39–40, who claims Spalatin was already busy with this task by May 1, 1512.

19. *Christoph Scheurls Briefbuch*, ed. J. K. F. Knaake (Potsdam, 1867), 1:105; cf. also Letters 45 and 63.

20. Gillert, 1:374; cf. also p. 398.

21. The fact that Mutianus, in his letter to Aldus, speaks of the library in the upper *Hofstube* as being adorned implies that meanwhile there had been preparation in that room by introducing bookcases, chairs, and perhaps even some pictures of which there were ample ones, as was shown in this study (vol. 1, chap. 13). Spalatin must have kept Mutianus informed of their progress after the old teacher of his had helped him with his purchases.

22. Schwiebert, *Wittenberg Library*, 10:510.

23. Mylius, 37.

24. Mylius, 37.

25. Mentz, *Friedrich der Groszmütige*, 1, Dritter Teil, 103–4.

26. Mentz, *Friedrich der Groszmütige*, 108–11; Mylius, 27.

27. Mentz, *Friedrich der Groszmütige*, 108–11; Mylius, 27.

28. Mentz, *Friedrich der Groszmütige*, 108–11; Mylius, 27.

29. Mylius, 31–32.

30. Friedensburg, *Urkundenbuch*, 1:297.

31. Friedensburg, *Urkundenbuch*, 1:297, n. 2. Cf. Mentz, *Friedrich der Groszmütige*, vol. 1, pt. 3, p. 256, n. 2. He quotes Bolte that there were 3,132 volumes in the library, while Mylius, 37, writes: "The summary of all the books in the Electoral library totaled: theological, 1040, legal 562, medical 545, philosophical, 964. The sum of all the books in the Electoral library 3,111 and in music 21," which means the total in the entire collection was 3,132.

32. Mentz, *Friedrich der Groszmütige*, vol. 1, pt. 3, p. 256.

33. Friedensburg, *Urkundenbuch*, 1:300. There seems to be an error on the part of Mylius here in giving the date 1548, when he, p. 33, claims the books reached Jena at that date; Grohmann, 1:97, is more accurate giving the date 1558, the year when the University of Jena was founded.

34. Schwiebert, *Wittenberg Library*, 501.

35. Mylius, 2.

36. Grohmann, 1:97.

37. Hildebrandt, *Bibliothek Wittenberg*, 39.

38. Spalatin, *Ephemerides*, for years, 1512, 1525, 1532, 1536.

39. Friedensburg, *Urkundenbuch*, 1:68.

40. For a detailed account, see chap. 17.

41. Drews, "Spalatiana," *ZKG* 19:88. Cf. doc. 24, in which he speaks of the "dren Jahrmetckte zu Leyptzick gute bücher in der Librey zu Wittemberg aufm Scholsz kauffen von Jar zu Jar zu bessern."

42. Friedensburg, *Urkundenbuch*, vol. 1, has the full text of the Statutes of 1533 and 1536.

43. As stated above, the library until 1536 was housed in an upper large room of the castle. Now it was to be made even more attractive by being placed in a large "alte Hofstube," on the second floor of the castle. For a more detailed discussion, see the section below.

44. A reprint of this text in the original may be found in Israël, 113, and Friedensburg, *Urkundenbuch*, 1:181.

45. Drews, "Spalatiana," *ZKG* 19:506. In a letter of Spalatin, Feb. 11, 1533, he writes, "Zu foderung R. Chf. G. Librey zu Wittenberg." This should not come as a surprise, as in the sixteenth century, the electors all regarded the lands over which they ruled, their mines, and subjects as belonging to them. They regarded their lands, subjects, and possessions as entrusted to them by God and for which they were responsible.

46. Drews, "Spalatiana," 88. "Gute bucher in die Librey zu Wittenberg aufm Schlosz zu kauffen."

47. Friedensburg, *Urkundenbuch*, 1:186.

48. Friedensburg, *Urkundenbuch*, 1:186.

49. Lukas Edenberger was the new librarian under the 1536 Statutes, but Spalatin was still the superintendent of the library. Cf. the

elector's letter, in Friedensburg, *Urkunden-buch,* 1:186, Oct. 12, 1536.

50. Friedensburg, *Urkundenbuch,* 1:234.

51. Friedensburg, *Urkundenbuch,* 1:236, n. 1.

52. Mylius, 2.

53. See the section below covering the contents of the Wittenberg Library in manuscripts and books.

54. Friedensburg, *G.U.W.,* 238, n. 2: "Melanchthon, der die Bücherauswahl in erster Linie besorgte, wünschte, dasz möglichst mannigfaltige Werke angeschaft würden, etc." Cf. Mylius, 17ff.

55. Melanchthon, CR, 2:625, no. 1089.

56. Drews, 88; Mylius, 14. The Leipzig "Fairs" had been given a wide range and variety of privileges under Emperor Maximilian I and thus were flourishing. See Hasse, *Geschichte der Leipziger Messen* (1885).

57. Friedensburg, *Urkundenbuch,* 1:221; Drews, 506; Mylius, 14. Nürnberg was another book center where works could often be purchased.

58. Schwiebert, *Wittenberg Library,* 504. Drews, 506.

59. See Enders, 7:29, n. 1. Edenberger had served as a tutor in the electoral court and now was the librarian.

60. CR 2:625.

61. Drews, 506.

62. For a good discussion of Luther's translations of the Bible and its subsequent editions, see M. Reu, *Luther's German Bible* (Columbus, 1934), 221–56; for an exhaustive source study, see the WA, "Die Deutsche Bibel," 7 vols.

63. Friedensburg, *G.U.W.,* 239, n. 5.

64. Schwiebert, *Luther,* 222, in which drawing by Wilbert Seidel under the author's direction, buildings 2 and 3 are the ones cited.

65. Grohmann, 173–98, refers to an electoral "Erlass of 1544" by John Frederick himself, three years before it was moved to Weimar. The prince refers to it as "die Bibliothek der Hochschule."

66. See chaps. 13 and 16.

67. For a description of the architecture of libraries and equipment during this period, see Clark, *Libraries,* 31ff.; for the classic description, also see Clark, *Care of Books;* and for an exhaustive study of medieval libraries, see Thompson, *Medieval Library,* especially

the chapter on "Library Administration and the Care of Books," 613ff.

68. Müller, 13; Clark, *Libraries,* 19ff. Most monasteries were not equipped to house rare volumes even if the monks were permitted to take them to their private cells for a period of time.

69. The practice of distributing books among the monks, which already existed among the English Benedictines in the days of Archbishop Lanfranc in 1070, became quite common, says Clark, *Libraries,* 35. For the origin of catalogs as records, see Thompson, *Medieval Library,* 64, 74, 78, 87, 142, 614. For a similar practice at Wittenberg, see Friedensburg, *Urkundenbuch,* 1:186.

70. Cf. Schwiebert, *Wittenberg Library,* 508, n. 78.

71. For examples of older types and Renaissance furniture for libraries, see Clark, *Libraries,* 39, 47–48; also Clark, *Care of Books,* 193ff.

72. Schwiebert, *Wittenberg Library,* 508.

73. Heubner, 28, writes: "Im wierten Geschosz werden im Inventar von 1611 ein Unzahl von Stuben und Kammern angegeben, die in ihrer Lage zu bestimmen unmöglich ist, und die wenig interesse erwecken." Nor does the enumeration of 1539 assist in locating the rooms, although many are mentioned, among them "ein Zimmer für den Bibliothekar, Dr. Spalatin" furnished like the others.

74. Friedensburg, *Urkundenbuch,* 1:181. It adds, "An einen bequemen ort in unsern Schlosz zu Wittenberg, als in der oberb grossen hoffstuben, zu legen und vormittelst götlicher hulf ausrichten lassen entschlossen, etc."

75. Professor Heubner was very helpful in 1936 when the author was attempting to reconstruct the town of Wittenberg, as shown in *Luther and His Times,* 246. For more details about the castle, see Heubner.

76. Dr. Gottfried Krüger, though a medical doctor, had spent a lifetime in the reconstruction of the original Wittenberg and was the best informed man about the town in 1936. He was extremely helpful in my construction of Wittenberg's environment. The institution cited here was founded by the citizens of Wittenberg under Krüger's leadership in 1910. The "Verein" was located in the north end of the west wing of the castle and adjoins the Castle Church.

77. Heubner, 20–21.

78. Heubner, 21; Schwiebert, *Wittenberg Library,* 509, n. 88.

79. Heubner, 21.

80. Heubner, 21.

81. Hausleiter, 27–28. He tells about their trip into the castle, in explanation to Reinhardt, "The first room that they enter is the *aestuarium commune,* which in common parlance is known as the room of agitation."

82. This is a museum of creative work that has come from the homes of clergymen to prove their worth to the Nazi state under Hitler.

83. Heubner, 21.

84. Schwiebert, *Wittenberg Library,* 510.

85. Friedensburg, *G.U.W.,* 154; Hildebrandt, 40.

86. Since we know that the "alte Hofstube" housed the entire collection in 1547, we can make our estimates on the basis of what size room was required to house 3,132 volumes, about half of which were large folio manuscripts with pigskin over board covers.

87. Schwiebert, *Wittenberg Library,* 510, n. 94.

88. Drews, "Spalatiana," *ZKG* 19:506.

89. Clark, *Libraries,* 27–28.

90. Clark, *Libraries,* 27–28. Universities patterned their libraries after those of monasteries. The library of the Sorbonne, for example, was housed in a room 120 by 36 feet and contained 28 desks, 5 feet high and so arranged that they were separated by moderate intervals. They were loaded with books, all of which were chained on top so that no thief might carry them off. These chains were fastened to the righthand cover of the books so that they might be readily moved from side to side and would not interfere with other readers (pp. 38–40). For the view that books were not chained before 1217, with the exception of service books, see Thompson, *Medieval Library,* 625. It appears that even some printed books were chained shortly after the invention of printing as they were copies of rare books.

91. The original of this may be seen in the "Sachsische Landesbibliothek" in Dresden and another one in the Halle-Wittenberg University at Halle, Germany. The author made a special trip to Dresden in 1936 to handle the Dresden copy. Walter Köhler made a reproduction of the Dresden one for his "Martin Luther," in *Im Morgenrot der*

Reformation (Hersfeld, 1915), 360. Even though it is reduced in size, it gives one some idea of the appearance of the south wall of the castle with its windows. Cf. Schwiebert, *Luther,* 158ff., for a description of the buildings of the town.

92. For a good picture see *Martin Luther,* in Atlantis Verlage (1933), 282.

93. Thulin, *Lutherstadt,* plate no. 39. For the best description of the Luther home, see Hermann Stein, *Geschichte des Lutherhauses* (1883); for the Melanchthon home, see Friedensburg, *Urkundenbuch,,* 1:165, n. 2.

94. Heubner, 19; Krüger, *Lutherstadt,* 22.

95. This building of churches for the elector by Konrad Pfleuger and the castle and Castle Church, see chap. 13.

96. *Dialogus of 1507,* chap. 8; Hausleiter, 27–32; Heubner, 19–20.

97. Friedensburg, *Urkundenbuch,* 1:68.

98. See above, n. 20.

99. Kolde, *Analecta Lutherana,* 310, implies there had been previous discussion of this matter. It implies they would think it over and at a meeting in Torgau it would be further discussed and decided upon.

100. As seen in chap. 14, above, many of the attractive paintings that hung in the castle had been done in the workshop of Albrecht Dürer and transported by wagons to Wittenberg. Some may also have been by the painter Lucas Cranach in Wittenberg. The castle was filled with very attractive paintings which the prince had ordered done.

101. Friedensburg, *G.U.W.,* 238.

102. Friedensburg, *Urkundenbuch,* 1:186. This is but a summary of the original he used in Weimar, Reg. O. N. 491, Bl 5.

103. Friedensburg, *Urkundenbuch,* 1:187.

104. Schwiebert, *Wittenberg Library,* 495ff. The author used these catalogue copies in 1936 and made the above copies, which then were still in the Jean library. Cf. Grohmann; Mylius, 10–11.

105. We possess no exact information as to whether these desks and benches were purchased or made locally. It may have been in the castle, as, according to Heubner, 28, it had a "Dreschalerei mit sieben Tischen." Since Wittenberg was deeply influenced by the Renaissance culture, in all likelihood the furniture would reflect that influence. For illustrations of this type, see Clark, *Libraries,* 47–48.

These bookcases were usually from five to six feet in height placed at moderate intervals.

106. Schwiebert, *Wittenberg Library*, 514–15; Kolde, 310; Friedensburg, *Urkundenbuch*, 1:186–87.

107. Clark, *Libraries*, 45, claims the walled bookcases began to be introduced about this time; also, Clark, *Care of Books*, 265ff.; for a more detailed account of the origin of this type of furniture, see Thompson, *Medieval Library*, 624ff.

108. Müller, 15; "One must think more about the preservation and the keeping of the pieces than their great possibility of much use. There are many directives stressing that: referring to annual revisions, setting up inventories (catalogues), references to their value, payment for a loan, and keeping of records of loaned books.

109. We possess no records of these visits, their frequency, etc., in the early years. Mylius, p. 9, thinks these did occur at least annually. From Spalatin's correspondence with Warbeck, ARG, 1:22–223, we learn that in 1525 he visited twice that year.

110. Drews, 88.

111. Friedensburg, *Urkundenbuch*, 1:160–61.

112. Schwiebert, *Wittenberg Library*, 516.

113. Friedensburg, *Urkundenbuch*, 1:160–61, does not give the letter but just a resume.

114. See chap. 14.

115. Müller, 68.

116. Mylius, 2.

117. Mutian, 374.

118. Friedensburg, *Urkundenbuch*, 1:181, 186–87.

119. Friedensburg, *Urkundenbuch*, 1:222. There is a possibility that Edenberger was not appointed until 1539 and that the Christopher Nicolas who copied the catalogues of 1536 mentioned above was the first librarian. Mylius speaks of him as Spalatin's "Famulus," who copied the catalogues. Since this person received no salary but merely expected a new "Hofcleid" in return for his work, we prefer to believe he was merely an assistant.

120. Friedensburg, *Urkundenbuch*, 1:221–22; 234–35, 236.

121. Mylius, 10–11.

122. Schwiebert, *Wittenberg Library*, 494.

123. Schwiebert, *Wittenberg Library*, 497, n. 18.

124. Mylius, 21–26. After pointing out that the library was enlarged in three ways, he added: "The library appears to have received even some very large additions, because without doubt entire libraries of various monasteries, especially Saxony (and containing codices), were added to the library in Wittenberg."

125. Friedensburg, *G.U.W.*, 87.

126. G. Berbig, "Georgi Spalatini," 28.

127. Enders, 1:86: "Nihil ita ardet animus (n.um), quam histrionem illu, qui tam vere Graecca larva ecclesiam lusit, multis revelare ignominiamque ejus cunctis ostender etc."

128. Schwiebert, *Wittenberg Library*, 251.

129. Enders, 1:170.

130. Schwiebert, *Luther.*

131. Enders, 1:220. P. Paulsen, 1:117–19, for an estimate of the famous address.

132. Enders, 1:237. The translation is by Albert Hyma, *Landmarks in History* (New York, 1928), 42.

133. Schwiebert, *Luther.*

134. See below, chap. 22.

135. Spalatin, *Ephemerides*, 56.

136. See for the effect of the Worms trial, Schwiebert, *Wittenberg and Other Universities*, for the statistical effects in student enrollment.

137. Walter Koehler, "Martin Luther," *Im Morgenrot der Reformation.*

138. See above, chap. 18.

139. Drews, 88.

140. Drews, 88.

141. Mylius, 7. Cf. Spalatin's letter to Warbeck, May 22, 1525, G. Mentz-Jena, ARG, 1:222.

142. Schwiebert, *Wittenberg Library*, 522–23.

143. Friedensburg, *Urkundenbuch.*

144. See vol. 1, chap. 14.

145. See vol. 1, chap. 14.

146. Schwiebert, *Luther.*

147. Schwiebert, *Luther.*

148. Friedensburg, *Urkundenbuch.*

149. Friedensburg, *G.U.W.*, 237.

150. Friedensburg, *G.U.W.*, 238, cf. also additions in n. 135 above, Mylius, 21–26.

151. Friedensburg, *Urkundenbuch*, 1:187–88.

152. Friedensburg, *Urkundenbuch*, 1:188, n. 1.

153. Friedensburg, *Urkundenbuch*, 1:188,

n. 1, doc. 203, offers the background for this Grimma library transfer of books.

154. Friedensburg, *Urkundenbuch*, 1:188, n. 1.

155. Friedensburg, *Urkundenbuch*, 1:221.

156. Duke Henry was a very different type of person from his brother Duke George. Duke George had studied for the priesthood for a while, which he had to drop when his father Albert died and he had to assume the reign. Duke Henry was an evangelical Catholic of the same type as Frederick the Wise. We find him later in the Protestant camp as he had married the sister of Philip of Hesse. When Duke George died, the Albertine lands passed over to Henry and Lutheranism soon spread throughout the lands. For a picture of religious conditions there, see Burckhardt, especially 225ff.

157. Friedensburg, *Urkundenbuch*, 1:221.

158. Friedensburg, *Urkundenbuch*, 1:221.

159. Berbig claims this visit was in 1535, in Spalatin, *Ephemerides*, for that year.

160. Since Henry seemed agreeable, the elector's predictions seem logical, but the sources do not record what happened about the interview.

161. Friedensburg, *Urkundenbuch*, 1:225. "He did not permit any books of the Talmud to be purchased in Venice, as there the princes had been raised too much."

162. Friedensburg, *Urkundenbuch*, 1:234.

163. Friedensburg, *Urkundenbuch*, 1:234–35; cf. Mentz, 2:388ff., who claims that John Frederick arrived in Speyer, February 18, 1544, but was so involved with political problems of the times that he had little time for the library; also Mylius, 26–27.

164. Friedensburg, *Urkundenbuch*, n. 6.

165. Friedensburg, *Urkundenbuch*, 1:236.

166. Friedensburg, *Urkundenbuch*, 1:236.

167. Mylius, 36. "De Bibliotheca electorali Wittbergensi, tanquam primo Bibliothecae academicae Jenensis fundamento specialis tractatio."

168. Mylius, 36–37. In this connection the author gives the sizes and numbers of volumes in the library in footnote summaries. Cf. Schwiebert, *Wittenberg Library*, 500, n. 36.

169. Mylius, 8–37.

170. MS, 22B, 2–3.

171. The theological books cover pp. 2–31; while pp. 30–31 cover the works of Erasmus; cf. pp. 2–3 and n. c.

172. Mylius, 34–42.

173. Mylius, 26; pp. 43–53 cover the books in Civil and Canon Law. What roles these played while in Wittenberg can be well estimated from the *Statutes of 1508* treated above in chap. 17.

174. Mylius, 53–61.

175. Mylius, 61–69.

176. Mylius, 69–76; cf. p. 18 for a book in medicine bought from Christoff Schramm by Cornelius Celsus, Qv. Serenus Aldus, and Dryandrius, which was expensive.

177. MS 22B, Mylius, 77–83.

178. Mylius, 83–95.

179. Mylius, 95ff.

180. Mylius, 38.

181. Mylius, 8–37.

182. Mylius now enters into a citation of the library holdings in chapter 2, pp. 38–143, where he covers the rare manuscrips and the counting of each in the many disciplines.

183. Mylius, 144–257.

184. Mylius, 258–69.

185. Mylius, 270–99.

186. Mylius, 300–410.

187. Mylius, 579–640.

188. Mylius, 39–44.

189. Mylius, 39–44.

190. Mylius, 42.

191. Mylius, 44–47.

192. Mylius, 57–83.

193. Mylius, 88–120.

194. Mylius, 127–43.

195. Mylius, 127–43.

196. Mylius, 144–73.

197. Mylius, 144–83.

198. This will be shown in the next chapter.

199. Mylius, 188–99.

200. Mylius, 244. This criticism seems somewhat strange according to modern works. See Warren Chappell, in his a *Short History of the Printed Word* (New York, 1970), 59ff.; D. J. Geanakopolos, *Greek Scholars in Venice* (Cambridge, 1962), who tells all about the Aldine Press, pp. 116ff.; Elizabeth Eisenstein, *The Printing Press as an Agent of Change* (Cambridge, 1979), 1:218ff., especially 221, about the ducal library. It is difficult to know what Mylius means with this criticism unless he limits it to publications of the Church Fathers and any doctrinally related manuscripts in which Rome objected to citations from earlier views of the Fathers and histories of the church.

201. Mylius, 240.
202. Mylius, 240, at the bottom.
203. Mylius, 240, at the bottom.
204. See above, chap. 16.
205. Geanakopolos, 116ff.: Chappell, 81ff.
206. Mylius, 13–14, in his introduction, praises the zeal of Spalatin, who claims he purchased "nearly all the Latin and Greek Classics." Cf. also p. 52.
207. Mylius, 251–52.
208. Mylius, 258–59. Title, *Index Locorum ubi Libri Antiqui Prodierunt,* an index of the titles of books and where they were printed in chronological order.
209. Mylius, 258ff.
210. Mylius, 258–69.
211. Berkowitz, 269ff.
212. Schwiebert, *Luther;* cf. chap. 14 above.
213. Mylius, 270.
214. Mylius, 270.
215. Mylius, 270.
216. Mylius, 270ff.
217. Mylius, 270ff.
218. Mylius, 270ff.
219. Mylius, 39.
220. Berkowitz has perhaps the best coverage of Hebrew publications available.
221. Berkowitz, 97.
222. Mylius, 39.
223. Berkowitz, 97.
224. Berkowitz, 97.
225. Berkowitz, 97, n. 165.
226. Berkowitz, 97, n. 165.
227. Berkowitz, 97, n. 165.
228. Berkowitz, 97, n. 165.
229. Mylius, 39.
230. Berkowitz, 97.
231. Berkowitz, 97.
232. Berkowitz, 97.
233. Mylius, 39.
234. Mylius, 39.
235. Geanakopolos, 238ff.
236. Geanakopolos, 239–42.
237. Geanakopolos, 244–45.
238. Schwiebert, *Luther.*
239. Mylius, 40. He adds that this consisted of nine volumes and had a psalter in Hebrew, Greek, and Latin.
240. Mylius, 40.
241. Mylius, 40.
242. Mylius, 49.
243. Mylius, 49–50.
244. Mylius, 53.

245. Mylius, 55.
246. Mylius, 56.
247. Mylius, 57. This terminates Mylius's list of rare books in jurisprudence and from there passes to the books of the School of Medicine.
248. Mylius, 57.
249. Mylius, 58.
250. Mylius, 58.
251. Mylius, 59.
252. Mylius, 59.
253. Mylius, 60.
254. Mylius, 60.
255. Mylius, 61.
256. Mylius, 61.
257. Mylius, 62.
258. Mylius, 66.
259. Mylius, 66.
260. Mylius, 69.
261. Mylius, 69.
262. Mylius, 69.
263. Mylius, 70.
264. Mylius, 70.
265. Mylius, 71.
266. Mylius, 73.
267. Mylius, 74.
268. Mylius, 78.
269. Mylius, 80.
270. Mylius, 81.
271. Mylius, 81–82.
272. Mylius, 82–83.
273. Mylius, 88–92. In later chapters of this volume the significance of this library build-up will become all the more apparent, when the university program became reoriented toward Biblical Humanism under Luther and Melanchthon's leadership from 1516 to 1536.
274. Mylius, 88–89.
275. Mylius, 88–89.
276. Mylius, 90.
277. Mylius, 91.
278. Mylius, 92.
279. Mylius, 94.
280. Mylius, 97–98.
281. Mylius, 98–99.
282. Mylius, 107.
283. Mylius, 108–9.
284. Mylius, 109.
285. Mylius, 111.
286. Mylius, 112.
287. Mylius, 113.
288. Mylius, 117.
289. Mylius, 119.

290. Mylius, 124.
291. Mylius, 125.
292. Mylius, 126.
293. Mylius, 230–31.
294. Mylius, 131.
295. Mylius, 132.
296. Mylius, 134.
297. Mylius, 135.
298. Mylius, 135.
299. Mylius, 136.
300. Mylius, 139.
301. Mylius, 140–41.
302. Mylius, 141.
303. Mylius, 142–43.
304. Mylius, 144.
305. Mylius, 145.
306. Mylius, 148.
307. Mylius, 1445–46.
308. Mylius, 149.
309. Mylius, 150–52.
310. Mylius, 152.
311. Mylius, 155.
312. Mylius, 157–58.
313. Mylius, 158–59.
314. Mylius, 160–61.
315. Mylius, 164–65.
316. Mylius, 167.
317. Mylius, 168.
318. Mylius, 169.
319. Mylius, 170.
320. Mylius, 171.
321. Mylius, 171–72.
322. Mylius, 172–73.
323. Mylius, 174.
324. Mylius, 174–75.
325. Mylius, 176.
326. Mylius, 177.
327. Mylius, 177–78.
328. Mylius, 179–80.
329. Mylius, 181–82.
330. Mylius, 182–83.
331. Mylius, 183–86.
332. Mylius, 186–87.
333. Mylius, 188.
334. See below, chap. 22.
335. Mylius, 192–93. The titles on oratory, rhetoric, etc., have been summarized in the same pages.
336. Mylius, 194–95. This covers the printed books and commentaries on Aristotle available to the Liberal Arts professors and students in the ducal library.
337. Mylius, 195.

338. Pliny the Elder wrote a *Historia Naturalis* between A.D. 23 and A.D. 79 on a wide range of aspects of the universe, but his science is not regarded as too reliable. He died of asphyxiation investigating the eruption of Mount Vesuvius. He was highly regarded in the Middle Ages, which carried on into the sixteenth century.
339. Mylius, 196.
340. Mylius, 197–99.
341. Mylius, 200.
342. Mylius, 200–201.
343. Mylius, 201.
344. Mylius, 201.
345. Mylius, 202.
346. Mylius, 205. For a good account of Bessarion, see Geanakopolos, *Greek Scholars,* who has much information on this former Greek scholar.
347. Mylius, 205–8.
348. Mylius, 208–12.
349. Mylius, 212–13.
350. Mylius, 212–13.
351. Mylius, 214–15.
352. Mylius, 216.
353. Mylius, 217–18.
354. Mylius, 219. For Gaza, see Geanakopolos, n. 346 above, who refers to him a number of times among the Greek scholars in Venice.
355. Mylius, 219. The author has a long commentary on the uniqueness of this work, citing authorities of later years.
356. See chap. 23 for Melanchthon's role in the introduction of Greek into the Wittenberg curriculum.
357. Mylius, 220–221.
358. Mylius, 222. This grammar was prepared by young Melanchthon while still at Tübingen and gave him the reputation as a Greek scholar to join the Wittenberg faculty in 1518.
359. Mylius, 222.
360. Mylius, 222–26.
361. Mylius, 225–26. See also Mylius's commentary on the works of Hutten.
362. Mylius, 226–27.
363. Mylius, 227.
364. Mylius, 228–29.
365. Mylius, 230–33.
366. Mylius, 234–35.
367. Mylius, 235–37.
368. Mylius, 237–38.

369. Mylius, 238–39.
370. Mylius, 239–41.
371. Mylius, 241–42.
372. Mylius, 242–44.

Chapter 22
Luther's Transformation of the University

1. Lortz, *HRC*.
2. Obermann. Since Martin Luther was trained in the school of the *Via Moderna* both at Erfurt and at Wittenberg, this study of Biel should prove very useful to many students concerned with Luther's monastic struggle that led to his later development as a reformer.
3. Jaroslav Pelikan, Sterling Professor at Yale University, has made an excellent contribution to the history of Christian dogma in *The Christian Tradition*. In his fourth volume, *Reformation of Church and Dogma* (1300–1700), published in 1984, he begins the first chapter with the title "Doctrinal Pluralism in the Later Middle Ages," which points to a wide range of interpretations by scholars in this period on basic scholastic doctrines that made the reforms of Martin Luther a little easier.
4. Friedensburg, *Urkundenbuch*, 1:56. In chapter 10 the Statutes of the Faculty of Liberal Arts states, "Let each professor teach freely his course in the way of St. Thomas, Duns Scotus or Gregory and present his view without any prejudice." Thus, says Friedensburg, in footnote t that someone in the original Scheurl document struck out the word Gregory and wrote "Occam" instead. When a student entered the Graduate School of Theology, he had to state how he wanted to study theology: *viam Thome, viam Scoti,* or the *Via Moderna.* Luther had studied Occam and Biel quite thoroughly and was promoted to the doctorate as a member of the *Via Moderna* à la Biel, which later also caused his monastic struggle as we shall see in this chapter.
5. Obermann, 5, 116. There he claims that Biel had really probed all the late nominalistic theological traditions and harvested those fruits that were ripe to nourish the Christian tradition of faith in search of understanding and to build up the unity of the church under

Christ and its vicar. Thus he reaped the harvest from not a declined but improved scholasticism.
6. A good illustration is the work by Hugh Thomson Kerr, Jr., from Princeton Theological Seminary, *A Compend of Luther's Theology* (Philadelphia, 1943). One cannot take any quotation of Luther, such as on Holy Communion, Baptism, and Justification, and mix the quotations of the evolving biblical humanist with those of his later life when he had fully developed his biblical exegesis.
7. Löwenich, *Martin Luther, Der Mann und das Werk,* chapter 7, "Die Werdezeit der reformatorische Theologie," 89ff. He was the dean of theological faculty at Erlangen University in 1949–1950, when I taught as Gast Professor in the faculty, and he is eminently qualified to treat this theme as the earlier author of Luther's theology of the Cross.
8. The mature Luther wrote an excellent tract in 1538, now in the Folger "Haus der Bücher" collection from Basel, entitled *Die dray Symbola oder Bekenntnis des gaubens Christi in der kircheneinttrechtiglich gebraucht* (Wittenberg, 1538). This is an original in which he not only accepts the great Ecumenical Creeds but discusses in detail how it applies to true Christianity in his day. When Melanchthon drafted new statutes for the theological faculty, he stated the same basic truth of the first real Lutheran faculty, when he says they are opposed to all the heresies of the early church but do accept the three great Ecumenical Creeds. See Friedensburg, *Urkundenbuch,* 1:154. The Augsburg Confession presented to Charles V shall be their guide in matters of faith and pure gospel preaching in the church of God.
9. Schwiebert, *Luther,* 309–12. For references see p. 795, n. 21.
10. Lortz, *HRC,* 50.
11. Vermanüg / an die geistlichen / versamlet auff dem / Reichstag zu Augs/burg. Anno 1530 / Wittemberg Bl 34; Hans Lufft, 1530, 36.Bl. (die letzen 2 leer. Benzing designated it as an Urdruch, which in spite of the Kaiser's *Verbot* arrived in Charles' camp. What influence, if any, it had remains unknown. In the *Haus der Bücher* printed catalog, "Reformation," it is number 509, which is now in the Folger collection.
12. This region has been treated in much

detail under the Ludowinger dynasty, in volume 1 of this account, based on medieval monks' chronicles. For a description of the *Erbzinsleute*, who had the five Höfe as a group in Möhra, see Boehmer, *Luther*, 21.

13. Oskar Thulin, *Martin Luther, Sein Leben in Bildern und Zeitdokumenten* (München, 1958), in illustrations, no. 2.

14. Löwenich, 36, points out that scholars formerly held that Martin Luther's mother was Margarethe Ziegler, but subsequent research has established that she was also a Lindemann. It was her mother who was a Ziegler.

15. As shown in vol. 1, in the coverage of the later house of Wettin, mining had really boomed in the Erzgebirge, where they became rich through gold and silver mines. Copper mining also flourished in the Harz Mountains region. So Luther's father decided to move there.

16. For a good picture of the house where Luther was born, see Thulin, *Martin Luther*, in illustrations, no. 6 and the Mansfeld home, no. 7.

17. CR, 6:156–57; Scheel, *Martin Luther*, 1:8, 265, n. 41.

18. Scheel, *Martin Luther*, 1:264–65, n. 25; WA Tr, 1:500–503; WA, 49:322.

19. There have been many views expressed about whether the nominalism of the fourteenth and fifteenth centuries was a decline in scholasticism. Obermann, in his concept of the harvest, holds that the nominalism of Occam and Biel was an advancement of Thomism; while Lortz, in his view believes Luther never would have had the soul struggle had he been taught *viam Thome*. We will face this problem in the young Luther in his courses in his *Lectura in Biblia*.

20. The *Liber Decanorum*, 4, has the following entry: "Die nona de Marcio (1509) Magister Martinus ad bibliam est admissus, sed vocatus Erphoriam adhuc non satisfecit facultat." Later there is an entry in Luther's hand by way of an explanation: "Non faciet. Quia tunc pauper et sub obedientia nihil habet. Soluet ergo Erffordia."

21. See Herbert Rommel, *Luthers Randbemerkungen. A Thesis*, 5ff., also WA, 9:10ff. This offers much insight for the theological development of Luther. Löwenich, 64, points out how thoroughly the young Augustinian

studied Augustine, but he adds that he still saw all his material through the eyes of Occam. However, he is already becoming quite critical. He also points out that Luther began to study Hebrew using Reuchlin's text.

22. *Liber Decanorum*, 13, "Religiosus pater frater Martinus lüder ordinis f. Emeritarum sancti Augustini Sacre theologie licentiatus."

23. See chap. 17.

24. Walther von Löwenich, *Martin Luther: The Man and His Work* (Minneapolis, 1986), Part One.

25. Löwenich, 64–68. Still the best coverage of the larger picture; see Heinrich Böhmer, *Luthers Romfahrt* (Leipzig, 1914), 1–177; also Otto Scheel, *Martin Luther*, 2:248–97; Schwiebert, *Luther*, 174–93.

26. The dean of Theology in the winter semester 1512–1513, when Luther was promoted October 18–19, 1512, but the officiant was Bodenstein von Carlstadt. See Otto Scheel, 2:311; Reu, 331, n. 51; Schwiebert, *Luther*, 193–96. The 50 Gulden were worth $3,750, which Luther picked up in Leipzig in person of the elector's treasury.

27. For references see Oscar Thulin, "Das Anlitz des Reformators," *Die Lutherstadt und Wittenberg und Torgau* (Berlin, 1932), 38; H. Böhmer, *LLRR*, 5–6, and n. 3. A former curator of the Lutherhalle, Julius Jordan, writes in "Luthers Bild," *Luther Mitteilungen der Luthergesellschaft* (1919), 1:67: "Nothing is so certain as the fact that neither Holborn, d.J. nor Albrecht Dürer came in contact with Luther." For a more recent review of the problem, see Oskar Thulin, "Das Lutherbild der Gegenwart" (Sonderdruck), *Luther Jahrbuch*, 23 (1941): 123ff.

28. Ficker, *Exposition of Luther's Pictures*, 13:69.

29. Ficker, *Exposition of Luther's Pictures*, 13:65ff.

30. Schreckenbach and Neubert, *Martin Luther*, 100.

31. For the original of Cranach, which was copied, see Schwiebert, *Luther*, 572.

32. Schreckenbach and Neubert, 108.

33. Schwiebert, *Luther*, in frontispiece.

34. Schreckenbach and Neubert, 127.

35. Thulin, *Martin Luther*, in picture section, nos. 46 and 47.

36. Thulin, *Martin Luther*, shows him as

Thulin's frontispiece. Here Luther looks quite
composed and dignified in his doctoral gown
and beret. Luther does not have a corpulent
figure as he is always portrayed by his son
Lucas Cranach d.J. Good examples are the
Nordhausen *Reformationsgruppe,* no. 65 and
the one in the Weimar Stadkirche, n. 68.

37. Thulin, *Lutherstadt,* numbers 22 and
23, have the two sides of Luther preaching
and Catherine and little Hans in the audience;
number 50 has part of the real Luther pulpit,
now on display in the Lutherhalle.

38. Thulin, *Martin Luther,* 93.

39. Thulin, *Martin Luther,* Ills. no. 61.

40. Thulin, *Martin Luther,* Ills. no. 63.

41. Thulin, *Martin Luther,* Ills. no. 22, the
copper etching of Luther of 1520 by the Elder
Cranach, and Mosellanus at the time of the
Leipzig Debate claims Luther was so thin that
every bone in his body could be numbered.

42. Boehmer, *LLRR,* 205.

43. Thulin, *Martin Luther,* Ills. 46, 47, 58,
for the frontispiece of the Elder Cranach;
while for the later larger Luther, see ill. 65.
There is also a free drawing of Luther at the
time of his death by Famulus Reifenstein in a
book belonging to Melanchthon, which has
Melanchthon's note about Luther's death. This
proves Luther then was still not the heavy man
of the Flügelatäre of L. Cranach the Younger.

44. See the source collection, *Martin
Luther,* by the Atlantis Verlag (1933), 81. It is
perhaps the most complete description we
possess of the young Luther while still a monk.

45. *Nuntiaturberichte,* 1:539–40.

46. Atlantis Verlag, *Luther,* 93–97.

47. Atlantis Verlag, *Luther,* 98–100.

48. Atlantis Verlag, *Luther,* 102–4.

49. Atlantis Verlag, *Luther,* 84–86.

50. Atlantis Verlag, *Luther,* 102ff. ZRG,
4:326.

51. Atlantis Verlag, *Luther,* 81.

52. Atlantis Verlag, *Luther,* 102–3.

53. Atlantis Verlag, *Luther,* 103.

54. Atlantis Verlag, *Luther,* 103–4.

55. Atlantis Verlag, *Luther,* 101. He did
admit he found Luther to be a forceful personality, but he did not appreciate his biting
criticisms of the Roman pontiff.

56. Atlantis Verlag, *Luther,* 85.

57. Chap. 14 has a detailed analysis of the
question: "Why did Frederick the Wise protect Luther?" See especially 121ff.

58. Jordan, "Luthers Bild," 1:66.

59. Jordan, "Luthers Bild," 1:66.

60. Myconius, *Historia Reformationis,* 35.
For a detailed story of the Augsburg Encounter, see chap. 14.

61. Kalkoff, *Depeschen,* 133.

62. Atlantis Verlag, *Luther,* 104. Cf. ibid,
81 for Mosellanus's views.

63. Atlantis Verlag, *Luther,* 104.

64. Atlantis Verlag, *Luther,* 306.

65. Schwiebert, *Luther,* 389ff.

66. Atlantis Verlag, *Luther,* 104.

67. Seeberg, *Greifwalder Studien,* 1ff.

68. Hagen, *Hebrews,* 15. See also Seeberg,
Greifwander Studien, 20, 35–36.

69. See Hagen, *Hebrews,* 15, n. 67.

70. This note becomes very pronounced in
Hagen, *Hebrews,* as he analyzed the various
medieval exegetes cited in the text.

71. Paul Wernle, *Die Renaissance,* 26,
30–31.

72. This thesis was never published. For
Whitefield's art of preaching, see Adams, 70.

73. Atlantis Verlag, *Luther,* 103–4.

74. Schwiebert, *Luther,* 367 and n. 27.

75. WA Br 2:453–57. The elector was worried as Dr. George in Nürnberg had stirred up
the Reichsregement to issue a mandate to terminate all evangelical preaching by Luther
and his supporters. Meanwhile Carlstadt and
the Zwickau prophets had stirred up the city
to violence, and Luther says the members of
the Pfarrkirche had begged Luther to return
from his captivity and bring peace to their
congregation. Luther then felt this was a call
from heaven to stop the devil's activities in
spite of the dangers involved. The Weimar
editors described the letter Luther wrote the
elector from Borna, March 5, 1522, as "eins
der merkwürdigsten Dokumente seines Glau-
bensmutes und einer Freimütigkeit wie sie
Fürsten selten zu hörem bekommen." In this
letter he told H.E.F.G. that he must remember "sasz ich das Evangelium nicht von
Menschen soldern ellein vom Himmel durch
unsern Herrn Jesum Christum habe." Since
he was God's servant, he could not do otherwise than to return; and the elector would
have to remember "ich kommen gen Wittenberg in gar viel einem hohern Schutz den des
Kürfursten." Then he adds that he detects the
elector's faith is still weak, how can he protect
him. In fact, the elector needs Luther's pro-

tection far more than the reformer needs that of the prince.

76. WA, 7:838. See chap. 14 above; Kuehn, *Wormser Reichs,* 75, n. 2; *Deutsche Reichstagsakten,* 2:555–56 Anm.

77. Atlantis Verlag, *Luther,* 289–301.

78. Atlantis Verlag, *Luther,* 302–17. The Latin text was translated into this German by his fellow professor Kaspar Kreuziger.

79. For a good view of the Catholic Luther picture prior to World War II, see Werner Beyna, *Das moderne katholische Lutherbild,* for an acquaintance with the vast literature involved, before World War II and since (Essen, 1969).

80. This was really Dr. Dobeneck from Wendelstein, one of the members of the Court of Duke, who after 1517 came out almost annually with an attack on Luther. He is the author of the *Septiceps Lutherus* in Schreckenbach and Neubert, *Martin Luther,* 89. It was this man's smear tactics that Herte really investigated in his three-volume study.

81. Adolf Herte, *Die Lutherbiographie des Johannes Cochlaeus, eine Quellenkritische Untersuchung.* Diss. (Muenster, 1915). This was just the beginning of Herte's investigations, which he extended all over Europe before he wrote his influential study in 1943.

82. He investigated the "Devil Story" about Luther's mother, that Luther's mother and a neighbor woman had met the Devil in a public bath, and the Devil was really Luther's father. A woman with her had told a priest in the confessional about this, and thus it had remained a Catholic secret. Herte found the story to be pure fabrication on the art of Cochlaeus. Likewise, the claim of Catherine carrying on with Wittenberg students were found to be without any foundation, pure fabrications by the Albertine Saxon court of Duke George.

83. In a seminar at the University of Iowa, my graduate students found the three-volume study of Adolf Herte full of amazing revelations.

84. Adolf Herte, *Das katholische Lutherbild in Bann der Lutherkommentare des Cochlaeus* (Muenster, 1943), 3 vols. He beings with Cochlaeus and in subsequent volumes carries on to today.

85. The author had access to their records during the German occupation from 1548 to 1949 and also had many conversations with these men in Munich.

86. Lortz, *HRC,* 10.

87. Lortz, *HRC,* 10–11. He suggests that Joseph Lortz says that Catholics will have to rethink their sixteenth-century views about what type of a reformer he really was.

88. Lortz, *HRC,* 9.

89. Lortz, *HRC,* 7.

90. *Reformata Reformanda* was a *Festausgabe,* edited by Irwin Iserloh and Konrad Repgen, in honor of Hubert Jedin, the expert on the Council of Trent, printed in Münster in 1965. It is really a two-volume work of Catholic scholars among which they included the final work of Joseph Lortz, "Martin Luther," in which he finally admitted that Luther had been one of the church's greatest theologians, for whom he wished there were place in Catholicism today, as through his works and teachings the church would be greatly enriched.

91. Lortz, "Martin Luther," 227–29. He says Redeweise it was Luther's way of bringing out an inner truth in the form of a paradox, like Abelard in his *Sic et Non* of Gratian in his work on canon law.

92. Lortz, "Martin Luther," 215.

93. Lortz, "Martin Luther," 215.

94. Lortz, "Martin Luther," 218.

95. Lortz, "Martin Luther," 218.

96. Lortz, "Martin Luther," 218.

97. Lortz, "Martin Luther," 218.

98. Lortz, "Martin Luther," 220-21.

99. Lortz, "Martin Luther," 219 and scattered observations throughout the whole chapter.

100. Lortz, "Martin Luther," 220.

101. Lortz, "Martin Luther," 245.

102. Lortz, "Martin Luther," 245.

103. Lortz, "Martin Luther," 245.

104. Friedensburg, *G.U.W.,* and *Urkundenbuch.* There are many related studies dealing with Luther's development as the reformer as will be observed below.

105. Löwenich, *Martin Luther,* 89.

106. The literature on this is overwhelming. See, e.g., Marilyn J. Harran, *Luther on Conversion* (Ithaca and London, 1985), 15ff. She begins with Karl Holl, Heinrich Böhmer, Emanuel Hirsch, and Erich Vogelsang and later cites the vast modern literature, 18–19 and notes.

107. *Liber Decanorum,* 4.

108. We saw that Luther did not have the necessary funds to be promoted and Erfurt was willing to advance the necessary fees for his Biblicus promotion and those which followed, up to his *Licentiatus* degree. See above, n. 20.

109. This theme was very ably developed by the keynote speaker Professor Jaroslav Pelikan of Yale University at the "Luther Jubilee" held in Washington, D.C., at the celebration of the five-hundredth anniversary of the birth of Martin Luther. It was recorded on tape and may be purchased. For further information contact Folger Shakespeare Library in Washington, D.C.

110. Friedensburg, *G.U.W.,* 90.

111. Friedensburg, *G.U.W.,* 90. Friedensburg based his material on the first Luther biographer but adds that since he did not come to Wittenberg until 1529, he must have gotten his information from Valentin Mellerstadt.

112. Friedensburg, *G.U.W.,* 94.

113. Friedensburg, *G.U.W.,* 94.

114. See above, chap. 19, on humanism at Wittenberg, 91–92. Men like Epp and Henning were dissatisfied with the past course offerings. Many of the men in the Law School and Medicine were sympathetic and wanted changes.

115. Boehmer, *Der Junge Luther,* 148.

116. Löwenich, *Martin Luther,* 89, under the theme "Der Werdegant," or Luther's formative period.

117. Friedensburg, *G.U.W.,* 94–95.

118. Boehmer, *LLRR,* 94; Ficker, *Römerbrief,* vol. 1, intro. 53.

119. Löwenich, *Martin Luther,* 90.

120. See chap. 19, on Humanism at Wittenberg, 104–5. John Lang had become a close friend of Luther while at Wittenberg and taught Luther Greek, but scholars are not as certain about Phylinus, who appears to have been converted to Luther's Biblical Humanism.

121. Friedensburg, *G.U.W.,* 64–68.

122. Luther wrote a letter to his friend in Erfurt, John Lang, about the Disputation, found in WA, Br, 1:64-68. Carlstadt's brief recording of this as dean is found in the *Liber Decanorum,* 19. The theses which Bernhardi used are printed in WA, 1:42. Bernhardi was later probst of Kemberg.

123. Schwiebert, *Luther,* 294–95.

124. *Liber Decanorum,* 19.

125. A doctorate of canon and civil law from a leading Italian university could not be acquired academically without years of work in residence; yet Carlstadt's ambition drove him to go to Italy, and in a matter of months he returned with a doctorate of Laws. It was also possible in that day to purchase degrees without attending any courses. He, as related above about the Wittenberg faculty in an earlier chapter, appeared on the campus of Wittenberg wearing a new Doctor of Laws gown. As related also about the mistreatment of the Erfurt professor, Jodocus Trutfetter, by Polich von Mellerstadt and Carlstadt, tells also the doubtful action by which he had become a deacon and canon of the Castle Church.

126. Friedensburg, *G.U.W.,* 98.

127. WA Tr, 4:187. Even then Luther said he at the time was already on the right course.

128. Barge, *Karlstadt,* 1:70–71. For the Theses, see ibid., 73–74.

129. Friedensburg, *G.U.W.,* 99.

130. Barge, *Karlstadt,* 73–74. Grane, *Contra Gabrielem,* 31, holds that this very work opened Luther's eyes to the *Gnaden lehre* of the early church.

131. Schwiebert, *Luther,* 295.

132. The Theses for this *Disputation* are printed in WA, 1:224ff. See *Liber Decanorum,* 20. See also Luther's letter about the debate to John Lang, Sept. 4, 1517, WA Br, 1:103–4, and n. 2.

133. The text is now also available in a Professor Harold J. Grimm translation, in "Career of the Reformer," 1, *Luther's Works,* 1:5–16. This text in vol. 31 is also introduced with a short introduction.

134. WA Br, 1:88–89. The letter was really written for Luther's former teachers at Erfurt, Jodocus Trutfetter and Usingen in an attempt to get them to give up their scholastic studies. The Weimer editors add, n. 4, that Luther's commentary on Aristotle's Physics was perhaps never completed. Nothing of it has remained. Until then Trutfetter had not replied to Luther's letter. See Enders, 1:85.

135. WA Br, 1:98–99.

136. Friedensburg, *G.U.W.,* 100.

137. Friedensburg, *G.U.W.,* 100.

138. Barge, 1:74.

139. Grane, *Contra Gabrielem,* 19ff.

140. Schwiebert, *Theses,* 126ff.

141. Grane, *Contra Gabrielem,* 369–70. For the source, see LW, 31:9–15, for an English version.

142. Grane, *Contra Gabrielem,* 370–71.

143. Grane, *Contra Gabrielem,* 272. LW 31:9–15.

144. Grane, *Contra Gabrielem,* 272. LW 31:9–15.

145. Grane, *Contra Gabrielem,* 272. LW 31:9–15.

146. WA, 1:221–28; LW 31:12.

147. LW, 31:13.

148. Grane, *Contra Gabrielem,* 376.

149. Schwiebert, *Luther,* 295.

150. Friedensburg, *G.U.W.,* 100.

151. Friedensburg, *G.U.W.,* 100.

152. Luther wrote Trutfetter in Erfurt, May 9, 1518, that the learned men of the Wittenberg faculty were on his side, citing Carlstadt, Amsdorf, Schurff, Stehelin, Bernhardi, and Lupinis as his supporters.

153. Friedensburg, *G.U.W.,* 53, 84, 141.

154. See above, chaps. 14 and 16.

155. Friedensburg, *G.U.W.,* 101.

156. For Spalatin as the builder of the Wittenberg Library, see chap. 21.

157. Gilbert, 490.

158. WA Br, 1:77–79. In this period there developed a lively correspondence between Luther and Spalatin. In these letters there was a lively exchange of how God's Holy Word should be studied and interpreted. These can be traced in WA Br, 1. Since there were over four hundred exchanges in the formative years, details are not possible.

159. Friedensburg, *G.U.W.,* 104. Later he also published his *Urkundenbuch,* in which he (1:64ff.) summarized the material and made some changes.

160. Friedensburg, *G.U.W.,* 104.

161. Friedensburg, *G.U.W.,* 105.

162. Bauch, *Geschichte und Altertums Schelesians,* 26:226–28.

163. Friedensburg, *G.U.W.,* 106–7, and n. 1, p. 107.

164. Friedensburg, *G.U.W.,* 106–7. n. 2.

165. Friedensburg, *G.U.W.,* 108.

166. Friedensburg, *Urkundenbuch,* 1:74–75, contains the report the university gave to the lawyers of the court on April 9, 1516.

167. Friedensburg, *G.U.W.,* 108.

168. Friedensburg, *G.U.W.,* 108–9. It seems the incomes of the Arts faculty were very low.

169. Friedensburg, *Urkundenbuch,* 1:76.

170. Friedensburg, *Urkundenbuch,* 1:76–84.

171. Friedensburg, *G.U.W.,* 112.

172. Friedensburg, *Urkundenbuch,* 1:85–86. See also the author's notes, p. 86.

173. Friedensburg, *Urkundenbuch,* 1:85–86.

174. Enders, 2:265.

175. Friedensburg, *G.U.W.,* 115.

176. WA Br, 1:174; Enders, 1:181.

177. Friedensburg, *G.U.W.,* 115.

178. WA Br, 1:175, n. 17, contains this entry: "Reuchlin am 25 April erhielt einen Brief von Friedrich den Weisen mit der Bitte, ihn bei der Versehung seiner Hochschule mit Lehrern des Hebräischen und Grieschen zu beraten und antwortete am 7.Mai." (Geiser, 294, Friedensburg, *G.U.W.,* 115–16).

179. Friedensburg, *G.U.W.,* 115–16.

180. Friedensburg, *G.U.W.,* 116.

181. The literature of Philip Melanchthon has grown to tremendous proportions during the last few decades. Heinz Scheible in the *Forschungsstelle* in Heidelberg is attempting a new edition of Melanchthon's correspondence in the *Corpus Reformatorum;* many young scholars have worked on various aspects of the Bretten Humanist. Since in this study our chief concern is the universities and the German Reformation, our Melanchthon coverage needs to be limited to that theme. Thus our references will concentrate on sources rather than on private studies. Yet since in the reorganization of the University of Wittenberg, in the twenties and thirties, he played such a vital role, that later Germans gave him the title of *Praeceptor Germaniae.* The still very useful biography is still that of Dr. Karl Hartfelder, *Philip Melanchthon als Praeceptor Germaniae* (Berlin, 1889). The best recent biography of the young Philip is by Wilhelm Maurer of Erlangen University, *Der junge Melanchthon zwischen Humanismus und Reformation,* 2 vols. (Göttingen, 1967–1969). Vol. 1 covers "Der Humanist," and vol. 2, "Der Theologie." Bretschneider and Bindseil, *Corpus Reformatorum, 28 Volumes of the Nineteenth Century,* is still useful, though Scheible has found a number of errors in the text. During his investigation Scheible discovered nearly a thousand new letters that were previously unknown. He began to prepare a series of *Registen,* offering dates and names of the new sources, with

some brief summaries that were based on the
Latin and Greek originals.

182. Maurer, 1:14.
183. Maurer, 1:14–15.
184. Maurer, 1:14–15.
185. Maurer, 1:23.
186. See chap. 19, on Humanism.
187. Maurer, 1:23.
188. Maurer, 1:28.
189. Maurer, 1:28.
190. Maurer, 1:26–27.
191. Maurer, 1:25.
192. Hartfelder, 29.
193. Hartfelder, 29. Hartfelder claims that
Professor Palles died in July 1512, based on
CR 10:260.
194. Hartfelder, 35.
195. Maurer, 1:36.
196. Maurer, 1:30.
197. Maurer, 1:33.
198. Maurer, 1:30.
199. CR, 11:14.
200. Hartfelder, 46.
201. CR, 20, 3, 180. This friendship could
not continue after he died, July 20, 1519.
202. Hartfelder, 48.
203. Hartfelder, 50.
204. Hartfelder, 50.
205. CR, 4:716.
206. CR, 1:26.
207. Maurer, 1:37.
208. Maurer, 1:35.
209. CR, 1:31–32; Scheible, *Briefwechsel,*
1:48.
210. CR, 1:31–32.
211. CR, 1:32–33.
212. CR, 1:34.
213. Friedensburg, *G.U.W.,* 117. On his
way from Augsburg, after meeting the elector,
Philip also spent some time in Nürnberg,
where he was graciously welcomed by
Pircheimer. Whether he also met with the
Staupitz circle is unknown. It is also doubtful
that on his hurried trip to Wittenberg he met
Christopher Scheurl. Then he also stopped
briefly in Leipzig and visited Mosellanus and
deepened their former friendship in person.
Luther also recorded in one of the Bibles in
the Wittenberg Library when Philip did arrive
in the Lutherstadt.
214. Friedensburg, *G.U.W.,* 212.
215. Friedensburg, *G.U.W.,* 116–18.
216. Enders, 1:220.
217. WA Br, 1:203, dated Sept. 16, 1518;

Enders 1:237. Cf. Melanchthon's letter to
Christopher Scheurl in Nürnberg, Sept. 24,
1518 (CR, 1:48), in which he tells him about
their Greek and Hebrew studies and that the
elector and Luther would like to have him
send them a Greek Bible, as he needs it for his
commentaries of Greek and Hebrew and
Latin Bible texts.
218. Friedensburg, *G.U.W.,* 118.
219. Friedensburg, *G.U.W.,* 118.
220. The coverage of Melanchthon's role
in theological lectures at Wittenberg, while he
had his battle with Rome and the kaiser at the
Diet of Worms in 1521, must be reserved for
the next chapter.
221. For an account of the revision and
refounding of the University of Wittenberg in
1533–1536, see chap. 22.
222. Friedensburg, *G.U.W.,* 118.
223. WA Br, 1:195–97; Enders 1:225.
Melanchthon in a letter, Sept. 5, 1518; also
CR, 1:50, "Audior frequenti Schola." Then
Spalatin wrote Veit Bild in Augsburg, Dec. 10,
1518, that Philip "Philippus Melanchthon
graecam illic legens plus minus cccc habet
auditores."
224. Friedensburg, *Urkundenbuch,* 1:126–
27.
225. Friedensburg, *Urkundenbuch,* 1:109.
226. See chap. 14.
227. Schiesz, *Briefwechsel der Brüder
Ambrosius und Thomas Blaurer,* 1:29–30; cf.
30–32 and 34; Friedensburg, *G.U.W.,* 152.
228. Friedensburg, *G.U.W.,* 152.
229. Friedensburg, *G.U.W.,* 152.
230. Friedensburg, *G.U.W.,* 152.
231. Friedensburg, *G.U.W.,* 152.
232. Friedensburg, *G.U.W.,* 152.
233. Bauch, *Monatsschrift,* N.F. 12, 22ff.,
77ff., 145ff., 214ff., 228ff., 461ff.
234. Bauch, *Monatsschrift,* 224–25.
235. Jews did not agree with Luther in
how Hebrew should be taught purely as a language.
236. Bauch, *Monatschrift,* 26.
237. Bauch, *Monatschrift,* 26.
238. Bauch, *Monatschrift,* 27.
239. Bauch, *Monatschrift,* 29–30.
240. Bauch, *Monatschrift,* 30.
241. WA Br, 1:404. The translation is taken
from *Luthers Works,* 45, "Letters," 1:123.
242. WA Br, 1:405, n. 2.
243. WA Br, 1:405, n. 2.
244. WA Br, 1:203; also n. 6. There is

Luther's observation about Melanchthon in his Galatian commentary, WA, 2:295.

245. WA Br, 1:212–13, dated Oct. 11, 1518.

246. Friedensburg, *G.U.W.*, 112.

247. Friedensburg, *G.U.W.*, 212–13.

248. Friedensburg, *G.U.W.*, 212–13.

249. Friedensburg, *G.U.W.*, 122.

250. Friedensburg, *G.U.W.*, 123.

251. WA Br, 1:228–29, and n. 11.

252. Bauch, *Monatschrift*, 155.

253. WA Br, 1:229 and n. 11. Carlstadt's reactions to Böschenstein was similar to that of Luther. He described him as being lazy, unfriendly toward his students, always aloof and unapproachable.

254. Freidensburg, *G.U.W.*, 123.

255. WA Br, 1:405 and n. 2; Bauch, *Monatschrift*, 286ff.

256. Bauch, *Monatschrift*, 41.

257. Bauch, *Monatschrift*, 41–42.

258. Bauch, *Monatschrift*, 42.

259. Bauch, *Monatschrift*, 43.

260. Friedensburg, *G.U.W.*, 133.

261. Bauch, *Monatschrift*, 46.

262. Bauch, *Monatschrift*, 45–46; *G.U.W.*, 123.

263. For a brief sketch of Werner Eichorn, see *Luther's Works* 1:154, n. 3.

264. WA Br, 2:82–83.

265. *Luther's Works*, 1: 160, based on WA Br, 2:82–83.

266. CR, 1:161–62.

267. WA Br, 2:93–95.

268. WA Br, 96.

269. WA Br, 96.

270. Enders, 2:395; 2:460.

271. Bauch, *Monatschrift*, 400.

272. Bauch, *Monatschrift*, 404–5.

273. WA Br, 2:104–5.

274. Bauch, *Monatschrift*, 405.

275. WA Br, 2:265; Enders 2:447.

276. Enders, 2:417; Bauch, *Monatschrift*, 465.

277. WA Br, 2:192; Bauch, *Monatschrift*, 465.

278. WA Br, 2:192.

279. Bauch, *Monatschrift*, 466.

280. WA Br, 2:193, n. 16; Friedensburg, *G.U.W.*, 124.

281. Bauch, *Monatschrift*, 466.

282. WA Br, 2:2, and n. 9.

283. CR, 1:358.

284. CR, 1:358.

285. Bauch, *Monatschrift*, 469ff.; Friedensburg, *G.U.W.*, 125.

Chapter 23
The New Reformation University

1. Friedensburg, *Urkundenbuch*, 1:166–87; also found in Dr. Friedrich Israël, *Das Wittenberger Universitätsarchiv, seine Geschichte und seine Bestände* (Halle a.d.S., 1913), pp. 104–111. (Cited below as Israël, *Fundationsurkunde*).

2. See above, chap. 22, where the incorporation of the *Stift* of the Castle Church in its original form is treated, the partial incorporation of 1525 under the Elector John the Constant and its completion under John Frederick in 1536.

3. Friedensburg, *Urkundenbuch*, 1:162–165. In this year the Pest broke out again and Wittenberg faced another problem of its transfer to Jena or elsewhere.

4. Friedensburg, *Urkundenbuch*, 1:172, No. 192.

5. Friedensburg, *Urkundenbuch*, 1:173–184; Israël, *Fundationsurkunde*, pp. 104–110. The original document is still at Halle, WUA, Tit. III, No. 12. Also in Weimar is a parchment copy of its final form, Weimar, Ges. Archiv, Reg, O.237, Bl. 42–58.

6. Friedensburg, *Urkundenbuch*, 1:173; Israël, *Fundationsurkunde*, p. 104; Friedensburg, *G.U.W.*, p. 180.

7. Israël, *Fundationsurkunde*, pp. 173–174.

8. Israël, *Fundationsurkunde*, 106; Friedensburg, *G.U.W.*, p. 108; Freidensburg, *Urkundenbuch*, I, 174–175.

9. It must be remembered that this document did not mean to limit its regulations to the present but also to generations to com. Hence there is not reference as to who will teach these prescribed courses.

10. Here we have the theoretical positions which were to be maintained by future generations.

11. There is a little confusion between theory and practice in Chancellor Brück's records, between the preparatory documents in 1535 and the *Fundationsurkunde*, for if it were met, there would be six members in the

theological faculty, four regular members plus Luther and Melanchthon without definite assignments.

12. Israël, *Fundationsurkunde,* pp. 177–178. See, also, Schwiebert, "The Theses and Wittenberg," *Luther for an Ecumenical Age* (St. Louis, 1967), pp. 120–143.

13. Friedensburg, *Urkundenbuch,* 1:163.

14. Friedensburg, *G.U.W.,* p. 186.

15. *Liber Decanorum,* pp. 152–157; also, in Paulson, G.G.U. (1896), pp. 211f.

16. Friedensburg, *G.U.W.,* p. 187.

17. Friedensburg, *G.U.W.*

18. Luther ordered the introduction of

Ordination by 1537, in which the candidates were examined by the faculty in the Town Church before they were sent out to be ordained by the congregations to which they were called.

19. W.A. 34, 575.

20. Friedensburg, *G.U.W.,* p. 194.

21. C.R., I, 784; Enders, V. 319.

22. Friedensburg, *G.U.W.,* p. 200.

23. C.R., II, 784; Enders VI, 319.

24. Friedensburg, *G.U.W.,* p. 195.

25. Friedensburg, *G.U.W.*

26. Friedensburg, *G.U.W.,* p. 196ff.

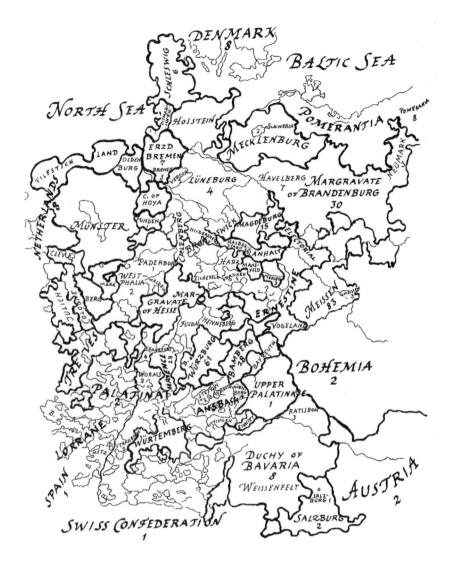

Germany and environs 1520

Germany and environs 1530

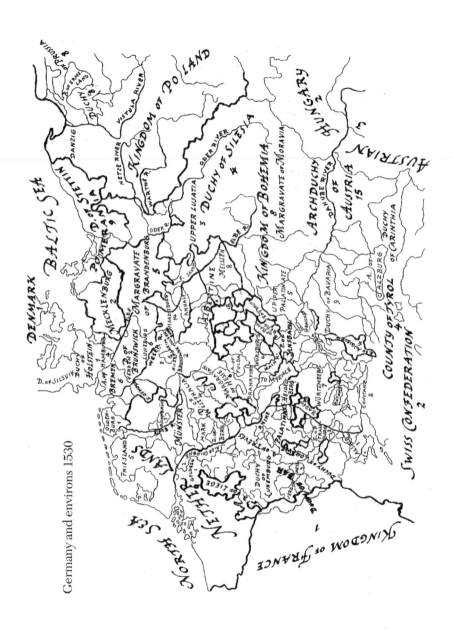

Germany and environs 1540

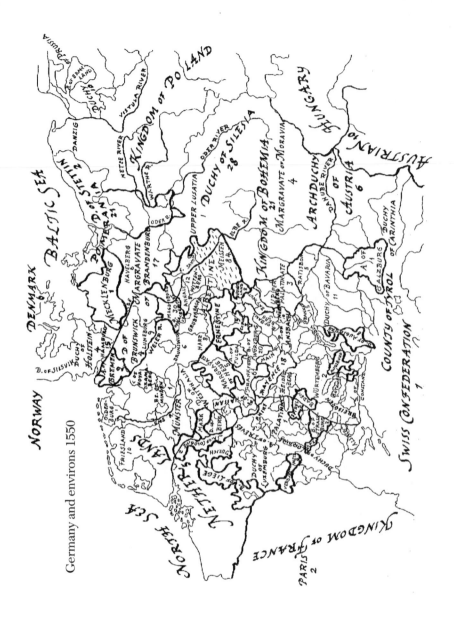

Germany and environs 1550

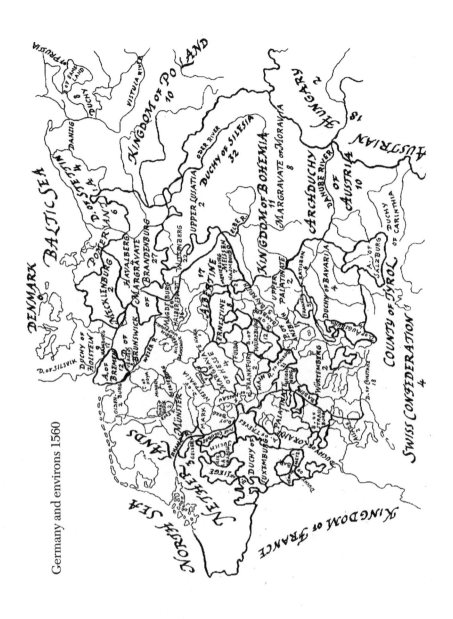

Germany and environs 1560

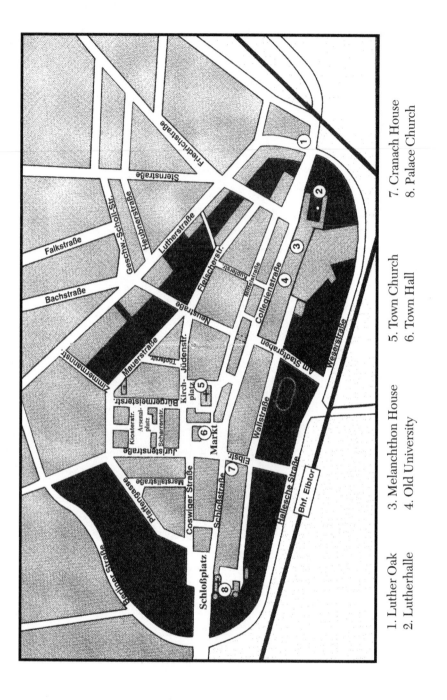

1. Luther Oak   3. Melanchthon House   5. Town Church   7. Cranach House
2. Lutherhalle   4. Old University   6. Town Hall   8. Palace Church

The Reformation:

Index

Bavarian plateau, 4-5
Bayer, 460
Bayso, Guido de, *Super Decretales,* 406
beadles, 191, 203-4, 225-26, 331, 337,
  339, 341, 343
Beatrix (wife of Frederick Barbarossa),
  36
Beauvoir, Armand von, 252
Bebel, Heinrich, 465, 467
Beckau, Mathäus, 229, 237, 242, 249,
  329, 451
Beckmann, Otto, 253, 306, 460
Bede, Venerable, 400; *Historia Ecclesi-
  astica gentis Anglicorum,* 414; *De sex
  aetatibus huius seculi,* 419
Bellini, 268
Bellunensis, Urban, *Institutiones graece
  Grammatices,* 417
Bembus, Petrus, *Epistolae,* 399
Ben Chayyim, Jacob, 392
Bender, Ulrich, 331
Benedicius, Alexander, *Anatomice et
  Aphormi medecinales,* 409
Benedict XII (pope), 145
Benedict XIII (pope), 473
Benedicti de Benedictis, *Consilia ultim,
  volunt,* 406
Benedict Paulus, 331, 334
Benivieni, Antonio di Pagolo, 275
Berendt, Friedrich, xiv, 43
Berilius, *Discernendi causas et differen-
  tias febrium,* 409
Beringer (brother of Ludwig der
  Springer), 77, 79
Berkowitz, D., xiv, 391, 392
Bernard of Clairveaux, *Opus complec-
  tens sermones de tempore et sanctis,*
  401
Bernard von Göppingen, 476
Bernhard of Ascania (youngest son of
  Albrecht the Bear; duke of Saxony),
  15, 28-38, 43; downfall of Henry the
  Lion and, 32; Gelnhausen charter
  and, 40-42; as elector of Saxony, 24,
  43, 50, 102-3
Bernhardi, Bartholomeus, 237, 249,
  452-54, 461
Bernward of Hildesheim (bishop), 68

Bero, Abbot, 58
Beroaldus, Philippus, 414, 415, 423;
  Orationes epigrammata et alia, 419
Berthold, xiv, 61, 111, 115, 117, 119, 120
Bertrucius of Bologna, *Collectorium
  totius medicinae,* 409
Bessarion, 272, 273, 414
Bessarius, Cardinal, *De sacramento
  Eucharistiae,* 404
Beyer, Christian, 329, 331
Bible, 278, 281, 283, 295, 302, 306, 345,
  353, 358, 360, 377, 385, 392-93, 438,
  444, 450, 453, 455, 458, 461-62;
  ancient versions of, in library of
  Wittenberg, 391-92
Biblia Rabbinica, 391-92
Bickel, Dyonisius, 237
Biel, Gabriel, 222, 242, 245, 249-50,
  295, 401, 402, 403, 426, 429, 450,
  453, 456, 467
Billican, Theobald, 465
Billung, Hermann, 38, 71
Black Cloister, 199, 207, 214, 215, 341,
  345-59, 435, 437, 448, 451, 469, 471,
  472
Black Death, 269-70
Blanche of Castile, 189-90
Blarer, Ambrosiua, 466
Blaschke, Karlheinz, xiv
Blaurer, Ambrosiua. *See* Blarer,
  Ambrosiua
Blaurer, Thomas, 471-72
Block, Dietrich, 237
Blondus, *Pii Pontificis epitome in Deca-
  des Blondi, ab inclinatione imperii,*
  397
Boccaccio, Giovanni, 260, 268, 270-71,
  276, 384, 398
Boccatius, 416
Bockenheim, Johannes, 461
Boedler, Karl E. F., xiv, 40-43, 50-52
Boehmer, Heinrich, xiv, 294, 433, 441
Boethius, 198, 271, 277, 383, 384; *De
  consolatione Philosophias,* 413
Bohemian Massive, 4-6, 156
Bohemis, 276
Böhmer, Heinrich. *See* Boehmer,
  Heinrich

588   The Reformation

Mutianus, Conrad, 274, 276, 278, 279,
  294, 301, 309, 363, 369, 372, 374, 376
Mutius, Henr., *De Gamanorum prima
  origine, moribus, institutis, legibus,*
  397
Myconius, xx
Mylius, M. J. C., xx, 274; *Memorabilia
  Bibliothecae,* 360; *Index Auctorum,*
  385; library of University of
  Wittenberg and, 360-424
Mynsingerus, Joachim, 398

nations: divisions of the University of
  Paris, 189-92; divisions of the
  University of Bologna, 203-4
Naumburg settlement, 159, 161
Nazis, 440-41
Nebrissensus, Antonius, *Legal Lexicon,*
  394
Nemorarius, Jordanus, *Elementa arith-
  metica,* 412
Neuenburg, 82, 85
Neuglaubigen (new believers), 427-28,
  435, 438, 447, 492
Neurkt, Johann von, 277
New Friderici College, 213, 216, 231,
  308, 339, 340, 341, 359, 368, 454,
  471, 486
"New Theology" of Wittenberg, 257,
  259, 293, 333, 343, 377, 426, 428,
  435-37, 447, 451, 452-53, 456, 458,
  481, 488-89, 491-92
Niavis, Faulus, 290
Nicander, *De Theoriaca,* 408
Nicholas V (pope), 272
Nicholas of Blonius, *Sermones de tem-
  pore et sanctis,* 401
Nicholas of Cusa, 60, 277, 279, 402
Nicholaus von Lyra, 300, 473; *Operum
  partes IV,* 401; *Postilla seu expositio
  litteralis moralis super epistolas et
  evangelia quadragesimalia,* 403
Nickel von Magdeburg, 155
Nicolaus de Lyra, 198
Nicoli, 272
Nigri, Petrus. See Petrus Nigrus
Nikolaus von Siegen, 59

Ninety-five Theses, 257, 296, 343, 344,
  360, 425, 426, 447
Niphus, Augustinus, 411
Nobles War, 146, 151
nominalism, 252, 279, 283
Nordheim family, 82
Novelia, Andreas, 407
Nuhm, Johannes, 63
Nürnberg, 5

Obermann, Heiko, xx, 426, 441
Obermann school, 425
Obsopaeus, Vincentius, 399
Occam, William, 228, 240, 241, 242,
  245, 249-50, 252, 282, 283, 295, 401,
  426, 429, 446, 450, 453, 455, 456, 467
Odofredus, 405
Oecolampadius, 466, 476, 477
O'Hanlen, Daniel J., 443
Oldradi de Ponte, *De Laude Consilia,*
  407
Order of St. Francis, 112
Order of Teutonic Knights, 124
ordinarius, 198-99, 229, 235, 251, 258
Oribasius of Sardinia, *Opera medica,*
  395
Orosius, 291, 383
Orsoy, Gosein von, 224
Osiander, Andreas, 475
Ostermeyer, Wolfgang, 228, 447
Ostrogoths, 8, 12
Otto (brother of William IV), 72
Otto (son of Otto of Hesse), 142
Otto I, 66
Otto II, 66
Otto IV (son of Henry the Lion), 42, 60,
  104, 105, 106
Ottokar of Bohemia, 102-3, 105, 134
Otto of Brandenburg (Markgraf), 137
Otto of Meissen, 100
Otto of Wittelsbach, 38, 107
Otto the Great, 38, 65, 66, 70
Otto the Rich, 32, 42
Otto the Square, 150, 152
Ovid, 198, 272, 280, 289, 291, 302, 424,
  450; *Metamorphoses,* 415; *Epistolae,*